THE FOOTLOOSE GUIDE

PARIS

Paris

DEIRDRE VINE

Series Editor: Andrew Sanger

SIMON & SCHUSTER

LONDON·SYDNEY·NEW YORK·TOKYO·SINGAPORE·TORONTO

First published in Great Britain by
Simon & Schuster Ltd in 1992
A Paramount Communications Company

Simon & Schuster Ltd
West Garden Place
Kendal Street
London W2 2AQ

Simon & Schuster of Australia Pty Ltd
Sydney

A catalogue record for this book is
available from the British Library
ISBN 0–671–65326–1

Typeset in Sabon & Futura by
Falcon Typographic Art Ltd, Fife, Scotland
Printed and bound in Great Britain by
HarperCollinsManufacturing, Glasgow

Illustrations by Julian Abela-Hyzler

CONTENTS

Acknowledgements

The author would like to thank the following for their invaluable help and contributions:

Jennifer Bouquet, Judith Carter, Joan Cousins, Peter France, Anne de Girard, Sian Parkhouse, Greg and Julie Pitt-Nash, Philippe Vidal, Richard Wigmore.

To Tomas

To Tomas

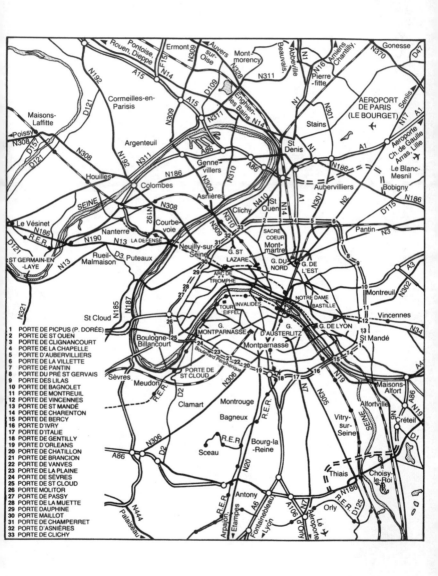

1 PORTE DE PICPUS (P. DORÉE)
2 PORTE DE ST OUEN
3 PORTE DE CLIGNANCOURT
4 PORTE DE LA CHAPELLE
5 PORTE D'AUBERVILLIERS
6 PORTE DE LA VILLETTE
7 PORTE DE PANTIN
8 PORTE DU PRÉ ST GERVAIS
9 PORTE DES LILAS
10 PORTE DE BAGNOLET
11 PORTE DE MONTREUIL
12 PORTE DE VINCENNES
13 PORTE DE ST MANDÉ
14 PORTE DE CHARENTON
15 PORTE DE BERCY
16 PORTE D'IVRY
17 PORTE D'ITALIE
18 PORTE DE GENTILLY
19 PORTE D'ORLEANS
20 PORTE DE CHATILLON
21 PORTE DE BRANCION
22 PORTE DE VANVES
23 PORTE DE LA PLAINE
24 PORTE DE SÈVRES
25 PORTE DE ST CLOUD
26 PORTE MOLITOR
27 PORTE DE PASSY
28 PORTE DE LA MUETTE
29 PORTE DAUPHINE
30 PORTE MAILLOT
31 PORTE DE CHAMPERRET
32 PORTE D'ASNIÈRES
33 PORTE DE CLICHY

PARIS TODAY

PARIS TODAY

Parisians exude self-sufficiency and self-confidence, leaving simpering self-disparagement to *les anglais*. While we go on about how everything at home is so much worse than anywhere else and moan about how awful things are – the poverty, the litter, the scandals, shambolic public transport – Parisians have an obstinate loyalty to their city, even though the problems are the same as, or even worse than, London's.

There are far more beggars and homeless in Paris than in London; the social security system is harsher – if people don't find work within a set time, their lifeline is disconnected. Depravity stalks the Parisian streets, where children flog their bodies for drugs, where immigrants live right at the bottom of the human heap in tumbledown tenements. There's a level of teenage suicide and delinquency equal to any in the developed world. The French seem to see all these problems as an inevitable part of the urban fabric, compatible with their city's image of refinement, cultural and intellectual hegemony. Their reputation for a superior sense of style, whether we're talking Epicurianism, wine, architecture, fashion or sex, need not, in their eyes, be tarnished by these social niggles.

Then again, it's useless trying to explain to a Parisian why we find it so peculiar that the most chic café should have the most primitive plumbing imaginable; and why there are so many places where all the chairs face the traffic, making voyeurism *de rigeur*, why we feel so grateful to have survived a day with life and limbs intact in the city's suicidal traffic, why it's so puzzling that everyone drives round with their hands on their horns . . .

They're so sure they've got it *right* and that their way of doing things is the only proper or civilised way, and, in any case, they're certainly not going to knock it. And here lies the secret of the city's greatest achievement – the ability to sustain such epic civic pride.

The buildings and the people breathe self-esteem, inhaling the city's confidence, they exhale self-love. Which brings us to the stress-inducing Parisians themselves. A 1988 campaign tried to persuade the French to polish up their unfriendly-to-tourists image, and to be more charming. Arrogant waiters were advised to become more deferential; taxi drivers less disdainful; porters were told to smile and to refuse tips. Did it work? A recent Thames TV survey showed that Brits still expect a ruder welcome from the French than from any other nation except Spain. *L'Expres* magazine writing about *la ville grimace* passed judgment on Parisians by describing them as "distrustful by nature and instinctively unhelpful".

Parisians remain true to their tribal tradition of being offhand to everyone, provincials, tourists, and yes, especially offensive to each other. They are, on the whole, as you've doubtless heard, a snooty bunch, prone to be foul about one's faulty French, making little effort with outsiders. Stuart Wavell reported in *The Sunday Times*, November 1991, that Parisian behaviour "can make the Japanese contemplate suicide and drive the British into profound depression". The disorder has even been named "the Paris syndrome" by a Dr Hiroaki Ota, a psychiatrist who has treated, or hospitalised, 139 disturbed Paris-dwelling Japanese in the past few years. If the pressure gets to you, think of what it does to the French – could this be why they pop more tranquillisers than anyone else in Europe?

But I digress. Everyone will tell you that the golden rule is not to be intimidated. Some swear the secret is simply to throw the rudeness back with knobs on – that way they'll regard you as one of them. An exception here is the police. They're probably a lost cause and the best advice is simply to stay on the right side of them.

Admittedly, Parisians have much to be proud of. Their food, of course. You *can* eat badly in Paris, but cookery is considered an art form, part of the French national heritage, and so something to be taken very seriously. Top chefs are more famous than footballers. When Jack Lang, the 55-year-old hip Minister of Culture, heard that today's French children didn't appreciate the republic's gastronomic arts, he sent packs of chefs into the primary schools of Paris to awaken their taste buds.

Then there's the obvious beauty of the city. Paris has retained its ancient character in a way that many other important European cities have not. The homogeneity of architectural appearance lingers, almost in spite of the zest for modernising – which continues briskly. And the city still remains, to a surprising degree, an alliance of villages, precious parts of which retain their traditional character, although almost engulfed by rapidly accelerating gentrification. One person's revival is another's ruin.

The city's past is reflected in its morphology – the Centre Rive Droite is still referred to, the ancient administrative centre on the right bank, the Ile de la Cité and Ile St Louis. There is the Paris of Catherine de Medici at the Tuileries, of Henri II at the Hôtel de Ville, of Louis XIV at Les Invalides, Louis XVI at the Panthéon and Napoleon at the place Vendôme. And of course there's the Paris of everyone else.

Quite apart from its status, beauty and assets, the city also happens to be efficiently run, prosperous and well-serviced. Due credit should land at the door of Mayor Chirac's dynamic administration. The Gaullist Jacques Chirac was briefly Prime Minister during the ill-starred coalition years of 1986–88. He took a beating at the hands of François Mitterrand in the last presidential election in 1988, yet within Paris itself, he's extremely popular. The capital may well be surrounded by left-wing outlying areas, but most Parisians are right-wing when it comes to local elections. When Chirac last ran for mayor he bulldozed the high-profile socialist candidate Pierre Joxe in 20 out of 20 *arrondissements* – a repeat performance of his achievement four years earlier. Often accused of turning Paris into a city for the rich, he's known as *le bulldozer* because of his awesome energy. He has, during his term as Mayor of Paris, relentlessly promoted and enhanced the city, especially as competition became more fierce for the position of Number One Eurocity *après* 1992.

Paris may have been pipped to the post as financial capital,

Who Runs Paris?

Like even the smallest commune in France, Paris is overseen by its elected mayor. For a century Paris was ruled directly by the national government, through a Prefect of Paris and so the citizens had no direct control over its running. Then, in 1977, mayors were reintroduced, the rôle being won by right-wing Jacques Chirac (who has also been twice prime minister). Chirac controls the purse strings of the 20 mayors of inner Paris.

The city's administration is overseen by a city council whose members are elected for a 6-year term. They meet in the palatial Hôtel de Ville in the Marais (see page 361), which is also the mayor's official residence. The mayor heads the council, and he also serves for a 6-year stint. The Mayor of Paris shares his powers with the Préfect of Police.

but it still has the strongest claim to the title on the arts front. And for evidence of how seriously culture is taken in the city, you only have to look at the lengthy queues outside galleries and museums. This is, after all, a country where new French films and plays are announced on the national news, a TV books programme, called *Apostrophes*, gets some of the highest ratings and an average of 4.5 recognised literary prizes are awarded every day. Minister of Culture, Jack Lang once tried to ban American soap operas from French TV – an initiative that bit the dust when several wives of political notables publicly protested their own addiction to them. Not so much a demagogue as a man always one step ahead of a trend, with his funds at the ready, waiting for it to catch on, his Ministry subsidises rap music and subway graffiti. A book which appeared in the autumn of 1991 by Marc Fumardi, entitled *L'État Culturel* (Éditions de Fallois) had a real go at the mindset of the Socialist government and was particularly merciless about Jack Lang. "We're living in a culture-saturated society and over-organised culture kills creativity," says designer Karl Lagerfeld, a fan of the book, "street culture may be culture too, but I don't think we need a Ministry for it." Cultural headaches Lang has to cure include the newish but still controversial £250-million Bastille Opera complex with its insatiable appetite for soaking up money.

Over the last 10 years there's been a huge boom in the city's museum space; the exhibition area in the Louvre has doubled; the d'Orsay and Picasso museums opened; the Parc de la Villette, on the old slaughterhouse site in the once down-at-heel 19e, is the most extravagant cultural complex in Europe today. Other huge cultural landmarks commissioned include the Institut du Monde Arabe, with its façade of giant lenses that open and close with the sun. All this adds up to billions of francs' worth of investment, the results of which are energetically debated in public and in private.

Unlike plan-less London, which seems to lack a civil intelligence shaping its city culture, Paris today (like so many other national and regional European capitals), is very different from the scruffy, trampled-on city of the post-war years. It gives the impression of confronting its problems with confidence and with optimism.

In the mid sixties, under Charles de Gaulle, an ambitious *grand plan* for the Paris region was implemented. It resulted in the tearing down of shabby inner-city districts and their reconstruction, the creation of new suburban business zones and huge new conurbations on the outskirts, all linked by motorways and a brand new transportation system – the RER, or *Réseau Express Regional*. The Métro system, too, was turned round from almost complete collapse.

In 1977, when Chirac first took over as mayor, there was a major change of policy and the development of skyscrapers and office blocks was curtailed. During the previous decade, the equivalent of ten times La Défense (see p. 428) had been built within the city. It was now time to call a halt in order to preserve the very characteristics which throughout history have represented the great charm of Paris. A pledge was made to maintain the balance in every part of town between residential and employment needs. As all of Paris is lived in, there are none of the vast shopping, business or administrative wildernesses that you get in so many cities, and there are precious few dead zones or tatty tourist wastelands.

In 1990 a completely new strategic plan to take the capital through the next quarter of a century was unleashed. And the opinions of the citizens themselves were canvassed. In

---

Keeping Paris Clean

Armies of Parisian cleaners wage constant war on litterbugs, pigeons, graffiti-artists (35,000 square metres of the stuff removed each year) leaves and dogs. Especially dogs. Paris has more dogs per square metre than any other capital. One guesstimate says there's one fully-functioning pooch for every four of us. French dogs eat more than the human population of Spain. (Dogs are well catered for in Paris, with 24-hour dog emergency hospitals, even doggie dating agencies, analysts, undertakers.) Shoes have a dirty time in dog-loving Paris where they're likely to land in something messy every 1123 steps. So Gallic ingenuity has come up with the *caninette* – a Honda motorcycle specially equipped with vacuum cleaners stuck on the back which follows *les chiens* and scoops up their poops.

The most sophisticated weaponry the municipal cleaning industry can supply is in the hands of the 8000 or so cleaners. The battalions of spruce troops wear green uniforms designed by Thierry Mugler, drive 1600 vehicles and use some 42,000 broomsticks a year (of which 12,000 are of birch twigs, 30,000 of plastic) in their ritual early morning washing of the streets. Paris is certainly *clean*. Many of the city's most important buildings have been cleaned up too, in honour of the 1989 bicentennial celebrations. Yet in spite of the pristine sewers and all the street ablutions, Paris is a smelly city: a mélange of body odours, baking, smoke, strong coffee mingling with gas, garlic, perfume, and a hint of drains. Per capita they spend twice as much as Brits do on scent each year; the same is probably true of the cleaning budget.

---

the summer of 1991, everyone who lived in Paris received a handout bearing the invitation to "Design Yourself A City". This referendum was the brainchild of Chirac who wanted to elicit views on everything from parking rules to licensing laws and the type of paintings that should hang in the city's museums. The response was staggering, and could also be seen as a shrewd political move, as the populace was also quizzed on issues over which Chirac's fiefdom has partial or no jurisdiction, thus furnishing him with handy ammunition to use against his arch-enemies in the socialist-controlled national government. For while Chirac has, to a large extent, shaped Paris, authority over many of the nuts and bolts that keep the city running is in the Prime Minister's court. "Paris is not a museum," declares Chirac, who has ensured that major buildings are cherished, that litter is picked up almost before it hits the pristine streets (see box feature) and that the city, thanks to the great bicentenary clean-up of '89, looks more bright and beautiful than ever.

The public transport network, one of the city's main glories, has been extended and updated. The Métro, where trains arrive every 90 seconds, is cheap, thanks to subsidies (by the government 27%; local authorities 13%; Paris employers 14%) and efficient, carrying 4 million passengers a day. The bright green buses seldom cause waits of more than a few minutes. Yet despite their special lanes, buses are snarled up in traffic jams. Central Paris claims some of the highest air pollution in western Europe, with a constantly jammed ring-road and average peak time speeds of 8mph.

For years there have been proposals to tunnel under the southern *périphérique* and build a subterranean motorway system and, although they periodically get taken out and dusted down, the plans tend to remain on the shelf because of the exorbitant cost.

Over 3 million cars are estimated to be clogging the city streets, of which some 65,000 park illegally in the centre at any one time. Parking fines are generally £22, but tougher measures for persistent offenders could mean the loss of licenses. And a recent innovation – the designation of *axes rouges*, six routes where no parking is allowed for 17 miles – has halved the time it takes to cross the city on a north-south or east-west axis. In 1991, 100,000 street parking places were abolished, to be replaced with underground and private parking; the latest building laws state that every new block of flats must allow for one car space per apartment.

And when Parisians aren't grumbling about the traffic, you might well hear them moan about skyrocketing rents and the high cost of property. An average of 20,000 Parisians left the city for the suburbs each year from 1982–1990. According to the Institut National de la Statistique des Études Economiques (INSEE), the capital's population stood at 2,057,000 in 1988; compared with a figure of 2,178,000 in 1982. Housing subsidies may help stem the fall in the city's population, but rents in the private sector in the capital are double those of anywhere else, a situation which is particularly tough for those on low incomes, including single-person households – one in two in the city.

While the population of the area within the *périphérique* is getting progressively more bourgeois, social disparities are increasing. The city's wealth has always gravitated to the west and, to help redress the imbalance, the Paris Project was born, a long-term scheme involving government, local authority and private money. Three developments, Bastille, Bercy and Villette, anchor the development of eastern Paris, and have given President Mitterrand ample opportunities to indulge in architectural vanity.

French Presidents since the second World War have been smitten with the desire to build, especially in their capital, and each has left its mark on the city. Brian Appleyard, writing in *The Times* four years ago, put it very neatly: "Paris is obsessively adorned by her lovers. The Eiffel Tower, the Opéra, Louvre and the Centre Pompidou are the costly trinkets offered by one proud fool after another. The world is invited to wonder at these lovers' excesses and to gasp at the generosity of a French *grand passion*, their profligacy in pursuit of *la gloire*."

Apart from his most controversial monument, the Centre Pompidou, Georges Pompidou planned even higher tower blocks than his predecessor's, not to mention a network of fast roads within the city – including a motorway along the left bank. But it's perhaps just as well that along came Valéry Giscard d'Éstaing, who stopped the road works, limited

---

Paris – Facts and Figures

"Greater Paris" covers 185 square miles (479 square kilometers) and has a population of some 8 1/2 million. Just over 2 million inhabit "Inner Paris", the compact area of 41 square miles (106 square kilometres) contained within the ring road or *périphérique*. Unlike sprawling London, or New York where you might not dare, you could walk comfortably right across Paris in a day. There are over 12,000 restaurants, cafés and clubs, 80 municipal libraries, over 60 theatres, more than 450 cinemas, over 40 concert halls.

the height of buildings, added green spaces. Projects for the d'Orsay Museum, La Villette and Arab Institute were launched and subsequently swallowed up by Mitterrand's media-grabbing *grands projets* which he sees as suitable memorials to his long term of office.

Initiated during his first term as president were the Pyramid and revamping at the Louvre, the triumphal Grande Arche at La Défense and the further two schemes which, with La Villette, were intended to develop eastern Paris – the Bastille Opera and Bercy. His zeal for building has been compared to Napoleon III's when he assigned Paris planning to Baron Haussmann.

A short reach down the Seine from the Pont de Bercy, at Tolbiac, on a particularly dismal stretch of eastern Paris, Mitterrand's latest architectural wonder is taking shape. The most advanced library in the world is due to open in the Spring of 1995 (which would provide Mitterrand, a true bibliophile, with a retirement fanfare when his second term of office expires). The design – four monumental, 20-storey glass towers, each shaped like an open book, cap each corner of a giant garden – won an international competition. This, the last of Mitterrand's *grands projets* where entry was open to foreigners, was in fact won by a 36-year-old Frenchman, the rank outsider Dominique Perrault. To the affront of Parisian chauvinism, previous projects had been scooped up by foreign architects and the final major building – a conference centre – is to be chosen exclusively from entries by French architects. Declares Perrault: "I wanted to give East Paris its Place de la Concorde."

With just a few misgivings about the wisdom of storing 12 million tomes in separate towers when particularly intricate cross referencing might lead to accessibility problems, and a few worries about the noise factor due to the neighbouring Gare d'Austerlitz, the billion-pound library development has met with considerable enthusiasm and interest. The *très grand bibliothèque* will be open to anyone who wishes to use it and is clearly seen as idealistic urban planning.

Paris never becomes old hat; when it plans it plans big, showing no sign that it intends ever to be stranded as a footnote or exiled on the margins of history.

KEY DATES IN THE HISTORY OF PARIS

BC

3rd century: A Gallic tribe called the Parisii make Ile de la Cité their capital.

52:   Julius Caesar's legions conquer the fortified island and it becomes an important Roman centre.

AD

360:   Lutetia is renamed Paris.

508:   King Clovis of the Franks makes Paris his capital.

800:   Charlemagne crowned Holy Roman Emperor.

885–86:   Difficult times for Paris: Norman pirates raid the city, ending in a 13-month siege. Finally the Normans are defeated.

987:   Hughes Capet, Count of Paris, becomes King of France. Paris established as French capital.

1163:   Notre-Dame begun.

1180–1223:   Philippe II sets about building the Louvre fortress, a defensive wall around the city, lays the foundation of the University of Paris and paves the streets.

1257:   Robert de Sorbonne founds the Sorbonne.

1348:   Black Death: it is estimated that a third of the French population was wiped out.

1358:   Étienne Marcel leads popular uprising against the Dauphin due to economic strife caused by the plague. He is assassinated.

1364–80:   Charles V (the Wise) builds the Bastille and a new city wall.

1420:   Treaty of Troyes makes Henry V of England heir to French throne. He takes Paris.

1431:   Henry VI of England crowns himself King of France in Notre-Dame.

1436: Charles VII recaptures Paris.

1453: The English withdraw from France except Calais.

1461–83: Louis XI comes to throne. During his reign the city prospers: school of medicine opened and the first printing press set up at the Sorbonne.

1515–47: François I reigns. He supports the arts with vigour, introducing the Italian Renaissance to France and stocks up the Louvre with their first masterpieces.

1531–70: Fontainebleau decorated.

1547–59: Henry II killed in jousting accident; Catherine de Medici, his wife, authorises the building of the Tuileries palace.

1559–89: Bloody confrontation between the Catholics and the Protestants, ending in the St Bartholomew's Day massacre (1572) when 3000 Huguenots were slain in Paris.

1577: Pont Neuf begun.

1589–1610: Henry IV creates the Place Royale (now Place des Vosges), the first square in Paris to be regular in design. Also construction of the first covered sewer in the city. Pont Neuf completed.

1610–43: *Grand Siècle* when Paris acquires much beautiful architecture; Luxembourg Palace built by Maria de Medici as a dower house; much of the Ile St Louis created.

1643–1715: Reign of Louis XIV. The royal court is transferred in 1670 to the newly built Versailles. Paris sees the creation of Les Invalides, the Salpêtrière Hôpital (a refuge for beggars), the Gobelins (tapesty factory), the Louvre colonnade and the Comédie Française.

1758: Church of Ste Geneviève (Panthéon) begun by Soufflot.

1789: The beginning of the French Revolution. The formation of the National Assembly.

1792: France declared a republic. Louis XVI imprisoned, and executed in 1793 along with Marie Antoinette.

1794: Execution of Robespierre.

1804: Napoleon crowns himself Emperor in Notre-Dame. Cemetery of Père-Lachaise opens.

1806: Arc de Triomphe and Arc de Triomphe du Carrousel begins. Napoleon introduces a system for numbering the city's houses.

1814–21: Allies enter Paris and Napoleon abdicates at Fontainebleau and is exiled to the island of Elba. He escapes, but his final campaign ends at Waterloo. Napoleon dies in exile in 1821 on the island of St Helena.

1815–48: During the restoration, in the reign of Louis XVIII, a time of modernisation: canal systems of St Denis and St Martin built; the French railway starts in 1837 with a line from Paris to St-Germain-en-Laye; gas lighting installed. But 19,000 deaths from cholera in 1832. In 1848 Louis ousted in the "Year of Revolutions". Civil war in the streets.

1852–70: Second Empire under Napoleon III. Haussmann lays out modern Paris, constructing his wide boulevards through the city, which was divided into the present 20 *arrondissements*. Outlying villages are annexed to Paris in 1860, including Montmartre which becomes an artistic centre. Other new buildings include the Opéra and Les Halles.

1875: The Opéra opens.

1876: Work begins on Sacré-Coeur, Montmartre.

1887–89: Eiffel Tower built for the World Exhibition.

1890: Heavy industry begins to establish itself around the outskirts of the city.

1895: First performance of a film by the Lumière brothers takes place in Paris, which becomes the centre of the film industry.

1900: The Second Summer Olympics takes place as part of the World Fair. The Grand and Petit Palais are built for the exhibition; Pont Alexandre III constructed. The Métro opens.

1900s: Belle Époque: Paris is Europe's fashion and entertainment centre.

1914: First World War begins. Battle of Marne saves Paris from a German invasion. The French government moves to Bordeaux.

1937: Palais de Chaillot is built.

1940–44: German Occupation.

1949: Founding of NATO.

1958: De Gaulle proclaimed first president of the Fifth Republic.

1959: EEC founded, with France as one of the six members.

1960: Work underway on La Défense, a vast commercial and residential complex west of Paris.

1968: Student uprisings in Paris; street fighting and barricades on the left bank.

1969: Les Halles market transferred to Rungis in the suburbs.

1970: De Gaulle dies.

1973: Montparnasse Tower built; ring road (*périphérique*) opens.

1974: Pompidou dies; Giscard d'Estaing elected President.

1977: Pompidou Centre opens; Jacques Chirac is elected as the first mayor of Paris since 1871.

1981: Mitterrand's socialist government is elected.

1984: Paris plagued by strikes.

1985: Picasso museum opens.

1986: Conservative Jacques Chirac appointed as Prime Minister, under the leadership of Mitterrand. Musée D'Orsay opens; also Science City at La Villette.

1988: Re-election of Mitterrand and appointment of a socialist prime minister, Michel Rocard. Renovated Les Halles area finished.

Paris celebrates bicentary of French Revolution. Bas-
 designed by Carlos Ott opens. "Grande Arche" at
efense and Louvre's Pyramid unveiled.
1991: Edith Cresson appointed Prime Minister by Mitterrand – the first woman to hold the job in France.

THE PRACTICAL SECTION

BEFORE YOU GO

Apart from information from the travel agent and this guide, you can write to or visit the French Government Tourist Office, 178 Piccadilly, London, W1V 0AL. Tel. 071 499 6911, for leaflets on entertainments, events, etc. in Paris and the Ile de France region. More comprehensive information (maps, brochures, etc.) is available from the Central Tourist Information Office (Office du Tourisme de Paris), 127 avenue des Champs-Élysées, Paris 75008. Tel. 47 23 61 72. Open 9am–8pm, Mon–Sat; 9am–6pm Sun. See also **When in Paris**, page 32.

The main FGTO offices abroad are:

Australia: BWP House, 12 Castlereagh Street, Sydney, NSW 2000. Tel. 612 2315244.

Canada: 1840 Ouest rue Sherbrooke, Montreal, Quebec H3H 1E4. Tel. 514 931 3855; 1 Dundas Street W, Suite 2405 (Box 8) Toronto, Ontario, M5G 1Z3. Tel. 416 693 4717.

Eire: c/o CIE Tours International, 35 Lower Abbey Street, Dublin 1. Tel. 35 07 77.

USA: 610 Fifth Avenue, New York, NY 10020. Tel. 212 757 1125.
646 N.Michigan Avenue, Suite 630, Chicago, IL60611. Tel. 312 337 6301.
2305 Cedar Springs Road, Dallas, TX 75201. Tel. 214 720 4010.
9401 Wilshire Boulevard, Beverley Hills, CA 90212. Tel. 212 272 2661.

360 Post Street, San Francisco, CA 94108. Tel. 415 986461.

FOR DISABLED TRAVELLERS

Over 300 railway stations in France have wheelchairs and mobile steps, so it's worth enquiring about exactly what's available, if you're travelling by train, before you leave home. The French Government Tourist Office in London, address above, publishes special information sheets and there's an excellent booklet in their series *Touristes Quand Même* (Tourists Nonetheless) from the Comité National Francais de Liaison pour la Réadaption des Handicapés – see below – giving details of facilities at major attractions.

The French government have a *Guide des Hôtels* where a wheelchair symbol denotes facilities for the disabled, although unfortunately it's not always possible to establish just what these facilities are. Although a hotel may offer rooms specially located on the ground floor, there's still a chance that a wheel-chair may have to negotiate an extremely narrow entrance door in the foyer.

Organisations which not only provide information for, but are compiled by, disabled travellers, include: The Royal Association for Disability and Rehabilitation (RADAR), 25 Mortimer Street, London W1N 8AB. Tel. 071 637 5400; Comité National pour la Réadaption des Handicapés, 38 boulevard Raspail 75007. Tel. 45 48 90 13. Open 9am–12 noon, 2–6pm. Phone for an appointment to get advice and info on matters as diverse as social and health provisions to travel facilities; the Association de Paralysés de France, 17 boulevard Auguste-Blanqui, Paris 75013. Tel. 45 80 82 40.

The Pauline Hephaistos Survey Projects Group, 39 Bradley Gardens, London W13 8HE, publish a guide to Paris detailing easy access to hotels etc. Researched by disabled people, it costs £3.

The Paris transport authority (RATP) has a free escort ser-vice for handicapped travellers called *Voyages Accompagnés* – Tel. 40 02 37 25 for details.

When to Go?

It's really up to you — there's plenty to see and do throughout the year. Paris is not particularly prone to touristic peaks and troughs. It is busy all year round, but especially so at Christmas and Easter. Tourism visibly perks up between April and October, but Paris tends to empty of many residents during French summer holidays (from mid-July to end of August) when you'll also find that some shops and restaurants close. Major fashion shows, trade fairs and conventions all have an effect on availability of services and accommodation and you'd be well advised to book ahead wherever you choose to travel. Quietest times are likely to be immediately before or after Christmas or early spring if you can put up with poor weather. (According to the Office of Tourism in Paris the most heavily booked dates are 2–6 February, 2–10 March, 1–2, 4–7 April, 5–10 June, 4–10, 17–26 September, 18–22 October, and 17–22 November.) Climatically, Paris is not dissimilar to London.

Average daily maximum and minimum temperatures in Paris

	Jan		**Feb**		**Mar**		**Apr**	
	F	C	F	C	F	C	F	C
Max	43	(6)	45	(7)	54	(12)	60	(16)
Min	34	(1)	34	(1)	43	(6)	49	(10)

	May		**Jun**		**Jul**		**Aug**	
	F	C	F	C	F	C	F	C
Max	68	(20)	73	(23)	76	(25)	75	(24)
Min	49	(10)	55	(13)	58	(15)	58	(14)

	Sep		**Oct**		**Nov**		**Dec**	
	F	C	F	C	F	C	F	C
Max	70	(21)	60	(16)	50	(10)	44	(7)
Min	53	(12)	46	(8)	40	(5)	36	(2)

FRENCH TIME

In common with most western European countries, France is 1 hour ahead of GMT in winter and 2 hours in summer — that's to say, 1 hour ahead of the UK for most of the year. The French use the 24-hour system so 6am is *six heures*, 4pm is *16 heures*, midnight is *24 heures*, etc.

ENTRY

EEC nationals – a passport will suffice. Visitors ...e USA, Canada or Switzerland don't need visas either ...less intending to stay more than 3 months. Nationals from other countries should ask at the French Consulate/Embassy before leaving home. The French Consulate in London is at 24 Rutland Gate, SW7. Tel. 071 581 5292.

Immigration officials keep a beady eye on young people with little money hoping to find casual work.

LONGER STAYS

No matter which document you've got (see above) you're supposed to get a *carte de séjour* after a 90-day stay. Contact the Immigration Service (*Service des Étrangers*) at the Préfecture de Police, 7–9 boulevard de Palais, Paris 75004. Tel. 43 29 21 55. They'll arrange for a *carte de séjour* to be issued on completion of the formalities (present a valid passport, half a dozen application forms – in French, financial guarantee and, if under 18, parental authorisation allowing you to stay).

Public Holidays

On *jours feriés*, or French national holidays, buses do not run, banks, museums, many shops and some restaurants are closed.

1 January: New Year
Good Friday
Easter Monday (*Pâcques*)
1 May: May Day (*Fête du Travail*)
8 May: VE Day (*Victoire 1945*)
Ascension (*Ascension*)
White Monday (*Pentecôte*)
14 July: Bastille Day (*Fête Nationale*)
15 August: Assumption (*Assomption*)
1 November: All Saints (*Toussaint*)
11 November: Armistice (*Armistice 1918*)
25 December: Christmas (*Noël*)

If you know in advance that your stay will be longer tha 3 months, you should enquire at the French Consulate before leaving home.

INSURANCE

It's sensible to take out good travel insurance (available from a local travel agent or from airports before departure) which will cover the cost of dealing with emergencies, lost valuables and so on. It usually covers medical expenses too, but see **Health** below. It goes without saying that whatever policy you choose, do pick your way through the small print to ensure you've got what you need.

HEALTH

No inoculations are required for France. All EEC citizens may take advantage of each other's health service, so while in France, Britons are entitled to the same medical attention as a French citizen as long as they have form E1.11. Good news you might think – but under the French social security system, everything has to be paid for, right down to the ambulance ride to the hospital. In France you can get a refund of about 70–75% of the medicinal costs. The DHSS in Great Britain advises travellers to take out a fully comprehensive insurance policy to cover all medical costs (see above) rather than simply relying on form E1.11. Nevertheless, British nationals before leaving their country should get hold of a CM-1 form from the Department of Health and Social Security – it's on the back of leaflet 8A28/30 *Medical Treatment During Visits Abroad*. Having returned your completed form, you then receive an E1.11 (or E1.12 if you're already in treatment).

Should you need to see a doctor while in France, you pay your bill and obtain a receipt or *feuille de soins*. At the pharmacy, if you've been given a prescription, you'll receive little stickers or *vignettes* which you must then apply to your *feuille de soins*. Post this with your prescription and E1.11 form to a French Sickness Insurance Office (*Caisse Primarie d'Assurance Maladie*) as listed in the telephone book under *Securité Sociale*. There's little point in taking it in person as

on-the-spot payments and procuring your refund
ugh patience to put up with the bureaucratic
s of the French social security system. However,
being well, you should get the refund (approx. 70%) for
medical expenses within 6−8 weeks. There's one snag, in that
if you post off your E1.11 you won't be able to visit a doctor
again under the insurance scheme. Wise then to take a note
of the Caisse Primaire's address and keep the documents until
the end of your stay.

All other nationals should check before departure to see
whether their country has reciprocal health arrangements with
France.

For more information see the section on medical attention
in **When in Paris**, p. 32.

MONEY

Cash

The French unit of currency is the Franc (f) divided into 100
centimes (c); bank notes in circulation (they increase in size
according to their value): 20f, 50f, 100f, 500f; coins: 5c, 10c,
20c, and 1/2f, 1f, 2f, 5f and 10f.

There's no limit to the amount of currency you can bring
into France, but there are restrictions on the amount of francs
and foreign currency that can be taken out, unless the large
sums were declared on arrival.

If you find it hard going converting values in your head,
especially after a couple of glasses of wine, you could buy an
"x-changer" (from Boots or department stores, for around a
fiver) − it will tell you just how much you've spent in the
restaurant.

There are bureaux de change at all points of entry, but
it's always wise to buy a few French francs before leaving,
preferably in smaller denominations as small shops and taxis
may not be able to change large notes. Most banks throughout
the UK offer exchange facilities.

Traveller's cheques are the safest way of carrying money
and they can always be replaced if lost or stolen − keep a
separate note of the serial numbers and the number to call in
emergencies. They're available from any British bank, branch

of American Express or Thomas Cook for a small commission and are widely recognised.

Eurocheques are an alternative for British citizens and other Europeans. Backed up with a Eurocheque Encashment Card, they may be used like an ordinary cheque book for settling bills. International Giro cheques from main British post offices work in a similar way to ordinary bank cheques except that they're cashed through post offices.

Credit Cards
Major international credit cards – Visa (known in France as Carte Bleue), Eurocard (Master Card), American Express, Diner's Club – are widely accepted, but don't take it for granted, as some smaller establishments may not take them.

It's an idea to insure yourself against loss of your cards. Credit Card Sentinel, Tel. 0705 472234, have insurance cover specifically for charge cards. They'll replace lost cards and advance £400 in cash (interest free) if your money has been taken with your cards.

The main numbers in Paris for reporting loss of credit cards are as follows:

American Express	Tel. 47 77 72 00
Diner's Club	Tel. 47 62 75 00
Eurocard/Master Card	Tel. 43 23 46 46
Visa/Carte Bleue	Tel. 42 77 11 90

NB: You should also report the loss to the nearest police station and get a written statement from them to support the claim.

GETTING THERE

BY AIR

Flying time from London is just over an hour (around 40 minutes actually in the air), from New York 7 hours. There are flights to Paris from most parts of the world and major cities in the States.

Scheduled services from Heathrow to Paris operated by British Airways/Air France run almost hourly. Air France planes also depart from Gatwick; both Air France and Air UK (Tel. 0345 666777) operate flights to Stanstead. Brymon Airways (Tel. 0345 090000) fly from London City Airport in Docklands and from Bristol. Add to that list the departures from other UK provincial airports (Aberdeen, Birmingham, Bristol, Cardiff, Edinburgh, Glasgow, Manchester, Newcastle and Southampton) and charter services and you'll see there's bags of choice.

British Airways, Tel. 081 897 4000 (London), 47 78 14 14 (Paris); Air France Tel. 071 499 9511 (London), 42 99 23 64 (Paris); Jersey European (Tel. 0345 078400) fly from Bournemouth, Exeter, Guernsey and Jersey; British Independent (Tel. 0679 21633) operate a coach/air service from London via Lydd in Kent; Dan Air (Tel. 0293 820700) fly from Gatwick; British Midland (Tel. 0332 810552/071 589 5599) fly from Heathrow and East Midlands.

Special offers on flights change all the time and it's a good idea to shop around, checking what's available in the classified travel sections of the quality Sundays. The weekly listings guide, *Time Out*, and the *Evening Standard* will also provide Londoners with good leads.

Some flight deals seem to be widely available almost any time and savings can be made on the regular fare by choosing a charter or a Superpex/Late Saver scheduled flight on British Airways/Air France. Advice and up-to-date prices can be obtained from STA Travel, 86 Old Brompton Road, London SW7, tel. 071 937 9921 or from Nouvelles Frontières, 1–2 Hanover Street, London W1, tel. 071 629 7772. STA Travel has 20 offices round the UK. Students represent 50% of their business but STA do not sell to students alone, catering rather for the independent traveller.

If you live outside London you might find it more cost effective to travel to London and fly from there, but don't let this deter you from checking for local departure bargains.

The Airline Advisory Board, Morley House, 320 Regent Street, London W1, tel. 071 636 5000 or at 59 Royal Exchange, Manchester, tel. 061832 2000, give free information regarding agents who offer cheap flights worldwide from the UK or Ireland. They can save you countless phone calls by investigating flight deals for you.

BY RAIL

Trains depart daily from London's Victoria Station (to connect with boats or hovercrafts) or from Charing Cross (to link with hovercrafts) and arrive at the Gare du Nord in Paris between 6 and 10 hours later, depending on how you've made the sea crossing.

The fare structure depends on when you go, how long you're staying and whether you qualify for reduced rates – which you do if you're young enough, a student or a senior citizen. Students and those under 26 can make big savings by buying BIGE tickets from travel agents and British Rail Centres, Eurotrain and most of the student travel agents whose addresses are given above.

The hovercrafts cross the Channel from Dover to Boulogne, with special fares for those eligible for concessions, as well as 5 day excursions. Ferry crossings are made from Dover or Folkestone to Calais or Boulogne. Fast trains (about 2 hours from Calais or Boulogne) then whisk you to Paris where you'll arrive at the Gare du Nord.

For more information contact British Rail International, Tel. 071 834 2345 (24 hours a day). Eurotrain, 52 Grosvenor Gardens, London SW1W 0AG, Tel. 071 730 8518. Credit card reservations are accepted by telephone on 071 834 2345 or in person at a British Rail Travel Centre.

BY BUS

The cheapest way of getting to Paris, with a sea crossing either by ferry, hovercraft or tunnel. Hoverspeed, Maybrook House, Queen's Gardens, Dover, Kent, CT17 9UQ, Tel. 0804 240241, operate a year-round daytime "Sprint Service", departing from Victoria Coach Station, crossing at Dover to Calais/Boulogne. Bookings and details of fares from travel agents, or call Hoverspeed. There are concessions for under 18s or under 26s in full-time education, children and under 14s.

For more details of daily departures of coach and ferry

options contact Euroways Eurolines at Victoria Coach Station, 52 Grosvenor Gardens, London SW1W 0AU, Tel. 071 730 0202/071 730 8235. You can choose between day or night travel. Journey time is approximately 8 hours. Again there are student/youth concessions. The journey is slower than by hovercraft due to the longer crossing time.

Eurolines and Hoverspeed "Sprint Service" are bookable in person at any National Express office or at the Coach Travel Centre, 13 Regent Street, London SW1 4LR. Credit card reservations on 071 824 8657.

BY CAR

Numerous car ferry services cross the Channel, the most popular links for Paris-bound motorists or hitchhikers being Dover-Calais/Boulogne, Folkestone-Boulogne or Ramsgate-Dunkerque. The Dover-Calais route includes the shortest Channel crossing (1 hour 15 minutes by ferry, 35 minutes by hovercraft), then driving time from the port is around 3 hours on the toll road, the A1 autoroute; about an hour longer on the toll-free N1.

Driving Do's

France-bound UK motorists need to have:

- a valid national (or international) driving licence. Drivers' licences issued in the USA and Canada are valid in France.

- International Green Card insurance (from any insurance company) which must be signed by the policy holder.

- nationality plate/sticker.

- first aid kit.

- warning lights and/or a red warning triangle.

- seat belts.

- headlamps properly adjusted and either fitted with yellow discs or painted yellow.

- Remember to take some French currency for the toll roads (*péages.*)

The longer Newhaven-Dieppe crossing (4 hours) involves a shorter drive through France and might be more convenient, depending on where you live.

Some Ferry Crossings

Dover-Calais	*P&O European Ferries*, Channel House, Channel View Road, Dover, Kent CT17 9TJ. Tel. 0304 223000. 75-minute crossing approx. Up to 15 sailings daily.
	Sealink British Ferries, Charter House, Park Street, Ashford, Kent TN24 8EX. Tel. 0233 47022. 90-minute crossing approx. Up to 18 sailings daily.
	Hoverspeed, Maybrook House, Queen's Gardens, Dover, Kent CT17 9UQ. Tel. 0304 240202. 35-minute crossing approx (by hovercraft). Up to 23 crossings a day.
Dover-Boulogne	*P&O European Ferries* 100-minute crossing approx. Up to six sailings a day.
	Hoverspeed 40-minute crossing. Up to six sailings a day.
Ramsgate-Dunkerque	*Sally Line*, Argyle Centre, York Street, Ramsgate, Kent CT11 9DS. Tel. 0843 595522. 2-hour crossing. Up to five crossings a day.
Newhaven-Dieppe	*Sealink Dieppe Ferries* 4-hour crossing. Up to four sailings a day.
Portsmouth-Le Havre	*P&O European Ferries* 5-hour crossing. Up to three sailings a day.

Other crossings you may wish to investigate, depending on

where you're starting your journey from include: Weymouth-Cherbourg (Sealink: 3 hours 55 mins); Portsmouth-Caen (Brittany Ferries: 5 hours 45 minutes. Tel. 0705–827701); Poole-Cherbourg (Brittany Ferries: 4 hours); Plymouth-Roscoff (Brittany Ferries: 6 hours. Tel. 0752–21321); Felixstowe-Zeebrugge (P&O European Ferries: 2 hours 55 mins); Portsmsouth-Cherbourg (Sealink, P&O European Ferries: 4 hours 45 mins).

HITCHING

Hitching to Paris is no easy option, especially during peak holiday periods, and when you take a closer look at the cheap coach fares around you might think it not worth all the hassle. If you're determined to do it, the usual rules of thumb apply. Look clean and respectable. Stay alert. Travel light and keep your luggage with you. If you're female, don't hitch alone. If you feel at all nervous about the lift, don't get in – or if it's too late for that, get out at the first chance you have. Always pick a place where a driver can stop easily and safely. Hitching is forbidden by law on motorways. Carrying a destination sign may be helpful. You can always try to negotiate your ride on the ferry/hovercraft or at a service station to gain an advantage.

Hitching out of Paris is a pain, with much competition for lifts on the motorway slip roads. You can try and miss out on this depressing experience by taking a local bus/train out to Montmorency.

Alternatively, you might be able to link up with a hitching companion or find a ride by vetting message boards in student travel offices or other student hangouts, or follow the example of many French students and contact Allôstop, 84 passage Brady, 75010 Paris, Tel. 47 70 02 01; 42 46 00 66 for departures from Paris. This hitching organisation, with offices in many major cities, links up riders with drivers to share expenses for a small introduction charge. Try to ring or write a few days in advance and enquire about annual subscription rates if you're a frequent traveller.

ARRIVAL

TRAVELLING FROM THE AIRPORTS

There are several ways of reaching central Paris from the two airports. Below we outline the possibilities and pick out our recommended option, although you may settle for a different one depending on your ultimate destination.

Charles de Gaulle/Roissy

Airport is 16 miles (26km) to the north-east of the city. Telephone number for airport information 48 62 22 80; for lost baggage 48 62 12 12.

Recommended route into Paris: easiest and quickest is Roissy-Rail, a bus-rail link. Courtesy buses shuttle (look for the word *navette* which means shuttle) between the two terminal buildings and the Roissy Aeroport RER station where they connect with RER Ligne B suburban express train to the Gare du Nord. Trains leave for town every 15 minutes from 5.30am–11.30pm and journey time is roughly 35 minutes.

Buses operated by Air France run every 12 minutes from 5.45am–11pm between the airport and the Air France terminal at Porte Maillot (where you can pick up the Métro) half a mile west of the Arc de Triomphe and handy if you happen to be staying in the 16e or 17e. Journey time is an optimum 45 minutes but traffic snarl-ups can and frequently do cause delays. Other services run by the RATP (*Réseau Autonome du Transport Parisien*) from the airport, including the 350 to the Gare du Nord and Gare de L'Est (which leaves every 15 minutes from 6am–11pm) and the 351 to place de la Nation, which leaves every 30 minutes from 6am–11pm, tend to be slow and quite expensive.

Orly

Located 12 miles (20km) to the south of the city. Telephone number for airport information: 48 84 52 52; for lost baggage 46 75 40 38.

Recommended route into Paris: easiest and quickest is,

once again, the bus-rail combination. Orly-Rail consists of free shuttle buses from the two terminals, Orly-Sud and Orly-Ouest, to pick up the RER Ligne C train to the Gare d'Austerlitz and other left bank stations which in turn connect with the Métro. There are train departures every 12–15 minutes from 5.30am–11.30pm and the journey time is approximately 30 minutes.

Buses operated by Air France go to Les Invalides Air France terminal in the 7e, leaving every 12 minutes from 5.50am–11pm. Traffic conditions dramatically affect journey time which takes between 40 minutes and an hour. The Orly bus leaves every 15 minutes and stops at Denfert-Rochereau in the 14e, but the journey is also likely to be slow (up to an hour) as is the public bus 215, also to Denfert-Rochereau, which leaves every 10 minutes from 6.05am–11pm.

Taxis may easily be picked up at both airports and are tempting propositions at the end of a journey. However the ride will be costly (around 200f from Charles de Gaulle, less from Orly – about 120f – plus luggage supplements) and will probably not be any quicker than using one of the services

---

Airline Information

Flight information is only available during normal working hours. Outside business hours, telephone the airport.

	Tel.	
Aer Lingus		42 66 93 61
Air Canada		42 20 12 00
Air France		45 35 61 61
Air Inter		45 39 25 25
Air UK		42 56 11 93
Alitalia		40 15 00 21
American		42 89 05 22
British Airways		47 78 14 14
Canadian		49 53 07 07
EL AL		47 42 41 29
Iberia		47 23 00 23
Lufthansa		42 65 37 35
Pan Am		42 66 45 45
Quantas		42 66 53 05
Sabena		47 42 47 47
Swissair		45 81 11 01
TWA		47 20 62 11

mentioned above. From Charles de Gaulle the journey will take at least 45–50 minutes, about 30 minutes longer and more francs during rush hour, while Orly is roughly a 30–40 minute ride.

ARRIVING BY TRAIN

Trains from the Channel ports of Calais and Boulogne arrive at the Gare du Nord; those from Dieppe at the Gare St Lazare. Railway stations can be disorientating at the best of times and for the travel-weary the following tips might be useful:

- Hopefully you'll have a few francs in your pocket by this stage of your journey, but if not, you'll find a *bureau de change* at the train station where you can cash some money. You'll probably get a better exchange rate at one of the large banks though, so it's not worth changing a lot of money. Bureaux de change are open from 8am–9pm at railway stations, daily at the Gare de Lyon and Gare du Nord, but closed on Sunday at the Gare Saint Lazare and Austerlitz.

- All mainline stations are served by several Métro lines, so by studying the map and explanatory section **Getting Around** pp. 49–64 you should be able to make your way to your destination. Remember that at railway stations, airports and major Métro stations you can buy *Paris Visite* or *Carte Orange* cards (see **Getting Around**) and start saving money instantly.

- If you're really weighed down by bags, take a taxi from the ranks you'll find outside all stations/terminals. (See advice on taxis on p. 55 and tipping on p. 36.) If you're feeling too fagged out to force yourself to speak French you can always write your destination on a piece of paper for the driver.

- If you're not completely wiped out by your journey think about stashing your bags in the *consigne* or left luggage (a large locker costs up to 10f or you can check them in) and then have a short wander round the area or collapse in a café. By avoiding the tempting little place slap opposite the station, you'll save yourself some money as prices will invariably be lower a street or two away.

• Save yourself energy and the fixed charge of 7.50f per bag levied by the porters by grabbing yourself a free luggage cart.

Hôtesses de Paris

You'll find multi-lingual *hôtesses de Paris* at the main railway stations who'll provide a clear map, directions, advice on how to use the telephone, the Métro (although you could always read the relevant section in this book for that kind of info, see pp. 48–63) or, for those unwise enough not to have sorted something out before leaving, they'll track down accommodation. Admittedly, they're not interested so much in finding you a room in a place of your specific choice (on the grounds that if you've singled somewhere out you can get on with booking it) but they will ring – for a small fee – relentlessly round until they've tucked you up in a place in your price range. It may not be the best value to be found but it'll do until you can sort yourself out. The *hôtesses de Paris* work for the Office du Tourisme de Paris whose railway branches are listed below:

Gare d'Austerlitz (arrival hall)	*Mon–Sat, 8am–3pm*
Terminal for trains from	*(10pm Easter –*
south-west France	*Nov 1)*
Tel. 45 84 91 70	
Gare de L'Est (departure hall)	*Mon–Sat, 8am–1pm,*
Terminal for trains from eastern	*5–8pm (10pm*
France	*Easter – Nov 1)*
Tel. 46 07 17 73	
Gare de Lyon (arrival hall)	*Mon–Sat, 8am–1pm,*
Terminal for trains from	*5–8pm (10pm Easter –*
south-east France	*Nov 1)*
Tel. 43 43 33 24	
Gare du Nord (mainline hall)	*Mon–Sat 8am–8pm*
Terminal for trains from northern	*(10pm Easter –*
France	*Nov 1), 1–8pm Sun*
Tel. 45 26 94 82	

You can pick up maps, leaflets, details of sightseeing tours, a list of hotels and restaurants listed by *arrondissement* and so on, from these offices.

Youth Accommodation at the Gare du Nord
There's always competition to get a clean, safe bed in a youth centre and to get a place in the Acceuil des Jeunes en France centre (AJF) at the Gare du Nord you'll need to present yourself at the office as early as possible and even be prepared to queue. The AJF Gare du Nord office is inside the Gare Banlieu, the suburban station, Tel. 42 85 86 19, and open Mon–Fri, 9.30am–7pm, from May–September.

ARRIVING BY BUS

You may well find your journey ending at the main *gare routière* in place Stalingrad where the Métro will whisk you into the centre. For details of coach departures ring VIA International on 42 05 12 10.

ARRIVING BY CAR

Circle the *périphérique* or ring road until you reach the exit or *porte* nearest to your final destination rather than attempting to cross Paris to get to it.

CUSTOMS/DUTY FREE ALLOWANCES

Passing through customs is usually uneventful, unless you resemble someone they're after or they pick you out at random to check your bags and baggage, leaving you to rearrange your packing. France takes a tough line when it comes to the import of narcotics. Penalties are severe, invariably involving heavy fines and imprisonment. Other prohibited and restricted goods include contraband, firearms (except for hunting guns with permits), pornography, explosives. Some guide books tell you to carry dated receipts for any valuable items you have with you (cameras, watches) to avoid any chance of your being charged duty on your return – fine if you can get yourself organised, but if not, and customs officials do pick on you,

you'll usually be given a certain length of time to provide proof of purchase. Do familiarise yourself with your duty free allowances – all of which apply to travellers over 17 years of age. Those returning to Britain from France, or any EEC country, are allowed to bring goods in these amounts purchased in France: 300 cigarettes, 75 cigars or 400 grams of pipe tobacco, 3 litres of wine, 1 litre of spirits, and other goods to the value of £35. If you made your purchases at a duty free shop, customs allowances are less – check on the spot.

WHEN IN PARIS

TOURIST INFORMATION

The main tourist office in Paris is at 127 avenue des Champs-Élysées 75008. Tel. 47 23 61 72. It's open every day except 25 December and 1 January from 9am–8pm. Don't take it personally if the staff seem brusque towards the end of the day – they work unbelievably hard dealing efficiently with every enquiry, no matter how asinine.

In addition to the Champs-Élysées office there are branches at the four principal railway terminii (Austerlitz, Est, Lyon and Nord) and from May–September, 11am–6pm, at the Eiffel Tower, Champs de Mars 75007. Tel. 45 51 22 15.

Recorded tourist information (in English) 24 hours a day is available on 47 20 88 98, with suggestions of things to do and see in Paris.

American Express Travel Service, 11 rue Scribe 75009. Tel. 42 66 09 99. For advice, help or emergency services.

MAPS

More detailed than any of the *plans* you get for free on request at Métro stations, highly recommended is the clear Michelin *Atlas Paris par arrondissements* with a street index, bus routes and so on. It also covers the outskirts. Though lightweight it's hardly pocket-sized. The excellent Michelin map 10, the *Plan de Paris*, is hopeless on windy street corners but otherwise sound. If you're staying for more than a few days, the A-Z, *Paris-Éclair* is a worthwhile investment. *Paris Éclair* has a pull-out environs of Paris map, though if you're going to need more detail, the Michelin No. 196 map *Environs de Paris* will be useful, or there are four separate *Banlieue de Paris* maps 18, 20, 22 and 24 covering the north west, north-east, south-west and south-east of the city respectively.

French bookshops and stationers stock street maps. In England you could try the French Bookshop, 28 Bute Street, London SW7. Tel. 071 584 2840.

BANKS/CHANGING MONEY

Banks are generally open on weekdays from 9am till noon and 2–4.30pm, but there are no standardised banking hours. All close on the afternoon before a Bank Holiday.

Not all French banks have exchange facilities. Some bureaux de change may be temptingly located in or close to airports, railway stations or hotels and they stay open late and at weekends, but do check their exchange rates/commission charged – they may be OK for survival money, but you'll probably get a better deal at one of the large commercial banks. Larger hotels will also change money but, once again, the rate won't be as good.

The following agencies take no commission:

Europullman: 10 rue d'Alger 75001. Tel. 42 60 55 58. Open 9am–7pm, Mon–Sat.

Société Générale de Change: 112 rue de Richelieu 75002. Tel. 42 96 56 13. Open 9am–6pm, Mon–Fri

Barclays: 33 rue 4 Septembre 75002. Tel. 42 66 65 31. No charge for cashing Barclays' travellers cheques here. Phone for opening hours.

International Westminster Bank: 18 place Vendôme 75001. Tel. 42 60 37 40, for details of opening hours.

Lloyds: 43 blvd des Capucines 75002. Tel. 42 61 51 25 for opening hours.

Midland 6 rue Piccini 75016. Tel. 45 02 80 80 for opening hours.

American Express 11 rue Scribe 75009. Tel. 42 66 09 99 for opening hours.

Metric Equivalents

Distance/Length

1 inch	25.4 millimetres
1 foot	30.5 centimetres
1 yard	0.9 metres
1 mile	1.6 kilometres
1 millimetre	0.03 inches
1 centimetre	0.03 feet
1 metre	1.09 yards
1 kilometre	0.62 miles

Driving Speeds

10	20	30	40	50	60	70	80	90	100 m.p.h.
16	32	48	64	80	96	112	128	144	160 k.p.h.

Tyre Pressures

Pounds per square inch	Kilogrammes per square centimetre
10	0.7
20	1.4
25	1.7
30	2.1
35	2.4
40	2.8

Weight

1 ounce	28 grammes
1 pound	0.45 kilogrammes
1 stone	6.4 kilogrammes
1 ton	1.02 tonnes
1 gramme	0.04 ounces
1 kilogramme	2.2 lbs
1 kilogramme	0.16 stone
1 tonne	10.98 tons

Volume

1 pint	0.57 litres
1 gallon	4.55 litres
1 litre	1.76 pints
1 litre	0.22 gallons

Temperatures

Celsius	Fahrenheit
10	50
15	59
20	68
25	77
30	86
35	95

Chase Manhattan Bank 18 boulevard Malesherbes, 75008, Tel. 40 17 13 00 for opening hours.

Banks offering exchange facilities at competitive rates with branches throughout Paris include BNP (Banque Nationale de Paris), Credit Agricole, Credit Lyonnais and Banco Central.

● Rates of exchange and commission levied vary from bank to bank.

● You need your passport when changing money.

● Cheques backed by a Eurocheque Encashment Card can be cashed at all banks displaying the sign.

Where to Change Money at Weekends
CCF: 115 avenue des Champs-Élysées 75008. (Open 9am–8pm, Mon–Sat)
UBP: 154 Champs-Élysées 75008 (Open 9am–5pm, Sat; 10.30am–6pm, Sun)
CIC: Gare de Lyon (Open 6.30–9pm daily)
CIC: Georges Pompidou Centre (Open 12–7pm, Mon–Fri; 10am–7pm Sat–Sun. Closed Tuesday)

OPENING HOURS

Standard shop opening hours in Paris are from around 9 or 10 in the morning until 6.30–7 in the evening. They're generally closed on Sunday and sometimes on Mondays too. You might well find shops and businesses closed for lunch for an hour or more between 12 and 2pm.

National Museums mostly shut on Tuesdays, except Versailles and the Musée d'Orsay which close on Mondays.

Churches are generally open from around 8am until 6pm or 7pm though some close at lunchtime or earlier in winter. Regional châteaux often close from October–May.

The annual holidays can bring complete closure for 4 weeks around July–August.

ELECTRIC CURRENT

This is 220V (50 cycles AC). Plugs are two-pin, round. Standard European Adaptors (*transformateurs*) can be bought either before you leave home or in Parisian general department stores.

TIPS/SERVICE CHARGE

The words *service compris* will tell you that service has been included, but here's a general guide to who expects what, as tipping is still widely practised in France.

Bars/Cafés: see restaurants below. 15% is included for table service in the prices. At the counter leave some change in the saucer on the bar.

Restaurants: service (at 15%) is normally *compris* but where it isn't included in the prices (*service non compris*) they'll add it on to the bottom of your bill for you. If the service has been particularly brilliant, you can show your appreciation by leaving a small extra tip for the waiter.

Hotels: service is added automatically but you should tip anyone else who has helped out (carrying luggage, getting taxis).

Cloakroom Attendants: 1–2f.

Porters/Left Luggage: set price – per piece of luggage. No tip necessary.

"Savoir Faire"

While the younger generation are a law unto themselves, older Parisians as a whole tend to be extremely conscious of good manners. The use of *tu* and *vous* immediately makes a statement of the degree of intimacy in the relationship. (The rule is never use the former form unless you're a member of the family or a very close friend.) Parisians like shaking hands – briefly, but always once the acquaintance has been established. Close friends kiss each other on alternate cheeks a couple of times. It'll help you to bridge the Parisian distance by adopting safe forms of *politesse* – remembering the *s'il vous plaîts and excusez-mois*, and when addressing someone, adding "*Madame/Mademoiselle/Monsieur*" without using a surname.

Even the stoniest Parisians warm up after a compliment, so if you're having a nice time, enjoying a meal, your accommodation, their city, no matter how clumsily you express it, the sentiment's bound to be appreciated.

Taxis: 10–15%.

Hairdressers: 10–15% depending on how pleased you are with what they've done.

Theatre and Cinema Ushers/Tour Guides: if for the cinema and theatre, 1–2f per person.

TOILETS

All but a few of the old urinals or *pissoirs* have been replaced by sanitised unisex booths which take a couple of francs and flush with a vengeance. Other mod cons are found in many Métro stations and public parks.

Toilet paper in the more low-rent bars or restaurants may be as rough and unbearable as brown paper – if you're lucky enough to get any at all, so be warned.

In hotels, stores and other loos where there's an attendant, you're expected to tip.

POSTAL SERVICE

If it's stamps you want you can buy them from *tabacs* indicated by the "T" sign as well as from post offices (*bureaux de poste*). If you're posting a letter abroad and there is more than one opening, look for one labelled *départements étrangers*.

Post offices are open from 8am–7pm, Monday–Friday and from 8am–noon on Saturday – all are listed in the phone book, under *Administration des PTT* in the Yellow Pages and under *poste* in the White Pages.

The main post office, open 24 hours a day for Poste Restante and telephones, is at 52 rue du Louvre 75001. If you have mail sent here you'll need to show a passport or similarly credible identification when you collect it and there'll be a small charge. (An alternative *poste restante* service is provided by American Express, 11 rue Scribe 75009.)

The post office at 71 avenue des Champs-Élysées 75008, Tel. 43 35 60 00, has extended opening hours – until 11.30pm weekdays, on Saturday it's open from noon until 11pm, and on Sunday from 2–8pm.

HOSPITALS

See telephone directory (White Pages) for listings under *Hôpital Assistance Publique* or ring 40 27 30 00. All have an emergency section open 24 hours a day. You will usually be able to find someone who speaks English, but virtually all members of staff speak English at the following hospitals, both of which offer a 24 hour service year-round.

The Hertford British Hospital: 3 rue Barbes, Levallois-Perrett. Tel. 47 58 13 12.

Medical treatment only (telephone first for an appointment). No dental care.

American Hospital: 63 boulevard Victor-Hugo, Neuilly. Tel. 47 47 53 00 or 47 45 71 00.

Telephone first for an appointment. Emergency treatment only on Sundays – no appointments. Dental as well as medical care.

CHEMISTS

Should you need to obtain a prescription or buy something for a minor ailment there are a number of chemists or *pharmacies* used to dealing with tourists. They are well stocked with English and American brands of medication and have English speaking staff. These include:

Pharmacie Anglaise des Champs-Élysées: 62 avenue de Champs-Élysées 75008. Tel. 43 59 22 52 and 42 25 25 13 Open 8.30am–10.30pm, Mon–Sat, Closed Sunday

British American Pharmacy: 1 rue Auber 75009. Tel. 47 42 49 40 Open 9am–8pm, Mon–Sat. Closed Sunday

Pharmacie Anglo-Americaine 6 rue Castiglione 75001. Tel.42 60 72 96 Open 9am–7.30pm, Mon–Sat.

Pharmacie des Arts 106 boulevard Montparnasse 75014. Tel. 43 25 44 88 Open 8.30am–midnight, Mon–Sat; 9am–1pm, Sun and Public Holidays.

Pharmacie des Champs-Élysées, 84 avenue des Champs-Élysées, 75008. Tel. 45 62 02 41 Open 24 hours a day, seven days a week. Very small but handy in emergencies with multi-lingual staff.

Pharmacie le Drugstore, boulevard St Germain (corner of rue

de Rennes) 75006. Tel. 45 48 04 55. Open 10am–2am,
daily.

DENTAL CARE

A complete list of practitioners is found in the telephone
directory (look under *"chirurgiens dentistes"*). To obtain
your social security refund do make sure you choose one
registered with the National Health. In an emergency you
could contact Urgences Dentaires on 47 07 44 44, any time
day or night for an appointment to see them at 9 boulevard
St Marcel 750013.

MEDICAL EMERGENCIES

For Paris's 24-hour service Tel. 45 67 60 50 or 47 07 77 77,
or for SOS Médicin (24 hrs) 43 37 77 77. House calls only;
fees from 150f. Specialist medical help listed below.

AIDS Hotline (SIDA AD) – Free advice on 45 82 93 39 from
9am–5pm, Mon–Fri; 9am–12 noon, Sat.

Alcoholics Anonymous – Tel. 46 34 59 65. Daily meetings.
English spoken.

Burns/Children – Hôpital de l'Assistance Publique Trousseau, 26 avenue Dr Arnold Netter 75012. Tel. 42 05 63
29.

Burn Centre (24 hours emergency number) – Tel. 42 34 17
58.

Dog Bites – **Institut Pasteur**, 213 rue de Vaugirard 75015. Tel.
45 67 35 09.

Drugs – Hôpital Marmottan, 19 rue d'Armaillé 75017.
Tel. 45 74 00 04.

Enfance et Partage (Hotline for kids in trouble, 24 hours) –
Tel. 45 05 12 34.

Hand Injuries – Hôpital Boucicaut, 78 rue de la Convention,
75015. Tel. 45 54 92 92. Or CHU Bichat (a University
hospital), 46 rue Henri Hûchard 75018. Tel. 40 25 80 80.
Both have emergency hand injury help.

SOS Handicap – Tel. 47 41 32 32. Medical help strictly for
the handicapped.

HIV Testing – **Centro Medico-Social**, 218 rue de Belleville

75020. Tel. 47 97 40 49. Open 5–7.30pm, Mon–Fri; 9.30am–12 noon Sat; 3–5 rue de Ridder 75014. Tel. 45 43 83 78. Open noon–8pm, Mon–Fri; 9.30am–12.30pm. Free, anonymous service.

Mouth Injuries/Ailments – 24-hour emergency help. Hôtel-Dieu, place de Parvis Notre Dame 75004. Tel. 42 34 80 36, 8am–11pm and 42 34 83 69 11pm–8am.

Emergencies

Police – Tel. 17.

Ambulance – Tel. 43 78 26 26.

Fire – Tel. 18.

Hospitals – See separate entry, p. 36.

All night chemist – See separate entry (p. 37) or call the *mairie* of the *arrondissement* where you're staying to find out where the nearest *pharmacie de garde* (all-night chemist) is.

Lost passport – Inform the police and your consulate at once.

Lost traveller's cheques – Contact the local police straight away and then consult the instructions accompanying your traveller's cheques or get in touch with the issuing company. If you're left with no money, contact your Consulate.

SOS Help – English crisis hotline. Tel. 47 23 80 80. Open daily 3–11pm

Legal Advice – Avocat Assistance et Recours du Consommateur, 15 place du Pont Neuf 75001, Paris. Tel. 43 54 32. 04. Open 2–6pm, Mon–Fri. Minimal fees are charged by lawyers here – around 180f for a consultation.

Palais de Justice, Galerie de Harlay, Escalier S, 4 blvd du Palais 75004. Tel. 46 34 12 34. Open 9.30am–noon, Mon–Fri. Free legal consultations but it gets busy so get there early to collect a numbered ticket.

For free legal advice over the phone, contact SOS Avocats on 43 29 33 00 between 7.30 and 11.30pm, Mon–Fri.

You can also get legal questions answered at town halls – ask for their *Consultations juridiques* – see the telephone directory under *mairies*.

Housing – Sous direction du logement, Tel. 427421 21, dish out free info on housing exchange, rents, financial assistance and so on.

Birth Control – The Mouvement Français pour le Planning Familial, 4 place St Irénée 75011, Tel. 48072910, also provides AIDS information. Open 9am–noon, 2–6pm, Mon–Fri.

Poisoning – Hôpital Fernand-Widal, 200 rue du Faubourg St Denis 75010. Tel. 42 05 63 29

Poison Centre (24 hours) – Tel. 40 37 04 04

Rape Crisis Hotline – Free call from anywhere in France. Tel. 05 05 95 95.

Sexually Transmitted Disease – Croix Rouge, 43 rue de Valois 75001. Tel. 42 61 30 04 and 35 rue Claude-Terrasse 75016. Tel. 42 88 33 42. Institut Vernes, 30 rue d'Assa 75006. Tel. 45 44 38 94. Free consultations for all STD except HIV/AIDS. No appointments, so expect queues.

THE TELEPHONE

There are plenty of telephone kiosks around, in the street or at stations. The old coin-operated kind were so badly vandalised that you now need a plastic card, called a *Telecarte*, to use in public phones. You simply slip them into the slot and a digital display tells you how much credit is left. Buy them from post offices, *tabacs*, or ticket windows at SCNF or Métro stations.

There are often public phones in bars, cafés and brasseries where you may need a *jeton*, a token you buy over the counter, or there may be a meter and you settle up after making your call. Post offices may have both coin and card phones. Charges depend on when you're calling and the duration of the call. Local calls cost 1f for about 6 minutes, standard rate.

To Make International Calls

You can make these from any kiosk and receive them as well if there's a blue logo of a ringing bell and a clearly displayed telephone number. You can also call from some post offices where you pay afterwards.

Dial 19, wait for the low-pitched tone, then dial the country code as below. Omit the initial "0" from the UK number when you dial.

UK	44
Australia	61
New Zealand	64
USA/Canada	1
Ireland	353

Reduced rates to the UK/Ireland apply from 9.30pm–8am,

Telephone Services
Operator assistance, directory enquiries (in French): 12
International directory enquiries (24 hours): 19 33 12, followed by country code
Alarm calls (24 hours): dial 36 88. You'll be asked to dial your phone number and then the time you wish to be woken using the 24-hour clock, e.g. to get the alarm call at 6.30am, dial 0630
News: recorded international news in French (24 hours) 36 65 44 55
Traffic News (24 hours): 48 99 33 33
Weather (24 hours): recorded summary for Paris and region 36 65 02 02; recorded summary for throughout France 64 09 01 01; specific enquiries on worldwide weather (3–6pm, Mon–Fri) 45 56 71 71

Mon–Fri; from 2pm Saturday and all day Sunday/Public Holidays. Reduced rates to the USA/Canada apply from 2am – 12 noon, Mon–Fri. There's another cheap band from 12 noon–2pm and from 8pm–2am, Mon–Sat; from 12 noon–2am, Sunday and Public Holidays.

To Make Local Calls
Simply dial the number after inserting your card/money/*jeton*. The French ringing tone is a series of little regular bleeps.
NB: Paris phone numbers have eight digits and central Paris numbers begin with a 4; suburban ones might begin with a 3 or a 6.

To Make Calls to Within France but Outside Paris
Dial 16, wait for the low-pitched tone, then dial the eight-digit telephone number which begins with the area code.

To Call Paris from Outside the City
Precede the number you need with 161.
Phone Books are kept in all post offices. The White Pages run to three volumes and list names of people and businesses alphabetically, while the two volumes of Yellow Pages list businesses under category headings.

Telegrams

To send a telegram by phone, in English, call 42 33 21 11. Seven words are the minimum and the address counts as part of the message.

THE PRESS

Paris has no local papers as such, but useful publications listing current events, entertainment, sports fixtures and so on include the weekly *Pariscope* and *L'Official des Spectacles* or *7 Jours à Paris*. They're in French but this isn't too much of a hindrance as information is very clearly presented. You can pick up a free copy of the monthly *Paris Selection* magazine from the tourist office.

French newspapers tend to take themselves seriously, none more so than *Le Monde*, established in 1944 and the most respected paper in Paris. *Le Figaro* is older (1866), traditionally right-wing and stronger on fashion coverage. *France Soir* is supposedly an evening paper whose first edition appears in the morning, carries little hard news and much more feature/consumer affairs material. *Libération* or *Libe* is left of centre, independent and very fashionable. Originally founded by Jean-Paul Sartre in the early '70s, it has good arts coverage.

Published in the morning, the Communist party newspaper *L'Humanité* was founded before World War I by leading socialist Jean Jaurés; not surprisingly, it no longer enjoys the huge readership it once had. There are no Sunday papers so Parisians tend to pick up the weekend reading on Thursdays when the weekly news mags come out.

The *Nouvel Observateur* is a wide-ranging weekly magazine which leans to the left, while *Le Point* and its traditional rival *L'Expres* lean the other way. Trenchant investigative journalism is found in the satirical weekly *Le Canard Enchaîné*.

Comics in France are elevated to art status and enjoy a huge following. *A Suivre* is one to pick out amongst the many you'll see at the news-stands, some more adult in taste than others.

PARIS ON THE CHEAP

While life in Paris is more costly than in the French provinces, it needn't cost megabucks if you're careful. It depends of course on how comfortably you want to live and how much you want to do. Accommodation (especially youth hostels) and food can be found reasonably cheaply with economies made by picnicking, using takeaways, drinking your beers or coffee standing at the bar (a lot cheaper than sitting down). To some extent the area reflects what you pay. You're likely to find more for your money in the more studenty Latin Quarter (5e) than in the ultra chic 8e around the Champs-Élysées and Faubourg St Honoré. Equally, the 7e and 16e will tend to be more costly than the eastern Paris *arrondissements*, the less obvious touristy bits of Montmartre and the little streets off the beaten tourist track. Avoid bars/cafés on popular streets like the boulevard St Germain – back street bars are a better bet.

- If you're eligible for one, be sure to carry your International Student Card as it will get you into most places at reduced price and offer savings on public transport.

- If you're going to be travelling around the city a lot get a *Carte Orange* (see p. 54) as it gives a week's unlimited use of buses and metro. Or get a *carnet*: single tickets are never the most economical way to go if you plan to use the metro regularly.

- Admission fees to museums can gobble up the budget. If you don't have an ISIC card, serious sightseers should invest in a *Carte Intermusées* (see box below). Valid for 1, 3 or 5 days, they entitle you to free admission to over 60 Parisian museums and monuments – and there's no need to queue.

Buy it in advance from the tourist office or from Métro stations. Alternatively, join the Sunday line-up when many museums offer free admission.

Useful Cards
Students and younger travellers can get various discounts and services on production of recognized identification. The

---

Museum Pass

There's reduced price admission on production of ID at many Parisian museums for students and/or younger travellers, but if you don't have these credentials and intend to do some serious museumological exploring, consider buying a *Carte Intermusées*. Costing 50f for 1 day, 100f for 3 days, 150f for 5 days, the card gives you instant admission (no queuing up) at over 60 museums and monuments in and around the city. It can be purchased in advance from the Tourist Office or at Métro stations.

- Allo Musées on 42 76 66 00 is a telephone information line (in French) giving information about French museums.

---

benefits include cheaper fares, reduced price entry into movies, museums, galleries, use of student accommodation, etc. To take advantage of them get yourself one of the following. Some are available before you leave home, others when you're in France:

International Student Identity Card (ISIC): internationally-acknowledged verification of student status, though not the only form of student ID accepted in France. To get an ISIC, produce college ID plus a passport-sized photo at a STA office. It costs around a fiver.

Carte d'Étudiant: essentially a student card that you'll receive from the enrolment office if you're studying at a French college.

Carte Jeune: entitles under 25s to a 50% discount on rail fares between June–December. Turn up in person at the Centre d'Information et de Documentation Jeunesse (CIDJ) to buy your Carte Jeune at 101 quai Branly, 75015. Tel. 45 67 35 85. Mo Bir Hakeim/Champs de Mars. Open 9am–7pm, Mon–Fri; 10am–6pm Sat.

International Youth Hostel Card: international membership brings access to cheap hostel accommodation and meals. Obtained from and used in any STA travel office worldwide. You'll need to produce a passport photo, plus proof of your age to get reduced price membership, but there's no age limit to international YHA membership.

Youth International Education Exchange Cards (YIEE): issued to anyone under 26 by the Federation of International Youth Travel Organisations (FIYTO). Internationally recognised, the FIYTO/YIEE card opens up some 8000 price reductions throughout Europe. For more information, write to FIYTO, 81 Islands Brugge, DK-2300 Copenhagen, Denmark. Tel. 01 54 32 97. The FIYTO card is also issued by STA agencies all over Europe.

EMBASSIES AND CONSULATES

- Phone and check opening hours before you go; you may need to make an appointment.
- All close on French public holidays and those of their own country.
- For a complete list refer to White or Yellow Pages in the telephone directory, under *Ambassades et Consulars*.

Australia: 4 rue Jean Rey 75015, Tel. 40 59 33 00. Visa section, Tel. 40 59 33 07.

Austria: 12 rue Edmond Valentin 75007. Tel. 47 05 27 17.

Belgium: 9 rue de Tilsitt 75017. Tel. 43 80 61 00. Visa section 1 avenue Macmahon 75017. Tel. 42 27 45 35.

Canada: 35 avenue Montaigne 75008. Tel. 47 23 01 01. Visa section, Tel. 47 23 52 20.

Germany (West): 13/15 avenue F.D. Roosevelt, Tel. 42 99 78 00 Consulate: 34 avenue d'Iéna 75016. Tel. 42 99 79 57.

Ireland: 12 avenue Foch 75016. Tel. 45 00 20 87.

Netherlands: 7 rue Eble 75007. Tel. 43 06 61 88 Consulate: 9 rue Eble (same phone number as embassy).

New Zealand: 7 rue Leonard-de-Vinci 75016. Tel. 45 00 24 11.

Sweden: 17 rue Barbet-de-Jouy 75007. Tel. 45 55 92 15.

United Kingdom Embassy: 35 rue du Faubourg-St-Honoré 75008. Tel. 42 66 91 42. Consulate: 16 rue d'Anjou 75008. Tel. 42 66 38 10.

United States Embassy 2 avenue Gabriel 75008. Tel. 42 96 12 02 Consulate: 2 rue Saint Florentin 75001. Tel. 42 61 80 75.

LIBRARIES

American Library: 10 rue Général Camou 75007. Tel. 45 51 46 82. Primarily for American students. Take passport and photo for annual membership. Non-members can read in library for a daily fee of 30f. Also summer membership available.

Bibliothèque Publique d'Information: Beaubourg Centre, entrance via rue Renard 75004. Tel. 42 77 12 33. Extensive English language collection – but you'll need to hunt for novels in translation as they're arranged alphabetically.

British Council Library: 9–11 rue de Constantine 75007. Tel. 45 55 95 95. Collection of books originally published in Britain. One day consulting fee payable. Also tea-shop.

Documentation Française: 31 quai Voltaire 75007. Tel. 40 15 70 00. French government's central reference library. ID needed. Small fee payable.

Bibliothèque Mazarine: 23 quai de Conti 75006. Tel. 43 54 89 58. Join the scholars at work by getting a *carte d'entrée* for half a dozen visits – take a couple of photos and ID. Free to the public.

RELIGION

Churches and religious centres are in the telephone directory (see Yellow Pages under *Églises* and *Culte*).

The Religious Information Centre (CIDR), 8 rue Massillon 75004, Tel. 46 33 01 01, has details of religious activities of every faith, as well as concerts and meetings in Paris. English is spoken. Open from 9.30am–noon and 2–6 pm, Mon–Fri.

Anglican
American Cathedral: 23 avenue George V 75008. Tel. 47 20 17 92. Services 9am, 11am, Sunday.
Saint George's Church: 7 rue Auguste-Vacquerie 75016. Tel.

47 20 22 51. Services 8.30am, 10.30am (with the excellent choir) Sunday.

Saint Michael's English Church: 5 rue d'Aguesseau 75008. Tel. 47 42 70 88. Services 12.45pm Thur. 10.30am, 6.30pm Sun.

Buddhist
Temple Bouddhique: 40 rue de Ceinture du Lac Daumesnil 75012. Phone for details on 43 41 86 48.

Catholic
Cathédral de Notre Dame de Paris: 6 Parvis Notre Dame 75004. Tel. 43 26 07 39. Services 8am, 9am, noon, 6.10pm (6.30pm Sat), Mon–Sat. 8am, 8.45am, 10 am (sung mass), 11.30am, 12.30pm, 6.30pm Sun. Free concert 5.45pm Sun.

Sacré Coeur of Montmartre: 36 rue du Chevalier de la Barre 75018. Tel. 42 51 17 02. Services 7am, 8am, 9am, 10am, 11am, 6.30pm (6pm Sat), 10.15pm Mon–Sat 7am, 8am, 9am, 9.45am, 11am (sung mass), 11.30am, 12.30pm, 6pm, 10.15pm Sun.

Lost and Found

An incredible 10,000 wallets, keys, suitcases, jewellery, brief-cases, umbrellas, items of clothing and other *objets trouvés* find their way each month to the Préfecture de Police's lost property office in the 15e. There's a distinctly '40s ambience to the depot with its dark wood tables and heavy counters. Until recently, items were neatly labelled with handwritten tags before being stacked on the shelves of the Service des Objets Trouvés. Amongst the usual clobber there are also cameras, televisions, a glass eye and a human skull, affectionately called Arthur by his keepers. Now all details of stuff handed in is entered '90's-style on computer. Items are held for 4 months to a year depending on their value. Any still unclaimed after that are destroyed or sold to flea markets.

The Bureau des Objets Trouvés, 36 rue des Morillons 75015, is open from 8.30am–5pm Mon–Fri. Nearest Métro station is Convention. The phone number is 45 31 14 80 but they don't deal with enquiries by telephone — you have to turn up to fill out a form.

Jewish
Orthodox: 44 rue de la Victoire 75009. Tel. 45 26 95 36.
Reform: Union Liberale Israelite Synagogue (English Rabbi),
24 rue Copernic 75016. Tel. 47 04 37 27.

Moslem
Grande Mosquée: 39 rue Geoffroy-St-Hilaire 75005. Tel.
45 35 97 33. Service (Moslems only) Friday prayers
12.30pm.

Orthodox
Greek Cathedral of Saint-Étienne: 7 rue Georges Bizet 75016.
Tel. 47 20 82 35. Service 9.45am Sun.
Russian Cathedral Sainte Alexandre: 12 rue Daru 75008. Tel.
42 27 37 34. Services 6pm, Sat; 10.15am Sun.

Protestant
American Church in Paris: 65 quai d'Orsay 75007. Tel. 47 05
07 99. A community centre as well as a church whose notice
board is full of ads offering rides, or rooms in exchange
for work/teaching. After the 11 am interdenominational
services on Sunday there's a half hour coffee break and then
an informal hearty lunch at 12.30pm for around 30f for
students, 45f non-students. Also international counselling
service – ring 45 50 26 59.
Church of Scotland: 17 rue Bayard 75008. Tel. 47 20 90 49.
Service 10.30am Sun.

GETTING AROUND

Being a newcomer in any bustling capital city is ghastly,
initially, but Paris is a lot easier to get to know than most.
It's compact for a start and has an efficient, easy-to-grasp,
user-friendly public transport system.

The highly-efficient Métro (underground/subway) is one
of the best in the world, there's a spider's web of bus
routes that criss-cross the city and also a suburban express

train network (RER). The Métro and RER are run by the Paris Transport Authority or RATP (Réseau Autonome du Transport Parisiens). Tickets cover all the services and if you're going to be staying for a day or two you should consider buying a *carnet* (see box below **Tickets/Travel Passes**)

It goes without saying that a Métro map is essential – you'll find one in this book – but you might want to supplement it with a colour version, *un plan de* Métro, available at ticket-office windows. For a general description of the layout of the city, see the section on **Getting your Bearings**, p. 300.

MÉTRO

There are Métro stations in virtually every part of Paris to deposit you within easy walking distance of any attraction. No part of the city is more than 440 yards/400 metres from a Métro station and trains are far more frequent than, say, on the London Underground.

Each station is identified by a huge "M" at its entrance. Reassuringly, you're greeted by a map with the station's location circled to remind you where you're starting from. At larger ones there are electric maps – you push a button indicating your destination to illuminate the line or lines you wish to take. A few stations even have computerised route finders – key in the name of the street you need to get to and out spews a print-out to tell you the quickest ways of getting there, on foot or by public transport.

Lines on the Métro are designated by colours and numbers. Once underground, in order to navigate your way successfully, you simply need to know the appropriate terminus on the line you require, then take the Métro in that direction.

Information Phoneline

The RATP have an information phoneline, open 24 hours a day (in French only), giving advice on how best to get from A to B, plus all you need to know about passes and tickets. Tel. 43 46 14 14.

How to Use the Métro

- Each Métro line is known by its end stations. It's a good idea to work out your route in advance so you know which signs you need to follow.

- Validate your ticket by inserting it into the turnstile – an automatic punching machine. Reclaim it when it pops up and keep it with you until you leave the Métro, passing the point marked *Limite de Validité des Billets*. The Métro is regularly patrolled by *Contrôleurs* who may ask to see your ticket. If you have to change lines, follow the orange/white *correspondence* for connecting lines at the station junction. If you keep plodding single-mindedly in the direction of the appropriate terminal you can't go wrong.

- Trains begin running at 5.30am and the last stops around 1am.

- Trains run every day, but with reduced services on Sundays, holidays and later in the evening.

- Individual tickets are good for one trip, but that trip can take in the entire length and breadth of the Métro system, irrespective of how many changes you make.

- A single ticket costs 5.50f. Tickets are also valid for the bus.

- Smoking is not allowed on the Métro.

- Rather than buying an individual ticket each time you travel on the Métro, it's better value and more convenient for a short stay to purchase a *carnet* or booklet of ten single tickets at a reduced rate (34.50f). Better still, invest in one of the special tickets detailed below.

- The blue/white sign *Sortie* indicates the exit. The one saying *Accès aux Quais* points the way to the platforms.

- While the Parisian Métro is generally safe – violent crime being the exception rather than the rule – pickpockets are not uncommon, so watch out.

RER

Welded on to the Métro is the subterranean RER service, (Réseau Express Régional) first opened in 1969 to speed out to suburban areas, such as Versailles, as well as the airports. You can use the same tickets as on buses or the Métro within the city limits. Outside the metropolitan area RER has a ticket system of its own and you must purchase a separate ticket unless you have a travel pass card that covers the area.

The four main RER lines are as follows:

Line A goes from St Germain-en-Laye to Boissy-St-Léger.

Line B goes from Robinson St-Rémy-les-Chevreuse to Roissy and Mitry-Claye.

Line B3 goes to Charles de Gaulle.

Line C goes from Versailles and St-Quentin-en-Yvelines to Dowdon.

Line C2 goes to Orly; Line C5 to Versailles.

Line D goes from Châtelet to Villiers.

An easternbound extension to Line A is planned to link Paris with Euro Disneyland.

RER services begin at 5.30am with trains running every 15 minutes until around 12.30am.

BUSES

Not by any means the most nippy way of getting you from A to B, due to the city's traffic-clogged arteries, but you obviously get to see a lot more by bus. The service creeps into every crevice of the city. Although the system might seem confusing at first glance, bus route maps are displayed at all bus stops (and in Métro stations) with each line numbered and your current position indicated. Bus stops are yellow – many have shelters – with a red disc on a standard above them. On the buses one ticket is valid for up to two fare stages (*sections*) and two tickets for three stages or more within the city limits.

GUIDED TOURS

You might fancy taking one of these to help you get your bearings but they're not cheap, at about 100–150f a go.

The RATP organise out of town excursions to all sorts of places departing from place de la Madeleine, including

Exciting Bus Routes

The RATP leaflet *Paris Bus Métro RER* lists many bus routes that go through historic or enticing districts and pass by major sights. It also gives directions to major monuments, museums and churches. A handful of routes take in enough sights to turn them into leisurely, cut-price sightseeing tours. And if you stay on the bus long enough you'll probably end up in a part of Paris most tourists rarely see. Examples are:

20 From Gare St Lazare to the Opéra, Montmartre-Poissonière, République, Bastille. Approx. time: 50 mins. Takes in the *grands boulevards*.

21 From Gare St Lazare to the Opéra, Palais Royale, Louvre, the Pont Neuf, St Michel, Gare du Luxembourg, Porte de Gentilly. Approx. time: 40 mins.

52 From Opéra to Concorde, Étoile Charles de Gaulle, Auteuil, Pont de St-Cloud. Approx. time: 50 mins.

82 From Gare du Luxembourg to Gare Montparnasse, École Militaire, Champs-de-Mars, Tour Eiffel, Porte Maillot, Neuilly. Approx. time: 45 mins.

83 From place d'Italie along boulevard Raspail, Gare des Invalides, Rond Point. Approx. time: 50 mins.

95 From Montparnasse Tower past St Germain-des-Prés, the Louvre, Palais Royal, the Opéra and to Montmartre near Sacré-Coeur. Approx time: 50 mins.

Montmartrobus: a scenic ride from Pigalle to the end of the line at Jules Joffrin Métro. See section on the 18e for details.

guided tour buses to Versailles, Paris by night, etc. but your French will have to be quite good to keep up with the commentary. Compared with commercial operators, their prices are modest. Pick up their leaflet *Excursions* from Métro or railway stations.

The following companies run bus tours of Paris lasting about 2 hours and starting in the centre. There'll either be a guide on board or they'll use a pre-recorded commentary in various languages. All coaches are non-smoking. Some tours might include a trip on the Seine.

American Express: 11 rue Scribe 75009. Tel. 42 25 22 55.

Cityrama: 4 place des Pyramides 75001. Tel. 42 60 30 14.

Tickets/Travel Passes

Buying tickets one at a time is costly. Better to consider one of the following:

Carnet

A wodge of ten tickets, the *carnet* costs 34.5f and works out cheaper than buying the tickets individually. Good for short stays.

Coupon Jaune

A week's Métro/bus pass, the *Coupon Jaune* costs 50f and is valid from Monday morning to Sunday night, irrespective of when you buy it. You'll need a passport-sized photo, but tickets are available on the spot after a short wait while they process your application. Buy it at Métro stations and from the tourist office.

Carte Orange

A monthly Métro/bus season pass costing 177f, this is valid from the first day of the month. Again you'll need a passport-sized photo. This is the best value if you're staying for a week or so and intend to do quite a bit of travelling about.

Like the *Coupon Jaune* you'll need a passport photo but the pass is issued on the spot.

Paris Visite (tourist ticket)

A single ticket for tourists entitling them to unlimited travel for 3 days at 80f and 5 days at 150f throughout Paris and its immediate suburbs.

For additional travel to Roissy/Charles de Gaulle or Orly airports and places further afield, like Versailles, it will cost 135f and 190f respectively).

You can use the pass on the Métro, bus, RER, SNCF trains in Ile de France and on the Montmartre funicular railway and there are peripheral discounts on such things as cycle hire. Buy it from main Métro and RER stations and at the RATP sales office, 53 bis quai des Grands Augustins 75006, or in the place de la Madeleine 75008.

How to Use the Bus

- Work out your route by seeing which bus lines come nearest to your destination.

- Buses don't stop automatically. Wave a bus down at the bus stop (*arrêt*). If you're in it, press one of the "stop" buttons to activate a sign in front of the bus, *Arrêt demandé*).

- Get in through the door at the front where you cancel your ticket in the machine by the driver's seat. NB: if you've a *Paris Visite or Carte Orange* travel pass (see **Tickets/Travel Passes** page 54) flash it at the driver, but on no account insert it into the machine as it will render it useless.

- Keep track of where you are by glancing at the route maps inside the bus.

- As on the Métro there are sometimes *contrôleurs* who'll ask to inspect your ticket, so keep it until you get off.

- Buses run roughly every 10 minutes from 7am until 8.30 pm, with slightly reduced services from 9pm until after midnight and on Sundays and public holidays.

- If in doubt about the correct fare it's better to tell the driver where you want to go at the start of your journey rather than risking a verbal battering about failing to get off when your ticket expired.

- Most buses with three digit numbers come or go to the sub-urbs; those with two digits operate exclusively within Paris.

Bus numbers in the 20s come/go to Gare St Lazare
     "   "   "   "   30s   "   "   "   Gare de L'Est
     "   "   "   "   30s   "   "   "   Gare du Nord
     "   "   "   "   30s   "   "   "   Châtelet/Hôtel de Ville
     "   "   "   "   30s   "   "   "   Luxembourg

- Night buses (*Noctambus*) run all night, starting from Châtelet whence they depart every hour on the half hour from 1–1.30am–5.30am (at 5.30am normal service resumes) running in two lines on avenue Victoria and rue St Martin. There are ten routes running in various directions, all following Métro routes. You can pick up a night bus map from Métro stations. Allow three Métro tickets, four if you use two buses.

Paris-Vision: (France-Tourisme): 214 rue de Rivoli 7500. Tel.
42 60 31 25.

RATP Offices: 53 bis quai des Grands Augustins 75006. Tel. 40
46 44 50 Kiosk, place de la Madeleine. Tel. 40 06 71 45.

WALKING TOURS

The best way to explore Paris is on foot (take comfortable
shoes). To make the most of your wanderings, you could
contact the following:

Caisse Nationale: 62 rue Saint Antoine 75004. Tel. 42 74
22 22. M Bastille/Saint Paul. Phone for details of the tour
programme which concentrates on museums, monuments
and, in the tourist season, tours of historic parts of town.
English-speaking guides available.

Paris Secret: 50 rue du Four 75006. Tel. 40 16 07 44. M
St Germain-des-Prés. Tours March–October from 2.30pm
daily. English spoken, reservations essential for these explorations of "unknown" Paris. Groups of about 20 escorted.

TAXIS

There are allegedly over 14,000 taxis in Paris, which may
seem hard to believe if you happen to be looking for one.
Theoretically, you should be able to hail them on the street
when the entire sign on the cab's roof is illuminated or wait
at a rank (signposted *arrêt taxis or tête de station*) for one to
pull up. You won't be popular though if you hail one within
a few yards of a rank – in fact the driver's not obliged to stop
if you're less than 165ft (50m) from a taxi rank.

The following radio taxi companies accept telephone bookings (an extra charge is added to the fare according to the
distance travelled by the cab to make the pick-up):

Alpha	45 85 85 85
Taxis bleus	42 02 42 02
Taxis Radio "G7"	47 39 47 39
Taxis-Radio Étoile	42 70 41 41

To find the numbers of taxi ranks in the telephone directory,
see under "*Taxis-Appel*".

Tariff A, the basic rate, is in effect from 7am–8pm (2.58f

per km); Tariff B from 8pm–7am (4.02 per km). Note: rate B is applicable the whole of Sunday and Bank Holidays.

Tariff C, the highest (5.39) is in effect from the airports and outer areas of Paris from 8pm–7am. At other times Rate B is charged.

If you've a complaint about a taxi, keep the receipt (*bulletin de voiture*) for your journey, and contact *Service des Taxis de la Préfecture de Police*, Tel. 45 31 14 80, Ext 4243.

BICYCLE

Cycling around Paris is no joyride. But if you want to live dangerously, and can accept that on the motorists' list of priorities cyclists come last, after dogs, here's a list of some companies who'll hire out sturdy bikes. The most pleasant places to pedal about are of course les Bois, whether it's de Boulogne or de Vincennes. Hire companies ask for a refundable deposit and a fee towards insurance cover. Average cost is 20f per hour, 350f per week. Daily, weekend, weekly and monthly hire charges are usually possible. Minors should show written parental authority.

Paris Vélo: 2 rue du Fer-à-Moulin 75005. Tel. 43 37 59 22.

Bicyclub de France: 8 place de La Porte-Champeret 75017. Tel. 47 66 55 92. Bicyclub rents bikes from rural spots like St Germain-en-Laye and Versailles too.

You can hire a scooter from Scoot 'Heure, 6 rue d'Arras 75005. Tel. 43 25 69 25.

BOAT TRIPS

While Paris doesn't have a riverbus service there is the Batobus, a boat service which runs from April until the end of September. There are five stops, although more are planned: port de la Bourdonnais (Eiffel Tower), port de Solférino (d'Orsay Museum), quai Malaquais (Louvre), quai de Montebello (Notre Dame), and quai de L'Hôtel de Ville. Boats run between 10am and 7pm daily with boats calling at each stop about every 40 minutes.

You can see Paris from the river on a fat, glass-topped *bateau-mouche* (also called *vedettes*). A sightseeing tour (with a commentary in English) is considerably cheaper than having lunch, dinner or even tea on board. A number of different companies depart regularly from different points along the Seine. You can pick up brochures and timetables from the tourist office on the Champs-Élysées or the main stations.

Bateaux-Mouches: departures from Pont d'Iéna (left bank) 75015. Tel. 47 05 50 05, 45 51 33 08. M Bir-Hakeim/Iéna.
    Lunch, tea, dinner cruises as well as straightforward sightseeing ones. Boats leave every hour, on the hour from 10am until 6pm (except 1 pm), with additional 8.30pm dinner cruises.
Vedettes de Pont Neuf: Departures from square du Vert Galant, Ile de la Cité 75001. Tel. 46 33 98 38. M Pont Neuf. Boats leave at 10am, 11.15am, 12 noon, and from 2–5pm every half hour.
Vedettes de Paris: Ile-de-France, Port de Suffren 75007. Tel. 47 05 71 29.
    Less touristy than taking a *bateau-mouche* is barging along the canals which cut through and run out of the city. La Villette and Cité des Sciences et de l'Industrie is one of the most popular destinations.

Canauxrama: Half and full day canal cruises in flat-bottom barges along the pretty and untouristy canal St Martin between Port de l'Arsenal (opposite 50 boulevard de La Bastille 75012, M Bastille) and the science park at La Villette (5 bis quai de la Loire, M Jaurés). Departures 9.30am, 2.30pm. Times do vary so it's best to telephone to check; you can only book cruises from Nov.15 – March 15. Telephone reservations on 42 39 15 00.

CAR

Paris can be hell for motorists – anyone who has tried to drive there knows there are a lot of Formula 1 *manqués* ready to carve you up on the boulevards. Local driving style is frequently idiosyncratic. The accident rate is high and it's almost impossible to park – there are few free parking areas in the city and competition is fierce to procure places. The clampers and towers-away are very zealous and you run a high risk of one or the other if you park illegally (on a bus lane/loading bay/pedestrian crossing, etc.) In the case of clamping, contact the local police station. If you're unfortunate enough to have the car towed away you'll have to fork out a 450f removal fee plus a 21f storage charge per day as well as a parking fine of 230–900f. Car pounds (*fourrières*) cover several *arrondissements*.

1er, 2e, 3e, 4e, 8e, 9e	Tel.	42 21 44 63
5e, 12e, 13e		43 46 69 38
6e, 7e, 14e,		43 20 65 24
15e, 16e, 17e, 18e		42 63 37 58
8e, 16e		45 01 80 13
10e, 11e, 19e, 20e		42 00 76 99

In place of parking meters you'll find *Eurodateurs* – usually one per street – which take coins (from 4f upwards per hour, depending on location). The machine will present you with a ticket to display inside your windshield. You may well find signs saying you may only park on one side of the street or giving other instructions to make life harder.

If all this hasn't put you off, it's only fair to point out that a car is very useful for out of town excursions and that sharing a hired car, if there's a group of you, might work

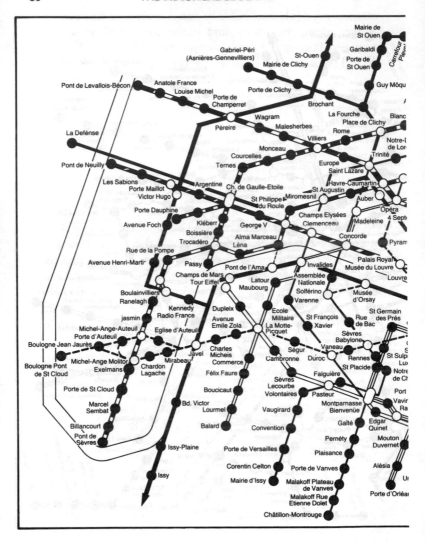

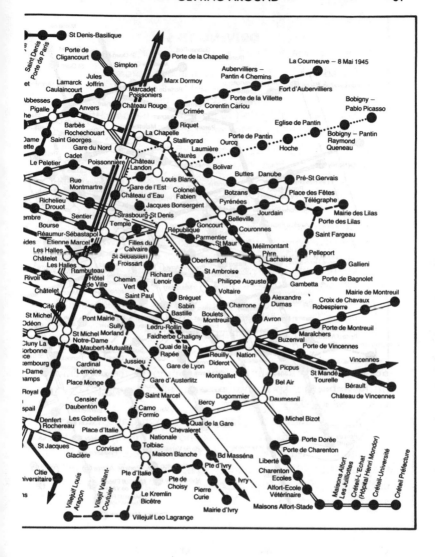

DRIVING TIPS

- Drive on the right and remember to overtake on the left!

- Speed limit is 60km/h (37 mph) in built up areas
  Speed limit is 90km/h (56 mph) in other areas
  Speed limit is 130km/h (80 mph) on urban stretches
  Speed limit is 80km/h (50 mph) on the *périphérique*
  Weather conditions may affect speed limits.

- Petrol is graded as *Normale* (80 octane) or *Super* (98 octane): do take care to use a grade in the range recommended for your vehicle. Unleaded petrol is sold in France as *Essence Super* (95 octane) with the pumps dispensing it clearly branded as *super sans plomb*.

- Do carry the original registration document with your car. If it's not in your name, you should have a letter of authorisation from the owner. If you're driving a UK-registered hired vehicle you could get a Hired/Leased Vehicle certificate (VE103A) from the AA.

- Familiarise yourself with road markings – a solid white or yellow line on the centre of the road shouldn't be crossed. Most road signs are international.

out cheaper than public transport. But given the convenience of the public transport system, a car in Paris might not seem worth the hassle.

Should you indeed decide to motor around, at least invest in a good map such as Michelin 12 showing the one way streets – without it you'll find it very tricky indeed. The Michelin map number 11 considerably marks with a P underground car parks, as does the excellent Michelin Atlas *Paris par arrondissements* 15.

Car Hire

Car hire is costly, with little to choose from between the major names on price – only the usual advice of "shop around" holds good here as much will depend on special promotions available at the time you want a car. All the major international car rental firms have offices in the airports and many national companies have Paris offices as you'll see from the telephone directory.

Parking

You can get information about parking by phoning 43 46 98 30 from 9am–5pm, Mon–Fri. If you're driving to Paris it could be a good idea to leave your car in one of the long-term car parks just outside the *périphérique* as they tend to be cheaper than ones in the city.

Below we list Paris garages. The ones marked with an asterisk* have 24-hour petrol stations. Charges vary from about 10f per hour.

Parking Concorde: place de la Concorde, 75001
Parking Vendôme: place Vendôme, 75001
Parking Parc Pont Neuf: quai des Orfèvres, 75001
Parking Saint-Honoré: 58 place du Marche St Honoré, 75001
Parking Hôtel de Ville: rue Lobau, 75004
Parking Notre Dame: parvis du Notre Dame, 75004
Parking Mazarine: rue Mazarine, 75006
Parking St Germain: 169 boulevard St Germain, 75006
Parking St Sulpice: place St Sulpice, 75006
Parking Tour Eiffel: place Joffre, 75007
Parking Invalides: rue de Constantine, 75007 (*until 1am)
Parking Berri Washington: 5 rue de Berri, 75008
Parking George V: 101 avenue des Champs-Élysées, 75008
Parking Rond-Point: avenue Matignon/Champs-Élysées, 75008 (*)
Parking Opéra: 4 rue Chaussée d'Antin, 75009
Parking Tour Montparnasse: 17 rue de l'Arrivée, 75015
The Shell Station: rue Colonel-Driant, 75001 (*)

Some French agencies include:

Autorent	Tel.	45 55 53 59
Europcar		45 00 08 06
Mattei		43 07 07 07

You'll need to have a current full driver's licence which you must have held for 12 months or more. Do check that the car is fully insured, even if it means making separate arrangements for insurance against damage to other vehicles and injury to your passengers.

Car Breakdown
The following garages provide 24-hour repair service:

Aleveque Daniel: 116 rue de la Convention 75015. Tel. 48 28 12 00/42 50 48 49. (Credit: AE, MC.V)

Alfauto: 69 bis rue Briancon 75015. Tel. 45 31 61 18/48 56 29 38. (No credit cards).

Assist-Auto: 10 rue René Villerme 75011. Tel. 43 38 44 08. (No credit cards).

TRAVEL OUT OF PARIS

BY DOMESTIC AIRLINES

Air France, the national carrier, has some flights to major French cities. The major internal airline in France is Air Inter.

Air France are at 119 avenue des Champs-Élysées 75008. Tel. 45 35 61 61. Open 9am–6pm, Mon–Sat.

Air Inter's central office is at 12 rue Castiglione 75001. Tel. 45 39 25 25. Open 9am–midnight, Mon–Sat; noon-midnight, Sun.

BY BUS

Where buses and trains cover the same routes, as a rule the bus is cheaper and slower. Generally, though, buses just run where there are gaps in the very thorough train service, with SCNF buses sometimes covering routes where it's not profitable to run their trains. The local tourist office or *gare routier*/bus station – often next to the railway station – keeps details of routes and fares.

BY TRAIN

The national rail company is the Société Nationale des Chemins de Fer (SNCF) which runs a vast and efficient network of train services to every corner of France.

Fares depend on when you travel. There are red, white and blue periods, red being busy times or "rush hour", "blue" the

---

Train Tips

There are a few things to remember about using trains in France:

- If you buy your rail ticket in France, you must validate it (*compostez votre billet*) in the orange ticket punch (*composteur*) at the entrance to the platforms. If the ticket has been purchased in the UK/USA/Canada, this requirement may be waived. Failure to do this can incur a hefty on-the-spot fine from an assiduous inspector. Pass holders must validate their tickets otherwise the same applies. You must keep your ticket with you during the journey as you may have to present it while on the train and on leaving it.

- Each Parisian station cover specific areas of France:
  Gare d'Austerlitz (south-west France; Spain)
  Gare de L'Est (east; southern Germany)
  Gare de Lyon (south-east)
  Gare Montparnasse (west)
  Gare du Nord (north, Belgium, northern Europe) including some UK destinations
  Gare St-Lazare (north-west; some UK destinations)

---

quiet time, while "white" comes in the middle. Discounts are offered to groups of people as incentives to tempt them to travel during the off-peak/blue period – for example, to senior citizens (*Carte Vermeille*); students (see below); parents with children; salaried employees. Those under 26 may get a *Carte Jeune*. It is valid all over France from 1 June–30 September, offering reductions of 50% on all "blue" period trains, except those in Paris and its suburbs. The card also entitles you to a 50% reduction on one round-trip ferry journey and discounts on entry to discos, museums, campsites and so on. You can also, if you're aged 12–26, buy a *Carré Jeune*. It covers four one-way journeys at half price during the blue period and 20% off during the white period. (Journeys must start in the relevant period, but can end in another.) Valid for a year, on both first and second class services, it costs about 140f.

A France Railpass (once known as a *France Vacances* special pass) allowing unlimited travel within a certain period covers transfer from Orly/Roissy to Paris and back, and a Métro pass allowing travel on the city's underground, buses and RER trains for a day. Enquire at the French Railways office in London or at travel agents.

There are all sorts of other passes available to those who want to do a lot of travelling by train, such as the Eurail pass, Eurail Youth pass, Eurail Saver pass and Inter Rail pass – SNCF offices, or their representatives in France have details, as should tourist offices and travel agents.

For general information call 45 82 50 50; for reservations call 45 65 60 60 (credit card booking possible by Visa). Open 8am–8pm daily.

TGV

Pride and joy of the SNCF is the ultra-fast *Train à Grande Vitesse*, acknowledged the world over as the most outstanding symbol of France's technological progress. Once upon a time even the most ambitious SNCF engineers reckoned the top speed would be less than 175mph, but TGVs now regularly hit 200mph, and a souped up model has effortlessly achieved speeds of more than 300mph. By the year 2000 the TGV could well be running through most of France. If the SNCF have their way (and it's under dispute at the time of writing) and get the TGV running all the way down to Marseilles, it would bring that city, 500 miles from Paris, to within 3 hours of the capital, and Nice (400 miles further away) a mere four hours. Irrespective of the colour periods, on TGVs you have to pay a supplement.

WHERE TO STAY

HOTELS

The range of accommodation in hotels throughout Paris is vast. In general, you get what you pay for, but even the most basic and cheapest hotel provides a satisfactory standard of cleanliness and efficiency. Yes, there are sleazy hotels in unsalubrious quarters of Paris, but unless a property has slipped downhill very suddenly, you shouldn't find them in our directory. On the other hand, while prices were double-checked at the time of going to press, hotels do tend to change, tart themselves up, re-price with amazing speed.

Do check the tariff for yourself before making a reservation. We should also point out that two people sharing a room will pay little more than one, and since Paris is a relatively small city and transport is quick and efficient, it's no great hardship to make one of the outer, cheaper, or less fashionable *arrondissements* your base.

The price of every room in any Parisian hotel vetted by the Office du Tourisme must be displayed at the registration desk and again in the room.

The cheapest room will be described as *chambre avec e.c* (*eau courante*), a room with hot and cold water from a basin but no bidet. *Chambre avec cabinet de toilette*, a room with washbasin and bidet, is the next cheapest and the best bet for impecunious travellers, since the ubiquitous bidet obviates the need to shell out a further 15f or so for the use of the hotel's public shower room. *Chambre avec douche* will give you a washbasin, bidet and shower; *chambre avec douche/bain et W.C.* comes with a basin, bidet, shower or bath and lavatory.

A double room with a *grand lit* (double bed) is normally cheaper than one with twin beds. Rooms with private bathrooms usually cost the same for both single or double occupancy. Before registering, do ask to be shown the room on offer. When leaving, remember to vacate your room by noon, or whatever time is requested, unless you've a prior agreement with the proprietor, or you will be charged a further night's stay.

BOOKING

If you don't fancy making bookings yourself or aren't rash enough to risk arriving bedless in Paris, you can ask one of the Paris Tourist Offices to make a reservation for you. See page 15 for list of addresses and phone numbers. The central office is at 127 Champs-Élysées 75008. Tel. 47 23 61 72. It's open every day from 9am–8pm except December 25 and January 1. The *Guide des Hôtels* produced by the Tourist Office is another useful source of information. We've included many properties that they list in our guide. They will charge a small booking fee (around 20f). The months of June, September and October tend to be the busiest for Parisian hotels, so if you're planning on travelling then, or at Easter or Christmas, it's wise to book well ahead.

BED AND BREAKFAST

This is not big business in Paris, but there is an organisation covering 300 or so Parisian homes that welcome visitors. The minimum stay is 2 nights. It's best to phone or write in advance, but you can phone or turn up at their office to check out possible accommodation for the same day.

Annual membership costs 50f per person, per year, and is included in the charges for the first reservation. Rates are from 240f for a double room in a central location close to a Métro station, and include breakfast.

Bed and Breakfast 1, 73 rue Notre-Dame-des-Champs 75006. Tel. 43 25 43 97. M Notre-Dame-des-Champs. Open every day except Sunday 9am–1pm, 2–7pm.

A bed and breakfast booking agency called Café Couette operates throughout France and has recently set up in Paris. The cost of bed and breakfast for two in a double room is from 120f. Their office, tucked away at the back of a little courtyard (keep looking), usually has English-speaking staff on hand.

Café Couette, 8 rue d'Isly 75008. M St Lazare.

You can also book bed and breakfast accommodation in Paris in advance through an English-based organisation.

Bed and Breakfast (France), PO Box 66, 94 Bell Street, Henley-on-Thames TG9 1XS. Tel: 0491 578 803.

STUDENT/YOUTH ACCOMMODATION

Paris scores high in this field with plenty of cheap, basic places to stay. During the summer holidays, students are often able to rent short stays in the halls of residence belonging to the city university.

Cité Universitaire, 18 boulevard Jourdan 75014. M Cité-Universitaire. Telephone 45 89 13 37 for details. The rate is around 90f per night, and you'll need to have an international student identity card (see page 45 for details of how to obtain this).

Countrywide, the Acceuil des Jeunes en France (AJF) has 8000 beds, and 11,000 in the summer when they use vacated student accommodation at universities (including the Cité Universitaire). In theory the age limit is 18–30 and groups of eight or more may book in advance at the office below; smaller groups or individuals have to go along to one of the AJF centres listed below, as early as possible, as rooms are on a first come, first served basis.

The head office and central booking office of the AJF is at 12 rue des Barres 75004. Tel. 42 72 72 09. M Pont Marie/bus. Office open 9.30am–7pm, Mon–Sat.

Once you're in Paris you can visit the AJF offices at the Gare du Nord arrival hall (March to November); at AJF Beaubourg opposite the Pompidou Centre, 119 rue St Martin, 75004. Tel. 42 77 87 80 (open all year); at 139 boulevard St Michel 75005. Tel. 43 54 95 86 (March to October); at AJF Marais, 16 rue du Pont Louis-Philippe 75004. Tel. 42 78 04 82 (June to September) and at AJF Saint Michel, 139 boulevard Saint Michel 75005, Tel. 43 54 95 86.

The AJF offices also provide an information service, student restaurants, meal vouchers and reduced price tickets for rail and coach. All the AJF offices are open Monday to Friday, except the one opposite the Pompidou Centre which is open on Saturdays too.

The youth centres in the Marais (Maubuisson, Fauconnier, Fourcy), are open all year round and are located in converted 18th-century town houses. Cost is around 80f a night including breakfast, sleeping one to eight to a room.

Le Fauconnier: 11 rue du Fauconnier 75004. Tel. 42 74 23 45. M St Paul. Open 7am–1am daily. No credit cards. One of the best and most popular of the AJF residences.
Fourcy: 6 rue de Fourcy 75004. Tel. as above. M St Paul. Open 7am–1am daily. No credit cards. Each of the 224 rooms sleeps two to eight.
Maubuisson: 12 rue des Barres 75004. Tel. 42 72 72 09. M Hôtel de Ville Open 6am–1am daily. No credit cards. Excellent location; converted town house, smallest of the Marais trio.
Résidence Luxembourg: 270 rue St Jacques 75005. Tel. 43 25 06 20. M Luxembourg. Only open July–September. 24-hour reception, no curfew.
AJF Bastille Résidence: 151 avenue Ledru Rollin 75011. Tel. 43 79 53 86. M Bastille/Voltaire. No credit cards.

Centre International de Séjour de Paris (CISP) have a couple of residences as follows. They're open to all ages with prices from 80f a night depending on whether you have a single room, share, or doss down in a dorm.

Maurice Ravel: 6 avenue Maruice Ravel 75012. Tel. 43 43 19 01. M Porte du Vincennes. Credit: AE, MC, V. Slightly less convenient location but 225 beds available, mostly catering to groups. Excellent facilities. No maximum stay.
Kellerman: 17 boulevard Kellerman 75013. Tel. 45 80 70 76. M Maison Blanche. Open 6.30am–1.30am daily. Credit: V. Half or full board is also available at this hostel. There's a park across the way.

OTHER HOSTEL ACCOMMODATION POSSIBILITIES

Association des Étudiants Protestants de Paris (AEPP): 46 rue de Vaugirard 75006. Tel. 46 33 23 30 or 43 54 31 49. M Luxembourg. Near the Luxembourg gardens; excellent facilities. Reservations accepted July–September (arrive before 10am at other times). Nominal rule of 3 days minimum, 13 week maximum stay, but it's negotiable either way.

The Union des Centres de Rencontres Internationales de France (UCRIF): run 16 hostels or foyers in Paris and throughout France. There's a UCRIF office in the Gare du Nord (next to AJF in the new building). You can get a complete list of the hostels from the Maison de l'UCRIF, 4 rue Jean-Jacques Rousseau 75001. Tel. 42 60 42 40. M Louvre. Open 10am–6pm, Mon–Fri, or at any of their hostels.

While the smaller *foyers* may take one and all, priority is given to group bookings and they're most popular with student back-packers. There's often a crowded, noisy and convivial atmosphere and a foreign clientèle. Breakfast and showers are almost always included in the room rate which hovers around the 80f mark. Credit cards aren't accepted. Call ahead to check availability or turn up early to procure a room: all are open 6am–2am daily.

The most central residences are as follows:

Centre International de Paris/Louvre: 20 rue Jean-Jacques Rousseau 75001. Tel. 42 36 88 18 or 40 26 66 43. M Louvre/Palais Royal. The largest – 200 beds – with some single rooms.

Paris Opéra: 11 rue Thérèse 75001. Tel. 42 60 77 23. M Pyramides. Bigger rooms than above, only 68 beds, some singles.

Paris les Halles: 5 rue Pélican 75001. Tel. 42 60 92 45. M Palais Royale. Smallest of these four. Some single rooms available.

Paris Quartier Latin: 44 rue Bernadins 75005. Tel. 43 29 34 80. M Maubert. Bigger rooms with more beds in each one.

Association des Foyers de Jeunes: Foyer de Jeunes Filles: 234 rue de Tolbiac 75013. Tel. 45 89 06 42. M Tolbiac. Well-equipped single rooms in large modern residence aimed at women students or workers aged 18–25. In July and August short stay reservations are accepted, but from September to June there's a one-month minimum stay. A nominal registration fee is required for longer stays. In summer expect to pay around 100f. There's a garden, TV room, washing machines, common rooms.

Foyer International des Étudiantes: 93 boulevard St Michel. Tel. 43

54 49 63. M Luxembourg. Spacious, spotless single/double room accommodation in a great location. From October to June only women studying in Paris are eligible to stay, but from July to the end of September it accepts men too. Very good facilities. Prices from 80f per night to include breakfast and showers. This is a popular base and reservations should be made several weeks ahead in writing and followed by a deposit and then confirmation.

Foyer International d'Acceuil de Paris: 30 rue Cabanis 75014. Tel. 45 89 89 15. M Glacière. Modern, massive, high-rise residence in an untouristy corner of Paris. There are 500 rooms, large and well-maintained, some with 4–6 beds and bathroom, suitable for families. Meals available too. Prices vary according to accommodation, but are modest. Postal bookings taken up to a month before arrival.

UCJF (Union Chrétienne de Jeunes Filles) or **YWCA**: 22 rue Naples 75008. Tel. 45 22 23 49. M Europe/Villiers. Women guests only; accepted during the summer for a minimum stay of 3 days. (At other times half-board and a 3 month minimum stay is required.) Reservations accepted by telephone in summer. There's a curfew and strictly no chaps allowed. Rooms sleep 1–4 and are priced from 80f per person.

YOUTH HOSTELS

International youth hostel membership is required, but some hostels can sell you a one-night membership for 15f. Several hostel organisations in Paris sell IYHF cards, as do student travel agencies.

There are only two Youth Hostels proper in Paris, well booked up in the peak months, so make a reservation if you're planning on being a summer visitor. The other two are in the suburbs and unless that's where you actually want to be, by the time you add in transport costs, you might be better off staying in a modest city hotel. Prices are around 70f a night to include generally a shower and breakfast.

Jules Ferry: 8 boulevard Jules Ferry 75011. Tel. 43 57 55 60. M. République. The most conveniently located hostel, but it fills up by 9am in the summer so get in early! Clean, large rooms, adequate kitchen facilities. Open 6am–2am, 4-day maximum stay, 2–6 per bedroom; laundry at extra cost. To reserve send a IYHF voucher well in advance; phone reservations accepted when there's lots of space.

D'Artagnan: 8 rue Vitruve 75020. Tel. 43 61 08 75. M Porte de Montreuil/Porte de Bagnolet. Seven floors of dormitory-type accommodation – 431 beds. Good facilities. Open 24 hours, rooms closed for cleaning 10am–4pm. 4-day maximum stay. Double rooms, 3–8 bed rooms. Reservations only accepted with IYHF vouchers.

If you have International Youth Hostel Association membership, contact the Ligue Française des Auberges de Jeunesse (LFAJ), 38 boulevard Raspail 75007. M Sèvres-Babylone. They will try to find you basic, cheap accommodation, often for a minimum stay of three nights. Their other hostels are at Choisy-le-Roi, 12 kilometres from Paris, and in the suburbs at Chatenay Malabry.

RENTING A FLAT

If you're going to be in Paris for at least a week (usually the minimum rental period) and have people with whom you can share an apartment, this can work out relatively low in cost and high in convenience. In some cases you should expect to pay a refundable deposit (up to around 2000f). Remember that self-catering options are also offered by many inclusive tour operators to Paris.

Englishman Ray Lampard offers a personalised accommodation service with a selection of fully furnished central apartments to let for a minimum of 1 week. Reckon on being charged from 350f a night for two in a studio flat, less per person in larger flats for up to six. This includes a weekly cleaning service, fresh flowers on arrival, and the kitchen stocked with essentials like tea, coffee, milk and sugar. Lampard's organisation is:

Rothray, 10 rue Nicolas-Flamel 75004. Tel. 48 87 13 37. M Pont Marie. Office open 9.30am–7pm, Mon–Sat.

Residence-hotels provide apartments and studios with kitchenettes, usually weekly maid service, towels, bedlinen and kitchenware, plus facilities ranging from restaurants and bars to swimming pools and jacuzzi. Four such places are:

Le Claridge: 74 avenue des Champs-Élysées 75008. Tel. 43 59 67 97. M Franklin D. Roosevelt. AE, DC, MC, V. Modern, functional apartments in what was one of the grandest mansions of the Champs-Élysées. Studios from 5500f a week; one-bed flats from 9000f; two-bed flats from 14,000f a week.

Home Plaza: 74 rue Ameloty 75011. Tel. 40 21 20 00. M St Sébastien Froissart. AE, DC, MC, V. Newly-opened development with 270 units. You can rent by the day, week or month. Bar, restaurant, garden, health spa, jacuzzi and sauna. All apartments have TV. Studios 1–2 people 400f per night, 3 people 500f a night, 4 people 600f. Cheaper if you stay longer.

Pierre et Vacances Montmartre: 10 place Charles Dullin 75018. Tel. 42 57 14 55. M Anvers. AE, MC, V. Apartments sleep from one to six. All have TV and cost between 480f and 1,060f. Discounts for longer stays.

Pierre et Vacances de Versailles, 20 rue Oradour-sur-Glane 75015. Tel. 45 54 97 43. M Porte de Versailles. AE, MC, V. On the southern edge of Paris, 188 units, all with TV. There's a bar, garden, *salon* and sauna. Two-room apartments for 4 people 570f to 690f a night, less for longer stays.

For much longer stays (a minimum of two months) try contacting Paris Promo SARL, 18 rue du Cardinal Lemoine 75005, or Inter Urbis, 1 rue Mollien 75008.

Flat-hunting in Paris isn't much fun – as in London it's an owner's market. The most reasonably-priced finds are likely to be in the 10–13e and 18–20e *arrondissements*. Trendiest places are the Marais (3e, 4e) and, increasingly, Bastille (11e). The 5e and 6e tend to be overpriced. Start by scouring newspaper ads – the *International Herald Tribune* especially and *Le Figaro* list furnished and unfurnished retals. Best days for listings are Tuesday to Thursday but the *Trib* has a property supplement on Fridays. Check out *France Soir*, too.

You can obtain more information from the Association Départementale pour l'Information sur le Logement. Tel. 45 49 14 14 (located in each *arrondissement*), or the Centre d'Information sur l'Habitat de Paris, 95 rue Cherche-Midi 75006. Tel. 45 49 25 26. M Rennes. By appointment only.

The Centre Interministeriel de Renseignements Administratifs, Tel. 43 46 13 46, has a helpline in English for administrative problems.

CAMPING

The only main campsite in the Paris area is in the Bois de Boulogne. It's open all year, but as you can imagine the only real demand is in the summer when you have to queue up to get in as there's a no-reservations policy.

Camping d'Ile de France, allée au Bord de l'Eau, Bois de Boulogne 75016. Tel. 45 24 30 00. M Porte Maillot. Connected in summer by a courtesy bus to the camp site/bus 43. Traveller's cheques are accepted.

Credit Cards

When a hotel accepts credit cards, we've used the following abbreviations:

AE	American Express
DC	Diners Club
MC	Mastercard
V	Visa

Also:
TC Traveller's cheques
EC Eurocheques

HOTEL ACCOMMODATION
GUIDE BY ARRONDISSEMENT

1er

Hôtel Agora: 7 rue de la Cossonnerie 75001. Tel. 42 33 46 02. M Les Halles.★★

Sparkling clean hotel with lots of antiques, lacy curtains and an air of quiet gentility. Rooms all well sound-proofed. 29 rooms all with shower or bath. Lift. Five rooms have TV. Brilliant, central location in Les Halles. AE.

Ducs d'Anjou: 1 rue Ste Opportune 75001. Tel. 42 36 92 24. M Les Halles.★★★

Pleasant, two-star hotel overlooking a pretty square. Rooms (480f) have TVs, are quiet, but many are dark. Lift. 39 rooms, 33 with bath/shower. Sound choice if peace and quiet a priority. AE, DC, MC. V.

Family: 35 rue Cambon 75001. Tel. 42 61 54 84. M Madeleine.★★★
You'd hardly expect a modest, family-run hotel in this fashionable area between the rue St-Honoré and La Madeleine, and we wait to see if this remains a "find" after the renovations under way in 1990. The friendly and courteous husband and wife team are smartening up the huge bedrooms. All now have bathrooms, TV and phone. Air of tranquillity. AE, MC, V.

Henry IV: 25 place Dauphine 75001. Tel. 43 54 55 53. M Pont Neuf.★
Well-loved, extremely popular hotel overlooking the beautiful place Dauphine on the Ile de la Cité. The building itself is 400 years old. Absolutely no frills – *en suite* loo the tops. Must book months in advance.

Lille: 8 rue du Pélican. Tel. 42 33 33 42. M Louvre/Palais Royal.★
In a small street moments from the Louvre, rather dilapidated state more than compensated for by location and low prices. Only 14 rooms, so must book well in advance.

Lion d'Or: 5 rue de la Sourdière 75001. Tel. 42 60 79 04. M Tuileries.★
Small, friendly hotel on a quiet street, currently in the process of redecoration and a general smartening up. Marvellous location, close to the Louvre, Palais Royal, Tuileries. Patron, M Damane, speaks excellent English. V, AE.

Hôtel d l'Ouest: 144 rue St Honoré 75001. Tel. 42 60 29 89. M Louvre/Palais Royal.★
Extremely modest, rooms small and not at all smart. Popular if only because of its close proximity to the Louvre. Advisable to book 2 weeks ahead.

Hôtel du Palais: 2 quai de la Mégisserie 75001. Tel. 42 36 98 25. M Pont Neuf Châtelet.★
Basic, but welcoming and clean. Rooms facing the Quai have a broad view of the river but at a hidden price: the constant noise of traffic. Redecoration and renovation imminent, but at the time of going to press you could still get a double room for 200f.

Prince Albert: 5 rue St Hyacinthe 75001. Tel. 42 61 58 36. M Pyramides.★★★
Most of the 31 rooms have a bathroom and some surprising extras: TV, phone, mini-bar and safe. There's also a sitting room and if the corridors are dim, the rooms are comfortable and clean. Borrowing from Victorian England in ambience, this two-star hotel is popular with Brits. Very central – roughly midway between Louvre and Opéra. MC, V.

Richelieu – Mazarin: 51 rue de Richelieu 75001. Tel. 42 97 46 20. M Palais Royal/Pyramides.★–★★

Good value small hotel with only 14 rooms, all with some private facilities. Clean and recently decorated, with friendly staff and a loyal following – so book in advance. Very central, front-facing rooms consequently noisy.

St Honoré: 85 rue St Honoré 75001. Tel. 42 36 20 38. M RER Châtelet-Les Halles/Louvre.★

Absolutely basic, nothing special, very cheap.

Prices

All French hotels are officially graded from one to four star *de luxe*, based theoretically on amenities. We have used a "star" system purely to indicate price. The hotels listed in this guide fall into one of four price bands, indicated by either one, two, three or four stars, with the emphasis on the cheaper price bands when possible. However if there's a particularly special hotel in a higher bracket, we've included that too.

★	**from under £25**
★★	**from under £35**
★★★	**from under £45**
★★★★	**from under £60**

When we have, put ★–★★, for example, next to a hotel entry, this indicates that there is cheaper accommodation available in the hotel, but that the majority of rooms will fall into the two-star price band. Obviously the cheaper rooms will in all likelihood be smaller, with fewer private facilities and the least pleasant aspect, but the general facilities, like lifts, breakfast room, and *salon*, will be rather more upmarket.

These prices are for two people sharing a room. Unless stated otherwise, they do not include the cost of breakfast which most of our hotels offer at a charge of between 20f and 50f per person. It is often a better bet to breakfast in a nearby café or *salon de thé* where the *patron* is catering for discerning Parisians and not just for overnight tourists. In a local bar-tabac or brasserie a coffee and croissant eaten standing at the bar will be half the cost of a hotel breakfast. Make it clear to the hotelier when you book in, if you don't require breakfast. Breakfast may be served in your room or in the breakfast room. In the case of our cost-conscious hotel listings, the hotels, as a rule, do not have restaurants.

2e

Hôtel de Bayonne: 41 rue d'Aboukir 75002. Tel. 45 08 40 09. M Sentier.★
Rock-bottom basic.

Tiquetonne: 6 rue Tiquetonne 75002. Tel. 42 36 94 58. M Étienne Marcel.★
There's a lift, 47 rooms, 32 with private facilities and that's about it. Handy for les Halles.

3e

Bellevue et Chariot d'Or: 39 rue de Turbigo 75003. Tel. 48 87 45 60. M Étienne Marcel.★★–★
Conveniently situated for Les Halles, the Pompidou Centre and the Beaubourg, this two-star hotel is good value in our middle price range (275–320f for a double room). Rooms are imaginatively decorated and there are 6 that sleep 4 at a bargain 400f a night. AE, DC, MC, V.

Hôtel de Cambrai: 30 rue de Turenne 75003. Tel. 42 72 73 47. M Bastille/St-Paul.★
Basic. No charm, but clean and adequate.

Chancelier Boucherat: 110 rue de Turenne 75003. Tel. 42 72 86 83. M Filles du Calvaire.★
Clean, unpretentious hotel in a quiet street. Slightly shabby rooms are being upgraded and a washer/dryer installed for guests' use. Cheerful, sunny breakfast room. Room prices are reduced between November and May. MC, V.

Grand Hôtel Arts et Métiers: 4 rue Borda 75003. Tel. 42 72 01 66. M Arts et Métiers.★
Simple 35-room hotel with double rooms from 135–180f. In tiny street. MC, V.

Hôtel du Marais, 2 bis rue des Commines 75003. Tel. 48 87 78 27. M Filles du Calvaire.★★–★★★
All rooms have small, private bathrooms, radio, TV and mini-bar, adding a touch of luxury to an otherwise simple but civilised two-star hotel. Well-situated for the Marais, but the street is fairly busy. AE, DC, MC, V.

4e

Castex: 5 rue Castex 75004. Tel. 42 72 31 52. M Bastille/Sully-Morland.★★
Family-run hotel renovated from top to bottom in 1989. Superb location in the Bastille/Marais area, charming, sociable *patrons* M

and Mme Bouchan, spotlessly clean rooms with private bathrooms, telephone and evidence of tender loving care. MC, V.

Hôtel de Célestins: 1 rue Charles V 75004. Tel. 48 87 87 04. M Sully-Morland.✶✶✶

Historic building (hence no lift) which, in the 18th-century, belonged to the Célestins Convent. The rooms are small but have bags of historic charm, including wooden walls, beamed ceilings, chintzes and antiques – allow 360–380f for a double. No sitting room, but friendly atmosphere. The narrow Marais street is quiet except during the early morning traffic chaos. AE, DC, MC, V.

Hôtel des Deux Iles: 59 rue St-Louis-en-l'Ile 75004. Tel. 43 26 13 35. M Cité.✶✶✶✶

Marvellous position in the quiet street that runs the length of the smaller and less bustling of the Seine's two islands. The building is 17th-century, the rooms modest in size, but very comfortable, with smart bathrooms, TV and phone. In the winter an open fire burns in the cellar bar; voluptuous sofas make this a cosy place to hole up of a winter's evening. Slightly more expensive than most of our selection (630f for a double) but its character and location makes it special.

Fauconnier: 11 rue du Fauconnier 75004. Tel. 42 74 23 45. M St Paul.✶

Not a hotel, but a government-subsidised establishment offering inexpensive accommodation to young people. The upper age limit used to be 30, but anyone willing to share a room with strangers of the same sex is welcome. Rooms sleep from 2 to 6 people. Spotlessly clean, welcoming and, here comes the bonus, historic surroundings (17th-century) with beams, original floor tiles and antique furniture. (See also **Student/Youth Accommodation**, page 70.)

Grand Hôtel Jeanne d'Arc: 3 rue de Jarente 75004. Tel. 48 87 62 11. M St Paul.✶✶

Charming, small hotel in a peaceful street leading towards the rue de Turenne. All rooms clean and neat with spacious bathrooms. *Patron* M Aymard speaks a little English. V.

Grand Hôtel Malher: 5 rue Malher 75004. Tel. 42 72 60 92. M St Paul.✶–✶✶

Marvellous location in the Marais with great restaurants all around, but the street is busy – ask for a room at the back. Immaculate rooms with old-fashioned furniture. Some English spoken.

Maubuisson: 12 rue des Barres 75004. Tel. 42 72 72 09. M Hôtel de Ville.✶

More of a hostel than hotel in a quiet location in a tiny street behind the church of St Gervais-St Protais. Another 17th-century building, simple, cheap accommodation, spotlessly clean. (See also **Student/Youth Accommodation**, p. 70.)

Hôtel de Nice: 42 bis rue de Rivoli 75004. Tel. 42 78 55 29. M Hôtel de Ville/St Paul.*—**

Superbly situated, minutes from the Beaubourg, clean and immaculate rooms, friendly staff, English spoken. . . but the rue de Rivoli is noisy. Apparently this is no deterrent to the hotel's loyal following and at peak times you need to book two weeks in advance. MC, V.

Hôtel de la Place des Vosges: 12 rue de Birague 75004. Tel. 42 72 60 46. M Bastille.**

Situated in a quiet street off one of the city's loveliest squares, this hotel has plenty of historic charm. The building is 17th-century, the *salon* a medley of stone walls, wooden beams and tapestry-hung windows, but the bedrooms, all with private facilities and phone, are more modern in style. AE, DC, MC, V.

Pratic: 9 rue d'Ormesson 75004. Tel. 48 87 80 47. M St Paul.*

Recently renovated, clean and still inexpensive. Doors close at midnight.

St Louis: 75 rue St-Louis-en-l'Ile 75004. Tel. 46 34 04 80. M Pont-Marie.****

Converted from a 17th-century townhouse, this is a chic, family-run hotel, friendly and, for its location, not too expensive (double rooms are 470–570f). All rooms have phone and shower or bath; breakfast is served is the stone-vaulted basement *salon*. Busy street.

Sévigné: 2 rue Malher 75004. Tel. 42 72 76 17. M St Paul.**

Well-run, clean and tidy, all rooms with bath or shower. Price includes breakfast. English spoken. Don't be put off by the strange, mirrored décor in the lobby, but be warned that the location is a little noisy. Rooms facing rue Malher are quietest, but most on busy rue St Antoine have a nice view of the church of St Paul-St Louis. Some rooms sleep 3 for 400f.

Stella: 14 rue Neuve-St-Pierre 75004. Tel. 42 72 23 66. M St Paul.**

Good location in a quiet street just south of the rue St Antoine. Simple, clean and recently renovated, it represents value for money when you consider the location. English spoken. TC, EC with 10% surcharge.

Hôtel du Vieux Marais: 8 rue du Plâtre 75004. Tel. 42 78 47 22. M Rambuteau.***

Stylish, comfortable accommodation in a now fashionable part of Paris. Thirty recently refurbished bedrooms all have light, modern and airy bathrooms and phone. Quiet situation, very convenient for sightseeing on the right bank. Friendly welcome by the Rumiels family. V.

5e

Hôtel des Alliés: 20 rue Berthollet 75005. Tel. 43 31 47 52. M Censier-Daubenton.★
42 Spruce, simple rooms, 7 with bath/shower, 29 with *cabinet de toilette*, with prices from 130–220f for a double. MC, V.

Hôtel le Central: 6 rue Descartes 75005. Tel. 46 33 57 93. M Cardinal Lemoine.★
Simple, inexpensive base near the Sorbonne.

Esmeralda: 4 rue St-Julien-le-Pauvre 75005. Tel. 43 54 19 20. M St Michel/Maubert-Mutualité.★★
In the heart of the city's oldest quarter, the Esmeralda occupies a fine building dating from the 16th century. *Patronne* Michele Bruel is an ex-sculptress, which explains the artistic flair that predominates among stone walls, tiled floors and old beams. Plenty of Gallic charm. Most of the bedrooms are small, dark and cosy with en suite bathrooms, although at the time of writing a few, cheaper rooms without facilities were available for less than 150f.

Hôtel des Grandes Écoles: 75 rue de Cardinal Lemoine 75005. Tel. 43 26 79 23. M Cardinal Lemoine.★★
This is a real find, but it's not exactly a secret, and it's wise to book at least a week in advance at peak times (telephone bookings taken between 2pm and 6pm). Close to the Sorbonne and Faculté des Sciences, this unpretentious hotel looks like a country mansion, surrounded as it is by lovely gardens at one end of a rustic, cobbled courtyard. There are two annexes to the main building. Almost all the simple bedrooms have shower or bath, all have a phone, overlook the peaceful garden and score high on charm. Third star must be imminent. AE, DC, MC, V.

Hôtel des Grands Hommes: 17 place du Panthéon 75005. Tel. 46 34 19 60. M Luxembourg.★★★★
At the top of our price range we include this comfortable and friendly 32-room hotel not just for its great location opposite the Panthéon and its three-star amenities, but because it claims to be the place where Surrealism was created – and has a marble plaque to substantiate it. André Breton and other surrealist painters are amongst the *grands hommes* who used to stay here. Rooms furnished in authentic, period style, 580–650f. Reduced rates in low season. AE, DC, MC, V.

Grand Hôtel d'Harcourt: 3 boulevard St Michel 75005. Tel. 43 26 52 35. M St Michel.★★
Busy street, but what a location, facing the St Michel fountain, and within walking distance of Notre-Dame, the Cluny Museum and Luxembourg Gardens. Recently renovated, this place is clean,

comfortable and welcoming but not at all grand. Spacious breakfast room. *Patron* M. Abed speaks good English. V, MC.

Plaisant: 50 rue des Bernadins 75005. Tel. 43 54 74 57. M Maubert-Mutualité.☆

Welcoming and homely two-star hotel where rooms with *cabinet* cost 190f; with bath, WC 350f.

6e

Hôtel des Academies: 15 rue de la Grande Chaumière 75006. Tel. 43 26 66 44. M Vavin.☆

One-star, no-frills. Twenty-one rooms, 17 with shower/bath (220f), 4 with *cabinet* (163f).

Alsace Lorraine: 14 rue des Canettes 75006. Tel. 43 25 10 14. M Mabillon.☆–☆☆

Modest hotel occupying a *monument historique* whose popularity in former times waxed and waned with visiting artists and writers. Quiet street, views of the towers of St Sulpice, comfortable rooms with rustic furniture and a preponderance of "I love Paris" Americans among the clientèle. V, DC, AE.

Delhy's: 22 rue de l'Hirondelle 75006. Tel. 43 26 58 25. M St Michel.☆

Pint-sized hotel in tiny street just off the place St Michel. Small but pleasant rooms, comfortable and popular. MC, V.

La Louisiane: 60 rue de Seine 75006. Tel. 43 29 59 30. M Odéon.☆☆☆

Functional Rive Gaucherie at budget price: double-glazing protects from the bustle of the rue de Buci market down below. Juliette Greco once lived here. Simone de Beauvoir, Hemingway, Sartre used to stay here. Rooms 400f. DC, MC, V.

Hôtel des Marronniers: 21 rue Jacob 75006. Tel. 43 25 30 60. M St-Germain-des-Près.☆☆☆

Tall, gracious hotel in the heart of St Germain, yet quiet thanks to its courtyard setting and chestnut tree-hung little garden. A glazed verandah overlooks the garden and breakfast is served in the stone-vaulted cellars. Fresh flowers everywhere. All bedrooms have shower or bath and phone and the public spaces have plenty of cosy sofas and chairs for lounging. Bathrooms are small. Rooms are 480–525f.

Nesle: 7 rue de Nesle 75006. Tel. 43 54 62 41. M Odéon. ☆Footloose favourite.

Extraordinary place much loved by students and footloosers, run by a redoubtable *patronne*. Each room is individually decorated in a wide range of styles: some have bathrooms, most have thin walls. Breakfast is served on brass trays to the sound of Arab music. There's a Turkish bath, a small garden, and a great sense of fun. Washer and dryer for guests' use. Cash only, in advance.

Pension de Famille Poirier: 120 boulevard Raspail 75006. Tel. 45 48 24 15. M Notre-Dame-des-Champs.★★

Authentic *pension* whose paying guests include students. Warm welcome, homely. Half board from 280f for one person, 360f for two; reduced terms for a stay of a month.

Perreyve, 63 rue Madame 75006. Tel. 45 48 35 01. M Rennes.★★★

Quiet location close by the Luxembourg Gardens. Recently renovated, comfortable bedrooms with smart if small bathrooms for 335–350f. Rather proper in style. All rooms have TV and phone. AE, DC, MC, V.

Récamier, 3 bis place St Sulpice 75006. Tel. 43 26 04 89. M St Sulpice.★★★

Don't be put off by its austere exterior – this is a cheerful resting place close to the Luxembourg Palace and the boulevard St Germain. Most of the small bedrooms have bath or shower *en suite* and are newly redecorated. Unremarkable but welcoming, with two little sitting rooms.

Regent's Hôtel: 44 rue Madame 75006. Tel.45 48 02 81. M St Sulpice.★★★

Pretty, quiet, calm and spacious with two-star comforts and a lovely garden (breakfast served here in good weather). MC, V.

St-André-des-Arts, 66 rue St-André-des-Arts 75006. Tel. 43 26 96 16. M Odéon.★★★

The owner of this historic hotel reckons that people stay here before they get famous and boring. The building is 17th-century, once the residence of the Musquetaires du Roi, and is little changed. Friendly welcome; lively, often noisy guests; and an equally noisy street (as much from strolling musicians as traffic). Accommodation nothing special but good fun.

Hôtel de Seine: 52 rue de Seine 75006. Tel. 46 34 22 80. M St-Germain-des-Prés/Odéon/Mabillon.★★

Close by the Latin Quarter in a quiet back street, this place is a find. No frills, but clean, efficient and welcoming. Good value: all bedrooms have bath/shower and phone, and breakfast is brought to your room. Plenty of return visitors, so book 2 weeks in advance in peak periods. AE, DC, MC, V.

Stanislas: 5 rue Montparnasse 75006. Tel. 45 48 37 05. M Notre-Dame-des-Champs.★–★★

Aged but welcoming, with clean if undistinguished rooms with double-glazing and TV.A room with a shower for 250f, shower/bath and loo for 270f or 290f. V.

7e

Bac St Germain: 66 rue du Bac 75007. Tel.42 22 20 03. M Rue du Bac.★★★

Immaculate, with a touch of luxury, in a brilliant location close to shops, museums and clubs. Bedrooms a little on the small side, but all have bath or shower, TV and radio/alarm. Breakfast is served on the seventh-floor glassed-in terrace (yes, there is a lift). Double rooms from 600f. AE, DC, MC, V.

Hôtel du Champ de Mars, 7 rue du Champ-de-Mars 75007, Tel. 45 51 52 30. M École Militaire.★★★

Clean, comfortable, friendly not spectacular but rooms more spacious than most comparable hotels in the area. All rooms have shower or bath. The street – plenty of bars and *tabacs* – is quiet by night. Recommended to eat breakfast in one of the neighbouring bars. MC, V.

Lenox St Germain: 9 rue de l'Université 75007. Tel. 42 96 10 95. M Rue du Bac.★★★★

Comfort and elegance three minutes' walk from the Seine and boulevard St Germain. This place may stretch the budget (rooms 400–560f) but it's marvellously situated, and has friendly, helpful staff. The Lenox began as a 19-century pension, accommodating literary lions like James Joyce. Elegant bedrooms, bar and sitting room. AE, DC, MC, V.

Grand Hôtel Leveque: 29 rue Cler 75007. Tel. 47 05 49 15. M École Militaire.★–★★

Marvellous location in a pedestrianised street lined with shops and stalls and wonderfully quiet by night. Small, cosy rooms recently redecorated.

Malar: 29 rue Malar 75007. Tel. 45 51 38 46. M Latour Maubourg.★★

A warm welcome, a loyal following, well-kept and modest, this is good value. Most rooms with shower/bath, TV. Prices from 210f.

Muguet, 11 rue Chevert, 75007. Tel. 47 05 05 93. M École Militaire.★

From some rooms of this friendly, family run hotel there are views of the Eiffel Tower or the dome of Les Invalides. Simple double room for 220f, with a shower 250f, add a WC and it'll be around 320f. AE, V.

Le Pavillon: 54 rue St Dominique 75007. Tel. 45 51 42 87. M Invalides/Latour Maubourg.★★★–★★★★

No public rooms, hence breakfast is served promptly in what are mostly small bedrooms, but the location is good (roughly midway between the Eiffel Tower and Les Invalides) and the ambience charming. In the 18th century this was a convent, set back from the bustle of the main street beyond a little courtyard and wrought-iron gates. All bedrooms have bath/shower and phone and are prettily decorated. A double costs from 390f. MC, V.

Prince: 66 avenue Bosquet 75007. Tel. 47 05 40 90. M École Militaire.★★

Small, especially good value, hence booked up in peak periods weeks in advance. All rooms have bath or shower, TV. Those facing the charming avenue Bosquet are double-glazed. English spoken. Cheerful jolly *patron*, M Roussel. AE, V.

Quai Voltaire: 19 quai Voltaire 75007. Tel. 42 61 50 91. M Wolférino.★★★★

Brilliant views over the Seine to the Tuileries Gardens beyond, brilliant past (frequented by Oscar Wilde, Charles Baudelaire), but noisy. The small bar is still the haunt of contemporary literati and a bedroom at the front of the building affords dreamy views. Double rooms from 430f. Take earplugs. AE, DC, MC, V.

Le Royal Phare: 40 avenue de la Motte-Picquet 75007. Tel. 47 05 57 30. M École Militaire.★★

All bedrooms have shower or bath, and renovations and redecorations were underway as we wrote. A warm welcome, nice atmosphere and good value in a brilliant shopping area. The street is quiet at night but bursts into action early in the morning. AE, MC, V.

Solférino: 91 rue de Lille 75007. Tel.47 05 85 54. M Solférino.★★★★

On a quiet street close to the Seine and a couple of minutes from the d'Orsay museum, this is one of the few medium-priced hotels in a smart, expensive area. (Double rooms from 486f.) Family-run, it scores high on comfort and a cheerful welcome. The bedrooms are prettily furnished and have bath/shower and phone, and there's an appealing little *salon*. The breakfast room is light and summery. MC, V.

Suède: 31 rue Vaneau, 75007. Tel.47 05 00 08. M Sèvres-Babylone.★★★★

Elegant, backing on to the Prime Minister's official residence (ask for a room on the second or third floor for a view). Spacious lounge and pretty inner courtyard where tea is served in summer. All bedrooms have bath/shower and phone; a double costs from 445f. AE, MC, V.

Hôtel de l'Université: 22 rue de l'Université 75007. Tel. 42 61 09 39. M Rue du Bac.★★★★

Antique, tapestries, plush comfort and a wide range of rooms from 510f to luxury apartments with private terraces. All bedrooms have shower/bath and phone. Quietest rooms at the back. Breakfast is served at marble tables in a lovely inner courtyard with flowers and fountain. The hotel occupies what was once a 17th-century mansion near the Seine. Bags of style and popular, so book well in advance.

Hôtel de Varenne: 44 rue de Bourgogne 75007. Tel. 45 51 45 55. M Varenne.★★★

Excellent location beside Les Invalides and close to the boulevard St

Germain. Well cared for, not particularly stylish but peaceful. Plenty of fresh flowers around and a small courtyard for summer breakfasts. All bedrooms have phone, TV and bathroom; prices from 410f.

8e

Argenson: 15 rue d'Argenson 75008. Tel. 42 65 16 87. M St Augustin/Miromesnil.★★★★
Good value in an expensive *arrondissement*, off boulevard Haussmann.

Bradford: 10 rue St-Philippe-du-Roule 75008. Tel. 43 59 24 20. M St-Philippe-du-Roule.★★★
Expensive (double room – 600f) but has its regulars who are addicted to its old-fashioned charm. Large, pleasant rooms, brand new bathrooms, friendly staff, and in a quiet street close to the rue du Faubourg-St-Honoré and the Champs-Élysées.

Marigny: 11 rue de l'Arcade 75008. Tel. 42 66 42 71. M St Lazare.★★
Charming, modest hotel, prettily furnished and sparkling clean five minutes' walk from the place de la Concorde. Double rooms 360f. V.

Hôtel du Ministère: 31 rue de Surène 75008. Tel. 42 66 21 43. M Madeleine.★
Modest hotel with 32 rooms, half a dozen of which are cheaper at 215f; for a double with private bath/shower expect to pay more. Rue de Surenne runs down to La Madeleine; Concorde is a few minutes' walk away. AE, V.

9e

Hôtel des Arts: 7 Cité Bergère 75009. Tel. 42 46 73 30. M Rue Montmartre.★★
Immaculate rooms with TV, phone, radio. Free parking is a bonus if you need it. Rooms with private facilities around 300f. AE, DC, V.

Hôtel de Berne, 30 rue de Châteaudun 75009. Tel. 48 74 37 66. M Le Peletier.★
Recently redecorated, very helpful attitude (they'll muster ham and eggs for breakfast if you want), but most rooms suffer from noisy traffic. Not to be confused with hotel of same name but very different prices in the 8e *arrondissement*.

Chopin: 46 passage Jouffroy 75009. Tel. 47 70 58 10. M Rue Montmartre.★★
Unusual, attractive and restful location in one of those traffic-free arcades close to the Opéra quarter. Most of the rooms are small but all have bath and phone, and the hotel itself, built in the mid-19th-century, has plenty of charm. MC, V.

Fénelon: 23 rue Buffault 75009. Tel. 48 78 32 18. M Le Peletier/Cadet.✩

TV and phones in 38 rooms, either with bath/shower or *cabinet de toilette*, and costing 180–340f for a double. Near the Folies Bergère. AE, V.

Grand Hôtel Lafayette-Buffault: 6 rue Buffault 75009. Tel. 47 70 70 96. M Le Peletier/Cadet.✩–✩✩

Two-star amenities – phones, TV in rooms, and there's a lift. Cheaper rooms (210f) have *cabinet*; you'll pay up to 390f for a private bath/shower. V.

Hôtel de Lille: 2 rue Montholon 75009. Tel. 47 70 38 76. M Cadet.✩

Rock-bottom prices, basic, clean and neat rooms. Don't be put off by the gloomy entrance.

Riboutté Lafayette: 5 rue Riboutté 75009. Tel. 47 70 62 36. M Cadet.✩✩✩

Quiet, prettily furnished hotel with a small *salon*. The bedrooms are individually decorated, some overlooking the courtyard. Those facing the street have double glazing. All have bath/shower, TV and phone, and prices are from 350f. MC, V.

10e

Hôtel du Centre: 4 rue Sibour 76010. Tel. 46 07 20 74. M Gare de l'Est.

Something of a find for budget travellers, this is five minutes from the Gare de l'Est. Clean and spacious, with large bedrooms, many with *en suite* bathrooms (mostly new and spotlessly clean). Don't expect the latest in carpets and decoration.

Hôtel Gare du Nord: 33 rue de St Quentin 75010. Tel. 48 78 02 92. M Gare du Nord.✩✩

Of the 49 rooms in this three-star establishment within shunting distance of the Gare du Nord, half a dozen come with *cabinets* at 280f. (The rest are priced up to 450f for a double.) AE, MC, V.

Jarry: 4 rue Jarry 75010. Tel. 47 70 70 38. M Château d'Eau.✩

Pleasant, clean and recently refurbished cash-only hotel where the concierge speaks good English. Close to the Gare de l'Est.

Hôtel du Jura, 6 rue Jarry 75010. Tel. 47 70 06 66. M Château d'Eau.✩

Basic, very cheap (double with shower 170f including breakfast) and cheerful, although it's in need of some redecoration. Cash only.

Hôtel de la Nouvelle France: 23 rue des Messageries 75010. Tel. 48 24 70 74. M Poissonière.✩

Inexpensive, yet has spacious, quiet bedrooms; staff are friendly and speak a little English.

Residence Magenta: 35 rue Yves Toudic 75010. Tel. 42 40 17 72. M Jacques Bonsergent.*–**

Two-star, 32-room hotel with prices ranging from 240–280f. All rooms have TV, phone. Location is unpromising but it's near a Métro. AE, MC. V.

Terminus Nord: 12 boulevard Denain 75010. Tel. 42 80 20 00. M Gare du Nord.****

Really big hotel (220 rooms) opposite the Gare du Nord with a range of prices from around 400f for a double. Bedrooms with private bath have a TV too. All those facing the street are insulated against noise. There's a bar, phones in all rooms, and a curious bonus – no charge for local calls. AE, MC, DC, V.

11e

Camélia: 6 avenue Philippe Auguste 75011. Tel. 43 73 67 50. M RER Nation.*

No frills, one-star, simple but adequate rooms from 120f.

Notre-Dame: 51 rue de Malte 75011. Tel. 47 00 78 76. M République.*

Peaceful, pleasantly decorated with homely touches, and inexpensive, this is a good find ... but you'll have to book well in advance throughout the high season. Closed in August. V.

Pax: 12 rue Charonne 75011. Tel. 47 00 40 98. M Ledru Rollin.*

Spruce and simple one-star, 47-room hotel. Some rooms 250f; some take three or four people. V.

Residence Alhambra: 11 bis rue de Malte 75011. Tel. 47 00 35 52. M Oberkampf.**

Good value on the eastern fringe of the Marais. 50 rooms, with bath or shower, TV, phone for 260f. Credit: AE, DC, MC, V.

Bethia: 3 rue Général-Blaise 75011. Tel. 47 00 47 18. M St Ambroise.*

In the heart of a quiet and peaceful bourgeois quarter, out of the way of the bustle of Paris, inexpensive and good value. Rooms are all recently redecorated.

Sans-Souci: 113 boulevard Ménilmontant 75011. Tel. 43 57 00 58. M Ménilmontant/Maur.*

Nice atmosphere, unpretentious, clean, and except for the few rooms facing the boulevard, quiet. Renovations underway. Double rooms currently 120–140f.

Hôtel de Vienne: 43 rue de Malte 75011. Tel. 48 05 44 42. M Oberkampf.*

Clean, modestly-priced rooms from 120f, incredible value on the fringe of the Marais.

12e

Hôtel de Marseille: 21 rue d'Austerlitz 75012. Tel. 43 43 54 22. M Gare de Lyon.⋆

Basic (no rooms have private loo) but clean, tidy and pleasant. Close to the Gare de Lyon.

13e

Hôtel des Arts: 8 rue Coypel 75013. Tel. 47 07 76 32. M Place d'Italie.⋆

No frills establishment; rooms have phones, private facilities. Cost 130–170f for a double.

Pacific: 8 rue Philippe-de-Champagne 750013. Tel. 43 31 17 06. M Place d'Italie.⋆

Comfortable, somewhat old-fashioned hotel right next to a *gendarmerie*, but conveniently close to the avenue des Gobelins (marvellous selection of small, inexpensive restaurants).

Rubens: 32 rue de Banquier 75013. Tel. 43 31 73 30. M Campo-Formio.⋆

Quiet location, with no through traffic, minutes' walk from the avenue des Gobelins and its selection of good restaurants. Nice rooms, big baths. Take your cash.

14e

Hôtel des Bains, 33 rue Delambre 75014. Tel. 42 20 85 27. M Edgar Quintet.⋆⋆

Recently renovated and upgraded. Pleasant, unremarkable base in a relatively quiet street (good for bargain clothes and food) within walking distance of the Tour de Montparnasse, the Gare Montparnasse and the legendary cafés of the boulevard du Montparnasse.

Le Châtillon: 11 square de Châtillon, 75014. Tel. 45 42 31 17. M Alésia.⋆⋆

Quirky little hotel five minutes from Alésia Metro (good for catacombs, discount clothing, exploring left bank), with apparently Anglophile owners, Monique and Daniel Lamouret. Comfortable beds, creaky floors. Quietly located in a cul-de-sac. Great value for money and highly recommended. V.

Fred: 11 avenue Villemain, 75014. Tel.45 43 24 18. M Plaisance.⋆–⋆⋆

Two-star comforts from 235–375f for three. AE, DC, V.

Hôtel du Parc: 8 rue Jolivet, 75014. Tel. 43 20 95 54. M Edgar Quintet, Montparnasse-Bienvenue.⋆

Within 5 minutes' walk of both the Tower and the Station in

Montparnasse, this little hotel is nevertheless quiet. It overlooks a tiny, triangular park just off the rue de la Gaîté, and has double-glazing. Basic, clean accommodation.

Hôtel de la Loire, 39 bis rue du Moulin-Vert 75014. Tel. 45 40 66 88. M Alésia/Plaisance.★

Quiet situation, in narrow cobbled street. Relaxed atmosphere. Small rooms downstairs (185f) face a pretty little garden; large rooms upstairs (320f) sleep up to four people. V.

15e

Tourisme: 66 avenue de La Motte-Picquet 75015. Tel. 47 34 28 01. M Dupleix La Motte Picquet.★★

Large (60 rooms) undistinguished two-star hotel, but immaculate rooms have phones, TVs, private facilities, 230–350f. Near the Eiffel Tower. Good value.

16e

Le Marois: 18 rue le Marois 75016. Tel. 46 51 13 14. M Porte St Cloud.★

Well-kept small hotel with basic amenities, rooms from 200f, to include, unusually, breakfast.

Hôtel du Ranelagh: 56 rue de l'Assomption 75016. Tel.42 88 31 63. M Ranelagh.★

Family-run, quiet and pleasant hotel with everything sparkling clean, comfortable and friendly. Well off the beaten tourist track, yet close to the good cafés and shops of the lovely avenue Mozart. Closed last 2 weeks of July.

Stella: 133 avenue Victor Hugo 75016. Tel. 45 53 55 94. M Victor-Hugo.★

This is such a good deal that you need to book one month ahead in the summer, and advance reservation is advisable at other times of the year. Prettily decorated rooms, generously sized bath towels, small but comfortable bathrooms from 160f for two. Need we say more?

17e

Hôtel de Banville: 166 boulevard Berthier 75017. Tel. 42 67 70 16. M Porte de Champerret/Pereire.★★★★

Lift, two lounges, bar, breakfast room – three-star facilities in this very friendly, agreeable, family-run 40-room hotel which is popular with out-of-town French people. Yes, it's in the boring 17e but near a Métro and 10 minutes' walk from l'Étoile. Rooms are 520f. AE, DC, MC, V.

Étoile: 3 rue de l'Étoile 75017. Tel. 43 80 36 94. M Ternes.★★★★

A touch of luxury close to the Arc de Triomphe. Rooms are 540–590f. Thick wall-to-wall carpets, TV, phone, mini-bar and smart bathrooms to all rooms. There's also a bar and small library in the lobby. AE, DC, MC, V.

La Régence-Étoile: 24 avenue Carnot 75013. Tel. 43 80 75 60. M Charles de Gaulle Étoile.★★★

Family-run three-star hotel in a listed 1875 house, spacious, traditionally furnished with smart bathrooms, TV and phones in all rooms (375–520f). The avenue Carnot is busy so that rooms at the front, though bigger, are somewhat noisy. Close to the Arc de Triomphe, this is also convenient for the Champs-Élysées, the avenue Foch and Bois de Boulogne. EC, DC, MC, V.

Regent's Garden: 6 rue Pierre-Demours 75017. Tel. 45 74 07 30. M Ternes.★★★★

Situated in a quiet, residential area, this has a thoroughly bourgeois setting: a real garden, complete with fountains and statues, and lofty, spacious rooms appropriately furnished with big mirrors and brass bedsteads. All have well-equipped modern bathrooms, phones and TV including cable, costing from 610f for a double. Arc de Triomphe close by. AE, DC, MC, V.

18e

André Gill: 4 rue André Gill 75018. Tel.42 62 48 48. M Pigalle.★

Very close to the sleazy Pigalle, but in a quiet cul-de-sac lined with trees. Recently completely renovated, all bedrooms are pleasant, some made memorable by pretty stained glass windows. They range from 160–250f for a double. AE, MC, DC, V.

Prima-Lepic: 29 rue Lepic 75018. Tel. 46 06 44 64. M Blanche.★★

In the heart of Montmartre, 10 minutes' walk from Sacré-Coeur, this is a family-run hotel. Bedrooms, modest in size, are individually decorated and all have bath/shower, TV and phone. A generous buffet breakfast is served in a *trompe-l'oeil* indoor garden room. MC, V.

19e

Le Laumière: 4 rue Petit 75019. Tel.42 06 10 77. M Laumière.

You may not be keen on staying so far from the centre, but this friendly two-star family-run hotel between the Buttes Chaumont park and Bassin de la Villett provides good value. V.

20e

Palma: 77 avenue Gambetta 75020. Tel. 46 36 13 65. M Gambetta.

Very close to the Père Lachaise cemetery, you get TVs in the rooms of this modest but comfortable two-star hotel, where a double room with private bath/shower is 290–335f. AE, V.

LA CRÈME DE LA CRÈME

Paris has some of the most prestigious and palatial hotels in the world. A night at one of these will cost upwards of 1800 francs.

Le Bristol: 112 rue du Faubourg St-Honoré 75008. Tel. 42 66 91 45. M Miromésnil.

Traditional, luxurious, discreet; stuffed full of oil paintings, sumptuous carpets and tapestries. Built in 1924 with a new no-expense-spared wing added in 1975. Vast garden overlooked by the summer restaurant.

Guests may take a dip in the roof-top pool, designed to the specifications of Aristotle Onassis' yacht designer.

Le Crillon: 10 place de la Concorde 75008. Tel. 42 65 24. M Concorde.

The only French-owned grand hotel in Paris was built by the same architect who designed Le Petit Trianon in Versailles – Jacques-Ange Gabriel. You might well *be* at Versailles in the mirrored splendour of the Ambassadeurs restaurant. Magnificent views from the hotel, across the place de la Concorde to the Seine from suites.

Georges V: 31 avenue Georges V 75008. Tel. 47 23 54 00. M Georges V.

More international in atmosphere; majestic public areas and a pretty inner courtyard.

Grand: 2 rue Scribe 75009. Tel. 40 07 32 32. M Opéra.

A massive restoration programme completed 3 years ago has transformed the 19th-century palace: Art Nouveau style predominates. Huge (471 rooms) and popular with international business jet setters.

Intercontinental: 3 rue Castiglione 75008. Tel. 42 60 37 80. M Tuileries.

One of the largest of the grand hotels (424 rooms), designed by Garnier of Paris Opéra fame (also the Grand, above).

Meurice: 228 rue de Rivoli 75001. Tel. 42 60 38 60. M Tuileries. Opened in 1816, the Meurice has strong connections with 19th-century English travellers, but more recently it's the international jet set who enjoy its opulence.

Plaza Athénée: 25 avenue Montaigne 75008. Tel. 47 23 78 33. M Franklin D. Roosevelt.

Glamour of the old-fashioned Hollywood kind permeates every corner, providing an opulent backdrop to American movie stars and European royals who are loyal to this grand hotel. Mata Hari and Katharine Hepburn have stayed there.

Prince de Galles: 33 avenue Georges V 75008. Tel. 47 23 55 11. M Georges V/Alma Marceau.

A star in the American Marriot chain, with Art Deco mosaics in the original 1928 bathrooms and a columned interior patio.

Ritz: 15 place Vendôme 75001. Tel. 42 60 38 30. M Tuileries.

Synonymous with luxury, the image created by César Ritz, enhanced by the patronage of Coco Chanel, Hemingway and Proust. Beautiful and not over-the-top period furnishings, a delightful inner garden, huge and splendid original baths – you name it, the Ritz has got it right.

Royal Monceau: 37 avenue Hoche 75008. Tel. 45 61 98 00. M Étoile.

Midway between the Arc de Triomphe and the bucolic Parc Monceau, this gracious hotel attracts those who appreciate privacy and attentive service. Serene "un-hotel-like" bedrooms and varied restaurants.

There's a health spa and a pool surrounded by greenery as well as a state-of-the-art business centre.

Luxury Paris

If you've money to blow on a luxurious night or two, Paris remains the ultimate city in which to live regally. The luxury, elegance, service and high style of the city's "palace" hotels are unrivalled, but you don't have to stay at the Ritz or the Crillon to find it, nor do you have to pay top-whack prices (that's between 2500f to 3500f a night). Listed below are some of Paris' more quietly glittering hotels where the cost of a double room is under the 2000f mark per night. Remember that a few may be featured in inclusive tour operators' short breaks programmes at attractive rates, so check the brochures. (VFB, for instance, offer the Relais Christine.)

Hôtel Balzac: 6 rue Balzac 75008. Tel. 45 61 97 22. M George V. 1500–19090+f

Discreet (you can sometimes spot certain royals keeping a low profile), immaculate service, 70 recently refurbished rooms including 14 suites. Some of these have terraces and views of the Eiffel Tower. Marble, heavily mirrored bathrooms have Nina Ricci toiletries. AE, DC, MC, V.

Hôtel Duc de Saint-Simon: 14 rue de Saint-Simon 75007. Tel. 45 48 35 66. M Rue du Bac. 850–1890f

Four of the 34 individually decorated rooms have terraces and several overlook the peaceful inner garden. Antiques, bowls of roses, countryside quiet. Traveller's cheques and cash only.

Relais Christine: 3 rue Christine 75006. Tel. 43 26 71 80. M St Michel/Odéon. 1050–1900f

A massive gateway leads to the cobbled courtyard of what was a 16th-century convent. All the 51 bedrooms maintain an air of quiet calm; some lead on to a grassy inner courtyard. Free underground car park but you must reserve a place in advance. Air-conditioning, marble bathrooms, open fires, elegant *salon* and a spectacular breakfast room made from the 16th-century arched cellar. AE, DC, MC, V.

Relais St-Germain, 9 Carrefour de l'Odéon 75006. Tel. 43 29 12 05. M Odéon. 850–1250f

A tiny hotel with only nine bedrooms and one suite occupying a medieval house. Owners M and Mme Laipsker are interior designers. Attentive staff, marble bathrooms, air-conditioning and a breakfast of pastries, breads, cheese, fruit and fruit juices included in the cost. AE, DC, MC, V.

La Résidence du Bois, 16 rue Chalgrin 75016. Tel. 45 00 50 59. M Argentine/Étoile. 850–1890f.

Run like a well-staffed private home, with a wide range, and cost, of rooms. Antiques, paintings, porcelain and wall hangings in abundance, and a quiet, grassy, tree-shaded garden with terrace, chairs and tables. No credit cards.

Le Saint-Grégoire: 43 rue de l'Abbé Grégoire 75006. Tel. 45 48 33 95. M St Placide. 850–1250f

Small, privately-owned hotel occupying a late 18th-century town house and decorated by David Hicks. Some of the 20 bedrooms have their own terrace or little garden. Some rooms are air-conditioned. Owners Lucie Agaud and Michel Bouvier also own the neighbouring restaurant "La Marlotte" – fine food in a medieval setting. AE, DC, MC, V.

San Régis, 12 rue Jean Goujon 75008. Tel. 43 59 41 90. M Franklin D. Roosevelt/Champs-Élysées/Clemenceau. 1500–1900+f

Intimate and exclusive in atmosphere – more like a stately private home than hotel. Chandeliers, marble and antique furniture contribute to its grandeur, though some of its 47 rooms are predominantly modern. Discreet, impeccable service. AE, DC, MC.

WHERE TO EAT

For all its reputation as the culinary capital of the universe, you cannot count on being able to eat well in Paris wherever you happen to unfurl your napkin. Having said that, with care you can eat extremely well even on the most modest budget.

Of the thousands of restaurants in the city, some are the most exalted and expensive in the world. In appropriately reverent tones we'll mention L'Ambroisie, Lucas-Corton, Taillevent (gastronauts claim this is the best in Paris), Tour d'Argent, Jamin. We're talking nourishment at its most sublime here — book weeks in advance and set aside a month's salary for the bill.

But its reputation as an Eating City is not entirely founded on the grand style. It was earned in the kitchens of French households and translated into the traditional, family-owned bistros and local brasseries, plenty of which you can still find in Paris. Many are mentioned in the guide that follows, places where flair and *savoir-faire* do not necessarily influence the size of the bill. And, on the subject of bills, even though prices have risen quite a bit in the last few years, you can, on the whole, have a satisfying meal for less than half the price of a comparable one in London or New York.

The area you choose to eat in, as well as the type of establishment, have a dramatic bearing on the prices, which vary a great deal: a sandwich and drink in a tourist trap on or around the Champs-Élysées, for example, could easily set you back as much as a set menu in a Latin Quarter backstreet. As a rule, the more bourgeois districts like the 8e will tend to be more pricey than less chic *arrondissements*, or ones like the 5e where there are places catering for the local student crowd.

Snacks can take a huge chunk out of a daily budget so you'd be wise to follow our suggestions below for takeaways and fuel-stops.

There's an incomparable range of eateries and cosmopolitan styles of cooking. A lot of very good restaurants aren't even French – you can try virtually every country's cuisine in Paris. There are Greek tavernas, Vietnamese and Japanese restaurants, displaying windows of whole glazed ducks, many varieties of couscous, piled high with spicy sausage or served with chicken or shellfish. Wander down some streets, like rue Mouffetard or St Séverin in the 5e, and you'll find almost every kind of cuisine. Because of France's West African colonial empire, Paris has a sizeable black African community – quite apart from the trendy Beur (North African) movement. There are countless North African eateries all over Paris but they're especially concentrated in the Belleville-Ménilmontant district. You can discover Senegalese food at African restaurants where, despite imperialistic excesses of the past, the welcome is never less than friendly.

There are no such things as Parisian specialities, but you will find a wide range of regional cooking from all over France, so you might sample *oeufs bourguignons* (eggs poached in red wine sauce) or *boeuf bourguignon* (a wine-sodden beef stew), a Marseilles-style *bouillabaisse*, *choucroute* Alsatian-style, or a simple plate of perfectly smoked Auverge ham.

Some *quartiers* are particularly known for their concentration of ethnic or French regional restaurants. A little bit of seaside Normandy surrounds the Gare St Lazare where the restaurants specialise in seafood brought in on the early morning trains; you'll find *Lyonnais* food near the Gare de Lyon. In the Marais there are many Jewish restaurants. Asian restaurants are ubiquitous, but the 13e "Asia in Paris" and 20e have loads of them.

Restaurants serve meals (not drinks by themselves) and usually only within the midday and evening meal times, but there are other options if you want a drink or a mid-afternoon snack – (See **Cafés**, page 158). Even a very unpretentious restaurant will be reluctant to serve you with just one dish, unless it's a main course and includes a side salad or other trimmings.

Styles of Cooking

Even in the regions there are different types of cooking. Top of the league is *haute cuisine*. This is food for treats, where it becomes an art form with its own rules and rituals and, as you'd expect, it doesn't come cheap. The French generally spend a large proportion of their income on food and drink and build such occasional indulgences into their budgets as gastronomic special events.

Although it can, in a different way, be as enjoyable as *haute cuisine*, the other main style of French cooking is family-style, or *cuisine bourgeoise*, the hearty fodder that gets eaten every day. Mundane ingredients are used imaginatively, herbs and other seasonings help out a lot. In fact *cuisine bourgeoise* has seen an upsurge in Parisian restaurants almost eclipsing pure *nouvelle* and *haute* cuisine in popularity, though the great classic dishes will survive all changes of fashion.

Nouvelle cuisine (not exactly "new" as the term crops up in earlier culinary history) initially provided a useful corrective to some of the excesses of classic French cooking and when it is at its best is lighter than traditional French cuisine, juxtaposing unusual, top-quality ingredients, meticulously presented in smaller portions. The trend now is for chefs to eschew labels and pursue their own individual style.

RESERVATIONS

Except for some of the very cheap restaurants where you might not be able to, it's imperative to book. The best ones – which are not necessarily the most pricey – get booked up quickly. Some restaurants have imposed official limits of up to 40% on bookings for foreigners, to keep their xenophobic regulars happy. If you happen to have booked at a very posh restaurant weeks ago, do ring the day before to reconfirm the reservation.

TIPPING

All restaurants, cafés and bars in France now have to include a service charge in the bill, so no additional tip is expected, although if you've eaten especially well or are pleased with the service you can always drop an extra few francs on the table.

OPENING HOURS

Some restaurants in Paris open only for lunch *or* for dinner and Parisians tend to lunch early, between midday and 2pm. Arrive before 12.30 to be sure of getting a table. In the evening last orders in some places may be 9.30–10pm. In the smarter restaurants business doesn't tend to pick up before 8.30–9.30pm. Brasseries stay open later. Many Paris restaurants are closed on Sundays and public holidays. Those restaurants which do open at Sunday lunchtime tend to be busy, as it's traditionally the time French families eat out together. They may well then be closed all day Monday. It's not unusual for places to close down for a whole month in the summer – sometimes for the whole of August, sometimes from July–August. However, there's no hard and fast rule; restaurants that don't want to miss the tourist business may stay open but close in January or February instead.

FOOD GUIDES

We've given our value for money selection below but it cannot hope to be definitive. The *Michelin Red Guide to Paris* and *Gault Millau* are both highly regarded, and the restaurant section of *Paris Pas Cher* (Flammarion, 99f) is particularly useful. The best guide we've come across to *salons de thé*, ice-cream parlours and places serving light lunches is *Paris Sucré* (Hachette, 79f). Both are only available in French.

MENU TIPS

If you're looking at the fixed price menu (*menu à prix fixe* or *menu conseillé*) does it include drink (*boisson comprise* or *bc, vin comprise* or *vc*)? Are there any *supplements* on

Restaurant Tips

- Don't be diffident when it comes to asking what some of the arcane, or perhaps illegible, names are on the menu. Maybe it's a dish invented by the chef and baffling even to the French diners at the adjoining table.

- Don't be alarmed if you're not exactly pandered to in French restaurants. Traditionally Parisian workers put up a convincing show of accepting customers only on sufferance and quite often there's a grumpy *patron* around. The golden rule — and it's easier said than done — is do not be intimidated by their disdainful looks. It's nothing personal and highly possible that the waiter doesn't understand anyone else's French either.

- More restaurant mores — bite your tongue if you get the urge to call the waiter *garçon*, even if he *is* young. Use Monsieur, Madame or Mademoiselle, and it's polite to say *Bonjour* or *Bonsoir, Monsieur/Madame* as you go into a restaurant and throw an *Au revoir* into the air as you leave.

- You can avoid the disdain of anyone within earshot by not ordering tea, coffee, milk or any alcoholic beverage except wine with your food. The French usually, but not *always,* drink wine with their meals and, contrary to myth, it's perfectly OK to order mineral water — or even a jug of tap water instead which would also save you money. (*Une carafe d'eau, s'il vous plaît.*)

- Don't be afraid to share a dish you want to try — unless, of course, that's the only thing you're ordering.

- Children and dogs are welcome in a great many restaurants but they are expected to be well behaved.

- In humbler restaurants: there may be paper tablecloths which the waiter might use to do his sums on; you may well be expected to use the same knife and fork throughout the meal.

- A great many restaurants have two types of menu, *à la carte* and fixed price — known as *un menu,* sometimes *menu conseillé*. Prices soon mount up if you order *à la carte*. Stick to the fixed price *menu* (which offers a number of courses with limited choice) and the house wine (*carafe*) in the places we mention and the sight of your bill won't give you dyspepsia. Some *menus* will include a quarter of a litre of wine or mineral water. You may see the words *"formule"*

— a two-course *menu* (choice of starter and main course or main course and dessert).

- Some of the cheaper *prix fixe* menus (i.e. under 80f) are brilliant value, but others all but toss out quality to keep the price at rock bottom — fine if you need to have a good feed to stop yourself falling over, but disappointing gastronomically. It might be a good idea to have a picnic or snack lunch instead and re-allocate your funds to a really splendid dinner.

- Wine and other drinks might easily send the price soaring. If you have an aperitif or two, drink during the meal and take a cognac after, you'll probably need another drink to steady you when you get the bill. Hedonistic paupers can save money by taking their preprandial drinks and cognacs at a little bar. The French do not always have an aperitif before a meal and it's unusual for them to have drinks at the table in a restaurant before dining.

- All French restaurants must, by law, display their menu outside. Check that the prices include service (*service compris* or *prix nets*). If not, it will be added to your bill automatically. Incidentally, a handwritten menu in French rather than a printed one, tends to be a promising sign, especially if it hasn't been translated.

- Don't take the decor as an indication of likely standards in the kitchen. In France good food often comes from unpretentious, basic, or uninspired settings.

certain dishes? If so, the bill could end up bigger than you'd expected.

Not all feasts will be five-coursers; the composition varies a great deal according to regional tradition, the chef's whim or how much you're paying. But as a rough guide, a sample meal could go like this:

Hors d'oeuvre

The first course, or starter, could be simply a soup or choice of *charcuterie* (*rillettes, pâtés*), *crudités* (raw vegetables with a dip), or a salad dish. Further up the price scale *foie gras*, snails or shellfish might be on offer.

Menu Talk

A French menu may well appear daunting, but take a deep breath and ask what things are if you're not sure. It's worth watching out for the following – they don't appeal to everyone's taste and are words that are easily confused:

aile: bird's wing   *ail*: garlic
anguille: small eel   *aiguillette*: thin slice of meat
brochet: pike   *brochette*: food cooked on skewers
cervelles: brains   *cervelas*: type of sausage
chevreau: baby goat   *chevreuil*: venison
oreille: pig's or calf's ear   *oseille*: sorrel
ris: sweetbreads   *riz*: rice
rognons blancs: testicles   *rognons*: kidneys
steak tartare: *sauce tartare*:
raw minced steak   mayonnaise sauce

Entrée

Top flight dining rooms will offer *menus gourmands* to include an additional course between the starter and the main course. Usually fish, presented in any number of possible ways, it could be lobster, salmon, or even frogs' legs or snails.

Main course

Traditionally the meat course, perhaps the *plat du jour*, but you could have fish poultry, offal or game, poultry. Apart from a little garnish it will probably sit alone on its plate with vegetables served separately.

Salad

This may well not make an appearance, but if so it does refresh your taste buds and make up for any lack of green vegetables until now.

Cheese

Always served before desserts in France, it could be a board full or a whole trolley groaning with regional/local varieties.

Dessert

Sorbets and ice creams, often home-made, chocolate mousse, fruit or caramel custard, with tarts, gâteaux and *pâtisserie* supplementing these standard dishes, are the norm. The more sophisticated restaurants, as you'd expect, offer more elaborate confections.

A *menu dégustation*, found in the more pricey establishments, consists of perhaps seven or eight courses – literally a "sampling" of what the chef can offer – small helpings of his specialities.

When you order meat, do bear in mind it'll usually be served very rare (*saignant*). If you want it almost raw ask for it *bleu*; if you prefer it to be rare, but not bloodily so, request *saignant*; for medium, *bien cuit*, means well-cooked.

TYPES OF PLACES TO EAT

BRASSERIES

You eat as much, or as little, as you like in these restaurant-cum-cafés and because of their size (they're generally big and bustling) you're more likely to get a table without a reservation – though that's not watertight advice since some brasseries – Bofinger for instance – the city's oldest, are always packed.

Alsace is homeland of the brasserie (which means "brewery") where brew pubs became known for their hearty yeoman's fare, like thick goose *cassoulets* or *choucroute*. The blossoming of smart brasserie culture came after the Franco-Prussian war of 1870 when exiles from the "lost" eastern territories relocated to Paris. The traditional taste for simple food is mostly maintained, with staples being *grillades, gigots*, glistening *fruits de mer* (artistically displayed seafood are often clustered round the brasserie entrance), strong dark coffee. Service is brisk, the customers are mixed; many brasseries, unlike restaurants, serve meals after midnight and open every day, weekends included.

CAFÉS

There are cafés and cafés – more than 10,000 of them spread through all parts of Paris. Some are extremely famous, almost national institutions (see the section **Café Society** in the

Some Types of Café

Buvettes: essentially a kiosk where you can get a drink and maybe a snack. Almost a thing of the past these days are the wine merchants or grocery stores with a zinc counter but usually no tables.

Café tabacs: telltale sign is a red lozenge. They are little cafés that sell a range of smoking materials, as well as stamps, postcards, state lottery tickets. The letters PMU outside indicate that the café tabac turns into a betting shop on certain days, letting punters have a flutter via the state tote system. Generally cheaper than larger cafés, they're often quite lively with pinball machines, tinny juke boxes, maybe even French billiards or American pool.

Salons de thé: some we'd probably call "coffee houses"; others are more definitely elegant little tea shops; some are exotic, boldly modern or cosy; some, like Fauchon in place de la Madeleine, attached to a pâtissier's shop. Mostly they open from noon until the early evening to serve irresistible cakes, ice creams, sometimes light meals, sandwiches, savoury snacks; occasionally alcoholic drinks — usually sweet ones — can be ordered too. Some serve good, though not the cheapest, breakfasts.

Check the menu displayed outside before diving into the tempting-looking *salon de thé* — they can be expensive, but they often serve divine hot chocolate, an excellent cup of coffee (which cannot be taken for granted at many cafés) and an interesting range of teas.

chapter on the 6e on page 392) and grossly overpriced while others might be anonymous and wonderful locals where you can get breakfast, a snack, a midday *plat du jour* (often handwritten on the window) and a glass of wine, or just about any other drink — soft or alcoholic, hot or cold — you fancy.

All the main squares and boulevards have pavement cafés, where prices tend to creep higher than those in less public locations. In very touristy or very chic spots you can get really stung as prices reflect the price of the real estate you're temporarily renting while you sit and sip. Bear in mind, too, that the majority have a two-tiered price system, depending on whether you drink at the bar or enjoy table service, inside or out. *La terrasse*, in connection with anywhere to eat or drink, means the tables and chairs are set outside, but not necessarily on a terrace.

BARS

Like cafés – and some are more café-like than others – Parisian bars come in every description from the grand and plush piano bars of top hotels to the dingy and cacophonous locals where everyone props up the counter. The majority of bars serve coffee and food of some kind, to blur the distinction even further; some stay open as late as 2am.

A lot of French beer is sold in bottles and is lager-like. It's cheaper to ask for *une demie* or *une pression*, and generally it's cheaper to drink wine or beer than mineral water.

As with cafés, you can save yourself money by standing up at the bar, and avoiding ones on the main boulevards and very public spots like the Beaubourg and around the Opéra where prices can be double or triple those in bars tucked away round the corner.

There are English and Irish style pubs, beer cellars, American cocktail bars and a number of wine bars in Paris. Wine is taken seriously at the wine bars, which tend to be yuppified

Snacks

- Some ethnic snackeries are open 24 hours a day. They're thick on the ground in the Latin Quarter, in rue Huchette, rue Mouffetard and so on.

- Many department stores have decently priced coffee shops serving snacks and reliable restaurants, as do the museums and galleries. Monoprix in the avenue de l'Opéra has a self service restaurant, as do Galeries Lafayette and the Printemps store in boulevard Haussmann. There are terrific views of the Seine from the tenth floor of magasin 2 of La Samaritaine, 2 quai du Louvre, 1er. The restaurant at the Picasso museum gets very busy, but is recommended for lunch if you get there early or are prepared to queue.

- There are *Les Selfs* or self-service restaurants all over town and most are inexpensive. Their great advantages are of course that you don't have to speak French, since the food is displayed at the counters, and also they're very quick.

- Drugstores — quite pricey — combine reasonable brasserie-type food service all day with a sort of mini shopping centre selling books, newspapers, tobacco, odds and ends.

and costly — a glass of really fine or interesting wine might set you back as much as a whole bottle of its less coveted cousin in a brasserie. The food is not the main point but it's usually available in the form of cheeses, *pâté, saucisson* and the like.

SNACKS, TAKEAWAYS, FAST FOOD

Parisians eat unabashedly in the streets — few French baguettes make it home with their ends unnibbled — so don't feel shy about picking up a snack to eat as you go along or after finding a quiet corner in a square or park to perch while you munch. The great thing about France is that the simplest things, like bread with a ripe cheese, are so good that they make an impromptu picnic meal.

Charcuteries/traîteurs are good providers of take-away snacks — they may stuff a baguette, or sell you a piece of quiche and they dish out salads in little cartons which may, or may not, come with their own handy plastic cutlery —

worth saving for the next picnic, although the really organised amongst you will already carry a handy plastic knife and fork in a pocket.

Of course there are the inevitable branches of Macdonalds and Burger King as well as pizzeria in most parts of Paris, and other imported flavours – but why settle for a limp hot dog when there are tasty indigenous snacks like the ubiquitous *croque monsieur* (a toasted cheese and ham sandwich) or *croque madame* (ditto but with the addition of a fried egg), or a crisp hot *croissant au jambon*, stuffed with ham and topped with a crust of baked cheese? Or try a *sandwich Grec* – French bread filled with lamb – followed by a brightly coloured pastry-like cake from a Moroccan or Tunisian coffee house. All these snacks are easily available on the left bank, in the little streets running down to the Seine. You'll also see *crêperie* stands – providers of thin pancakes made while you watch, plain or with various flavoured fillings.

FOOD AND DRINK

WINE

Wine, in all its glorious variety, is to be enjoyed – though you'd never believe it from the way some oenophiles go on. Rather than get bogged down in the rituals and lore, sample a variety, get to know what you like. Although the French as a whole are as interested in it as they are in good food, wine tends to be treated more casually in France than in Britain, with the possible exception of the major wine-producing areas. In fact, the French are less particular and more adventurous than many tourists in exploring the possibilities of matching wines to food. Ideally the aim is to complement the food in strength, richness and style.

Stringent controls govern French wines, especially top-quality ones. *Appellation contrôlée* is the top classification, the certificate granted to wines produced subject to certain regulations governing methods of cultivation and wine-making. Not every AC wine is necessarily a great one but all the top French wines have AC status. An *appellation* may be limited to wine from a particular village, vineyard or region – as a rule the more specific the limits, the higher the quality of wine. *Vin Delimité de Qualité Supérieure* (VDQS) is the second category (now being phased out), whose wines are of medium quality and whose area of origin is always shown on the label. VDQS wines adhere to less strict criteria and prices reflect this.

Below these come the *Vin de Pays* – literally "country wine" often labelled according to their grape variety, "Chardonnay" etc.

The largest category is *Vin de Table*. Often sold under a brand name, these are blended wines from different areas, even different countries. You take pot luck when you order these in a carafe or *pichet*.

Wine: A Brief Guide
Dry White

Alsace	(Gewurztraminer, Riesling)
Bordeaux	(Entre-Deux-Mers, Graves)
Britanny	(Muscadet)
Burgundy	(Chabis, Macon, Pouilly-Fuissé, Pouilly-Fumé)
Loire	(Coteaux de la Loire, Jasnières, Sancerre Vouvray)
Northern Rhône	(Crozes-Hermitage)

Sweet White

Alsace	(Gerwurztraminer)
Bordeaux	(Barsac, Sauternes)
Perigord	(Monbazillac)
Languedoc	(Frontignan, Lunel)
Loire	(Coteaux de Layon)
Southern Rhône	(Beaumes de Venise)
Rouissillon/Pyrenées	(Benyuls, Jurançon, Muscat de Rivesaltes)

Sparkling White

Alsace	(Crémant d'Alsace)
Burgundy	(Crémant de Bourgogne)

Champagne
See *marque* or brand name of maker (e.g. Bollinger, Krug,

Cheese

There's more to French cheeses than Camembert, Brie and Roquefort. In fact there are enough French cheeses for you to sample a different one on every day of the year, as France is the biggest producer of cheese in the world, after the USA. Each region produces specialities, including the Ile de France, the area around Paris, which is known for its rich, soft creamy cheeses like Boursin as well as Brie de Meaux, Brie de Melun, Brie de Coulommiers, and Chevru.

If you've never had a nibble, don't be put off by the "goat" in goat's milk cheese (*Chèvre*). Generally fairly dry in texture, they're neither necessarily strong nor "goaty" and they go very nicely with a glass of red wine. It's often said that a good cheeseboard is a sign of a good restaurant – the least you can expect is a choice of half a dozen; at best there'll be a tray or trolley loaded with them in all sorts of shapes, sizes and wrappings. Below we list some of the ones you're most likely to be offered:

Bleu d'Auvergne – blue mould cheese created by a nineteenth-century peasant, usually made from a blend of goat's, ewe's and cow's milk.

Brie – soft cow's cheese in round discs of varying size. A good one should be yellow, creamy but not runny. It's often called by the name of the area where it is made, for example Brie de Meaux or Brie de Melun.

Brillat-Savarin – mild, creamy cow's cheese from Normandy, named after the famous 18th-century gastronome.

Lanson, Mercier, Moet & Chandon, Mumm, Pol Roger, Tattinger). Many make a *de luxe* champagne as well (e.g. Moet & Chandon's Dom Pérignon).

Brut zéro – no sugar

Brut – very dry

Extra sec – dry

Sec – slightly sweet

Demi-sec – sweet

Doux – very sweet   (Crémant de Loire – Saumur
                                                        Mousseux)

Loire Note: *Blancs de Blancs* is champagne made from white grapes only, light and delicate. *Pink Champagne* (*rosé*) has a little red wine added in, *Crémant* has less fizz than the standard.

Camembert — small circular soft cheese invented in about 1790 by a farmer's wife, Madame Harel. You can see a statue of her in the small village of Camembert, in Normandy.

Dauphin — soft, herby cow's cheese thought to have been from the Champagne-Ardennes area, named after Louis X1V's son.

Livarot — soft, strong cylindrical cow's cheese from a small market town in Normandy.

Munster — softish round cow's cheese with orange rind, matured for 3 to 6 weeks, with strong smell and tangy flavour. Made in the Munster valley in Alsace. Sometimes cumin or caraway added to make *Munster au Cumin*.

Olivet Bleu—small, rich, cow's cheese with bluish skin, sometimes leaf-wrapped; it comes from the Loire.

Pont-l'Éveque — small, square pungent cow's cheese, ripened in cellars, usually for 3 to 4 months.

Port-Salut — round, supple, yellow, whole-milk cow's cheese, first made at the Trappist Monastery of Port du Salut in Brittany.

Reblochon — soft, flat cow's cheese from Savoie, with mild, creamy taste.

Roquefort — real Roquefort, from the town of the same name in the Massif Central, is made exclusively from ewe's milk. Pungent, with a blue mould.

You can always ask the waiter if you can have a few small samples (*petits morceaux*) of a number of different types. Cheese is eaten by itself, or with bread but rarely with biscuits.

Rosé

Burgundy	(Marsannay)
Champagne	(Rose de Riceys)
Jura	(Arbois)
Loire	(Cabernet/Rosé d'Anjou)
Provence	(Côtes de Provence)
Southern Rhône	(Lirac, Tavel)

Red

Bordeaux (Haut-Médoc, Médoc, Pomerol, St Émilion)
Burgundy (Beaujolais, Vosne-Romanée, Nuits-St-Georges, Beaune, Pommard, Volnay, Santenay)

Languedoc	(Corbières)
Loire	(Chinon, Saumur-Champigny)
Northern Rhône	(Côtes du Rhône)
Perigord	(Bergerac, Cahors)
Provence	(Côtes de Provence)
Southern Rhône	(Chateauneuf-du-Pape, Côtes du Rhône Villages, Côtes du Ventoux Gigondas)
Rouissillon & Pyrenees	(Côtes de Rouissillon, Madiron)

WHERE TO EAT IN PARIS

Every restaurant has been carefully selected for providing value for money; with some entries the ambience is more interesting than the food – or vice versa. Happily the two coincide quite often. We've avoided mentioning any places where anything other than good cooking at reasonable prices can be found. However, even as we went to press, changes were afoot. Restaurants open and close with the frequency you'd expect in any major city. Prices creep up and closing times are prone to change. While we've been as accurate as possible, it's advisable to ring the restaurant to check when it's open before setting off.

Credit cards, especially Visa (Carte Bleue) are widely accepted but this can certainly not be taken for granted at some smaller, simpler establishments, where they insist on cash – so be prepared.

The Footloose Guide has used following broad price categories:

Cheap: up to 100f per head.
Moderate: 100–200f per head.
Expensive: 200f+ per head.

Where, for instance, there's a very good value set menu but a considerably more pricey *à la carte*, the price classification might well fall between two categories i.e. moderate to expensive.

1er

André Faure   *cheap to moderate*
40 rue du Mont-Thabor. Tel. 42 60 74 28. M *Concorde*
Open noon–2.30pm, 7–10pm. Cl. Sunday.
Country-style menu served in the evenings, at this typical cosy bistro.
About 85f.

L'Ami Léon   *cheap to moderate*
11 rue Jean-Jacques Rousseau. Tel. 42 33 06 20. M Louvre
Open noon–2pm, 8–11pm. Cl. Saturday and Sunday.
Two panelled dining rooms serving excellent food. Try the duck breasts
with potatoes fried in goose fat. Menu 80f.

Au Pied de Cochon   *expensive*
6 rue Coquillière Tel. 42 36 11 75. M Les Halles.
Open every day, 24 hours a day
One of the historic *Belle Époque* brasseries in Paris; apart from the
eponymous pig's trotters, you could have *fruits de mer*, a pork chop,
or maybe its famous onion soup. Allow about 200–250f.

L'Atelier Bleu   *cheap*
7 rue des Prouvaires. Tel. 42 33 74 47. M Les Halles
Open noon–3pm, 6.30pm–12.30am. Cl. Sunday.
Large, busy, and the set menu is excellent value at 52f.

Aux Deux Saules   *cheap*
91 rue St Denis. Tel. 42 36 46 57. M Châtelet
Open noon-midnight daily.
Traditional bistro with set menu 56f.

Aux Rendezvous des Camionneurs   *cheap*
72 quai des Orfèvres. Tel. 43 54 88 74. M Cité, Pont-Neuf.
Open noon–11pm. Cl. Saturday and Sunday.
Booking is advisable at this popular, friendly restaurant where family
cooking pulls in local lawyers, journalists, as well as tourists. Menu
65f.

Caveau François Villon   *moderate*
64 rue de L'Arbre-Sec. Tel. 42 36 10 92. M Pont-Neuf.
Open noon–2.30pm, 7pm-midnight. Cl. Sunday and Monday.
Casual eating place near the Louvre, good fish dishes. Allow 100f.

Le Châtelet Gourmand   *moderate*
13 rue des Lavandière. Tel. 40 26 45 00. M Châtelet.
Open 12.15–2.30pm, 7.30–10.30pm. Cl. Sunday and Monday.
Known for its grilled meats. Menu 130f.

Le Comptoir   *moderate*
14 rue Vauvilliers. Tel. 40 26 26 66. M Châtelet.
Open every day, noon–1am.

"Re-past Times"

Culture and gastronomy have always been enjoyed with almost equal gusto in Paris, so it's no surprise that you can ingest both at a single sitting.

Over two dozen Parisian restaurants are, like the Arc de Triomphe, also officially designated historical monuments. Some are palatial, with sky-high prices, like the 230-year-old Grand Véfour beneath whose flickering chandeliers Napoleon wooed Josephine, or the Lucas-Carton with its *belle époque* interiors carved from maple, sycamore and white citrus. Prunier, the aristocratic 19th-century fish restaurant in the avenue Victor-Hugo is listed, plus left bank institutions like the legendary Montparnasse La Coupole, the Brasserie Lipp and Le Vagenende, a spectacular Art Nouveau brasserie built around 1902.

Fouquet's, on the avenue des Champs-Élysées, was endowed with protected status just in time to beat the bulldozers but on the strength of its "historical associations" rather than its architectural merits.

Benefiting from the upward mobility of the now trendy Bastille is one of the oldest and most beautiful of Parisian eateries, Bofinger, across from the new opera house, and always packed. Dripping with Art Deco, it opened in 1864, the first place in Paris to serve draft beer. No less popular is Julien in the rue du Faubourg St Denis, brimming with Mucha-inspired stained glass and burnished woods, built to coincide with the great Paris fair of 1989.

Whether the décor eclipses the food — or vice versa — is for you to decide ...

Tapas, *pot-au-feu* and couscous in this Les Halles bistro. Allow 100f.

Chicago Meatpackers   *moderate*
8 rue de la Coquillière. Tel. 40 28 02 33. *M Châtelet/Les Halles*
Open 11am–1am, Monday–Friday; 11am–1.30am, Saturday–Sunday.
American style eatery, burger, ribs and the like. Allow 120f.

La Fauvette   *cheap*
46 rue St Honoré Tel. 42 36 75. 85. *M Louvre Les Halles*.
Open 11am–3pm. Cl. Saturday and Sunday.
This original small market restaurant serves simple but delicious food. For 50f you can eat a selection of starters, roast beef or chicken and tarts or cheese. Go early!

La Feuillade   *moderate*

6 rue de la Grande Truanderie. Tel. 40 39 93 02. M *Étienne-Marcel*.
Open daily 12.30–2.30pm, 8pm–midnight. Cl. Sunday lunch.
Tiny Les Halles bistro serving satisfying, reasonably priced meals in
an area where unappealing tourist *formules* are the norm. 100f wine
included usually does it.

Foujita   *cheap to moderate*
41 rue St Roch. Tel. 42 61 42 93. M *Pyramides, Palais Royal*.
Open noon–10.30pm. Cl. Sunday.
The best sushi bar in the district. Décor is pretty and plain. The
lunchtime menu for 60f includes a bowl of soup, a generous plate of
superior raw fish with rice, vegetables and tea, all exquisitely presented.
Service is fast and efficient but you can also eat at the counter if you're
in a particular hurry. Count on 150f *à la carte*.

L'Incroyable   *cheap*
26 rue de Richelieu. Tel. 42 96 24 64. M *Palais-Royal*.
Open 11.45am–2.15pm, 6.30–8.30pm. Cl. Monday and Saturday
evening and Sunday.
Crowded, much-admired eaterie in a little passage whose clientèle
appreciate rock-bottom prices. In summer you can fight for a table
outside. Menu 45f (lunch), 60f (dinner).

Joe Allen   *moderate*
30 rue Pierre-Lescot. Tel. 42 36 70 13. M *Étienne-Marcel*.
Open noon–1am daily.
Eschew the traditional bistro fare for black bean soup and barbecued
chicken at this New York style restaurant. Allow 150f.

Kinkeliba   *moderate*
5 rue des Déchargeurs. Tel. 45 08 96 61. M *Les Halles*.
Phone for opening hours.
Gabonese restaurant; smoked fish, yassa chicken and stuffed crab.
Allow 100f.

Le Pasadena   *cheap to moderate*
7 rue du 29 Juillet. Tel. 42 60 68 96. M *Tuileries*.
Open 12.30–2.30pm, 7pm–1am. Cl. Sunday.
Smartly-run restaurant with 80f menu.

La Petite Moisanderie   *cheap*
52 rue de Richelieu. Tel. 42 96 92 93. M *Pyramides*.
Open 11.45am–2pm, 6.45–9.30pm. Cl. Sunday.
Neatly decorated and comfortable restaurant on three floors where
you can experience traditional food, e.g. peppered steaks and duck *à
l'orange*.
Allow 100f.

Le Petit Ramoneur   *cheap*
74 rue St Denis. Tel. 42 36 39 24. M *RER Châtelet-Les Halles*.
Open until 9.30 pm Cl. Saturday and Sunday.

Basic 50f menu in good bistro tradition, good wine, busy and friendly atmosphere.

La Potée des Halles   *cheap to moderate*
3 rue Étienne Marcel. Tel. 42 36 18 68. *M Étienne Marcel/Réaumur – Sebastopol.*
Open noon–2.30pm, Monday–Friday; 7pm–10.30pm, Saturday. Cl. Saturday lunchtime, Sunday.
Turn-of-the-century bistro retaining its original, wonderful Sarreguemines ceramic decorations. The food's OK too – generous helpings and the 89f menu served at lunchtime and in the evenings includes three courses. Advisable to book in advance.

Le Potiron   *cheap*
16 rue du Roule, Tel. 42 33 35 68. *M Louvre.*
Open till 11pm. Cl. Sunday and Monday.
An establishment run by women with exhibitions by women artists. Creative cooking leans towards *nouvelle cuisine*. Menu 62f.

La Poule au Pot   *moderate*
9 rue Vauvilliers. Tel. 42 36 32 96. *M Les Halles.*
Open until 6am. Cl. Monday.
Atmospheric old bistro serving *poule au pot*. Good for nocturnal eaters. Allow 150f.

Le Relais du Sud-Ouest   *cheap*
154 rue St Honoré. Tel. 42 60 62 01. *M Louvre.*
Open 11.30am–2.30pm, 7pm–11pm. Cl. Sunday.
Old Paris at its best. Solid bistro fare from the South West. Three courses, wine and service: 60f.

Le Stado   *cheap*
150 rue St Honoré. Tel. 42 60 29 75. *M Louvre.*
Open noon–2.30pm, Tuesday–Saturday.
Good stop-off before, during or after the Louvre. Go for the 60f lunch menu, wine and service included.

La Tourelle   *cheap*
2 rue de la Vrillière, off rue Croix des Petits-Champs. Tel. 42 61 35 41. *M Bourse.*
Open 11.30am–2.30pm, 6–11pm. Cl. Sunday.
Good terrines and steaks. Menu 59f.

2e

L'Amanguier   *moderate*
110 rue de Richelieu. Tel. 42 96 37 79. *M Richelieu-Drouot.*
Open noon–2.30pm, 7pm–midnight daily.
Pretty, garden-style décor makes this a pleasant place to enjoy a good traditional three-course meal. Menus from about 110f including wine.

Aux Crus de Bourgogne   *moderate*
3 rue Bachaumont Tel. 42 33 48 24. *M Sentier*.
Open noon until 10.30pm. Cl. Saturday and Sunday.
A discreetly fashionable clientèle appreciate the traditional Les Halles
atmosphere: there's brown panelling, mirrors, *coq au vin* and the kind
of hearty meat stews which used to sustain the market traders. In the
evening you must reserve a table. Allow 140–170f.

Chez Pierrot   *moderate*
18 rue Étienne-Marcel. Tel. 45 08 17 64. *M Étienne-Marcel*.
Open lunch and dinner. Phone for opening hours. Cl. Saturday
and Sunday.
This restaurant with all its traditional décor is a fun place to eat. Neatly
dressed staff, smiling faces and great food. Allow 150f.

Claude Brisse Moret   *moderate*
5 rue St Marc. Tel. 42 36 91 72. *M Rue Montmartre/Bourse*.
Open noon–2pm, 8–10pm. Cl. Saturday and Sunday.
Shambolic bistro providing some of the best food in the area at
reasonable prices. Allow 130f.

Dona Flor   *moderate*
10 rue Dussoubs. Tel. 42 36 46 55. *M Étienne-Marcel*.
Open until 2am. Cl. Monday.
Stylish Brazilian restaurant with a South American version of cassoulet
called Feijoada. Dinner only. Allow 160f.

Dow Jones   *cheap to moderate*
6 rue St Marc. Tel. 42 36 63 09. *M Bourse*.
Open until 11.30pm. Cl. Saturday, Sunday lunch.
Trendy 1950s-style restaurant inspired more by Wall Street than the
nearby Bourse, full of yuppies and fashion fatalities. Good fixed price
menu 90f.

Le Drouot   *cheap*
103 rue de Richelieu. No telephone number available. *M Richelieu-
Drouot*.
Open 11am–3pm, 6–9.30pm daily.
Same management as Chartier, delivers the same good value for money
but better food; drinkable cheap wine too. Menu 50f.

La Gentilhommière   *moderate*
10 rue Chabanais. Tel. 42 96 54 69. *M Pyramides*.
Open lunch and dinner. Phone for opening hours. Closed Sunday.
Delightful restaurant with specialities from Lyons. The 91f menu, service
included is very tempting.

Le Grand Cerf   *cheap*
10–12 passage du Grand Cerf (145 rue St Denis). No telephone. *M
Réaumur-Sébastopol*.
Open noon–10pm. Cl. Sunday.

This tucked away Spanish-cum-French eaterie dishes up cheap and honest fare. Menu around 40f.

Hollywood Savoy   *expensive*
44 rue Notre-Dame-des-Victoires. Tel. 42 36 16 73. *M Bourse*.
Open 8pm–2am (Catch the show from 10pm–2am). Cl. Sunday.
American specialities served by flamboyant staff swaying to the music, who are employed more for their vocal talents than manual dexterity – but at least they won't drop the *canard en sauce* all over you. Allow 200f.

Le Macadam   *cheap to moderate*
23 rue de Turbigo. Tel. 42 36 52 32. *M Étienne-Marcel*.
Open 8am–1am. Cl. Saturday, Sunday.
Packed with mediati; delicious *fondant au chocolat*. Lunch menu best value at 95f.

La Maisonette   *cheap*
59 rue Montmartre. No telephone number available. *M Sentier ob. Les Halles*.
Open noon–2.30pm, 7.30–midnight. Cl. Sunday.
Traditional tiled floors and walls, hearty food and quaffable wine; lunch menu including service 55f.

Pile ou Face   *expensive*
52 bis rue Notre-Dame-des-Victoires. Tel. 42 33 64 33. *M Bourse*.
Open noon–2pm, 8–10pm. Cl. Saturday and Sunday.
Popular place with the "in crowd"; inventive dishes, intimate surroundings. Allow 250f.

Le Vaudeville   *moderate to expensive*
29 rue Vivienne. Tel. 42 33 39 31. *M Bourse*.
Open 11–2am (last orders 3.30pm and 1.30am) daily.
A Parisian institution, now one of the Jean-Paul Bucher group – he who rescued many historic brasseries, including Flo, Le Boeuf sur le Toit, Julien. Marvellous original features, including grandiose marbles; good classical cuisine. Late opening makes it handy for after a show. Cheaper at lunch, *prix fixe* 105f.

3e

L'Alisier   *moderate*
26 rue de Montmorency. Tel. 42 72 31 04. *M Rambuteau*.
Open until 10pm. Cl. Saturday lunch, Sunday.
Typical bistro serving above average food in terms of quality, value and interest. Allow 150f.

L'Ambassade d'Auvergne   *expensive*
22 rue du Grenier-St-Lazare. Tel. 42 72 31 22. *M Rambuteau*.
Arts-et-Métiers

Open noon–2pm, 7–11pm. Cl. Sunday.
Paris-based natives and fans of the Auvergne come here when they
hanker for hearty regional cooking. Distinctly rustic ambience – smoked
pork in the stews *and* hanging from the ceiling. Expensive but worth it.
Superb Auvergnat cheeses too. Allow 200f.

L'Ami Louis   *expensive*
32 rue du Vertbois. Tel. 48 87 77 48. *M Temple*.
Open noon–2pm, 8–10.30pm. Cl. Monday and Tuesday.
Always full. Excellent, rich, traditional South-Western cooking in this
marvellous slightly run-down bistro. Allow 350f.

Chez Jenny   *cheap to moderate*
33 boulevard du Temple. Tel. 42 74 75 75. *M République*.
Open until 1am daily.
One of the oldest brasseries in Paris where authentic Alsatian dishes are
served by costumed waitresses. Homemade sausages, terrines, onion
soup and one of the most authentic *choucroutes* in town – nice
juicy sausage with sharp sauerkraut, just as it should be. Fixed price
70f or 90f.

L'Helium   *cheap*
3 rue des Haudriettes. Tel. 42 72 81 10. *M Rambuteau*.
Open noon–3pm, 7pm–midnight. Cl. Sunday.
While there's no fixed price menu, you can still eat well and
very reasonably. French or international dishes. Allow 75f including wine.

L'Orée du Marais   *cheap*
29 rue des Francs-Bourgeois. Tel. 48 87 81 70. *M St Paul*.
Open noon–2.30pm, 7–10pm.
Open every day of the year and definitely worth a visit if you are in
the northern Marais as the menu, at 59f, is quite a find in a yuppified
area. Standard bistro food; wine rather pricey.

Taverne de Nicolas Flamel   *moderate*
51 rue de Montmorency. Tel. 42 72 07 11. *M Arts-et-Métiers*.
Open 12.15–2.30pm, 7.30–10.30pm. Cl. Sunday.
Flamel, a medieval alchemist, lived here in one of the oldest houses
in Paris, built in 1407. Today the chef works his alchemy producing
traditional meals at moderate prices. Allow 130f.

4e

L'Ardelene   *cheap to moderate*
24 rue des Lombards. Tel. 42 77 71 71. *M Châtelet*.
Open noon–2pm, 7–11.30pm.
Open every day and handy for the Pompidou Centre, cheery local with
reasonable menus 70–130f.

Au Franc Pinot *moderate*
1 quai de Bourbon. Tel. 43 29 46 98. *M Pont-Marie*.
Open noon–2pm, 7.30–11pm. Cl. Sunday and Monday.
Excellent, pricey *nouvelle cuisine* served in 17th-century surroundings.
Menu (lunch only) 150f.

Bofinger *moderate*
3–7 rue de la Bastille. Tel. 42 72 87 82. *M Bastille*.
Open noon–3pm, 7.30pm–1am daily.
A stone's throw from the long gone prison, this is the oldest brasserie
in Paris, last renovated in 1919 when the stunning glass dome was put
up. Paris's first draft beer was served here in 1864, at the long zinc
bar. Immaculate black-jacketed waiters administer to loyal regulars and
post-opera diners. Seafood is good; sauerkraut only if you must. Menu
155f including wine.

Cinq Bis *cheap to moderate*
5 bis rue St Paul. Tel. 42 71 98 28. *M Saint Paul*.
Open noon–3pm, 7.30–9pm. Cl. Monday evenings and Tuesdays.
During the week a restaurant serving homemade *pâtés* and homely veal
stew, it becomes a tea room on Saturday and Sunday afternoons. Allow 90f.

Le Cristal *cheap*
13 rue Beautrellis. Tel. 42 72 38 34. *M St Paul/Bastille*.
Open noon–2.30pm, 7–11.30pm. Cl. Saturday lunch and Sunday.
Tiny restaurant, only a few tables, but nicely decorated and extremely
decent food. Salad with hot goat's cheese, pork fillet in prune sauce,
good desserts. Menu 58f.

L'Excuse *cheap to moderate*
14 rue Charles V. Tel. 42 77 98 97. *M St Paul*.
Open noon–2pm, 7–11pm. Cl. Sunday.
Sophisticated restaurant with inventive cooking: calf's liver with crayfish
and *beurre blanc*, figs stewed in champagne. Menu 90f.

Le Faste Fou *cheap to moderate*
36 boulevard Henry IV. Tel. 42 72 17 09. *M Bastille*.
Open lunch and evening till 10.30pm. Cl. Sunday.
Menu changes every day in this Manhattan-y, minimally decorated
eaterie; e.g. good cold carrot soup, fish loaf and pork with mushrooms.
Allow 90f with wine.

Jo Goldenberg's *cheap to moderate*
7 rue des Rosiers. Tel. 48 87 20 16. *M St Paul*.
Open daily from 9am–12pm.
Paris's best known Jewish restaurant in the heart of the Marais Jewish
quarter: pastrami, bortsch and blinis. Live music most nights. Deli and
tea room too. Menus around 65f.

L'Oulette *moderate*
38 rue des Tournelles. Tel. 42 71 43 33. *M Chemin Vert*.

Open 8–10pm. Cl. Saturday and Sunday
Justifiably popular Marais bistro which comes into its own serving regional food like *foie gras*, rabbit; good pear tart. Menu 120f.

La Petite Chaumière   *moderate*
41 rue des Blancs Manteaux. Tel. 42 72 13 90. M *Rambuteau*.
Open till 10pm. Cl. Sunday lunch.
Warm and wholesome and reasonably priced, not far from the Pompidou Centre. Allow 150f.

Le Pot   *cheap*
27 rue du Temple. No telephone. M *Hôtel de Ville*.
Open 11–2pm.
Very French, homey, conventional food. Menu 35f.

Le Relais St Gervais   *cheap*
13 rue François Miron. Tel. 40 29 07 52. M *St Paul*.
Open noon–2pm, 7–11pm. Cl. Tuesday.
Located in a 14th-century building. Food is unpretentious but delicious. Menu 65f.

La Taverne du Sergent Recruteur   *cheap to moderate*
41 rue St Louis-en-l'Ile. Tel. 43 54 75 42. M *Pont Marie*.
Open dinner only until 12.30am. Cl. Sunday
On the romantic Ile-St-Louis, this old 18th-century recruiting post has wooden beams, stone arches and floors. Food to fuel a march round Paris. Basket of sausages and bread to start, main dishes and dessert. No menu. Allow 80f.

Le Trumilou   *cheap*
84 quai de l'Hôtel de Ville. Tel. 42 77 63 98. M *Hôtel de Ville*.
Open noon–3pm, 7–10pm. Cl. Monday.
Extrovert eaters enjoy this bustling bistro serving simple good and filling food. A Footloose favourite – it's one of the best value for money bistros in Paris. Menus 54f, 70f.

5e

Atelier de Maître Albert   *expensive*
1 rue Maître Albert. Tel. 46 33 06 44. M *Maubert-Mutualité*.
Open 7.30–midnight. Cl. Sunday.
Fancy décor and food, in this *nouvelle cuisine* stronghold. The four-course menu with wine, although 210f, is good value.

Aux Savoyards   *cheap*
14 rue des Boulangers. Tel. 46 33 53 78. M *Jussieu*.
Open noon–2.30pm, 7pm–10.30pm. Cl. Saturday evening and Sunday.
Student haunt which means low prices, generous helpings and passable wine all for 56f.

Le Baptiste *cheap*
11 rue des Boulangers. Tel. 43 25 57 24. *M Jussieu.*
Open noon–2pm, 7–10.30pm. Cl. Saturday lunch and Sunday.
Rustic interior, friendly service; simple but impeccable cooking. Menu
57f without wine, which is pricey.

Le Bouche Trou *cheap*
20 rue des Boulangers. No telephone number available. *M Jussieu.*
Take a gamble on this, it's friendly and crowded with students and serves
typical bistro grub and cheap wine (7f for a ¼ litre). Menu 52f.

Brasserie Balzar *moderate*
49 rue des Écoles. Tel. 43 54 13 67. *M Maubert-Mutualité.*
Open 8am–1am daily.
Around the corner from the Sorbonne, a '30s restaurant, cosy and busy,
where the waiters wear smart white aprons. The food is unremarkable,
traditional: onion soup, grilled pig's trotters, roast lamb with white
beans. Popular with thespians, celebs, literati. Small café section too.
Allow 150f.

Le Jardin des Pâtes *cheap to moderate*
4 rue Lacépède. Tel. 43 31 50 71. *M Monge.*
Open noon–2.30pm, 7–10.30pm. Cl. Monday.
Homemade pasta made from flour ground on the premises which
accompanies mouth-watering dishes. Allow 90f.

Perraudin *cheap*
157 rue St Jacques. Tel. 46 33 15 75. *M Luxembourg.*
Open noon–2.30pm, 7.30–10.15pm. Cl. Saturday evenings and Sunday.
Simple, sound and great value menu 60f.

Le Port du Salut *moderate*
163 bis rue St Jacques. Tel. 43 54 32 03. *M Gare du Luxembourg.*
Open noon–2.30pm, 7–10.45pm.
Open every day for excellent food, the 89f menu is incredible value.

Taverne Descartes *cheap*
35 rue Descartes. Tel. 43 25 67 77. *M Cardinal Lemoine,. Monge*
Open noon–2pm, 7–11.30pm. Cl. Saturday lunch.
Straightforward menu, cheerful atmosphere. Menu 37f, 48f, including
service and wine.

6e

Assiette au Boeuf I *cheap to moderate*
22 rue Guillaume-Apollinaire .Tel. 42 60 88 44. *M St-Germain-
des-Prés.*
Open till 1am daily.
One of a successful chain. Lots of mirrors, stained glass and traditional
French cuisine. Menu 60f.

L'Assignat *cheap*
7 rue Guénégaud. Tel. 43 54 87 68. M *Odéon*.
Open 11am–4pm. Cl. Sunday.
Unobtrusive bistro tucked away in a quiet St Germain street. Liked by
workers from the nearby Mint and the students of the School of Beaux
Arts. Friendly atmosphere and with simple but sound dishes from 40f.
The bill shouldn't exceed 80f.

Aux Charpentiers *moderate to expensive*
10 rue Mabillon. Tel. 43 26 30 05. M *Mabillon*.
Open lunch and dinner until 11.30pm. Cl. Sunday.
Classic bistro once frequented by members of the Carpenters' Guild.
Dependable stews and succulent roasts dominate the menu, along with
homemade fruit tarts. It has been said that anyone who hasn't been
here hasn't seen the real Paris! Allow 180f.

Bouch *cheap to moderate*
12 rue de l'Éperon. Tel. 43 26 51 43. M *Odéon*.
Open 11.30am–midnight daily.
Brightly lit, lively, restaurant-cum-grill with music. Baked potatoes,
hamburgers and other simple dishes. Allow 95f. There's a special menu
for children 35f.

Brasserie Lipp *moderate to expensive*
151 boulevard St Germain. Tel. 45 48 53 91. M *St-Germain-des-Prés*.
Open Tuesday–Sunday until 12.45am.
Once upon a time Picasso and Sartre ate here. Today it's popular with the
Élysée Palace set, prone to impromptu lunchtime political conventions.
The showbiz élite like it too. Unknowns get shoved upstairs, but the
brave insist on being seated downstairs where the fun is. *Plats du jour,
pot au feu*, and pepper steak all worthwhile. Fixed price menu 150f or
allow 180–200f.

Bistro de la Gare *moderate*
59 boulevard du Montparnasse. Tel. 45 48 38 01. M *Montparnasse-
Bienvenue*.
Open until 1am daily.
OK so you can't eat it, but the big attraction here is the Art Nouveau
glass window (an historic monument). The food is passable and service
efficient. Allow 100f.

Bistro de la Grille *cheap to moderate*
14 rue Mabillon. Tel. 43 54 16 87. M *Mabillon*.
Open noon–5.30pm, 7.30–midnight daily.
The dining room is a typical 19th-century one with Eugène Atget
photographs on the walls. The food is inventive: fresh fish with lime,
raw sirloin ribbons and olive oil. Very busy, go early. Menu 80f.

Claude Valentino/Monteverdi *cheap to moderate*
5–7 rue Guisarde. Tel. 43 29 53 04. M *Mabillon*.

Open noon–2pm, 6pm–midnight. Cl. Sunday.

A Franco-Italian restaurant with two rooms connected by an archway. A trio plays in the Monteverdi room. Menu 75f served at lunch and until 9pm.

La Closerie des Lilas   *moderate*
171 boulevard du Montparnasse. Tel. 43 26 70 50. *M Port Royal.*
Open noon–4pm, 8pm–midnight (Brasserie 2pm) daily.
Old-style grand café and a little less touristy than some. Tables bear plaques inscribed with the names of artists who sat there, Hemingway and Scott Fitzgerald amongst them. The food is unpretentious and good; the lively atmosphere and the terrace in summer make it a place to be. Go for the Brasserie lunch menu 110f – the restaurant is expensive.

L'Ecaille de P.C.B.   *moderate*
5 rue Mabillon. Tel. 43 26 73 70. *M Mabillon.*
Open noon–3.00pm, 7.30–11.30pm. Cl. Sunday.
A very expensive *à la carte*, so the 90f menu here seems like a bargain. Each day there is a different, exciting *plat du jour*, such as salt cod with cream and garlic.

L'Enfance de Lard   *cheap to moderate*
21 rue Guisarde. Tel. 46 33 89 65. *M Mabillon.*
Open noon–2.30pm, 7–11pm. Cl. Sunday.
Go early to this popular establishment or be disappointed and miss the savoury profiteroles stuffed with snails and garlic cream. Menu 75f.

Jacques Cagna   *expensive*
14 rue Grands Augustins. Tel. 43 26 49 39. *M Latour-Mauborg.*
Open Monday–Friday until 11pm.
Don't pass this one by – although the lunchtime menu is 260f, it is seriously good. Just think, at dinner you could be spending 550f *à la carte*. Set in a 17th-century building.

Orestias   *cheap*
4 rue Grégoire-de-Tours. Tel. 43 54 62 01. *M Odéon.*
Open noon–2.30pm, 6.30–11.30pm. Cl. Sunday.
Good value, copious servings of Greek specialities. 49f menu. Wine 7f quarter litre.

Le Papadam   *cheap to moderate*
27 rue Madame. Tel. 45 48 69 57. *M St Sulpice.*
Open noon–2pm, 7–10pm. Cl. Saturday lunch and Sunday.
Indian specialities, chicken tandoori, lamb madras, lassi and mango sorbet. Cheap lunch menu 69f. Dinner 109f.

Le Petit Zinc   *moderate*
25 rue de Buci. Tel. 46 33 51 66. *M Mabillon.*
Open noon–3am daily.
Fresh seafood in this turn-of-century cheerful brasserie as well as tasty

country dishes. It is always crowded. Try it after the Buci market. The terrace tables are especially popular in summer. 137f menu.

Le Polidor *cheap*
41 rue Monsieur-le-Prince. Tel. 43 26 95 34. *M Odéon.*
Open noon–2.30pm, 7pm–1am (11pm Sunday).
A Footloose favourite; its tiled floor has been worn away since 1845 by satisfied customers including Verlaine, Joyce and Hemingway, or, more recently Claire Bretécher. The friendly service and lace curtains make it a comforting place to eat classic country cooking. Lunch menu 50f, wine 7f, otherwise 80–100f. *Go early.*

Le Procope *expensive*
13 rue de l'Ancienne Comédie. Tel. 43 26 99 20. *M Odéon.*
Open noon–2am daily.
The oldest café in the world, or so they say (1686), has been recently renovated, but past habitués (Napoleon, Balzac, Voltaire and Rousseau amongst them) would not be ashamed of it today. The lunch menu is 98f, otherwise 300f *à la carte.*

Restaurant des Arts *cheap*
73 rue de Seine. No telephone. *M Odéon.*
Open noon–2pm, 7–9pm. Closed Friday pm, Saturday, Sunday.
Family-run establishment near Saint-Germain-des-Prés, little changed

since it opened in 1921. Well-cooked food, the 64f menu offers three courses, including *blanquette de veau, boeuf bourguignon, boeuf à la mode*. You can't book.

Restaurant des Beaux-Arts   *cheap*
11 rue Bonaparte. Tel. 43 26 92 64. *M St-Germain-des-Prés*.
Open noon–2pm, 7–11pm daily.
An absolute bargain in such a pricey area. Simple and hearty food with lots of choice, the 60f menu, which includes wine, is a favourite with locals, art students from across the road and Footloose researchers. Huge canvases cover the walls to help make the Beaux-Arts crowd feel at home.

Le Vagenende   *moderate*
142 boulevard St Germain. Tel. 43 26 19 14. *M Odéon*.
Open noon–3pm, 7pm–1am daily.
Overlooking the boulevard Saint Germain this spectacular Art Nouveau brasserie is a listed historic monument, built around 1902. Its curious name, pronounced by Parisians in different ways, comes from the restaurateur who bought it in 1920, before which time it was known as the Bouillon Chartier. Oh yes and they serve food as well. Menus 98f (lunch) 128f (dinner).

7e

Au Babylone   *cheap*
13 rue de Babylone. Tel. 45 48 72 73. *M Sèvres*.
Open lunch only. C1. Sunday.
Popular old-style French bistro with industrious waitresses, simple and inexpensive. *Pâtés*, salads, steaks and staples, all well prepared. Three courses, wine and service about 65f.

Au Pied de Fouet   *moderate*
45 rue de Babylone. Tel. 47 05 12 27. *M Vaneau/Sèvres-Babylone*.
Open noon–2pm, 7–9pm. C1. Saturday dinner and Sunday.
Perennially popular (with Parisians, not tourists) minuscule bistro-ette, there are only four tables seating 16 people; good home cooking. Allow around 100f for a meal.

Le Bourbon   *cheap*
1 place du Palais Bourbon. Tel. 45 51 58 27. *M Chambre des Deputés*.
Open 11.30am–3pm, 6–10pm. C1. Sunday evening.
Alsatian specialities. Good 70f menu.

Café Max   *moderate*
7 avenue de la Motte-Picquet. Tel. 47 05 57 66. *M Latour-Mauborg*.
Open lunch and dinner until midnight. C1. Sunday, Monday lunch.
Dimly-lit old bistro whose intimate atmosphere is enjoyed by local residents, especially those in the 20- and 30-something range. There's a more

restrained atmosphere during the week, it gets more animated towards the weekend. Famous salad and warm apple tart. Allow 120f.

Le Divellec *expensive*
107 rue de l'Université. Tel. 45 51 91 96. M *Invalides*.
Open noon–2pm, 8–10pm. Cl. Sunday and Monday.
One of the best fish restaurants in Paris. Lunch menu 250f, *à la carte* 600f.

Chez Germaine *cheap*
30 rue Pierre Leroux. Tel. 42 73 28 24. M *Vaneau*.
Open 11.30am–2.30pm, 6.30–9pm. Cl. Saturday dinner and Sunday.
One of the better cheap restaurants in Paris, whose standards have never faltered. The menu changes daily. Pork and lentils, *pot au feu*, *tartes* and mousses. Allow 50f including wine and service.

Jules Verne *expensive*
2nd floor Tour Eiffel. Tel. 45 55 61 44. M *Champ de Mars*.
Open 12.30–2pm, 7.30–10.15pm.
Perched on the second floor of the Eiffel Tower, gain access by the restaurant's own lift. The food is very sound, the attraction of the setting and the stylish décor of grey and black makes it one of the best places to eat in Paris. The fixed price menu is on weekday lunchtimes only 220f.

L'Oeillade *moderate*
10 rue de St Simon. Tel. 42 22 01 60. M *Bac*.
Open 12.15–2pm, 7.30–9.45pm. Cl. Sunday.
Charming little restaurant, delicate cooking by women; marinated salmon, duck with peaches, lemon tarts with lime ice cream. Menus 99f/135f.

La Petite Chaise *moderate*
36 rue de Grenelle. Tel. 42 22 13 35. M *Sèvres/Babylone*.
Open noon–2.15pm, 7–11pm daily.
Once an old coaching inn, now a cheerful rustic eatery, one of the most popular in Paris. Excellent value, allow 150f.

Relais des Mandarins *cheap*
17 rue Augereau. Tel. 47 05 28 75. M *École Militaire*.
Open noon–2.30pm, 7.30–10pm. Cl. Sunday
Vietnamese restaurant. Good value menu at 80f.

La Source *cheap*
49 boulevard de Latour-Mauborg. Tel. 47 05 51 34. M *Latour-Mauborg*.
Open 11am–midnight. Cl. Sunday.
Traditional cuisine with a 77f menu, 39f for children.

Le Roupeyrac *cheap*
62 rue de Bellechasse. Tel. 45 51 33 42. M *Solférino*.

Open noon–2.45pm, 7–9.30pm. C1. Saturday dinner and Sunday.
Near the Museum d'Orsay, genial atmosphere, generous and delicious
food at 58f for three courses. Wine and service extra.

Le Télégraphe   *expensive*
41 rue de Lille. Tel. 40 15 06 65. M *Solférino*.
Open until 12.45am. C1. Sunday.
A stylish restaurant which has become very fashionable with journos and
publishers and the occasional princess from Monaco. À *la mode* cuisine
which is reasonably priced considering the terrific quality. Allow 300f.

Thoumieux   *moderate*
79 rue St Dominque. Tel. 47 05 49 75. M *Latour-Maubourg*.
Open noon–3pm, 7–11.30pm. C1. Monday.
Ultra traditional 1930s bistro, featuring family cooking from south-west
France, served by immaculately turned out waiters. Spotted on the menu:
*tripes à la mode de Caen, cassoulet, confit de canard, pieds de porc sauce
au vin*. Set lunch menu 70f, à *la carte* 120f.

8e

Androuet   *expensive*
41 rue d'Amsterdam. Tel. 48 74 26 93. M *Liège*.
Open noon–2pm, 7–10pm. C1. Sunday.
A famous *fromagerie* where you can buy and taste cheeses in the
shop and sample cheesey gastronomy in the restaurant. Menus 190f,
200f, 250f.

L'Assiette Au Boeuf II   *cheap*
123 avenue des Champs-Élysées. Tel. 47 20 01 13. M *George V*.
Open 11.30am–1am daily.
The latest addition to Michel Olivier's successful chain serving grills
and numerous desserts. Pianist at weekends. Menu 51f, 90f, 104f.

Au Jardin du Printemps   *expensive*
32 rue de Penthiève. Tel. 43 59 44 48. M *Miromesnil*.
Open until 11.30pm. C1. Sunday.
Upmarket Chinese and as stylish as they come. Crisp and appetising
offerings. Allow 250f.

Buffet Paris Saint-Lazare   *cheap*
Salle Alize. 11 rue d'Amsterdam. Tel. 42 93 05 41. M *St Lazare*.
Open noon–2.30pm, 6–9pm. C1. Saturday and Sunday.
Traditional cuisine with 88f, 120f, 165f menus.

Chez André   *moderate*
12 rue Marbeuf. Tel. 47 20 59 57. M *Alma Marceau*.
Open noon–3.30pm, 7pm–midnight daily.
Charming 1930s bistro specialising in shellfish, fish and game. Allow
150f.

Chez Martin   *moderate*
(Hôtel du Printemps) 1 rue de l'Isly. Tel. 42 94 12 12. *M St Lazare.*
Open noon–2.30pm, 7–10pm. C1. Saturday and Sunday.
The clientèle has no complaints about the cordial atmosphere and
traditional fish dishes. Menu 98f, 160f.

The Chicago Pizza Pie Factory   *moderate*
5 rue de Berri. Tel. 45 62 50 23. *M George V.*
Open noon–1am daily.
Chicagoan turned anglophile Bob Payton opened this Paris branch
of his highly successful themed pizzeria some years ago. Pizzas are
usually big enough for two but lone diners can take home a doggy
bag. The garlic bread speaks for itself. Usually packed during happy
hour. Allow 150f.

Chez Germain   *cheap*
19 rue Jean Mermoz. Tel. 43 59 29 24. *M Miromesnil.*
Open noon–3pm, 7–10.15pm. C1. Saturday dinner and Sunday.
No frills, honest cooking at prices you can't argue with. No menu but
the *à la carte* offers fish soup, *pot au feu*, cheese or homemade tarts
with wine for about 85f.

Circus Line   *cheap/moderate*
32 rue Marbeuf. Tel. 42 89 54 54. *M Franklin D. Roosevelt.*
Open 8am–2am.
An elegant theatrical setting with a jolly pianist, open for breakfast,
lunch and dinner. Inventive lunch menu, monkfish and coriander, 60f.

Le Drugstorien   *moderate*
1 avenue Matignon (1st floor). Tel. 43 59 38 70. *M Franklin D.
Roosevelt.*
Open noon–2.30pm, 7–12.30am daily.
Nice view of the Jardin des Champs-Élysées; children can eat for 56f,
big people for 140f. *Fruits de mer* recommended.

Hippopotamus   *cheap*
6 avenue Franklin D. Roosevelt. Tel. 42 25 77 96. *M Champs-Élysées.*
Open till 1am daily.
One of a chain, very busy till closing time serving steaks, burgers, fries,
drinkable plonk. Menu 65f.

Le Moka   *cheap*
25 rue d'Artois. No telephone number available. *M George V.*
Open 11.30–3pm. Cl. Saturday and Sunday.
Heavy on atmosphere, low on prices, this down to earth noisy
bar-cum-restaurant has a daily changing menu, always packed. Quite a
find in the overpriced 8e. Starter, steak, salad, wine and service, 60f.

Le Relais   *cheap*
44 rue de Londres. Tel. 43 87 46 15. *M St Lazare.*

Open noon–2.30pm, 7.30–9.30pm. Cl. Saturday and Sunday.
Intimate, inexpensive local bistro for conventional but sound dishes and
guzzleable vino. Menu 75f.

Le Volnay *cheap*
6 rue de Laborde. No telephone. *M St Lazare.*
Open 11.45am–2.30pm, 6.45–8.30pm. Cl. Saturday and Sunday.
Hard to spend too much money here – very sound and simple dishes,
no menu but allow 85f.

Le Verger *cheap*
84 avenue des Champs-Élysées. Tel. 45 62 00 10. *M George V.*
Open noon–2.30pm, 7–10.30pm daily.
Eat well and cheaply here. Starter, main course, cheese, dessert, wine
and service for about 75f.

White House *cheap to moderate*
37 rue Washington. Tel. 45 63 66 22. *M George V.*
Open 11.30–3pm, 7–10.30pm. Cl. Saturday and Sunday.
Noisy, casual, fun. Lunch may include steak tartare, lamb chops, lasagne,
at about 60f. Dinner is a little more upmarket – steak with Roquefort or
John Dory with sorrel sauce. Allow 80–120f.

9e

Au Petit Riche *moderate*
25 rue le Peletier. Tel. 47 70 68 68. *M Le Peletier.*
Open: lunch and dinner. Cl. Saturday (14 July – 2 Sept) and Sunday.
Décor and ambience upstage the food, but the typical dishes (with
emphasis on the Loire region) are sound. Famed for its apple pie.
180f menu.

L'Auberge des Temples *cheap*
74 rue de Dunkerque. Tel. 48 74 84 41. *M Gare du Nord.*
Open 11.45am–2.45pm, 6.45pm–10.45pm daily.
Cambodian, Chinese, Japanese, Thai and Vietnamese dishes. Menu 58f,
90f, 72f, 80f.

Au Pupillin *cheap*
19 rue Notre-Dame-de-Lorette. Tel. 42 85 46 06. *M Saint Georges.*
Open noon–3pm, 6pm–2am. Cl. Saturday lunch.
Saturday brunch is good value at 80f or the lunch menu at 54f, which
includes starter and main course. There is a wine bar downstairs ensuring
a good selection.

Bistrot Ste Cécile *cheap/moderate*
15 rue Ste Cécile. Tel. 42 46 48 18. *M rue Montmartre.*
Open 11.45am–2pm, 7–10pm. Cl. Sunday.
A popular buffet (as much as you can eat), rich desserts and wine from
a barrel. Allow 85f.

Boeuf Bourguignon   *cheap*
21 rue de Douai. Tel. 42 82 08 79. *M Pigalle*.
Open noon–3pm, 7–9.45pm. Cl. Saturday evening and Sunday.
Boeuf bourguignon more often than not, and a superb *fondant au chocolat*. Lunch menu 55f.

Brasserie Flo   *moderate*
Au Printemps (Printemps de la Mode).
64 boulevard Haussmann. Tel. 42 82 58 81. *M Havre Caumartin*
Open noon–7pm. Cl. Sunday.
Recover from the rigours of shopping amidst the stylish Art Deco interior. Allow 200f. (Also in-store, Café Flo: closed Monday, 100f.)

Casa Miguel   *the cheapest*
48 rue St Georges. Tel. 42 81 09 61. *M St Georges*.
Open noon–1am, 7 to 8pm. Cl. Sunday evening.
In the Guinness Book of Records. Believe it or not, you can eat a starter, main course, cheese or dessert, wine and bread for, wait for it, 5f. Better leave a good tip!

Chartier   *cheap*
7 rue de Faubourg. Tel. 47 70 86 29. *M rue Montmartre*.
Open 11am–3pm, 6–9.30pm daily. A restaurant for the people, serving simple food very quickly. A bustling atmosphere and huge yet stylish interior (1896). Allow 60f with wine and service but be prepared to add up your own bill – and get your order rehearsed off pat as the waiters (who have formidable memories) don't hang around long to take it.

Chez Maurice   *cheap*
44 rue Notre-Dame-de-Lorette. (No telephone number available). *M St Georges*.
Open noon–2pm, 7–10.30pm daily.
Hearty eating here with good fish dishes, open every day of the year. Menus from 60f to 100f.

Chez Vincent   *cheap*
56 rue St Georges. Tel. 42 85 02 79. *M St Georges*.
Open 11.45am–2pm, 6.45–10pm. Cl. Saturday lunch and Sunday.
This local bistro tries very hard to be inventive with its food. There's a friendly atmosphere and the three-course menu for 75f is a must.

Les Diamantaires   *cheap*
60 rue Lafayette. Tel. 47 70 78 14. *M Cadet*.
Open lunch and until 11pm. Cl. Monday evenings and Tuesdays.
Eat borek, fresh breads, kebabs and other Greek delights in quite possibly the oldest established Greek restaurant in Paris. Allow 80f.

L'Entrecôte   *cheap*
101 rue St Lazare. Tel. 48 74 74 90. *M St Lazare*.

Open 11.30am–12.30am daily.
A 1930s bistro serving traditional cuisine with an excellent 49f menu
for children. Big people – 72f.

La Galatée   *cheap*
3 rue Victor Massé, Tel. 48 78 55 60. *M Pigalle.*
Open 11.30am–2.30pm, 6.30–11pm.
Air-conditioned 1900s restaurant, an ideal place to recover after walking
round Pigalle/Montmartre. Straightforward food with menus at 65f,
120f, 165f.

Le Gavroche   *cheap*
3 rue Rougemont. Tel. 47 70 57 67. *M Bonne Nouvelle.*
Open 11.30am–2pm, 6.30–9.30pm daily.
Large, rustic eatery providing robust regional dishes. Menus 62–140f.

Hatelet   *cheap*
23 rue Maubeuge. Tel. 42 81 22 66. *M Cadet.*
Also at 16 rue Notre-Dame-de-Lorette. Tel. 42 85 23 82. *M St Georges.*
Open 11.30am–3.30pm. Cl. Sunday.
Light and agreeable meals, skewers of fish or meat with salad and gratin
vegetables. Menu 48f, 56f, 65f. Express service between 11am–3pm.

Kazatchok   *cheap to moderate*
7 rue Manuel. Tel. 48 78 74 81. *M Notre-Dame-de-Lorette.*
Open 7pm–2am. Cl. Sunday.
Spicey Russian menu: goulash, Kiev cutlets and vodka. Allow 100f.

Natraj   *cheap*
28 rue Godot de Mauroy. Tel. 42 65 04 65. *M Madeleine.*
Open noon–3pm, 7–11pm daily.
After a visit to La Madeleine, pop in to this small Indian curry house
which has a 69f lunch menu.

Nine rue Choron   *cheap*
9 rue Choron. No telephone. *M Notre Dame de Lorette.*
Open noon–2pm, 7–10pm daily.
One of the best value eateries in Paris: it's possible to eat for about
35f including wine. The snag is there's not much choice.

Pagoda   *cheap to moderate*
50 rue de Provence. Tel. 48 74 81 48. *M Chaussée d'Antin.*
Open 11.30am–2.30pm, 7–10.30pm, Mon–Fri; 7.30–11pm Sat.
Cl. Sunday.
Serves dishes from all over Asia, and does it very well. Menus
85f, 95f.

Le Petit Doué   *cheap*
65 rue de Douai. Tel. 45 96 06 81. *M Place de Clichy.*
Open noon–2pm, 7–11pm. Closed Saturday and Sunday lunch; Monday. Cheerful local serving the usual bistro grub. Menu at lunch, 80f.

Le Roi du Pot-au-Feu *moderate*
34 rue Vignon. Tel. 47 42 37 10. *M Madeleine.*
Open noon–9.30pm. Cl. Sunday.
Charming bistro serving substantial beef stews, soups and pies.
Allow 100f.

Sam Kearny *cheap*
100 rue St Lazare. Tel. 42 80 31 41. *M St Lazare.*
Open 11.30am–1am daily.
American Brunch on Saturday and Sunday for 85f. Children's menus 45f. Jazz.

10e

L'Atlantique *cheap*
51 boulevard Magenta. Tel. 42 08 27 20. *M Gare de L'Est.*
Open noon–2pm, 7.30–10.30pm. Cl. Saturday lunch and Sunday.
Food spills from the sea; aromatic *bouillabaisse* and fresh shellfish.
Menu 78–139f.

Brasserie Flo *moderate*
7 cour des Petites-Ecuries. Tel. 47 70 13 59. *M Château d'Eau.*
Open noon–3pm, 7pm–1.30am daily.
One of five brasseries owned by historic restaurant rescuer Jean-Paul Bücher, this specialises in Alsatian cuisine and has an oyster stand on the street. The interior (1886) is stunning with brass luggage racks and hat stands, stained glass and wooden floors. Beer from the barrel too. Allow 100f.

Brasserie Le Gymnase *cheap*
44 boulevard Bonne Nouvelle. Tel. 47 70 50 43. *M Bonne Nouvelle.*
Open 11am–midnight daily.
Near to the Theâtré du Gymnase Marie Bell. Reliable, traditional menu 48f, 130f.

Buffet Frantour Paris Est *cheap*
Cour d'honneur de la Gare de L'Est, 4 rue du 8-Mai-1945. Tel. 45 23 23 24. *M Gare de L'Est.*
Open 11.30am–3pm, 6.30–10pm daily.
1930s bistro which pours onto an open *terrasse*; restorative meals for the spent traveller. Try the sauerkraut. 45f menu for kids. Allow 90f.

Chez Justine *cheap*
96 rue Oberkampf. Tel. 43 57 44 03. *M Parmentier.*
Open noon–2.30pm, 7–10.30pm. Cl. Sunday and Monday lunch.
Impressive selection of very fresh *hors d'oeuvres*, main course, a piece of brie and lemon tart for 63f. (74f in the evening.)

Doucet Est *cheap*
8 rue du 8-Mai-1945. Tel. 40 38 40 62. *M Gare de L'Est.*

Open 11.30am–3pm, 6.30pm–midnight daily.
Plates of seafood and sauerkraut in this 1900s eaterie; corner reserved
for non-smokers. Allow 85f.

Le Fleury   *cheap*
139 ave Parmentier. Tel. 42 38 36 97. *M Goncourt.*
Open noon–3pm, 7pm–10.30pm. Cl. Tuesday evening and Wednesday.
Classic, well-prepared dishes: fish cassoulet, steak and creamed onions
served cheerfully. *Menu formule* 98f.

Hatelet   *cheap*
89 rue d'Hauteville. Tel. 47 70 35 19. *M Poissonnière.*
Also at 96 rue d'Hauteville. Tel. 47 70 35 19.
Open 11.30am–3.30pm. Cl. Sunday.
At both establishments light and agreeable meals, skewers of fish or
meat with salad and gratin vegetables. Menu 48f, 56f, 65f. Express
service between 11am–3pm.

Julien   *moderate*
16 rue du Faubourg St Denis. Tel. 47 70 12 06. *M Strasbourg-
St Denis.*
Open noon–3pm, 7pm–1.30am daily.
Walk off the busy street market into one of Paris's most beautiful
Art Deco interiors. Excellent brasserie food more delicate than usual,
specialities include *foie gras* and fish dishes. 99f menu at lunch, 139f
at dinner.

La Moutardière   *cheap/moderate*
12 ave Richerand. Tel. 42 05 96 80. *M Goncourt.*
Open noon–2.30pm, 8–10.30pm. Cl. Sunday and Monday evenings.
Sturdy daily specials, plentiful *hors d'oeuvres*, unlimited cheese and as
much wine as you can drink! Lunch menu 90f.

Le Pot d'Étain   *moderate*
27 rue Yves Toudic. Tel. 42 02 37 43. *M République.*
Open lunch and dinner until 10pm. Cl. Saturday and Sunday.
Family-run neighbourhood restaurant, good fish and poultry with wine
and service. Allow around 130f.

Le Saulnier   *cheap*
39 boulevard de Strasbourg. Tel. 47 70 08 31. *M Château d'Eau.*
Open 11.30am–2.30pm, 6.30–9.30pm daily
Decorative 1930s bistro with an open terrace serving good traditional
grub with menus at 55f to 105f.

Terminus Nord   *moderate*
23 rue de Dunkerque. Tel. 42 85 05 15. *M Gare du Nord.*
Open 11am–12.30am daily.
Another Bucher brasserie (see Brasserie Flo, 10e) though probably the
least impressive of the group. *Fruits de mer* and menus from 98f.

11e

L'Artisan *cheap*

9 rue de Charonne. Tel. 47 00 54 53. *M Ledru Rollin.*
Open lunch and dinner until midnight. Cl. Saturday and Sunday.
Cheery bistro-ette serving fish, duck and pork in a classic French manner.
Menu 55f.

Anjou-Normandie *cheap*

13 rue de la Folie-Méricourt. Tel. 47 00 30 59. *M Saint-Ambroise.*
Open 11.45am–2pm, 7.30–9.15pm. Cl. Saturday and Sunday.
The menu announces that it's traditional cooking – *artisanal* as they
say, no colourings or additives. Fresh *moules* and fish with a bottle of
house Muscadet should be no more than 95f.

Astier *cheap*

44 rue Jean-Pierre Timband. Tel. 43 57 16 35. *M Parmentier.*
Open 12.15–2pm, 8–10pm. Cl. Saturday and Sunday.
Likeable restaurant serving heart-warming home cooking with touches
of class. Go for the fish dishes or game and a bottle of Loire wine.
Allow 90f.

Au Trou Normand *cheap*

9 rue Jean-Pierre Timbaud. Tel. 48 05 80 23. *M Oberkampf.*
Open noon–2.30pm, 7–11.30pm. Cl. Saturday evening and Sunday.
Plain but pretty, serving inexpensive and tempting dishes. Allow 60f for
dinner including wine and service.

Caves Mélac *cheap*

42 rue Léon Frot. Tel. 43 70 59 27. *M Charonne.*
Open 8.30am–8pm (until 10.30pm Tues & Thurs). Cl. Saturday
and Sunday.
Listed in the bar section but worth a visit for the *charcuterie*, omelettes,
cheese and crunchy *Poilâne* bread. *Pot au feu* for something hot. 52f.

Chardenoux *moderate*

1 rue Jules Vallès. Tel. 43 71 49 52. *M Charonne.*
Open noon–2pm, 8–10.30pm. Cl. Saturday lunch and Sunday.
This backwater restaurant with its authentic 1900 décor, zinc and marble
bar, is near to Père Lachaise cemetery. When the chef has a night off,
owner Marc Souverain produces his speciality *Gigot Brayaud*, a mutton
stew cooked for 7 hours. Allow 180f.

Cinq Points Cardinaux *cheap*

14 rue Jean Mace. Tel. 43 71 47 22. *M Charonne.*
Open noon–2pm, 7.30–10pm. Cl. Saturday and Sunday.
Old photographs of Paris adorn the walls of this charming rendezvous.
As with many bistros in this area it serves lots of sweetbreads, but

there will be something that takes your fancy. Menu 48f at lunch, 90f at dinner.

La Courtille   cheap
16 rue Guillaume Bertrand. Tel. 48 06 48 34. *M St Maur*.
Open for lunch and dinner until 10pm. Cl. Sunday.
Inventive cooking, sort of *nouvelle*, lots of purées, mousses and fine cuts of meat and fish. Menu 80f.

La Galoche d'Aurillac   moderate
41 rue Lappe. Tel. 47 00 77 15. *M Bastille*.
Open lunch and dinner until 10pm. Cl. Sunday and Monday.
A place to visit when the weather turns chilly, as the dishes are rich and robust. Specialising in duck, game and beef. Great plonk. Allow 160f.

Hamilton's Noted Fish & Chips   cheap
51 rue de Lappe. Tel. 48 06 77 92. *M Bastille*.
Open noon–2.30pm, 6–11.30pm. Cl. Sunday lunch.
Home-from-home fish and chips, mainly takeaway. Allow 40f.

Hatelet   cheap
54 rue de Malte. Tel. 48 06 40 24. *M Oberkamf*.
Also at 32 rue St Sébastien. Tel. 43 57 97 51. *M Richard Lenoir*.
Open 11.30am–3.30pm. Cl. Sunday.
Light and agreeable meals, skewers of fish or meat with salad and gratin vegetables. Menu 48f, 56f, 65f. Express service between 11am–3pm.

Le Jardin de l'Artisan   cheap
9 rue de Charonne. Tel. 47 00 54 53. *M Ledru Rollin*.
Open noon–3pm, 7–10.30pm. Cl. Saturday and Sunday.
Friday evenings catch the live singing. On other nights the salmon and sorrel (not Saturday or Sunday) will draw you back.
Lunch menu 45f. Evening 150f.

1929   cheap
90 bis, rue de la Roquette. Tel. 43 79 71 55. *M Voltaire*.
Open noon–3pm, 8pm–2am. Cl. Sunday lunch.
Traditional cuisine and accordion music in the evening; chitterlings in Riesling is the house special. Menu at lunch 60f.

Le Nioullaville   cheap
32–34 rue de l'Orillon. Tel. 43 38 95 23. *M Belleville*.
Open noon–3.30pm, 6.30pm–1am, Monday–Saturday; noon–1am Sunday.
In a pocket of Chinatown, it specialises in Chinese, Thai and Vietnamese food. Allow 85f.

L'Occitanie   cheap
96 rue Oberkampf. Tel. 48 06 46 98. *M St Maur/Ménilmontant*.
Open lunch and dinner until 10.30pm. Cl. Saturday lunch and Sunday.

Give your wallet a rest at this little restaurant serving flavours of the south: roast rabbit, *cassoulet*, Toulouse sausages, also curious omelettes made with tasty cheeses. Menus 48f, 85f.

Le Péché Mignon   *moderate*
5 rue Guillaume-Bertrand. Tel. 43 57 02 51. *M St Maur*.
Open noon–2pm, 7.15–10pm. Cl. Sunday and Monday.
Follow the discerning eaters of Paris here, where you'll find an informal atmosphere and a six course *menu gourmand* for 195f. Lamb and basil, fish with coral sauce, oysters in champagne, and delicious desserts. Worth every centime.

Pho Dong Huong   *cheap*
14 rue Louis Bonnet. No phone number available. *M Belleville*.
Open 11.30am–10.30pm. Cl. Tuesday.
Small and packed with Asian eaters, large Vietnamese noodle soups and satay. No set menu but around 26f a dish.

La Ravigotte   *moderate*
41 rue de Montreuil. Tel. 43 72 96 22. *M Faidherbe-Chaligny*.
Open noon–2.30pm Monday to Saturday. Dinner Thursday, Friday, Saturday until 9.30pm.
An inviting neighbourhood restaurant for earnest eaters. The 100f menu copes with most appetites.

Le Slickaphonic   *moderate*
1 impasse Gandelet. Tel. 40 21 04 84. *M Parmentier/Ménilmontant*.
Open 7.30pm–midnight daily.
Mouth to ear contact as you eat accompanied by jazz. Allow 100f.

Taco Loco   *moderate*
25 rue Jean-Pierre Timbaud. Tel. 43 57 90 24. *M Oberkampf*.
Open 11.00am–midnight. Cl. Sunday.
Mexican grub, guacamole, tacos, Chilli Mexican Rose, tequila and imported beers. Allow 100f.

Tokaj   *cheap*
57 rue du Chemin Vert. Tel. 47 00 64 56. *M Saint Ambroise*.
Open noon–3pm, 7.30–10.30pm. Cl. Sunday and Monday.
Likeable Hungarian restaurant with lots of paprika, veal and goulash to the sounds of traditional music. Lunch menu 60f. 130f for dinner.

Val de Loire   *cheap*
149 rue Amelot. Tel. 47 00 34 11. *M Oberkampf*.
Open noon–2.30pm, 6.30–9.45pm. Cl. Sunday
Warm and endearing, this eaterie offers a great menu for 52f: soup and escalope of chicken, fruit tart. Wine inexpensive and good.

12e

Au Trou Gascon
expensive

40 rue Taine. Tel. 43 44 34 26. *M Daumesnil.*
Open noon–2pm, 7.30–10pm. Cl. Saturday and Sunday.
A guide book favourite; even though pricey it's always full of contented eaters. Inventive dishes from Gascony and an impressive wine list. *Dégustation* menu 200f.

Brasserie l'Européen
cheap

21 bis boulevard Diderot. Tel. 43 43 99 70. *M Diderot.*
Open 11am–1am daily.
Comfortable Belle Époque brasserie serving seafood. Allow 80f.

Brasserie Luneau
cheap to moderate

5 rue de Lyon. Tel. 43 43 90 85. *M Gare de Lyon.*
Open 11am–1am daily.
Alastian specials, *fruits de mer* and sauerkraut. Menu 69f, 130f.

Caviar and Co
cheap to moderate

5 rue de Reuilly. Tel. 43 56 13 98. *M Faidherbe-Chaligny.*
Open noon–2.30pm, 7pm–3am daily. Cl. Saturday and Sunday lunch.
The three great luxuries in life: caviar, *foie gras* and smoked salmon. Predominantly gay clientèle. Set menu 85f.

Chez Adé
cheap to moderate

35 rue Traversière. Tel. 43 07 27 70. *M Gare de Lyon.*
Open evenings only until 10.30pm.
Small *Antillais* restaurant, with West Indian menu of fish soups, curries, rice and peas. Allow 90f.

La Closerie Sarladaise
moderate

94 boulevard Diderot. Tel. 43 46 88 07. *M Reuilly Diderot.*
Open noon–2.30pm, 7–10.30pm daily.
Rustic eaterie with Périgord specialities; there's a room for parties. Menu 150f.

La Connivence
moderate

1 rue de Cotte. Tel. 46 28 46 17. *M Gare de Lyon.*
Phone for opening times.
Convivial little restaurant with interesting cuisine, e.g. *filet mignon* with ginger and walnuts. About 125f. Wine good but not cheap.

Le Cyrnos
cheap

228 rue de Charenton. No telephone number available. *M Porte Dorée/Michel Bizot.*
Take pot luck at this tiny bistro, tiny bills, menu 34f.

Le Limonaire
cheap

88 rue de Charenton. No phone number available. *M Ledru-Rollin/Gare de Lyon.*

Open noon–2.130pm, 8–10pm daily
Full of bric-à-brac, with a handsome zinc bar this small restaurant serves
hearty and delicious country food. A *plat du jour* at lunch with starter
45f. No menu.

Le Parrot   *cheap*
5 rue Parrot. Tel. 43 43 05 64. *M Gare de Lyon.*
Open noon–3pm, 7–10pm. Cl. Sunday.
Good value food with two menus at 48f and 54f. Beefy and fishy.

Le Terroir   *cheap to moderate*
22 rue Chaligny. Tel. 43 07 47 66. *M Reuilly-Diderot.*
Open until 9.30pm. Cl. Saturday dinner and Sunday.
Busy bistro serving solid *cuisine bourgeoise* and *sud-ouest* specialities.
Allow 80–110f.

La Tour de Lyon   *cheap*
1 rue de Lyon. Tel. 43 43 88 30. *M Gare de Lyon.*
Open 11–1am daily.
Pretty 1900s bistro with covered terrace, fresh fish and *fruits de mer*.
Formule 76f.

Le Train Bleu   *expensive*
20 boulevard Diderot Gare de Lyon. Tel. 43 43 09 06. *M Gare
de Lyon.*
Open noon–2pm, 7–10pm, daily.
Marvel at the *fin-de-siècle* frescoes, and wood panelling – now declared
an historic monument, and eat traditional and well-presented dishes.
Allow 200f.

13e

Auberge Etchegorry   *moderate*
41 rue Croulebarbe. Tel. 43 31 63 05. *M Gobelins.*
Open noon–2.30pm, 7.30–10.30pm.
Cl. Sunday.
Up-market Basque bistro but the *menu gastronomique* is remarkable
value. Duck and pork feature strongly; watch out for the *gâteau basque*.
Menu 185f with half bottle of wine.

Bangkok-Thailand   *cheap*
35 boulevard Auguste-Blanqui. No phone number available. *M
Corvisart.*
Open noon–2.30pm, 7–10.45pm.
Tantalising but subtle Thai dishes flavoured with coconut, spices and
coriander. Soup, meat dish and dessert with tea, 65f.

Chez Bernard   *cheap*
9 rue Esquirol. Tel. 45 85 00 23. *M Nationale.*
Open noon–2.30pm, 7–10pm. Cl. Saturday dinner and Sunday.

Good and simple cooking, terrines, pan-fried veal, plus yummy tarts. Menu 65f.

Chez Françoise   *cheap*
12 rue de la Butte aux Cailles. Tel. 45 80 12 02. M *Corvisart*.
Open noon–2pm, 7.30–10.30pm. Cl. Saturday and Sunday.
Décor rustique, agreeable and classic dishes, *cassoulet*, duck with cider and mega-calorie tarts. Lunch menu 60f. Dinner 80f.

Entoto   *moderate*
143–145 rue Léon M. Nordmann. Tel. 45 87 08 51. M *Glacière*.
Open 7.30–10pm. Cl. Sunday and Monday.
Probably the only Ethiopian restaurant in Paris; *azifa* – a lentil dish with a delightful flat bread, spicey mutton stew and sherberts for dessert. Allow 130f.

Fortune des Mers   *moderate to expensive*
55 ave d'Italie. Tel. 48 85 76 83. M *Tolbiac*.
Open lunch and dinner until 11pm. Cl. Sunday and Monday.
One of the biggest restaurants in Paris, stylish and all fish. There are three sections, "Homard Bleu", "L'Ataphoes", and "Lady Jane" where you can eat for about 80f; elsewhere will cost you an arm and a lobster.

Jadorie   *moderate*
103 rue de Tolbiac. Tel. 45 82 88 77. M *Tolbiac*.
Open till 10.30pm. Cl. Monday.
Attractively presented Chinese food with a nouvelle cuisine influence. Allow 150f.

Maï Soïse   *cheap*
90 rue du Dessous des Berges. Tel. 45 83 46 15. M *Chevaleret*.
Open noon–3pm, 7.30–10pm. Cl. Sunday.
More snack bar than restaurant, very edible savoury tarts, terrines and salads. Menue 45f. wine 8f quarter litre.

Le Ménéstrel   *cheap to moderate*
10 rue de l'Ésperance. Tel. 45 89 14 08. M *Corvisart*.
Open lunch and dinner until 11pm.
Looks plain, but the simple exterior belies the inventive kitchen. Try monkfish with green peppercorns, or a plate of salmon, herring, smoked haddock, caviare and ice cold vodka. Eat well for 95f.

La Nouvelle Gare   *cheap*
49 boulevard Vincent Auriol. Tel. 45 84 74 29. M *Chevaleret*.
Open 24 hours a day. Cl. between Sunday 6am to Monday 6am.
For hungry and poor insomniacs, not much décor but good atmosphere for eating fish, rabbit, beef and chicken with *frites*. Menu 35f.

Le Palais de Cristal   *cheap*
70 rue Baudricourt. Tel. 45 84 81 56. M *Tolbiac*.

Open 11am–3pm, 6.15–11pm. Cl. Wednesday.
Enormous helpings of Asian foods, lacks style but great value. The soups
and main dishes arrive at the same time, as is traditional. Dishes 30f.

Le Petit Marquery   *expensive*
9 boulevard du Port Royal. Tel. 43 31 58 59. M *Gobelins*.
Open noon–2pm, 7.30–10.30pm, Tuesday–Saturday.
Increasingly popular bistro with people in the know, serving classic
dishes. Menu 290f.

Le Rozes   *cheap*
Centre Galaxie 30 avenue d'Italie. Tel. 45 80 66 34. M *Tolbiac*.
Place d'Italie.
Open 11.30–3.30, 7pm–1.30am daily.
Excellent *fruits de mer*. Menus 80f, 130f.

Le Rhône   *moderate*
40 boulevard Arago. Tel. 47 07 33 57. M *Gobelins.*
Open noon–2.30pm, 7–9.45pm. Cl. Saturday and Sunday.
Small, friendly family restaurant; onion tarts, Lyon sausages, lamb and
haricot beans. Menu 98f.

Le Temps des Cerises   *cheap*
18 rue de la Butte aux Cailles. Tel. 45 89 69 48. M *Corvisant*.
Open noon–2pm, 8–11pm. Cl. Sunday.
A co-operative restaurant with several set menus to cater for all
pockets.

14e

Auberge du Centre   *cheap to moderate*
10 rue Delambre. Tel. 43 35 43 09. M *Edgar Quinet*.
Open noon–2pm, 7–11.45pm. Cl. Sunday.
There's an attractive 1920s bar in this small eating place serving
traditional and regional cuisine. Menus at 50f, 98f, 160f.

Au Feu Follet   *moderate*
5 rue Raymond Losserand. Tel. 43 22 65 72. M *Gaîté*.
Open daily for lunch and dinner. Cl. Sunday.
Small, hospitable eaterie serving homely dishes. Little choice but very
good. Allow 80f.

Aux Iles Marquises   *moderate*
15 rue de la Gaîté. Tel. 43 20 93 58. M *Gaîté*.
Open noon–2pm, 7pm–midnight. Cl. Saturday lunch and Sunday.
Near to the cemetry of Montparnasse, this small bistro serves fish and
fruits de mer. Menus 130f, 150f.

Au Rendezvous des Camionneurs   *cheap*
34 rue des Plantes. Tel. 45 40 43 36. M *Alésia*.

Open noon–2.30pm, 7–9.30pm. Cl. Saturday and Sunday.
Enjoyable bistro with a 54f menu (starter, *plat du jour*, cheese or dessert).
Stray away from the *menu conseillé* and try the sardines, lamb with herbs
for 73f including wine.

Au Vin des Rues *cheap*
21 rue Boulard. Tel. 43 22 19 78. M *Denfert-Rochereau*.
Open 1–3.30pm, 9–11pm Wednesday and Friday. Cl. Sunday and
Monday.
After picking your way through the rue Daguerre street market, stop
off here for filling, tasty fare. 75f including wine.

Bar à Huitres *expensive*
112 boulevard de Montparnasse. Tel. 43 20 71 01. M *Vavin*.
Open noon–2am daily.
A restaurant specialising in different types of oysters and shellfish.
Allow 200f.

La Bergamote *cheap to moderate*
1 rue Niepce. Tel. 43 22 79 47. M *Pernety*.
Open lunch and dinner until 10.30pm. Cl. Sunday and Monday.
Inventive *nouvelle* food in a relaxed atmosphere, e.g. pieces of fish in
saffron sauce, veal in coriander and good sorbets. Lunch menu 99f.

Canard au Pot *moderate*
2 rue Boulard. Tel. 43 22 79 62. M *Denfert-Rochereau*.
Open 12.15–2.30pm, 7.15–10pm. Cl. Wednesday and Saturday lunch.
No ducks in the pot here but a great deal of veal, beef and fish.
Allow 160f.

La Cagouille *expensive*
10–12 place Constantin Brancusi. Tel. 43 22 09 01. M *Gaîté*.
Open noon–2pm, 9.45–10.30pm. Cl. Sunday and Monday.
Fantastically fresh fish at a price. Allow 300f.

Les Comestibles *cheap*
10 rue de la Sablière. Tel. 45 45 47 12. M *Alésia*.
Open noon–4pm. Cl. Saturday.
Main dishes such as roast beef, salmon or chicken for 50f, *crudités* 10f
and good plonk for 15f. Sunday menu of soup, ham, chicken, cheese or
dessert. 100f.

La Coupole *expensive*
102 boulevard Montparnasse. Tel. 43 20 14 20. M *Vavin*.
Open 7am–2am daily
More talking than eating in this trendy café brasserie – landmark where
Sartre once sat and existentialised. It has the largest fish stand in Paris.
(See also page 112)

Le Dôme *expensive*
108 boulevard du Montparnasse. Tel. 43 35 25 81. M *Vavin*.

Open until midnight. Cl. Monday.
Another classic café that's more of a restaurant these days.

Le Duc   *expensive*
243 boulevard Raspail. Tel. 43 22 59 59. *M Denfert-Rochereau*.
Open until 10.30pm. Cl. Saturday, Sunday and Monday.
Regarded as one of the best fish restaurants in Paris. Maximum
freshness, maximum cost. Allow 550f.

Le Flamboyant   *cheap to moderate*
11 rue Boyer-Barret. Tel. 45 41 00 22. *M Pernety*.
Open until 11.30pm. Cl. Sunday dinner, Monday, Tuesday lunch.
Caribbean flavours mainly fishy and fruity with pepper and spice.

Jeroboam   *cheap to moderate*
72 rue Didot. Tel. 45 39 39 13. *M Plaisance*.
Open noon–2.30pm, 7.30–10pm. Cl. Sunday and Monday evening.
Small but reliable restaurant, excellent 87f menu featuring such dishes
as haddock with cress sauce and lamb curry. Desserts from 13f. Lunch
menu 62f.

Le Maison du Cantal   *moderate to expensive*
82 boulevard du Montparnasse. Tel. 43 35 24 29. *M Montparnasse*.
Open noon–2.30pm, 7–10.30pm. Cl. Sunday and Monday lunch.
Eat marvellously well for 102f. (Other menus 148f, 247f.) Auvergne
cuisine dishes of ham and cheese, trout and bacon and yummy tarts.

Mandarin des Vanves   *cheap*
10 boulevard Brune. Tel. 45 39 93 76. *M Porte-de-Vanves*.
Open 11.30am–10pm. Cl. Sunday evening.
Oriental cuisine with good value 45f and 65f menus. Go on Sunday
after the flea market in the avenue Marc Sangnier.

La Moule en Folie   *cheap to moderate*
5 rue du Maire. Tel. 43 20 03 42. *M Edgar-Quinet*.
Open noon to 3pm, 7–11pm daily.
Lots of mussel in this seafood restaurant; lunch is around 90f
including wine.

Natacha   *expensive*
17 bis rue Campagne-Première. Tel. 43 20 79 27. *M Raspail*.
Open 8pm–1am. Cl. Sunday.
Media folk gather here, others stargaze.

L'Olivier Ouzerie   *cheap to moderate*
9 rue Vandamme. Tel. 43 21 57 58. *M Gaîté*.
Open noon–2.30pm, 6.30pm–midnight. Cl. Monday.
Dependable Greek eaterie with the usual moussaka, pastries and retsina.
Menu 80f. Lunch menu 50f.

Les Petites Sorcières   *moderate*
12 rue Liancourt. Tel. 43 21 95 68. *M Denfert-Rochereau*.

Open noon–2pm, 8–10.30pm. Cl. Saturday and Sunday.
Culinary concoctions such as sole and green lemon and chocolate gâteau with custard. Lunch menu 125f.

La Route du Château   *cheap*
123 rue du Château. Tel. 43 20 09 59. *M Pernety.*
Open until 12.30am. Cl. Sunday and Monday lunch.
The décor is pretty, plain and traditional as is the food. Menu 70f.

Télémaque   *moderate*
15 rue Roger. Tel. 43 20 66 38. *M Denfert-Rochereau.*
Open noon–2.30pm, 7–11pm. Cl. Saturday lunch and Sunday.
Great Greek cooking, no frills, lamb, cod, grills, pastries, retsina and more. Menu 65f.

L'Univers   *moderate*
73 rue d'Alésia. Tel. 43 27 17 71. *M Alésia.*
Open lunch and dinner until 10pm. Cl. Sunday.
Impeccable brasserie, faultless food; haddock in lemon juice, classic *pot-au-feu*, chocolate gâteau and custard. Allow 140f *à la carte.*

N'Zadette M'Foua   *cheap*
152 rue du Château. Tel. 43 22 00 16. *M Pernety/Gaîté.*
Open dinner only.
Cl. Sunday.
Congolese restaurant with stuffed snakes (that's the décor) but the food is quite exotic too. Plantains, manioc and kebabs of beef, African style. Menu 70f.

15e

L'Amanguier   *moderate*
51 rue du Théâtre. Tel. 45 77 04 01. *M Charles Michels.*
Open noon–2.30pm, 7pm–midnight.
See page 114 in the 2e section.

Aux Artistes   *cheap*
63 rue Falguière. Tel. 43 22 05 39. *M Pasteur.*
Open noon–3pm, 7.30pm–1am. Cl. Sunday.
Small, bohemian and a lot of choice, 25f starters and 30f main courses. The 68f menu features for example brawn, *boeuf bourgnignon* and cheese.

Le Bélisaire   *cheap*
2 rue Marmontel. Tel. 48 28 62 24. *M Vaugirard.*
Open noon–2pm, 7.45–10pm.
Cl. Saturday and Sunday.
Typical Parisian bistro with cuisine from the south-west. Try the duck gizzard salad, duck breast in fruit sauce and chocolate mousse. 115f with wine. Lunch menus 62f, 75f.

Bistro Bourdelle   *cheap*
12 rue Antoine Bourdelle. No telephone. *M Montparnasse.*
Open noon–2pm, 8–10pm. Cl. Saturday and Sunday.
Sturdy 74f menu, starter and *plat du jour*, steaks, stews and fish. Dessert
is extra from 30f.

Bistro D'Andre   *moderate*
232 rue Saint Charles. Tel. 45 57 89 14. *M Balard.*
Open noon–2.30pm, 7.30–10.30pm.
For 110f poached salmon in butter sauce, or a 59f menu at lunch.

Café Pacifico   *moderate*
50 boulevard du Montparnasse. Tel. 45 48 63 87. *Montparnasse-
Bienvenue.*
Open noon–4pm, 6pm–midnight.
Busy Mexican cantina, good Sunday brunch. Allow 150f.

Le Clos Morillons   *moderate*
50 rue des Morillons. Tel. 48 28 04 37. *M Convention.*
Open lunch and dinner. Phone for opening hours.
Good game and seasonal dishes. Lunch menu 195f.

Le Commerce   *cheap*
51 rue du Commerce. Tel. 48 28 77 01. *M Émile-Zola.*
Open noon–2.45pm, 6.30–9.30pm daily.
A slightly more sophisticated menu than its sister establishments Chartier
(9e) and Le Druout (2e), but it's less of a touristic honeypot due to its
location. Prices slightly higher too but still very reasonable. Eat up on the
green gallery, look down on eaters below. Allow 60f all in.

La Criée   *cheap*
54 boulevard du Montparnasse. Tel. 42 22 01 81. *M Place du 18
Juin 1940.*
Open noon–3pm, 7pm–1am daily.
Fish and *fruits de mer* menus at 69f, 85f. Children 50f.

Le Jardin du Maine   *cheap*
32 avenue du Maine. Tel. 45 44 63 53. *M Montparnasse-Bienvenue.*
Open 11.30–3pm, 6.30pm–1am daily
Terraced restaurant serving traditional dishes. 72f menu.

Les Jardins de Shah Jahan   *cheap*
179 rue de Vaugirard. Tel. 47 34 09 62. *M Pasteur Montparnasse.*
Open noon–2.30pm, 7–11.30pm.
Tandoori specialities; lunch menu 55f.

Le Kikana   *moderate*
3 ave du Maine. Tel. 45 44 71 88. *M Montparnasse.*
Open noon–7am daily.
Eat to the thump of the drum, traditional African dishes, root vegetables,
spicey goat meat. Allow 160f.

L'Océan
cheap to moderate

24 rue du Docteur-Finlay. Tel. 45 77 14 59. *M Bir-Hakeim.*
Open 9am–2.30pm, 7–10.30pm.
Fishialities. Menus 85f, 155f.

Le Pavé de la Halle
cheap

330 rue de Vaugirard. Tel. 45 33 91 38. *M Convention.*
Open 11.45am–3pm, 7pm–midnight daily.
Meat grills with menus at 69f, 79f and children for 46f.

Pizza Les Artistes
cheap

98 boulevard de Grenelle. Tel. 45 77 79 70. *M La Motte-Picquet.*
Large selection of pizzas; also fritters, salads and ice cream galore.
Menus 70f, 110f.

La Pomme de Reinette
cheap

48 rue Dutot. No phone number available. *M Vaugirard.*
Open noon–2.30pm, 7–10.30pm. Cl. Sunday.
Mouthwatering savoury *crêpes*, salads and sweet *crêpes* for dessert.
70f menu.

Sampieru Corsu
very cheap

12 rue de l'Admiral Roussin. No phone number available. *M Cambronne.*
Open noon–1.30pm, 7–9pm. Cl. Saturday and Sunday.
You're invited to pay 31f for a starter, daily special, dessert and wine.
If you are down-at-heel there's no bill. Over 55,000 free meals have
been served in 20 years.

Ty Breiz
cheap

52 boulevard de Vaugirard. Tel. 43 20 83 72. *M Montparnasse.*
Open 11.45am–2.45pm, 7–9.45pm. Cl. Sunday.
Ham and gruyère *crêpes* with a glass of cider will set you back 62f.

L'Univers
cheap

37 quai de Grenelle. Tel. 45 77 55 52. *M Bir Hakeim.*
Open 11am–2.30pm, 6.30–9.30pm. Cl. Sunday.
Honest eaterie with a Seine-side view. Children's 40f menu, big
people 85f.

16e

Auberge du Bonheur
moderate

Carré four de Longchamp, Bois de Boulogne. Tel. 47 72 66 00.
Bus 244.
Open noon–2.45pm, 7.30–10.45pm. Cl. evenings from October to
April.
A pleasant place to eat in the summer, outside under the trees. The
124f menu is simple and sound. Kids 55f.

Au Clocher du Village *moderate*
8 bis rue Verderet. Tel. 42 88 35 87. *M Église D'Auteuill.*
Open until 10.30pm. Cl. Saturday lunch and Sunday.
A very special restaurant, villagey atmosphere with classic dishes well
prepared. Allow 160f.

Le Beaujolais d'Auteuil *cheap*
99 boulevard de Montmorency. Tel. 47 43 03 5. *M Porte d'Auteuil.*
Open until 10.30pm. Cl. Saturday lunch and Sunday.
Rustic and homely. The 99f menu includes wine, rabbit terrine, grills
or stews and very chocolatey mousse.

La Brasserie de la Poste *moderate*
54 rue de Longchamp. Tel. 47 55 01 31. *M Trocadéro.*
Open noon–3pm, 7–1am daily.
Alsatian specialities in this brasserie located handily for the Trocadéro
and the Palais de Tokyo. Allow 150f.

Les Chauffeurs *Cheap to moderate*
8 Chaussée de la Muette. Tel. 42 88 50 05. *M La Muette.*
Open noon–10pm daily.
Reasonably priced classic dishes; fish delivered direct from Concarneau.
Menu 54f.

Le Conservatoire Rachmaninoff *cheap*
26 avenue de New York. Tel. 47 20 65 17. *M Alma-Marceau.*
Open noon–2.30pm, 7–9.30pm. Cl. Sunday, Monday, lunch.
Russian food at its best and cheapest in this friendly basement restaurant.
For three courses, allow 65f.

La Criée *cheap*
29 bis rue St Didier. Tel. 47 27 20 70. *M Boissière.*
Open noon–3pm, 7pm–midnight daily.
Worth a visit after "doing" the Trocadéro with menus at 69f and 85f.
Fish and *fruits de mer* a speciality.

La Ferme du Golf Jardin d'Acclimatation *cheap*
Avenue du Mahatma Gandhi. Tel. 45 01 21 34. *M Sablons.*
Open Wednesday, Saturday and Sunday and holidays from noon–6pm
(telephone to be sure).
Adored by children and the grown-ups, you eat in a restaurant-cum-
farm, *pot-au-feu*, salads and tarts. Menu 90f, kids 45f. (1.5 million
people visit the Jardin d'Acclimatation every year so go early.)

Le Jouvenet *cheap*
1 rue Jouvenet. No phone number available. *M Exelmans-Chardons
Lagache.*
Open noon–3pm, 7–10pm. Cl. Sunday.
Multi-choice *hors d'oeuvres*, fish and beef dishes with sauces, desserts
and wine for 65f.

Le Malakoff *cheap*
6 place du Trocadéro. Tel. 45 53 75 27. *M Trocadéro.*
Open 11.30am–12.30am. Cl. Sunday.
Friendly brasserie with terrace and traditional home cooking. From 60f.

Le Mathusalem *cheap to moderate*
5 bis boulevard Exelmans. Tel. 42 88 10 73. *M Boulevard Victor.*
Open 11.30–3pm, 7.30–10.30pm. Cl. Sunday.
Same management as Jeroboam in the 14e. See p. 141

Mexico Café *moderate*
1 place de Mexico. Tel. 47 27 96 98. *M Trocadéro.*
Open noon–midnight daily.
French and Tex-Mex cuisine. Menu 125f

Le Paris Passy *cheap*
3 place de Passy. No phone number available. *M Muette.*
Open 7am–midnight, every day of the year.
Unusually cheap for the area, this hectic eaterie offers two courses for
56f. Desserts and wine extra.

Restaurant Phoenicia *cheap*
19 rue Le Marois. Tel. 45 24 20 80. *M Porte de St Cloud.*
Open noon–2.15pm, 7.30–10.30pm. Cl. Sunday.
Marvellous Lebanese food, chicken with lemon and spice, pancakes and
milky ice cream. Allow 80f.

Le Relais d'Auteuil *moderate*
31 boulevard Murat. Tel. 46 51 09 54. *M Porte d'Auteil.*
Open for lunchy and dinner until 10pm. Cl. Saturday and Sunday.
The refined and imaginative cooking of Patrick Pignol makes the 170f
menu worth every centime. There's also a *menu-dégustation* with eight
dishes for 340f.

Le Rude *moderate*
11 avenue de la Grande Armée. Tel. 45 00 13 21. *M Charles-de-
Gaulle-Étoile.*
Open noon–4pm, 7pm–midnight daily.
A menu at 138f serving Spanish food.

Le Scheffer *moderate*
22 rue Scheffer. Tel. 47 27 81 11. *M Trocadéro.*
Open noon–2.30pm, 7.30–10.30pm. Cl. Sunday.
Excellent steaks, mutton, crème caramel and superb wines. Menu
120f.

Le Totem *cheap*
Musée de l'Homme. 1 place du Trocadéro. Tel. 47 27 74 11. *M
Trocadéro.*
Open noon–2.30pm, 8–10.30pm. Cl. Tuesday.
Terrific terrace, right above the Trocadéro gardens, overlooking the
Eiffel Tower. A buffet with a daily special. Menu 75f and 95f.

17e

L'Amanguier
43 avenue des Ternes. Tel. 43 80 19 28. *M Ternes.*
(See Page 114 in the 2e).

L'Appolon   *cheap*
27 rue Salneuve. Tel. 47 66 03 12. *M Malesherbes.*
Open noon–2.30pm, 7.30–11.30pm. Cl. Sunday.
Greek goodies, taramaslata, moussaka and kebabs. Three courses for
59f and the retsina and wine cheap too.

Le Beudant   *moderate*
97 rue des Dames. Tel. 43 87 11 20. *M Victor Hugo.*
Open noon–2.30pm, 7.30–10.30pm. Cl. Saturday lunch and Sunday.
Fish is the speciality. Menu 135f.

La Bonne Cuisine   *cheap*
17 rue Biot. No phone number available. *M Place de Clichy.*
Open noon–2pm, 7–9.45pm. Cl. Saturday lunch and Sunday.
Loads of atmosphere, low prices, this friendly restaurant serves a
three-course 70f menu at lunch.

Bistrot d'à Côté   *moderate*
10 rue Gustave Flaubert. Tel. 42 67 05 81. *M Péreire.*
Open 12.30–2pm, 7.30–11pm. Cl. Saturday and Sunday.
Charming bistro owned by Michel Rostang who cooks around the
corner in his eponymous restaurant for 680f a go. Here somewhat
less – allow 180f.

Bistrot de L'Étoile   *moderate*
75 av Niel. Tel. 42 27 88 44. *M Péreire.*
Open lunch and dinner. Phone for opening hours.
Guy Savoy (like Michel Rostang above) is a chef-proprietor of his own
two-star restaurant. Now he has opened this bistro near to his first
establishment. Menu 170f.

Brasserie du Pont Legendre   *cheap*
135 rue de Rome. Tel. 47 63 66 13. *M Rome.*
Open 11.45am–2.45pm, 6.30–10pm. Cl. Sunday evening.
Pickled white cabbage, quiches, ham and lentils. Menus 67f, 75f

Cafétéria Monte Carlo   *cheap*
9 ave de Wagram. Tel. 43 80 02 20. *M Charles-de-Gaulle-Étoile.*
Open 11am–11pm every day.
After appraising the Arc de Triomphe, head for this *self* where the food
is beautifully prepared, cheap and tasty. Menu 50f

Chez Fred   *moderate*
190 bis boulevard Pereire. Tel. 45 74 20 48. *M Péreire.*

Open noon–2pm, 7.30–10.30pm. Cl. Saturday lunch and Sunday.
Sausages and *andouillettes* eaten outside if the weather is fine.
Menu 145f.

Churrasco   *cheap*
277 boulevard Péreire. Tel. 40 55 92 00. *M Neuilly Ponte Maillot.*
Open 11.45am–midnight, 1.00am Saturdays, daily.
Argentinian meats, grilled and fried. Menus 50f/73f, 25f for children.

La Cloche à Fromage   *cheap to moderate*
71 boulevard Gouvion-St-Cyr. Tel. 45 72 50 06. *M Neuilly Porte
Maillot.*
Open noon–2.30pm, 7–11pm daily.
Cheese, breads and wine. Menu 99f. Children 50f.

Four à Pain   *moderate*
19 rue Guy Moquet. Tel. 42 29 07 30. *M Brochant.*
Open noon–3pm, 7–11pm. Cl. Saturday lunch and Sunday.
Lavish buffet with menus at 100f, 130f, 150f.

Goldenburg   *cheap*
69 ave de Wagram. Tel. 42 27 34 79. *M Ternes.*
Open until 11pm daily.
A little room at the back of this deli is open daily for Jewish delicacies,
pastrami, salt beef, pickles, bagels with a bumper Sunday brunch. Allow
25f–100f. Brunch 110f.

Le Jardin d'Ez Zahra   *moderate*
18 rue Jouffroy. Tel. 47 63 82 18. *M Malesherbes.*
Open noon–3pm, 7.30–10.30pm. Cl. Saturday and Sunday.
Dishes and wines from 17 Mediterranean coastal countries. Allow
150f.

Le Melrose   *cheap to moderate*
5 place de Clichy. Tel. 42 93 61 34. *M Place Clichy.*
Open noon–2.30pm, 7.30–10.30pm. Cl. Saturday lunch and Sunday.
Busy local with excellent terrines of fish and meat. Two courses 75f.
Regular menu 155f.

Mère Michel   *moderate*
5 rue Rennequin. Tel. 47 63 59 80. *M Ternes.*
Open lunch and dinner. Phone for opening hours. Cl. Saturday
and Sunday
With its lace-curtained windows it is as French as you can get. Famed
for its *beurre blanc* and fish. Three courses 200f.

Natacha   *cheap*
35 rue Guersant. Tel. 45 74 23 86. *M Porte Maillot.*
Open noon–2pm, 7–11pm. Cl. Sunday.
Uncomplicated bistro, *hors d'oeuvres*, grilled meats, tarts, and as much
wine as you can drink for 75f.

Sormani   *expensive*
4 rue du Général Lanrezac. Tel. 43 80 13 91. *M Charles-de-Gaulle-Etoile.*
Open 12.15–2pm, 7.45–10pm. Cl. Saturday and Sunday.
Probably the best Italian in Paris, with prices that testify to the fact. 270–400f.

Le Sushi Bar   *moderate*
Hôtel Meridien, 81 boulevard Gouvion-St-Cyr. Tel. 40 68 30 82. *M Porte Maillot.*
Open lunch and dinner. Phone for opening hours.
Over 20different types of raw fish on the menu. Lunch 155f.

La Verre Boutelle   *moderate*
85 avenue des Ternes. Tel. 45 74 01 02. *M Porte Maillot.*
Open noon–3pm, 7.30pm–5am. Cl. Saturday and Sunday.
Unusual décor, board games on the walls, the cuisine plays safe but well. Very friendly atmosphere. Allow 100f.

18e

Un Africain à Paris   *cheap*
9 rue Marcadet. Tel. 42 23 87 98. *M Marcadet-Poissonières.*
Open 7.30pm–midnight. Cl. Sunday.
There's no *menu* at this North African restaurant, so pick carefully through the *à la carte*, maybe the nicely spiced chicken for 65f.

L'Anniversaire   *cheap to moderate*
103 rue Marcadet. Tel. 42 55 08 77. *M Jules Joffrin.*
Open noon–2pm, 7.30–10.30pm. Cl. Saturday lunch, Monday.
Trusty grills and traditional cuisine with menus at 70f/99f/140f.

Au Poulbot Gourmet   *moderate*
39 rue Lamarck. Tel. 46 06 86 00. *M Lamarck-Caulincourt.*
Open lunch and dinner, phone for opening hours. Cl. Sunday.
You must book at this little seafood eaterie – it's very popular. Allow 150f.

Beauvillers   *expensive*
52 rue Lamarck. Tel. 42 54 54 42. *M Lamarck-Caulincourt.*
Open 12.15–2.00pm, 7.30–10.45pm. Cl. Sunday and Monday lunch.
A laudable luxury restaurant with *nouvelle* dishes, the 175f lunch menu makes it bearable, otherwise pay 600f.

La Butte aux Moulins – le Montmartre   *cheap*
74 rue des Martyrs. Tel. 42 64 74 28. *M Pigalle.*
Open noon–2.30pm, 6.30–10.30pm.
French traditional cuisine with 59f/98f menus.

Butte en Vigre   *cheap*
5 rue Poulbot, place du Tertre. Tel. 46 06 91 96. *M Abbesses*.
Open noon–2pm, 7–10.45pm. Cl. Wednesday.
Burly, beefy stews in a rustic setting by the Basilique.

Les Chauffeurs   *cheap*
11 rue des Portes-Blanches. Tel. 42 64 04 17. *M Marcardet-Poisonnière*.
Open noon–3pm, 7–10pm daily.
Hefty dishes of good food, no menu but a terrine to start, a succulent
steak and homemade ice cream will set you back 75f.

Chez Ginette   *cheap*
101 rue Caulaincourt. Tel. 46 06 01 49. *M Lamarck-Caulaincourt*
Open noon–2.30pm, 7.30–11.30pm. Cl. Sunday.
Hearty home cooking in a comfortable and friendly eaterie, grilled
meats, curried pork, all served with couscous. Menu 75f.

La Crémaillère 1900   *cheap to moderate*
15 place du Tertre. Tel. 46 06 58 59. *M Abbesses*.
Open noon–11pm daily.
Stylish décor, and reliable fish and meat dishes which, weather
permitting, can be eaten on the terrace or in the garden. 77f menu.

L'Etrier   *cheap to moderate*
154 rue Lamarck. Tel. 42 29 14 01. *M Guy-Môquet*.
Open 7–11pm. Cl. Sunday.
Argentinian meats a speciality. Menu 92f.

Flunch   *cheap*
1 rue Caulaincourt. Tel. 45 22 39 52. *M Place de Clichy.*
Open 11am–2.30pm, 5.30–11pm.
Self-service with a non smoking area. 40–90f

Da Graziano   *cheap to moderate*
83 rue Lepic. Tel. 46 06 84 77. *M Abbesses*.
Open noon–3pm, 8pm–12.30am.
Authentic Italian restaurant with garden for summer eating. Lunch menu
65f, otherwise pricey.

Le Lampadaire   *cheap*
106 rue Lepic. Tel. 42 54 02 21. *M Abbesses*.
Open lunch and dinner till 11pm. Cl. Sunday.
Fresh, well-prepared dishes mainly seafood and duck, excellent cheese
and desserts. Menu 85f.

Le Maquis   *moderate*
69 rue Caulaincourt. Tel. 42 59 76 07. *M Larmarck-Caulaincourt*.
Open noon–2.30pm, 7.30–10.30pm. Cl. Sunday and Monday.
One of the better places to eat in the 18e. It's tiny, so book. Lunch
menu 110f.

La Petit Chose   *cheap*
41 rue des Trois Frères. Tel. 42 64 49 15. *M Abbesses.*
Open 11.30–2.30pm, 7–11pm. Cl. Monday, Tuesday lunch.
Old artists' studio serving fish with a 59f menu at lunch, 89f/140f at dinner. Children 40f.

Le Petit Moulin   *cheap*
17 rue Tholozé. Tel. 42 52 46 16. *M Abbesses.*
Open 7pm–midnight. Cl. Wednesday.
The menu changes daily at this little mill, good food for about 60f.

Le Poirier Sans Pareil   *moderate*
195 rue Championnet. Tel. 46 27 29 14. *M Simplon.*
Open lunch and dinner until 11pm. Cl. Sunday and Monday lunch.
Fishy fare such as bass, trout and lobster salad. Remarkable 80f menu, where the *à la carte* can be 350f.

La Poutre
10 rue Trois-Frères. Tel. 42 57 45 04. *M Abbesses.*
Open noon–3pm, 6pm–1am.
Pretty restaurant specialising in *Périgord* cuisine. Menu 50f.

Le Restaurant   *moderate*
32 rue Veron. Tel. 42 23 06 22. *M Abbesses.*
Open noon–2.30pm, 8–10.30pm. Cl. Sunday and Monday.
This young chef, former student of Senderens' at Lucas Carton, is a hit with the media folk. Menu at lunch 98f.

Wepler   *moderate*
14 place de Clichy. Tel. 45 22 53 24. *M Place de Clichy.*
Open noon–1am.
If it lives in the sea you can eat it here, elbow to elbow. Menu 140f (continuous service).

19e

Au Rendez-vous de la Marine   *moderate*
14 quai de la Loire. Tel. 42 49 33 40. *M Jaurès.*
Open lunch and dinner until 9.30pm. Cl. Sunday and Monday.
Once frequented by bargemen, you'll still find solid bistro food: *coquilles Saint-Jacques*, duck, lemon tart. There's a *bouillabaisse* for four which must be ordered eight hours in advance.

Le Cargo   *cheap to moderate*
41 bis quai de la Loire. Tel. 42/41 34 34. *M Laumière.*
Open daily until 12.30am.
Spartan interior with the warmth provided by the yuppy media type clientèle who enjoy this old converted warehouse with its modern cuisine. Menu 70f at lunch.

Le Chaumont-Laumière   *cheap*
20 ave Laumière. Tel. 46 07 83 04. *M Laumière*.
Open 8am–10.30am, noon–2.30pm, 7–10pm. Cl. Sunday.
Friendly local eaterie near the pretty Parc des Buttes Chaumont. 60f
menu includes three courses and wine.

Ferme de la Villette   *cheap*
180 avenue Jean-Jaurès. Tel. 42 41 71 35. *M Porte de Pantin*.
Phone for opening times.
The restaurant moved to its present address during the building
of the science museum but it maintains its traditional dishes and
atmosphere.
Tasty Thai and Chinese food. Allow 100f.

Le Sancerre   *moderate*
13 ave Corentin-Cariou. Tel. 40 36 80 44. *M Porte de Pantin*.
Open noon–10.30pm daily.
Reliable homely cooking: boiled beef, carrots, etc. Allow 180f.

Sushiya   *cheap*
12 rue Pradier. Tel. 42 02 85 82. *M Pyrénées*.
Open noon–2.30pm, 6.30–10pm. Cl. Saturday and Sunday.
Raw fish, rice and sake. Menu 55f.

Tai Yien   *cheap to moderate*
5 rue de Belleville. Tel. 42 41 44 16. *M Belleville*.
Open every day until 1am.
Huge Chinese decorated with traditional lanterns, with mostly Asian
clientèle – always a good sign. Allow at least 75f a head.

20e

Aux Fins Gourmets   *cheap to moderate*
15 rue du Surmelin. Tel. 43 64 39 63. *M Gambetta*.
Open noon–7pm. Cl. Saturday lunch, Sunday and Monday dinner.
Very French bistro with 69f, 125f menus. Allow 150f.

Chez Nous   *cheap*
81 rue de Bagnolet (at junction of rue Lesseps). Tel. 43 70 77 93. *M
Alexandre-Dumas*.
Open lunch and dinner until the last client staggers out. Cl. Sunday.
Authentic little neighbourhood restaurant, popular with locals.
Menu 50f (includes wine), 79f.

Chez Roger   *moderate*
145 rue d'Avron. Tel. 43 73 55 47. *M Porte-de-Montreuil*.
Phone for opening times. Cl. Wednesday evening, Thursday.
Small authentic restaurant: reliable staples include grilled salmon, rabbit
sautéd in Sauvignon. Allow 120f per person.

The Top Five

Where to go for a once in a lifetime gastronomic orgasm. All the restaurants below have three Michelin stars, impeccable food and top prices. You'll need to book several weeks in advance!

L'Ambrosie

9 Place des Vosges 75004. Tel. 42 78 51 45. M Bastille
Open noon—2pm, 8—10pm. Closed. Sunday and Monday.
A lunch menu for a mere 300f but pay around 700f *à la carte*. The smallest and newest of the big five.

Jamin

32 rue de Longchamp 75016. Tel. 47 27 12 27. M *Trocadéro*.
Open 12.30—2pm, 7.30—10pm. Closed Saturday and Sunday.
Joël Robuchon is the brightest light in the firmament of brilliant young French chefs. Allow 900f.

Lucas-Carton

9 place Madeleine 75008. Tel. 42 65 22 90. M *Madeleine*.
Open 12.30—2.30pm, 8—10.30pm. Closed Saturday and Sunday.
Owned by Remy Martin, Alain Senderens is *chef de cuisine*. Stunning *Belle Époque* décor, but the kitchens are amongst the most up-to-date in Paris. The *menu* is 800f, *à la cartes à remortgager*.

Taillevent

15 rue Lamennais 75008. Tel. 45 63 39 94. M *Georges V*.
Open 12.30—2pm, 8—10.30pm. Closed Saturday and Sunday.
This 1850s mansion is a suitably reverential and attractive setting for some of the best food in France, with the most extensive and expensive wine list in Paris. Allow 750f.

Tour d'Argent

15—17 quai de la Tournelle 75005. Tel. 43 54 23 31. M *Maubert-Mutualité*.
Open noon—2.30pm, 8—10.30pm. Closed Monday.
Long-established Paris institution famed for its duck Tour d'Argent. Enjoy if you can the 400f lunch menu or the 800f *à la carte*.

Chez Vincent *moderate*
60 boulevard de Ménilmontant. Tel. 46 36 07 67. *M Père Lachaise*.
Open noon–2pm, 7–9.45pm daily.
Friendly family-run restaurant where a starter, T-bone steak with
bearnaise sauce, chocolate mousse and wine costs 70f.

Egée *moderate*
19 rue de Ménilmontant. Tel. 43 58 70 26. *M Ménilmontant*.
Open noon–2.30pm, 7.30–11.30pm daily.
Authentic Greek and Turkish cooking, excellent *hors d'oeuvres*.
Allow 100f with wine.

Lyanes *cheap*
16 rue des Lyanes. Tel. 43 61 41 64. *M Gambetta*.
Open lunch and evening until 9.30pm. Cl. Saturday lunchtime,
Sunday.
Recent renovation and enlargement has not spoilt this agreeable,
welcoming bistro. Allow 80f per person.

Royal Bangkok *cheap to moderate*
4 rue du Cher. Tel. 46 36 46 24. *M Gambetta*.
Cl. Sunday.
Tasty Thai and Chinese food. Allow 100f.

VEGETARIAN RESTAURANTS

1er

Végétarien Lacour *cheap*
3 rue Villedo (off rue Richelieu). Tel. 42 96 08 33. *M Pyramides*.
Phone for opening hours.
Simple but wholesome food: three courses and delicious coffee for
40f.

2e

Country Life *cheap*
6 rue Danou. Tel. 42 97 48 51. *M Opéra*.
Open (restaurant) 11.30am–2.30pm, Monday–Friday.
Daily changing menu featuring delicious help-yourself buffet of hot and
cold dishes.
No wine, alcohol, smoking. There's an organic grocery shop too.

La Patata *cheap*
25 boulevard des Italiens. Tel. 42 68 16 88. *M Opéra*.
Open 11am–midnight every day.
Enormous jacket potatoes with 19 different garnishes (between 38f–76f)
some of which are vegetarian. Accompany the filling fare with a glass

(9f) or bottle (from 56f) of wine. Quick, friendly service. Before noon and between 5pm and 7pm, there's a free drink offered to early eaters. See also **Verdeau** in the 9e.

4e

Aquarius   *cheap*
54 rue Ste-Croix-de-la-Bretonnerie. Tel. 48 87 48 71. *M Hôtel de Ville*.
Open noon–9.45pm daily. Cl. Sunday.
Refuel on light vegetarian fodder for 60f. (Also a branch in the 14e.)

Piccolo Teátro   *cheap*
6 rue des Écouffes. Tel. 42 72 17 79. *M St Paul*.
Open noon–3pm, 7–11pm daily. Cl. Monday.
Inventive cuisine (e.g. carrot caviar) at this excellent vegetarian restaurant. Allow 120f maximum *à la carte*. There's a *menu* (lunchtimes only) for 49f.

Top Vitamines   *cheap to moderate*
61 rue de Quincampoix. Tel. 40 27 92 78. *M Rambuteau/Étienne Marcel*.
Open 12.15–3pm, 6.30–10pm Monday–Saturday.
Ionised air in this trendy non-smoking vegetarian eaterie set in vaulted *caves*. Special lunch menu 49f, regular menu 149f, or allow about 130f *à la carte*.

5e

L'Auberge In   *cheap*
34 rue du Cardinal Lemoine. Tel. 43 26 43 51. *M Cardinal Lemoine*.
Open noon–2pm.
Organic produce turned into vegetarian temptations. Also at 88 rue Rochechouart, 9e.

Aux Abeilles d'Or   *cheap*
12 rue Royer-Collard. No phone number available. *M Luxembourg/Odéon*.
Vegetarian *nouvelle cuisine*.

Le Grenier de Notre-Dame   *cheap*
18 rue de la Bûcherie. Tel. 43 29 98 29. *M Maubert-Mutualité*.
Open noon–2pm, 7.30–11.30pm daily.
Macrobiotic specialities and "protein platters" opposite Notre-Dame.

Le Jardin des Pâtes   *cheap*
4 rue Lacépède. Tel. 43 31 50 71. *M Monge/Jussieu*.
Open noon–2.30pm, 7–9.30pm. Cl. Monday.
Pasta made on the spot from a range of different cereals (they even grind

the flour) served with a wide and imaginative variety of sauces, including fishy and veggie options. Organic wine too and art exhibitions. Allow 100f for a three-course meal.

Le Petit Légume *cheap*
36 rue des Boulangers. Tel. 40 46 06 85. *M Cardinal Lemoine*.
Open 9.30am–10pm.
Eat in or take out. Adjacent shop sells vitamins, wholesome ingredients.

Roselight *cheap*
29 quai de la Tournelle. No telephone numbers available. *M St Michel*.
Riverside *salon de thé*. Open noon–4pm, 7pm–1am.

6e

La Macrobiothèque *cheap*
17 rue de Savoie. Tel. 43 25 04 96. *M St Michel/Odéon*.
Open noon–2pm, 7–9.30pm daily. Cl. Sunday
Agreeable setting for macrobiotic vegetarian cooking: salads, tofu, tarts, cereals and pulses. An adjacent shop sells vitamins and health foods. Allow 80f dinner. There's a lunch menu at around 42f. No alcohol served.

7e

Le Jardin *cheap to moderate*
100 rue du Bac. Tel. 42 22 81 56. *M Bac Rhede*.
Open noon–3pm, 7–10pm daily. Cl. Sunday.
Exciting food served in a bright and airy conservatory dining room. Calories are listed next to the dishes on the menu which includes various salads, gratins, savoury flans, ices, cakes. There's also a shop. Allow 150f *à la carte*. Dinner menu 94f. In the afternoon it becomes a tea-room.

8e

Royal Monceau *moderate*
39 avenue Hoche. Tel. 42 25 06 66. *M Charles-de-Gaulle-Étoile*.
Open 11.30am–3pm. Cl. Sunday.
Different kinds of health food brunches for just under 200f, beside the swimming pool on Sundays from 11.30am–3.30pm. Book in advance.

9e

La Fermette d'Olivier *cheap*
40 rue du Faubourg Montmartre. No phone number available. *M Peletier/Montmartre*.

Open noon–4pm, 6–10pm, Monday–Friday.
Macrobiotic as well as regular fare.

Verdeau   *cheap to moderate*
25 passage Verdeau. Tel. 45 23 15 96. *M Richelieu-Drouot.*
Open 11.30am–3pm. Cl. Sunday.
Perfect lunch stop after a spot of dry weather shopping in the arcades
or visiting the Grévin: superior stuffed baked potatoes is the fare,
some with vegetarian fillings. Sister establishment **La Patata** in the 2e.
Allow 120f.

13e

Le Bol en Bois   *cheap*
35 rue Pascal. Tel. 47 07 27 24. *M Gobelins.*
Open noon–2pm, 7–9.30pm.
Rather austere macrobiotic restaurant/natural food shop and one of the
oldest in France.

14e

Aquarius   *cheap*
40 rue de Gergovie. Tel. 45 41 36 88. *M Pernety.*
Open noon–3pm, 7–10.30pm daily. Cl. Sunday.
Same management as **Aquarius** in the 4e.

15e

Grain Sauvage   *cheap*
15 rue Letellier. Tel. 45 79 63 43. *M Grenelle.*
Open noon–2pm, 6–9pm daily. Cl. Sunday.
Macrobiotic vegetarian cooking as well as natural food shop, information and conference centre, cookery school, courses.

17e

L'Epicerie Verte   *cheap*
5 rue Saussier Leroy. Tel. 47 64 19 68. *M Ternes.*
Open noon–2.15pm, 7.15–9.30pm, Mon–Fri.
Behind the health food *épicerie* is an organic and vegetarian restaurant.
Mixed salads, vegetable tarts, a *gratin d'endives*, goat cheeses, good
chocolate cake. Allow around 70f for a wholesome three courses.
Wine served.

Les Fines Herbes   *cheap*
38 rue Nollet. Tel. 43 87 05 41. *M Place de Clichy.*
Open 11.30am–3pm, Tue–Sat. Cl. Sun–Mon.
Exclusively vegetarian food – you can have a vitamin-packed lunch here

for around 50f. Bread is baked on the premises, wines from 9f for a quarter. No smoking permitted.

Le Pitchou   *cheap*
2 rue Truffaut. Tel. 43 87 96 79. *M Brochant*.
Open 11.30am–2pm, 6.30–11pm. Cl. Wed, Thur lunchtimes.
Useful vegetarian restaurant near the Batignolles.

Yamato   *cheap*
38 rue Nollet. Tel. 43 87 05 41. *M Place de Clichy*.
Open 11.30am–3pm. Cl. Sun–Mon.
Yamato is a dish of rice, vegetables, cold fish mayonnaise and salad.
No meat but other fishy dishes available.

Grain de Folie   *cheap to moderate*
24 rue la Vieuville. Tel. 42 58 15 57. *M Abbesses*.
Open 12.30–3.30pm, 7–11pm.
Halfway up the Butte Montmartre is this Anglo-American restaurant with an attractive stone interior and welcoming staff. The 65f menu includes soup or salad, vegetable flan or a cereal pulse-based dish, dessert. Fish included on the liberal menu, organic wine too. Smoking is permitted. Allow 150f *à la carte*.

Naturalia   *cheap*
107 rue Caulaincourt. Tel. 42 62 33 68. *M Lamarck-Caulaincourt*.
Open 11.30am–3.30pm, Mon–Fri.
Attached to a health food shop, the eaterie has a lunchtime vegetarian menu and takeaway service. Fish and chicken also appear a couple of times a week on the menu; alcohol served with full meals only. Organic wines.

Rayons de Santé   *cheap*
8 place Charles Dullin. Tel. 42 59 64 81. *M Anvers*.
Open 10am–10.30pm, Sun–Thur; 10am–3pm Fri.
Simple vegetarian café near the Basilique du Sacré-Coeur; good value *formule* (no drink, no dessert) at 40f.

SALONS DE THÉ AND CAFÉS

1er

Angelina
226 rue de Rivoli.
Open 9.30am–7pm daily.
Founded in 1903, and still one of *the* places to be seen at teatime. Art Deco lanterns apart, the interior's little changed since the turn of the century. Marcel Proust, King George V and Coco Chanel all enjoyed the delicious hot chocolate and rich pastries.

Cador
2 rue de L'Admiral-Coligny.
Open 9am–7.30pm, Tue–Sun.
Chic Louis XVI-style backdrop, complete with white and gilt panelling and original tiled floor for tea or a light lunch; good brunches too. Handy for the Louvre.

Café Costes
4 rue Berger, place des Innocents.
Open 8am–2am daily.
Chic, trendy, and so not cheap. There's plenty of space to be seen in this sea of designer chairs, tables and coffee cups. When Café Costes opened in 1985 its interior by Philippe Starck sparked off a rash of imitations.

Fanny Tea
20 place Dauphine.
Open 1–8pm Tue–Sat; 3.30–8pm Sun. Cl. Mon.
Tiny (seats 18) rustic tearoom, flavoursome teas, poetry books for browsing through.

Rose-Thé
91 rue St Honoré.
Open noon–6.30pm. Cl. Sun.
Very welcoming tearoom: near a courtyard of antique shops. Good light meals (salads, savoury tarts) and brilliant cheesecake.

Verlet
256 rue St Honoré.
Open noon–6.30pm, Tue–Fri. Cl. Sun–Mon.
A coffee shop since 1880, selling and serving tea and coffee, popular with actors and journalists.

2e

A Priori Thé
36 galerie Vivienne.
Open for breakfast 8.30–11am. Lunch from noon. Tea 3–7.30pm daily.
Welcoming, pastel, glass-roofed salon de thé serving English tea. (Also lunch and good Sunday brunch.) Located in the city's most beautifully restored arcade, off rue des Petits Champs.

Pandora
24 passage Choiseul.
Open 11.30am–7pm, Mon–Fri. Cl. Sat.
Open Sun, Oct–March, noon–7pm.
Two pretty rooms in which to enjoy tasty snacks and teas. Reasonably priced, copious Sunday brunch.

Le Paradis du Fruit
28 bis rue Louis-le-Grand.
Open 11.30am–1.30am daily.
Paradise found: light, refreshing and exotic fruit concoctions. Also branches in the 4e and 6e.

Thé Au Fils
80 rue Montmartre.
Open noon–6pm, Mon–Fri.
Relaxing small *salon* where you can pore quietly over the papers with a coffee and a sandwich.

3e

Brocco
180 rue du Temple.
Open 8am–7pm daily.
Pretty tea room very near place de la République; good value, yummy pastries and super café crème.

Le Petit Salé
97 rue Vieille-du-Temple.
Open noon–5pm, 8pm–midnight, Wed–Fri; All day Sat and Sun. Cl. Mon–Tue.
Handy refreshment stop after treking around the Picasso Museum, for chocolate, tea, cake, a light lunch or supper.

Quartier de Jour
103 rue Vieille-du-Temple.
Open 10am–6pm daily except Sat; 10am–10pm in summer.
Useful snack-stop with aviation themed décor. *Très branché* clientèle.

4e

Au Lys d'Argent
90 rue St-Louis-en-l'Isle.
Open 11am–7pm. Cl. Mon.
The Ile St Louis has many tea rooms, but this one is particularly pleasant. Teas (36 kinds), cakes and generous brunch.

La Charlotte de l'Isle
26 rue St-Louis-en-l'Ile.
Open 2–8pm. Cl. Mon–Tue.
Tiny, pretty tea room ruled by Charlotte whose two passions are poetry and chocolate. Drunk or eaten, her chocolate is excellent. On Wednesdays from 5.30pm–7.30pm there's a *piano-thé*.

L'Ébouillanté
6 rue des Barres.

Open noon–9pm, Tue–Sun. Cl. Mon.
Friendly down-to-arth doll's house-sized café serving heavenly chocolate cake. Brunch on the terrace in summer is lovely.

Les Enfants Gâtés
43 rue des Francs-Bourgeois.
Open noon–7pm daily.
Friendly tea room, scrummy chocolate and orange tart, brownies and light lunches. Brunch on Saturday and Sunday between noon and 4pm.

Eurydice
10 place des Vosges.
Open 10.30am–7.30pm, until 11pm in summer. Cl. Mon.
Imaginative light meals, salads, cakes and tea under the arcades of the place des Vosges, next to the Victor Hugo museum.

Le Flore en l'Ile
42 quai d'Orléans.
Open 10am–2am daily.
Sample the rich cakes, Berthillon ices and sorbets overlooking the Seine and Notre-Dame. Not the cheapest prices, but you're paying for the location.

Les Fous de l'Ile
33 rue des Deux-Ponts.
Open 3–7pm daily.
Large but welcoming tearoom, country furnishings, old wooden tables with flowers on them, games, magazines and exhibitions of unknown painters and photographers' work, excellent cheesecake and carrot cake too.

Le Loir dans la Théière
3 rue des Rosiers.
Open noon–7pm. Cl. Mon.
Just by the Hammam on the rue des Rosiers, the Alice in Wonderland mural helps explain the tearoom's name (dormouse in the teapot); delicious cakes, lemon tart and good Sunday brunch.

Ma Bourgogne
19 place des Vosges.
Open 7am–1.30am daily.
A Marais institution where the in-crowd meet under the red brick arches of the *place*, for b reakfast, lunch and dinner; wine bar upstairs. Inspector Maigret, apparently, was a former regular here.

Marais Plus
20 rue des Francs-Bourgeois.
Open 9am–midnight; Sun 9am–7pm.
Tuck yourself away with a newspaper in this art bookshop-cum-tearoom with old tables, plants and posters. Superb lemon tart and brownies.

Mariages Frères
30 rue du Bourg-Tibourg.
Open noon–7.30pm, Tue–Sun. Cl. Mon.
Colonial atmosphere softened by greenery. Celebrated teas (almost 300 kinds) and excellent brunches with inventive menus.

La Pomme de Pain
76 rue de Rivoli.
Open 10am–8pm. Cl. Sun.
Useful refuelling-stop for the sandwiches filled with all sorts, salads and tarts.

Le 4e Sans Ascenseur
8 rue des Écouffes.
Open noon–7pm, Sat. and Sun. only.
Restful teahouse; rich and generous *tartes*.

Café Beaubourg
100 rue St Martin.
Open 8am–2am daily.
Roomy, hip, cosmopolitan (newspapers in several languages) trendies oscillate between here and Café Costes above, though some say the Café Beaubourg crowd is not as chic.

5e

Café de la Mosquée
39 rue Geoffroy-St Hilaire.
Open 10am–10pm daily.
Part of a mosque built in 1922. Idyllic setting for a Moorish café (fountains, patio) for mint tea, sticky and exotic Middle Eastern pastries. Studenty and Muslim clientèle mostly.

Café Mouffetard
118 rue Mouffetard.
Open 7am–9pm, Tues–Sat; 7am–noon Sun.
Collapse here after visiting the local market or the Panthéon; croissants made on the premises.

Caramelle
6 rue de l'Arbalète.
Open 11.30am–7pm. Cl. Sun.
Irresistible homemade cakes and savories, in a rustic atmosphere; art exhibits and musical performances.

La Fontaine d'Ana
42 rue Pierre-Nicole.
Open 10am–10pm, Mon–Fri; 10am–4pm Sat.
Interesting salads as well as delectable cakes and tea.

La Fourmi Ailée
8 rue Fouarre.
Open noon–7pm. Cl. Tue.
Not a place for slimmers; rich and impressive apple crumble, muffins,
scones and flans. The bookshop holds monthly exhibitions.

La Passion du Fruit
71 quai de la Tournelle.
Open 11am–2am daily in summer; noon–1am Tue–Sun in winter.
Fruit shakes, teas and juices with romantic view of Notre-Dame.

Tea Caddy
14 rue Saint-Julien-le-Pauvre.
Open noon–7pm. Cl. Tue.
Originally run by an English woman, the tradition for English tea is
preserved except that the cinammon toast, muffins, scones and buns
are, if anything, better.

6e

La Cour de Rohan
59–61 rue St-André-des-Arts.
Open noon–6pm, Tue–Thur; noon–midnight Fri–Sat; 2.30–8pm Sun.
Chintzy, cosy tea-room, off the boulevard Saint Germain.
Good light lunches too.

Les Deux Magots
170 boulevard St Germain.
Open 7.30am–1.30am daily.
Paris café *par excellence* (see box feature in 6e) opposite the Church
of St Germain. Excellent jugs of hot chocolate.

Dalloyau
2 place Edmond-Rostand.
Open 9.30am–7.30pm; 9am–7pm Sun.
Little upstairs tea-room overlooking the Luxembourg Gardens. Good
tea, coffee, pastries, excellent macaroons. Crowded at weekends.

Le Flore
172 boulevard St Germain.
Open 7am–1.30am daily.
Lynch-pin of café life. Like Les Deux Magots above, it's a café
with a past. Literary patrons included Sartre, Camus, Apollinaire.
People-watching from the terrasse is a *Flore* tradition.

La Paradis du Fruit
27 quai des Grands-Augustins.
Open noon–2am daily.
See listing in the 2e.

Le Select
99 boulevard du Montparnasse.

Open 8.30am–2am daily.

Old-style 1920s café, retaining some of its former glory with the in-crowd, directly opposite La Coupole.

La Tchaïka

9 rue de l'Eperon.

Open 11.30am–3pm, 7pm–10.30pm. Cl. Sat–Sun.

Cosy Russian tea-room serving light meals and chocolate cake. Also does lunch and dinner. Another establishment at 7 rue de Lappe, 11e.

Village Voice

6 rue Princesse.

Open 11am–7pm. Cl. Sun–Mon.

Cultural tea-room, books, art and brownies (the edible kind).

Café des Hauteurs

Musée D'Orsay. 1 rue de Bellechasse.

Open 10.30am–6pm, Tue–Fri and Sun; 10.30am–9pm Thurs; 9am–6pm Sat. Cl. Mon.

Stop here after d'Orsay art-gazing; good view over Paris.

Christian Constant

26 rue du Bac.

Open 9.30am–7pm daily.

Christian Constant is generally acknowledged as one of the best *pâtissiers* in Paris. You can test his reputation for yourself in his small and antiquated *salon de thé*; delicious hot chocolate too.

Concertea

3 rue Paul-Louis-Courier.

Open 11.30am–7pm (until 4pm Mon), Mon–Sat. Cl. Sun.

Arty place to compose a new song or enjoy a masterpiece of confectionery, like the house *tarte au chocolat*. A variety of fragrant teas served in huge teapots.

La Pagode

57 bis rue de Babylone.

Open 4am–10pm, Mon–Sat; 2–8pm Sun.

Delightful cinema with tearoom and ornamental Chinese garden to sip away the hours even if you're not film-watching.

Le Petit Boulé

16 avenue la Motte-Picquet.

Open 9am–7pm. Cl. Mon.

Bon chic, bon goût rules. Madame Rochas is amongst the celebrities who have been spotted here. Excellent chocolate.

Sugar

3 rue Paul Louis Couvier.

Open noon–7pm. Cl.Sun.

Busy, friendly and pretty tea-room.

8e

La Boulangerie Saint-Philippe
73 avenue Franklin-D. Roosevelt.
Open 8am–6.30pm (9am Sun). Cl. Sat.
Old established tearoom-cum-bakery serving mega-calorie tarts.

La Boutique à Sandwiches
12 rue du Colisée.
Open 11.45am–11.30pm. Cl. Sun.
Every sandwich imaginable.

Daru
19 rue Daru.
Open 9am–11pm. Cl. Sun.
Old Russian deli by the Orthodox Church, quick bites, caviar, vodka and tea.

Drugstore Élysées
133 avenue des Champs-Élysées.
Open 9am–2am daily.
Stop off for snacks, meals, newspapers and tobacco.

Fauchon
26 place de la Madeleine.
Open 9.45am–6.30pm. Cl. Sun.
Stand in a hectic self-service café eating wonderful sandwiches and cakes.

Ladurée
16 rue Royale.
Open 8.30am–7pm. Cl. Sun.
Excellent chocolate croissants and macaroons.

Le Fouquets
99 avenue des Champs-Élysées.
Open 9am–2am daily.
Landmark terrace coffee-stop.

Mollard
113 rue St Lazare.
Open noon–1am daily.
Go for the sumptuous and ornate Art Moderne décor and stained glass windows.

La Maison du Chocolat
52 rue François 1er.
Open 9.30am–6.30pm. Cl. Sun.
No tea here but wonderful varieties of hot chocolate; fresh juices, pastries or a light savoury lunch for chocophobes.

9e

Café de la Paix
12 boulevard des Capucines.
Open 10am–1.30pm, 2.30pm–midnight daily.
Designed by Garnier (of the Opéra) and now a national monument.
Classic café fare, but expensive. A place to linger and crowd watch.

Tarte Julie
12 rue Vignon.
Open 9am–7.30pm. Cl. Sun.
Busy at lunchtime with local workers; teatime is more sedate.
Classic and herbal teas, savouries, salads and tarts.

Tea Follies
6 place Gustave-Toudouze.
Open 9am–9pm Mon–Sat; 9am–7pm Sun.
Art gallery-cum-café on a tree-filled square; tea and scones in the
afternoon; light meals and Sunday brunch. Lively atmosphere: stacks
of newspapers and a monthly changing art show, with works accepted
from patrons. Brunch on Sundays 12.30–4pm.

11e

Agnès et Guillemette
10 rue St Sébastien-Froissart.
Open 11.30am–3pm, Mon–Fri.
Laid back *salon de thé* popular with parents and their offspring; serves
light lunches.

Pause Café
41 rue de Charonne.
Open 8am–2am daily.
Laid back resting spot in a yuppified stretch of Bastille.

La Tchaïka
7 rue de Lappe.
Open 11.30am–3pm, 7pm–10.30pm. Cl. Sat–Sun.
Cosy Russian tea-room serving light meals and chocolate cake.
Also does lunch and dinner.

14e

La Bouffothèque
27 rue Campagne Première.
Open 9am–7pm daily.
Ideal for breakfast, afternoon tea or a weekend brunch (Sat, Sun
10am–3pm). Around 10 salads to choose from (prices from 35f–40f).

Midi-Trente
56 rue Daguerre.
Open 11am–6pm daily. Cl. Sun.
Get a quick meal or linger over a calorie-unconscious tea at this fresh, bright spot, popular with models and photographers working at the nearby studio. The fruit crumble is especially good.

15e

Je thé . . . Me
4 rue d'Alleray.
Open 9am–11am, 3pm–6pm. Cl. Sun.
Set in former 19th-century grocery store, 30 tea varieties, good caramelised apple tart.

16e

Carette
4 place du Trocadéro.
Open 8am–7pm. Cl. Tue.
Once a local café now patronised by the young, chic and hip.
Attractive setting.

Le Coquelin Aîné
1 rue de Passy.
Open 8.30am–7.30pm, Mon–Sat; 8.30am–12.30pm Sun.
Old style comfortable tearoom, named after the 19th-century actor. The rum baba and *mille-feuille* are particularly recommended.

Le Kléber
place du Trocadéro.
Open till dawn daily.
Young hangout; recover from a hangover over a coffee. Romantic views and the Eiffel Tower.

Thé Cool
10 rue Jean-Boulogne.
Open 12 noon–7pm; Sun. brunch 11am–6pm.
Charming tea-room on a small, quiet square, a refuge from the noisy rue de Passy. Terrific Sunday brunches, popular with the *seizième* set. Actresses Isabelle Adjani and Fanny Ardant have been spotted here.

17e

Aux Delices de Scott
39 avenue de Villiers.
Open 9am–9pm, Tue–Sat; 9.30am–9pm Sun. Cl. Mon.

Founded in 1904 and as lively as ever. seventeen traditional teas, cakes and light meals.

Le Stübli.
11 rue Poncelet.
Open 10am–6.30pm (until 1 pm Sun). Cl. Mon.
Viennese *pâtisserie* serving sweet and savoury snacks or meals (70f–100f). Tea-time treats include Viennese éclairs, Viennese tea and chocolate.

18e

Patachou
9 place du Tertre.
Open 8am–midnight daily.
All things sweet: ice cream, chocolate and pastries. An agreeably, soothing bolt hole from the Montmartre tourists.

BARS, PUBS, COCKTAIL AND WINE BARS

1er

Au Caveau Montpensier
15 rue de Montpensier.
Home-from-home English Pub.

Aux Bon Crus
7 rue des Petits-Champs.
Local bar for neighbourhood workers.

Bar du Meurice
228 rue de Rivoli.
Sink into the sumptuous décor and dry Martinis.

La Cloche des Halles
28 rue Coquillière.
Historically entrenched in Les Halles; named after the bell which opened and closed the market, great wines and good food.

L'Écluse
rue Mondétour.
Fashionable wine bar, excellent wines and foie gras. Also at 15 quai des Grands-Augustins 6e.

Front Page
58 rue St Denis.
Long bar serving American food and drink.

Guinness Tavern
31 rue des Lombards.
Guinness and live music Mon, Tues and Thurs.

Juvenile's
47 rue de Richelieu.
Tapas bar with well chosen wines.

Le Normandy
7 rue de l'Echelle.
Warm and inviting especially in winter; great cocktails.

Le Rubis
10 rue du Marché-St-Honoré.
Enjoy splendid wines, daily hot dish and sandwiches in this famous old wine bar.

Taverne Henri IV
13 place du Pont-Neuf.
Oak and brick tavern, mature wines, Poilâne bread and charcuterie.

Taverne de Rubens
12 rue St Denis.
Bavarian beers and Sauerkraut, open till late.

Tribulum
62 rue St Denis.
Star bar of the astrological sort, zodiac cocktails.

Willi's Wine Bar
13 rue des Petits-Champs.
Good wines, posh nosh in this English-run bar.

2e

Café Noir
65 rue Montmartre.
Worthwhile local bar.

Le Duc de Richelieu
110 rue de Richelieu.
Join the journos who come here for the fine Loire wines and *plats du jour*.

L'Entre-Deux-Verres
48 rue Ste Anne.
Lunch time only; well chosen wines from small, family vineyards.

Fitzcarraldo
8 rue Dussoubs.
Lively local bar with cinemagraphic décor.

Harry's New York Bar
5 rue Daunou.
A classic bar, a hangout for Hemingway and Fitzgerald in their day.
Try a Mint Julep in summer and a Manhattan in winter.

Jéroboam
8 rue Monsigny.
Tastings every Monday of rare vintages.

Kitty O'Shea's
10 rue des Capucines.
Sounds Irish and is, Guinness and whiskies.

Le Manneken-Pis
4 rue Daunou.
Lively bar serving Belgian beer in jugs.

La Micro-Brasserie
106 rue de Richelieu.
Brews a beer on the premises called Morgane; there's also a good
set menu.

3e

Bleue Nuit
9 rue des Vertus.
No fuss English-cum-French bar.

L'Helium
3 rue des Haudriettes.
High-tech décor, open until 1am every day of the week. Good cocktails
and milk shakes at reasonable prices.

The Quiet Man
5 rue des Haudriettes.
One of the many Irish pubs in Paris and one of the best – they pull a
good Guinness here.

Taxi Jaune
13 rue Chapon.
An in-crowd bar.

4e

Au Franc Pinot
1 quai de Bourbon.
Marvellous selection of wines, some rather good value, plus tasty cold
platters. Restaurant below.

Le Coude Fou
12 rue de Bourg-Tibourg.
Wine bar-cum-bistro: good, unusual French wines; excellent food.

Ma Bourgogne
19 place des Vosges.
The bar at this famous café has great Burgundy.

Le Mousson
9 rue de la Bastille.
Colonial look bar attracting trendy media types. Tropical cocktails and
jazz add to the heady mix.

Pacific Palissades
51 rue Quincampoix.
Once mega-trendy but still popular bar, even though the groupies have
moved on.

La Perla
26 rue François-Miron.
Mexican hot spot; Margaritas, tequila and snacks.

Le Petit Gavroche
15 rue Ste-Croix-de-la-Bretonnerie.
Welcoming local bar; useful 39f menu.

Le Piano Zinc
49 rue des Blancs-Manteaux.
Gays and hetereos come here to enjoy themselves; there's a cabaret in
the cellar on some evenings. When punters play the piano, the *patron*
has been known to dance.

La Tartine
24 rue de Rivoli.
Old-fashioned bar, former Trotsky watering hole but now comman-
deered by the Marais hip.

5e

Académie de la Bière
88 bis boulevard de Port Royal.
Over 100 different beers, some on tap.

La Bourgogne
144 rue Mouffetard.
Cheerful local bar/bistro with tables outside. Inexpensive Belgian beers;
good selection of wines.

La Café de la Nouvelle Mairie
19 rue des Fossés-St-Jacques.
Small and friendly bar near the Panthéon with tables outside in the
summer. Good wine.

Connolly's Corner
12 rue de Mirbel.

One of the best Irish pubs in Paris, popular with Brits; low on tables, high on atmosphere, especially at the weekend.

Le Crocodile
6 rue Royer-Collard.
Comfortable and traditional bar serving cocktails to the sounds of the 60s.

Finnegan's Wake
9 rue des Boulangers.
The name says it all – another Irish pub with cosy "snug" corners.

Le Flamingo
184 rue St Jacques.
Popular with young jazz fans.

Le Piano Vache
8 rue Laplace.
Studenty bar complete with loud rock and videos.

Polly Magoo
11 rue St Jacques.
Student haunt in the Latin Quarter, 60s relived, open late for beer and wine.

6e

Birdland
8 rue Guisarde.
Low lights, low prices and jazz.

Caveau de la Bolée
25 rue Hirondelle.
Set in a seventeenth-century cellar, *bar de nuit* with jazz and cabaret.

Chez Georges
11 rue des Canettes.
A popular left bank bar; lively and late.

La Closerie des Lilas
171 boulevard du Montparnasse.
Smart bar, cocktails and old time piano player. Hemingway and others exercised their elbows here.

L'Ecluse
15 quai des Grands-Augustins.
New chain of wine bars, traditional style but lacks the rough edges.
(See also 1er).

London Tavern
3 rue de Sabot.
English beers, piano and jazz.

Le Mazet
61 rue St-André-des-Arts.
Lively bar full of buskers.

Millésuimes
7 rue Lobineau.
Rather splendid wines at cheap prices served with charcuterie.

La Paillote
45 rue Monsieur-le-Prince.
Miles Davis, Miles Davis and bamboo décor.

La Palette
43 rue de Seine.
An art mob bar, pretty terrace outside, murals inside.

Pub Saint-Germain
17 rue de l'Ancienne-Comédie.
Open 24 hours a day for hundreds of different beers. Doctor "don't lose your head" Guillentin, once lived here.

7e

Au Sauvignon
80 rue des Saints-Pères.
Opens very late; small, fun and down-to-earth wine bar.

Sancerre
22 avenue Rapp.
Attractive wine bar with wood panelling, serving Sancerre with light meals.

Twickenham
70 rue des Saints-Pères.
British-style pub, where rugby fans like to prop up the mahogany bar. International beers and a *plat du jour*.

8e

Bar Alexandre
53 avenue George.
You can smell the polished wood and leather in this smart watering hole.

La Cervoise
11 rue du Colisée.
Comfortable bar off the avenue des Champs-Élysées.

Chez Jeannot
4 bis rue La Boétie.

Arty Parisian pub.

Le Forum
4 boulevard Malesherbes.
Top-class bar steeped in tradition with a peaceful and cosy atmosphere.

Le Fouquet's
99 avenue des Champs-Élysées.
The great and good and even the bad frequent this beautiful bar, steer away from the costly cocktails.

Newstore
63 avenue des Champs-Élysées.
Divided into booths serving over 100 beers mostly Belgian.

Washington Square
47 rue de Washington.
Small, elegant yet cosy cocktail bar, popular with the young.

9e

Au Général la Fayette
52 rue la Fayette.
Busy, jovial *Belle Époque* bar, Guinness and draught beers.

Bar Romain
6 rue Caumartin.
1900s bar with romantic frescoes, sometimes rowdy, full of showbiz people. Choose from 200 cocktails.

Bar du Scribe (Hôtel Scribe)
1 rue Scribe.
Plush and posh bar popular with Americans staying at the hotel.

La Cave Drouot
8 rue Drouot.
Well-priced, great wines especially Burgundies with cold platters.

Cockney Tavern
39 boulevard de Clichy.
Restaurant-cum-bar, serves bacon, sausage and eggs for breakfast.

Le Dépanneur
27 rue Fontaine.
1930's bar with distinctive chromework, popular with young thespians and musicians.

Le Moloko
26 rue Fontaine.
Newly opened bar with pre-war interior, drinks from 25f. Jazz and blues on Tuesdays and Thursdays.

10e

Le Petit Château d'Eau
67 rue Château d'Eau.
Bar-cum-café with a traditional half-moon zinc bar.

11e

Au Métro
138 rue de la Roquette.
Friendly vocal bar with Belgian beer on tap.

La Casbah
18–20 rue de la Forge-Royale.
New back street Bastille bar, movie set interior of the "if you can play it for her you can play it for me" type.

Le Clown Bar
114 rue Amelot.
Filled with memorabilia from the Cirque d'Hiver which is at No. 110.

L'Entre Pots
14 rue de Charonne.
Shoot pool and sink the cocktails.

H_2O
50 rue Godefroy-Cavaignac.
The water's fine but the wine and beer is better. Near to the Bastille.

Jacques Mélac
42 rue Léon-Frot.
Friendly down-to-earth wine bar, excellent wines and tasty food. One of Paris's favourites.

Objectif Lune
19 rue de la Roquette.
Tequila bar, stays open late.

12e

Le Baron Rouge
1 rue Théophile-Roussel.
Shop and bar: try before you buy. Take your own bottles and they will fill them for around 10f a litre.

China Club
50 rue Charenton.
Comfortable colonial bar for the Chanel and Hermés brigade.

Le Train Bleu
1st floor Gare de Lyon, 20 boulevard Diderot.
Fabulous *Belle Époque* décor makes waiting for a train a pleasant experience.

14e

Le Père Tranquille
30 avenue du Maine.
Good wines, irascible *patron*.

Le Rallye
6 rue Daguerre.
Small bar, big cellar, specialising in Beaujolais; drop in after a visit to Cimetière de Montmartre.

Le Rosebud
11 bis rue Delambre.
Well established and comfortable Bohemian wine bar, a nice place to be. Open until 2am.

Tahonga Club
PLM Saint Jacques Hôtel. 17 boulevard St Jacques.
Live jazz several nights a week; zappy cocktails.

15e

Ciel de Paris
Tour Montparnasse, 33 avenue du Maine.
Amazing view, vertigo sufferers may need an extra drink after whizzing up the tower on one of the world's fastest lifts.

Le Toit de Paris
Hôtel Hilton, 18, avenue de Suffren.
Momumental cocktails, Eiffel, Opéra and Trocadéro for around 55f.

16e

Pub Winston Churchill
5 rue de Presbourg.
Huge, but still crowded, serving Watneys, and pub-grub. Live jazz in the cellar. Open until 2am.

La Péniche
1 avenue du Président Kennedy.
A bar on a barge, admission 270f includes dinner and cabaret.

Bar Raphaël
17 avenue Kléber.
Very English interior, Tudor oak panelling, well-prepared cocktails.

17e

Bar Belge
75 avenue de St Ouen.
Old Belgian pub offering 30 different brews.

Bar du Concorde-La Fayette
3 place du Géneral-Koening.
The Bois de Boulogne as seen from the 32nd floor of the Concorde-La Fayette, mixes well with a drink. 56f before 9.30pm.

Hurlingham Polo Bar
Hôtel Meridien, 81 boulevard Gouvion-St-Cyr.
Whisky galore and cocktails from 45f.

Jazz Club Lionel Hampton
Hôtel Meridien as above.
Piano bar until 10pm then jazz.

Le Pain et le Vin
1 rue d'Armaille.
The cruover (keeps open wine bottles drinkable) enables you to taste great vintages by the glass.

18e

Aux Négociants
27 rue Lambert.
Near to Sacré Coeur, this pretty bar serves good wines and hot meals at lunch.

Lux Bar
12 rue Lepic.
Busy market bar which has outstanding ceramic murals of the Moulin Rouge.

ENTERTAINMENT

Parisians know how to enjoy themselves and tend to spend a lot of francs doing so. The city caters for all tastes, from the smoky jazz cellars to perfect-pitch concert halls, state-of-the-art discos to seedy sex shows.

You can't single out any specific area for nightlife, although some parts are particularly lively after dark. On the left bank, the streets in St Germain and the Latin Quarter stay awake till late, especially the bars, cafés and clubs of the insomniac boulevard St Michel.

Some specific streets stand out as night-owl nests – rue de la Huchette, for instance, with its ethnic restaurants and famous jazz club. A bit further south, in the 14e, the boulevard Montparnasse and the rue de la Gaîté are a microcosm of the gaudy, neon Pigalle patch on the right bank. Spilling into the 9e and 18e, Pigalle is synonymous with sequin-smothered bosoms, its side streets full of tattoo parlours and sex shows that leave nothing to the imagination. It's the Parisian equivalent of London's Soho. Around the boulevard Clichy is one of the city's reddest light districts, and so is the nearby infamous rue St Denis, though its lower half is more sanitised and yuppified these days, dipping as it does towards one of the city's most hip late late-night spots, the Les Halles area. Rue des Lombards is a street of jazz clubs and the easterly neighbour of Bastille has an up-and-thrusting nightlife, with a less homogeneous clientèle than other areas (see chapter 11e) and reminders of Paris's erstwhile popular dance hall tradition.

Aside from a rich and varied selection of cultural offerings, clubs and other diversions, there are the pleasures of simply enjoying being in Paris at night – most of the major sites are helpfully illuminated so you could wander the streets doing a little nocturnal sight-seeing, go people-watching from a well positioned perch, take a moonlight river trip . . .

For a small price, there are many bars where buying a drink licenses you to listen to the band for as long as you like, and some cafés have entertainers too. So, apart from the clubs we mention below, it's worth checking the bars/cafés section of this book (pp. 158–177) for more ideas.

Eating out is still the most popular Parisian evening diversion and the restaurant section on page 110 will point you in dozens of different directions.

Without wanting to sound like party-poopers, there are a few purely practical points the Sensible Guide Book Writer must make.

SECURITY

Pickpockets are as prevalent and as skilled in Paris as they are in any other capital city, so when you're out clubbing or on the town, make sure no one can get at your dosh.

SEX

Be careful. Paris has become the Aids Capital of Europe with more recorded HIV infection than any other major city on the Continent. After road accidents and cancer, among Parisians aged 25–44, Aids is the third major killer. In 1988 it caused one in every two deaths of single men aged 25–44 who worked in the arts, media and entertainment sectors in Paris.

Should you need condoms late at night and not be near a handy dispensing machine, try the 24-hour *Pharmacie des Champs* on the Champs-Élysées or one of the late opening ones as listed in the general information section of this guide.

WHAT'S ON

Nightclubs come and go. Slave as we might to make this section accurate, truthful and topical, Parisian nightlife is notoriously volatile, so it pays to check that a club/venue is still operating and offering what we say. Details of entertainment and nightlife options are given in *Pariscope* or *L'Officiel des Spectacles*, both published on Wednesdays. You can also ring France Information Loisirs (FIL) an English-speaking service on 47 20 88 98 for information on concerts, cinemas, theatres.

GETTING HOME

Métros stop at around 12.45am; all bus services cease at midnight. Taxis are the best bet, but if you're very patient, sooner or later a Noctambus should come along. The buses follow Métro routes and they start running at 1am from place du Châtelet (avenue Victoria). Those with season tickets (*Carte Orange*) travel free; otherwise you buy a ticket on the bus. Full details from RATP, tel. 43 46 14 14, or get a night bus map from a Métro station, or see pages 52–5 of this guide. And see page 55 for numbers of taxi companies which take telephone bookings around the clock.

NIGHTCLUBS AND DISCOS

Dancing the night away in Parisian night clubs might be easier than in early-bird London, but it's perhaps not as much fun as in Barcelona, Milan or New York. Partly it's the steep admission prices (80–120f, often to include one drink) and the hefty price of drinks thereafter – on average twice the price of drinks in London clubs.

The strict vetting policy of the doormen doesn't add to the fun. The prevailing idea seems to be that the best party is one made up of the same kind of folk, so the *noctambuler* will only rarely run into a colourful variety of people, rather than a crowd of stereotypes: *BCBGs* (Bon Chic, Bon Genre – the French equivalent of a Sloane), weirdos, arty types, etc. Nevertheless, once you've decided on the type of club you want to slip into and once you've dressed accordingly, there's an abundance of choice.

Discos and clubs are found all over town, but many are ephemeral, disappearing as quickly as they start up as they dip out of fashion. Some are garish, some gimmicky, some glitzy. There are four big names in the night club firmament: Les Bains, Le Palace, and for the seriously moneyed or affluent greys, the exclusive Castel and Régine. All the other clubs orbit these four big stars.

The majority open their doors between 10 and 11pm, but things don't really get rolling until after midnight. Only Castel and Régine stick firmly to the "Members Only" rule – although a personal recommendation from a respected regular might help ease you in. The others are less strict, but nevertheless they are likely to let you hang about for a bit outside before allowing you in. It's all a question of principle really. Club managers believe it's good for the *Image de Marque* of the club – the club seems more exclusive, the punters more important. Best to look on the positive side – spending 20-minutes on the pavement in summer might be the start of some interesting new friendships. Those too proud to queue, and smile ingratiatingly at doormen, should show up early or after 3am when there's a less humiliating entrance procedure.

Most clubs have once-a-week theme bashes, making every night a different kind of escapade. These "one night stands" change quickly and often, so we're not copping out when we suggest that you'd best check what's going on by phoning or looking in one of the listings mags.

Here is a selection, by *arrondissement*, of popular clubs "in" at the time of writing, worth trying for the music or atmosphere or both if you're lucky.

1er (LES HALLES)

Black and White
32 bis rue des Lombards. Tel. 45 08 94 48. M Châtelet.
From 11pm. Entrance 100f with drink.
Cosmopolitan Chic Africa in Paris – you might well find yourself dancing away between the Senegalese Trade Minister and a Franco-Iranian real estate developer.

Distrito
49 rue Berger. Tel. 40 26 91 00. M Les Halles/Louvre. From midnight.
Entrance free, beer 40f.
Trendy restaurant-cum-jazz and rock club featuring the best of the local bands in the cellar. Expensive, but there's happy hour from 8–10pm when drinks are half-price.

Néo Japonesque
21 rue Montorgueil. Tel. 42 36 87 87. M Les Halles/Étienne Marcel.
From 11pm. Entrance free, drinks 50f.
Tiny dance floor for jostling with other clubbers to rock and trash classics.

La Scala de Paris
188 bis rue de Rivoli. Tel. 42 60 45 64. M Palais-Royal Tuileries.
From 10.30pm. Entrance 80f with drink; free for women Mon, Wed, Thur. Admission for women 60f Fri.
Three floors of pop accompanied by all the very latest electronic wizardry for a predominantly sixteeny to eighteeny clientèle, plus tourists.

3e (LES HALLES/MARAIS)

Les Bains
7 rue Bourg-L'Abbé. Tel. 48 87 01 80. M Étienne Marcel.

From 11.30pm daily. Entrance 120f with drink; additional drinks 100f.

Behind the turn-of-the-century façade, the former Turkish Baths remain the most poseur-y nightclub in the city: there are more people to be found standing hopefully outside than enjoying themselves within. Watch out for the intimidating doorlady who decides whether or nor you'll be allowed to join in. Proust used to have a steam here, but today Polanski dines at Les Bains. (He likes the club so much that he recreated it in a studio for a scene in his film "Frantic".) Age-defying celebs, movie stars, starlets and models, including Inès de la Fressange and couturier Christian La Croix's former muse Marie Seznec, are amongst the high-profile dressed-to-kill clientèle. Like other clubs, different nights have different themes: Wednesday night is a live music night, at the time of going to press.

Le Tango
13–14 rue du Maire. Tel. 42 22 17 78. M Arts-et-Métiers. From 11pm.
Entrance 80f with drink.

Practise your sambas and cha-cha-chas: Africans, South Americans, Parisians are sandwiched together on the dance floor of this intimate, informal club. No vetting and the drinks are cheap. Just dance away and enjoy it.

5e (LATIN QUARTER)

Au Nocambo
31 rue de l'échaudé. Tel. 43 29 41 80. M Mabillon. From 11pm every night but Mon. Entrance 70f with drink; free for women Thur and Sun.

Funk and Latino music; relaxed atmosphere. Brazilian nights are especially good.

Chez Félix
23 rue Mouffetard. Tel. 47 07 68 78. M Monge. From 11pm every night until dawn except Sunday and Monday. Closed August.

The oldest Brazilian club in Paris. Dinner and a show from 8.30pm until 2am, 250f during the week, 270f on Saturdays. The Brazilian band plays from 11pm, Fri and Sat. 100f a drink; 80f weekdays. Free for women Tue–Thur. Also impersonators, poets, pianists. Good samba. Every Brazilian staying in Paris has been here at least once.

Le Saint
7 rue St Séverin. Tel. 43 25 50 04 (at night). M St Michel.
From 11pm. Closed Mon. Entrance 50f weekdays, 70f Sats (includes drink).

In the heart of St Michel, a likeable cave-like club where people dance unselfconsciously to new wave or rock music. No ego shoot-outs here

– you get the impression clubbers are more interested in enjoying themselves than staring at each other or admiring themselves a rarity in Parisian discos. Second drinks aren't costly (between 15f and 70f) when compared to Les Bains, for instance.

Zed Club

2 rue des Anglais. Tel. 43 54 93 78. M Maubert-Mutualité.

From 10.30pm. Closed Sun, Mon, Tue, August. Entrance 90f with drink; drinks 40f thereafter.

Live bands from time to time in this white-washed cavern, otherwise there's lively dancing. Rock only evenings, Brazilian samba, bebop, '60s music and jazz. Smart dress.

6e (ST GERMAIN)

Castel

15 rue Princesse. Tel 43 26 90 22. M Mabillon/St Germain-des-Prés. Members only.

About as upmarket as a Parisian supper club can get; three floors of élitist good-timers – only a dinner booking gets a non-member in (and makes it easier to dance later) unless you can talk your way past the snooty custodian at the door. The plush restaurant is on the first floor (wall-to-wall French VIPs) and the entire club is overseen by Jean Castel, known as the King of the Paris Night.

Epsom Bar

1 rue St Benôit. Tel. 42 84 07 77. M St-Germain-des-Prés.

From 10pm–2am. Free

Private, comfortable, clubby-type atmosphere to this bar where there's music every night, from classical piano to jazz.

L'Escale

15 rue Monsieur le Prince. Tel. 43 54 63 47. M Odéon. From 11pm. Phone for details.

Salsa in the basement (disco on Wed) with other live Latin American sounds on the ground floor.

Flash Back

18 rue des Quatre-Vents. Tel. 43 25 56 10. M Odéon. From 11pm. Closed Mon. Entrance 60f, free for *"dames et les jeunes filles"* from Tue–Thur. Drinks from 60f.

Crowded dance floor, but not suffocating.

O'Brasil

10 rue Guénégaud. Tel. 43 54 98 56. M St Michel.

From 10.30pm. Entrance (to the club) 60f for women Mon–Thur, 95f men; 90f for all at weekends.

Brazilian music and ambience pervades both the discothèque and restaurant.

Ruby's Club
31 rue Dauphine. Tel. 46 33 68 16. M Odéon.
From 10pm. Entrance (includes drink) 70f weekdays, 80f Fri, Sat.
A famous Latin Quarter *cave* of the post-war period used as a backdrop
for Sartre, Simone de Beauvoir and Juliette Greco to discuss and refine
their existentialist theories.

8e (CHAMPS ÉLYSÉES)

Keur-Samba
79 rue de la Boétie. Tel. 43 59 03 10. M Miromésnil/Franklin
D. Roosevelt.
From 11pm. Entrance 120f with drink. NB: no credit cards.
Very select – and therefore hard to get into – club featuring African
music. Comfortable sofas, small dance floor, smart clientèle, predominantly 25–35ish. Not a place to bring the jeans; to get in you'll need
to be in your smart threads.

Là Bas (*Lord Byron*)
6 rue Balzac. Tel. 45 63 12 39. M Georges V.
From 11pm. Entrance 120f. No credit cards. Closed Sun.
A favourite amongst Parisian BCBGs. Distinctive Art Deco interior. It's
small and not easy to get in, but worth a try, to mingle with the mainly
young and lovely crowd.

Le Central 102
102 avenue des Champs-Élysées. Tel. 42 89 31 41. M Georges V.
From 11pm–dawn daily. Entrance 80f with drink, Mon; 120f with
drink at weekends; 100f other days.
Disco with film-set backdrop popular with yuppies from affluent western
Paris suburbs.

Le Garage
41 rue Washington. Tel. 45 63 21 27. M George V. From 11pm. Entrance
120f (includes drink). Free for women during the week.
Another famous "in" Parisian club with a bar/disco and accompanying
light show, an expensive but banal décor, flashy/tacky clientèle. There's
a slightly older crowd here, mid-twenties to fifty somethings, with most
of those over 35 being male.

Olivia Valère
40 rue du Colisée. Tel. 42 25 11 68. M St-Philippe-du-Roule, Franklin
D. Roosevelt.
From 11pm. Entrance: members only (3500f per year).
If you get in, a drink will set you back 140f, so be warned.
Heavy red décor hangs over this swish, exclusive club, popular
with models, middle-aged celebs, French Sloanes and their escorts,
older sophisticates.

Régine's

49 rue Ponthieu. Tel. 43 59 21 60. M Franklin D. Roosevelt.
From 11pm. Entrance: membership required.
Middle-aged international jet-setters, major and minor celebs loll around
the piano bar, dance floor and restaurant. It's expensive, swanky, and
it's *not* easy to get into.

Studio A

51 rue de Ponthieu. Tel. 42 25 12 13. M Franklin D. Roosevelt.
From 10.30pm on Mon, Wed, Fri, Sat. Entrance varies according to
theme night. 100f (with drink) Wed.
Favourite lesbian hangout, a stone's throw from the Champs-Élysées:
good dancing to house and hip hop. Wed night is for heteros, popular
with 18–25s. Occasional live bands.

9e OPÉRA (GRANDS BOULEVARDS/PIGALLE)

Bus Palladium

6 rue Fontaine. Tel. 48 74 54 99. M Blanche/Pigalle. From 11.30pm.
Closed Mon. Entrance 110f during the week, 130f weekends. Sun: free
for all. Tue: free for women.
On the edge of Montmartre, this is one of the most famous rock/soul
clubs in Paris, and a favourite. The size of the club is just right. You
don't have to search for your friends for hours, but you can also
dance without bumping into your neighbours all the time. You'd be
overdressed in evening gear – smart means chic here. If you don't like
the music (doubtful) there are always the pinball machines. The DJ has
been here for over a decade and never gets carried away by the latest
music fads – unless he happens to think they're good. Live music (some
nights) until midnight. Every Wednesday there's a battle of the bands
with aspiring new artists playing 20-minute sets in front of a jury.

La Chance

26 rue Fontaine. Tel. 48 74 03 70. M Blanche/Pigalle. From 10pm Fri
and Sat only. Brunch served on Sunday from 2pm. Entrance 100f with
drink Fri, Sat, Sun. 2pm–10pm 80f with drink/brunch.
Newly opened venue with two dance floors.

La Nouvelle Eve

25 rue Fontaine. Tel. 48 74 69 25. M Blanche/Pigalle.
From 1am. Book in advance.
Plush, red-velvety joint with prices to suit expense account pockets, this
is actually a supper club with cabaret (540f) except on Fridays when it's
a night club with an entrance fee of 100–120f. Young, smart *BCBGs*
and *NAPs* (Neuilly-Auteuil-Passy) set. Strict vetting at the door.

Le Palace

8 rue du Faubourg Montmartre. Tel. 42 46 10 87. M Rue Montmartre.

From 11pm daily. Entrance weekdays 120f, weekends 130f. Free for women on Sunday. No credit cards.

One of the best known discos in Paris (it holds 2000), this former theatre was given a state-of-the-art facelift in 1987 which certainly revived its popularity: now everyone goes there to gyrate on the multi-level dance floors under the latest lasers. Roller skating in the basement on certain afternoons, tea dances too, and an expensive restaurant. Thematic nights change the mood, which is never short of exuberant. Downstairs is the more select Kit Kat Club which has its regulars – showbizzy types mostly, lower music, no flashy lights.

This is not a place for dressing down – your most outrageous party clothes will do nicely!

Shéhérezade

3 rue Liège. Tel. 48 74 85 20. M Liège Europe.

From 10pm (Thur), 11pm (Fri–Sat). Entrance 100f with drink.

This old and famous Russian cabaret, founded in 1927, had to close at the end of 1988. Now it has been rescued and the cabaret, with its plush baroque décor, is skipping to a new beat as a very trendy nightclub open from Thur–Sat nights and soon, the owners hope, to open every night with the possible addition of a restaurant. Music is a mix of hip hop, soul and salsa – it's fun and it's an in place to be, for now at any rate.

Rex Club

5 boulevard Poissonière. Tel. 42 36 83 98. M Bonne-Nouvelle.

From 11pm, Tue–Sat. Entrance 60f with drink, but varies according to theme.

Next door to the Grand Rex (see **Live Music** below) there's a relaxed atmosphere; a young crowd come to the changing theme evenings. It's a prime venue on Sundays (3–10pm) for live artists to be given a try out. The best bands in Paris can be found playing here after midnight on Tuesday and Friday nights.

10e (RÉPUBLIQUE)

El Globo

8 boulevard Strasbourg. Tel. 42 01 37 33. M Stasbourg-Saint-Denis Château-d'Eau.

From 11pm Fri only. Entrance 70f with drink.

This bodega club is a rarity – you'll actually see *BCBGs*, punks, Latinos, and just about anyone dancing to old Stones' records or Vanessa Paradis or a Piaf classic – and all played consecutively. Subdued delirium and contentment prevails.

La Java

105 rue du Faubourg du Temple. Tel. 42 02 20 52. M Goncourt, Belleville.

Fri/Sat from 9.30pm; Sun 2–7pm; Mon 2.30–7pm. Entrance Fri 70f, Sat 80f, Sun 55f, Mon 30f. No credit cards.

Young clientèle dance to songs they first heard in the womb – Stones and Beatles oldies at this dance hall where Piaf first made her name.

11e (BASTILLE)

Le Balajo

9 rue de Lappe. Tel. 47 00 07 87. M Bastille.

From 10pm Fri, Sat, Sun, Mon (also 3pm–6pm on those days). Entrance 100f with drink. No credit cards.

Echoing old dance hall with fabulous period décor intact, the bar which once gave elbow space to Piaf and Jean Gabin. Beware though – Saturdays are given over to French popular songs and tunes, not *Top Cinquante* but accordion/*bal musette* melodies. The Monday crowd is an eclectic group that dances to '70s funk, retro tracks, current dance hits.

Le Chappelle des Lombards

19 rue de Lappe. Tel. 43 57 24 24. M Bastille.

From 11.30pm. Entrance: 70f weekdays, 80f weekends.

In the heat of the hot Bastille, salsa and samba *sans interruption* in this former women's prison and erstwhile *bal musette*. The place for tropical dancing. (See also **Live Music** below.)

Le Gibus

18 rue du Faubourg du Temple. Tel. 47 00 78 88. M Bastille.

Music starts around 11pm. Closed Sun and Mon. Entrance 60f with drink weekdays, 70f with drink weekends.

Your actual rock and roll club featuring raw, exciting bands in an intimate setting. Clash and Police played their first Paris gigs here. Drinks are affordable.

14e (MONTPARNASSE)

Bobino

20 rue de la Gâieté. Tel. 43 27 24 24. M Gâieté Edgar-Quinet.

Entrance 100f with drink.

Flamboyant nightclub also occasionally used as a concert venue. Reggae artists who've played there recently include Jimmy Cliff.

16e

5e Avenue

2 avenue Foch. Tel. 45 00 00 13. M Étoile.

From 11pm. Entrance: phone for details.

Expensive, underground, snooty hangout with a couple of bars and three dance floors. Popular with professional dancers who show off their tango and bossa nova techniques. A free breakfast is served around dawn.

17e

La Main Jaune
place de la Porte de Champerret. Tel. 47 63 26 47. M Porte de Champerret.
From 10pm–5am, Fri–Sat; 2.30pm–6am, Thur. Entrance 70f (includes drink) Thur: 110f Friday. No credit cards. Phone for details of possible student discounts.
Celebrated its tenth anniversary in 1990 with a glitzy new look. (Philippe Starck décor). Teens on roller skates whizz round a dance floor. On Fridays a young crowd bounces to a mix of funk and hip hop.

Salle Wagram
39 avenue de Wagram. Tel. 43 80 30 03 M Ternes. From 10pm Sats.
Entrance (includes drink) 75f. Further drinks from 20f.
Huge discothèque.

18e (MONTMARTRE)

La Locomotive
90 boulevard de Clichy. Tel. 42 57 37 37. M Blanche. From 11pm.
Closed Monday. Entrance (includes drink) 60f. 100f on Fri, Sat. Free for women Sun. 2nd drink between 30f–50f.
Very different from its next-door neighbour (the Moulin Rouge) the lively Locomotive is often used for rock concerts; otherwise the three tiers of this popular nightspot throb with trendies. Young, relaxed, no one cares what you look like – dance floor is *hugissimo*.

LIVE MUSIC

French rock bands simply do not have anything like the reputation of their home-grown jazz musicians, and it's probably true to say that the best French rock is imported. Jazz aside, there's a lively live music scene, the undistinguised overall quality of the rock more than compensated for by the ethnic sounds from reggae to salsa of city-based or touring bands.

Among the venues we list below, you'll find plenty of spunky alternatives to schmaltz. The music scene is volatile though and as clubs close new ones spring up fast, so it's best to check the listings mags or phone first for up to the minute info. Bear in mind too that some of the clubs given in the discos/nightclubs section often have live bands too.

MAJOR VENUES

Large concert spaces that do not have their own box office might sell tickets through the chain called FNAC. Call 40 26 8 18 for details of the branch closest to you. Concerts held at major venues tend to command high ticket prices – 150f is average and they're often higher.

La Bataclan:
50 boulevard Voltaire 75011. Tel. 47 00 30 12. M Oberkampf.
No credit cards. Box office open 10.30am–7pm.
Round hall with large stage hosting concerts once a week. Kitsch Sunday tea dances for all (4–9pm) at 60f.

Casino de Paris
16 rue de Clichy 75009. Tel. 42 85 26 27. M Trinité.
No credit cards. Box office open 11am–7pm, Mon–Sat.
In spite of the name, this is a former vaudeville theatre where there's no gambling, except on how good the band is. Concerts most evenings – some of which are rock and roll. Seats 1500. Wonderful acoustics.

La Cigale
120 boulevard Rochechouart, 75018. Tel. 42 23 38 00. M Pigalle.
No credit cards.
Old Vaudeville theatre with decent acoustics, nicely renovated to make one of the best concert venues in town, with concerts two or three times a week – call box office for details.

Élysée-Montmartre
72 boulevard Rochechouart 75018. Tel. 42 52 25 15. M Anvers.
No credit cards. Box office open noon–7pm, Mon–Fri.
Behind the historic façade of the turn-of-the-century theatre is the city's major venue for rock and roll music. Once a month there's a free concert.

Forum des Halles
Niveau 3 Porte Rambuteau, 15 rue de l'Equerre-d'Argent 75001. Tel. 42 03 11 11. M Châtelet.
Not just a rock venue, but also used for other performances, including theatre.

Grand Rex
1 boulevard Poissonière 75002. Tel. 42 36 83 93. M Bonne Nouvelle.
No credit cards.

Holding 3000, this claims to be Europe's largest movie theatre and is now a popular venue for big name concerts. Seat prices start at around 120f. Comfortable seats, if short on leg room.

Olympia
28 boulevard des Capucines 75009. Tel. 47 42 25 49. M Opéra.
Aznavour and Yves Montand sang here and now this comfortable, turn-of-the-century, renovated venue occasionally hosts concerts by the likes of Elvis Costello, the Rolling Stones or Lou Reed. Performances every evening – phone to check the programme. Admission varies from 150–180f. Tickets also available from FNAC or Virgin Megastore.

Palais des Omnisports de Bercy
8 boulevard de Bercy 75012. Tel. 43 41 72 04. M Bercy.
No credit cards. Box Office open 11am–6pm daily.
The big names play here in front of the biggest audiences – 16,000 is the max. this huge stadium holds, which means the chances are you'll be paying sky high prices to see dwarf-sized versions of your favourite rock stars. Ticket prices are the highest – from 160f depending on who's on.

Le Zenith
211 avenue Jean-Jaurès 75019. Tel. 42 08 60 00. M Porte de Pantin.
No credit cards.
Leading English and American groups that don't play Bercy play at this cavernous (seats 6500) inflatable auditorium, designed especially for rock and pop performances. Telephone for details of weekly concerts and prices (which vary). Tickets available at all FNAC outlets or Virgin Megastore.

CLUBS WITH LIVE MUSIC

Listings are given by *arrondissement*: see also section on jazz clubs.

1er

Le Baiser Salé – see Jazz.

Les Trottoirs de Buenos Aires
37 rue des Lombards. Tel. 42 33 58 37. M Châtelet.
From 8.30pm–1am, Tue–Sun. Shows at 8.30pm, 10.30pm (10.30pm only on Mon). Entrance 90f, half price after midnight.
Tango in a dinner-theatre setting. Solo guitar recitals Sat, 6pm. Tango classes and tea dances on Sundays.

2e

Rex Club – see Nightclubs and Discos.

Le Discophage

11 passage du Clos-Bruneau, off 31–33 rue des Écoles. Tel. 43 26 31 41. M Maubert-Mutualité/Cardinal Lemoine. From 9pm–3am. Closed Sun and whole of August. Music starts 10pm. Entrance 85f with a drink. Call answering machine or after 6pm for dinner reservations.

Small, crowded, but worth the discomfort for some of the best Brazilian music; sambas, bossas, guitar duos, the works.

Les Tois Mailletz

58 rue Galande. Tel. 43 54 00 79. M Maubert-Mutualité/St Michel. From 6pm, Wed–Sun. Entrance 60f for music downstairs; drinks from 30f.

Cosmopolitan studenty set seem to like the really odd mix of music in this wonderful cellar-bar – varies on any given night from different kinds of jazz, rock and roll to Latin or blues. Tiny piano bar upstairs where food is also available.

6e

L'Éscale – see **Nightclubs and Discos**.

8e

Studio A – see **Nightclubs and Discos**.

9e

Bus Palladium – see **Nightclubs and Discos**.

New Moon

66 rue Pigalle. Tel. 45 95 92 33. M Pigalle. From 11pm, Mon–Sat. Closed. Sun. Entrance weekdays 50f (includes one beer: subsequent beers 30f); same deal at weekends for 60f.

Along with Le Gibus in the 11e (see **Nightclubs and Discos**) this is one of the most popular small rock venues, mainly featuring French and German bands. It seats only 200 and the atmosphere hasn't been ruined by a recent facelift.

Le Palace – see **Nightclubs and Discos**.

11e

Chappelle des Lombards:

19 rue de Lappe. Tel. 43 57 24 24. M Bastille. From 10.30pm, bands Thur–Sat. C1. Sun–Mon.

Rumba, flamenco, soul and rhythmn and blues are the more usual sounds to come out of this former *bal musette* these days. It has also become the top place to hear African music.

Le Gibus – see **Nightclubs and Discos.**

18e

Éspace Ornano
78 boulevard Ornano. Tel. 42 55 57 57/42 41 18 12. M Porte de Clignancourt.
Doors open 7.30pm; music from 8pm–2am.
Very wide and varied programming at this concert venue – watch for advertising posters on Métro walls.

JAZZ

In the words of the jazz pianist Floris Nico Bunink: "Jazz can be loud and boisterous, but it can also *whisper*." This pioneer of bebop opened Paris' legendary Blue Note Club in 1957 with Zoot Sims. Today you'll find every variety of jazz at varying velocity and volubility in the clubs which have sprung up to replace the old standards like the Blue Note and Le Chat qui Pêche.

Jazz has enjoyed a marked revival in Paris in recent years, collecting a following as devoted as that of the '50s and '60s, and many renowned jazz musicians still live in the city. Nostalgia freaks in search of the smoky jazz *caves* of yesteryear should be prepared to put up with damp cellars and excruciatingly uncomfortable seating.

Jazz and all sorts of blues are also performed at piano bars, and sometimes in ordinary bars and cafés with just a late-night surcharge on drinks. Admission prices to the clubs and the piano bars are as varied as the clientèle, but on average entry and a first drink costs around 120f. As in Britain, the price goes up according to the programme – you'd expect to pay more to see an internationally known artist.

In late October/early November a jazz festival takes place in the city and in July jazz is featured in a nine-day programme of contemporary music.

Here by *arrondissement* is our selection of the best jazz spots in town.

1er

Le Baiser Salé

58 rue des Lombards. Tel. 42 33 37 71. M Châtelet. Bars open at 8.30pm. Entrance 65–90f.

Right in the middle of Beaubourg, this is *the* place for live Brazilian rock, as well as blues, funk and hard/contemporary jazz, every day from 11pm–4am.

Bistro d'Eustache

37 rue Berger. Tel. 40 26 23 20. M Les Halles. Entrance 45f; drinks 38–52f. Live music until 12 midnight or 1am. Reasonably priced food. Open from 10.30pm–4am.

Some of the cheapest jazz in town at this typical little Parisian bistro. Concerts every evening except Sunday.

Les Bouchons

19 rue des Halles. Tel. 42 33 28 73. M Châtelet.

Colonial, clubby feel to this dimly-lit venue where you can dine while listening to American jazz. There are live bands three or four times a week – ring for details. No entry charge; reasonably priced drinks. Recommended.

Magnetic Terrasse

12 rue de la Cassonie. Tel. 42 36 26 24. M Les Halles.

Situated in a recently converted Catholic church. The clientèle here is very arty, the jazz very contemporary. Good restaurant on the ground floor. Entrance charge depends on who's playing but can vary from 60–100f. There's a restaurant too (about 150f per person).

Le Petit Opportun

15 rue de Lavandières-Ste-Opportune. Tel. 42 36 01 36. M Châtelet. Entrance 120f (with drink), subsequent drinks 60f.

Run by Bernard and former trapeze artist/stunt woman Marianne, this highly recommended, friendly basement jazz club is the best in Les Halles, regularly presenting top calibre musicians (Johnny Griffin, Clark Terry, Art Farmer). Cognoscenti arrive early to nab a decent seat – there are only 60 of them. Upstairs tapes play in the bar which opens at 9pm and closes at 4am. Live music from 11pm–3pm.

Le Slow Club

130 rue de Rivoli. Tel. 42 33 84 30. M Louvre/Châtelet/Pont-Neuf. Open 9.30pm–2.30am/3am Friday; 4am Saturday. Closed Sunday and Monday. Entrance 50–70f, drinks extra but not obligatory.

Basement jazz club – one of the oldest in town. Endure the rather uncomfortable seating to enjoy jazz classics as well as bebop.

Le Sunset

60 rue des Lombards. Tel. 40 26 46 60. M Châtelet. Open from 10.30pm–4am. Entrance from about 70f. Closed Sunday.
Small (too small for some) and popular haunt with bar, restaurant and cellar jazz club specialising in modern jazz. Monday night jam sessions are particularly recommended (10.30pm).

5e

Le Caveau de la Huchette

5 rue de la Huchette. Tel. 43 26 65 05. M St Michel.
Open every day from 9.30pm–2.30am (4am on Saturdays). Entrance 40f weekdays, 50f weekends. The price of the first drink is about 15f.
The real thing – probably the best-known jazz club in town, and certainly one of the very oldest, on what was once known as the street of jazz. A lugubrious, subterranean, rather crammed, smoky *cave* with stone ceiling, spiral staircase and a dance floor where you can bop away. Irresistible.

Le Petit Journal

71 boulevard St Michel. Tel. 43 26 28 59. M Port Royal Odéon.
Open every day except Sun, 5pm–2am. Entrance 70–80f.
Mainly New Orleans jazz at this small, studenty and highly recommended Latin Quarter venue.

6e

Le Bilboquet

13 rue St Benoît. Tel. 45 48 81 84. M St-Germain-des-Prés.
Music from 10.30pm–2am every day except Sunday. Entrance 120f with drink.
Jazz bar that's also a restaurant where musicians play (for example the George Arvanitas Trio) in a coffin-shaped Art Nouveau room on the ground floor of a hotel.

Le Montana

28 rue St Benoît. Tel. 45 48 93 08. M St-Germain-des-Prés.
Open 10.30pm–2.15am nightly. Entrance 85f (bar), 100f with drink (club).
The club was founded during the golden age of jazz in St Germain. Although the live music stops at 2am, you can stay till the club closes at 5am. Closed Sunday.

Latitudes St Germain

7–11 rue St Benoît. Tel. 42 61 53 53. M Montparnasse/Vavin.
Open 5pm–2am. Music from 10.30pm.
One of the newest, classiest, jazz places on the left bank, close to the Bilboquet and the Montana, with bebop and good standard jazz programmes. Tickets available from FNAC outlets. Recommended, but drinks are costly.

10e

Le New Morning

7–9 rue des Petites Écuries. Tel. 45 23 51 41. M Château d'Eau.

Phone for details of opening hours; generally open from 9pm with concerts starting from 10pm. Entrance varies from 80–100f with soft drink, extra 30–50f for an alcoholic drink.

A world away from the smoky jazz cellars, this famous club was founded in 1981 after the success of a similar venture in Geneva, and is a major centre of jazz life in the city. One of the bigger, most comfortable and popular venues with capacity of around 400 people, it attracts the really big names on the international circuit in jazz as well as African, Brazilian and salsa bands.

14e

Le Petit Journal Montparnasse

13 rue du Commandant-Mouchotte. Tel. 43 21 56 70. M Gaîté Montparnasse.

Open 10pm–2am, Mon–Sat. Entrance 90f with drink.

A spin-off from the original, smaller Petit Journal St Michel, this branch under the Hôtel Montparnasse is more modern and tends to pull in the bigger, visiting names, mostly traditional jazz but sometimes contemporary, funk and rhythm and blues. Excellent views from just about anywhere in the place.

17e

Jazz Club Lionel Hampton

Hôtel Meridien, 81 boulevard Gouvian-St-Cyr. Tel. 47 58 12 30 or 40 68 34 34 and ask for jazz club. M Porte-Maillot.

From 10pm–2am nightly. Entrance about 140f.

Rather characterless (hotel lobby-like) though very upmarket, laid-back setting for top notch jazz, or you can get jazz with your Sunday lunch. Guest appearances by Lionel Hampton, Memphis Slim, Cab Calloway.

CLASSICAL MUSIC

Not a day slips by without a concert or recital being given in one or another of the city's main concert halls – and in many less obvious venues too. For centuries Parisian musical life has been enriched by church acoustics and by composers who have come to the city to play in them. In fact, probably the greater number of classical concerts in Paris are performed in churches (see below). Ticket prices are considerably less than the major concert halls and many recitals are free. The concerts in Notre-Dame and candlelit ones in Ste Chapelle are exceptional, and you'll need in the case of the latter to reserve well ahead. Look out for posters around town or check the magazines *Pariscope* or *Le Monde de la Musique*. Remember that performances in churches usually have unnumbered seats – arrive early for the choicest backdrops of ecclesiastical architecture to the organ recitals or choral pieces.

The following venues regularly have concerts or recitals. Except for foyer events, they are not cheap: reckon on between 100f and 180f for orchestral concerts, 90f and 130f for recitals. Tickets are best bought at the box offices, although a proportion of seats are always pre-booked by subscribers. The major venues will usually give a discount on ticket prices if you have a valid student card. Inexpensive or free classical concerts also take place at Radio France (see below).

1er

Auditorium Les Halles
Porte St Eustache, Forum des Halles. Tel. 42 33 00 00. M Les Halles.
Comparatively recent addition to the regular classical music venues, presenting generally excellent (though not always famous) artists. The acoustics here have met with some flack.

Auditorium du Louvre
Louvre Museum (entrance via Pyramid), 34–6 Quai du Louvre. Tel. 40 20 52 99. M Palais Royal.
Newly-constructed auditorium with evening and lunchtime programme of concerts.

Théâtre Musical de Paris Châtelet
1 place du Châtelet. Tel. 40 28 28 40. M Châtelet.
Two big halls for concerts and operatic productions, plus foyer for recitals and chamber music.

4e

Centre Georges Pompidou/IRCAM: main entrance on rue St Martin. Tel. 42 77 12 33. M Hôtel de Ville/Rambuteau.

The permanent home of IRCAM, a set up that's devoted to the development of and experimentation in contemporary music, under the direction of Pierre Boulez, the best known living French composer. You can attend a performance by the resident L'Ensemble Inter-Contemporain—check *Pariscope* etc for details, or enquire at the Beaubourg information desk. L'Ensemble Inter-Contemporain will, from 1993, be based at the new Cité de la Musique in the 19e.

7e

Musée d'Orsay: 1 rue Bellechasse. Tel. 40 49 48 14. M Solférino.
Infrequent concerts, often free with museum ticket.

8e

Salle Gaveau: 46 rue La Boétie. Tel. 49 53 05 07. M Miromesnil.
1000 seat plush concert hall, plus chamber music hall.

Salle Pleyel: 252 rue du Faubourg St Honoré. Tel. 45 63 88 73. M Ternes.
2300 seats; home of the Paris Symphony Orchestra (Orchestre de Paris) and before the Opéra de la Bastille, the city's main home of classical music.

Théâtre des Champs-Élysées: 15 avenue Montaigne. Tel. 47 20 36 37. M Alma-Marceau.
Performances range from opera to quartets and orchestral works; also a dance venue.

Théâtre Renaud-Barrault: avenue Franklin D. Roosevelt. Tel. 42 56 60 70. M Champs-Élysées/Clemenceau.
International chamber music.

16e

Maison de la Radio-France: 116 avenue du Président Kennedy. Tel. 42 30 23 08. M Ranelagh.
Philharmonic orchestra organised by the French National Radio Service. Inexpensive seats, sometimes free concerts.

17e

Centre de Musique Baroque de Versailles: 51 rue de Prony. Tel. 47 66 30 49. M Wagram/Malesherbes.
Chamber music, voice.

Salle Cortot: 78 rue Cardinet. Tel. 47 63 80 16. M Malesherbes.

19e

Cité de la Musique: avenue Jean-Jaurès. Tel. 42 40 27 28. M Porte de Pantin.

The national music academy, the Conservatoire National Supérieur de Musique, is the city's newest concert venue (information and bookings on 40 40 46 46 or 40 40 46 47) while the adjacent, state of the art auditorium, the Salle de Concert, should be up and running in 1993. It will be the new home of the IRCAM (see **Centre Georges Pompidou**)

CHURCHES WHERE CONCERTS ARE REGULARLY HELD

1er

Église St Eustache
2 rue du Jour. M Les Halles.
Famous organ in this great cathedral-like church of Les Halles. In 1855, Berlioz conducted the first performance of his *Te Deum* here, with 950 performers. A bust of Liszt in the church commemorates his conducting there.

Église St Roch
296 rue St Honoré. M Pyramids.
The musician's church of Paris.

Saint-Chapelle
4 boulevard du Palais. M Cité St Michel.
Extraordinary acoustics, candlelit concerts a speciality.

4e

Église des Billettes
24 rue des Archives. M Hôtel de Ville.

Notre-Dame de Paris
place du Parvis Notre-Dame. M Cité.

Notre-Dame-des-Blancs-Manteaux
12 rue des Blancs-Manteaux. M Hôtel de Ville.

St-Louis-en-l'Ile
19 bis rue St-Louis-en-l'Ile. M Pont l'Ile.

St-Merri
76 rue de la Verrerie. M Hôtel de Ville.

5e

St-Julien-le-Pauvre
rue St-Julien-le-Pauvre. M St Michel.
Intimate church, perfect for summer recitals of chamber music.

St-Médard
141 rue Mouffetard. M Censier-Daubenton.

6e

St-Germain-des-Prés
3 place St-Germain-des-Prés. M St-Germain-des-Prés.

St Sulpice
place St Sulpice. M St Sulpice.
The exceptional organ in this church (which is sometimes called the
"cathedral of the left bank") is bigger even than that of Notre-Dame,
with 6588 pipes. Charles Widor, a great organist, was based here,
succeeded by his most distinguished pupil, Marcel Dupré.

7e

Chapelle des Catéchismes de Ste Clotilde
29 rue Las-Cases. M Solférino.
Fine organ here, as used by celebrated Bégian organist César Franck
for nearly 40 years. He lived ascetically, like a saint; Debussy called
him "one of the greatest".

Eglise Américaine
65 quai d'Orsay. M Invalides.

8e

La Madeleine
place de la Madeleine. M Madeleine.
Concerts held several times a week, including free Sunday afternoon
concerts twice a month during the academic year. Saint-Saëns and his
pupil Gabriel Fauré became organists here.

St Augustin
46 boulevard Malesherbes. M St Augustin.

9e

Eglise Allemande
25 rue Blanche. M Trinité.

10e

St Vincent de Paul
place Franz Liszt. M Poissonnière.

11e

Eglise Réformée de la Bastille
7 rue du Pasteur-Wagner. M Bastille.

18e

St Pierre de Montmartre
place du Tertre. M Anvers.

20e

St Germain de Charonne
place St Blaise. M Porte de Bagnolet.

The following venues sometimes have concerts or recitals of
classical music:

3e

Centre Culturel Suisse
38 rue des Francs-Bourgeois. Tel. 42 71 38 38. M St Paul.

Musée Carnavalet

23 rue de Sévigné. Tel. 42 72 21 13. M St Paul.

4e

Le Mécène
6 rue des Lombards. Tel. 42 77 40 25. M Châtelet.

5e

Amphithéâtre de la Sorbonne
17 rue de la Sorbonne. M Cluny.

Schola Cantorum
217 rue St Jaques. Tel. 43 54 15 39. M Luxembourg.

6e

Mairie du Ville
78 rue Bonaparte. Tel. 43 29 12 78. M St-Germain-des-Prés.

7e

Institut Néerlandais
121 rue de Lille. M Bac.

Maison de l'Amérique Latine
217 boulevard St Germain. Tel. 42 22 97 60. M Bac.

Salle André Marchal
56 boulevard des Invalides. Tel. 47 34 11 91. M Duroc.

8e

Maison du Danemark
142 avenue des Champs-Élysées. Tel. 47 23 54 20. M Charles de Gaulle-Etoile.

9e

Hôtel Scribe
1 rue Scribe. Tel. 47 42 03 40. M Opéra.

10e

Opus Café
167 quai de Valmy. Tel. 40 38 09 57. M Château Landon.
Café with quartets, chamber and solo recitals.

12e

Centre d'Activités Sportives et Culturelles
143 rue de Bercy. Tel. 40 04 20 85. M Bercy.

13e

Mandapa
6 rue Wurtz. Tel. 45 89 01 60. M Glacière.

14e

Fiap
30 rue Cabanis. M Glacière.

Fondation Heinrich Heine
27c boulevard Jourdan. Tel. 45 89 92 20. M Cité Universitaire.

Maison d'Italie
7a boulevard Jourdan. Tel. 45 89 92 20. M Cité Universitaire.

Théâtre 14, Jean-Marie Serreau
20 avenue Marc-Sangnier. Tel. 45 45 49 77. M Porte de Vanves.

16e

Conservatoire Rachmaninoff
26 avenue de New York. Tel. 47 23 51 44. M Passy.

17e

Madigan
22 rue de la Terrasse. Tel. 42 27 31 51. M Villiers.

OPERA

Mitterand's *grand projet*, the building of a new home for opera in the traditionally proletarian Bastille, was intended to make the art more accessible and affordable. Its first production, in 1990, the 6-hour-long *Les Troyens* by Berlioz, called this objective into doubt and, while procuring seats at the old Opéra Garnier was difficult and expensive, at least people wanted them. However, what the new venue lacks in opulence, it makes up for in efficiency and some of its earlier

arcane programming traits have been dropped in favour of
a more balanced repertoire. Performances also take place at
the Opéra Comique and at the multi-purpose venues. (See
Classical Music section, or check topical listings guides for
details.)

1er

Théâtre Musical de Paris
1 place du Châtelet. Tel. 40 28 28 40. M Châtelet.
Opera – as well as ballet – for a wide audience.

2e

Opéra Comique (Salle Favart)
5 rue Favart. Tel. 42 96 12 20. M Richelieu-Drouot.
Hosts visiting opera companies, as well as dance performances,
concerts.

4e

Le Roseau Théâtre
12 rue de Renard. Tel. 42 72 23 41. M Hôtel de Ville.
Opera, as well as dance and music, classical and contemporary. (This
venue was formerly known as the Épicerie-Beaubourg, but changed its
name in 1988.)

12e

Opéra Paris Bastille
2 place de la Bastille. Tel. 40 01 16 16 (box office), 43 43 96 96
(programme details), 43 42 92 92 (administration). M Bastille.
Principal opera venue in the city, mounting full-scale, new productions.
Two auditoriums: one for *opéra lyrique* repertoire and the other for the
work of contemporary composers. Tickets (40f–520f) available Mon–
Sat, 11am–6pm or from the ticket offices Mon–Sat, 11am–6.30pm
within two weeks of the performance. The cheapest seats can only
be purchased by personal callers; unsold seats are sold at discounted
prices to students 5 minutes prior to curtain up.

DANCE

Modern dance in a glorious variety of styles has been enjoying
a revival in France, though many of the companies aren't

Paris-based. Names to look for are Roland Petit's from Marseille, Dominique Bagouet's from Montpellier, Jean-Claude Gallota's from Grenoble; creative choreographers working in or near Paris include Jean-François Duroure, Maguy Marin, Karine Saporta.

The work of the new wave of small, innovative companies may often be seen in the 11e, at places like the Café de la Danse or Centre Pompidou before they scale the heights of the Théâtre de la Bastille or Théâtre de la Ville.

With operatic life now revolving around the Opéra Bastille, the vast old Opéra Garnier has been given over to contemporary and classical dance. Ballet was invented in France – Louis XIV himself was an early performer – and, as well as its home-grown companies, Paris draws in the world's finest dancers. Visitors include the Bolshoi, the Kirov and the New York City Ballet. Highlight of the balletic calendar is the autumn Festival International de Danse de Paris, bringing together a variety of traditions and dance forms. Other festivals which bring together theatre, dance, mime, classical and contemporary music include the Féstival du Marais in June and the Féstival "Foire St-Germain" in June and July.

1er

Théâtre Musical de Paris
1 place du Châtelet. Tel. 40 28 28 40. M Châtelet.
Ballet, as well as opera productions, are held here. It was the venue where, in 1910, Diaghilev staged the first season of Russian ballet, helped by Cocteau, Proust, Rod and others.

2e

Opéra Comique (Salle Favart)
5 rue Favart. Tel. 42 96 12 20. M Richelieu-Drouot.
Dance, as well as concerts and opera, usually of the classical kind.

3e

Le Déjazet
41 boulevard du Temple. Tel. 48 87 97 34. M République.
Experimental dance and mime.

4e

Le Roseau Théâtre
12 rue de Renard. Tel. 42 72 23 41. M Hôtel de Ville.
Dance venue in Beaubourg.

Théâtre de la Ville
2 place du Châtelet. Tel. 42 74 22 77. M Châtelet.
Venue almost entirely given over to dance, with two shows nightly. Wide range of visiting companies and styles, though mostly contemporary, including well-known international names. Good value early evening review performances.

Théâtre Contemporain de Dance
9 rue Geoffroy-l'Asnier. Tel. 42 74 44 22. M Pont Marie.
Innovative dance performances.

7e

Palais de Unesco
125 avenue de Suffren. Tel. 45 68 10 00. M Ségur.
Frequently hosts international dance artists.

8e

Théâtre des Champs-Élysées
15 avenue Montaigne. Tel. 47 20 36 37. M Alma Marceau.
International dance festivals are held in this plush theatre, as well as concerts and opera.

9e

Opéra de Paris Garnier
place de l'Opéra. Tel. 47 42 53 71. M Opéra.

Opulent home of the Paris Opéra Ballet, under the directorship of young star Patric Dupoud. It's usually well booked in advance, largely filled by subscribers, but 300 tickets are available 13 days before each performance. Be there, or phone early, or apply for tickets in writing to: Théâtre de l'Opéra, Service de location par correspondance, 8 rue Scribe, 75009, Paris. The rear seats of the boxes go on sale from 1.30pm on the day prior to the performance, while any seats left are sold off to students, dramatically reduced, just before the performance.

11e

Café de la Danse
5 passage Louis-Philippe. Tel. 48 05 57 22. M Bastille.
Tiny venue with big name for modern, innovative dance and "alternative" musicals.

Théâtre de la Bastille
79 rue de la Roquette. Tel. 43 57 42 14. M Bastille.
Dance and mime as well as more traditional theatre.

13e

Centre Mandapa
6 rue Wurtz. Tel. 45 89 01 60. M Glacière.
Traditional dances from around the world performed here.

THEATRE

Theatregoers in Paris really are spoilt for choice, but quantity tends to eclipse quality and most drama will leave you untouched unless your French is pretty good. If you're blowing money on a night out it's safer to opt for the dance, *chansonniers* or the lively atmosphere of a café-théâtre than to sit soberly in a conventional theatre. With around 100 theatres serving up productions varying from mega-glitz extravaganzas to the light entertainment of the *théâtre du boulevard*, from classical drama to one-man shows, all tastes are catered for.

Most venues close on Monday and conventional theatres tend not to play on Sunday evenings. Evening performances usually begin at 8.30pm. Tickets usually go on sale 2 or 3 weeks before the performance and individual box offices open at around 11am until 6 or 7pm. Even if a show is supposed to be sold out, it's worth checking at the box office as cancellations are returned directly to the venue. Booking agencies (see below) charge the usual commission of 22%, but can save on hassle. If you have sufficient time, it's worth queueing at the Kiosque Théâtre for half-price tickets for same-day performances. Remember that you'll also be charged a 12f booking fee per ticket.

Ticket prices vary enormously. Expect to pay 60f to 240f at a national or large independent theatre, 40f to 150f at smaller venues. The Comédie Française puts 112 cheap seats on sale before each performance – line up for them at 7.45pm; the Odéon theatre has 99 seats at reduced prices 30 minutes before curtain-up.

Half-price tickets for many plays and shows are on sale from midday at the two Kiosque-Théâtres: Place de la Madeleine and Châtelet-Les Halles Métro station.

The listing below covers a wide range of venues from the big "national" theatres (marked *) to the small studios where you just might discover a bright young Gallic star in the making. The Comédie Française (1er) is the most important venue in Paris for classical theatre, whether it be Molière or Shakespeare (in French). Over on the left bank, the Comédie Française holds other seasons at the Odéon, an impressive theatre which was occupied by rioting students in the uprisings of '68. The theatre has had its name changed several times according to the ruling régime. In 1959 it was called the Théâtre de France and, more recently, became the Théâtre de l'Europe, underling its rôle as the European base for international theatre seasons. Attached to the Odéon Théâtre de l'Europe, the Petit Odéon also hosts and mounts foreign language productions of modern and classical European plays and is a forum for new works. Still on the left bank, La Maison des Cultures de Monde (6e) is devoted entirely to world theatre, verging at times on the esoteric. We recently came across a performance there in the language of 16th-century Portugal.

The Odéon and Comédie Française are both among the state-subsidised theatres in Paris. The other very prominent one is the TNP or Théâtre National Populaire, founded in 1920 and housed in the Trocadéro Palace.

The Palais des Glaces (10e) has a reputation for interesting and avant-garde programmes, including mime and visual theatre. The Théâtre de Paris (9e) normally hosts musical shows, such as the French version of "Cats". Light farce and operettas can often be found at the Olympia in the 9e.

For details of current productions check the local press, or the usual entertainment listings publications, like *Pariscope*.

Booking Agencies

Agence Chèque-Théâtres: 2nd Floor, 33 rue Le Peletier 75009. Tel. 42 46 72 40. M Le Peletier. Open: 10am to 7pm, Mon to Sat. No Credit Cards.

Makes bookings for all forms of entertainment by phone, post or in person.

Alpha-FNAC: 3rd level down Forum des Halles 75001. Tel. 40 26 81 18. M Châtelet-Les Halles. Open 2–7.30pm, Mon; 10am to 7.30pm, Tues–Sat.

Speedy, efficient service covering all kinds of entertainment. Phone here to find the branch nearest to you.

Jeunesses Musicales de France: 56 rue de l'Hôtel de Ville 75004. Tel. 42 78 19 54. M Hôtel de Ville. Open: 10am – 7pm, Mon to Sat; 10am – 6pm, Sun.

No credit cards. Rates: 150f over 30s; 80f age 18 to 30; 15f under 18s.

Membership organisation offering 50% discount at all major theatres on certain days. Reciprocal arrangement with members of the British organisation "Youth and Music" (78 Neal Street, London WC2H 9PA). Helpful, friendly staff.

Kiosque Théâtre: across from 15 place de la Madeleine 75008. M Madeleine. Open: 12.30–8pm, Tues to Fri; 12.30pm Sat for matinées and 2–8pm for evening performances; 12.30–4pm, Sun. Closed Mon. No credit cards.

Sells same-day performance tickets for half-price. Good deal for those who don't mind queueing. The seats available are amongst the most pricey. Also at Châtelet RER station 75001.

1er

Comédie Française*
2 rue de Richelieu. Tel. 40 15 00 15. M Palais Royal.
Grand, classical venue for classic theatre, all well done. Bookings 14 days in advance.

Palais Royal*
38 rue Montpensier. Tel. 42 97 59 81. M Bourse Palais Royal.
Beautiful building, reasonable prices (20f to 260f) for exquisitely turned light comedy, principally bedroom farces. The very cheapest seats have rotten views.

Théâtre Musical de Paris (Châtelet)*

1 place du Châtelet. Tel. 40 28 28 40. M Châtelet.
Musical theatre, as well as dance and opera.

2e

Bouffes Parisiens
4 rue Monsigny. Tel. 42 96 60 24. M Quatre Septembre.
Reasonably priced, popular comedy and undemanding boulevard
drama.

Daunou
7 rue Daunou. Tel. 42 61 69 14. M Étienne Marcel.

Marie Stuart
4 rue Marie-Stuart. Tel. 45 08 17 80. M Étienne Marcel.

Opéra Comique (Salle Favart)*
5 rue Favart. Tel. 42 86 88 83. M Richelieu-Drouot.
Well-established theatre hot on musicals, though some productions are
excessively sentimental. Also hosts dance companies.

Potinière
7 rue Louis-le-Grand. Tel. 42 61 44 16. M Opéra.

Variétés
7 boulevard Montmartre. Tel. 42 33 09 92. M Rue Montmartre
Bourse.
Light, farcical boulevard entertainment.

3e

Éspace Marais
22 rue Beautreillis. Tel. 48 04 91 55. M Saint Paul.
Fringe theatre.

Marais
37 rue Volta. Tel. 42 78 03 53. M Arts-et-Métiers.
More fringe theatre.

Michodière
4 rue de la Michodière. Tel. 47 42 95 22. M Quatre Septembre.

4e

Essaion de Paris
6 rue Pierre-au-Lard, angle 24 rue du Renard. Tel. 42 71 30 20. M
Hôtel de Ville.

Théâtre de la Ville (Mairie de Paris)*
2 place du Châtelet. Tel. 42 74 22 77. M Châtelet.

Primarily a contemporary dance venue, but has dramatic offerings too.

5e

Huchette
23 rue de la Huchette. Tel. 43 26 38 99. M St Michel.
Specialists in Ionesco. *The Bald Primadonna* has been running here longer than *The Mousetrap* in London. The also stage double and triple Ionesco bills.

Nouveau Théâtre Mouffetard
73 rue Mouffetard. Tel. 43 31 11 99. M Monge.
Inexpensive Latin Quarter venue popular with students.

Vieille Grille
1 rue du Puits de l'Ermite. Tel. 47 07 22 11. M Monge/Censier Daubenton.
Bar-cum-theatre, erstwhile pioneer of radical comedy and experimental drama. Varied programme.

6e

Lucernaire Centre National d'Art et d'Essai*
53 rue Notre-Dame-des-Champs. Tel. 45 44 57 34. M Vavin, Notre-Dame-des-Champs.
Modern classics a speciality.

Maison des Cultures de Monde
101 boulevard Raspail. Tel. 45 44 72 30. M Notre-Dame-des-Champs.

Théâtre National de l'Odéon*
1 place Paul Claudel. Tel. 43 25 70 32. M Odéon.
Twin to the Comédie Française, with well-done contemporary productions in the main house and, in the Petit Odéon, an interesting programme of European plays performed in all European languages other than French.

Poche Montparnasse
75 boulevard du Montparnasse. Tel. 45 48 92 97. M Montparnasse-Bienvenue.

8e

Comédie des Champs-Élysées
15 avenue Montaigne. Tel. 47 23 37 21. M Alma Marceau.
One of the city's most fashionable theatres, also used for dance during the winter season and well known for its classical music concerts.

Marigny
Carré Marigny. Tel. 42 56 04 41. M Champs Elysées/Clemenceau

Michel
38 rue des Mathurins. Tel. 42 65 35 02. M Havre-Caumartin.

Renaud-Barrault (Théâtre du Rond-Point)
2 bis avenue Franklin D. Roosevelt. Tel. 42 46 60 70. M Franklin
D. Roosevelt.
Two playhouses with adventurous and generally good programmes of
20th-century drama. Sponsors discussion series with public, performers
and writers. Founded by Jean-Louis Barrault and his wife Madeleine
Renaud, a famous French theatrical twosome, and now one of the
best-known theatrical companies in Paris.

Studio des Champs-Élysées
15 avenue Montaigne. Tel. 47 23 35 10. M Alma Marceau.

Tristan Bernard
64 rue du Rocher. Tel. 45 22 08 40. M Villiers.
Fashionable, contemporary plays.

9e
La Bruyère
5 rue la Bruyère. Tel. 48 74 76 99. M St Georges.

Comédie Caumartin
25 rue Caumartin. Tel. 47 42 43 41. M Havre-Caumartin.
Privately-funded theatre, wide range of productions.

Comédie de Paris
42 rue Fontaine. Tel. 42 81 00 11. M Blanche.

Edouard VII Sacha Guitry
10 place Edouard VII. Tel. 47 42 59 92. M Opéra.
Respectable productions for respectable audiences.

Fontaine
10 rue Fontaine. Tel. 48 74 74 40. M Pigalle.
Check out the programme – it's not always straight theatre.

Mogador
25 rue de Mogador. Tel. 42 85 45 30. M Trinité.
Sumptuous building, sound productions, with good views from all
the seats.

Nouveautés
24 boulevard Poissonnière. Tel. 47 70 52 76. M Rue Montmartre.

Oeuvre
55 rue de Clichy. Tel. 48 74 42 52/48 74 47 36. M Place de Clichy.

Olympia
28 boulevard des Capucines. Tel. 47 42 25 49. M Opéra/Madeleine.
Good for light farce, operettas and lightweight music programmes.

St Georges
51 rue St Georges. Tel. 48 78 63 47. M St Georges.

Théâtre de Paris
15 rue Blanche. Tel. 42 80 09 30. M Trinité.
Well-established independent theatre, a safe bet for whatever's popular
such as *Cats*. Don't confuse with the national theatre, Théâtre
de la Ville.

10e

Antoine-Simone Berriau
14 boulevard de Strasbourg. Tel. 42 08 77 71/42 08 76 58. M
Strasbourg-St Denis.
Boulevard theatre with a difference, a pioneer at the turn-of-the-century
of "realism" in theatre. More likely to find homegrown playwrights
performed here than foreign imports. Mostly middlebrow.

Bateau Théâtre
opposite 188 quai de Jemmapes. Tel. 40 51 84 53/42 08 68 89. M
Jaurès Château Landon.
Light drama and farce executed on a floating stage (the boat is
moored).

Bouffes du Nord
37 bis boulevard de la Chapelle. Tel. 42 39 34 50/46 07 34 50. M La
Chapelle.
Good, professional adaptations of foreign plays and interesting, contem-
porary work. This is Peter Brook's stamping ground: his cross-cultural
French company is based here.

Porte St Martin
16 boulevard St Martin. Tel. 42 08 00 32. M Strasbourg-St Denis.
Even quality productions in a dodgy area.

Renaissance
20 boulevard St Martin. Tel. 42 08 18 50. M Strasbourg-St Denis.

11e

Arcane Théâtre
168 rue St Maur. Tel. 43 38 19 70. M Goncourt Belleville.

Akteon Théâtre
11 rue du général Blaise. Tel. 43 38 74 62. M St Ambroise.

Bataclan

50 boulevard Voltaire. Tel. 47 00 30 12. M Oberkampf.

Bastille
76 rue de la Roquette. Tel. 43 57 42 14. M Bastille.
Inexpensive venue (tickets 90f) that's often the launch pad for high-flying directors and companies. Shows new dance and theatre.

Théâtre du Berry
63 boulevard de Belleville. Tel. 43 79 71 70. M Couronnes.

Le Bourvil
13 rue des Boulets. Tel. 43 73 47 84. M Nation.

Café de la Danse
5 passage Louis-Philippe. Tel. 48 05 57 52. M Bastille.

12e

Cartoucherie
Route de Champs-de-Manoeuvres, Bois de Vincennes. Tel. 43 74 24 08. M Château de Vincennes then shuttle bus 112.
Avant-garde multi-theatre complex in attractive forest setting: well worth a visit if your French is up to it. Excellent attendance record – and it's inexpensive: 40–90f.

13e

Châpiteau Compagnie Foraine
109 quai de la gare. Tel. 43 41 80 69. M Quai de la Gare.

Cinq Diamants
8 rue des Cinq Diamants. Tel. 45 80 51 31. M Place d'Italie.
Light drama/farce; inexpensive.

14e

Cité Internationale Universitaire
21 boulevard Jourdan. Tel. 45 89 38 69. M Cité-Universitaire.
Relatively unsophisticated with good mixture of cultures and performance styles. Inexpensive: 35–100f.

Comédie Italienne
17 rue de la Gaîté. Tel. 43 21 22 22. M Edgar Quinet.
Not the best in town, but nor is it the most expensive: classics and modern works.

Gaîté-Montparnasse
26 rue de la Gaîté. Tel. 43 22 16 18. M Gaîté.
Hot on comedy and good one man shows.

Le Grand Edgar

6 rue de la Gaîté. Tel. 43 35 32 31/43 20 90 09. M Edgar Quinet.

Guichet-Montparnasse
15 rue du Maine. Tel. 43 27 88 61. M Montparnasse-Bienvenue.

Montparnasse
31 rue de la Gaîté. Tel. 43 22 77 74. M Gaîté/Edgar Quinet.
The main theatrical puller in Montparnasse – a duo of playhouses for reliable imported and French productions.

16e

Théâtre National de Chaillot*
1 place du Trocadéro. Tel. 47 27 81 15. M Trocadéro.
Expensive, stylish, mainstream theatre.

Ranelagh
5 rue des Vignes. Tel. 42 88 64 44. M La Muette.
Quality productions of some of the best contemporary work in town.

17e

Éspace Européen
5 rue Biot. Tel. 42 93 69 68. M Place de Clichy.

Hebertot
78 boulevard des Batignolles. Tel. 43 87 23 23. M Villiers.

18e

Atelier
1 place Charles Dullin. Tel. 46 06 49 24. M Anvers.
Large-scale productions, including musicals.

18 Théâtre
16 rue Georgette Agutte. Tel. 42 26 47 47. M Guy Moquet.

20e

Amandiers de Paris
110 rue des Amandiers. Tel. 43 66 42 17. M Ménilmontant.

Théâtre National de la Colline
15 rue Malte-Brun. Tel. 43 66 43 60. M Gambetta.
Adventurous programme of contemporary plays that occasionally verge on the incomprehensible even to those fluent in French.

CAFÉ-THEATRES

There are around 150 café-théâtres in Paris, usually small-scale places where a successful show will run for a long time. Ticket prices are lower than at other theatres, averaging 50f, and there's usually the option of an all-in price for supper and show. There are often reduced prices for students. The alternative humour widely on offer may well elude those with less than an incredible grasp of the language; traditional fare of sketches and songs are easier on effort for those with imperfect French. Performances usually begin late, between 9.30pm and 10.30pm, and a couple of different shows may be given each evening.

1er

Au Bec Fin
6 rue Thérèse. Tel. 42 96 29 35. M Palais Royal.

2e

Sentier des Halles
50 rue d'Aboukir. Tel. 42 36 37 27. M Sentier.

3e

Le Movies
15 rue Michel le Comte. Tel. 42 74 14 22. M Rambuteau/Les Halles.

Petit Casino
17 rue Chapon. Tel. 42 78 36 50. M Arts-et-Métiers.

4e

Blancs-Manteaux
15 rue des Blancs-Manteaux. Tel. 48 87 15 84. M Hôtel de Ville.

Café de la Gare
41 rue du Temple. Tel. 42 78 52 51. M Hôtel de Ville.

Points Virgule
7 rue Ste-Croix-de-la-Bretonnerie. Tel. 42 78 67 03. M Hôtel de Ville.

Le Sunset
60 rue des Lombards. Tel. 40 26 46 60. M Châtelet.

5e

Les Trois Mailletz
56 rue Galande. Tel. 40 46 93 60. M Maubert-Mutualité.

13e

Théâtre de l'Arlequin
13 passage du Moulinet. Tel. 48 46 60 69. M Tolbiac.

14e

Café d'Edgar
58 boulevard Edgar-Quinet. Tel. 43 20 85 11. M Edgar Quinet/
Montparnasse.

Cave du Cloître
19 rue St Jacques. Tel. 43 25 19 92. M St Michel.

17e

Au Grenier
3 rue Rennequin. Tel. 43 80 68 01. M Ternes.

REVUE REVIEW

Paris after dark still has a risqué but glamorous reputation,
evoked by the names Folies Bergère and the Moulin Rouge.
These cabarets, which once inspired Toulouse Lautrec, along
with their successors, the Lido and Paradis Latin, attempt to
turn voyeurism into a performing art. They're magnets to
tourists but are not, in fact, patronised exclusively by foreign
visitors. If you get your kicks looking at the high kicks of
topless ladies plastered in plumes doing a good impersonation
of an X-rated Busby Berkeley movie, here's a brief guide to
where to find the fun.

A multitude of overpriced, tatty shows come under the
revue heading. All the major revues – as opposed to the
tawdry bump and grind jobs – are highly professional, slick
and rather soulless, and feature some sort of can-can. While
the showgirls are slipping in and out of their rhinestones,

the audience gets treated to speciality acts like juggling or ventriloquism. Champagne is often included in the ticket price for the show, which might fall into one of three formats.

At the Folies Bergère, for instance, you may have a pre-show dinner and then you see the performance as in a theatre; at the Lido and Moulin Rouge you dine during the first performance, drink during the others; at a third kind of cabaret you just watch and drink, such as at the Crazy Horse. It's always necessary to reserve in advance.

There are many other so-called "revues" in Paris of varying respectability. Some are essentially no more than tacky sex shows, especially those around the rue St Denis and Pigalle, without any gloss or glamour whatsoever.

Folies Bergère
32 rue de Richer 75009. Tel. 42 46 77 11. M Cadet Rue Montmartre. From 9pm, Tue–Sun. Closed Jan. Entrance: **show only standing behind stalls: 82f; show only stalls: 360f.** Telephone for details of dinner. Smart dress.

The oldest cabaret – it opened in 1869 – it is actually frequented by French people too. The show, in the style of the 19th-century musical, is a vast 3-hour spectacular of variety acts and bare breasts smothered in a sea of sequins and ostrich feathers. Punters have the choice of a pre-revue Grand Siècle dinner (a new addition in 1990) in the spacious ante room served by becostumed waiters.

Moulin Rouge
82 boulevard de Clichy 75011, Tel. 46 06 00 19. M Blanche.
From 8pm. Shows at 8pm, 10pm, midnight daily. Entrance: dinner and dance at 8pm, from 530f per person, to include tourist menu and half-bottle champagne. Show only, at 10pm and midnight, from 36f per person (includes half bottle champagne). Smart dress.

Toulouse Lautrec has a lot to answer for, but the can-can is strictly peripheral to the show with supplementary wholesome fun in the form of variety acts. Lavish costumes, lighting effects, décor . . . but it's all a bit dated.

Le Lido
116 avenue des Champs-Élysées 75008. Tel. 45 63 11 61. M George V.
Shows 8pm, 10.15pm, 12.30am daily. Entrance dinner at 8pm, 510f. Show only: 10.15pm and 12.30am, 350f.

The famous Bluebell girls have been jump-led into the 21st century as the Lido has discovered laser technology and computerised choreography. Less traditional than the others, but no less lavish:

dancers, acrobats, a conjuror and flesh add up to an expensive, slick and strangely asexual experience. It's very popular with the Japanese who are no fools when it comes to getting their yen's worth by day or night. Smart dress required.

Paradis Latin

28 rue Cardinal-Lemoine 75005. Tel. 43 25 28 08. M Cardinal-Lemoine.
From 8.30pm Mon, Wed–Sun. Entrance and dinner 510f (includes half bottle champagne).

Lots of male (and foreign) spectators at the dinner spectacle which has long had a reputation for being the best show in town – but then that's what they all say. The theatre was built by Gustave Eiffel. Smart or evening dress.

La Belle Époque

36 rue des Petits-Champs 75002. Tel. 42 96 33 33. Phone for all the glossy trappings, yet a less traditional more raunchy show, with some acts in very questionable burlesque taste.

Alcazar

62 rue Mazarine 75006. Tel. 43 29 02 20. M Odéon. Show 10pm, Mon–Sat. Closed mid-July to end-Aug. Entrance and dinner (8pm) 510–900f includes half bottle champagne; show only (10pm) 350f (includes half bottle of champagne).

Newly renovated, but not enjoying the reputation it had in the '70s as one of the funniest (in the sense of most entertaining) shows, it features a glitzy boobs and plumes revue, the ubiquitous can-can as well as some hit and miss modern touches, a dash of transvestism and political satire. Parisians actually do go to this one. Smart or evening dress.

Crazy Horse

12 avenue George V, 75008. Tel. 47 23 32 32. M Alma Marceau.
Shows at 9pm, 1.30pm, Mon–Thur, Sun; 8.15pm, 10.35pm and 12.45am, Fri, Sat. Entrance standing at bar 195f (includes one drink), seated 495f (includes half bottle champagne).

Less of a theatrical experience than an upmarket sex show, yet for all the lighting pyrotechnics, it's not erotic – the taped music and blatant commercialism see to that. American and Japanese businessmen don't seem to be put off by the lack of sophistication, and seem to enjoy the racey spectacle provided by *déshabillé* dancers with unsubtle epithets like Vanilla Banana, Betty Buttocks and Friday Trampoline. No can-cans.

MORE IDEAS FOR NIGHTS OUT

Cafés, alternative cabaret, food with entertainment . . .

L'Ane Rouge

3 rue Laugier, 75017. Tel. 45 62 52 42. M Ternes. From 9pm daily, show 10.30 daily. Entrance: dinner 150f, 250f, 350f (not including wine), Mon–Fri, Sun; 200f Sat, public holidays. No credit cards.

Popular with bunches of people, birthday parties, outings, as a lot of audience participation is involved at this smartish dinner-cum-cabaret spot. Lots of celebrants and business types in the audience. Slick comedy, magic, ventriloquism and music is the entertainment menu.

Au Lapin Agile
22 rue des Saules 75018. Tel. 46 06 85 87. M Lamarck-Caulaincourt. Open Tue–Sun until 2am. Entrance and drink 10f. Subsequent drinks 25f. Reductions for students.

Tourists have long supplanted the artists who used to hang out here in the days of old Montmartre. Arrive early for a decent seat; shows start at 9pm featuring French folk songs. If you're in good voice, you can join in – at least it'll keep you awake. You'll need to have pretty agile French to get the jokes.

Caveau des Oubliettes
11 rue St-Julien-le-Pauvre 75005. Tel. 43 54 94 97. M St-Michel. From 9pm (Show 9pm), Mon–Sat. Entrance 100f with one drink No credit cards.

Nostalgic nose-dive in the cellar of the old prisons of Châtelet where you can wallow in renditions of nostalgic ballads by minstrels and troubadours from the 11th to 19th centuries. After the show you can have a grisly tour of the dungeons. Popular with tourists.

City Rock
13 rue de Berri 75008. Tel. 43 59 52 09. M Georges V. From 6pm daily; bands from 10pm daily. Entrance free, drinks 50f. Popular with Americans. Upstairs for hamburgers and ribs, downstairs for rock and roll or country music.

Club des Poètes
30 rue de Bourgogne 75007. Tel. 47 05 06 03. M Invalides. Telephone for times, prices.

Only in Paris? Poetry in motion with the help of singing, acting, dance and mime.

Le Corail
140 rue Montmartre 75002. Tel. 42 36 39 66. M Bourse. Music from 10pm, Wed–Sat. Entrance 50f, beer 30f.

Round the clock bar, open 24 hours a day, with a subterranean samba/salsa shrine plus small dance space.

La Coupole
102 boulevard Montparnasse 75014. Tel. 43 20 14 20. M Monparnasse-Bienvenue.
(See page 140, Dancing in the basement.)

Hollywood Savoy

44 rue Notre-Dame-des-Victoires 75002. Tel. 42 36 16 73. M Rue Montmartre. From 7pm, Mon–Sat. Entrance free, drinks from 50f.

A supper club with a dash of entertainment: popular with preppies and *nouveau yuppies* yearning for Transatlantica. Mon, Thur, Sat are rock nights; jazz on other nights.

(See also **Restaurants** p. 114.)

Le Limonaire

88 rue de Charenton 75012. Tel. 43 43 49 14. M Ledru-Rollin.
From 8pm, Mon–Sat. Closed Sunday and August. Show 10–11pm, Wed–Sat. Entrance: no fee but donations requested after show. No credit cards.

Convivial neighbourhood bistro in *branché* Bastille with resident mime artist/street singer. You usually get musical entertainment while you sup (excellent value *à la carte* meal for around 90f a head) but from time to time it's over to the comics and poets.

Madame Arthur

75 bis rue des Martyres 75018. Tel. 42 64 48 27. M Pigalle.
From 1pm. Show 10.15pm daily. Entrance: dinner 8.30pm, 250f, includes wine; show only 10.15pm, 165f (includes one drink, second drink 95f). Must reserve in advance.

Highly-acclaimed, award-winning transvestite show with nonstop line-up of camp impersonations of female singers and worse. Relentless attempts to involve audience either innocuously – by getting them to do the conga – or insidiously as Madame Arthur hurls abuse at the spotty, the bespectacled, or anyone who happens to be sitting near the front.

Nostalgie

27 avenue des Ternes 75017. Tel. 42 27 65 27. M Ternes Porte Maillot.
From 9pm, Tue–Sat. Closed. Aug. Show 10pm, Tue–Sat. Entrance: dinner 350f includes wine; drink and show from 100f.

Lively cabaret and good food are hallmarks of this trendy, large '50s-style restaurant with a good sound system. Aspiring amateurs in the audience are given their chance up on the stage; otherwise sit back and enjoy the conjurors, ventriloquists, *chanseurs*.

Le Piano Zinc

(See **Gay Paris**, page 293.)

René Cousinier ("La Branlette")

4 impasse Marie Blanche (off rue Lepic) 75018. Tel. 46 06 49 46. M Blanche.
From 10pm, Tue–Sun. Entrance free but must buy drink, with prices from 80f. No credit cards.

A grimy cellar bar is the setting for a French Lenny Bruce, René Cousinier, who fires his anecdotes and jokes into the young audience

Chansonniers

A very Parisian entertainment — satirical sketches and witty parodies of French political life are staples. Two well-known venues are:

Caveau de la République, (1 boulevard Saint Martin 75003. Tel. 42 78 44 45. M République) and **Les Deux Anes** (100 boulevard de Clichy 75018, Tel. 46 06 10 26. M Blanche).

Performances begin around 9pm, with matinées on Sundays. To get the jokes you'll need to be very *au fait* with the news and have an impeccable grasp of the lingo.

like bullets. He's rude, waspish, incredibly funny, but you'll need good French to keep up with him.

Tintamarre

10 rue de Lombards 75004. Tel. 48 87 33 82. M Châtelet-Les Halles.
From 8pm, Tue–Sat. Entry 60–80f show. Auditions on Sat. 2.30pm, 30f. No credit cards.

Budget-conscious spectators go to the Saturday auditions where talented hopefuls do their best to impress the audience with their singing/jokes/acting to gain a regular spot in the theatre in the evening.

La Vieille Grille

1 rue du Puits de l'Ermite 75005. Tel. 47 07 22 11. M Censier Daubenton.
From 8pm, Tue–Sat; show 8.30pm. Entrance 80f. No credit cards.

Snug bar-theatre that was once a pioneer of fringe cabaret/-theatre/comedy, still presenting a varied programme from stand-up comics to classical music on different evenings. A pre-recorded message gives information about what's appearing on any given week.

CINEMA

Parisians are movie-mad and for *cinéastes* Paris is unrivalled. During a typical week, over 300 different films will be showing on the 350 plus screens within the city's limits. You can choose from the newest releases, varied programmes at the Pompidou Centre (the National Film Theatre) and all over town there are many cinemas showing previous runs (*réprises*)

Film Language

Watch out for the initials VO (standing for *Version Originale*) and VF (*Version Française*) following the film listing. Foreign movies are either dubbed in French (VF) or presented in their original version with French subtitles (VO). So if you want to see a British or American movie in English, look for a VO, or possibly a VA (*Version Anglaise*) which denotes an English language film made by a French-speaking director.

---

or cinemas holding seasons based around a particular actress, actor, director, period or theme.

Commercial cinemas showing mostly major first runs are found all along the Champs-Élysées – you'll expect to pay a slightly higher price for your seat, and also on the *grands boulevards*, especially boulevard des Italiens. As in Britain, for a new, much-hyped blockbuster expect queues – somehow, miraculously, everyone nearly always gets in. The independents of the left bank, notably those in the Action chain, present a cross section of revivals from worldwide cinemas.

Programmes change on Wednesdays, the day that the weekly entertainment guides, like *Pariscope* (3f) which lists movies by category and *arrondissement*, are published.

Major cinema chains these days employ salaried personnel who no longer expect a tip, but elsewhere in smaller set-ups the ushers still rely totally on tips for their income – a couple of francs is about the decent minimum to give. Seat prices range from 35–45f with weekday discounts of approximately 10f for students and senior citizens at most venues – a few places also offer the *tariff reduit* at weekends too. Seats are cheaper by 30% at the majority of cinemas on Mondays. There are bargain matinées (around 25f) at certain cinemas, including the Forum Horizon, Forum Orient Express and Gaumont Les Halles in 1e; Racine and 14 Juillet Odéon in 6e; and the George V and Triomphe in 8e. Ardent cinema-goers, or long-term visitors, could invest in a magnetic debit card from UGC or Pathé for use only in their theatres – perks include savings on entry and priority admission.

Programmes are from 1pm onwards at many places and go on until late, with the last show usually starting at 10pm, or midnight on Friday and Saturday. The majority of places give a couple of starting times for each programme – the first, known as the *séance*, is kicking-off time for commercials and coming attractions and is only worth sitting through if you want to be sure of one of the best seats.

English language epics are shown at many of the smart Champs-Élysées establishments. Screens listed as *grande salle, salle prestige* or *Gaumont Rama* are worth watching out for – a large screen, highly respectable standards of seating, sound and projection are all guaranteed. A handful of other cinemas also show the latest offerings in English: the THX *Grande Salle* at Forum Horizon (1er), Max Linder Panorama (9e), Kinopanorama (15e).

Aside from the smart main cinemas of the Champs-Élysées, which you can't miss, here's a brief summary by *arrondissement* of some of the most interesting commercial cinemas:

1er

Forum Horizon
7 place de la Rotonde, Nouveau Forum des Halles. Tel. 45 08 57 57. M RER Châtelet-Les Halles.
Student reductions daily.
Six-screen, subterranean, air-conditioned centre where you can see the latest releases in the lap of luxury. The 600-seat *Grande Salle* THX is the showpiece, with the most expensive seats. Every day of the week, from 11.30am–1pm, there's a discount for the first show of the day. Midnight shows on Saturdays.

2e

Le Grand Rex
boulevard Poissonnière. Tel. 42 36 83 93. Mo Bonne-Nouvelle.
Student reductions 1–5pm, Tue–Fri. UGC debit card accepted.
Grand Rex is the city's largest cinema with 2800 seats. An enormous screen, and magnificent kitschy décor–complete with projected clouds wafting across the ceiling–make it a one-off. Should the feature film be being presented in Grand Large, you must sacrifice the comfy stall seats and take to the balcony since the management has installed a retractable huge screen that supercedes the proscenium screen. Mostly dubbed movies here. Late shows are on Friday and Saturday nights.

5e

Accatone
20 rue Cujas. Tel. 46 33 86 86. M Luxembourg/Cluny-La-Sorbonne.
Reduced price tickets 6pm, Mon–Fri.
Outward-looking repertory programming with varied selection of movies showing at this small screen 115-seater. Good specialised books on sale, smallish exhibition space.

Action
Mini-chain. This independent group has been keeping ciné addicts happy since its opening in 1967. Retrospectives are a speciality as are old movie classics. The flagship is Action Rive Gauche and there are three other screens in the 5e, four in the 6e, and the Mac-Mahon in the 17e. A free *carte de fidélité*, stamped each time you buy a ticket, entitles you to a sixth film free of charge for every five paid admissions. Action honours student ID cards 7 days a week.

Action Écoles
23 rue des Écoles. Tel. 43 25 72 07. M Maubert-Mutualité Cardinal-Lemoine.

Action Rive Gauche
5 rue des Écoles. Tel. 43 29 44 40. M Cardinale-Lemoine.
The flagship of the Action chain with 240 seats, panoramic screen and Dolby sound system.

Le Champo
51 rue des Écoles. Tel. 43 54 51 60. M Odéon St Michel.
Truffaut was one of the many fans of this cinema, which celebrated its fiftieth anniversary in 1989. Recently redecorated to pay tribute to the French comic Jacques Tati. Two small screen-rooms fill up fast for theme retrospectives.

Panthéon
13 rue Victor-Cousin. Tel. 43 54 15 04. M Luxembourg. Tickets reduced Mon–Fri. One-screen cinema with 229 seats, wonderful décor and Dolby stereo, showing art films.

Studio Galande
42 rue Galande. Tel. 43 54 72 71. M St Michel. Tickets reduced Mon–Fri.
Intimate 92-seater where you can see *The Rocky Horror Picture Show* from Thursday through to Sunday night, with an extra post-midnight show on Friday and Saturday evenings.

Studio des Ursulines
10 rue des Ursulines. Tel. 43 26 19 09. M Luxembourg Port-Royal.

The Blue Angel had its world première here in the city's oldest art house which opened on 21 January 1926.

6e

Action Christine
4 rue Christine and 10 rue des Grands-Augustins. Tel. 43 29 11 30. Odéon St Michel.
See Action Chain above.

Le Bretagne
73 boulevard Montparnasse. Tel. 42 22 57 97. M Montparnasse. Tickets 40f; reduced 30f Mon–Fri. Air-conditioned. The *Grande Salle* with 860 seats, a large screen and Dolby stereo, is a good place to catch the major releases, provided they're in VO.

Cosmos
76 rue de Rennes 75006. Tel. 45 44 28 80. M St Sulpice.
Large one-screen cinema specialising in Soviet films.

Lucernaire Forum
53 rue Nôtre-Dame-des-Champs. Tel. 45 44 57 34. M Nôtre-Dame-des-Champs.
Tickets reduced Mon–Fri.
Three small cinemas, consistently screening the best art films, which are part of an arts complex which also includes a couple of theatres, a bar, restaurant and gallery space.

St-André-des-Arts
30 rue St-André-des-Arts. Tel. 43 26 48 18 & 12 rue Gît-le-Coeur 75006. Tel. 43 26 80 25. M St Michel.
This complex is renowned for its stimulating, quality features shown in the medium-sized theatres.

St-Germain-des-Prés
place St-Germain-des-Prés. Tel. 42 22 87 23. M St-Germain-des-Prés.
Bargain show at noon; student reductions daily.
One decent-sized screen here with emphasis on the anti-new and re-releases.

Les 3 Luxembourg
67 rue Monsieur-le-Prince. Tel. 46 33 97 77. M Luxembourg Odéon.
Student reductions daily.
Three scruffy screening rooms but the movies make up for the lack of comfort.

7e

La Pagode
57 rue de Babylone. Tel. 47 05 12 15. M St François Xavier.

Early Screening

The tradition for movie-mania in the city goes back a long way. Back as far as 1895, in fact, which is when the Lumière brothers held an enormously successful public screening – the first ever at a cinema. A plaque at 14 boulevard des Capucines, 75001, marks the spot, almost opposite the place where, 2 decades earlier, the first Impressionist exhibition was held.

Tickets reduced Mon–Fri. *Salon de thé* open 4pm–10pm, Mon–Sat; 2pm–8pm, Sun.

The most beautiful and exotic cinema in Paris – and the only one left in this *arrondissement* – the Pagode was reconstructed at the turn of the century as a party place for one of the directors of the nearby department store, Bon Marché. (See 7e, page 417.) Most of it was actually shipped in from Japan. The wall panels of the *Grande Salle* are embroidered in silk, while golden dragons and elephants support the candelabra. It became a cinema in 1931 and in 1982 was declared a historical monument. If you don't want to see a movie, you can always have tea here.

8e

The *arrondissement*'s slick, well-equipped cinemas include the **Gaumont Ambassade** (Gaumont Rama), the **George V**, the **Pathé Marignan Concorde** and the **Publicis Élysées**. The large Balzac – the only cinema concentrating on "art" films in the area – is also comfortable and worth checking out.

9e

Max Linder Panorama

24 boulevard Poissonnière. Tel. 48 24 88 88. M Rue Montmartre Bonne Nouvelle.

This brilliantly equipped, air-conditioned cinema with a huge screen is one of the best places in town to catch the latest English language blockbuster.

11e

République Cinéma

18 faubourg du Temple.

Tel. 48 05 51 33. M République.

It has seen better days, but the 200-seat cinema is comfortable and has a fine selection of films showing in repertory.

13e

Escurial Panorama
11 boulevard du Port Royal. Tel. 47 07 28 04. M Gobelins.
Dandified establishment combining massive screen with VO.

14e

Recommended are the Gaumont Rama *salles* of the **Gaumont Alésia**
(73 avenue du Général-Leclerc), which sometimes show films in VO,
and the **Gaumont Parnasse** (82 boulevard du Montparnasse), which
always shows films in VO, both in this *arrondissement*.

Denfert
24 place Denfert-Rochereau. Tel. 43 21 41 01. M Denfert-Rochereau.
Tickets 34f, reduced to 25f daily. Wheelchair access.
Outstanding repertory programming at this 120-seater.

L'Entrepôt
7–9 rue Francis de Pressensé. Tel. 45 43 41 63. M Pernety.
Air-conditioned. Restaurant (open noon–midnight daily). Shop (open
2–8pm, Mon–Sat). Three screening rooms, each with 100 seats,
showing art films including imaginative retrospective.

15e

364 rue Lecourbe. Tel. 45 54 46 85. M Balard.
Two cinemas, the 130-seat Tribord and the 160-seat Babord, showing
a mixture of art and popular films.

Kinopanorama
60 avenue de La Motte-Piquet. Tel. 43 06 50 50. M La *Motte-
Piquet/Grenelle*.
Tickets reduced Mon–Fri, last two shows Sun. Air-conditioned.
This popular cinema has one of the widest screens in Paris, and 620
seats; tickets for 250 of them can be purchased up to three days in
advance for each show.

St Lambert
6 rue Péclet. Tel. 45 32 91 68/48 28 78 87. M Vaugirard.
Tickets reduced Mon–Fri (including under-18s).
A good selection of children's films, along with adult offerings, feature at
this family-run local cinema. And, unusually for Paris, seats are cheaper
for kids.

16e

Ranelagh

5 rue de Vignes. Tel. 42 88 64 44. M Muette.

Tickets 35f, reduced to 25f, Mon–Fri. Wheelchair access.

The only commercial cinema in the affluent 16e *arrondissement* showing movie classics and occasionally providing the venue for plays and concerts.

17e

Mac-Mahon

5 avenue Mac-Mahon. Tel. 43 29 79 89. M Étoile.

Traditional local which celebrated its 50 birthday in 1989 and is part of the Action chain, now just open for public screenings at weekends.

18e

Studio 28

10 rue Tholozé. Tel. 46 06 36 07. M Abesses, Blanche. Tickets reduced Wed–Fri; block of five tickets (valid 2 months).

The only VO cinema in the 18e and the least expensive place in town, this family-run theatre was started up in 1928 – hence the name. Bunuel's "L'Age d'Or" premièred here in 1930. Closed on Mondays and Tuesdays, and during most of August.

19e

La Géode

26 avenue Corentin-Cariou. Tel. 42 46 13 13. M Porte de la Villette.

OMNIMAX cinema in glorious geodesic dome (see 19e). Hourly shows run from 10am to 9pm, Tuesday through to Sunday. It's advisable to book and reservations are accepted. Buy a combination ticket for the film and the adjacent Science and Industry Museum.

Cinémathèques

Serious film buffs will enjoy the following venues where many movies are screened that wouldn't be shown commercially.

1er

Vidéothèque de Paris
2 Grand Galerie, Porte St Eustache, Forum des Halles. Tel. 40 26 34 30. M RER Châtelet-Les-Halles.
Stay as long as you like at the Vidéothèque for just 18f. It was opened in 1988 as a public archive of film and video documents on Paris. Screening rooms are named after the number of seats it contains. There's a café here too.

4e

Pompidou Centre – Salle Garance
Centre Pompidou. Tel. 42 78 37 29. M Rambuteau Hôtel de Ville.
The box office is at the back of the Pompidou Centre and the theatre itself is two flights up. Varied Programme.

16e

La Cinémathèque Française
Palais de Chaillot, place de Trocadéro (avenue Albert de Mun & avenue du Président Wilson). Tel. 47 04 24 24. M Trocadéro.
A remarkably varied selection of original language films with French subtitles shown daily from the archives. There are plans to open additional screening rooms at the nearby Palais de Tokyo in 1993, when the Cinémathèque's exceptional film reference library and stills collection will be under one roof.

Also in the Palais de Chaillot is the **Musée du Cinéma – Henri Langlois** (Tel. 45 53 74 39) Admission 20f. The designers of London's Museum of the Moving Image were inspired by this museum of cinemabilia. There are 90-minute guided tours in French at 10am, 11am, 2pm, 3pm, 4pm.

WHERE TO SHOP

If you live to shop, as opposed to shop to live, you'll be at home in Paris. So diverse and copious are the retail temptations that unless you walk around blindfolded you have to fight hard to trim expenditure to fit your credit limit. Should you be lucky enough to possess a few newly emancipated francs, then you'll be in the right place to blow the lot on the latest/smartest/best of whatever takes your fancy.

Giant emporia stuffed to the ceiling with consumer durables have their place, but it's the smaller specialist shops, the *bijoux* boutiques, the flea and fragrant food markets, that make shopping in Paris such a pleasure.

SHOPPER'S NOTES

DÉTAXE/EXPORT SCHEME

Value added tax (*TVA*) is levied on nearly all goods and services in France. Foreign visitors should ask for the *détaxe*, a refund, returnable on departure from the country with the purchases. Non-EEC residents may claim the refund if their buys total over 1200f; EEC residents may claim if purchases are over 2400f.

Obtain a *détaxe* form from the sales assistant. You then present this to French customs on departure where it will be officially stamped. You keep one copy and send the other back to the store. Allowing for the meanderings of bureaucracy you should receive the refund within 2 or 3 months. Large department stores will take it off your bill on the spot – you just have to take all your buys to the *détaxe* desk with your passport and plane ticket.

SALES

Some shops have sales when they feel like it but the biggest waves of sales fever hits every January and July. Watch for the word "*soldes*" plastered on windows.

OPENING HOURS

These vary according to season/type of shop. In most cases shops open on Saturday and may shut on Monday or at least open up slightly later. Food shops generally close later than others, often at 7-ish in the evening and open on Sunday and Bank Holiday mornings.

As a rule, all small shops close for an hour or two at or soon after midday; many close completely for up to a month July/August.

It's always worth ringing to check the opening times before setting off to visit a specific shop.

DEPARTMENT STORES AND DRUGSTORES

Department stores are useful things for visitors: you can avoid the one-to-one intimidating confrontation with snooty sales people; you can avoid practising your French – both **Printemps** and **Galeries Lafayette** distribute shopping guides to departments in English; the shops are great for browsing around if you don't know what you want, or good if you *do* know and want to find it quickly. Both Galeries and Printemps have multilingual hostesses to help confused shoppers orientate themselves.

Drugstores do have chemists but are less American-style drugstores than small shopping emporia. They stock books, fragrance, food, toys, videos, gifts, magazines, tobacco, and are open all hours.

Au Bon Marché: 22 rue de Sèvres 75007. Tel. 45 49 21 22. M Sèvres-Babylone. Open 9.30am–6.30pm, Mon–Sat; food department 9.30am–7.30pm.

Art Nouveau building houses the city's oldest department store

Shopping Areas

It's easy enough to wander from area to area and enjoy the shopping diversity of central Paris, but if you're in a hurry you might want to concentrate on particular districts with a density of shops.

On the right bank, the area around the Opéra has large department stores, with many clothing and jewellery shops in the surrounding streets. From Opéra to the Madeleine church, the shops and their merchandise become smarter. The most exclusive district for elegant fashion and luxury goods centres on the avenue Montaigne and the rue du Faubourg St Honoré. More affordable and trendier clothing is found in the boutiques of the Marais and the lively subterranean arcades of the Forum des Halles.

On the left bank you'll unearth all kinds of fascinating specialist shops. For fashionable, chic clothes, check out the boulevard St Germain and its neighbouring streets. This is also the epicentre of French publishing and you'll find a large number of bookshops.

To find everything under one roof, there's the vast shopping complex at the Palais de Congrès at 2 place de la Porte Maillot, 17e, or the eight-level Montparnasse-Maine centre near the enormous Tour Montparnasse skyscraper.

(founded 1852) with the largest food halls in Paris, excellent Oriental rugs (a specialist since 1871), good classic fashion and costume jewellery.

Au Printemps: 64 boulevard Haussmann 75009. Tel. 42 82 50 00. M Havre-Caumartin/Auber. Open 10am–7pm, Mon–Sat.

Largest fragrance department in town; the selection of cosmetics and womenswear (in the Nouveau Magasin) is particularly strong; good for bathing costumes – they stock just about every make. Stronger on menswear than Galeries, with one shop, Magasin Brummell, devoted to them. The store's turquoise dome is a historical monument: you can have lunch under it.

Bazar de l'Hôtel de Ville (BHV): 52–64 rue de Rivoli 75004. Tel. 42 74 90 00. M Hôtel de Ville. Open 9am–6.30pm Mon–Fri, 9am–10pm Wed, 9am–7pm Sat. Everything for the home; this is one of the largest hardware stores in the world, with a reputation for DIY equipment, garden tools, quality household and sporting goods. Also has a book and music department (stereo equipment, radios CDs and so on).

Galeries Lafayette: 40 boulevard Haussmann 75009. Tel. 42 82 34 56. M Chaussée d'Antin/Auber. Open 9.30am–5.45pm, Mon–Sat.

Also at Maine-Montparnasse Centre 75014. Tel. 45 38 52 87. M Monparnasse-Bienvenue. Open 9.15am–7.15pm, Mon–Sat.

Traditional, but not behind the times, with a good reputation as a fashion store: on the 1st and 2nd floors there's a wide choice of men's and women's well-known brands in individual boutiques. Superb lingerie department on 3rd floor of G.L. Haussmann. Strong on chic, arty clothes, sporting goods and togs, household items. Check out the Galeries own label wear "Galfa-Club".

Printemps and Galeries have their respective fans. Printemps claims to be the most "Parisian" store and some say it's slightly more upmarket, but then again, others give this accolade to Galeries. Both are wonders of Belle Époque architecture and have excellent views from their top floor terraces; both have convenient restaurants – five in the case of Galeries.

La Samaritaine: 75 rue de Rivoli 75001. Tel. 40 41 20 20. M Pont Neuf. Open 9.30am–7pm, Mon, Wed, Thur; 9.30am-8.30pm, Tue, Fri.

Four old enormous and imposing buildings of utilitarian thrills for trendies who come to buy *ouvrier's* overalls or uniforms with a matching gardener's *pannier*. Samaritaine was founded with the workman and his gear in mind and still has a huge range of goods at low or reasonable prices. Motto: "*On trouve tout à la Samaritaine.*" From the tenth floor of Magasin 2 there's a panoramic view of Paris. (NB: it's only open from April–September 9.30am–7pm, Mon–Sat; 9.30am–8.30pm, Tue and Fri.)

Monoprix and Prisunic
There are branches of these two stores all over Paris selling food, cosmetics, clothes, toiletries, stationery. Their clothes are cheap and used to be naff, but if you look carefully you can sometimes spot some well-designed bargains. Good buys for children, household items, undies, costume jewellery. A centrally-located Monoprix is at 21 avenue de l'Opéra. Open 9am–7pm, Mon–Sat.

The biggest Prisunics are on the corner of the avenue des Champs-Élysées (open 9am–midnight); 109 rue la Boétie and 56 rue de Caumartin. Open Mon–Sat, but times vary from branch to branch.

Marks and Spencer: 35 boulevard Haussmann 75009. Tel. 47 42 42 91. M Chausée d'Antin. Open 9.30am–6.30pm Mon, Wed–Sat.

Inexpensive baby and children's clothing, woollies, lingerie, scotch eggs, bacon, fresh egg and watercress sarnies.

Drugstore Élysées (Drugstore Publicis): 133 avenue des Champs-Élysées 75008. Tel. 47 23 54 34. M Charles-de-Gaulle-Étoile. Open 9am–2am, Mon–Sat; 10am–2am, Sun.

Drugstore Matignon: 1 avenue Matignon. Tel. 43 59 38 70. M Franklin D. Roosevelt. 10am–2am.

Drugstore St Germain: 149 boulevard St Germain 75006. Tel. 42 22 92 50. M St-Germain-des-Prés. Open 10am–2am.

MARKETS (NON-FOOD)

ANTIQUES

Prices tend to be on the high side but it doesn't cost you anything
to browse.

La cour aux Antiquaires: 54 rue du Faubourg St Honoré 75008. M
Concorde. Open Mon–Sat.

One of the smallest but smartest collections of antique shops selling
a variety of old and precious items, from icons to paintings.

Le Louvre des Antiquaires, 2 place du Palais 75001. M Palais Royal.
Open Tue–Sun.

Around 250 galleries or antique shops in a grand arcade. Exquisite
china, lamps, furniture, etc.

Village St Paul: off the rue St Paul and the rue Charlemagne 75004.
M St Paul. Open Thur–Mon.

Collection of antique shops in and around streets and courtyards of
the Southern Marais. Wide price range, but not flea market level.

Village Suisse: reached from the avenue de La Motte-Picquet or
the avenue de Suffren 75015. M La Motte-Picquet/Grenelle. Open
Thur–Sun.

Independent dealers with quality goods all opening up at different
hours to suit themselves.

On the left bank too, antique hunters head for **Carré Rive Gauche** where
there's a concentration of small dealers in the streets rue du Bac, de Lille,
Jacob and quai Voltaire.

BOOKS

Marché aux livres: parc Georges Brassens, rue Briançon 75015. Open
9.30am–6pm, Sat–Sun. M Porte de Vanves.

Antiquarian and second-hand books – be prepared to do some hard
bargaining.

Books and print stalls also line the riverside opposite the Ile de la Cité
and Ile Saint Louis. Bibliophiles should check out the following spots
in particular: **quais des Grands Augustins, Conti, Malaquais** in the 6e
(M St Michel); **quais de Louvre et Mégisserie** in the 1er (M Port Royal
Pont Neuf); **quai Voltaire** in the 6e (M rue-du-Bac).

FLOWERS, PLANTS & BIRDS

Plant and Pet Market: quai de la Mégisserie 75001. M Pont Neuf. Open 9am–6pm daily.

Marché aux Fleurs: place Louis-Lépine, Ile de la Cité, 75004. M Cité. Open 8am–4pm, Mon–Sat.

Marché aux Oiseaux: place Louis Lépine, Ile de la Cité, 75004. M Cité. Open 9am–7pm, Sunday. A bird market ousts the flower-sellers in place Louis Lépine on Sundays: both tame and wild birds, some extremely rare, most quite pricey. Other flower markets are beside the church in **place de la Madeleine** in the 8e (M Madeleine) and **place des Ternes** in the 17e (Mo Ternes). Both are open daily except Monday.

POSTCARDS

Marché aux Cartes Postales: corner boulevard Gambetta and rue Vaudetard, Issy-les-Moulineaux. M Corentin Cariou. Open 9.30am–7pm, Tue and Thur.
Old documents, coins, stamps, as well as postcards.

Marché aux Cartes Postales Anciennes: 3 rue Mabillon, marché St Germain 75006. M Mabillon. Open 11am–6pm, Wed.
Great selection of fine, faded old postcards.

STAMPS

Marché aux Timbres: cour Marigny 75008. M Champs-Élysées.
The stamp market is a philatelist's dream: buy sell or trade all day, Thursday, Saturday, Sunday, public holidays from 10am–6pm. Find it on the corner of avenue Marigny and avenue Gabriel overlooking the gardens at the bottom of the Champs-Élysées. The scores of stalls are run by licensed dealers and you'll find that prices vary enormously.

FLEA MARKETS (*Marché aux Puces*)

The golden rules are to go early – the dealers do – before the best buys have been grabbed. Flea markets don't yield the bargains they used to, but you never know your luck. Do remember to take your cash to the markets – cheques aren't particularly welcome and most probably won't be acceptable at all. There are lesser known fleas at **Porte de Vanves** and **Porte de Montreuil**, but the big one is just across the *périphérique* in the moribund suburb of **St Ouen**.

Marché d'Aligre place d'Aligre, 75012: M Ledru-Rolling. 9.30am–1pm daily. Closed Mondays.
Bric-à-brac, some clothes, jewellery, silver, silver-plate, books, glassware, old photos.

Marché aux Puces, Porte de Montreuil: 75020 M Porte de Montreuil. 6.30am–1pm, Sat, Sun, Mon.
Less choice but less touristy than Clignancourt. Antique clothing, odd bits of furniture. Old leather jackets and shoes are worth a second look.

Marché aux Puces, Porte de St Ouen: 75018 M Porte de Clignancourt or Porte de St Ouen. Between portes de St Ouen and de Clignancourt. 7.30am–7pm, Sat, Sun, Mon.
The famous Paris flea market (and the world's biggest) with 4 miles (6km) of crammed full stalls, selling everything from genuine junk to genuine good buys, but no longer at unbelievably cheap or unbeatable prices. Those adept at haggling will have the advantage: combine this knack with fast-fire French and you're on to a winner.
The market splits into various parts: there's a more authentic flea market atmosphere in the inner areas: ancient, antique and antiquated *objets* and collectibles, old accessories, clothes, glass. Marché Biron has more substantial, posher items; check out Marché Jules Valles for old books, curios, souvenirs.

Marché aux Puces Porte de Vanves: avenue Marc Saingnier 75014. M Porte de Vanves. Dawn–7pm, Sat, Sun.

Little of real value to be unearthed here, but persistent rummagers might pick up some interesting bric-à-brac; old, but not particularly collectable books, oddments of silver, china, postcards, pots, costume jewellery of the '40s and '50s. From October–March painters and sculptors display their work here on Sunday afternoons.

Marché St Pierre: rue Paul Albert 75018. M Anvers. Close to Sacré-Coeur. 9.30am–6.30pm, Mon–Fri.

Best textile bargains in Paris, both old clothes and furnishing fabrics, including household linen. Bargain shoes too.

Marché du Temple: Carreau du Temple 75003. M Hôtel de Ville. 9am–12noon, 2–7pm, Tues–Sat; 9am–1pm, Sun.

Not strictly a flea market but ensconced in a beautiful building where new clothes are sold at wholesale prices.

FOOD MARKETS

Good French meals begin at the best food markets. Every *quartier* has one, some are exceptional. Most local open air food markets are normally open for just a few days a week: the most likely day to find one closed (apart from Sunday) is Monday.

Good housekeepers appear just towards closing time at the end of a market day to sniff out any possible price reductions. On the other hand, of course, the choice is best first thing in the morning, from around 8am onwards. Markets usually bustle away till lunchtime then reopen around 4pm, to wind down 2^1/2 to 3^1/2 hours later.

A comprehensive free list of Parisian street markets, *Les Marchés de Paris*, is available from the Mairie de Paris (Tel. 42 76 49 61). Here are some of the best or best known:

Rue Cler (1e): from avenue de La Motte-Picquet to rue de Grenelle, M École Militaire.

Neat and proper streetmarket with quality foods – perfect picnic materials at the shops which lie behind the stalls too.

Rue de Seine/Buci (6e): M Odéon.

An animated, aromatic, food market stuffed into the centre of the Latin Quarter. Runny Brie, glossy fish, mounds of fruit and veg. On Sunday mornings there's background live music.

Marché d'Aligre (12e): M Ledru-Rollin.

A weekend market (and Monday mornings), un-touristy and inexpensive, with fruit, vegetables, meat and seafood. Stalls reflect the social and ethnic mixtures in the area. Mountains of chilli peppers, exotic fruit, bags of almonds and dried flowers. (See also **Fleamarkets** p.237.)

Marché rue Lepic (18e): M Blanche.

Runny Brie, pungent sausages; this is the place to pick up a picnic before clambering up the hill toward Montmartre. On Sunday, musicians provide entertainment while you and the locals shop in this long-established market.

Rue Mouffetard (5e): M Censier Daubenton/Monge.

At its most lively on a Saturday evening or Sunday morning, the food section starts a quarter of the way down this narrow, ancient street. La Mouffe is one of the oldest open air markets in Paris (reputedly there since the 14th century) and oozing *atmosphère*.

St Pierre (18e): rue Charles Nodier, M Anvers.

Big on textiles, but this market is also particularly cheap and has a wide selection of food, especially the exotic kinds.

WHERE TO BUY: A COMPLETE GUIDE

NB: where no opening hours are given, it's wise to phone before setting off to check.

BREAD

Ganachaud: 150–4 rue de Ménilmontant 75020. Tel. 46 36 13 82. M Gambetta. Open 7.30am–8pm Wed–Sat (2.30pm Tue, – 8pm, 7.30am–1.30pm Sun) Closed Monday

Much respected master baker Ganachaud produces some 30 types of bread from his huge wood-fired ovens; regional recipes are used; traditional cakes and pastries from all parts of France are also sold.

Poilâne: 8 rue du Cherche-Midi 75008. Tel. 45 48 42 59. M Sèvres-Babylone. Open 7.15am–8.15pm. Closed Sun. Also at 49 boulevard de Grenelle 75015. Tel. 45 79 11 49. M Dupleix.

In the land of the baguette, Lionel Poilâne is king, renowned for his huge round crusty loaves baked according to traditional methods and exported all over the place. In Paris, appreciative queues signpost his shops. Try the wholewheat bread with walnuts, the rye studded with raisins, heavenly butter brioches or rustic pastries.

CHARCUTERIE

There are hundreds of charcuteries in Paris and everyone has a favourite, but here are just a few:

Divay: 50 rue du Faubourg St Denis 75010. Tel. 47 70 06 86. M Strasbourg-St Denis. Open 7am–1.30pm, 4–7.30pm, Tue–Sat. Closed Sun pm, Wednesday pm.

Also at 4 rue Bayen 75017. Tel. 43 80 16 97. M Ternes. Open 7am–1.30pm, 3.30–7pm, Tue–Sat, Sun am.

Excellent value and quality: *foie gras* at 630f the kilo; tasty sausages; all meat smoked on the premises.

Goldenberg's: 7 rue des Rosiers 75004. Tel. 42 72 83 89. M St Paul. Open 10am–11pm.

A Parisian institution: Jewish deli and restaurant in heart of ancient Jewish quarter (see **Where to Eat**).

Mon Porc: 18 rue Cadet 75009. Tel. 48 24 65 95. M Cadet. Open 7.30am–1.30pm, 4–7.30pm, Tue–Sat; Sunday am. Closed Monday.

Some of the best prices in town for *foie gras* at 650f a kilo. Also cooked dishes, etc.

Villette Salaisons: 22 avenue Corentin Cariou 75019. Tel. 40 34 98 20. M Porte de la Villette. Open 6.15am–5.30pm, Mon–Fri.

Wide selection of goodies in this enormous shop, including parma ham, pizzas, quiches, salamis, also professional cooking utensils.

CHEESE

Androuët: 41 rue d'Amsterdam 75008. Tel. 48 74 26 93. M St Lazare. Open 10am–7pm, Tue–Fri.

Pierre Androuët (sound the *t*), *maître fromager*, is a Parisian institution, whose emporium sells nothing but cheese (and some wine), every known variety from cow, ewe and nanny. Upstairs is a cheesy restaurant (see **Where to Eat**).

Barthélémy: 51 rue de Grenelle 75007. Tel. 45 48 56 75. M Rue du Bac. Open 8.30am–1pm, 4–7.15pm, Tue–Fri; 8.30am–1.30pm, 3–7.15pm, Sat.

Purveyor of wonderful cheeses to celebs, the Presidential Élysée Palace and Harrods, Roland Barthélémy is one of the best *fromagers* you'll find. Farmhouse goat's cheese, fruity cantals, creamy camemberts, are just a few of over 300 varieties.

Marie-Anne Cantin: 12 rue du Champ de Mars 75007. Tel. 45 50 43 94. M École Militaire. Open 8.30am–1pm, 4–7.30pm, Tue–Fri; 8.30am–1pm, 3.30–7.30pm, Sat.

Traditional juice-provoking cheeses galore, aged in the shop's cellar and mostly farm-produced.

La Fromagerie Montorgueil: 32 rue Montorgueil 75001. Tel. 42 61 31 99. M Étienne Marcel/Les Halles. Open 5am–1pm, 4–7.30pm, Tue–Sat; 6am–1pm Sun.

A thriving wholesale business doesn't stop this supplier from selling cheeses to the public and at competitive prices. A variety of special offers are made at frequent intervals.

Maison du Fromage Radenac: Marché Beauveau, place d'Aligre 75012. Tel. 43 43 52 71. M Ledru-Rollin. Open 7.30am–1pm, 4–7.30pm, Tue–Sat; Sun am. Closed Sunday pm, Monday and throughout August.

Reasonably priced, exceptionally good cheeses from all over France. Almost 50 different kinds of goat's cheese.

CHOCOLATES AND CONFECTIONERY

Christian Constant: 26 rue du Bac 75007. Tel. 42 96 53 53. M Rue du Bac. Open 8am–8pm, Mon–Sat

Bitter chocolate freaks enjoy the low sugar content and purest ingredients used by this *pâtissier* who also happens to know a thing or two about chocolate.

Debauve et Gallais: 30 rue des Saints-Pères 75006. Tel. 45 48 54 67. M St-Germain-des-Prés. Open 10am–1pm, 2–7pm, Tue–Sat.

The shop itself is classified as being of historical interest and the chocs don't disappoint either. House specials are the dark chocolate crunchies.

Duc de Praslin: 44 avenue Montaigne 75008. Tel. 47 20 99 63. M Franklin D. Roosevelt.

A praline palace, plus other house chocs and confectionery dressed up in lavish wrappings; sweets from all over France.

Godiva: branches all over town – in the 1er, 6e, 8e, 9e, 16e, 17e – best to check the telephone directories for addresses.

Fans swear by them, others find they lack subtlety. *Chacun à son goût.*

La Maison du Chocolat: 225 rue du Faubourg St Honoré 75008. Tel. 42 27 39 44. M Ternes. Open 9.30am–7pm, Tue–Sat. at 52 rue François 1er 75008. Tel. 47 23 38 25.

Jean-Paul Belmondo and Carole Bouquet are amongst the celebs who enjoy the velvety, home-made, absolutely fresh chocolates from this supplier. Some say they're quite simply the best in town . . .

La Petite Fabrique: 12 rue St Sabin, 75011. Tel. 48 05 82 02. M Bastille. Open 10.30am–7.30pm, Mon–Sat.

Delicious, homemade, elegantly wrapped. Nougat and dark chocolate bars especially good.

Richart: 258 boulevard St Germain 75007. Tel. 45 55 66 00. M Solférino. Open 2–7pm Mon, 10am–7pm Tue–Sat.

Sublime, superfine chocs from a Lyon-based company.

COFFEE – see tea and coffee below

ICE CREAMS AND SORBETS

Berthillon: 31 rue St-Louis-en-L'Ile 75004. Tel. 43 54 31 61. M Pont Marie. Open 10am–8pm, Wed–Sun.

The most famous ice cream parlour in France. No need to remember the address – you can't miss the omnipresent long line of people queueing up on the tiny pavement whatever the weather, or season. Take your pick from 60 melt-in-the-mouth flavours of sorbets and ice creams.

Gelati: 45 rue Mouffetard 75005. Tel. 43 31 61 29. M Monge. Open noon–1am every day from 1 March until 31 October.

Home-made Italian ices with a particularly brilliant chocolate variety.

Romainville: 20 rue de Romainville 75019. Tel. 42 02 24 54. M Télégraph. Open 8.15am–1pm, 2–5pm, Tue–Sat.

Pâtisserie (passion fruit and strawberry tarts are delicious) as well as supplier of a wide variety of not expensive ices and sorbets.

Le Sorbet de Paris: 43 rue des Alouettes 75019. Tel. 42 49 35 83. M Buttes-Chaumont. Open 9am–7pm, Mon–Sat.

Sorbets at sensible prices and great ice cream made only with fresh cream and eggs. Jaded palates can wake up to the *Beaujolais nouveau* sorbet.

La Tropicale: 4 rue Jean du Bellay 75004. Tel. 43 29 82 79. M Pont Marie. Open 11am–midnight daily.

Date and nut, fig and cinnamon, sesame and banana ices; plus original, subtle sorbets – cream of cucumber, tomato and basil as well as tropical fruit flavours. Eat on the premises or take away.

PÂTISSERIE

Cador: 2 rue d'Amiral-de-Coligny 75001. Tel. 75 08 19 18. M Pont Neuf. Open 9am–7pm, Tue–Sun.

Monsieur Cador creates wonderful *petit Cador* (chocolate and orange peel short pastry).

Christian Constant: see **Chocolates** above.

Melting *Pont Royal* (sponge cake and hazelnut cream) and other impeccable confections.

Dalloyau: branches in the 6e, 8e, 15e (see telephone directory).

A famous Parisian *pâtisserie*, established in 1802, with acclaimed macaroons, mogador (chocolate sponge and mousse with rasberry sauce) and pear caprice (almond butter cake, mousse and slices of pear). Exquisite, expensive.

Lenôtre: branches in the 7e, 8e, 16e, 17e.

Legendary *pâtissier*; you won't forget his macaroons, *sablés*, Napoléons, fruit tartlets and desserts.

Lerch: 4 rue du Cardinal Lemoine 75005. Tel. 43 26 15 80. M Cardinal Lemoine. Open 7am–1.30pm, 3–7pm, Wed–Sun.

Tarts made with seasonal fresh fruits from cocktail size to big enough to fill 18 people. Reasonable prices. Also breads and Alsatian specialities.

Millet: 103 rue St Dominique 75007. Tel.45 51 49 80. M Solférino Open 9am–7pm, Tue–Sat; 8am–1.30pm, Sun.

Jean Millet has served as President of the National Association of French Pastry Chefs and is considered to be one of the best in town.

Le Moule à Gâteau: 111 rue Mouffetard 75005. Tel. 43 31 65 45. M Monge/Censier-Daubenton Open 8.30am–7.30pm, Mon–Sat; Sun am.

Typical, traditional *pâtisserie*. Savoury tarts can be bought by the slice – handy for picnics.

Peltier: 66 rue de Sèvres 75007 Tel. 47 34 06 62. M Sèvres-Babylon/Vaneau. Open 9.30am–7.30pm, Tue–Sat; 8.30am–7pm, Sun.

Another famous pâtisserie – Black Forest gâteau has never tasted so heavenly.

FOOD (Specialist)

A l'Olivier: 23 rue de Rivoli 75004. Tel. 48 04 86 59. M St Paul Hôtel de Ville. Open 9.30am–1pm, 2–7pm, Tue–Sat.

Walnuts, hazelnut, grape seed, pumpkin – if it's an oil, it'll be here, especially incomparable virgin olive oil.

Au Bon Marché: 38 rue de Sèvres 75007. Tel. 45 49 21 22. M Sèvres-Babylone. Open 8.30am–8.30pm, Mon–Sat.

The biggest gourmet supermarket in town.

Aux Cinq Continents: 75 rue de la Roquette 75011. Tel. 43 79 75 51. M Voltaire. Open 9.30am–1pm, 3.30–8pm, Mon–Sat; 9.30am–1pm, Sun.

Spices from all over the world.

Fauchon: 26 place de la Madeleine 75008. Tel. 47 42 60 11. M Madeleine. Open 9.45am–7pm, Mon–Sat.

One of the world's best known food shops – if it's delicious, it'll be here. Window displays are almost art and even the tins look tempting.

Faugais: 30 rue de la Trémoille 75008. Tel. 47 20 80 91. M Franklin D. Roosevelt.

Old-fashioned *épicerie* scented with freshly roasted coffee. Good selection of biscuits, oils, mustards, preserves.

Hédiard: 21 place de la Madeleine 75008. Tel. 42 66 44 36. M Madeleine. Open 9am–7.30pm, Mon–Sat.

Vintage sardines, cherry juice, rose petal jam, pistachio oil. Not a jaffa cake in sight, but the fresh fruit jellied candies are toothsome treats. Also other branches around town (see phone directory).

Herbier de Provence: 19 rue Daguerre 75014. Tel. 43 22 48 57. M Denfert-Rochereau. Open 10am–1pm, 4–7.30pm, Tue–Sat. Also at 25 rue de l'Annonciation 75016, Tel. 45 27 07 76.

Therapeutic and culinary herbs and spices dried and packed into pretty glass jars; also sold in bulk.

Izraël (*Le Monde des Épices*): 30 rue François-Miron 75004. Tel. 42 72 66 23. M St Paul. Open 9.30am–1pm, 2.30–7pm, Tue–Fri; 9am–7pm, Sat.

Exotic ingredients for all kinds of ethnic dishes: Turkish Delight, spices, cakes from South America, rice sold from massive sacks.

Maison de la Truffe: 19 place de la Madeleine, 75008.
M Madeleine. Open 9am–8pm, Mon–Sat.

The place for truffles (fresh when in season, November–April), otherwise dried or preserved. Other pricey gastronomic goodies sold here include smoked salmon, caviar, *foie gras.*

La Maison du Miel: 24 rue Vignon 75009. Tel. 47 42 26 70. M Madeleine Open 9.30am–7pm, Mon–Sat.

Over 30 kinds of honey in this turn-of-the-century honeypot.

A la Mère de Famille: 35 rue du Faubourg Montmartre 75009. Tel. 47 70 83 69. M Le Péletier. Open 7.30am–1.30pm, 3–7pm, Tue–Sat.

Traditional French delicatessen founded round 1761; the interior dates from the 1900s and still has the wooden display stands with enamel labels and a richly patterned tiled floor carrying the name of the shop. Multi-coloured rows of perfect home-made jams, as well as *bons-bons*, make good presents; prices are very reasonable considering the excellent quality.

Soirée Gourmande: 16 boulevard Richard-Lenoir 75011. Tel. 43 38 99 11. M Bastille.

Posh nosh for the discerning palate at some of the best prices you'll find in town.

Soleil de Provence: 6 rue du Cherche-Midi 75006. Tel. 45 48 15 02. M St Sulpice. Open 9.30am–7pm, Tue–Sat.

Fragrant dried herbs, honeys, oils, mild olive oil soap: a ray of Provençal sunshine.

La Table d'Italie: 69 rue de Seine 75006. Tel. 43 54 34 69. M Mabillon.

Excellent fresh pasta as well as less obvious Italian culinary delights.

Than Binh: 29 place Maubert 75005. Tel. 43 28 81 65. M Maubert-Mutualité. Open 9am–7pm, Tue–Sun. Also at 18 rue Lagrange 75005. Tel. 43 54 66 11.

Oriental delicacies – swallows' nests, soybean curds, etc.

TEA AND COFFEE

Brûlerie Maubert: 3 rue Monge 75005. Tel. 46 33 38 77. M Maubert-Mutualité. Open 9am–1pm, 3–7.15pm, Tue–Sat; 10am–1pm, Sun. Also at 14 rue des Poissonniers 75008. Tel. 46 06 01 57. M Château Rouge.

Reasonable prices, good choice of coffees, teas, English jams.

Cafés Méo: 95 rue St Lazare 75009. Tel. 48 74 36 77. M St Lazare. Open 8am–7pm, Tue–Sun; 2–7pm Mon.

Low prices for freshly roasted coffee and a choice of around 40 teas. Also branches in the 4e, 10e and 14e (see telephone directory).

Maison des Colonies: 47 rue Vieille du Temple 75004. Tel. 48 87 98 59. M St Paul.

Also at 26 rue Beautreillis 75004. Tel. 42 77 92 27. M St Paul. Both open 9am–7pm, Tue–Sun.

A selection of 13 different coffees from around the world, a dozen teas, cookies, jams. Also branches in the 15e and 17e.

Mariage Frères: 30–32 rue du Bourg-Tibourg 75004. Tel. 42 72 28 11. M Hôtel de Ville. Open 11am–7.30pm, Tue–Sun.

The place to buy green tea from Japan, white tea from China – over 300 different varieties from 30 countries, plus an assortment of teapots in all shapes and sizes, and various tea jams. Mariage Frères was founded in 1854 and still has its colonial wood-panelled counter and antique tea chests. Also *salon de thé*.

Verlet: 256 rue St Honoré 75001. Tel. 42 60 67 39. M Palais Royal. Open 9am–7pm, Mon–Fri.

Around 50 kinds of tea and a score of coffee blends in this little café/roasting shop. From midday you may sit and sample on the spot some of the remarkable blends before deciding on which to buy. Owner Pierre Verlet will always customise a blend for you if you can't make up your mind.

WINE

Cave de Beaugrelle: 11 rue du Théâtre 75015. Tel. 45 79 96 19. M Charles Michels. Open 10am–1pm, 3–8pm, Mon–Sat; also Sun am.

Come here for drinkable, everyday *vin de pays* from the Côtes du Ventoux (12.50f per litre for Ventoux rouge AOC). Agreeable bottled wines too and even the champagne is cheap at 85f (100f for rosé).

Cave de la Madeleine: cité Berryer, 25 rue Royale 75008. Tel. 42 65 92 40. M Madeleine. Open 9am–7pm, Mon–Fri; 10am–2pm, Sat.   This small mews is the domain of Englishman Steven Spurrier, who has built up a name and loyal following for well-chosen clarets and burgundies, as well as his exclusive own label champagne.

Club Amical du Vin Jean Christophe Estève: 10 rue de le Cerisaie 75004. Tel. 42 72 33 05. M Bastille. Open 9.30am–12.30pm, 2.30–7.30pm Tue–Sat.

Some tantalising buys, especially from the south-west, for under 50f a bottle; tastings and discussions are held on Saturdays.

Divinord: 10 rue Morice 92 Clichy. Tel. 47 30 30 56. M Mairie de Clichy. Open 10am–7pm, Tue–Sat.

Take a car – they deal only in Bordeaux and sell by case or half case. There's always a good range of cheap quaffable wine and special offers at discounts of 10%.

Hédiard: 21 place de la Madeleine 75008. Tel. 42 66 44 36. M Madeleine. Open Mon–Sat, 9.15am–7.30pm.

The famous gourmet's delight also has an excellent cellar so if you like the wine you drink in the upstairs restaurant, you can buy a bottle in the shop.

Legrand: 1 rue de la Banque 75002. Tel. 42 60 07 12. M Bourse. Open 8.30am–7.30pm, Tues–Sat.

Also at 12 galerie Vivienne 75002. M Bourse.

Behind the picturesque exterior is an oenophile's delight; great wines, good advice, and reasonably priced, little-known finds. Wine-tastings held on Saturdays, except July–August.

Nicolas: over 30 shops throughout greater Paris.

Since 1822 Parisians have counted on their neighbourhood branch of Nicolas for quality and value for money. They're generally open from 9am–1pm, 3–7pm, Tues–Sat. Closed Sun pm. Mon.

KITCHEN EQUIPMENT, HOUSEHOLD ACCESSORIES, CHINA, GLASS, SILVER ETC.

Au Bain Marie: 8 rue Boissy d'Anglas 75008. Tel. 42 66 59 74. M Concorde. Open 10am–7pm, Mon–Sat.

Superb collection of new or well-preserved china and porcelain, linens, tableware.

Baccarat: 30 bis rue de Paradis 75010. Tel. 47 70 64 30. M Château d'Eau. Open 9am–6pm, Mon–Fri; 10am–12.30pm, 2–6pm, Sat.

Huge showroom and shop showing off the prestigious glassware, vases, chandeliers, tableware. Also museum.

Christofle: 12 rue Royale 75008. Tel. 42 60 34 07. M Madeleine. Open 9.30am–7pm, Mon–Sat.

Top of the range silverplate – everything from escargot forks to fruit knives. Modern and retro designs on vases, champagne buckets and so on. Also branches in 2e, 6e, 16e.

Dehillerin: 8 rue Coquillière 75001. Tel. 42 36 53 13. M RER Châtelet-Les Halles. Open 8am–12.30pm, 2–6pm, Mon–Sat.

Great and aspiring chefs come to this 150-year-old shop for their *batterie de cuisine*: every imaginable kitchen utensil.

Lalique: 11 rue Royale 75008. Tel. 42 65 33 70. M Madeleine. Open 9.30am–12 noon, 2–6pm, Mon–Sat.

One of the world's foremost crystal manufacturers. Vases with flowered motifs, boxes, bottles etc – all little works of art.

Limoges – Unic: 12 and 58 rue de Paradis 75010. Tel. 47 70 54 49. M Château d'Eau. Open 10am–6.45pm, Mon–Sat.

No. 58 has more down-to-earth range of tableware; no. 12 is where to find the prestigious porcelain, as well as Lalique crystal, Chistofle silverware.

La Table Royale: 23 rue Vauvenargues 75018. Tel. 42 26 13 10. M Guy Moquet. Open 10.30am–12.30pm, 1.30–7pm, Tue–Sat.

Cut-price china outlet from famous manufacturers, plus glassware, silver-plated ware at discount prices.

Villeroy et Boch: No. 58 Usines Center, Paris Nord 11, 95 Gonesse. Tel. 48 63 25 23. RER Parc des Éxpositions. Open 11am–7pm, Mon–Fri; 10am–8pm, Sat, Sun.

End of line outlet with prices up to 50% below normal retail.

BOOKS

Albion: 13 rue Charles V 75004. Tel. 42 72 50 71. M Sully-Morland St Paul. Open 2–7pm, Mon; 9.30am–7pm, Tue–Sat.

Discounts offered in October (for the college *rentrée*) at this English bookshop.

Artcurial: 9 avenue Matignon 75008. Tel. 42 99 16 19. M Franklin D. Roosevelt. Open 10.30am–7.15pm, Mon–Sat.

Wonderful bookshop on three levels, the best of its type – specialising in art, architecture and design – in Paris, with over 10,000 titles, French and foreign. Also exhibition space, gallery, giftshop, lithographs and posters at regular prices.

Attica: 34 rue des Écoles 75005. Tel. 43 26 09 56. M Maubert-Mutualité. Open 2–7pm, Mon; 10am–1pm, 2–7pm, Tue–Sat.

American literature English books sold for the same price as in Britain.

Attica 2: 84 boulevard St Michel 75005. Tel. 46 34 16 30. M St Michel. Open 2–7pm Mon; 10am–1pm, 2–7pm Tue–Sat.

Videos, language tapes, dictionaries.

Attica Junior: 23 rue Jean-de-Beauvais 75005. Tel. 46 34 62 03. M Maubert-Mutualité. Open 2–7pm, Mon; 10am–1pm, 2–7pm, Tue–Sat.

Children's books in English, as well as teaching programmes.

Brentano's: 37 avenue de l'Ópera 75002. Tel. 42 61 52 50. M Pyramides Opéra. Open 10am–7pm, Mon–Sat.

An institution in the Opéra *quartier*, this Anglo-American bookstore also carries a sizeable selection of French titles.

Chambre Claire: 14 rue St Sulpice 75006. Tel. 46 34 04 31. M Odéon. Open 11am–7pm, Tue–Sat.

Books on photography in French and other languages.

FNAC *Librairie International*, 71 boulevard Saint Germain 75006 Tel. 44 41 31 50. M Cluny/Sorbonne/Maubert-Mutualité. Open 10am–8pm, Mon–Sat.

Opened in October 1991 on the site of the former Cluny theatre and cinema, this 1000 square metre bookshop on three floors carries no French books at all. Instead there are some 70,000 titles in English, German, Italian, Spanish, Portuguese, Dutch and many other languages. Thematic strengths from different countries are brought out: children's books from the UK, management books from the USA, art books from Italy. FNAC have book departments in 28 upmarket stores in France and are now the country's largest bookseller.

La Hune: 170 boulevard St Germain 75006. Tel. 45 48 35 85. M St Germain-des-Prés. Open 2–11.45pm, Mon; 10am–11.45pm, Tue–Fri; 10am–7.15pm, Sat.

Worth popping in as you come out of Les Deux Magots or the Flore to inspect this intellectually heavyweight book shrine.

Galignani: 224 rue de Rivoli 75001. Tel. 42 60 76 07. M Concorde. Open 9.30am–7pm, Mon–Sat.

Along with its near neighbour W.H. Smith, it supplies mostly English and American books. Established in 1800, this claims to be the "oldest bookstore on the continent".

Marais Plus: 20 rue des Francs Bourgeois 75001. Tel 48 87 01 40. M St Paul. Open 9am–midnight, Mon–Sat; 9am–7pm, Sun.

Tea room-cum-bookshop where you may both browse and brunch (Sat/Sun around 90f) or enjoy a light dinner (eg 40f for a slice of savoury tart with *crudités*). Large selection of books on Paris and intelligent books for children, plus beautiful to look at art books and lots of pretty or funny *objets*.

Mots et Merveilles: 7 boulevard de Port Royal 75013. Tel. 47 07 25 21. M Gobelins. Open 10am–1pm, 2–7pm, Tue–Sat.

Taped editions of over 2000 French titles (plays, stories etc.) and novelty postcards with Parisian sound effects on one side and with one side blank for you to record your own message.

NQL International: 18 boulevard St Michel 75006. Tel. 43 26 42 70. M RER Port Royal. Open 10am–7pm, Mon–Sat.

Bookshop specialising in foreign work including good choice of English (80%) paperbacks, dictionaries and so on. NQL stands for *Nouveau Quartier Latin*.

Shakespeare and Co: 37 rue de la Bûcherie 75005. Tel. 43 26 96 50. M St Michel. Open noon–midnight daily.

Literary landmark selling new/secondhand titles, with English library and reading room. (See also page 372, in the section on the 5e.)

W.H. Smith: 248 rue de Rivoi 75001. Tel. 42 60 37 97. M Concorde. Open 9.30am–7pm, Mon–Sat.

Over 8000 American and British titles; special subscription service too.

Le Verre et l'Assiette: 1 rue du Val-de-Grâce 75005. Tel. 46 33 45 96. M RER Port Royal. Open 2–7pm, Mon; 10am–2.30pm, 2–7pm, Tue–Sat.

Foodies are at home here–a great selection of gastronomy and wine titles, books on dietetics, children's books.

RECORD, TAPES, CDS.

FNAC: Forum des Halles, Pierre-Lescot entrance, 2nd level 75001. Tel. 40 41 40 00. M Châtelet/RER Châtelet-Les Halles

Also FNAC Étoile, 26 avenue de Wagram 75008. Tel. 47 66 52 50. M Charles-de-Gaulle-Étoile/Ternes FNAC Montparnasse, 136 rue de Rennes 75006. Tel. 49 54 30 30. M St Placide Montparnasse-Bienvenue; FNAC Défense, 2 place de la Défense 92 Puteaux. Tel. 46 92 29 00. RER Défense.

Well-known, popular discount store with brilliant selection of CDs (approx 80f) records, books, videos, concert tickets as well as TV, hi-fi, cameras.

Virgin Megastore: 52–60 avenue des Champs-Élysées 75008. Tel. 40 74 06 48. M Franklin D. Roosevelt. Open 10am-midnight, Mon–Sat; noon-midnight, Sun.

The latest of all genres in every format: CDs, tapes, videos etc. Stunning Parisian version of the British Virgin record stores. Prices are about the same as you'll find at FNAC (above).

SHOES

Carel: 22 avenue de Champs-Élysées 75008. Tel. 45 62 30 62. M Franklin D. Roosevelt. Open 11am–7pm, Mon; 10am–7pm, Tue–Sat.
Fashionable and good quality shoes.

Colisée de Sacha: 64 rue de Rennes 75006. Tel. 40 49 02 13. M St-Germain-des-Prés. Open 10.30am–7.30pm, Mon–Sat.
Fashionable, fun women's shoes. Also branches in the 2e and 17e.

Maud Frizon: 83 rue des Saint-Pères 75006. Tel. 42 22 06 93. M St-Germain-des-Prés.
Also at 7 rue de Grenelle 75007. See below too.
Imaginatively bebowed and buttoned sophisticated women's shoes, but at designer prices.

Miss Maud: 21 rue de Grenelle 75007. Tel. 45 48 64 44. M Sèvres-Babylone.
As above but at gentler prices.

Charles Kammer: 4 place des Victoires 75001. Tel. 42 36 31 84.
Haute shoe craft from the classical to fantastical for men and women.

Stéphane Kélian: 13 bis rue de Grenelle 75007. Tel. 42 22 93 03. M Sèvres-Babylone. Open 10.30am–7pm, Mon–Sat.
Wearable, comfortable, fashionable – if only the prices were more bearable. Smart pumps from around £95 a pair. Other branches in the 8e, 3e, 2e 16e.

Robert Clergerie: 46 rue Croix-des-Petits-Champs 75001. Tel. 42 61 49 24. M Bourse.
5 rue du Cherche-Midi 75006. Tel. 45 48 75 47. M Sèvres-Babylone.
Classic but chic and supremely comfortable styles for men and women in fine leathers from £90 a pair. Also at the Au Printemps store.

ACCESSORIES, LEATHER GOODS, LUGGAGE, COSTUME JEWELLERY: A MIXED BAG OF BARGAINS AND BEST BUYS

Accessoires à Soie: 21 rue des Acacias 75017. Tel. 42 27 78 77. M Argentine. Open 10.30am–2pm, 3–7.30pm, Mon–Sat.
Silk accessories (ties, throws) for men and women at very reasonable prices. Cashmere, presents, plus bargain box.

Agatha: Trendy chain specialising in good quality costume jewellery, watches, accessories, from 150f–1500f. The perfect compromise between a *BCBG* style and too way out.

Several shops, including ones at 1 rue Pierre Lescot 75001. Tel. 40 39 92 88. M Les Halles. Open 10.30am–7.30pm, Mon–Sat. 97 rue de Rennes 75006, Tel. 45 48 81 30. M St Placide. 12 rond-point des Champs-Élysées 75008. Tel. 43 59 68 68. M Franklin D. Roosevelt.

La Bagagerie: 41 rue du Four 75006. Tel. 45 48 85 88. M St-Germain-des-Prés. Also in the 8e, 15e, 16e. Open 10.15am–7pm, Mon–Sat.

Youthful shops selling purses, folding bags and travel bags to suit all tastes and budgets, in various colours and materials.

Bon Chic-Bon Prix: 4 place d'Estienne d'Orves 75009. Tel. 40 16 42 73. M Trinité. Open 10am (12.30pm Mon)–7pm, Mon–Sat.

Designer leather goods and accessories at bargain prices in this little boutique. Bags by Balmain, Cardin, Enny, Lapidus around 30% cheaper.

Didier Ludot: 23–4 galerie Montpensier 75001. Tel. 42 96 06 56. M Palais Royal. Open 11am–2pm, 3–7pm, Mon–Fri; 11am–1pm, 2–7pm, Sat.

Deluxe second hand leather goods shop selling lovingly reconditioned designer bags (Hermès Céline, Cartier, Morabito). Also suitcases, surgical bags. Mind you, some of the prices make you wonder what they'd have cost when new.

Fabrice: 33 and 54 rue Bonaparte 75006. Tel. 43 26 57 95. M St-Germain-des-Prés. Open 10am (11.30am at no. 33)–7pm, Mon–Sat.

Sophisticated modern costume jewellery using leather, wood, metal, shells, silk. Prices from about £50.

Georges: 104 rue St Maur 75011. Tel. 43 57 21 59. M St Maur. Open 10.30am–7pm, Tue–Sat.

Wholesaler offering discounts of 30–40% below retail prices on a huge stock of bags and small leather goods. Repair work undertaken too. There's another branch in the 18e.

Gucci: 2 rue du Faubourg St Honoré 75008. Tel. 42 96 83 7. M Concorde. Open 9.30am–6.30pm, Mon–Sat.

Three floors of chic and snobby Gucci, the Italian counterpart to Louis Vuitton; gift items under 500f.

Hermès: 24 rue du Faubourg St Honoré 75008. Tel. 42 65 21 60. M Concorde Madeleine. Open 10am–1pm, 2.15–6.30pm, Tue–Fri.

Classic silk squares, power ties, fine leather goods.

Jack Gomme: 12 rue Rochebrune 75011. Tel. 40 21 06 43. M St Ambroise. Open 10am–1pm, 2–7pm, Mon–Sat.

Not the easiest place to find, but worth seeking out for its fashionable and original stock of belts, bags, braces, backpacks in various materials.

Marie Mercié: 56 rue Tiquetonne 75002. Tel. 40 26 60 68. M Étienne Marcel. Open 11am–7pm, Mon–Sat.

In a boutique that resembles an old-fashioned millinery shop, Marie Mercié sells her handmade hats which are priced from 250f upwards, many costing around the 500f mark.

Monic: 5 rue des Francs Bourgeois 75004. Tel. 42 72 39 15. M St Paul. Open 10am–7pm (2pm Sun).

Around 10,000 pieces of costume jewellery ranging in price from 1f to 10,000f, and you can pick up costume pieces by Dior, Ricci, Saint Laurent at prices which are 30% below those seen elsewhere. Enormous stock of earrings from 35f a pair.

Paloma Picasso: 5 rue de la Paix 75002. Tel. 42 86 02 21. M Opéra. Open 10am–7pm, Mon–Sat.

Striking accessories, porcelain, crystal, stockings, red signature lipstick and scent.

Philippe Model: 33 place du Marché St Honoré 75001. Tel. 42 96 89 02. M Pyramides. Open 10.30am–7.30pm, Mon–Sat.

Caroline of Monaco is a fan of this milliner's extravagant creations – spectacular fantasy hats, gloves with crenellated edges, witty shoes and costume jewellery. Set aside at least £150 spending money. Boxy purses are 2500f.

Prélude: 135 rue de Sèvres 75006. Tel. 43 06 62 90. M Duroc. Open 10.45am–7pm, Mon–Sat.

Friendly staff at this marvellous little shop selling discontinued lines at discount prices. Gloves, silk scarves and ties, handbags by Cardin, Balmain and Lanvin. Assorted leather accessories at half price. (Also branches in the 14e and 15e.)

Sidonis: 42 rue de Clignancourt 75018. Tel. 42 57 77 38. M Château Rouge. Open 10am–7.15pm, Tue–Sat.

A patient rummage could unearth a bargain here – a Balenciaga or Nina Ricci bag from 325f or an Art Deco-style handbag for 579f; also belts, brollies, silk neckerchiefs, pretty hats (200–330f), and gloves at reasonable prices.

Toumain: 56 rue de Lancry 75010. Tel. 42 03 63 22. M République Jacques Bonsergent. Open 9am–7pm, Tue–Sat.

Studio-cum-boutique selling costume jewellery; '30s-style brooches 50–60f, earrings 120–150f, in gold and silver-plated brass and other materials.

Louis Vuitton: 57 avenue Montaigne, or 78 bis avenue Marceau 75008. Tel. 47 20 47 00 (for both). M Franklin D. Roosevelt.

Ultimate range of show-off luggage to impress at impressively high prices.

CLOTHES SHOPPING: HIS AND HERS

Agnès B: 2–6 rue du Jour 75001. Tel. 45 08 56 56. M RER Châtelet-Les Halles. Open 10.30am–7pm, Mon–Sat.

Also at 13 rue Michelet 75006. Tel. 46 33 70 20 (women); and at 17 avenue Pierre 1er de Serbie 75008. Tel. 47 20 22 44 (women) and at number 25. Tel. 47 23 36 69 (men).

Simple, chic classics – you'll find perfect T-shirts, skirts or shirts. Clothes for men, women and children in stylish adjoining shops at one end of the tiny rue du Jour.

Alain Figaret: 21 rue de la Paix 75002. Tel. 42 65 04 99. M Opéra. Open 10am–7pm, Mon–Sat.

Also at 14 rue Marboeuf 75008; 99 rue de Longchamp 75016.

Thousands of men's shirts in hundreds of fabrics (some exclusive).

Apostrophe: 54 rue Bonaparte 75006. Tel. 43 54 91 73/43 29 08 38. M St Germain-des-Prés.

Also at 93 rue du Faubourg St Honoré 75008. Tel. 42 66 30 35. M St-Philippe-du-Roule; 24 rue Cambon 75001. Tel. 42 61 50 81. M Concorde.

Fashionable, but not outrageously so, quality clothes for women. Moderately high to expensive prices (eg 1400–1600f for smart skirt/pants).

Benetton: Forum des Halles, niveau 375001. Tel. 40 39 95 10. M RER Châtelet-Les-Halles. Other branches of this popular chain in the 6e, 8e and 16e.

Biba: 18 rue de Sèvres 75006. Tel. 45 48 89 18. M Sèvres-Babylone. Open 2–7pm, Mon; 11am–7pm, Tue–Sat.

Odette Baché, who owns this shop, stocks the work of young *créateurs* (designers). Names to look for are Sophie Sitbon, Corinne Cobson, Yorke and Cole, Myrène de Prémonville. She also sells her own label perfectly-cut grey flannel suits (1950f).

Blanc Bleu: 6 boulevard de Sébastopol 75003. Tel. 42 77 59 59. M Châtelet.

Also at 189 rue de la Pompe 75016. Tel. 47 27 21 03. M Victor-Hugo; also in Galeries Layfayette.

Relaxed togs: jogging pants, sweaters, sweatshirts, T-shirts (see also below).

B.B. Stock: 12 rue du Bourg l'Abbé 75003. Tel. 42 72 80 80. M Réamur-Sébastopol. Open 9.45am–7pm, Mon–Fri; 11am–7pm, Sat.

Slight seconds and previous season's collection of Blanc Bleu wear at reduced prices, with discounts averaging 20–50%. Adult sweatshirts from 129–379f, tee shirts 89–179f. Also rucksacks and children's clothes to fit 4–14 years.

Browns: 182 boulevard St Germain 75006. Tel. 45 44 49 76. M St-Germain-des-Prés. Open 12 noon–7pm, Mon; 10.30am–7pm, Tue–Sat.

Prêt-à-porter wear from young designers; British clothes for men.

Cacharel: 51 rue Étienne Marcel 75001. Tel. 42 21 13 13. M Sentier;
Also at 34 rue Tronchet 75008. Tel. 47 42 12 61. M Havre-Caumartin; and shop for men at 5 place des Victoires 75001. M Étienne Marcel.

Classic, but not fogey, quality clothes that don't date; mid-price range. (see also Cacherel stock in **Bargain Clothing** section.)

Chantal Thomas: 11 rue Madame 75006. Tel. 45 49 41 29. M St Sulpice.
Also at 5 rue du Vieux Colombier 75006. Tel. 45 44 60 11. M St Sulpice; 12 rond point des Champs-Élysées 75008. Tel. 43 59 87 34. M Franklin D. Roosevelt.

Feminine, beguiling designer wear.

Chipie: 16 rue du Four 75006. Tel. 46 34 62 32. M Mabillon; 31 rue de la Ferronerie 75001. Tel. 45 08 58 74. M Châtelet.

Qualité, drôlerie: ie quality and fun, is the motto here; Chipie unisex and kid's jeans, jean-jackets, T-shirts are best sellers – not the cheapest, but they wear well.

Claudie Pierlot: 23 rue du Vieux Colombier 75006. Tel. 45 48 11 96. M St Sulpice/Sèvres-Babylone.
Also at 4 rue du Jour 75001. Tel. 42 21 38 38. M RER Châtelet-Les-Halles; and at Au Printemps, boulevard Haussmann 75009.

Classic quality women's basic fashion buys to coordinate with more adventurous additions to the wardrobe. Claudie Pierlot's biggest fans are 16-year-olds and their *BCBG* grandmothers.

Comme des Garçons: 40–2 rue Étienne Marcel 75002. Tel. 42 33 05 21. (women). Tel. 42 36 91 54 (men). M Bourse Étienne Marcel. Open 11am–7pm, Mon–Sat.

Men's wear at no. 40 (suits 75,000f, shirts 700–200f) shoes, accessories; women's shop at no. 42 (dresses and blouses from 2000f) minimal décor, minimum colours; Japan's Rei Kawakubo is one of the big names and the prices match the reputation.

Cowboy Dream: 16 and 21 rue de Turbigo 75001. Tel. 42 36 30 05. M Étienne Marcel. Open 9.30am–7.30pm, Mon–Sat.

Huge selection of western-syle clothes and accessories.

Creeks: 98 rue St Denis 75001. Tel. 42 33 81 70. M Étienne Marcel. Open 11am–7.30pm, Mon; 10.30am–7.30pm, Tue–Sat.   Philippe Starck was the architect responsible for the stainless steel shop-front concealing three floors of informal wear for men and women. Creeks jeans from 300f, bikers' jackets from 1500f. Check out the top floor for avant-garde threads for the female form. There are several other branches in the 6e and one in the 5e.

Daniel: 44 and 68 rue St Antoine 75004. Tel. 42 78 65 70/42 74 04 68. M St Paul.

Famous names sportswear for men at a discount – jeans from 300f. Parisian sources tell us this is where Bruce Springsteen buys his jeans when he's in town. Also branches in the 5e and the 12e.

Daniel Hechter: 146 boulevard St Germain 75006. Tel. 43 26 96 36. M Mabillon.

Classic well-cut casual and sportswear for men, women and children. Also branches at the 1er and 16e.

Dorothée Bis: 17 rue de Sèvres 75006. Tel. 42 22 00 45. M Sèvres-Babylone.

Also at 10 rue Tronchet 75008. Tel. 47 42 60 82. M Madeleine. Open 10am–7pm, Mon; 10am–7pm, Tue–Sat.

Mix and match inventive clothes in colours ranging from bright to sober (women only). Also branches in Forum des Halles.

Elisabeth de Senneville: 3 rue de Turbigo 75001. Tel. 42 33 90 83. M Étienne Marcel. Open 10.45am–7.15pm, Mon–Sat.

Also at 55 rue Bonaparte 75006. Tel. 46 33 57 90.

Big shop with departments for women and children to showcase talents of an innovative designer famous for adventurous yet practical clothes at not exorbitant prices.

Equipment: 46 rue Étienne Marcel 75002. Tel. 40 26 17 84. M Bourse. Open 1.30–7pm, Mon; 10.30am–7pm, Tue–Sat.

Top quality, roomy shirts for men and women; cotton from 550f, washed silk 950f.

Érès: 2 rue Tronchet 75008. Tel. 47 24 24 55. M Madeleine.

High fashion, state-of-the-art swimming costumes – at a price.

Et Vous: 62–6 rue de Rennes 75006. Tel. 45 48 56 93. M St Sulpice. Open 10.30am–7.30pm, Mon–Sat.

Also at 15 rue des Francs-Bourgeois 75004. M St Paul; Galeries Lafayette 75009. M Opéra.

Smart jeans, khaki trousers from 380f, quality chambray shirts from 550f, leather belts and Western-inspired nostalgia costume.

Façonnable: 25 rue Royale 75008. Tel. 47 42 72 60. M Madeleine. Open 2–7pm, Mon; 10am–7pm, Tue–Sat.

Also at 174 boulevard St Germain. Tel. 40 49 02 47.

A sort of French equivalent of Ralph Lauren for men with tasteful, good-looking suits at around 4500f, silk ties for 325f, plus less urbane gear, hunting jackets, jeans.

Fil à Fil: 8 rue Tronchet 75009. Tel. 47 42 55 24. M Madeleine. Open 10am–7pm, Mon–Sat. Other branches in 1er and 16e.

Smart range of shirts, ties, belts for men and women.

Frédérick Secordel-Martin: 8 place Vendôme 75001. Tel. 42 61 86 18. M Madeleine. Open 2–8pm, Mon–Fri.

A men's wear couturier who doesn't shoo away women who like good tailoring and is happy to adapt his nine classic jacket styles to the sexes. Wide choice of fabrics for the made to measure jackets priced from 3950f.

Gaultier Junior: see **Jean-Paul Gaultier**.

Gérard Darel: 176 boulevard St Germain 75006. M St-Germain-des-Prés.

Trendy but elegant styles – sample price for a pair of gaberdine cotton trousers is around 620f.

Georges Rech: 273 rue St-Honoré 75008. Tel. 42 61 41 14. M Concorde.

Also at 54 rue Bonaparte 75006 M. St-Germain-des-Prés. Tel. 43 26 84 11; 23 avenue Victor Hugo 75016. Tel. 45 00 83 19 M. Étoile. Open 10am (11am Mon)–7pm Mon–Sat.

Conservatively chic clothes for women; cheaper diffusion range Synonyme especially good at 23 avenue Victor Hugo.

Hémisphères: 1 boulevard Emile-Augier 75016. Tel. 45 20 13 75. M Muette. Open 10.30am–7pm Mon–Sat.

Also at 22 avenue de la Grande-Armée 75016. M Argentine.

Very good quality smart casual garb for men and women with a shoe department. Not cheap.

Henry Cottons: 52 rue Étienne Marcel 75002. Tel. 42 36 01 22. M Sentier. Open 10am–7pm, Mon–Sat.

If *Façonnable* is France's answer to Ralph Lauren, this is Italy's – yuppy casual wear at yuppy prices (5000f for a parka). Also shoes, accessories.

Jean-Paul Gaultier: 6 rue Vivienne 75002. Tel. 42 86 05 05. M Pyramides.

Exciting fashion ideas that don't always fit the budget – if that's the case try **Junior Gaultier** at 7 rue du Jour 75001. Tel. 40 28 01 91. M Les Halles. Open 10am–7pm, Mon–Sat.

Old favourites like desert boots and parkas get a new twist. Denim jackets from 900f.

Killwatch: 100 rue St Denis 75001. Tel. 42 21 99 37. M Étienne Marcel.

Gaultier, Yorke and Cole, English Eccentrics are among the Anglo-French designer mix represented here.

L'Idéale: 4 rue Ste Opportune 75001. Tel. 42 33 30 83. M Châtelet.

Also at 37 rue de Chartres, 92200 Neuilly. Tel. 47 45 19 06.

One for the chaps: casual, good quality classics at reasonable prices:

suits (from 1200f), jackets (100f), trousers (350f), shirts (295f), shoes (780f), and nice gift items too.

Il pour l'homme: 13 rue du Roi-de-Sicile 75004. Tel. 42 76 01 18. M St Paul.

The third branch of Il pour l'homme has a good selection of stylish shirts for women (around 670f) as well as fun silk ties for men (Eiffel Tower ones to remind you of Paris; a snooker game or a Picasso painting).

Irié: 8 rue du Pré-Aux-Clercs 75005. Tel. 42 61 18 28. M Bac. Open 10am–7am, Mon–Sat.

Kenzo was the mentor of Irié, the designer behind this exciting boutique.

Light: 92 avenue des Champs-Élysèes 75008. Tel. 43 59 83 72. M George V. Open 9.45am–7pm, Mon–Sat.

It looks like a tourist trap but smart Parisian women are just as likely to jump into this clever shop on their way to or from the avenue Montaigne. On the ground floor are the gentler prices of designers "diffusion" ranges – Gaultier Junior, Lolita bis, etc; but one floor up, the prices sneak up too. Spotted on the rails the latest from Patrick Kelly, Alaïa, Helmut Lang. Up one more floor and you're in the evening dress section. Worth popping in if you're passing, if only to check what's on offer in the permanent "sale" corner.

Max Mara: 37 rue du Four 75006. Tel. 43 29 91 10. M St-Germain-des-Prés.

Also at 265 rue St Honoré 75008. Tel. 40 20 04 58.

Classic, smart women's wear from this Italian company.

Marithé et François Girbaud: 38 rue Étienne Marcel 75002. Tel. 42 33 54 69. M Châtelet-Les-Halles.

Behind the rather intimidating hi-tech exterior is a unisex shop (and a children's line) which is worth slipping into for a glimpse of the remarkable interior. Marithé et François Girbaud own label shirts and separates are snapped up by yuppies, media trendies, and anyone else who can afford the prices. *Très chic* socks, jeans from 680f, jackets from around 150f upwards.

Martine Sitbon: c/o *Delya*, 9 boulevard Bonne Nouvelle 75002. Tel. 45 08 53 32. M Bonne Nouvelle. Or c/o Maria Luisa, 2 rue Cambon 75001. Tel. 47 03 96 15. M Concorde.

One of the best known younger French designers.

Moholy-Nagy: 2 galerie Vivienne 75002. Tel. 40 15 05 33. M Bourse. Open 11am–7pm, Mon–Sat; closed Sats in Aug.

The place to go for a white shirt (men and women) in cotton, viyella, silk, from 600f to around 800f.

Naf Naf: 5 rue des Cannettes 75006. Tel. 43 54 75 25. M Mabillon;

Young, fun, easy to wear clothes, but not cheap.

New Man: 14 rue de l'Ancienne Comédie 75006. Tel. 43 54 44 95. M Odéon.

Also at 84 avenue des Champs-Élysées 75008. Tel. 43 59 24 27. M Franklin. D. Roosevelt/Palais de Congrès.

Also at Porte Maillot 75017. M Porte Maillot.

Smart good quality classic casualwear for men, women and *enfants.*

Philippe Adec: 89 boulevard Beaumarchais 75003. Tel. 42 72 39 02. M Saint Sébastien-Froissart.

Also at 33 rue du Four 75006. M St-Germain-des-Près.

Women only clothier; classically trendy linen jacket 1800f, washed silk trousers 990f.

Scapa of Scotland: 71 rue des Saints-Pères 75006. Tel. 45 44 18 50/45 44 57 52. M Sèvres-Babylone.

This shop sells what the French call British style. Isabelle Adjani's navy sweaters have come from here. Also sells raincoats, overcoats, classic suits, blouses.

Scooter: 10 rue de Turbigo 75001. Tel. 45 08 09 31. M Étienne-Marcel. Open 2–7.30pm, Mon; 10.30am–7.30pm, Tue–Sat.

Young cheerful costume jewellery, multi-coloured bags and a bright young range, Madamoiselle Zaza.

Smuggler: 93 rue de Longchamp 75016. Tel. 47 04 23 27. M Rue de la Pompe/Trocadéro. Open 2–8pm, Mon; 10.30am–8pm, Tue–Sat.

Quality classics at moderate prices for would be preppy-looking twenty- or thirty-something men.

Surplus Bensimon: c/o Autour du Monde, 12 rue des Francs-Bourgeois 75003. M St Paul.

Also at 54 rue de Seine 75006. M St-Germain-des-Prés.

Jeans, denimwear, T-shirts, tennis shoes, all moderately priced.

Tant qu'il y aura des Hommes: 23 rue du Cherche-Midi 75006. Tel. 45 48 48 17. M St Sulpice Sèvres-Babylone. Open noon–7pm, Mon; 10.30am–7pm, Tue–Sat.

Men's shirts, sweaters, underwear, accessories.

Ventilo: 27 bis rue du Louvre 75001. Tel. 42 36 74 12/42 33 18 67. M Sentier. Open noon–7pm, Mon; 10.30am–7pm, Tue–Sat.

Three floors of women's wear from the Ventilo own label, good, sensible but not frowsy separates; men's range in the basement from Italian labels. Also *salon de thé,* open 12.30–6pm, Mon–Sat, except Aug.

Victoire: 12 place des Victoires 75002. Tel. 42 61 09 02. M Étienne Marcel/Les Halles. Open Mon–Sat, 10am–7pm.

Also at 38 rue François 1er 75008. Tel. 47 23 89 81. M Franklin.

D. Roosevelt; 1 rue Madame 75006. Tel. 45 44 28 14. M St Sulpice; 16 rue de Passy 75016. Tel. 42 88 20 84. M Passy.

Expensive, but always exciting, stock of wearable creations from established and new names; second skins from Alaïa, hats, shoes.

DESIGNERS' DIRECTORY

Designers' ready to wearables – not as costly as *haute couture* but still expensive, available from the following:

Azzedine Alaïa: 17 rue du Parc-Royal 75003. Tel. 47 72 19 19.

Balmain: 44 rue François 1er 75008. Tel. 47 20 35 34.

Céline: 38 avenue Montaigne 75008. Tel. 47 23 74 12.

Cerruti 1881 (for women): 15 place de la Madeleine 75008. Tel. 47 42 10 78.

Chanel: 31 rue Cambon 75001. Tel. 42 61 54 55; 42 avenue Montaigne 75008. Tel. 47 23 74 12.

Christian Dior: 30 avenue Montaigne 75008. Tel. 40 73 54 44.

Christian Lacroix: 73 rue du Faubourg St-Honoré 75008. Tel. 42 65 79 08.

Courrèges: 40 rue François 1er 75008. Tel. 47 20 70 44.

Givenchy: 3 avenue George V 75008. Tel. 47 23 81 36.

Guy Laroche: 29 avenue Montaigne 75008. Tel. 47 23 78 72.

Jean Patou: 7 rue St Florentin 75008. Tel. 42 36 81 41.

Kenzo: 3 place des Victoires 75001. Tel. 42 36 81 41.

Lanvin: 22 rue du Faubourg St-Honoré 75001. Tel. 42 65 14 40.

Lolita Lempicka: 3 bis rue des Rosiers 75004. Tel. 42 74 42 94.

Louis Féraud: 88 rue du Faubourg St-Honoré 75001. Tel. 42 65 27 29.

Montana: 31 rue de Grenelle 75007. Tel. 42 22 69 56.

Nina Ricci: 39 avenue Montaigne 75008. Tel. 47 23 78 88.

Pierre Cardin: Éspace Boutique 29 (women); 59 (men) rue du Faubourg St Honoré 75008. Tel. 42 65 36 91.

Saint Laurent: 38 rue du Faubourg St-Honoré 75008. Tel. 42 65 74 59. **Saint Laurent Rive Gauche:** 6 place St Sulpice 75006. Tel. 43 29 43 00.

Sonia Rykiel: 4 and 6 rue de Grenelle 75006. Tel. 42 22 43 22; 70 rue du Faubourg St-Honoré 75008. Tel. 42 65 20 81.

Ted Lapidus: 35 rue François 1er 75008. Tel. 47 20 69 33.

Thierry Mugler: 49 avenue Montaigne 7500. Tel. 47 23 37 62.

Valentino: 17–19 avenue Montaigne 75008. Tel. 47 23 64 61.

Versace: 11 rue du Faubourg St-Honoré 75008. Tel. 42 65 27 04.

Ungaro: 2 avenue Montaigne 75008. Tel. 47 23 61 94.

BARGAIN CLOTHING

Parisiennes and Parisians are famed for their sartorial style, but they can't all afford to spend a fortune on clothes. "*Impossible n'est pas français*" impoverished but fashion-conscious types tell us. The French invented "*Système D*", the "D" meaning "*débrouillardise*", a popular word that manages to imply "always managing to find what you want". Ever-resourceful, they get what they want by making good use of discount and thrifty second-hand outlets: *la fripe, les dépôts vente* or *les stocks*.

LA FRIPE

La Fripe, straightforward secondhand or retro garments, is the cheapest way to grow a wardrobe – prices will vary enormously but we've spotted secondhand tweed jackets for 200f, glam '80s evening dresses for 400f, a '60s coat for 300f. The flea markets aren't the only hunting grounds for glad rags. Try fishing around in the following.

L'Apache: 45 rue Vieille du Temple 75004. Tel. 42 71 84 27. M Hôtel de Ville. Open 2–7pm Mon; 11am–7pm, Tue–Sat.

Clothes for men and women from the '30s and '40s. Superb cashmere or wool coats, great felt hats – not cheap at 200f, but Madame Mireille, the owner, will tell you they're unique in Paris. Blouses between 100–150f. Men's suits approx 800f. Free alteration service.

Bucks: 142 rue de la Pompe 75016. Tel. 47 27 80 99. M. Pompe. Open 2–7.30pm, Tue; 10.30am–7.30pm, Wed–Sat.

Secondhand jackets, coats and raincoats a speciality, as well as new jeans-wear. Well organised over two floors with jackets categorised according to type of material. Tweedy jackets cost around 149f, Harris (200f), cashmere (500f).

Derrière les Fagots: 8 rue des Abbesses 75018. Tel. 42 59 72 53. M Abbesses. Open 11.30am–7.30pm, Tue–Sat.

1880s–1960s little worn clothes and accessories shoes/hats/purses/ gloves. Also hat makers. Sample prices: evening dresses 200–250f; real Burberrys 650f.

L'Empire des Fripes: 51 bis rue Lamarck 75018. Tel. 42 54 73 75. M Lamarck-Caulaincourt. Open 11.30am–1pm, 2–7.30pm, Mon–Sat.

Carefully selected period wear, including antique theatrical costumes plus costume jewellery (*bijoux fantaisie*). Also Art Deco crockery; hats (men and women) 50–150f. Men's waistcoats and shirts cost 80f, double-breasted suits around 500f.

La Halle aux Fringues: 16 rue de Montreuil 75011. Tel. 43 73 13 12. M Faidherbe-Chaligny. Open 2.30–7.30pm, Mon; 10am–1.30pm, 2.30–7.30pm, Tue–Sat.

American and European '40s *fripe*. Raincoats 150f; dresses 100–300f. Wide selection of men's suits (from 800f) and the cheapest Austrian jackets in Paris. Lots of hats 75–180f. Also new Levi 501s (320–380f) and kimonos.

Next Stop: 58 rue S-André-des Arts 75006. Tel. 43 25 13 36. M Odéon. Open 10am–7.30pm, Mon–Sat.

Also at 80 avenue de Clichy 75017. M La Fourche. Open 10am–7.30pm, Mon–Sat.

American *fripe* and new casual/sporty wear. Unwashed 501s, 250f, washed, 299f. Tweed jackets from 120f, Colombo-style raincoat, 149f.

Optas: 71 rue de Rome 75008. Tel. 45 22 60 37. M Europe. Open 2–7pm Mon; 9.45am–12.30pm, 2–7pm, Tue–Sat.

Military surplus a speciality. Coats around 250f, shirts 85f. Wide selection of binoculars and compasses, all secondhand, around 200–500f.

Retro Activité: 38 rue du Vert-Bois 75003. Tel. 42 77 64 43. M Temple. Open noon–7pm, Tue–Sat.

Little-worn, clean clothes from '30s–'60s. Blouses 30–150f. Silk or cotton nighties 80–100f. Evening dresses 100–250f. Also a selection of men's suits from the '50s and '60s for around 250f, and shirts 40–80f.

Square: 26 bis rue Charles Baudelaire 75012. Tel. 43 07 14 60. M Ledru-Rollin. Open 10.30am–1pm, 3–7pm Tue–Fri; 10.30am–7pm, Sat; 10.30am–1pm Sun.

American second-hands from the '50s–'70s, as well as other slightly used cheapies, fill this very individual little shop near the place d'Aligre market. Slip into a boned ball-gown (from 200–1000f) or a tweed jacket (100–400f). There's also a selection of new clothes from young designers and from "La Factory" as well as designer jewellery.

Tango Trog: see Dépôts Ventes.

Vertiges: 85 rue St Martin 75004. Tel. 48 87 34 64. M Rambuteau. Open 10am–8pm, Mon–Sat; 10am–noon, Sun.

It's worth looking here for men and women's wear of the '40s–'60s from Europe and the States. Average prices for tweed jackets and for raincoats 80f; blouses 30–50f, cocktail dresses 500f. Large selection of leather and suede jackets, averaging 150–200f.

DÉPÔTS VENTES

Translated literally, these shops deal in "deposits and sales". Clothes must be of good quality, look as good as new and bear a well-known or prestigious label to be accepted for sale by the *dépôt vente*. Well-heeled clothes-horses will often deposit their last season's cast-offs to be resold at 30–50% of their original value at these useful places.

Alternatives: 18 rue du Roi-de-Sicile 75004. Tel. 42 78 31 50. M S Paul. Open 10.30am–1.30pm, 2.30–7.30pm, Mon–Sat.

A friendly, young clientèle comes to ransack the stock of Kenzo jackets from 1000f, Agnès B jackets (around 50f), and check out the racks for Yamamoto and Gaultier. Lots of Kenzo in the chap's department, too.

Chercheminippes: 109 and 111 rue du Cherche-Midi 75006. Tel. 42 22 45 23. M Duroc. Open 10.30am–7pm, Mon–Sat.

New and secondhand, inexpensive and trendy clothes in the women's shop (at 109), unlabelled (*dégriffés*) from Chantal Thomas, Kenzo, Sonia Rykiel. A secondhand black silk shirt was spotted for 380f, a yellow linen Chantal Thomas suit, 590f. Designer's end of label

CHECK IT OUT!

While many of the establishments listed here have been going strong for a while, and were trading buoyantly at the addresses given at the time of going to press, the secondhand clothes/discount clothes scene in Paris is volatile. It's best to ring to check the shops are still selling the kinds of things we say they are before setting off to have a rummage.

lines sell for 25–35% of original price. In the men's shop (at 111) the majority of clothes are new with unlabelled suits selling at 1400f and parkas at 780f.

L'Eventail: 65 bis rue Lauriston 75016. Tel. 47 04 58 68. M Victor Hugo. Open 10.30am–6.30pm, Mon–Fri.

Stock changes swiftly here – the women's clothes are all recent deposits, all labelled. Cotton shirts sell for 80–160f, jackets from 500f, plus accessories and knick-knacks.

Fabienne: 77 bis rue Boileau 75016. Tel. 45 25 64 26. M Exelmans. Open 10.30am–1.30pm, 3–7pm, Tue–Sat.

The best *dépôt vente* for men in Paris: fashionable, labelled clothes in perfect conditions – from Kenzo shirts to Façonnable suits. Excellent sales every February. Sample prices (non-sale): Trousers 150–220f, cashmere coats 1500f, jackets 250–400f, suits 500–1000f. The best quality French shoes for men, Weston shoes, sell at approx 800f, whereas normally they'd retail at at least three times that much per pair.

Malvina: 47 bis rue Bénard 75014. Tel. 40 44 96 08. M Mouton Duvernet. Open 1–8pm, Sun; 10am–1pm, Tue–Sat.

This is the place to ransack Claudette Colbert's wardrobe: Madame Malvina's tiny shop specialises in theatrical and movie costumes from 1900–1970s. A slithery strapless silk number labelled "Saks Claudette Colbert" with its matching bolero top sells at 750f. Suits sell for 250–550f. And if you want to put on the glitz for a night out at Le Palace you can rent clothes here too, for 250–500f for 48 hours.

Opportune: 114 avenue Michel Bizot 75012. Tel. 43 44 54 50. M Michel Bizot. Open 10.30am–3pm, Mon; 10.30am–1pm, 3–7.30pm, Tue–Sat. Closed Wed am.

No prestigious labels here, but a very good selection of trendy clothes at bargain prices. Cotton/silk blouses 60–150f, a linen suit for 250f. Interesting retro corner with lacy nighties, gloves, pearly purses, hats, trinkets and odds and ends from the '30s and '40s.

Réciproque: 95, 101, 123 rue de la Pompe 75016. Tel. 47 04 30 28. M Pompe. Open 10am–6.45pm, Tue–Sat.

A great address these three large, side-by-side branches. No 95 has a wide selection of very good designer clothes worn either at fashion shows or only a few times by private clients. On the ground floor there's mega-smart stuff from Chanel, St Laurent, Nina Ricci, Balmain, Lacroix, with prices ranging from 700–300f. In the basement are masses of more casual clothes. Officially sizes 36–44 (8–16) are stocked, but actually 38–40 (10–12) predominate. The only drawback to this place, apart from the sizing, is the surly demeanour of the assistants who could be a little more helpful.

At the other two, less exciting, branches you'll find men's clothes and gifts at 101 while 123 stocks ladies coats, leather goods, jewellery, scarves and miscellaneous accessories.

Tango Trog: 6 rue Euryale-Dehaynin 75019. Tel. 42 06 89 77. M Laumière. Open noon–7pm, Tue–Sat; 6pm on Sat.

Although Madame Blanche's shop is in a *quartier* undergoing complete renovation, the emphasis is firmly on nostalgia. Her *dépôt vente* features fashionable unlabelled skirts (50–300f), dresses (300f) and jeans (80f), but best of all is her well-supplied retro department full of exciting little dresses (around 300f) – just the things to sling on for Le Balajo on Monday or Thursday nights.

Trocade: 5 and 9 avenue de Villiers 75017. Tel. 42 67 80 14. M Villiers Tel. 42 67 80 14. M Villiers. No. 5 (women's) open 10am–2pm, Monday, 10am–7pm, Tue–Sat. No. 9 (men's) open 10am–7pm, Tue–Sat.

Superb quality nearly-new women's wear in number 5, with a wide range of styles and designers including permanent selections from Chanel and Lolita Lempicka; cocktail dresses from 800f. We found an Ungaro cotton strapless dress for 600f. The boutique for blokes at number 9 is smaller, selling classic suits including tuxedos from 900f–1500f. There are shirts for 120f.

Troc Mode: 230 avenue du Maine 75014. Tel. 45 40 45 93. M Alésia. Open 11am–7pm, Tue–Sat.

No prestigiously labelled *vêtements*, but a great choice of *prêt-à-porter* women's clothes in good condition, for all tastes and sizes. Jeans cost 139f, skirts and blouses from 110f, suits 350–450f. Also accessories and an interesting selection of shoes.

Troc Parnass: 58 rue du Montparnasse 75014. Tel. 43 22 72 53. M Edgar Quinet. Open 11.30am–7.30pm Tue–Sat.

Always worth checking the *dépôt-vente* for impressively labelled trendiness from Alaïa et al. Spotted suits and blouses by Daniel Hechter with 50% discount. Only women's clothes.

"STOCKS"

With the fashion business not being as buoyant as it might, even the most established *prêt-à-porter* names can no longer clear their stock in bi-annual sales. This is where the open *stocks* help out – permanent sales of merchandise where anyone can buy the remains of a previous season's collection at a third or even half of the original price. None of the garments are secondhand – just second season. You could do worse than start your shopping spree in the rue d'Alésia in the 14e where many of the outlets are concentrated.

Cacharel Stock: 114 rue d'Alésia 75014. Tel. 45 92 53 04. M Alésia. Open 10am–6.45pm, Mon–Sat.

Wide selection of women's and children's clothing on the ground floor, and for men on the first floor, with 30–50% discount on the previous collection's retail price. Good prices for superior quality.

Fabrice Karel Stock: 105 rue d'Alésia 75014. Tel. 45 42 42 61. M Alésia. Open 10am–7pm, Tue–Sat.

Discount of 50% off Fabrice Karel's previous year's collections. The quality of the chic, classical designs and fine knitwear for women is excellent. Skirts around 280f, sweaters from 400f.

Stock Blanc Bleu: 82 rue d'Alésia 75014. M Alésia. Open 11am–7pm, Mon; 10am–7pm, Tue–Sat.

Sweatshirts from 199f, jumpers from 200f, plus lots of T-shirts, jackets, ski jackets.

Stock Daniel Hechter: 16 boulevard de l'Hôpital 75013. Tel. 47 07 88 44. M Austerlitz. Open 10am–7pm, Mon–Sat.

Large and pleasant shop offering Daniel Hechter's *"fin de séries"* for women, men and children, with 30–40% discount. Superb bargains: blouses and jumpers around 350f, coats 1450f, skirts 650–750f.

See also, *Stock 2 Daniel Hechter:* 92 rue d'Alésia 75014. Tel. 45 41 65 65. M Alésia. Open 10am–7pm, Mon–Sat.
Stock Daniel Hechter: 83–85 rue de l'Ourcq 75019. Tel. 42 41 77 69. M Crimée. Phone for opening hours. *Paris Nord Diffusion-Stock Daniel Hechter:* 34–62 rue de Pelleport 75020. Tel. 43 60 77 69. M Gambetta. Open 10.30am–7.30pm, Mon–Sat.

Marithé et François Girbaud: 5 rue Planchat 75020. Tel. 43 72 43 84. M Avron. Open 10.30am–6.30pm, Mon–Sat.

Extremely popular label in the States, lesser known in the UK. Here you'll get 30–50% off previous collection's prices. Jeans from 400f, jackets from 600f. Trousers 300–500f. You get a friendlier welcome here than in the "official" Girbaud boutique in the rue Étienne-Marcel. Only one snag – there's no changing room so go prepared, wearing a "body" if you're shy.

Salambô: 38 rue de la Roquette 75011. Tel. 47 00 06 30. M Bastille. Open 11am–8pm, Mon–Sat.

Talented Salambô's *tailleurs* (suits) cost from 1700f, coats 1400–2300f, and sexy evening dresses from 350f.

Bargain Alaïa

If you feel like splashing out, especially if it costs a lot less than it normally should, *"faire une petite folie"* at **Alaïa**: 60 rue de Bellechasse 75007. Tel. 47 05 13 18. M Solférino. Open 10am–6.30pm, Mon–Sat.

Discount of 50% on Alaïa's end of line (*fins de collection*) including leather and accessories, and a big 80% off previous collections. No changing room – you just wriggle into things in a corner of the showroom.

DISCOUNT PERFUMES AND COSMETICS

As with clothes, if you know where to go you can buy designer fragrances and cosmetics at a less than normal retail prices. There are at least 40 cut price *parfumeries*, mainly catering for tourists, and most give discounts below the airport prices. Here are a few examples:

American Perfumery: 31 rue de la Sourdière 75001. Tel. 42 61 37 16. M Pyramides. Open 10am–6.45pm, Mon–Fri.

Also at 34 place du Marché St Honoré 75001. M Pyramides; 21 rue de Rome 75008. M St Lazare; 12 boulevard Poissonnière 75009. M Bonne Nouvelle (all with same telephone number and opening hours).

Most of the most well-known cosmetic companies' products and fragrances are sold here at a 20–30% discount.

Parfumerie d'Arches: 27 rue Danielle Casanova 5001. Tel. 42 61 43 73. M Pyramides. Open 10am–7pm, Mon–Sat.

An average 25% off normal retail prices of most top brand name cosmetics and perfumes. Helpful shop assistants.

Centre Franco-Americain: 49 rue d'Aboukir 75002. Tel. 42 36 77 46. M Sentier. Open 9am–6.30pm, Mon–Sat (5.30pm on Sat).

Perfumes, 12 brands of cosmetics, plus gifts, accessories, clothes at 20% to 30% off.

Parfumerie Madame: 15 rue de Richelieu 75001. Tel. 42 96 24 54. M Palais Royal. Open 10am–7.30pm, Mon–Fri.

Between 25% and 30% off around 30 different fragrances and 20% off cosmetics by Dior, Lancôme and others. Welcoming staff more than willing to advise. At the same address there's a well-known beauty institute where treatments will only cost half the regular price if you're under 25 or have proof of student status.

Paris Look: 13 and 19 avenue de l'Opéra 75001. Tel. 42 60 52 82.

M Pyramides. Open 10am–7pm, Mon–Sat. Other branches too (see phone directory).

Wide choice of designer fragrances, cosmetics, accessories with 25% off.

OTHER BEAUTY/HEALTH SHOPS

Strictly for budget-unconscious sybarites . . .

Annick Goutal: 14 rue de Castiglione 75008. Tel. 42 60 52 82. M Tuileries.

Also at 16 rue de Bellechasse 75007. Tel. 45 51 36 13. M Solférino. Open 10am–7pm, Mon–Sat.

Shops in ivory and old gold selling wonderful fragrances. Annick Goutal is a rarity, a female "nose" who began the French fashion for little fragrant pebbles that you pile in decorative heaps or place in a holder over a light bulb which further diffuses their scent. A complete range of lotions and creams complement her fragrances.

L'Artisan Parfumeur: 5 rue des Capucines 75007. Tel. 42 96 35 13;

Also at 84 bis rue de Grenelle 75007. Tel. 45 44 61 57. Open 9.30am–7pm, Mon–Sat.

Parfumerie decked out like bijou antique shop: sachets of husky amber to scent your linen, effusive French fragrances (the *mûre et musc*, blackberry and musk, is very chic).

Caron: 34 avenue Montaigne 75008. Tel. 47 23 40 82. M Franklin D. Roosevelt. Open 10am–6.30pm, Mon–Sat.

Tiny shop, lavish in the Empire style, with lines of Baccarat crystal urns from which your dram of scent is decanted. There are perfumes from the past, not available elsewhere (225–270f, 7.5ml). Lacquer compacts (250f) and small, decorative perfume bottles (200–235f).

Guerlain: 68 avenue des Champs-Élysées 75008. Tel. 43 59 31 10. M Franklin D. Roosevelt. Open 9.30am–6.45pm, Mon–Sat.

The most glamorous spot on the Champs-Élysées; wonderful cosmetics and, of course, all the classic Guerlain scents, including some you can't buy anywhere else. Upstairs is an Institut de Beauté for pampering treatments. Other Guerlain boutiques in rue Tronchet, 8e; in the 1er, 16e and 15e.

Phu-Xuan: 8 rue Monsieur-le-Prince 75006. Tel. 43 25 08 27. M Odéon. Open 9am–6.45pm, Mon–Sat.

The Phan family have dispensed traditional cures of the Orient for 20 years. Phu-Xuan does not sell medicine or fill prescriptions *per se*, their treatments are intended to supplement conventional allopathic medicine. Half the shop is set aside for acupuncture accoutrements.

SERVICES

HAIR

Leading French coiffeur Jean-Louis David hit upon a winning idea in 1987 when he opened his "Quick Service Jean-Louis David" salons in Paris, offering the same faultless professionalism he'd built his reputation on, but at cut prices. The snag is that you can't make an appointment, no real hardship though, as the wait is never lengthy. A shampoo, haircut and finish costs around 135f (women), 75f (men), with 20% off if you're under 20. Open 10am–7pm. Closed Sunday and Monday.

Find Quick Service/Jean-Louis David at:

27 rue de la Ferronnerie (1er)	M Les Halles. Tel. 40 41 98 61
5 rue Cambon (1er)	M Concorde. Tel. 42 97 47 26
160 bis rue de Temple (3e)	M République. Tel. 48 87 75 47
58 rue St Antoine (4e)	M Lédru-Rollin. Tel. 40 29 08 39
7 rue Monge (5e)	M Maubert. Tel. 40 46 81 44
82 rue de Rennes (6e)	M St Sulpice. Tel. 45 44 91 63

And check the telephone directory for branches in all other *arrondissements*.

HAIR "DOCTORS": JEAN-FRANÇOIS LAZARTIQUE

Over the last couple of decades J.-F. Lazartique centres have mushroomed – there are now around 60 worldwide, dedicated to healthy hair. Detailed analysis of your scalp and locks is free in the ten futuristic Parisian institutes. The prescribed home treatment using their own excellent products is not cheap (between 1500–2000f for 3 months' supply). Really sick hair is treated at the salon, and other treatments are available – perming, straightening, colouring, without harming its health. Consultations by appointment only.

35 rue St Antoine (4e)	M Bastille. Tel. 42 72 86 00
3 rue de Monfauçon (6e)	M Mabillon. Tel. 43 29 33 44
5 rue du Faubourg St Honoré (8e)	M Concorde. Tel. 42 65 29 24
74 avenue des Champs-Élysées (8e)	M Franklin D. Roosevelt Tel. 45 63 36 71
44 rue de la Chaussée-d'Antin (9e)	M Chaussée-d'Antin Tel. 48 74 52 14
21 and 23 rue du Départ (14e)	M Montparnasse Tel. 43 21 56 35
306 rue de Vaugirard (15e)	M Convention Tel. 45 31 06 88
48 rue de Passy (16e)	M Muette Tel. 45 27 54 76
142 rue de Courcelles (17e)	M Péreire Tel. 42 27 87 12

1 rue Caulaincourt (18e)   M Place Clichy Tel. 45 22 39 46
10 rue du Château, 92–200
Neuilly   M Pont de Neuilly Tel. 47 45 36 17

GADGETS AND GIFTS

Small *objets* that are that little bit different, finishing touches for the home, cheap but exciting gifts – here are some places to look for gadgets and things:

Axis: 18 rue Guénégard 75006. Tel. 43 29 66 23. M Pont Neuf. Open 10.30am–1pm, 2–7.30pm, Mon–Sat.
  A famous shop, popular with classy present-hunters (gifts from 140f). Ceramics, glasses, designer jewellery, scarves, exclusive carpets made and signed by painters.

Bathroom Graffitti: Forum des Halles, Niveau 2, 15 passage de la Réale 75001. Tel. 40 13 03 03. M RER Châtelet-Les-Halles.
  Also at 98 rue de Longchamp 75016. Tel. 47 04 23 12.
M Trocadéro; 7 avenue des Ternes 75017. Tel. 43 80 52 38. M Ternes; 22 rue Madeleine Michelis 92200 Neuilly. Tel. 47 45 85 25. M Porte Maillot.
  Trendy, fun presents – brooches, pens, boxer shorts, cigarette cases etc. – plus expensive items (designer telephones, statues) as well as original, colourful bits for your bathroom.

Beauté Divine: 40 rue St Sulpice 75006. Tel. 43 26 25 31. M Mabillon. Open 2–7pm, Mon; 10am–1.15pm, 2–7pm, Tue–Sat.
  Rare, ancient, exquisite *objets* for the *soignée* bathroom or boudoir – ravishing perfume bottles, handsome brushes, with prices from 300f. Buy the incense as burned in Notre-Dame to remind you of Paris. Items from 50–2500f approx.

Blasphème: 52 rue Vavin 75006. Tel. 46 34 52 51. M Vavin. Open 3–7pm, Mon; 10am–7pm, Tue–Sat.
  Prices aren't always very competitive (150–300f), average for a present, but it's worth calling in here to find an exotic gift from ones gathered from all corners of the globe. The selection is inspiring, with attractive bags, jewellery, gadgets, fountain pens, elegant and modern stationery.

Calligrane: 4 and 6 rue de Pont-Louis-Philippe 75004. Tel. 40 27 00 74. M Pont Marie/St Paul. Open 2.30–7.30pm, Mon; 11am–7.30pm, Tue–Sat.
  Gift items from 50–1000f approx. All the writing materials imaginable: magnificent blotters, writing pads, diaries, letter racks, wrapping paper.

Cassegrain: 422 rue St Honoré 75001. Tel. 42 60 20 08. M Madeleine.

Genteel stationery shop with *raffiné* desk accessories, marbled papers, elegant photo frames.

La Chaise Longue: 30 rue Croix-des-Petits-Champs 75001. Tel. 42 96 32 14. M Palais Royal. Open 11am–7pm, Mon–Sat.

Also at: 20 rue des Francs-Bourgeois 75004. Tel. 42 96 32 14. M St Paul; 8 rue Princesse 75006. Tel. 42 29 62 39. M Mabillon (stays open till 1am).

A '30s and '50s influence prevails in these attractive gift shops where presents range in price from 15–5000f. Chrome, wood, glass objects, James Dean's sunglasses, a *Happy Days* toaster or *Seven Year Itch* percolator, '50s radio, colonial fans, are the sort of things you'll find here.

Destination Paris: 9 rue du 29 Juillet 75001. Tel. 49 27 98 90. M Tuileries. Open 10.30am–7.30pm, Mon–Sat.

Paris-abilia galore; funny, practical, even beautiful items, plus fashion accessories, scarves, toys, clothes, crockery from 5–5000f.

Diptyque: 34 boulevard St Germain 75005. Tel. 43 26 45 27. M St-Germain-des-Près. Open 10am–7pm, Mon–Sat.

Chic Parisians visit this shrine to bathroom and boudoir for stylish presents like wonderful scents or plump perfumed candles.

L'Écritoire: 61 rue St Martin 75004. Tel. 42 78 01 18. M Hôtel de Ville. Open 10.30am–1pm, 2–7.15pm, Mon–Sat.

Another shop which gives you the urge to write – although its hardbacked copy books and retro diaries, all made on the premises, look almost too good to use.

L'Éntrepôt: 50 rue de Passy 75016. Tel. 45 25 64 17. M Passy. Open 10.30am–7pm, Mon–Sat.

This shop is like a gift supermarket to the *BCBG*s who make regular raids on its booty of clothes, stationery, kitchen items, watches, gadgets, etc. The prices aren't particularly cheap but the choice on offer is particularly interesting. There's a café too (open shop hours) and a *détaxe* export scheme.

Jardins Imaginaires: 9 bis rue d'Assas 75006. Tel. 42 22 90 03. M Rennes. Open 2–7pm Mon; 10.30am–7pm, Tue–Sat.

Exclusive *cachepots* based on antique designs, a garden apron and gloves faithfully reproduced from an 18th-century document, plus gardening tools and less transportable items, like benches.

Letter Box: 7 rue d'Assas 75006. Tel. 42 22 40 03. M Rennes. Open 2–7pm, Mon; 10.30am–1pm, 2–7pm, Tue–Sun.

Very original stationery shop, good for seeking out simple, small, cheapish gifts. Fountain pens are in the 95–1500f range, notebooks, photo albums (95–385f), plus other paperwork.

La Maison des Boites: 18 rue des Grands-Augustins 75006. Tel. 43 25 11 66. M Odéon. Open 11am–6pm, Tue–Sat.

Unusual little shop in Latin Quarter specialising in boxes – not any old *boîtes*, you understand, but heart-shaped ones for pills, tobacco-leaved cigar boxes, animal-shaped ones for knick-knacks. Prices from around 50f.

MH Way: 17 rue des Saints-Pères 75006. Tel. 42 60 81 65. M St-Germain-des-Prés. Open 3–7.15pm, Mon; 10.30am–7.15pm, Tue–Sat.

Bring together a Japanese designer, Mario Hasuike, and Italian manufacturers and you get state-of-the-art items and office accessories like those featured in this shrine of contemporary design.

Miller et Bertaux: 17 rue Ferdinand Duval 75004. Tel. 42 78 28 39. M St Paul. Open 1–7pm, Mon; 10.30am–7pm, Tue–Sat.

Australian artists who sell all kinds of things, including wearables made out of natural materials – wood, silk, wool, muslin and so on. A vegetable fibre bow tie could be yours for 450f, a wooden badge for 50f.

Present-Perfect: 79 rue St-Louis-en-L'Ile 75004. Tel. 43 29 77 37. M Pont-Marie/Cité. Open 10.30am–midnight in summer; 10am–8pm winter.

Good quality selection of gift items at reasonable prices given the location. Watches from 290f.

Pyramide: 55 rue de Vaugirard 75006. Tel. 45 49 11 20. M Rennes. Open 12 noon-7pm, Mon; 10.30am–7.30pm, Tue–Sat.

Also at 97 rue de Courcelles 75017. Tel. 46 22 14 36, M Pèreire.

Hard not to find something covetable here from the tempting line-up of pens, watches, kitchen and bathroom accessories, phones, teapots and so on.

Ralph Lauren's Home Collection: 2 place de la Madeleine 75008. Tel. 47 03 45 52. M Madeleine. Open 10am–7pm, Mon–Sat.

On the newly renovated second floor of the men and women's wear fashion store, the flagship of all the European Polo stores is the Home Collection. You might spot the perfect china, earthenware, rattan, crystal or pot pourri here. All of the products are displayed in themed settings.

Saint Op: 10 rue des Halles 75001. Tel. 42 33 37 35. M Les Halles. Open 2–7pm, Mon; 10am–7pm, Tue–Sat.

Very trendy fun giftshop with all the usual present-y stuff, in the heart of Les Halles. Not too pricey.

PARIS SPORTIF

The possibilities for do-ers and watchers in and around Paris are given below. Facilities do sometimes have odd opening hours – it's a good idea to check they haven't changed before you set off.

For **sporting events**, check the listings mags like *Pariscope* or relevant pages of the daily press, especially *Le Figaro*'s Wednesday supplement, *Figaroscope*. The all-sports daily is called *L'Équipe*, for fluent French-speaking enthusiasts only. As with any major sporting events, if you go, be prepared to endure hordes and battle for seats.

Many private **fitness centres** do day or week passes, but the cheapest facilities are those in the multi-purpose leisure complexes run by the City of Paris.

A municipal phone line giving details of sports and events in the Paris area is *Allô Sports*. (Tel. 42 76 54 54) which is open 10.30am–5pm, Mon–Thur, 10.30am–4.30pm, Fri.

You can get a list of private multi-purpose clubs from *CIDJ*, 101 quai Branly 75015. Tel. 45 66 40 20.

Paris has two big woods, the **Bois de Boulogne** and **Bois de Vincennes**, which offer various sporting facilities/amenities. In addition there are the following:

Aquaboulevard: 4 rue Louis Armand 75015. Tel. 40 60 10 00. M Balard/RER Boulevard Victor. Open 8am–1am daily. Entrance Aquatic Park 60f adults; 45f 3–12s; under 3s free. Watersports plus gym: 140f. No credit cards.

Well-run, well-equipped new multi-sports complex near the *périphèrique* with a dozen tennis courts, half a dozen squash courts, putting greens, plus the pools and giant water slides.

Parc d'Antony: 148 bis ave du General de Gaulle 92160 Antony. Tel. 43 50 39 35. RER (Line B) Croix de Berny, then walk towards Parc de Sceaux.

Outdoor, olympic-sized pool (closed October–May), five soccer fields, ten tennis courts (open to public during the week), just 15 minutes from central Paris.

Parc de Puteaux: Ile de Puteaux 92800 Puteaux. Tel. 45 06 68 12; pool 45 0615 98. M Pont de Neuilly, then bus 144. Open dawn–dusk.

Still close to central Paris, yet feels countrified with an olympic-sized outdoor pool, (closed October–March) and good area for sunbathing, 24 tennis courts and five soccer fields.

ATHLETICS

Contact Fédération Française d'Athlétisme (10 rue de Faubourg Poissonnière 75010. Tel. 47 70 90 61). Or write for a list of stadiums to Bureau des Sports (17 boulevard Morland 75181).

BICYCLING

The nation that goes mad for the Tour de France (which finishes in Paris in July) loves cycles. If you're fearless enough to want to bike round Paris you can hire one (see **Getting Around**), or you can hire in both Bois where there are cycle trails to pedal along. (More info from Fédération Française du Cyclisme, 43 rue de Dunkerque 75010. Tel. 42 85 41 20.)

Remember that the SNCF have a great "*train plus vélo*" deal giving a day's train excursion with bicycle rental thrown in. Reservations should be made in advance to the relevant station.

BILLIARDS

The table in the French version has no pockets. You can try your hand for free or simply watch at **Académie de Clichy-Montmartre** (84 rue de Clichy 75009. M Clichy. Open 1.30–11.30pm daily). Alternatively there's the **Académie de Paris** (47 avenue de Wagram 75017. M Ternes. Open 12.30–11pm; 2–11pm weekends), and **Café les Sports** (108 boulevard Jourdan 75014. M Porte d'Orléans. Open 7.30am– 11.30pm. Closed Thur).

BOATING

Rent a pleasure boat in these parks:

Bois de Boulogne	M Porte-Dauphine
Bois de Vincennes	M Château-de-Vincennes
Parc de Buttes-Chaumont	M Buttes-Chaumont

BOULES

As French as Gauloises and berets. To watch a game, just take a look in any Parisian park on a weekend afternoon. The major annual tournament (*Tournai International de Pétanque*) takes place for 5 days in June in the Roman Arènes de Lutèce in the heart of the Latin Quarter. (More info from Ligue de l'Ile de France de la Fédération Française de Pétanque et de Jeu Provençal, 9 rue Duperré 75009. Tel. 48 74 61 63.)

BOWLING

Not a home-grown sport, but Parisians seem to like it. The largest, trendiest, alley is the **Bowling de Paris** in the Jardin d'Acclimation (Bois de Boulogne. Tel. 47 47 77 55. M Sablons). And there's a 16-lane alley at the **Gaîté Montparnasse Complex** (25 rue de Commandant René-Mouchotte 75014. Tel. 43 21 61 32. M Montparnasse-Bienvenue.) Cheaper, and popular with students, is **Bowling Mouffetard** (Centre Commercial Monge, 11 rue Gracieuse 75005. Tel. 43 31 09 35. M Monge). To check other venues for "*bowlings*" look in *Pariscope* or *L'Officiel*.

BOXING

More info about English boxing from Fédération Française de Boxe (62 rue Nollet 75017. Tel. 48 78 14 93) and about French boxing from the Fédération Française de Boxe Française – Savate et Disciplines Assimilées, (25 boulevard des Italiens 75002. Tel. 47 42 82 27).

CHESS

Played in cafés as well as clubs. The official body for more information is the Ligue d'Ile de France d'Échecs (33–37 quai de Grenelle 75015. Tel. 45 78 98 43).

DANCING

At the **Centre de Danse du Marais** you can take single lessons (around 60f a go) to brush up your modern dance, folk dancing or rock and roll; aerobics available at the **California Club** at the same address (41 rue du Temple 75004. M Hôtel de Ville. Open 9am–7pm). For details of other dance centres in Paris contact the Fédération Française de la Danse, (12 rue St-Germain-l'Auxerrois 75001. Tel. 42 36 19 61).

There are also afternoon dancing sessions in some *quartiers*, where you don't have to dress up or spend a lot of money. For instance, try **Balajo** (9 rue de Lappe 75011. M Bastille. From 3pm.) Where there is recorded music to tango, rock or waltz to. Or there's **Tchatch au Tango** (12 rue au Maire 75003. M Arts-et-Métiers. From 2.30pm. Entry free, just buy a drink.) Which this is one of the oldest dance halls in town with an un-yuppie cross-section of clients of all ages who come simply to dance. Also see listings under *"thé dansings"* in *Pariscope* and nightlife section listings for more dancing venues.

FISHING

Piscatorial types should contact Fédération Interdepartmental des Associations de Pêche et de Pisciculture (8 rue Léon Frot 75011. Tel. 43 48 36 34.) for advice on when, where and how to fish around Paris.

FOOTBALL

Soccer mecca is **Parc des Princes** (Porte de St Cloud, 16e) near the southern end of the Bois. It's here that the French cup final

is held. The Paris Clubs are Paris St Germain and Paris FC. Info
from Fédération Française de Football (60 bis avenue d'Iéna
75016. Tel. 47 20 65 40.) or the Ligue Parisienne de Football,
(5 place de Valois 75001. Tel. 42 61 56 47).

GOLF

At the Fédération Française de Golf (69 avenue Victor-Hugo
75016. Tel. 45 02 13 55. M Victor-Hugo. Open 9.30am–6pm,
Mon–Fri.) they'll answer all your queries and give you a list of
all the golf courses in France. The Aqua-boulevard has putting
greens (see introduction to this chapter). The brilliantly
equipped École de Golf de Paris (5 avenue des Ternes 75017.
Tel. 47 63 06 54. M Ternes. Open 8.30am–10pm, Mon–Fri;
9am–6pm, Sat.) lends equipment if you pay the steep fee to
register and play – over 300f.

GYMNASIUMS AND HEALTH CLUBS

There are gyms and fitness centres all over Paris – see notes at
the beginning of this section – or get a full list from Allô Sports.
Many are membership only and are expensive; some charge
for extra activities – so do check first; many are crowded
during lunch or rush hours.

The biggest chain is Gymnase Club, with a young and yuppy
clientèle. You can get a book of ten admission tickets for 500f
plus 220f registration fee. The Garden Gym chain does a book
of ten tickets for 450f – a good deal for visitors – or, better
still, a monthly pass for the same price. They're smaller and
more clubby than the Gymnase Club. The small Vitatop chain
are sophisticated, upmarket gyms with jacuzzis and pools,
offering a day pass for 150f. At Porte Maillot Vitatop (Tel.
40 68 00 21) you can brush up your cliff-scaling on a wall
or go jogging in the nearby Bois; their Sofitel gym – in a hotel
– has a rooftop pool; and their third branch, Vaugirard, is
in St Germain. See telephone directory for addresses. The
Fédération Française Education Physique et de Gymnastique
Volontaire (2 rue de Valois 75001. Tel. 42 96 12 80.) will
also supply a list of city gyms.

We'd recommend the **Éspace Vit'Halles** where, for around the same sort of outlay (150f), you can body-build, use a multi-gym, exercise or dancercise and then flop into a sauna, on to a sunbed, or collapse at the diet bar (48 rue Rambuteau 75004. Tel. 42 77 21 37. M RER Châtelet-Les-Halles. Open 9am–10pm, Mon–Fri; 10am–6pm, Sat; 11am–3pm, Sun.).

Of the city's many health clubs, the majority admit just members. There are lots of hotels with saunas and other facilities for residents. Perhaps if you're only in Paris for a short while you'd be better off exercising your feet on the pavements or going swimming instead. We prefer the easy-going rituals of the hammams (Turkish baths). A relaxing steam bath or sauna and a massage may be just what you need after a trek around the museums of Paris.

Hammam de la Mosquée: 39 rue Geoffroy-St-Hilaire 75005. Tel. 43 31 18 14. M Censier-Daubenton. Open: *Women* 11am–7pm, Mon, Wed; 11am–9pm, Thur; 10am–7pm, Sat. *Men* 11am–7pm, Fri, Sun. Admission 60f. No credit cards.

Hammam de St Paul: 4 rue des Rosiers 75004. Tel. 42 72 71 82. M St Paul. Open: *Women*–10am–8pm, Wed, Fri. *Men*–10am–8pm, Thur, Sat. Admission 95f. No credit cards. Beauty treatments of all kinds available for extra fees.

HORSE RACING

Hippodrome d'Auteuil: Bois de Boulogne 75016. Tel. 42 24 47 04. M Porte d'Auteuil. Closed during July, Aug.

Hippodrome de Longchamp: Bois de Boulogne 75016. M Porte d'Auteuil. Tel. 42 24 13 29. then shuttle service on race days. Closed during July, Aug.

Hippodrome de Vincennes: Bois de Vincennes 75012. Tel. 43 68 35 39; reservations for restaurant 43 68 64 94. RER Joinville, 10-minute walk.

Other *hippodromes* (grass tracks) close to Paris are at St Cloud, Chantilly, Énghien-les-Bains. (See **Ile de France**). Admission prices are reasonable. See daily press for details.

ICE HOCKEY

Yes, the French do play it. Catch the **Français Volants** every other Saturday afternoon at the Bercy Sports Complex (8 boulevard de Bercy 75012. M Bercy. Or call them on 43 46 98 37 for more information).

ICE SKATING

At both the following rinks you can hire skates; the Montparnasse one tends to be busier.

Gaîté Montparnasse: 27 rue du Commandant René Mouchotte 75015. Tel. 42 60 15 90. M Montparnasse.

Patinoire des Buttes Chaumont: 30 rue Edouard Pailleron 75019. M Bolivar.

JOGGING

Jog in the **Bois de Boulogne** or **Bois de Vincennes**, but watch out for the traffic when crossing a road – the drivers are merciless. Inner city dwellers circuit the **Champs de Mars**, running by the Eiffel Tower ($1^{1}/2$m). Shorter (around 1m) routes are in the **Luxembourg Gardens**, the **Tuileries, Parc Monceau** and, more challenging, the undulating **Parc Montsouris** in the 14e.

ROLLER SKATING

Watch or join in at the major roller skating rink in Paris, **La Main Jaune** (it becomes a disco in the evening), where you can hire skates for an extra 10f. (Porte de Champerret 75017. Tel. 47 63 26 47. M Porte de Champerret. Open 2.30–7pm, Wed, Sat, Sun. Admission 40f; 25f under 14s Wed.) There's also a free roller skating rink in the **Bois de Boulogne**, near the Porte Maillot.

RUGBY

As with main soccer matches, principal rugby fixtures (Triple Crown) are held at the **Parc des Princes**: see daily press for details. For information about rugby union contact the Fédération Française de Rugby, (7 Cité d'Antin 75009. Tel. 48 74 84 75).

SQUASH

Courts frequently require membership. Enquire at the ones at **Tour Montparnasse** (37 avenue de Main 75015. Tel. 45 38 66 20) and **Le Squash Front de Seine** (21 rue Gaston-de-Cavaillet 75015. Tel. 45 75 35 37). Or see **Aquaboulevard** earlier in this chapter.

SWIMMING

Details of the city's 26 municipal pools from *Allô Sports* (Tel. 42 76 54 54), or the local *Mairie*, or contact the Fédération Française de Natation – Comité de l'Ile de France (148 avenue Gambetta 75020. Tel. 43 64 17 02). *Pariscope* and similar list (under *Piscines*) pools with opening hours (which may be restricted as some times are given over to schools: Parisian kids tend to fill them up on Wednesday and Saturday afternoon). In addition, there are privately owned/run pools. See also **Aquaboulevard**, this chapter. Here's a small selection of some of the city's best:

1er

Piscine Suzanne-Berlioux: 20 place de la Rotonde. Tel. 42 36 98 44. M Les Halles.
New, indoor, stays open until late.

4e

Piscine St Merri: 18 rue de Renard. Tel. 42 72 29 45. M Rambuteau/ Hôtel de Ville.

Much smaller than Piscine Suzanne-Berlioux above, indoor and with solarium. Just behind the Pompidou Centre.

5e

Piscine de Pontoise: 19 rue de Pontoise. Tel. 43 54 82 45. M Maubert-Mutualité.

Nude swimming Monday and Thursday evenings from 8–10pm at this old pool with its period tiles and skylight. Solarium. Jacuzzi.

Piscine Jean-Taris: 16 rue Thouin. Tel. 43 25 54 03. M Cardinal Lemoine.

Two indoor pools, the smaller one for kids. No chlorine, thanks to electronic purification. Popular with students. No solarium.

6e

Piscine du Marché St Germain: 7 rue Clémont. Tel. 43 29 08 15. M Mabillon.

Small, subterranean pool with an extra deep diving part. No solarium.

7e

Piscine Déligny: 5 quai Anatole France. Tel. 45 51 72 15. M Solférino.

Freshwater open air pool near the Palais Bourbon. Owned by the management of the chic Les Bains nightclub, it's the smart place to swim or sunbathe on the vast deck above the Seine. Entrance is chic-ly steep too – 40f. It also has sports facilities and a restaurant.

11e

Piscine Oberkampf: 160 rue Oberkampf. Tel. 43 57 56 19. M Ménilmontant.

Two indoor, quiet, old-fashioned pools, one topped by a glass dome. No solarium.

13e

Piscine Buttes-aux-Cailles: 5 place Paul Verlaine. Tel. 45 89 60 05. M Place d'Italie.

Originally built in 1910, renovated in the '20s and in 1990, attractive indoor pool and an open air smaller one open in summer. No solarium.

15e

Piscine Armand-Massard: 66 boulevard du Montparnasse. Tel. 45 38 65 19. M Montparnasse-Bienvenue.

Huge subterranean complex under the Montparnasse Tower with three pools. No solarium but there's a gym.

16e

Piscine d'Auteuil: route des Lacs Bois de Boulogne. Tel. 42 24 07 59. M Ranelagh.

Underground, but not oppressive, pool with outside tanning area. Due to its location, in the centre of the racetrack, it closes at midday on race days.

18e

Piscine des Amiraux: 6 rue Hermann-Lachapelle. Tel. 46 06 46 47. M Simplon.

Indoor pool constructed in 1930 by the creator of the Samantaine department store.

20e

Piscine Georges Vallarey: 147 ave Gambetta. Tel. 40 31 15 20. M Saint-Fargeau.

This renovated indoor pool has a retractable roof for sunny swims from May–October. No solarium.

TENNIS

Private Parisian tennis clubs are both exclusive and expensive. Public pay-as-you-play courts have their own arcane rules. Along with many other expatriates you could take pot luck on the six concrete public courts at the **Luxembourg Gardens** (M Luxembourg) where it's a matter of first come first served.

There are other walk-on options – at, for example, the **Centre Sportific de Vaugirard** (2 rue Louis Armand 75015. Tel. 45 54 36 12. M Porte de Versailles); **Courts de Polygone de Vincennes** (Porte de la Pyramide 75012. Tel. 43 74 40 93. M Château de Vincennes); the **Centre Sportif de Lannes** (32 boulevard Lannes 75016. Tel. 45 03 03 64. M Porte

Dauphine). In all cases you should try to reserve 24 hours in advance. *Allô Sports* (Tel. 42 76 54 54) will supply more information or, alternatively, for a complete list of municipal courts – there are almost 200 – write to Bureau des Sports, 17 boulevard Morland 75181.

PARIS FOR KIDS

Paris is no better or worse than many other capital cities when it comes to catering for energetic children. Where it has the edge over London is that, providing they're well behaved, children are actually welcomed in the majority of cafés, restaurants and hotels. Few places have high-chairs, but many will serve children's portions on request. Cheap snacks, of course, can always be found easily in the many fast food outlets.

National museums admit under 18s free and there are children's discounts at most other attractions.

If you *and* the children are to enjoy Paris you'll need to plan extra carefully. Do check out the *pour les jeunes* section in one of the "What's On" guides like *L'Officiel*, *Pariscope* or *7 à Paris*, for topical news of children's events. Local town halls (*Mairies*) disseminate information on kids' activities in the *arrondissement*, and all *arrondissements* have public libraries with a children's corner and some books in English.

Here are some ideas for activities with children:

Aquaboulevard: aquatic wonderland with wonderful pool bordered by "Tahitan" village (4 rue Louis-Armand 75015. Tel: 40 60 10 00. M Balard. Free admission for under 3s).

Aquariums: even very young children like gazing at exotic fish. The two principal aquariums in Paris are **Aquarium de la Mer et des Eaux** (195 rue St Jacques 75015. Admission: 15f adults, 9f children. Open 10am–12.30pm and 1.15–5.30pm, Tues–Fri; weekends 10–5.30. M Luxembourg). **Aquarium Tropical** (293 avenue Daumesnil, in Musée National des Arts Africains et Océaniens, 75012.

Admission: 20f. 10f on Sun. Open 9.45am–noon and
1.30–5.15pm, Wednesday–Monday. M Porte Dorèe).

Boat Trips: a ride on the Seine on a *bateau-mouche* or
vedette is a fun way to get to know the capital. Boats are
large, covered, and there are commentaries in English. The
cost is 25–30f for adults, 12–15f for children under ten.
Departures every half-hour from: Square du Vert Galant
75001. M Pont-Neuf; Eiffel Tower 75007. M Bir Hakeim;
Pont de l'Alma 75008. M Alma Marceau. You can also
take a barge ride along the canals to La Villette – see
page 58.

Boating: Rent a rowing boat at the Lac Inférieur in the Bois
de Boulogne, at Lac des Minimes and Lac Daumesnil in the
Bois de Vincennes.

Circus: Language isn't such a barrier. Tickets range from
40F to 120f. There are evening and weekend matinée
performances: full listings are given in weekly guides or
check out the following:

Cirque Pauwels (Jardin d'Acclimation, Bois de Boulogne. M Les
Sablons.)

Cirque d'Hiver (110 rue Amelot 75011. Tel. 47 00 28 81. M Chemin
Vert. October–January).

Une Journée au Cirque (A day at the Circus) Le Cirque de Paris, avenue de la Commune de Paris/avenue Hoche 9200 Nanterre. Tel. 47 24 11 70. RER Nanterre Ville, line A. Sessions 10am–5pm, Wed, Sun, public holidays, school holidays. Closed during July–Oct. Show only 55–140f adults, 35–90f under-12s; day at circus and one meal 195–270f adults, 155–195f under-12s. No credit cards.) Children can spend a day training with the artists, clowning about, making up, having lunch in the ring followed by seeing the show at 3pm. The multi-lingual lion tamer takes the tots on a tour of the big cats.

MUSEUMS AND WORKSHOPS

At the **Centre Georges Pompidou** there's a children's library (*Salle d'Actualité de Jeunesse*) where the over 6s can be left unaccompanied to browse through books, comics and video films (a few in English). The children's workshop (*Atelier des Enfants*), run on a first come first served basis, enables you to deposit 6–12 year olds in the care of kindly assistants who oversee arty-crafty activities. A little knowledge of French will prevent the child from feeling totally bewildered. Enquire about the Wednesday and Saturday workshops with English-speaking playleaders.

Outside the Pompidou Centre the multifarious entertainers—juggling, fire-eating and so on—on the **Plateau Beaubourg** will amuse the kids, and they love the exterior, glassed-in elevators.

Other museums which don't ignore kids are the **en Herbe** museum (Jardin d'Acclimation), the **Parc Océanique Cousteau** in Les Halles, **L'Inventorium** at Cité des Sciences. Many museums have special programmes for children on Wednesday afternoons, but on the whole don't cater for non-French speakers. The newest attraction is **Planète Magique**. (3 bis rue Papin 75003. M Réamur-Sébastopol. Open 1–7pm, Mon; 10am–7pm, Tue–Sun during school holidays; Wed, Sat, Sun and holidays 10am–7pm; 1–7pm, Thur, Fri for the rest of the time). A series of themed game-rooms (Arthurian dungeon, Inca palace etc) will keep the kids spending francs till the fun's all over.

The most popular museum is likely to be the waxworks – especially the 9e branch with the dramatic sound effects and atmospheric cellar. **Musée Grévin Waxworks** (10 boulevard Montmartre 75009. Tel. 47 70 85 05. M Rue Montmartre. Open 10am–7pm daily. Admission 40f adults, 28f 6–14s, free under-6s. No credit cards).

OTHER OUTING IDEAS . . .

Don't forget the **Géode** with its 180-degree projection, the **catacombs** and the **sewers**, if, like most children, they have a taste for the creepy. Descriptions of these appear in the sections on the **19e, 14e** and **7e** respectively. Most children enjoy a climb, and the **Eiffel Tower, Tour Montparnasse, Arc de Triomphe, Notre-Dame** and **Sacré Coeur** provide the challenges. If you go to **Montmartre** they'll enjoy the brief ride on the funicular railway.

For details of swimming pools, ice-skating and roller skating rinks, see relevant sections in **Paris Sportif**.

In the Parisian suburbs, 22 miles (35km) from the centre, there's the **Parc Astérix** at Plailly. French children's first knowledge of the Roman Empire is gleaned from the adventures of Asterix and Obelisk and this themed amusement park aims to recreate the gladiator days. Rides, parades, music, puppeteers – kids love the lot. English is spoken. Expect long queues for the more exciting rides at the weekends and in high summer. See box on **Euro Disneyland** too.

Parc Astérix: (Tel.44 62 32 10. Off the Calais-Paris autoroute A1, exit Parc Asterix or by shuttle bus from M Fort d'Aubervilliers, every 30 minutes.) Open 10am–6pm, Mon–Fri, Sun; 10am–10pm, Sat, public holidays. Slightly longer opening hours July, Aug. Closed Nov–Mar. Admission charges are quite steep – around 140f adults, 100f 3–12s, under-3s free.

More thrills, courtesy of ghost trains, helter-skelters and white-knuckle rides lie in wait at **Parc Mirapolis** about 20 miles (30km) north-west of Paris. Find it on route de Courdimanche, Cergy-Pontoise. There's a free shuttle train from Cergy-St Christophe Station (RER line A3 terminus) to the entrance. (Open 10am–6.30pm daily, April–Aug;

10am—6.30pm, Sat and Sun, Sept. Admission 100f adults, 75f 5—13s, under-5s free.)

PARKS AND ZOOS

The **Jardin d'Acclimation**, while no bargain, is still the best place to take young children. Go in the afternoon if they want to ride the little train from Porte Maillot Métro. On Wednesday afternoons and at weekends there are special shows. The **Bois de Vincennes** also has lakes for boating, a little train, games area and a zoo (see **12e**).

A less brilliant zoo is in the **Jardin des Plantes** (5e) where in the Menagerie there are open enclosures with farm animals as well as the wilder beasts. Also in the Jardin des Plantes is the **Natural History Museum** – lots of skeletal dinosaurs. Over in east Paris, the **Buttes Chaumont** (19e), is a relaxed park where no one gets told off for walking on the grass; there are donkey rides, roller skating, boating.

Donkey rides and puppet shows are found in the shadow of the Eiffel Tower in the **Champ-de-Mars** (7e). The **Luxembourg Gardens** (6e) have a very good playground for young children with donkey rides, puppets and a pond for sailing toy boats and the **Parc Monceau** in the 8e is popular with families. In the 16e **Ranelagh Gardens** has a playground, cycling and roller skating track, merry-go-round and puppet shows – and you will also find the latter two in the Tuileries.

The open-air, supervised children's activity garden, slap in the centre of Les Halles (**Jardin des Enfants aux Halles**), caters for active 7—11 year olds with its slides, tunnels, rope swings and other paraphernalia. Grown-ups are banned, except on Saturdays between 10am—2pm when they may also bring smaller children. As numbers are restricted, best turn up early to book.

Jardin des Enfants aux Halles (Children's Garden in Les Halles): 105 rue Rambuteau 75001. Tel. 45 08 07 18. M Les Halles. Open May—October 9am—noon, 2—6pm, Tue, Thur, Fri; 10am—6pm, Wed, Sat; 1—6pm, Sun,

Euro Disney Resort

In Disneyspeak it's a "total destination resort"; in reality there's an almost baffling choice of things to do, see and eat at Europe's version of Disneyland, which opened Spring 1992, on a site one-fifth the size of Paris. Kids will love it — they'll want to stay a week or two — for their parents a couple of days would be about right. However long you choose to linger there are plenty of accommodation possibilities — six elaborately themed hotels, each saluting a different American lifestyle and time period (National Park historic lodges, a pueblo-style village, the Wild West, for instance) — plus a huge Davy Crockett camping ground which can accommodate over 12,000 guests. Enquiries about any of the Disney hotels should be directed to Euro Disney Reservations, PO Box 105, 94350. Villiers-Sur-Marne, France. Tel. 010 331 4941 4910 for information/reservations. They're predicting 15 million visitors a year.

No space here to detail all the activities, but if we hurl some words at you — stomach-churning rides (like the "runaway" Big Thunder Mountain mine train), a health club, marina, 36 themed shops, 1000-seat arena for the staging of a Wild West show, a disco, a Never Never Land Club for children, night clubs — you'll get the picture! There are five themed "lands" to explore: Main Street USA, tinkling with familiar Disney movie tunes, its cobblestones stroked with the tinsel they call "pixie dust"; Fantasyland; Frontierland; Adventureland and Discoveryland. There's a nod at European fairytales, featuring Peter Pan (the token Englishman), Cinderella (she's French) and Sleeping Beauty's Loire-inspired Château, complete with fire-breathing dragon.

Euro Disney is located along the A4 motorway that runs from Paris to Strasbourg. It's 35 minutes from Paris by RER and trains stop right outside the centre's front gate, as do public bus services. From June 1994 there'll also be a TGV high-speed rail link. Dormitory town for the new theme park is Marne-La-Vallée, a new town some 20 miles (32km) east of Paris.

For the first 3 months of operation the entry prices will be £20 per day for adults, £15 for children aged 3–9. The Wild West Show will cost about £30 for adults, £20 for children.

public holidays. November–April 9am–noon, 2–4pm, Tue, Thur, Fri; 10am–4pm Wed, Sat; 1–4pm Sun. public holidays, reserve a place in person, one hour before garden opens. Admission 2.20f per hour.

THEATRES, FILMS

Aside from puppet shows in the parks, many theatres have special children's productions – see the entertainment guides and also check the fringe (*cafe-théâtres*) where kids' shows may be staged at weekends and during school holidays.

One cinema in particular places the emphasis on children, **Le St Lambert** (6 rue Peclet 75015. Tel 45 32 91 68/48 28 78 87. M Vaugirard) specialising as it does in kids' films, including classics and comic strips all shown in VO (ie *version originale* or original language).

SHOPS FOR KIDS

BOOKS, TOYS . . .

The main stores, especially **Le Printemps**, have well-stocked toy departments and sell children's titles in their books department – the Trois Hiboux section of **Au Bon Marché** (ground floor, Magasin 1) is particularly good. **Chantelivre** at 13 rue de Sèvres 75006 (Tel. 45 48 87 90. M Sèvres-Babylone) is excellent for children's books and music in French and English. Privileged progeny receive their play things from the best-known toy emporium in Paris **Au Nain Bleu** (406–410 rue St Honoré 75001. Tel. 42 60 39 01. M Concorde). Three floors of toys of every type, including pocket money gadgetry. Scott Fitzgerald shopped here for daughter Sophie's tin soldiers. **Jouets et Cie** has costumes and party paraphernalia as well as every conceivable kind of toy (11 boulevard de Sébastopol 75001. Tel. 42 33 67 67. M Rambuteau).

Other top children's shops are listed below.

Si Tu Veux: 62–68 Galerie Vivienne 75002. Tel. 42 60 59 97.

Toys with a dash of nostalgia including teddy bears to turn-of-the-century designs, tin plate trains, while next door sells contemporary costumes (Babar, Tintin, etc.), games and playthings.

Ali Baba: 29 avenue de Tourville 75007. Tel. 45 55 10 85. M École Militaire St François-Xavier.

Farandole: 49 avenue Victor Hugo 75008. Tel. 45 01 72 32. M Victor-Hugo.

Jouets Extraordinaires: 70 rue d'Auteuil 75016. Tel. 46 51 15 70. M Porte d'Auteuil.

Jouets Montparnasse: 33 boulevard Edgar-Quinet 75014. Tel. 42 20 98 79. M Edgar Quinet.

Le Ciel est à tout le monde: 10 rue Gay-Lussac 75005. Tel. 46 33 21 50. M Luxembourg.

CLOTHES

French children's clothes are generally very stylish and very expensive. Many designers do a children's line. The leading department stores carry a wide selection; there are lovely, but pricey children's boutiques in **rue Jacob, 6e** and the following are worth investigating.

Un Après Midi de Chien: 10 rue du Jour 75001. Tel. 42 26 92 78. M Les Halles. Would-be Shirley Temples can look like Shirley Temple if they pick an outfit from this shop specialising in pre-teen girl's wear.

Benetton: 59 rue de Rennes 75006. Tel. 45 48 80 92. M St Supice.

Chipie: 31 rue de la Ferronerie 75001. Tel. 45 08 58 74. M Châtelet/Les Halles or 49 rue Bonaparte 6e. Tel. 43 29 21 94. M St Sulpice.

Trendy gear for 6m-pre teenies including versions of their retro jeanswear and denim jackets.

Elisabeth de Senneville: 38 place du Marché St Honoré 75001. Tel. 42 60 08 10. M Pyramides.

Exciting mini-clothing for 3-month to 12-year-olds in bold prints using computer graphics. Not a bunny or a bow in sight.

Miki House: 1 place des Victoires 75001. Tel. 40 26 23 00. M Bourse.

Discount Children's Clothing

As with adult fashion you can get great buys in nearly new, brand-named or designer children's wear if you know where to look. If new they might be "seconds", with tiny flaws, with the label torn out, or simply old stock. You'll probably have to rummage patiently and check the garments carefully. *Paris Pas Cher* (in French, Flammarion, 99f) is a very good source of outlets. A few of our favourites are:

Chercheminippes: 110 rue du Cherche-Midi 75006. Tel. 42 22 33 89. M Duroc. Open 10am–7pm, Mon–Sat. New and second hand clothes for 1–12 year olds, plus accessories.

Mouton à Cinq Pattes: 10 rue St Placide 75006. Tel. 45 48 50 77. M Sèvres-Babylone. Open 10am–7pm, Tue–Sat and 2–7pm, Mon. Also at 26 rue des Canettes 75006. Tel. 43 26 52 32. M Mabillon. Open 11am–7pm, Tue–Sat; 2–7pm Mon. Good quality at much lower prices than you'll find in smarter shops. Caters for babies and children up to 16.

Maman Troc: 6 bis rue Fourcroy 75017. Tel. 47 66 70 20. M Ternes. Open 10.30am–1pm and 3–7pm, Mon–Fri. Good choice of as-new baby and children's clothing (Chipie from 100f for trousers) plus maternity dresses. A few new items too.

Clothes, hats, accessories and shoes for the very young – up to 7 years – in pretty colours with appliqués.
Petit Bateau: 72 avenue Victor Hugo 75016. Tel. 45 00 13 95. M Kléber.

Quality, irresistible clothes for younger children.

CHILD MINDING

If you want a childless night out you can hire a babysitter. Fees vary according to when and for how long cover is needed. One of the oldest baby-sitting agencies in Paris, established over 20 years ago is: **Kid Service** (Tel. 42 96 04 16 or 42 96 '04 17. 9am–1pm, 2–8pm, Mon–Fri; 10am–2pm, 3–8pm, Sat. Closed Sun, public holidays. Rates around 25f per hour, depending on time of day. Booking fee charged).

You can rent baby equipment, a cot or pushchair, or a

babysitter from: **Âllo! Maman Poule** (Tel. 47 47 78 78. 24-hour service. Aprox 28f per hour plus booking fee).

Not a tourist service as such, but a helpful team provide a free telephone advisory service answering questions on babysitting and children's activities around town as well as kids' health, rights, sports activities: **Inter Service Parents** (Tel. 43 48 28 28. Open 9.30am–12.30pm, 1.30–5pm, Mon–Tue, Fri: 9.30am–12.30pm, Wed; 1.30–5pm, Thur. No credit cards).

More babysitting agencies are listed in the magazines *Pariscope* or *L'Officel des Spectacles* under *"Gardes d'Enfants"*.

GAY PARIS

There was a time when Paris did have clearly defined "gay" areas – St Germain for one. These days the gay quarters have shifted across the Seine to the Marais and Les Halles, but having said that, it's almost impossible to pinpoint any other area in particular in Paris where there's a greater or lesser concentration of gay residents. One of the oldest gay spots in the capital is the **Terrasse du Bord de l'Eau** in the **Tuileries**, popular for promenades for over 200 years. In summer **Tata Beach**, port des Tuileries, on the river bank is packed with half-dressed sun soakers.

What follows is a selection of gay, lesbian or sympathetic establishments and suggested organisations to contact when in Paris. The night spots do change quickly so it's wise to check in *Gay Pied* for up to the moment information or look in *Lesbia*. Gay men have much more choice when it comes to clubs than gay women – few lesbian clubs are exclusively female.

GENERAL INFORMATION/HELP

Centre du Christ Libérateur
3 bis rue Clairaut 75017. Tel. 46 27 49 36. M La Fourche.
The largest centre for gays in Paris, CCL sponsors various kinds of groups and activities. CCL is actually a Christian organisation, but the centre's services are available to all, regardless of religious affiliation. Information on gay weddings, trans-sexuality and a wide range of other gay issues. Christian services are held each Sunday at 12 noon and a bilingual candlelit meal is also held every Wednesday at 8.30pm. A CCL-sponsored discussion group for bisexuals meets the first Friday of each month at 8.30pm. *SOS Homosexualité*, a gay switchboard number 46 27 49 36, is open 10am-midnight daily.

Miel (*Mouvement d'Information et d'Expression des Lesbiennes*)
A friendly gay women's support group. Meets every Thursday at 7pm
and runs a very cheap club, **L'Hydromel**, each Friday 8pm–1am at the
Maison des Femmes, 8 cité Prost 75011. Tel. 43 48 24 91. (Phone first).
M Faidherbe-Chaligny. Information on current activities for women. Tel.
43 79 61 91 or 43 79 66 07.

Gage
c/o Les Mots à la Bouche, 6 rue Ste-Croix-de-la-Bretonnerie 75004.
Tel. 42 02 03 03. M St Paul.
Gay student group: men and women welcome.

Kid'logement
c/o Éspaces Libertés, BP468, 75527 Paris, Cedex 11.
A service that helps gays find lodging in Paris.

Act Up
177 rue de Charonne 75011, Tel. 42 63 44 78. M Charonne.
Leading anti-aids crusader. Anyone is welcome to go along to the weekly
Tuesday meetings at 7.30pm.

PUBLICATIONS/BOOKS

Les Mots à la Bouche
6 rue Ste-Croix-de-la-Bretonnerie 75004. Tel. 42 78 88 30. M Hôtel
de la Ville.
Situated in the Marais, this is the main gay bookshop in the capital, with
a wide international selection of gay literature, psychology magazines
plus art books and postcards. You can buy Weaver's *Gay Paris* here
– the English language gay guide to the city.
Open 11am–8pm, Mon–Sat. Credit: MC, V.

Des Femmes Librairie-Galérie
74 rue de Seine 75006. Tel. 43 29 50 75. M Odéon.
Feminist bookshop, including titles of particular interest to lesbians.
You can buy *Lesbia* here, the largest and most comprehensive magazine
for lesbians, published monthly. (Telephone number of *Lesbia*: 43
48 89 54.)

Gai Pied Hebdo
The main magazine for the gay community in France, published weekly.
New issues out each Friday. *Gai Pied* also produce an annual guide to
France – the most comprehensive available – which is published in
June. Buy it from newsagents, major bookshops or from *Les Mots à
la Bouche*, or by post from *Gai Pied*.

    Gai Pied Emploi is a gay employment agency associated with
the magazine. Mon–Fri. Gai Pied Emploi, c/o Gai Pied, 45 rue

Sedaine 75011. Tel. 43 38 18 00. M Breguet–Sabin. Office hours: 9.30am–12.30pm.

Gay News Kiosk
29 boulevard des Italiens 75002. M Opéra.
Open 8am-12 midnight, Mon–Sat.

Lesbian Archives ARCL (*Archives Researches et Cultures Lesbiennes*)
BP 362, 75526 Paris, Cedex 11. Tel. 45 05 25 89.
Books and magazines, to read there or to borrow – much in English.
Also videos, cassettes.

GAY VENUES

BH
7 rue de Roule 75001. No phone. M Louvre RER Châtelet-Les Halles.
Open 11pm–7am daily. Admission free Mon–Thur and Sun. Small charge at weekends. Credit: MC, V.
Upstairs bar, downstairs dance floor. Warm, even hot, atmosphere.

Le Boy
6 rue Caumartin 75009. Tel. 47 42 68 05. M Madeleine Opéra.
Open 11pm–6.30am daily. Admission free weekdays, charge at weekends.
Ever popular venue for mixed crowd to party and show off their designer threads.

Broad Café
13 rue de la Ferronnerie 75001. Tel. 42 33 35 31. M RER Châtelet Les-Halles.
Open 11.30am–3am, Mon–Sat; 2.30pm–3am, Sunday. Credit: MC V
Trendy cocktail bar-cum-coffee shop; shows video clips.

Bar Hôtel Central
33 rue Vieille-du-Temple 75004. Tel. 42 78 11 42. M St Paul/Hôtel de Ville. 4pm–2am daily. Credit: MC, V.
Well-known, popular bar – one of the oldest of the gay Marais with a friendly, laid back atmosphere. Mostly, but not exclusively, men. If you get there early prices are cheaper; they go up after 10pm.

Le Caveau de la Bastille
6 passage Thiéré 75011. Tel. 47 00 55 33. M Bastille.
Strictly women only bar with music and small games room for backgammon fans. Quality cabaret once a month.

La Champmeslé
4 rue Chabanais 75002. Tel. 42 96 85 20. M Pyramides/Les Halles.

Open 6pm–2am, Mon–Sat. Credit AE, DC, V.
Countrified (dark beams, wooden tables, flickering candles) women only bar with amateur cabaret night on Thursdays when customers get up and do a turn. Drinks aren't cheap, although cheaper before 10pm. The notice board here details current women's events and small ads.

Club 18
18 rue du Beaujolais 75001. Tel. 42 97 52 13. M Bourse.
Open 1.30pm–6am daily. Admission free Mon–Thurs, Sun. Charge Fri–Sat. Credit: MC, V.
Teenagers party to chart toppers in this small, pally nightspot. Mostly for the boys.

Coffee Shop Central
3 rue Ste-Croix-de-la-Bretonnerie 75004. Tel. 42 74 71 52. M St Paul.
Open every day 12 noon-midnight.
A mixed and happy blend of gays and straights makes this bistro-like place a relaxed spot to hang out and enjoy the recent videos imported from the United States. Light meals.

Le Duplex
25 rue Michel le Comte 75003. Tel. 42 72 80 86. M Rambuteau.
Open 8pm–2am daily. No credit cards.
Friendly little bar with young gay and lesbian clientèle. Avant-garde exhibitions held regularly.

H²O
50 rue Godefroy Cavaignac 75011. Tel. 40 09 90 92. M Voltaire.
Open 8pm–2am daily. Credit, MC, V.
An eccentric "in" place on the edge of the Bastille area, not exclusively gay. The main speciality of this slick bar is cocktails, although there's a decent selection of beers too.

Le Guet-Apens
10 rue Descartes 75005. Tel. 40 46 81 40. M Maubert.
Open 11am–2am, Mon–Sat: 6–11pm, Sun.
Quiet bar/café with terrace that serves cocktails, snacks; professional singer most Saturdays. Mostly women, men allowed.

Le Katmandu
21 rue de Vieux Colombier 75006. Tel. 45 48 12 96. M St Sulpice.
Open 11pm–6am daily. Admission 90f.
One of the oldest lesbian clubs in town (no men) with strict door policy, founded 15 years ago by a feminist writer. Wednesday and Thursday are the best nights. Drinks are expensive but the first is included in the admission charge.

Le Memorie's
78 boulevard Gouvion-St-Cyr 75017. Tel. 46 40 28 12. M Porte Maillot.
Open 11pm–dawn every night. One of the newest lesbian clubs. A few

men make it past the fierce *patronne*. Ring to book a table if you don't feel strong enough to fight your way in; small, packed dance floor.

Le Palace (Tea Dance)

8 rue du Faubourg Montmartre 75009. Tel. 42 46 10 87. M rue Montmartre.
Gay Parisian institution – the all male Sunday afternoon tea dance. 60f. Phone for times.

Objectif Lune

19 rue de la Roquette 75011. Tel. 48 06 46 05. M Bastille.
Open 6pm–2am daily. Credit: MC, V.
Cabaret at another "in" watering-hole in the newly trendy area close to the new Bastille Opéra.

Piano Zinc

49 rue des Blancs-Manteaux 75001. Tel. 42 74 32 42. M Hôtel de Ville.
Open 6pm–2am daily. Closed on Mon.
Friendly, always busy upstairs with a downstairs ebullient piano bar (from 10pm). The (mixed) audience are encouraged to join in the entertainment.

Le Quetzal

10 rue de la Verrerie 75004. Tel. 48 87 99 07. M Hôtel de Ville.
Open noon–2am, Mon–Fri; 2pm–2am, weekends.
Enormously popular – and so usually crowded – and very *loud* bar, complete with videos.

Le Soft

7 place Pigalle 75009. Tel. 42 80 64 64. M Pigalle.
Open 11pm–dawn, Wed–Sat.
Wednesdays are traditionally lesbian club time with cabaret and spaghetti party.

Studio A

51 rue de Ponthieu 75008.
(See **Night Clubs and Discos** p. 181.)

Le Swing

42 rue Vieille du Temple 75004. Tel. 42 72 16 94. M Hôtel de Ville.
Open noon–2am, Mon–Sat; 2pm–2am, Sun.
Small well-frequented 1950's-style bar where straight and gay crowd drink, read the papers and listen to the music.

Le Transfert

3 rue de la Sourdière 75001. Tel. 42 60 48 42. M Tuileries.
Open 11pm–5am daily. Credit: V. Leather dress.

The Trap

10 rue Jacob 75006. Tel. 43 54 53 53. M Saint-Germain-des-Prés.

Open 11pm–4am daily. Admission 50f.
Ground floor bar with an iron staircase leading to a busy, dark first floor. A door policy operates, bouncers can be quite choosy but friendly if you're not too pushy.

RESTAURANTS

Some listed here cater for a predominantly gay clientèle, others are mostly run by gay people for a mixed crowd:

Agnès et Guillemette
10 rue St Sébastien 75011. Tel. 43 55 27 31. M St-Sébastien-Froissart.
Open 11.30am–3pm, Mon–Fri.
Delightful tea room in quiet street between place de la République and place de la Bastille. Light lunches, cakes etc. from the hands of the eponymous proprietors; 17 kinds of tea, yummy chocolate gâteau and apple crumble. Allow 40f per person for a nice tea.

L'Amazonial
3 rue Ste Opportune 75001. Tel. 42 33 53 13. M Châtelet/Les Halles.
Open noon–3pm, 7pm–1am, Mon–Fri; 7pm–1am, Sat, Sun. Credit: MC, V.
Large (120 seats), exotically decorated, always crowded both inside and out on the terrace. Central Les Halles location makes it a popular post-show supper spot. Good French fare; set menus from around 80f.

Aux Mauvais Garçons
4 rue des Mauvais Garçons 75004. Tel. 48 87 96 98. M Hôtel de Ville.
Open noon–1.30pm, Tue–Sat; 7–11pm, Sun. Credit: AE, MC, V.
Informal, small restaurant serving traditional French cooking.

L'Aviatic
23 rue Ste-Croix-de-la-Bretonnerie 75004. Tel. 42 78 26 20. M Hôtel de Ville.
Open noon–2am daily. Credit: AE, MC, V.
High-tech décor and US-influenced food (burgers, big salads, ices). Expensive and trendy.

La Bolée
25 rue Servandoni 75006. Tel. 46 34 17 68. M St Sulpice/Odéon.
Open 11am–3pm, 6–10pm, Mon–Sat. Credit V.
Breton crêperie popular with assorted combinations of couples. Allow 50–60f.

Chez Nini Peau d'Chien

24 rue des Taillandiers 75011. Tel. 47 00 45 35. M Bastille.

Open: ring for times, Mon–Sat.

Mainly female clientèle, especially later in the week. Standard French fare with a 90f set menu.

L'Etrier

154 rue Lamarck 75018. Tel. 42 29 14 01. M Guy Moquet.

Open 7–11pm, Mon–Sat.

Run by lesbians, this fashionable eaterie specialises in French food with an Argentinian influence (Argentian chef). Set menu 92f. Ring for details of the monthly musical Argentinian soirée.

Au Petit Cabanon

7 rue Ste Apolline 75003. Tel. 48 87 66 53. M Strasbourg-St Denis.

Open lunchtimes Mon–Fri; 7pm–1am, Thur–Sat.

Reliable French cuisine appreciated by local lunchers; in the evenings 99% of the diners are female.

La Pierrot de la Butte

41 rue de Caulaincourt 75018. Tel. 46 06 06 97. M Place de Clichy/Lamarck-Caulaincourt.

Open noon–2pm, 7.30–11.30pm, Mon–Sat. Credit: MC, V.

People often come here after a show for the traditional French cooking. Set menus lunch (65f), dinner (95f).

Le Remedium

11 rue Rodier 75009. Tel. 48 78 27 80. M Notre-Dame-de-Lorette/Anvers.

Open 7pm–midnight, Mon–Sat. Credit: MC, V.

Not cheap but pleasant small Polish/Russian restaurant. Multilingual cosmopolitan staff.

GETTING YOUR BEARINGS

THE "PÉRIPH"

Paris is encircled by the infamous *périphérique*, a 22-mile ring road that wraps round the central sector of the city as tightly as an elastic band round a parcel.

The million vehicles that circuit it daily all have the same priority – to get round and off a.s.a.p. This is Europe's busiest (and, arguably, scariest) road. The figures say it all: around 14,000 crashes, 20 deaths and a quarter of a million speeding fines a year.

It was built on the site of the city fortifications – which helpfully doubled as a tax point for anyone who wanted to enter the capital. Tax is always fearsome, but today 20% of fatalities on the *"périf"* result from heart attacks. But when the average daytime traffic speed of 13mph trickles to a halt, you're more likely to feel you're going to die of old age before you get to your destination.

ARRONDISSEMENTS

Within the *périphérique*, central Paris is compact. You can cross it in half a day. In fact, the inner city measures just 6.5 miles (10.5km) from east to west, 5.4 miles (8.7km) from north to south.

It was Baron Haussmann, Prefect of the Seine district under Napoleon III, who drew a new boundary round Paris, bringing in parts of the forests of Boulogne and Vincennes, and outlying "villages" like Belleville, Montmartre, Auteuil and Passy. He sliced the city into 20 sections or *arrondissements*, each of which has its own *quartiers* which (mathematically) aren't quarters but districts. Each *arrondissement* has a distinctive personality and is dealt with in turn in this book, with a full description of what there is to see and do.

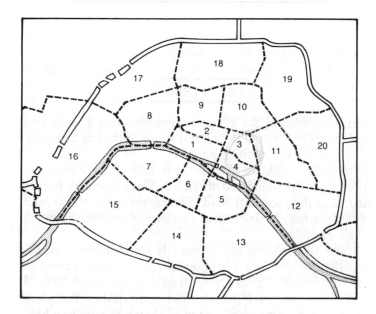

The first *arrondissement* (written 1er, the abbreviation for *premier*) is centred on the Louvre and the rest uncoil clockwise. (The most central segment of the city is contained within numbers 1er–8e.) Throughout this book we've used 2e for *deuxième*, etc.

Curving across town from east to west, with two islands in its centre (Ile de la Cité and Ile St Louis), is the river Seine.

THE RIGHT AND LEFT BANKS OF THE SEINE

Stand on one of the 33 bridges that sweep across the Seine and face the direction of the current: the right bank (*rive droite*) is on the right, the left bank (*rive gauche*) on the left. With ruthless French logic, the streets which are vertical in relation to the Seine have numbers beginning at the end nearest the river. Streets which run parallel to the Seine have numbers which run east to west, or as you head downstream.

Certain landmarks help you to keep your bearings as they pop up repeatedly on the horizon – the Eiffel Tower is to the west of the city, the Montparnasse Tower to the south-west, the white domes of Sacré-Coeur, Montmartre to the north.

When Parisians refer to the *rive droite* and *rive gauche* they're most likely using the tags to indicate direction rather than describe what an area's like. Nevertheless, each bank has its own characteristics and atmosphere.

The larger right bank is the more commercial – although in a city which changes constantly and rapidly, almost every generalisation needs qualifying, and some of the southern left bank *arrondissements* are also becoming important business centres. But it has major financial institutions, sober banks, grandiose buildings, spacious boulevards. Huge chunks of the right bank become a stage set for displays of chauvinistic nationalism – notably the Arc de Triomphe, Champs-Élysées and place de la Concorde.

As well as grandeur, the Paris beloved of ad agencies has glamour too – the stylish fashion shops and salons of the rue du Faubourg St Honoré, place Vendôme, Palais Royale and Opéra. There's seediness, too, in the Clichy/Pigalle and Sentier districts. And the discretion of "sealed-off" exclusive residential areas in the 16e, nesting place of the well-off, well-dressed French Sloanes, the *BCBGs* (*bon chic, bon genre*). The Marais is an unspoilt corner, like no other in the city, with a late medieval character.

Contrasts abound too on the left bank, which, generally speaking, has a more laid back, carefree, informal feel than its opposite number. To the north there's the *beaux arts* district with medieval façades; to the west the 18th-century Faubourg St Germain and famous cafés; to the south busy broad 19th-century avenues and the 20th-century Tour Montparnasse. To the east is the ancient abbey church of St-Germain-des-Prés, a reminder of when the area was meadowland.

The left bank was known for ages as the "*Université*" – the two other parts of Paris were "*Cité*" (the island) and "*Ville*" (the right bank) — and its reputation as the intellectual nest of Paris still clings. For centuries applied scepticism has filled the left bank streets, from the rhetoric of medieval teachers to 20th-century student riots over outmoded educational systems. Well trampled and touristy in parts, the left bank is nevertheless a compelling, characterful part of the city, rich in history and colour.

1ER:
Museums and Markets

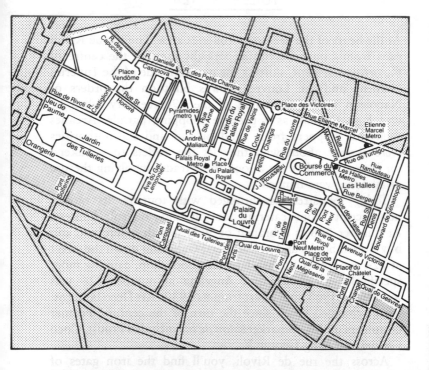

Old and new are dramatically juxtaposed in the first *arrondissement*. The square slab of central Paris encompassed by the 1er includes the monumental and the modern: the Louvre, Palais Royal and most of Les Halles. Strictly speaking, a segment of the Ile de la Cité is in the 1er too, but this has a section of its own with the Ile St Louis (see page 304.)

As well as having its fair share of the most historic buildings in the city, there's also the brash new Forum sitting cheek by jowl with the yuppified streets of the former central market of Les Halles; the resolutely modern glass pyramid defiantly squatting amongst the late-19th-century buildings of the Cour Napoléon at the Louvre. And it goes almost without saying that there are cohorts of tourists too.

TUILERIES AREA

At the heart of the 1er is the Tuileries area. The **rue de Rivoli** runs from Concorde cutting straight through the centre of the *arrondissement*, skirting the northern side of the Tuileries Gardens and the Louvre. It was built on the orders of Napoleon at the beginning of the 19th century when he was First Consul, as a prestige shopping parade. Arcades sheltered shoppers from wind or sun and the authorities were choosy about who they let the outlets to – bakers, for instance, didn't get a look in as trades involving the use of an oven were banned.

Today the street is thronged with tourists, its mostly nondescript shops catering for gift and souvenir hunters. At number 248 is a branch of **W.H. Smith** where you can buy British books and newspapers; **Galignani** down the street at 224 is another English-language bookshop, catering more specifically for Americans. **Angelina** at number 226 was founded in 1903 and, apart from its 1930s Art Deco lanterns, hasn't changed much since the turn of the century. Former customers of this upmarket *salon de thé* included Proust, Coco Chanel and King George V.

Across the rue de Rivoli, you'll find the iron gates of the **Jardins des Tuileries**, so called because it was once the site of an old tileworks (*tuileries*). The gardens were first planned in the 16th century by Catherine de Medici who missed the public promenades of her native Italy. But the present gardens owe all to André Le Nôtre, the designer of the gardens at Versailles, who introduced all his favourite formal elements – manicured, ruler-straight gravelly avenues, clipped trees, statues galore. The central avenue with its two ornamental ponds (popular with toy boat-sailing children) is neatly aligned with the Champs-Élysées and the Louvre. The Seine side of the park is a popular pick-up spot for gays, especially after dusk. On raised terraces at the far western end are twin large pavilions, the **Jeu de Paume** (formerly the real tennis court) and the **Orangerie** (formerly the greenhouse of the gardens) – both now art galleries.

The Jeu de Paume has been ransacked, its magnificent collection of impressionist paintings having been moved into the d'Orsay, and is being converted into a contemporary art gallery, due to open as we went to press. The Orangerie is one of Paris's small museum delights. It houses the Walter and Guillaume collection of paintings, one of the best presented in Paris, and famous artists you'll find well represented here are Renoir, Matisse and Cézanne; there are a few fine Picassos, and paintings by Rousseau, Sisley and Soutines. Pride of place goes to Monet's eye-soothing "Nymphéas", his waterlilies at Giverny murals which are on permanent display in beautifully-lit oval rooms.

Musée de l'Orangerie: place de la Concorde. Tel. 42 97 48 16. M Concorde. Open 9.45am–5.15pm, Mon, Wed–Sun. Closed Tue. Admission 23f adults; 12f 18–25s, OAPs, everyone on Sunday; free under-18s. No credit cards.

Before we leave this patch, it's worth mentioning that the designer of the Tuileries gardens, Le Nôtre, is buried five minutes' walk away in the **Church of St Roch**. A fine example of baroque architecture, the church is also the burial spot of the playwrights Corneille and Diderot. It's the artists' church of Paris, particularly musicians – the Sunday mid-morning mass is held in their honour. Concerts are held here periodically – phone for details.

Church of St Roch: 296 rue St Honoré. Tel. 42 60 81 69. M Pyramides/Tuileries. Open 8am–7.15 pm daily. Services: 11am, 12.15pm, 6.45pm, Mon–Fri; 11am, 6.30pm, Sat; 8.30am, 9.30am (in Latin), noon, 6.30pm, Sunday.

Walk down rue des Pyramides and you come to **place des Pyramides,** a focal point for coach tours of the city. (Cityrama is at number 4. Tel. 42 60 30 14.) The gilded equestrian statue is of Joan of Arc.

From here you're virtually on the doorstep of the **Louvre,** so if you're in the mood for tackling that, skip a few pages. To see another corner of the 1er, read on.

From majestic gardening to majestic urban planning – if you walk up the rue de Castiglione which leads off the rue de Rivoli, you'll come to the octagonal **place Vendôme,** an epicentre of style that's every bit as expensive as it looks. It exudes an aloof "look but don't touch-ness" from every elegant arcade, to deter impoverished interlopers. The Ministry of Justice, well-known bankers, jewellers (Cartier, Chaumet, Boucheron, Van Cleef and Arpels), perfumiers (Guerlain) and fashion houses are, however, all very opulently at home here.

Designed by Jules Hardouin-Mansart, construction of the place Vendôme began in 1685 during the reign of Louis XIV as a showpiece backdrop for the King's statue – originally it was just a masterly strip of façades with arches below, and classical pedimented pavilions at focal points. It wasn't until 33 years after work had started on the square that the last building behind the perfectly proportioned façades was added.

Come the Revolution, down came the aforementioned statue. In 1810, with a characteristic thrust of imperialist pomp, Napoleon erected a bronze column made from 1200 canons, captured from the Russians and Austrians at the Battle of Austerlitz 5 years previously, to commemorate his victories. With equally characteristic lack of modesty, he topped it with a statue of himself thinly disguised as Julius Caesar. In the following years statues were swapped and changed as they came and went out of fashion, all to be finally replaced by La Colonne, Napoleon's monument.

As you might imagine, the grand town houses of the *place* have provided a roof over the head of financiers and aristos galore. A plaque at number 12 records that the composer Chopin died there; at number 16 lived the inventor of Mesmerism, the Austrian F.A. Mesmer. No plaque is required at number 15 to remind us that "Winston Churchill, Greta

Garbo, Charlie Chaplin slept here" – instead the Ritz names its suites after some of its erstwhile illustrious guests like Coco Chanel who spent the last years of her life there. Once they'd hit the literary jackpot, F. Scott Fitzgerald and Ernest Hemingway also ensconced themselves here – but you're far more likely to see well-padded American tourists than up-and-coming writers at the famous Hemingway Bar (so called because it was the writer's favourite hangout) in the Ritz today.

From here if you double back to the rue de Rivoli, you'll confront the massive Louvre.

THE LOUVRE

The most famous art gallery on earth; the largest palace in Europe; the biggest museum in the world – the **Louvre** excels in superlatives. It's about Art with a capital "A"; art from the beginning of civilisation to the 19th century. The Louvre's statistics are staggering. It took 660 years to build, involving countless architects and rulers. A staff of 1000 minister to the 4 million visitors who came each year to eyeball the 300,000 works of art on display.

The new, improved, Louvre has never been so user-friendly, even though, its detractors say, it is still not user-friendly enough. Before we get on to how and why, and actually move inside, it's time to sneak in a quick word on the architectural merits of the palace itself – or perhaps that should be demerits.

EXTERIOR OF THE LOUVRE

The fact is that architecturally the Louvre is monotonous: it simply goes on and on and on. It's hardly any wonder that so many French monarchs preferred to live elsewhere – Louis XIV became so bored with it halfway through his rebuilding programme that he moved the court out to Versailles, leaving the Louvre as a rather posh storage depot and office block. But, to be fair, two parts in particular are worth a closer look.

A Little Louvre History

"Chequered" is the word that best fits the Louvre's history. Eight hundred years ago the French, worried about Richard the Lionheart's plans to sail up the Seine and capture Paris, built this edifice as a formidable fortress. It marked the city's limits on the right bank. From the mid-14th century onwards it became a royal mansion for successive generations of French monarchs, even though there was a less austere official residence already, on the Ile de la Cité. François I (1494–1547) rebuilt the Louvre to create a more palatial, less fortress-like, setting for his collection of Italian Renaissance art — which included the Mona Lisa — and the great museum was begun. Subsequent monarchs added to both the palace and the artworks haphazardly, and the latter swallowed up more and more of the former as the collection burgeoned.

With the Revolution under way and the monarchy no more, a decision was taken to open up the *Grand Galerie* part of the Louvre to the public, which it was, in 1793. Napoleon supplemented the existing private collections of kings and their courtiers with artistic plunderings from his Empire — and, hey presto, he had the largest art collection in the world on his hands. Some of these artworks were later returned, but an awful lot were not.

For the visitor this is probably beginning to sound like hard work. Even if you moved in tomorrow, you say to yourself, you'd die of exhaustion before you'd exhausted the art treasures. There's no doubt that up until a few years ago the Louvre was not an easy place to get to grips with. Since its radical revamp, however, the exasperation involved in tracking down favourite treasures has been greatly minimised.

The finest is the harmonious **Cour Carré** or square court, not much changed since Pierre Lescot designed it in the 16th century for François I in Renaissance style. Louis XIII extended the west façade in the same style 100 years later and Louis XIV built the remainder of the court. At the extreme eastern end of the Louvre, along the outside of this courtyard, like a screen, is a commanding **colonnade** of 52 columns, a great example of the neo-classical style carried out by Claude Perrault in 1673.

Facing this, across the road, is **St Germain l'Auxerrois**, the French royal family's parish church, used until the Revolution, when the Louvre was still a palace. It took 200 years to build and incorporates 13th-, 14th-, 15th- and 16th-century architecture.

You're now at the easternmost end of the Louvre and if you're flagging, there's a handy tea shop at **Cador**, 2 rue de l'Admiral-Coligny, where you can plan your route march round the museum or simply collapse. Its white and gilt panelling enriched with garlands and pilasters and an original green-and-white-tiled floor make a soothing setting.

At the opposite, westernmost, end of the Louvre there's a gentle reminder that Napoleon Bonaparte was one of the museum's greatest patrons. Erected in 1806, the **Arc du Carrousel**, a neater Arc de Triomphe, celebrates his military victories, including Austerlitz. There's a smashing view from the place du Carrousel, of the Arc de Triomphe itself, looking across the Tuileries, place de la Concorde and the Champs-Élysées.

THE PYRAMID

The main reason, of course, for visiting the Louvre is to see the treasures it contains. The principal entrance is through the Cour Napoléon via the spectacular 71-foot-high glass pyramid which caused such a rumpus when it was unveiled. Ironically, most Parisians have been to the Louvre only twice in their lives – once as schoolchildren on the old free Wednesdays (stopped in 1988), and once again in 1989 to see the Pyramid.

Designed by the Chinese-American architect Ieoh Ming Pei, the bold glass and metal monument has helped to bring the fossilised 19th-century museum into the 20th century. ("It was time to bring life to the Louvre, because if it sleeps, then the rest of Paris is asleep too," said the Pyramid's creator).

An alien's spaceship? A presidential ego-trip? An annexe to Disneyland? Whatever you think of it, the latest daring addition to 8 centuries of building, demolition, reconstruction and restoration, has made it a lot easier to get into and around the museum. Escalators sweep you down to a gigantic, incandescent entrance hall – which critics say looks like an

How to Survive the Louvre

- Make an early start: a thick queue starts draping itself around the courtyard well before opening time, 9am, and later on the Louvre is like the Métro at rush hour — except that it lasts all day.

- The Louvre Métro has nice murals, but the Palais Royale Métro is a little quicker and easier — head for the exit by the rue de Rivoli, through the arch to Cour Napoléon *et voilà* . . .

  If you've seen the Pyramid and can't face a long wait, go in through the lesser-known back door of the Louvre. De-Métro at the Tuileries Gardens stop, turn left into the gardens, past the fountain, bear left until you reach Porte Jaujard — the entrance used by Parisians in The Know.

- Unless you like the feeling of being at the first day of Harrods' sale, give Sunday at the Louvre a miss. Until February 1990 there was free access to the museum on Sunday, but price for entry is now *demi tarif*, as in all other national museums on the Sabbath. (The young, old and unemployed are still let in free.)

- You can spend your whole holiday (except Tuesdays) in the Louvre or just half an hour, but you'll enjoy it more if you allow as much time as possible. A quick ogle-and-be-off dash round isn't much fun.

- All those people with you in the queue wearing Reeboks can't be wrong — even with helpful lifts and escalators, there's a fair bit of footwork to be done.

- You might not like the idea of following an umbrella-toting tour guide round the Louvre, but it's not a bad idea on a first visit to get an overall view of the collections.

airport — where you can orientate yourself and plan your march through the masterpieces.

Pei created some 20 subterranean acres *beneath* the Pyramid to contain all the infrastructure needed to run the Louvre. The whole area had to be excavated carefully — and a valuable by-product of this was the cache uncovered: the remains of the medieval Louvre under the Cour Carré and some streets and houses under the Cour Napoléon. See them for yourself in the exhibition on the history of the palace.

In the **Hall Napoléon** (entrance to which is free and can also be reached via passage Richelieu from rue de Rivoli, from the underground car park or through the Tuileries) there are nearly all the facilities of an airport – phones, loos, a post office, a room with nursery facilities, a café, a restaurant, bureau de change, shops selling reproductions, videos and souvenirs. You can hire a cassette player (guided tours in six languages), or buy an official catalogue (pricey).

Check in at the information counter, at the bottom of the escalator, to pick up a copy of the free leaflet setting out the room numbers for each of the three colour-coded floors. These are U-shaped: the **Richelieu** wing is on one side, **Denon** on the other, **Sully** at the end, the Pyramid in the centre. These three territories are divided into sections, each marked by numbers in square panels, displayed outside the rooms. So every artwork has its own address. Here is a useful clue: the most popular masterpiece in residence, the Mona Lisa, is Denon 5 Purple. The other two most-ogled exhibits, the Winged Victory of Samothrace and the Venus de Milo, are equally clearly signposted. Thanks to the expansion, many previously undisplayed treasures are now on view: President Mitterand has stuck by his pledge to turn the Louvre into the biggest museum in the world.

THE EXHIBITS

The ministry of finance has been turfed out of its offices in the Richelieu wing to make more room for the artworks and the presentation of the collections has been much improved, exploiting the third of extra exhibition space they've gained. The **Applied Arts** section now joins up with the **Musée des Arts Décoratifs** collection on the second floor of the former finance ministry and the north wing of the Cour Carré.

Briefly, the collections subdivide into sections as follows below. The escalators, lifts, omnipresent maps and signs will deposit you directly at the place you want to be – or so the theory goes. A handful of major exhibits for each section are listed below.

THE LOUVRE: A BRIEF GUIDE

Note: the rearrangement of the Louvre is not complete so you can't be 100% certain what will be on show.

Oriental Antiquities (Ground Floor)
Mainly devoted to the Mesopotamian civilisation and treasures from Iran, Levant and the Orient (with the Eastern section being in the Musée d'Arts Asiatiques). Look out for: the **Code of King Hammurabi of Babylon**, a basalt stone inscribed with his 282 laws in the Akkad language (*c.*1750 BC); **Stele of The Vultures** which commemorates the victory of a Sumerian King at Lagash, (2450 BC); the impressive **Stele of Naram-Sin** (2250 BC), a rose-coloured sandstone showing the king and the defeated enemy.

Greek, Etruscan and Roman Antiquities (Ground and 1st Floors)

Representing every period, from early Hellenic times to the end of the Roman Empire, this is one of the most popular collections in the museum due to its two starlets. The **Venus de Milo** (*c*.3–2 BC) was discovered in 1820 by a farm worker, has vital statistics of 47.6, 33.2 50.8 inches, and she is almost 7 feet tall. The handsome but headless **Winged Victory of Samothrace** (*c*.3 BC) is the other big draw. Also watch out for the **Lady of Auxerre**, an early example of Greek sculpture, **Hera of Samos**, the **Rampin Horseman** (*c*.6 BC), the pre-classical bronze of **Apollo of Piombino** (*c*.5 BC).

Egyptian Antiquities (Ground and 1st Floors)

Begun in 1826 by the acclaimed Egyptologist Champollion, who decoded the Rosetta Stone, this collection is one of the finest in world with its figurines, jewellery and statues. Major exhibits include the flint-bladed **Gebel-el-Arak Knife** with delicately carved ivory handle (3400 BC), the bust of Amenophis IV, jewels of Rameses II, and a masterpiece in bronze, the **Statue of Queen Karomama**.

Sculptures (Ground Floor)

The least-visited section of the Louvre depicts the development of sculpture from its beginnings to the end of the 19th century, including seminal works by non-French greats such as Michelangelo's **The Slaves**, carved between 1513 and 1520 for the unfinished tomb of Pope Julius II, and the **Madonna and Child** by Donatello. A French offering by Jean Goujon is **Nymphs from the Fountain of the Innocents**. (NB: the French sculptures will be moved to Pavillion Richelieu when it is ready.)

Objets d'Art and Furniture (1st Floor)

Furniture and Objets d'Art from the middle ages to the 19th century are in the famous **Galerie d'Apollon** (1661, but much restored since the fire of 1871). Murals by Le Brun and Delacroix provide an ideal setting for the number one attraction, the **Crown Jewels,** which include the Regent Diamond (137 carats).

The Colonnade Galleries with their spectacular panelling and ceilings house decorative art from the middle ages to Napoleon, Notably the **Ivory Virgin,** and the **Maximilian Tapestries** woven in 1535.

Paintings (1st and 2nd Floors)

An incredibly rich section filling most of the first and second floors, encompassing six main schools: French, Italian, Spanish, Dutch and Flemish, German and English. Many of the masterpieces are in the **Grande Galerie** (1610), one of the world's longest rooms, where a quarter of a mile of fine art beckons.

French School

The Inspiration of the Poet, Poussin (1594–1665). **The Embarkation for the Island of Cythera** and **Gillies,** both by Watteau. (1684–1721). **The Coronation of Napoleon** and **The Turkish Bath** by David (1748–1825). **Scenes of The Massacres of Chios,** Delacroix (1798–1863). **The Raft of Medusa** by Gèricault (1791–1824) and **La Grande Odalisque,** Ingres (1780–1867).

Italian School

Virgin and Angels, Cimabue (*c.* 1280); **Coronation of the Virgin,** Fra Angelico; **Saint Sebastian** by Mantega; **St Francis of Assisi,** Giotto. As well as da Vinci's **Mona Lisa,** who sits securely behind armoured glass while bewitched tourists struggle to focus their Nikons illicitly. There are other Leonardos including **Virgin and Infant Jesus with St Anne, Bacchus, John the Baptist, Virgin of the Rocks** and **La Belle Ferronière.**

Spanish School

Crucifixion, E1 Greco; **The Club Foot,** Ribera; and Murillo's **Young Beggar.** Others by Velazquez and Goya.

Dutch and Flemish Schools

The detailed work of the Flemish masters: **Greeting of the Angel**, Van der Weyden; **Madonna with Chancellor Rolin**, Jan Van Eyck: Rembrandt's **self-portraits**; and other work by Memling, Breugel and Vermeer.

German and English Schools

Including Dürer's **Self-portrait, Erasmus** by Holbein, and fine works by Constable, Turner, Gainsborough and Burne-Jones.

Graphic Arts (First and Second Floors)

The Louvre has one of the world's largest and finest collections of old master drawings. Since works on paper are fragile and sensitive to light, only a few of the 80,000 drawings, engravings and watercolours are on permanent exhibition. You can get a glimpse of the tip of the iceberg at the temporary shows held year round which bring together works selected to illustrate a particular theme or period.

The Louvre: 34–36 quai du Louvre. Tel. 40 20 51 51/40 20 53 17. M Palais Royal/Louvre. Open (permanent collection) 9am–9.45pm, Mon and Wed; 9am–6pm, Thu, Fri, Sat, Sun. Closed Tue. Temporary exhibitions open noon–10pm, Mon, Wed–Sun. Admission: 25f adults; 13f 18–25s and OAPs; free under-18s.

DECORATIVE ARTS AND FASHION MUSEUMS

These two neighbours are within the Louvre but also reached directly from rue de Rivoli. The **Musée des Arts Decoratifs** at 107 rue de Rivoli has a collection of over 50,000 items, including furniture and applied arts from the Middle Ages to the present day. You can see the reconstituted private apartments of couturière Jeanne Lanvin, an Art Deco jewel, plus tapestries, silver, tableware, glass, pottery, sculpture. There's a gallery of contemporary design too, featuring crafts and toys, furniture and objects by designers such as Paulin, Starck, Wilmotte – the antiques of tomorrow.

Musée des Arts Decoratifs (Decorative Arts Museum): 107 rue de Rivoli. Tel. 42 60 32 14. M Palais Royal/Tuileries.
Open 12.30–6pm, Wed–Sat; 12–6pm, Sun; Closed Mon and Tue.

Guided tours from Sept–July. Tel. 42 86 98 18. for details. Admission
20f adults; 15f under-25s, OAPs.

Four centuries of fashion are followed at the neighbouring
Musée des Arts de la Mode at 109 rue de Rivoli. Exhibits
pay tribute to the greats of French fashion (and occasionally
elsewhere) with stunning displays – many fabrics, accessories
or costumes having been donated by famous names from
haute couture – Schiaparelli and Chanel included. At the
time of writing, the main collections are not on display, so the
museum is closed between temporary exhibitions. A reference
library is open 2–7pm by appointment (Tel. 42 60 32 14 for
details).

THE PALAIS ROYAL AREA

Across the hectic rue de Rivoli, north of the Louvre, is a
small piece of central Paris that is surprisingly solemn and
sedate, with several worthy and worthwhile sights all within
easy strolling distance of each other.

With its symmetrical gardens, fountain, and serene, arcaded
pavements, the **Palais Royal** presents a dignified picture,
belying the impropriety of its past. Few buildings in Paris
have had as many rôles.

Originally built in 1629 for Cardinal Richelieu and bequeathed by him to the royal family in 1642, the palace was
the childhood home of Louis XIV. He gave it to his brother, the
Duke of Orléans, who gave the place a bad name by holding
scandalous parties there.

In 1763 the palace was partly destroyed by fire. A later
Duc d'Orléans – who would receive the nickname "Philippe
Egalité" for his libertarian views during the Revolution –
decided to play speculator and raise funds for its restoration in the 1780s by enclosing the gardens with elegant
galleries of shops on the ground floor and building covetable apartments to let above. At the time it was considered outrageous for a member of the royal family to
become involved in anything so commercial as property
development.

In the late-18th and 19th centuries, the square became the

life and soul of Parisian partying. It acquired an extremely dodgy reputation when the arcades became brothels and seedy gambling dens, out of bounds to the police. Order was finally restored, but not for long. During the Commune of 1871, the Palace was set on fire and again badly damaged, but rebuilt shortly after. Today, decorum long since restored, the shops sell curios, antiques and stamps.

In more recent years Cocteau and the novelist Colette are amongst the famous to have lived in apartments overlooking the gardens – she liked to dine at **Le Grand Véfour**, at 17 rue Beaujolais, the Palais Royal's most famous (and, according to the *Gault Millau* guide "the world's prettiest") restaurant. It is the last example of the many restaurants that proliferated in the Palais gardens 200 years ago, and has been restored to its former glory. For the privilege of dining where Napoleon, King Louis Philippe and Victor Hugo have munched before, be prepared to book way in advance and don't expect too much change from £100 (including service).

The Palais Royal itself is now occupied by bureaucrats instead of aristocrats: various government offices are housed here and not open to the public. Their current use is perhaps not inappropriate, as historically the Palace Gardens were used for political speech-making. On the Sunday afternoon of 12 July, 1789 the revolutionary Camille Desmoulins jumped up on a café table and made the famous speech which, 2 days later, led to the storming of the Bastille and the beginning of the French Revolution.

The Palais Royal Gardens seemed almost bound to be left undisturbed after their hectic history, but in 1985 there was shock and horror when the palace courtyard became home to one of President Mitterand's dottiest public art commissions – Daniel Burens's **Les Deux Plateaux**, an extra-huge geometric extravagance of striped broken columns arranged over 3500 square yards where Cardinal Richelieu used to stroll. The overall effect of the Buren Columns is, at first glance, not unlike a car park.

If you carry on along the nearby rue des Petits Champs you come to one of the most attractive squares in Paris, the **place des Victoires**, built – like the place Vendôme – to show off

---

The Comédie Française

The most prestigious theatre in France stands in all its colonaded glory right alongside the Palais Royal, on the place André Malraux – named after the distinguished ex-minister of culture, who was a former resident of the Palais. Don't be taken in by the name, the company doesn't necessarily play for laughs. A bastion of traditional French drama, there are regular performances of classics by the likes of Molière, Corneille and Racine, with the occasional soupçon from modern, or even foreign, playwrights. The company was founded by Louis XIV in 1680 and moved to its present spot at the end of the 18th century.

Behind its discreet façade is an impressive building, worthy of a daytime guided tour, if not an evening visit. You might get the impression it's not so much a theatre as a crafts museum with wig makers, cabinet makers, cobblers, milliners and other artisans employed here alongside the actors.

On display in the upstairs foyer you can see, but not sit in, the chair in which Molière collapsed on stage just hours before he died, in 1673. Ironically, it was after a performance of *Le Malade Imaginaire*. Also in this foyer is a bronze cast of Houdin's statue of Voltaire. (You can see the original plaster in the Mansart Gallery of the Bibliothèque National, across from the Palais Royal gardens, at 58 rue de Richelieu in the 2e.)

Comédie Française: 2 rue de Richelieu 75001. Tel. 40 15 00 15. M Palais Royal. Open (box office) 11am–6pm daily.

---

a statue of a reigning monarch: in this case to commemorate the victories of Louis XIV.

The stately houses encircling the monument have been converted and the *place* has become one of the city's most chic fashion enclaves – Kenzo is at number 3, Thierry Mügler at number 10. Victoire at number 12 is an in place to find the work of several designers. Yet more upmarket designer shops spill out into the rue Étienne Marcel.

Place des Victoires is at the northern edge of the 1er. Just south is the great stone hulk of the Bank of France, and a little further east, the bulky, drum-shaped Commodity Market or **Bourse du Commerce** at rue de Viarmes. Built in the 18th century, it was once a corn exchange.

A few steps north of here, at number 2 rue du Jour, is a beautiful church which, during the Revolution, was turned into an agricultural hall. This is **St Eustache**, the huge, former parish church of Palais Royal and the old Halles, built between 1532–1640, in a mixture of Gothic and Renaissance styles. After Notre-Dame it's the largest church in Paris and, like the Cathedral, took over 100 years to complete.

Missed by many tourists who rush past to get to the brash Halles quarter, St Eustache is full of historical associations: Cardinal Richelieu, and the fishmonger's daughter Madame de Pompadour, (to be) were christened there; Molière's christening and funeral were held there; Louis XIV took his first communion there as he was living with his mother in the Palais Royal at the time. From time to time concerts are held – a good opportunity to let your eyes roam around the florid interior. (Telephone for details.) There's an early Rubens (Pilgrims at Emmaeus, 1611) and stunning stained glass, but pride of place goes to the organ upon which Berlioz used to play – it was here, in 1855, that he conducted the first performance of his *Te Deum*.

St Eustache: 2 rue du Jour. Tel. 42 36 31 05. M Les Halles. RER, Châtelet – Les Halles. Open 8.30am–7pm daily. Services 10am, 6pm, Mon–Sat; 8.30am, 9.45am, 11am, 6pm, Sun.

St Eustache clashes dramatically with the startling ultra-modern Les Halles *quartier*; it overlooks the Forum and the Jardin des Halles, a small green oasis in the concrete desert.

LES HALLES – THE PARISIAN'S COVENT GARDEN

One of the biggest, trendiest tourist baits in Paris these days is the lively, not to mention rapacious, **Les Halles** (say Lay Alle). For 8 centuries it was "the belly of Paris" – Emile Zola's words – the central food market, until the market traders were exiled to Rungis, out near Orly airport in 1969.

In the years of redevelopment that followed streets were pulled down and so were ten glass and cast iron *Halles*, or halls, built in the 1850s by Victor Baltard to shelter the vendors of fruit, vegetables, poultry, fish, butter and other victuals. (The only surviving hall, the **Pavillon Baltard**, has been re-erected as a theatre at Nogent-Sur-Marne, to the east of Paris.) This demolition left one hell of a hole. President Pompidou fancied filling it with grandiose offices, but Giscard d'Estaing preferred to give it back to the Parisians – which he has done with a vengeance.

The result is a very different kind of market – the ultimate dry-weather facility for shopaholics – a slightly gaudy **Forum** which descends to four levels, containing over 200 shops selling everything from bonbons to bed linen, plus restaurants, car parks and a Métro station. Above ground, the 54-acre site is a colossal glass, steel and concrete aggregate of offices, flats, fountains, landscaped gardens and a kids' adventure playground.

Since it opened in 1979, the futuristic Forum, like its neighbour the high-tech Pompidou Centre, has been the subject of controversy and censure. Whether it's an innovative triumph or an awful eye-sore, the Forum has been an unequivocal commercial success, whose popularity has infused new life into the area.

Rather like a subterranean airport, there are computerised maps in four languages to help keep shoppers and sightseers on the right track. Fashionable clothing and shoe shops predominate in the Forum arcades but, without wanting to cop out, outlets change hands so suddenly and so often that it's difficult to give a precise guide. Perennially popular though is the **FNAC** – always worth checking out for the best prices on books, cameras, records and hi-tech electronic or sporting goods – it's manic on a Saturday, so be warned.

To counterbalance the surfeit of commercialism, there are sporty and cultural diversions within the Forum, to the tune of ten cinemas, a glass-walled swimming pool and gymnasium, photographic and art galleries. On level minus one is a branch of the **Grévin Museum**. As well as waxwork figures from the cancan era of the Belle Epoque (Balzac, Hugo *et al*), areas of Paris are reproduced in model form at various points in history. (The main museum is at 10 boulevard Montmartre – see the section on the 9e.)

Musée Grevin: 1, Grand Balcon, rue Pierre Lescot. Tel. 40 26 28 05 M RER Châtelet-Les-Halles. Open 10am–6.45pm, Mon–Sat; 1pm–7.15pm, Sun and holidays. Admission 40f adults, 28f 6–14s, free under-6s. No credit cards.

The Forum also provides an appropriately state-of-the-art setting for the **Museum of Holography,** on the same level, with its small and un-mindblowing collection of 3-D wizardry.

Holography Museum: Level – 1, Forum des Halles. Tel. 40 39 96 83. M RER Châtelet-Les Halles. Open 10am–7.30pm, Mon–Sat; 1–7pm, Sun. Admission 28f adults; 22f students, OAPs; under-18s free. Credit (shop only): V.

You can follow in the flippers of deep sea diver Jacques Cousteau via videos and audio-visual devices at the **Cousteau Oceanic Centre.** Kids will love the 1½ hour tour of shipwrecks, sharks and sea-bed creepies, climaxing in being swallowed by a colossal blue whale.

Cousteau Centre: Forum des Halles, Tel. 40 28 98 98/99. M RER Châtelet-Les Halles. Open noon–7pm, Tue–Sun (last ticket 5.30pm). Admission 75f adults, 52.50f 5–14s, free under-5s, group discounts available. Credit: V.

The streets all around the Forum are lively, with many studenty bars, all kinds of restaurants – from the chi-chi to the cheap – and high-rent low-life. Nor is it an area that goes to bed early: some of the city's best rock and jazz pulses from this patch. In rue des Lombards is a **Guinness Tavern** where a pint, if you have to have one, will cost twice what you pay in Britain. Hotter spots in the same street include **Le Baiser Salé, Le Sunset, Les Trottoirs de Buenos Aires** (see Jazz, pp. 193–196). In the rue Berger, facing the Halles garden, is the jazz bar **L'Eustache** with the more expensive but very "now" **Distrito** down the street. There's another pub, the **James Joyce,** in the rue du Jour, and American-style cocktail bars dotted around the area, as well as the inevitable Burger King.

HISTORIC LES HALLES

In spite of the neighbourhood upheaval and loss, Les Halles has kept some of its historic heart, with a large number of

---

Video City

In the bowels of one the oldest parts of Paris, the wonders of technology can conjure up images of the past. Head for the **Paris Vidéothèque** where you can do some sedentary sightseeing. You descend deep underground into a kind of video catacomb where you take your pick from archival material – everything remotely connected with Paris on film or video is stashed here and for a couple of pounds you can lose yourself in the sights and sounds of old Paris. You don't even need to wear headphones since the sound comes out of your chair. Special screenings of films on a particular theme are also held from time to time, but it's best to ring for details.

Paris Vidéothèque: 2 Grande Galerie du Forum. Tel. 40 26 34 30. M RER Châtelet-Les Halles. Open 10.30am–9pm, Tue–Fri, Sun; 10am–9pm, Sat. Admission 20f. No credit cards.

---

buildings dating from the 17th and 18th centuries and even earlier still intact. For until Baltard's 19th-century replacement of the market, the plan of the district had hardly changed since medieval times.

Haussmann, the human bulldozer, who was Baltard's boss, had bashed his boulevards towards and around the new market, but left the core alone. Echoes of the old Les Halles reverberate in the smaller surrounding streets. Walk up **rue Coquillière** at the back of the new Les Halles early in the morning (it's by St Eustache) and waiters will be hosing down pavements and polishing glasses while oyster-sellers set out their stalls. Nothing breathtaking, just very French. **Au Pied de Cochon** at number 6 stays open night and day, just as it always has since 1946. The etchings on the walls are reminders of what it was like in the old days. The house speciality is fine if you like pork, including *all* its extremities. There's a famous 150-year-old kitchenware shop, **Dehillerin**, in this street stacked to the rafters with waffle irons and sauté pans. Just ahead is the wide, prosperous and tatty **rue Montmartre**, where there are still a few food merchants. Shifting into guidebook-speak, **Le Cochon à l'Oreille** at number 15 is the most complete example of a late-19th-century café in Paris, with walls decorated with glazed ceramic panels representing scenes

---

Latest in Les Halles

Newest, and most gruesome, crowd-puller in Les Halles is **Les Martyrs de Paris**. It's a 15-million-franc visual history of the terrible tortures endured by French prisoners and dissidents, accompanied by appropriate sound and special effects. (You not only *see* life-like mannequins being boiled alive, you *hear* their screams and *smell* the burning coal ...) It won't surprise you to hear that set decorators of *Indiana Jones*, *Superman* and *Alien* worked on the project.

In early 1992 yet another new attraction is due to open — the European Rock and Roll Hall of Fame, right next-door to Les Martyrs.

Les Martyrs de Paris: Forum des Halles, Porte de Louvre. Tel. 40 28 08 13. M RER Châtelet-Les Halles. Open 10.30am–6.30pm daily. 40f Adults; 26f children under 15; 30f students.

---

from the life of Les Halles. Actually it still keeps old market hours too – opening at 4am, closing at 3pm – and has original fitted benches, a tiled floor and a hand-beaten zinc counter.

Turn into **rue du Jour**, a pretty, rather yuppified shopping street almost entirely given over to Agnès B designs – one of Paris's great fashion secrets – excellent quality French chic for men, women and kids in three separate shops. The unspoilt **rue Montorgueil**, once the Paris oyster market, has shabbily elegant houses built by prosperous 18th-century tradesmen. Its colourful street market is one of the city's liveliest.

At number 25, the one with genteel wrought-iron balconies, lived a Madame Lecomte who for 35 years owned the **Escargot Montorgueil** restaurant across the way. Genuine Second Empire ceilings, wall mirrors, chandeliers and gold snails have hardly changed in a hundred years, which is more than can be said of the prices. The foyer ceiling came from Sarah Bernhardt's summer home. Snails, of course, are on the menu, cooked in half a dozen different ways; it's always crowded at lunchtimes and, in any case, nicer at night. It's also open on Sundays.

The pedestrian streets east of here are good wander-land:

Pet Quai-pers

You don't expect to hear hens clucking in the first *arrondissement*, but along the south-eastern edge of the right bank in the 1er, you'll find rows of rabbits, hamsters, pigeons and birds sitting in the car fumes beside a busy main road. The farmyard noises come from the **quai de la Mégisserie**, between the Pont Neuf and the Pont au Change which, once ripe with the smell of leather tonning, is now a noisy pet market.

---

rues **Pierre Lescot, de la Grande Truanderie** (*truand* is a crook or gangster) and **St Denis**. The latter is one of the oldest streets in Paris, renowned for being a centre for one of the oldest professions. Admittedly the Halles end has been a little yuppified, but the street gets progressively seedier the further north you go. Some of the houses still have 16th-century gables.

Step inside the friendly **Taverne de Rubens** at number 12 and you forsake the trendy Halles for a selection of serious German beers and sauerkraut. It's open until 5am at the weekend, so is a handy place to know about should hunger pangs strike early on a Sunday morning. At number 4 (just north of place du Châtelet) is **Le Trappiste**, another beery joint with 20 different international beers on draught and over 180 bottled.

Adjacent to the rue St Denis in a tree-lined square is the attractive Renaissance **Fontaine des Innocents**: built in 1549, it stands on the site of the medieval communal cemetery. The remains were eventually moved in the 18th century to the Catacombs – see the section on the 14e – it took years to transport over 3 million skeletons.

1ER AND 4E: ILES DE LA CITÉ AND ST LOUIS:
Birthplace of Paris

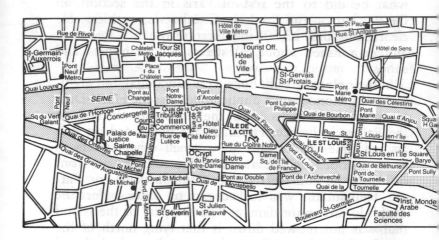

Along with the *quais* that overlook them on either side, these
two islands mark the origins of Paris. Together they make up
one of the most fascinating chunks of the city. Gaggles of
tourists come here to goggle at the glorious clichés: the gothic
core of **Notre-Dame** cathedral, gorgeous **Ste Chapelle**. The
historic islands are in the 1e and 4e, and lie in mid-Seine, joined
to each other and to the banks of the river by 14 bridges.

ILE DE LA CITÉ

The **Ile de la Cité** is where Paris began and it is still the
very heart of the capital. The city even got its name, Paris,

from the island, as around 200 BC Celtic fishermen of the Parisii tribe were the earliest settlers. But they called it "Lutetia" from the Celtic word for a "dwelling in the midst of the waters". In 52 BC it was overrun by the Romans, who built their own fortifications on the island and a temple, where Notre-Dame now stands. By the 4th century, though, the settlement had taken on the name of its founders: Paris.

The island's close-knit medieval centre remained almost intact until the reign of Napoleon III when his Préfect Haussmann was let loose on it. You can read about what he did to the rest of Paris in the section on the 9e, but on the Ile de la Cité he was ruthless. He cleared out some 25,000 inhabitants from the Cité centre and demolished about 90 streets full of homes and shops.

In their place he built huge, very functional, but architecturally monotonous public buildings: the Hôtel-Dieu Hospital, a barracks (now the Préfecture de Police), the Palais de Justice. He made the boulevard du Palais ten times wider and he widened other streets in order to open up the views of Notre-Dame in front of which he constructed the vast courtyard, or Parvis. Haussmann was kicked out of office before he could do any more damage and the part of the island that was not mowed down is that lying north of the rue de Cloître Notre-Dame, between the cathedral and the Seine.

The most painted (by artists that is) bridge across the Seine, the **Pont Neuf** slips over to the western (downstream) tip of Ile de la Cité. Don't be fooled by its name – there's nothing *neuf* about it. Started in 1578, completed 1604, it's the oldest bridge in Paris and although 400 years old, has never been enlarged.

It was inaugurated in 1607 by Henri IV whose equestrian statue (1818) overlooks the small, sylvan **Square du Vert Galant**, to the west of the Pont Neuf. Right on the triangular tip of the island, this is a lovely spot to be on a balmy summer's evening. It's especially popular with lovers, which is somehow appropriate since the square was named in honour of the King's prowess as a lover especially in later years. Translated literally "*vert galant*" means "evergreen gallant", i.e. a spry old dog.

Opposite, you can retreat from the traffic of the Pont Neuf into the traffic-less, tree-shaded **Place Dauphine**. Henri IV, the good lover, who gave the city the place des Vosges, also left this one behind and named it in honour of his son, who later became Louis XIII. In his novel *Nadja* André Breton described place Dauphine as "one of the most profoundly secluded places I know". Only the houses at numbers 14 and 26 are still in their original state since 18th century developers found it more profitable to remodel the properties. Until her death in 1985 Simone Signoret lived with Yves Montand in this square, next to the minute *salon de thé* **Fanny Thé**, where for over a decade, the lady-like Fanny has placed a teapot and a book of poems on each table. In summer you can lunch, snack, or take tea outdoors.

Further on, taking up the width of the island, bounded by the boulevard du Palais, is the huge historic block of buildings – the **Palais de Justice**, and the Conciergerie enfolding the gothic masterpiece of the **Ste-Chapelle**.

To the south of the Palais is the **quai des Orfèvres**, the gold and silversmith's quay, once the centre of the jewel trade before becoming (number 36) the HQ of the CID (Police Judiciare). More interesting is the **quai de l'Horloge**, on the north side of the Palais. At the corner of the quai and boulevard de Palais stands the square tower known as the **Tour de l'Horloge** – the first public clock in Paris – it has kept time since 1334.

Part of the great early 14th-century palace built on the north side of the Ile de la Cité, but now incorporated into the Palais de Justice complex, the macabre **Conciergerie**, at 1 quai de l'Horloge was a notorious prison during the Revolution, named after the royally appointed officer, or *concierge*, in charge of criminals. Victims of the Revolutionary guillotine sweated out their final gloomy hours in the Conciergerie,

---

Law and Order

The imposing and massive complex of the *Palais de Justice* contains the centralised legal machinery of modern France. The public are admitted to hearings of civil cases and trials for minor offences. In the thirteenth century this was a royal palace, but became for a time in the fourteenth the seat of parliament when the royal family moved out to the more secure Louvre. It was renamed during the Revolution and it was here that prisoners from the Conciergerie were hauled for trial. The Palais was rebuilt after a particularly serious fire in 1871 to resemble the original building.

Palais de Justice: boulevard du Palais 75001 M Cité. Tel. 43 29 12 55. Open Mon–Fri, 10am–6pm.

---

including Marie Antointette, Danton, Robespierre and St Just.

In the Salle des Girondins, you can see gruesome mementoes: one of the guillotine blades, the crucifix to which Marie Antoinette prayed before losing her head, and the lock from Robespierre's cell. More impressive than these though are the bits of the building that date back to the 14th century, including the vaulted Salle des Gardes (where you wait for the guided tours) the immense, late Gothic, Salle des Gens d'Armée, the former canteen and restroom of the royal household staff beyond it, and the massive kitchens from which over 3000 people could be fed.

The Conciergerie: quai de l'Horloge. Tel. 43 54 30 06. M Cité. Open summer 9.30am–6pm daily. Winter 10am–4.30pm daily. Admission 22f adults, 12f children. No credit cards.

In striking contrast to the gloomy Conciergerie, by taking the passage to the left of the Cour de Mai (the main public entrance to the Law Courts) you'll find tucked away in the precincts, the exquisite **Ste Chapelle**. This Gothic wonder was built by St Louis (Louis IX) between 1246 and 1248 to house relics believed to be of Christ's crown of thorns and the true cross. These and the reliquary made for them cost two and a half times more than the church itself and are now in Notre-Dame. St Louis acquired them – indirectly – from Baudouin, the last French Emperor of Byzantium, when he repaid Baudouin's creditors in 1239. Baudouin had pawned the crown in order to borrow money from the Venetians, but he couldn't pay them back in time.

Ste Chapelle is a two-tier chapel, with the many columns and arches of the dark lower chapel (originally intended for court officials and servants) supporting the upper chapel (intended just for the king and his retinue). A spiral staircase winds up to the upper chapel where the spellbinding stained-glass windows – the oldest in Paris, dating from the 13th century – virtually replace walls. They depict over 1000 scenes from the Old and New Testaments, over a glass area of 1500 square yards. Even the slimmest ray of sunshine illuminates the incredible detail and the vibrant colours. The Ste Chapelle is a magnet for tourists, so you'd be wise to get there early in the day to appreciate it fully.

Sainte Chapelle: boulevard du Palais. M Cité. Open 10am–4pm, Oct–Mar; 10am–5.20pm, April–Sept. Half price Sun and hols – admission ticket also admits to Conciergerie, see above.

Almost crushed by the imperious lines of the **Hôtel Dieu** hospital and Paris's equivalent of Scotland Yard (the **Préfecture de Police**), the **place Louis Lepine** bursts unexpectedly into the million tight-curled blooms of the flower market (catch it Mon–Sat; it becomes a bird market on Sundays) just by the Cité Métro.

From here, if you go back to the place du Parvis-Notre-Dame, you can visit the bizarre **Crypt Archéologique**. The entrance is at the western end of the Parvis. Don't be put off by the musty smell near the entrance – it's worth holding your nose and making the descent to see the spookily lit remains of the original cathedral, plus streets and houses of the Cité back as far as Roman times.

NOTRE-DAME

The Gothic core of the city is of course the cathedral itself – "a vast symphony in stone" is what Victor Hugo called it in his novel *Notre-Dame de Paris*, better known to British readers as *The Hunchback of Notre-Dame*. Too corny for words, yet so robustly beautiful that no matter how many times you've seen it in photographs, you can't help but be stopped in your tracks.

The shape and proportions are in striking perfect harmony, all the more remarkable given the gigantic dimensions – and what's more amazing, its stature and serenity never seem cheapened by the incessant camera-toting tourists crawling all over it.

The 19th-century historian, Jules Michelet, described Notre-Dame as "the Parish of French History", and its immense historical importance certainly extends beyond the capital. For 8 centuries many great moments in French history have been celebrated at the cathedral, including royal marriages and baptisms, state funerals and *Te Deums* sung in honour of great national victories – such as the liberation of Paris, 26th August, 1944. French Kings were crowned at Reims cathedral but one English King – Henry VI, at the age of nine – was crowned King of France here at Notre-Dame in 1431.

Its central role in French history is underlined too by a brass plaque just by the main entrance to the cathedral. It marks the zero point – *kilomètre zero* – from which all distances from Paris are measured.

The spot where Notre-Dame stands has been a place of worship for 2000 years, since the Romans built a temple there. Much later on there were two Christian churches on adjacent sites which were removed in the 12th century and Notre-Dame was built to replace them. It was conceived by the bishop of the diocese, Maurice de Sully, and the foundation stone laid in 1163 by Pope Alexander III, but the cathedral wasn't completed for 165 years.

Notre-Dame encapsulates all aspects of pure Gothic style, and even though it has seen a lot of change over the centuries, it still triumphs over all the embellishments and restoration work.

A great deal of damage was suffered as a result of the anti-clericalism of the Revolution (1789–99), when its treasures were plundered, bells melted down and many of the statues and carvings destroyed. Turned into a Temple of Reason, statues of Voltaire and Rousseau were put in place of the saints. Uprisings in 1830 and 1831 wreaked more havoc and such was the state of its architectural decay that it was under threat of demolition.

In 1841 the publication of Hugo's *Hunchback of Notre-Dame* stirred up so much public interest in the cathedral that the indefatigable restorer Viollet-Le-Duc was commissioned to recreate its former beauty for posterity. An archaeologist as well as an architect, he was a Gothic-oholic and, for the best part of the next quarter of a century, set to restoring Notre-Dame to his own vision of the masterpiece it had been in the 14th century.

He replaced hundreds of destroyed carvings and, because early engravings showed that the cathedral had a slender spire at one time, he added one to counterpoint the squat rectangular towers. But the 295-foot Viollet-le-Duc version of the spire lacks the sparseness and simplicity of the original. Then, OD-ing on medievalism, and with uncanny insight into the 20th century's mania for postcard-images, he proceeded to make the cathedral sprout sinister gargoyles all over the place: you can get a really good look at these if you climb the towers. Worse, he added the 16 copper statues which surround the base of the central spire – apostles and evangelists, amongst whom he immodestly included himself.

Before entering the cathedral, it's worth pausing on the *parvis* to take a look at the main three-storeyed **façade**, bearing in mind that most of its sculptures are clever copies or restorations by Viollet-le-Duc and his pupils. He was responsible for restoring the **Galerie des Rois** (Kings Gallery) – 28 statues across the top of the three doorways representing the Kings of Judah and Israel – which had been pulled down during the Revolution because they were thought to be Kings of France. The heads of the originals are now in the Cluny Museum (see page 377).

The great north **rose window**, 30 feet across – and the largest ever made in the 13th century – is in the centre, over the King's Gallery. Both the south and west rose windows were extensively restored, in the 18th and 19th centuries respectively.

The three richly carved entrances to the cathedral are known as **the portals of the Virgin Mary**, of **the last Judgement**, and of **Saint Anne**.

The Virgin Mary entrance dates from the 13th century and its bas reliefs illustrating the tasks of both the rich and the poor give an insight into daily life of the period. The central doorway of Judgement is dominated by the huge statue of Christ teaching, surrounded by the 12 apostles.

The other sides have fine carving too – with the most lavishly Gothic on the north façade of the transept. By the **Portal du Cloître** on the northern side is a famous and graceful late-13th-century statue of the Virgin. It is the original, and survived the Revolution, but for the loss of the child.

Inside the cathedral, tiers of arches rise to the vaulted ceiling, enhancing the building's breadth. (It can hold 9000 worshippers.) Once your eyes are accustomed to it, the first thing that strikes you is the marvellous play of light and colour from the three giant rose windows (the west one partly hidden by the largest organ in France).

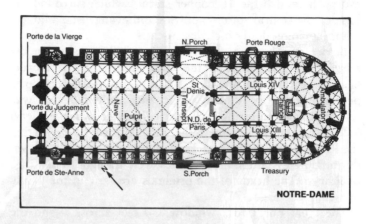

The finest of the many works of art in the nave, aisles, transepts and chapels is the 14th-century statue of the **Virgin and Child**, against the southernmost pillar at the entrance to the chancel. The **choir** is decorated with superb, early-18th-century panelling in its 114 carved stalls, and the stone **chancel screen** is decorated with 21 14th-century bas reliefs.

The **treasury** has a large collection of reliquaries, manuscripts and other treasures. It's open from 9am–5pm except Sunday and national holidays.

There are almost 400 worn and winding steps to the **high gallery** and to the top of the **south tower**, but it's well worth huffing and puffing your way for vertiginous views across Paris that will take the rest of your breath away, as well as allowing a closer look at the grim griffins and gargoyles.

In the south tower you can visit the **belfry** (with a guide) to see the 13-ton bell, rung only on special occasions and operated not by a latterday Quasimodo, but by an electronic system. There is also a room containing a **museum** of the cathedral's history.

Before leaving Notre-Dame, it's worth walking round the **gardens** on the east and south sides, from where there's a clear view of the famous fabulous flying buttresses. Dating from 1318–44, they're astonishing in the effortless way they support the apse at the east end of the cathedral, and were built on a principle entirely new to the 14th century. Across the road from the Cathedral is a **museum** with a small collection of pictures, manuscripts and miscellaneous objects illustrating its life story.

Notre-Dame: place de Parvis-Nortre-Dame. Tel. 43 26 07 39. M Cité. Open 8am–7pm daily. Towers open (entrance at foot of northern tower) 10am–5.30pm (4.30pm in winter) daily. Admission 22f.

Make your way north from Notre-Dame and you'll find a

In Memoriam

Following the river round the south side of the cathedral of Notre-Dame you'll come to the public garden of the little square de l'Ile de France. At its easternmost tip is a moving testimony to the Occupation and an underground memorial to the 20,000 French victims who died during the last war in Nazi concentration camps. The **Memorial de la Déportation** is barely visible above ground, a kind of bunker-crypt comprising concrete cells, some chains, a list of the many camps on the walls, and the tomb of the Unknown Deportee. Above the exit are the words "Forgive. Do not forget". The memorial is open daily from 10am–12 noon, 2–5pm. Admission free.

part of the Ile de la Cité that Haussmann didn't have a chance to get at. The houses of the Canons of Notre-Dame used to line rue Chanoinesse but only two of these remain intact – numbers 22 and 24, dating from the 16th century, although there are other interesting façades dating from later periods.

Off rue Chanoinesse is the shabby rue de la Colombe, where the ancient Gallo-Roman wall is traced in a line in the cobblestones. It was in this neck of the woods that the forerunner of the Sorbonne, the Cathedral School of Notre-Dame was founded. The monk Abélard, one half of that romantic duo Abélard and Héloïse, taught here around 800 years ago, until he fell out with the authorities and left, taking some of his pupils with him, to found an alternative centre of learning on the left bank – an embryonic University of Paris. Saunter over to the nearby quai aux Fleurs and you'll see a couple of stone heads and a memorial over the door to number 9, marking the place where he fell in love with his landlord's niece, the beautiful and clever Héloïse, who was more than 20 years his junior. The rest, as they say, is history. They were mad about each other, made clandestine love and when Héloïse discovered she was pregnant, they married in secret. This upset Uncle (who was a Canon of Notre-Dame) who, as revenge, had Abélard castrated. She became a nun, but even after she had entered the convent, Abélard wrote more than 100 love poems to her and immortalised their affair in his tender and sexy autobiography. Today they're entombed, together at last, in Père Lachaise cemetery in the 20e – see page 515.

The quai aux Fleurs leads east from here to the little **Pont St Louis**, which links the Ile de la Cité with its smaller neighbour, the lozenge-shaped Ile St Louis.

ILE ST LOUIS

While tourists crawl all over the Ile de la Cité, there are no major sights to see on the **Ile St Louis** and, by comparison, it's a peaceful backwater. Like an elegant model 17th-century village caught in a time-warp, it has the kind of self-assurance that comes with being, for 3 centuries, one of the city's most affluent and sought-after residential havens. There's nothing so modern or mundane as a Métro station or a supermarket, a post office or a cinema, and amongst the 30 restaurants you won't find any of the self-service or fast food kind. Since traffic is banned from the streets in the heart of the island (except for those who live there) it's a pleasant place to walk around – something that's rare in the heart of any metropolis this side of Bhutan.

The island was originally two islets – both uninhabited: the Ile Notre-Dame and, upstream, the Ile des Vaches, used as cow pastures and for the occasional early morning duel. The saintly King Louis IX (who became King at the age of 12, in 1226) used to come and pray here. He lived an exceedingly pious life, and after his death was canonised and the island named after him. Originally the two islands belonged to the Canons of Notre-Dame, but, early in the 17th century, they sold them off to three architects (Marie, Le Ragrattier and Poulletier), the canal separating them was filled in and the islands were joined together at what is now the rue Poulletier, and building commenced.

You can see the oldest buildings, dating from 1616, at the corner of the rue St-Louis-en-Ile and rue Le Regrattier. By the middle of the 17th century all the land had been built on and the French aristos were only too keen to slip across the Seine from the nearby Marais where they had been living, to settle in the magnificent houses (*hôtels*) which now stood on the island's sunny quays and in the streets behind them.

By and large, the fine houses remain intact, giving the whole island a rare sort of grand symmetry – though the harmony wasn't contrived as was the case with the architecturally-unified place des Vosges or place Vendôme.

Grandest of all the grand *hôtels* is the **Hôtel Lambert** at the far end of the rue Saint Louis en l'Ile. Built in 1640 by Louis XIV's architect, Le Vau, it was once the home of the Marquise de Châtelet, Voltaire's mistress. In the 19th century it was owned by Prince Adam Czartoryski who was only too pleased to take refuge there after the first uprising against the Russian occupation of Poland in 1843. His house became the centre of Polish social life – Chopin often played there. During the Second World War it was a transit point for escaping Allied airmen shot down over France.

Nowadays the building belongs to Baron Guy de Rothschild and is even more fortress-like than ever, with its high-tech security devices. It's not open to the public. On other buildings plaques commemorate former inhabitants. At number 12, we're told, Philippe Le Bon introduced gas lighting to France in 1799.

RUE ST LOUIS-EN-L'ILE

The Ile St Louis is sliced lengthways by the rue St Louis-en-l'Ile which has fishermen at the eastern Pont de Sully end, and Notre-Dame at the other. It's the equivalent of the village high street with useful or exciting small shops, the best of which will often have enough people outside in a queue to fill a bus. The perpetually crowded tiny bakery, **Haupois**, bakes brilliant *baguettes* in their wood-fired ovens and fills the street with the smell of fresh bread. You'll find dozens of varieties of the best homemade ice cream in Paris at the famous **Berthillon** (Open 10am–8pm, closed Monday, Tuesday and school holidays, except Christmas). Or you can get a nice cup of one of over 50 varieties of tea at number 81, the *salon de thé* **St Louis**.

This is a *quartier* where the *salons de thé* tend to outnumber the sites. **Au Lys D'Argent**, at 90 rue St-Louis-en-l'Isle, is a particularly pleasant one, where the brunches are also good. **La Charlotte de l'Isle** at number 24 is a tiny tea-room serving some of the best chocolate (to eat or drink) in Paris. **Les Fous** de L'Ile is a very French, very cosy tearoom with old wooden tables, games, magazines and flowers on the tables. Find it at 33 rue des Deux-Ponts.

Unfortunately, many of the former shopkeepers and crafts-people have sold out to luxury boutiques; the last hardware shop and shoemaker have gone and, as in so many other parts of Paris, question marks hover over the community as the slick restaurants and anonymous businesses muscle in.

Dominating the spindly street is the openwork spine of the stylish church, the **Église St-Louis-en-l'Ile**. The baroque interior is as elaborate as you'd expect to find in such an affluent parish, with a collection of Dutch, Flemish and Italian 16th- and 17th-century art, some fine 12th-century tapestries as well as a relic of saintly King Louis himself.

Engraved plaques along the **quai d'Anjou** (at the north-eastern corner to the left from the Pont Marie) are a guide to who has lived where – mostly aristos, politicos and artists. At number 17 is one of the best-known of the island's buildings, the stately **Hôtel Lauzun** – like the Hôtel Lambert, designed by Le Vau.

Built for a rich financier in the 1650s, it was later the home of the Duc de Lauzun who commanded the French army at the Battle of the Boyne. Since the late 1920s it has belonged to the City of Paris and its vast, sumptuous rooms are used for entertaining VIP visitors, the Queen of England included. In the mid-19th-century, less decorous soirées took place as it was the venue for the **Hashish Club**, amongst whose regulars were Théophile Gautier and Baudelaire – both of whom also lived in the building for a while at different times, as did the German lyric poet Rilke, the composer Wagner and the English painter Walter Sickert. The Hashish Club met in the small east room – you can see this and the rest of the obsessively rich interior of the Hôtel Lauzun for yourself at certain times, but must obtain prior permission from Syndicat du Conseil de Paris, Hôtel de Ville (Tel. 42 77 40 40).

On the **quai de Béthune** and **quai d'Orléans** in the south of the island there are yet more grandly porticoed houses. Number 6 quai d'Orléans, a former meeting place for expat Polish artist and writers, is now the **Adam Mickiewitz Museum** containing souvenirs of the poet Mickiewitz – considered to be the Polish Dante – and other well-known Poles, such as Chopin. (It is open on Thursday 2–5pm; closed July 14–September 15.)

President Pompidou lived further down the quais at 16 quai de Béthune. He liked to escape from the Élysée Palace as often as possible to this enclave, and, looking at it, you can hardly blame him. Should you be tempted to take up temporary residence with the elite, you'll find that accommodation on the Ile St Louis is always both in great demand and very limited.

The **Hôtel Deux Iles** and the **Hôtel Lutèce**, while not exactly cheap, are both medieval houses, 17 and 23 rooms respectively, with lots of character and modern comforts, but you'll need to book way in advance to get in. Both are situated on the rue St-Louis-en-l'Ile, as is the chic but slightly cheaper 21-room **Hôtel St Louis** – see our accommodation guide for details.

2E:
Money Making and Spending

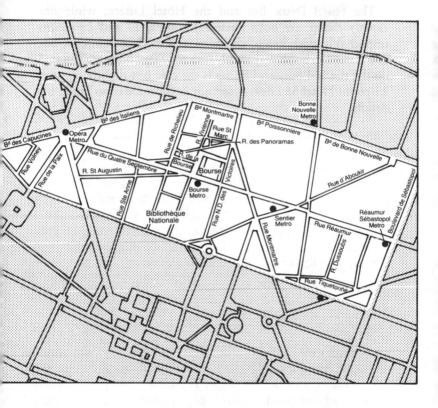

It's the smallest *arrondissement* in Paris. Just south of the
Opéra and *grands boulevards* and nudging the 1er north of
the Palais Royal, the 2e is enclosed within the boulevard
de Sébastopol and rue Étienne-Marcel. Commercial values
prevail in an area dominated by the rag trade, the stock

exchange and the city's main red light district. The chief attractions are the revitalised, 19th-century weatherproof **shopping arcades**, the **Bourse**, the **Bibliothèque National** and, on a more earthly level, the colourful **Sentier** district with its old *passages*.

RUE DE LA PAIX

The most stylish entrance you can make to the 2e is to walk along the exclusive and wildly expensive **rue de la Paix**, which leads from the equally exclusively expensive place Vendôme to the Opéra. Lined with jewellers, it's one of the most opulent streets in Paris.

For a further taste of the high life, you might slip into **Harry's Bar**, round the corner at 5 rue Daunou, where a Blue Lagoon, or a *Pétrifiant* – the house cocktail which lives up to its name – will knock you out in style. It's very much a Paris institution: Noël Coward, Hemingway, Scott Fitzgerald, James Joyce and Jacques Prévert, were amongst the literary patrons of yesteryear. The bar counter and mahogany wall panelling were shipped from New York to ensure an authentic ambience in time for the opening on Thanksgiving Day, 1911. Legend has it that when thirsty Americans came to Paris, they'd have at least one address – "sank roo doe noo" – and every taxi driver knew where to take them.

BOURSE ET BIBLIOTHÈQUE

Crossing over the avenue de l'Opéra and into the wide rue du Quatre Septembre, the stock exchange, Palais Brongniart, or **Bourse**, soon looms into sight. The 19th-century neo-classical exterior is outwardly calm if not oppressive. It's no surprise that its architect, Brongniart, was also chosen to create the Père Lachaise cemetery. Certainly the façade gives no hint of the freneticism within – there's been no Big Bang as yet, although plans to modernise the Bourse hover in the air like broken promises.

Feudal Tower

At the south-easternmost corner of the *arrondissement*, only a few steps from the Étienne Marcel Métro, at 20 rue Étienne-Marcel, the fortified Tower of Jean-sans-Peur is one of the last vestiges of feudal Paris.

It has been closed for restoration and is due to reopen as a museum sometime in 1991. Built in 1408 as a hideout for Jean, duc de Bourgogne – ironically known as Jean-sans-Peur – the tower is the sole remainder of a once extensive and magnificent medieval palace, Hôtel de Bourgogne, begun in 1270.

A spiral, 140-step staircase leads to a chamber with a remarkable vaulted carved ceiling – a rare example of medieval sculpture used in a domestic interior.

You can get a glimpse of the action from a gallery (12.30–2.30 pm at quotation time, is good for a visit). Tours take place throughout the day every half an hour or so – but be warned, they last an hour and a half. A shorter alternative is an audio-visual presentation explaining how the Bourse works.

La Bourse: place de la Bourse. Tel. 42 33 99 83. M Bourse. Open: tours lasting one and a half hours every half hour from 11am–1pm, Mon–Fri. July 1–Sept. 15. one tour at 12pm. Admission 8f (form of identification required).

A stroll south down rue Vivienne or the parallel rue Richelieu deposits you outside the world's largest library after London's British Museum. Established on its present site in 1721, the **Bibliothèque National** has several million books, some dating from the 15th century, shelved in exceptional splendour in various buildings, including the former town house of Cardinal Mazarin, with surviving interiors by Mansart dating back to the 1640s. Eventually (i.e. 1995 or 1996) this will move to the south-east of Paris as this is the proposed site of the TGB or **Très Grande Bibliothèque** as the new "world's biggest library" is to be called.

The library's *pièce de résistance* is its main reading room, built in the 1860s by Henri Labrouste, architect of the Bibliothèque Sainte Geneviève in the 5e. With its shallow, domed ceiling and cast iron colonettes, the interior was designed to be fireproof – you can take a peek at it through the glass doors, unless you have official scholarly accreditation to use the reading room. There are always good temporary exhibitions in the ground floor Mansart Gallery, Mazarin Gallery or the Photographic Gallery. On the first floor is a major collection (some 400,000) of coins and medals.

The Bibliothèque Nationale: 58 rue de Richelieu. Tel. 47 03 81 26. M Palais Royal/Bourse. Open noon–6pm, Mon–Sat. Phone for details of guided tours.

Musée du Cabinet des Médailles: Bibliothèque Nationale, 58 rue Richelieu. Tel. 47 03 83 30. M Palais Royal/Bourse. Open 9am–5pm, Mon–Sat. Admission 20f adults; 12f students, OAPs; free under-12s. No credit cards.

For a breath of air after the rarified Bibliothèque, there's an intimate park opposite in the **square Louvois**. It has chestnut trees and a voluptuous, cherub-adorned Visconti fountain.

ST DENIS & SENTIER

Over on the eastern side of the *arrondissement*, we take a nose dive from the highbrow to the low life. The stretch of the **rue St Denis** with it's pullulation of prostitutes is simply not as saintly as the name suggests. But only the sex shops are a 20th-century phenomenon – St Denis has been a well-used pick-up place since the Middle Ages.

Following Method Acting principles to the letter, Shirley Maclaine came to this particular street of shame to do her research for her role in *Irma La Douce*.

Business becomes less blatant at the porte St Denis which marks the *arrondissement* boundary of the 2e with the 9e.

Porte St Denis itself dates back to 1672. Replacing the old city gates, it was designed as yet another triumphal arch to commemorate Louis XIV's military victories. East of the rue St Denis, the busy area all around the Sentier Métro is devoted

Passages

Before the days of department stores and shopping malls, Parisians had chic 19th-century glass-topped arcades with marble or tiled floors where they could parade and spend money protected from the traffic and the elements. Almost a hundred of them remain and, in the 2e where they proliferated, many have been rescued from decay in recent years. They are still great places to give the crowds the slip, full of seductive shops and cafés.

The most easy on the eye, if not on the pocket, is the glorious **Galerie Vivienne** (entrances at rue des Petits Champs, 5 rue de la Banque, 6 rue Vivienne; M Bourse). Built in 1823, it has a dramatic Rotunda decorated with figures symbolising Plenty. Plenty of money essential if you nip into Jean-Paul Gautier (entrance at 6 rue Vivienne) for its wild avant-garde designs or one of the other little shops here.

Running off Galerie Vivienne is the renovated **Galerie Colbert** with impressive *faux marbre* columns. You can buy posters or postcards from the next door Bibliothèque Nationale's collection and it's worth slipping into the Grand Café Colbert as much for the turn-of-the-century décor as for *le café*.

Less affluent nowadays are the passages round **passage des Panoramas** full of bric-à-brac shops, tearooms, stamp dealers. Watch out for **Stern**, a company founded in the first half of the 19th century and once the largest printing and stationery business in France, even supplying bank notes to heads of state, at 47 passage des Panoramas. The interior is a really remarkable antiquarian confection.

Near the Richelieu-Drouot Métro station, connecting the boulevard des Italiens with rue de Richelieu is the tiny **passage des Princes** — worth a detour to see the renovated ironwork and tiled floor, and to look at the shopfront of the old pipemakers, **J. Sommer**. Craftsmen sculpt pipes in clay and fashion others in briar just as they've done for 150 years. **Passage Choiseul** (23 rue Augustin to 40 rue des Petits Champs) is a popular and lively shopping arcade; the unspoilt **Galerie Véro-Dodat** (off rue Croix des Petits Champs) has handsome mahogany shopfronts and a comfortable good, old-fashioned restaurant. Other passages are downright dilapidated but none the less appealing for that — like the three-storey **passage du Grand-Cerf**, at the bottom of rue St Denis. Others that run into the rue St Denis are best avoided after dark; **passage du Caire** has ancient gabled houses; **passage Beauregard** is dark, tatty, and slightly creepy.

to the clothing industry with **place de Caire** at its centre. The raucous, hurly-burly of loading and unloading deliveries makes for a more colourful, if seedier, street life than that of the more staid western side of the *arrondissement*.

3E AND 4E, THE MARAIS:
A Historic Goldfish Bowl

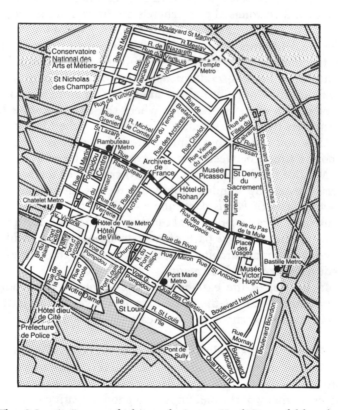

"The Marais," says fashion designer Karl Lagerfeld, who lives there some of the time, "is for middle-aged old money". Don't let this put you off – its charm may be enjoyed by all, irrespective of socio-demographic credentials. One of the most historic and homogeneous parts of Paris, the attractive district between Les Halles and the Bastille is, admittedly, a perfect stage-set for the arty and creative high-achievers who choose to work and play there. To *live* there, money is a must. Ongoing careful restoration and regeneration have dramatically transformed the rundown, working-class Marais of a couple of decades ago into a highly sought-after residential area: big-name natives include French Minister of Culture Jack Lang (who lives in the lovely place des Vosges) and Paloma Picasso when she's in town.

But the Marais is not just wall-to-wall middle-class media-philes and customised chic. There's an historic, undeveloped Jewish quarter around rue des Rosiers, the gay community of the rue des Blancs-Manteaux and its surrounding streets, and a dwindling number of long-established, small shops selling buttons or housing crafts people repairing handbags – or, come to think of it, just about anything. An authentic social life bubbles away in the cafés where the *patron* knows his customers by their first names. Tatty edges of the Marais still exist – you can catch a glimpse around the Jewish quarter, and the streets between rues de Sévigné and Turenne.

Most of the 3e is filled by the northern half of the Marais, criss-crossed by winding cobbled streets with magnificent town houses or *hôtels particuliers* – some of which are now museums, libraries or cultural centres. The Marais is fortunate in being one of the few parts of Paris which still has much of its pre-revolutionary architecture, having survived the wholesale redevelopment of Haussmann.

In the 4e, to the east of the state-of-the-art Beaubourg, the southern half of the *arrondissement* takes in the Jewish quarter and the city's first and least spoilt square, the place des Vosges.

Besides its outstanding individual buildings and museums, the Marais as an area is atmospheric and rewarding to wander around, by day or night (weekdays are best if you want to gain access to many of the buildings). It's good for eating out too – the varied street life is reflected in the culinary choice available – from vegetarian to Vietnamese, *nouvelle* to traditional.

Party time in the Marais is a fortnight in October (check press for precise details) when culture takes to the pavements by night throughout the neighbourhood – during the day it's business as usual. The first ever **Fêtes du Marais** were held in 1990, replacing the defunct Festival du Marais whose highbrow happenings in the *hôtels* were thought too élitist.

THE NORTHERN MARAIS

The starting point for a wander round is the northern tip of the Marais, by Temple Métro station in the historic goldfish bowl of the 3e. A little south of the Métro, by the Mairie du Temple, you'll find a secluded park, the **square du Temple**. It was on this spot, though you'd never tell, that the medieval Knights Templar built a fortress – the Temple – which was used during the Revolution as a prison, where the royal family were held.

Going east, you come in a minute or two to **rue Volta**, and what's claimed to be, at number 3, the oldest house in Paris. Four streets south number **51 rue de Montmorency** was built in 1407 as a lodging house, is now a restaurant, and is probably the second oldest house in the city.

The huge building two streets east of rue Volta, sandwiched between rue St Martin and rue Vaucanson, is the **Conservatoire des Arts et Métiers**, a technical college with a National Technical Museum for the technically-minded. The college itself was founded in 1794 and its first director was a M. Montgolfier, the inventor of the hot air balloon. Housed in the former medieval priory of **St Martin-des-Champs**, its early Gothic church is now part of the museum, brimming with vintage cars, aeroplanes, engines and bikes galore. Inventiveness is displayed in the thousands of exhibits from fridges to clocks and model trains. Nothing is left out – there's glasswork from Lalique, Baccarat and Murano, cameras used by Daguerre and the Lumière brothers, and the plane flown by Louis Blériot across the Channel in 1909.

Musée National des Techniques (*National Technical Museum*): 292 rue St Martin. Tel. 40 27 20 00. M Reámur-Sébastopol/Arts-et-Métiers. Open 10am–5.30pm, Tues–Sun. Closed Monday. Admission 20f adults; 10f students, OAPs, everyone on Suns; free under-12s. No credit cards.

Across rue Reámur from the Conservatoire at 254 rue St Martin is the church of **St-Nicholas-des-Champs**, a hybrid of features from different periods: a fine Renaissance doorway, a flamboyant Gothic façade and belfry.

Open 9am–7pm, Mon–Fri; 9.30am–noon, Sun.

The rue St Martin continues south down to the **quartier de l'Horloge,** a tarted-up pedestrianised shopping district within paint-flicking distance of the Beaubourg Centre in the 4e. You can't miss the enormous brass and steel mechanical clock overlooking the rue Bernard-de-Clairvaux. A lifesize "Defender of Time" fights on the hour one of the three animals, symbolising the elements: a dragon (earth), a bird (air) and a crab (water). At noon, 6pm and 10pm, all three attack together.

Opposite the passage des Ménétriers, in a little house at the far end of the impasse Berthaud, is the **Musical Instruments Museum,** a labour of love for the owner-collectors of phonographs, pianolas, music boxes and barrel organs, who also give demonstrations. An entertaining tour (in understandable French) lasts about an hour and a quarter.

Musée d'Instruments de Musique Mécanique (Musical Instruments Museum): impasse Berthaud. Tel. 42 71 99 54. M Rambuteau. Open 2–7pm, Sat, Sun, public holidays; other times by appointment. Admission 25f adults; 15f under 12s. No credit cards.

On the other side of rue Brantôme is **AS-ECO,** Paris's only all-night supermarket, but closed on Sunday.

Ease your way out of the narrow streets, cross rue du Temple into rue des Archives and round the corner at number 60 rue des Francs-Bourgeois is the early-18th-century mansion, the Hôtel Soubise. This is the grand home of the **National Archives** and the **Museum of French History.** There's paperwork beyond the wildest imaginings here – in the archives are 6000 million items spread over 175 miles of shelving. The nearby Hôtel Rohan acts as an overspill repository.

On the first floor of the Hôtel Soubise is the **Musée de l'Histoire de France,** where you can visit the rococo former apartments of the Princess de Rohan-Soubise. Decorated by such artists as Boucher and Van Loo, they give a glimpse of

Marais History

The word *marais* means a marsh, which is what it was until it was drained in the 12th century by monks and the Knights Templar. The reclaimed area soon became the site of many convents and monasteries — their legacy is reflected in some of today's street names — rue des Blancs-Manteaux, rue des Filles-du-Calvaire, rue Ste-Croix-de-la-Bretonnerie — alongside an embryonic Jewish community.

By the 15th century the Marais had begun to be a fashionable place to live — the rue St Antoine leading to the city gate at Bastille became a frequent venue for fêtes, processions and tournaments — it was here that Henry II lost his life in a jousting accident, in 1559.

Gentrification was given a push forward half a century later with the creation of the place Royale (now the place des Vosges) by Henri IV. A building boom had begun.

Beautiful town houses, usually built around a private court-yard at the front and with a formal back garden, and decorated by famous artists of the time, sprouted up to house the nobility. These mansions give the Marais its gracious char-acter today, thanks to Baron Haussmann's turning a blind eye to the area when he drove his boulevards through town.

By the 17th century the Marais was in its heyday, but with the building of Versailles and then the outbreak of Revolution, the district declined. The fashionable world went west and, with mansions emptied of aristocratic owners, the artisans moved in — jewellers, hatters, haberdashers, leather workers. There was little local money to invest so buildings became dilapidated, courtyards squalid and overgrown.

After the Second World War, property speculators even began demolition work here, building tacky apartments as cheaply as possible. Deterioration continued until 1962 when the then Minister of Culture, André Malraux, rescued the Marais from its slum landlords by declaring it a conservation area, thus preventing wholesale destruction. A renovation programme was instigated and since then the Marais has become sacrosanct.

The development of the Beaubourg sparked yet another phase of regeneration: buildings are cleaner, shops smarter than ever, prices higher. Property prices have escalated by about 30% a year over the last 3 years — the designer and gallery folk who can't meet the high rents have joined the migration eastwards to the Bastille (see **11e and 12e**).

the lifestyles of 18th-century French aristocrats. Amongst the documents on display dating from the Middle Ages to the Hundred Years War, in the Caran section, are the Edict of Nantes (1598), Napoleon's will, Louis XVI's diary showing the entry for July 14th 1789: "Rien". In fact the reason he wrote "Rien" was because he had not managed to catch a thing hunting that day.

Musée de l'Histoire de France (Museum of French History): Hôtel de Soubise, 60 rue des Francs-Bourgeois. Tel. 40 27 62 18. M Rambuteau/St Paul. Open 1.30–5.45pm, Mon, Wed–Sun. Admission 12f adults; 8f students, teachers, OAPs; free under-18s. No credit cards.

THE SOUTHERN MARAIS

The fashionable but not touristy **rue des Francs-Bourgeois** crosses the Marais from east to west, dividing the 3e from the 4e, and leads to the **place des Vosges**. A good shopping street for glassware, antiques, silverware and costume jewellery, it has a number of tempting refreshment stops too: try the **Marais Plus**, a bookshop and *salon de thé* at number 20, or **Les Enfants Gâtés** at number 43 – both serve scrumptious brownies. The curious name is medieval, meaning "street of the free citizens" – referring to the poor who lived in the almshouses built here in the 14th century. They were so hard up, they were exempt, or "free", of taxes.

Later on, the street was more affluent: the noble **Hôtel Carnavalet** is proof of that. This was the scene in the late 17th-century of the most dazzling salon in Paris, hosted by Madame de Sévigné, and now a museum, the Carnavalet. (See box feature.)

The main entrance to the Carnavalet is in one of the prettiest streets in the Marais, the **rue de Sévigné**.

At 41 rue des Francs-Bourgeois, the **Kwok-On Museum** houses an exotic private collection of oriental theatrical objects – masks, puppets, Chinese embroidered opera costumes in rich fabrics.

Kwok-On Museum: 41 rue des Francs-Bourgeois. Tel. 42 72 99 42. M St Paul/Rambuteau. Open 10am–5.30pm, Mon–Fri. Admission 10f adults; 5f under-12s, students under 25, OAPs. No credit cards.

Hotels and Hôtels

Q: When is a *hôtel* not a hotel? A: When it's a *hôtel particulier*. In French, long before it meant a place where you pay to spend the night, *hôtel* was used to describe a private town house.

The idea of a privately-owned, grand town residence — not a palace or château, simply an imposing domestic dwelling — was quite a novelty when architects Le Vau, François Mansart, Jules Hardouin Mansart and others built their beautifully-proportioned, homochromous houses. They took their inspiration not from the Gothic tradition, but from the classical style. More than 100 of the *hôtels* of the Marais have survived, some built in the 17th century by some of France's greatest architects. Unfortunately, over the years 29 have disappeared. Of the 100 that are left, all those left are protected from redevelopment owing to their historic or architectural assets.

Opposite the Carnavalet, at the corner of rue Pavée (one of the first paved streets of Paris) is one of the largest and oldest houses in the Marais, the turreted **Hôtel de Lamoignon**, originally built in 1555 and now a dignified home for the Paris Historical Library. Temporary exhibitions are also held here. In rue Pavée itself, at a number 20 is the **Pavé Glacé** where you'll find delicious home-made ice creams – at a price. The **synagogue**, built in 1913, at number 10, is the work of the famous Art Nouveau architect Hector Guimard, who was responsible for so many curly Métro entrances.

One 17th-century mansion follows another in this patch. Slip up the rue Payenne, alongside the Carnavalet, off rue des Francs-Bourgeois and there are a couple more – **Hôtel de Chatillon** (number 13) and next-door **Hôtel de Polaston-Polignac**, along with a refreshing patch of green, the **square Georges-Cain**.

On leaving the Carnavalet you could follow the rue de Turenne down to the place des Vosges, or else take a look at some of the other magnificent mansions near the Carnavalet. On rue de Turenne there's the **Hôtel de Montrésor** (now a school) and the **Hôtel de Grand-Veneur**, once a house of the master of the royal hunt. Symbols of hunting and a boar's head

Life is a Carnavalet

Proust's bedroom is just one of the tableaux of Parisian life depicted at the **Carnavalet Museum**, which chronicles the city's history like an intimate diary spanning the ages.

It was here in her old apartment overlooking the geometrical French gardens that Madame de Sévigné wrote many of her gossipy letters, between 1677 and 1696.

In 1880 Baron Haussmann decided that the Hôtel Carnavalet, a prime example of French Renaissance architecture, should become a museum of the history of Paris from Henry IV to the Belle Époque. More recently, in honour of the bicentennial, the Carnavalet's period rooms were refurbished and the collection allowed to grow into the neighbouring late-17th-century Hôtel Le Peletier de Saint-Fargeau. There's a fascinating collection of exhibits — antique furniture, beautiful *boiseries*, a 19th-century morsel of bread from the Siege of Paris, the pen of Alexandre Dumas fils.

Roman bronzes co-exist with daguerreotypes, vintage silver-coated copper plates showing facets of Parisian architecture and life that has long disappeared. (One, taken between 1845–50, is a panoramic view of the Louvre and quai Mégisserie; others show the barricades in the rue St Maur in 1845.) The section on the Revolution has models of the guillotines, placards, original execution orders and Declarations of the Rights of Man, as well as Marie Antoinette's lacy slippers. There's a reconstruction of her prison cell and several period interiors salvaged from demolished or remodelled buildings, the earliest being the mid-17th-century painted study from the Hôtel de Villacerf.

Most stunning of all are the reconstructed Art Nouveau interiors from the Café de Paris (1899) which disappeared from the avenue de l'Opéra in 1954, and the jeweller's shop Fouquet (1899), as well as the lavish ballroom from the old Hôtel Wandel townhouse. Amongst the numerous fine paintings is Francois Gérard's flirty portrait of Madame Récamier, the Carnavalet's "Mona Lisa", plus portraits of the Tout Paris of yesteryear by Boucher and Fragonard.

Carnavalet Museum: 23 rue de Sévigné. Tel. 42 72 21 13. M Saint Paul Chemin Vert. Open 10am–5.40pm, Tue–Sun. Admission 15f adults; 8.50f students, teachers; free under-7s. Credit (bookshop only): AE, V.

The Picasso Museum

The museum is impressive from the entrance onwards where the staircase, lavishly decorated with delicately carved honey-coloured stone, curls upwards to the galleries containing the largest collection of works by Picasso in the world.

Admittedly, many of the artist's well-known pieces are in other collections, but those amassed here cover all phases of his long, fecund, career. Aged 92 when he died, he continued to work through into his eighties. In the grand, bright, white rooms there are 158 sculptures, over 200 paintings, 3000 drawings and etchings plus collages, ceramics and personal memorabilia. The painter's precocious maturity is shown in amazing early work like the "Barefoot Girl", painted when he was only 14; his life and loves, crises and commitments, are chronicled in other paintings.

Picasso's own private collection of works by other artists, including paintings by Cézanne, Renoir, Matisse, Rousseau, a Balthus, a Miró and Modigliani are also on show. Furniture by Diego Giacometti is an unexpected extra. The museum is extremely popular so it's a good idea to get there early. The reasonably-priced restaurant is a good lunch stop.

Musée Picasso (Picasso National Museum): Hôtel Salé, 5 rue de Thorigny. Tel. 42 71 25 21. M Chemis Vert/St Paul/Filles du Calvaire. Open 9.15am–5.15pm, Mon, Thurs–Sun. 9.15am–10pm Wed. Admission 28f adults; 16f 18–25s, students, OAPs, free under 18s. No credit cards.

---

decorate the façade. Up along the street is the neo-classical church of **St-Denys-du-Sacrement**, built in 1835, containing a forceful Delacroix *Déposition* (1844) in the front right-hand chapel.

Cut through rue Ste Anastase to rue de Thorigny and you're almost face to face with the **Hôtel Salé**, built in 1656 by a salt tax collector (*salé* = salted). Between 1974 and 1980 the beautiful 17th-century house, one of the finest in the Marais, was restored. But you don't come here just to see the palatial building: it is also the **Musée Picasso** which opened in 1985 to show off a splendid and huge collection of his works donated to the State in lieu of death duties – a deal which was a first in French legal history. In fact the law was changed in 1968 in preparation for his death (1973) to make this possible. There's a great synergy between the surroundings and the

The Cognacq-Jay

Two streets west of the Carnavalet is the Cognacq-Jay museum. Transplanted in 1991 from the boulevard des Capucines to its Marais home in the Hôtel Donon, the collection was assembled by the founders of La Samaritaine department stores. Ernest Cognacq, by his own admission, was no art lover (he liked to boast that he'd never set foot inside the Louvre) but with expert guidance, he and his wife, Louise Jay, amassed a treasure trove of 18th-century furniture, *objets d'art*, porcelain and paintings, including works by Boucher, Chardin, Canaletto, Fragonard, early Rembrandt, Reynolds and Watteau.

Musée Cognacq-Jay, Hôtel Donon, 8 rue Elzévir. Tel. 42 61 94 54. M Chemin Vert St Paul/Rambuteau. Open 10am–5.40pm, Tue–Sun. Admission 12f.

works, the historic house counterpointing the modernity of Picasso exceptionally well.

Close to the Picasso museum, at place de Thorigny, is another majestic *hôtel* now housing a museum. The architect of Les Invalides (Libéral Bruand) built the Hôtel Libéral Bruand for himself in 1685, and it's now the **Bricard Museum** (also known as the Musée de la Serrure), devoted to locks, keys and other portal pieces from Roman times onwards.

Musée de la Serrure (Bricard Museum): Hôtel Libéral Braund, 1 rue de la Perle. Tel. 42 77 79 62. M St Paul/Chemin Vert. Open Tue–Sat, 10–12, 2pm–5pm. Admission 10f. Closed Sun, Mon, Aug, last week Dec. No credit cards.

Doubling back now, past the Bricard towards the Archives, you pass the Hôtel de Rohan, and at the corner of rue des Archives and rue des Fils is the beautifully restored François Mansart mansion, the **Hotel Guénégaud**, built 1648–51. It will not come as a surprise that there's a museum tucked away inside – devoted, in this instance, to hunting. Fine pictures (Brueghel, Rubens), every kind of weapon, decorated guns, interesting ceramics and two rooms of stuffed animals, the majority of which were killed before conservation caught, on, are arranged over three floors.

Museum of Hunting: Hôtel Guénégaud, 60 rue des Archives. Tel. 42 72 86 43. M Hôtel de Ville. Open 10am–12.30pm, 1.30–5.30pm, Mon, Wed–Sun. Admission 20f adults, 10f under-10s. No credit cards.

When you leave the building, if you turn left into rue des Archives and continue on rue Rambuteau to rue Beaubourg (also called rue du Renard), then turn left, you'll find on your right the famous **Pompidou Centre**.

BEAUBOURG

In spite of its name (*beau* meaning beautiful; *bourg* meaning village) Beaubourg was once a particularly smelly medieval village and, thanks to the detritus that was deposited here from Les Halles, remained one of the most squalid and insanitary parts of Paris up until the mid-1930s. These days it's not just the name of the area, but also of the high-tech tangle of tubes and drainpipes of the **Pompidou Centre**, officially the **Centre National d'Art et de Culture**.

Initiated by President Pompidou, a great lover of modernity, as part of the Les Halles redevelopment, the aim was to create a huge contemporary exhibition centre, a kind of mission-control dispensing wholesale culture.

When it opened in 1977, after Pompidou's death, there was outrage, admiration, lots of "disgusteds of Montpelliers" – a reception not dissimilar to that aroused by the Eiffel Tower a century earlier. Nothing like it had been seen in Paris – above all in the city's conservative museum cliques. Yet its very notoriety has helped to popularise modern art on an unprecedented scale and the Centre has become the most visited sight (20,000 each day) in Paris: it is as if the building had turned itself inside out to attract the public from the surrounding 17th-century streets. It is accessible, animated and deeply democratic. Gradually, olive branches have replaced outrage.

Designed by the Anglo-Italian team of architects Richard Rodgers and Renzo Piano, the five-storey building has its multi-coloured viscera – pipes, shafts, escalators, etc. – outside the walls. This exo-skeleton leaves great chasms of space inside to be manipulated freely by movable screens, well suited to the triumphant, vast exhibitions that have become a speciality of the Centre. Climbing through the perspex body of escalators outside the building gives an ever-changing panorama over the Paris rooftops: it's a place less devoted to contemplation than to the immediate. Inside too there's a sense of frenzy: you are never alone in the Beaubourg.

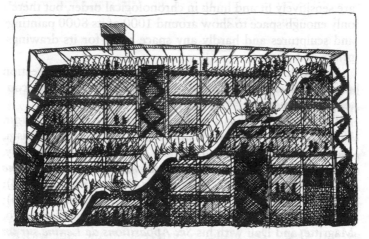

As well as housing the immensely impressive **National Museum of Modern Art**, the largest collection of its kind in the world, (see below) there are a number of other departments under the same roof:

- **Public Information Library** (*BPI – Bibliothèque Publique d'Information*)
  Reached from the second floor, there are a million books plus slides, videotapes, records, audio cassettes for auto didacts. Spreads over the third floor too. The only large open-shelf library in Paris.

- **Industrial Design Centre** (*CCI – Centre de Création Industrielle*)
  A ground floor gallery has exhibitions on diverse themes.

- **Institute for Contemporary Acoustic and Musical Research** (*IRCAM – Institut de Récherche et de Coordination Acoustique/Musique*)

Under the direction of composer Pierre Boulez. The subterranean lab isn't open to the public, but there are lectures and demonstrations.

The National Museum of Modern Art, (MNAM), on the third and fourth floors, the Beaubourg's greatest crowd-puller, covers all schools of contemporary art and sculpture. Works are sensitively lit and hung in chronological order, but there's only enough space to show around 1000 of its 8000 paintings and sculptures and hardly any space at all for its drawings, prints and photos.

On the third floor are works from 1965 onwards, a section which is often rearranged to accommodate even more contemporary pieces.

The fourth floor has a permanent exhibition of work from 1905, covering Fauvism, Cubism, Abstract, Expressionism, Dadaism, Surrealism, Pop – right up until the present day. Trace the progress of modern art movements though *Femme Assise*, Picasso (1909); *L'Homme à la Guitare*, Braque (1914); the abstract *Prismes Electriques*, Sonia Delaunay (1914); works by the expressionist Kandinsky; the Surrealists Miro, Magritte, and Dali with his *Six Apparitions de Lenine sur un piano* (1931); sculpture by Matisse, Moore and Modigliani; the works of Francis Bacon, Warhol and Lichtenstein.

Also on this floor are the **Salle d'Art Graphique** and the **Salon Photo**, both with changing exhibitions.

On the fifth floor are the **Grandes Galeries** where major temporary exhibitions are staged; the excellent **Salle Garance** cinema and a self-service cafeteria and restaurant where the view is better than the food. In addition, there's a children's library and workshop where you can leave the kids to sculpt and paint, supervised by English-speaking attendants.

Centre National d'Art et de Culture Georges Pompidou: Plateau Beaubourg. Tel. 42 77 12 33/recorded information Tel. 42 77 11 12. M Châtelet/Hôtel de Ville/Rambuteau. Open noon–10pm, Mon, Wed–Fri; 10am–10pm, Sat–Sun. Admission to MNAM: 23f adults; 17f 18–25s, OAPs; free under-18s;

Half the 5-acre site of the Pompidou Centre was left open as a large piazza for impromptu, informal art and displays.

You can spend a leisurely afternoon outside one of the many cafés which circle the plateau Beaubourg watching a modern medieval circus where buskers, vendors, bongo-drummers, fire-eaters, mime artists and all sorts of bizarre acts compete for audiences. It's a bit like Gerry Cottle's on a Bank Holiday.

FROM BEAUBOURG TO HÔTEL DE VILLE

In front of the plateau Beaubourg is the rue St Martin, lined with galleries, shops and places to eat, none more trendy than **Café Beaubourg** at number 100 rue St Martin, on the corner of rue St Merri. Spaciousness, light, and designer folk fill this stylish, high-tech café.

The **Church of St Merri**, a little south of the Pompidou Centre, is worth a look for its anachronistic use of 15th-century flamboyant Gothic style. Although completed in 1612, it has a particularly ornate west front in the earlier style and its bell, made in 1331, is said to be the oldest one in Paris. St Merri used to be the wealthy parish church of the Lombard money-lenders, who gave their name to the rue des Lombards nearby. Concerts are held here from time to time – phone for details on 42 74 42 96.

Behind rue St Martin is the slither of rue Quincampoix, and at number 37 **Zabriskie** is a must for photography buffs. Sister establishment of the New York gallery of the same name, Zabriskie has prints from some of the world's greatest lens-people, including some at prices to make you blink twice. (It is open 11am–7pm, Tue–Sat. No credit cards. Tel. 42 72 35 47).

South again, at the Seine and on the border of the 1er and 4e *arrondissements*, not *strictly* part of the Marais, is the **place du Châtelet** on the site of a vile medieval prison – said to be even worse than the infamous Conciergerie. Not a sign of this today, of course, although under the square is the world's biggest underground station and there's something very prison-like about its endless labyrinth of corridors. Back above ground you'll see there are a couple of symmetrical theatres built in 1862 in the *place*. The state-owned **Théâtre Musical de Paris** (formerly the Théâtre du Châtelet) had the biggest auditorium of any theatre, before Opéra Bastille came along. Opposite is the **Théâtre de la Ville** (formerly the Théâtre Sarah Bernhardt).

Taking the fat avenue Victoria (named after the well-upholstered British queen) you pass the **Tour St Jacques**, a Seine landmark. It's actually a Gothic belfry – the only remnant of the 16th-century church of St Jacques, one of the starting points of the pilgrimage (via rue St Jacques in the 5e on the left bank) to Santiago, Spain. The avenue Victoria slips into the **place de l'Hôtel de Ville** which, for hundreds of years, was the only really large square in Paris. Until 1830 it was known as the place de Grève. As well as being a site for public executions, it was a meeting place for the unemployed, to express their grievances, which is what the expression *faire la grève* once meant. Over the years the meaning has subtly changed and today it means "to go on strike".

On a more prosaic note, off the *place* you'll spot the **Bazar de l'Hôtel de Ville (BHV)** one of the largest hardware stores anywhere with more tools than the most imaginative DIY-er could dream up. Records, books, stereos and sporting goods are also sold here.

BHV: 52–64 rue de Rivoli. Tel. 42 74 90 00. M Hôtel de Ville. Open 9am–6.30pm, Mon–Tue; 9am–10pm, Wed; 9am–6.30pm, Thurs–Fri; 9am–7pm, Sat.

From the Hôtel de Ville, a short walk up the cobbled rue des Barres gives a good view of the buttresses of the intriguing Church of **St Gervais et St Protais**. The façade, finished in 1621, was the first to be built in the classical or Renaissance style in Paris and behind it is an attractive late-Gothic church which wasn't completed until 1657, and has the oldest organ in Paris, as well as pretty stained glass. Behind the church is a tableau of medieval building, but for a glimpse of medieval grandeur, take the rue de l'Hôtel de Ville to where it meets the tiny rue **de Figuier**.

Here you'll find one of the oldest Parisian mansions, the meticulously-restored 15th-century **Hôtel de Sens**. Originally a small, fortified castle built for the archbishop of Sens in 1475, it's now a fine arts library, the **Bibliothèque Forney**, with a gallery for temporary design exhibitions. Look for a hole above the portal that was used for dropping boiling oil on unwelcome visitors – note the past tense. (Admission is free, and it's open 1.30–8.30pm, Tue–Sat.)

Sidle east a little along rue Ave Maria passing the rue des Jardins St Paul and slip into the signposted **Village St Paul** for a look at a "New Marais" *quartier*. Cobbled, car-less, interlinked old courtyards with chi-chi flats above and pricey craft and antique shops below, it might strike you as charming or simply contrived.

If, by chance, your stomach is telling you it's time for a little something, there are two terrific-value stops near here. One means back-tracking a bit along the Seine to a little bistro at 84 quai de l'Hôtel de Ville called **Le Trumilou**; to get to the other, head up rue du Petit-Muse

Hôtel de Ville

Municipal authority has centred on the place de l'Hôtel de Ville since way back — the first town hall (city hall if you're American) was built in 1357 when one of the earliest mayors, Étienne Marcel, established the City Council here. (There's a statue of him by the south side of the Hôtel.)

For 100 years Paris was ruled directly by the government, but, in 1977, mayors were re-introduced. Today the Hôtel de Ville is the HQ of Jacques Chirac whose offices are at the river end of the building.

If there's a meeting of the City Council, when the public are admitted, or an exhibition, it's worth going inside the Hôtel de Ville (which was finished in 1882) to see the grandiloquent interior complete with Baccarat chandeliers and coffered ceilings — especially if you're interested in *fin-de-siècle* decor.

Guided tours take place on Mondays at 10.30am — telephone 42 76 40 40 to check. From 29 rue de Rivoli, the publicity department of the Hôtel de Ville distributes municipal information.

and on the corner at 31 rue de la Cerisaie is a dingy café, popular with locals, called Le Temps des Cérises, with a cheap lunchtime menu for around 50f. In both instances go before 12.30pm or after 1.30pm or you won't get squeezed in.

Otherwise you could point yourself north (go up rue St Paul or rue du Fauçonnier and along the tiny passage Charlemagne) and check out the OTT baroque-style 17th-century church of St Paul–St Louis. You'll find it where the eastern end of the rue de Rivoli (looking quite different from how it did an *arrondissement* ago) becomes the rue St Antoine.

On the opposite side of the wide rue St Antoine, at number 62, is the 17th-century Hôtel de Béthune-Sully, one of the best Marais *hôtels* and now the national monument's administrative offices, alias Caisse Nationale des Monuments Historiques, where temporary exhibitions on architecture and conservation are held. It's also the starting point for guided tours (in French) to sites and buildings all over the city.

Stop to take a look at the stately inner courtyard with intricately carved windows. Inside (it's open to the public on Wednesday, Saturday and Sunday afternoons) there are fine painted ceilings and panelling in Sully's basement study. The stone staircase was one of the first straight-angle ones built in France. Clearly the Duke of Sully did not want them sullied. He told his wife, "You may have your lovers, but keep the stairs clear." The duchess's many admirers had to use the back stairs. Visitors today can wander round the gardens and the bookshop by the gate has a wide selection of publications (including ones in English) and is open daily from 10am–12.45pm, 1.45 to 6pm.

From here, if you turn up the villagey rue de Birague, you come, via an archway, to the **place des Vosges** (see box feature). If you take a right as you leave the Hôtel Béthune-Sully, into rue St Antoine again past the church St Paul-St Louis and turn into rue François-Miron, which is flanked by doddery, timbered medieval houses, you will find the tottering **Hôtel de Beauvais** which dates from 1665 at number 68. The highly respectable façade hides a colourful history. It was built as a thank-you for Pierre Beauvais and his wife Catherine Bellier (known as one-eyed Kate) who was chambermaid to Queen Anne of Austria. The 40-year-old Catherine, at the Queen's request, provided sexual initiation for the 16-year-old Louis XIV. A hundred years later, the *hôtel* was the home of the Bavarian ambassador, and in 1763 it was here that the 7-year old Mozart gave his first Paris recitals.

Turning northwards over rue de Rivoli brings you to the heart of the Jewish quarter in rue des Rosiers.

THE JEWISH QUARTER

Six synagogues, Hebrew booksellers, kosher delis, Middle Eastern restaurants, Jewish supermarkets and butchers still fill the sinuous cobbled streets between the **rue des Rosiers** and the adjoining **rue des Écouffes**, in the centuries-old Jewish quarter. The community has survived both Revolution and Occupation. These days, when you're more likely to see Azzedine Alaia-clad Parisiennes than black-robed *chasidim*

Place des Vosges

From the Carnavalet Museum, if you take the rue des Francs-Bourgeois crossing the rue de Turenne, you'll come to the oldest square in Paris, **place des Vosges**.

The Marais is now one of the most densely populated parts of the city and this spacious and gracious tree-filled square is the only green expanse to speak of in the *quartier*, so it's no wonder that it's so popular with sandwich-munchers, toddlers and other pedestrians looking for parking space.

The place des Vosges was built on the orders of Henry IV in 1605 on the site of a horse market, but was not finished until 2 years after his assassination, in the reign of his son Louis XIII. He wanted a square on a monumental scale where fêtes and ceremonies could be held. it opened with a flourish in 1612 with a lavish, 3-day tournament in honour of Louis XIII's marriage to Anne of Austria and of his sister to a Spanish prince. Thereon, its fashionable status was guaranteed.

Originally known as the place Royal, the square lost its name in 1789 when its noble residents lost their heads and acquired its present name for the not very exotic but revolutionarily sound reason that the department of the Vosges in the east of France was the first to pay up all its taxes to support the new régime.

There's a dignified symmetry to the 36 houses, or *pavillions*, of red brick and golden stone façades which overlook the square – nine on each side, all of which are historic monuments. Building began with the King's Pavilion on the south side, counterbalanced on the north side by the Queen's Pavilion – the idea being that the King would live in the big house himself and his estranged wife, Marie de Medici, in the one on the other side. However, it was his concierge instead who lived in the King's Pavilion. At ground level are shady arcades housing galleries, shops, cafés. The brown-fronted café-brasserie **Ma Bourgogne**, on the north-western corner is a Marais landmark and particularly popular with locals for Sunday breakfast. There's also a good wine bar upstairs.

The square has always been an élite residential enclave: Richelieu lived at number 21 from 1615–27. Théophile Gautier at number 8. The *grande dame* of the Marais, Madame de Sévigné, was born in 1626 at 1 bis. It was while he was living in the place des Vosges in 1930 that Georges Simenon began to write his best-selling Inspector Maigret novels.

Past the Pavilion du Roi where the odd numbers end and the even numbers begin is number 6, the house where the Square's best known 19th-century inhabitant, Victor Hugo, wrote *Les Misérables*. He rented an apartment here from 1833–48 before his exile to Guernsey and you can visit the small museum devoted to him, from the windows of which, incidentally, there's a wonderful view of the Square. Surprisingly, amongst the miscellaneous Hugo memorabilia, there's a collection of the writer's paintings, distraught surrealist drawings and engravings, as well as the rather odd furniture he designed and carved.

Victor Hugo Museum: Hôtel de Rohan-Guéménée, 6 place des Vosges. Tel. 42 72 16 65. M St Paul Bastille/Chemin Vert. Open 10am–5.10pm, Tue–Sun. Closed Mon. Admission 16f. No credit cards.

in the *quartier*, this area is a precious pocket of un-yuppified Marais. All around designer boutiques and art galleries appropriate the bakeries and grocery shops. Nearby, sandwiched between Romeo Gigli's stunning new high-tech boutique and Stephanie Kélian's shop at 36 rue Sévigné, is a small Jewish museum. South, across the rue de Rivoli, at 17 rue Geoffroy l'Asnier, the sober 1956 **Memorial du Martyr Juif Inconnu** (Memorial to the Unknown Jewish Martyr) is an eternal flame commemorating Parisian Jews who were killed by the Nazis. The upper floors house a museum of the Holocaust and a reading room. Open 10am–12 noon, 2–5pm, Mon–Fri; also these hours on Sundays in July and August. Closed on May 1st and on Jewish holidays. Tel. 42 77 44 72 for more information.

Spinal cord of the Jewish quarter is the animated rue des Rosiers and at number 7 business is better than ever at the most famous Jewish restaurant in Paris. **Jo Goldenberg's** has been going since the beginning of the century, but more recently has also become a chic place to eat. Like the museum and synagogues in the area, it was the scene of a terrible terrorist attack in 1982, in which six people died. The reception given to visitors is not as guarded as you might expect. Entrance to the slightly kitsch split-level restaurant is through the busy, traditional delicatessen. There's a vast menu of simply prepared, moderately priced Jewish, Hungarian and Russian nosh, much enjoyed by President Mitterand who is a

frequent diner there these days. (Open 8.30am–11pm daily.
Tel. 48 87 20 16.)

At number 4 there's a not unfriendly atmosphere at
Hamman de St Paul sauna where, for 30 years, treatments
have been offered to soothe and relax (massage, manicure,
etc.) in Art Deco surroundings.

The Hamman de St Paul: Open 10am–10pm; women, Wed and Fri,
Men, Thus and Sat (9am–10pm). On Tuesdays the complex is open
from 5pm–11pm for those who hold a *carte naturiste*.

Continuing along the street **Kosher Pizza**, number 11, serves
up what it says, from 15f a slice. **Diasporama** at number
20 sells Judaic crafts, records, jewellery, and has temporary exhibitions with occasional guest artists. **Bibllophone** at
number 26 sells fiction and non-fiction on Judaism and has a
selection in English. **Chez Finkelsztajn** is at number 27 where
Sacha, a third generation baker, sells central European and
Russian pastries and Sunday bagels while his wife **Florence
Finkelsztajn** at neighbouring 24 rue des Ecouffes is also a
purvey of these, as well as Middle Eastern take-outs and
meats. You can get Sunday brunch, light lunches, and tea and
cakes all day at a pretend English tearoom, **Le Loir dans La
Théière** (Dormouse in the Teapot), 3 rue des Rosiers. *Falafel*
fast-food (delicious sandwiches), an Israeli favourite and an
inexpensive way of quietening a rumbling tum, is available
from at least half a dozen stands within two blocks along rue
des Rosiers.

Just off rue des Rosiers, in a street that's barely as long as
its name, **Chez Marianne** at 2 rue des Hospitalières-St-Gervais
is a 40-year old deli-restaurant with central European and
Israeli specialities. Next door the **Libraire du Temple** stocks
ceremonial artefacts as well as scholarly Judaic books.

Many of the trendy new shops have been opened up by
young Jews who are second or third generation in the fashion
business. **Costanza**, a high-fashion, handmade shoe shop in
rue des Francs-Bourgeois, is a "*gescheft de famille*", or family
business housed in a former butcher's shop which dates back
to 1860. Listed as a historic monument, there's a preservation
order on the green marble fascia. Two talented Jewish men,
Francis Miller and Patrick Bertraux, spotted the potential of

the Marais as a style centre in 1986 and their shop, **Miller and Bertraux** in rue Ferdinand Duval sells fashion, accessories and gifts, while a few doors away another Jewish duo, Vanessa Bruno and Philippe Bianco, make and design clothes for their shop **Zyga**.

5E, QUARTIER LATIN:
Students and
Perpetual Students

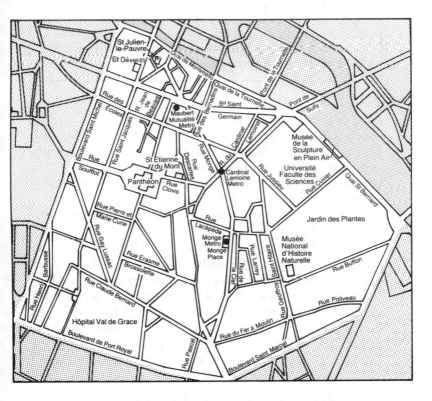

The great slab of the 5e bounded by the Seine and the boulevards
St Michel, Port Royal and St Marcel is best known for its medi-
eval Latin Quarter and the university complex of the Sorbonne.
Quartier Latin instantly evokes a liberal, Bohemian, intellectual
Paris. If the Latin Quarter didn't exist, someone would have to

Why "Latin" Quarter?

Until the 18th century only Latin was spoken in this scholar's *quartier* – hence the name we use today, though you'll be hard-pressed to find many students or academics still conversing in it.

The Latin Quarter didn't really get going until the 12th century when the scholarly monk Abélard (the one passionately linked to Héloïse) led the first student revolt. He rebelled against the rigid, ecclesiastical teaching pattern practised on the Ile de la Cité, formed a more liberal centre of learning on the left bank and his students followed him. In 1253, Robert de Sorbon, Chaplain to Louis IX, started a college there for poor theological students and the rest, as they say, is history. It eventually became one of the most formidable think-tanks in the world, with illustrious teachers.

invent it. As it is, the imagination has to work overtime these days, as the students seem to get harder to find amongst the cosmopolitan swarms. Nevertheless, the district as a whole still has the largest concentration of colleges and secondary schools in the country. So while the Latin Quarter's no longer the Paris University HQ (due to the decentralisation, after the turbulence of the 1968 student riots, into 13 various campuses) it's still a youthful, lively, colourful area, even though some of the students may be of the perpetual variety.

Many of the small, studenty hangouts, the raffish bars and bistros, have become pizza parlours or fast foodlets but there are still countless cheap, lively cafés and ethnic restaurants. You just need to choose with care as there is an equal number of the tourist-grasping variety. This isn't a district that drops dead after dark – small cinemas like **Action Écoles** (23 rue des Écoles. Tel. 43 25 72 07) and the **Studio Galande**, (42 rue Galande. Tel. 43 54 72 71) showing cult and classic films and the multitudinous discos, clubs and jazz cellars see to that.

NORTH OF THE SORBONNE

Until Baron Haussmann bulldozed his broad boulevards St Germain and St Michel through the left bank, it was a labyrinth of small, crowded streets. Pockets of the past can still be picked up in the evocative older streets in the north of the 5e – rue de la Harpe, rue Séguier, rue du Chat-qui-Pêche, rue Gît-le-Coeur. Before Haussmann, the main thoroughfare was the old medieval Gallo-Roman road of rue St Jacques, so named because it was the starting point for pilgrims to the shrine of St Jacques de Compostelle in northern Spain. At the northern end of the rue St Jacques, down rue St Séverin and left into rue des Prêtres, is **St Séverin** – one of the most attractive churches in Paris – complete with Romanesque tower, 13th-century porch, 16th-century spire, façade and ambulatory of the most amazingly flamboyant Gothic style.

Built on the site of an ancient oratory, St Séverin was the parish church for the whole of the left bank around the end of the 11th century, and is now the official Sorbonne University church.

Saint Séverin: rue Saint Séverin. M St Michel. Open 11am–1pm, 3–7.30pm, Tue-Fri. Admission free.

Across the rue St Jacques, almost next door to St Séverin, but on the opposite side of the street, is the small, quiet church of **St-Julien-le-Pauvre** which is the same age (1165–1220) as Notre-Dame, facing it across the river. Since 1889 it has been a Greek Catholic (Melchite) Church, whose Sunday morning High Mass is worth listening to; regular concerts are also held here. Throughout the Middle Ages, St Julien was the place where university assemblies and elections were held; in 1524 they became too rough and rowdy and were banned from the church for ever.

St-Julien-le-Pauvre: rue St-Julien-le-Pauvre. Maubert-Mutualité/Saint Michel.

The square René Viviani, next to Pont-au-Double, lies alongside St Julien and the Seine and it's worth pausing here for a minute or two to take in the remarkable view of Notre-Dame. In the garden is a twisted acacia brought back from North America and planted there around 1680, which makes it the second oldest tree in Paris – the most ancient being in the Jardin des Plantes (see page 382).

Shakespeare and Co.

In the shadow of Notre-Dame Cathedral, just across the river, at 37 rue de la Bûcherie, is the best-known and most unusual bookshop in town, Shakespeare and Company.

The book-crammed shop was opened in 1951 by American expatriate George Whitman, a relative of Walt's. He had been a friend of Sylvia Beach, whose greatest literary coup was to publish Joyce's *Ulysses* for the first time in book form. She had run a bookshop on rue de l'Odéon called Shakespeare & Co. In the '20s and '30s it had been a haunt of such ex-pat literary luminaries as F. Scott Fitzgerald, Ezra Pound, James Joyce and Hemingway. To quote the latter, it was "a warm, cheerful place with a big stove in winter, tables and shelves of books". After Sylvia Beach died, and on the anniversary of William Shakespeare's death in 1964, Whitman changed the name of his shop to hers. The homage went further — Whitman and his artist wife Felicity named their first child Sylvia after S.B.

Shakespeare & Co. has three storeys and 13 rooms full of browsers and buyers of books. There are some 30,000 second-hand and new volumes, mostly English and American literature, some autographed by well-known literati. But not all of the books are for sale, especially the antiquarian variety, though you're certainly allowed to look at them. Downstairs, in the cellar, is the press that was used to put out the first printing of *Ulysses*. These days a new generation of literary lion cubs prowl the floors — they come to meet fellow book freaks and exchange gossip — while outside the shop a blackboard broadcasts details of regular events like poetry readings, literary courses and debates. A "To Let" board lists apartments in both London and Paris.

Shakespeare and Co. :37 rue de la Bûcherie. Open noon—midnight.

You can get a glimpse of old Paris by peering down some of the neighbouring streets: rue St Séverin and the rue Galande — which was the ancient Roman route to Lyon — and the rue de Fouarre, named after bales of straw (*fouarre*) used as seats by students once upon a time when they attended the public University lectures given there. Out of the time-warp, around to the left from St Julien, is rue de la Bûcherie and the famous English bookshop, **Shakespeare and Co.** (see box feature).

Latin Paris

There's another good reason (apart from the Latin-speaking) for calling the area the "Latin Quarter". The Romans actually founded the Latin quarter in 50 BC when they built a colony in the district near the Panthéon, now called the Montagne-Ste-Geneviève. The governor lived on the Ile de la Cité, but it was here, in the 5e, that the forum, temple and baths were built.

Archaeologists have unearthed parts of a **forum** at rue Soufflot, between the boulevard St Michel and rue Monge and three **bath houses** at rue des Écoles, rue Gay Lussac and boulevard St Michel. The Romans, of course, were avid builders of baths and amphitheatres. On the principle that those who steam together stick together, they aimed to incorporate Celts and Gauls into Romanisation by letting them soak and also by entertaining them with fierce fights, as well as the gentler arts – dances, mimes, plays. It's the amphitheatre – the **Arènes de Lutèce** – Lutèce being the Roman name for Paris – and the **Cluny Baths** that really hint at the former glory of Gallo-Roman architecture, and it's these that the visitor can see.

No queues and no admission fee to inspect Les Arènes de Lutèce, between rues Monge and Navarre (M Jussieu) – you can view the arena at any time as it's now in a public park. So these days for gloating gladiators, read victorious boules players. The remains were uncovered in 1869 and, together with the Cluny Baths, they're the oldest Roman ruins in Paris.

On the ground floor of the **Cluny Museum**, the present ruins of the thermal baths cover about a third of the site that must have been taken up by a vast Gallo-Roman public bath house at the beginning of the 3rd century. Most impressive is the 50-foot high vast vaulted room which housed the cold bath or *frigidarium*; the warm bath (*terridarium*) and steam bath (*caldarium*) are all well preserved. In the cold bath room you can make out traces of the marble flooring, fresco work and mosaic décor. The ribbed vaulting of the *frigidarium* rests on consoles carved as ship's prows – giving rise to the theory that the baths were built by the rich and powerful boatman's guild which controlled all river traffic on and around Lutetia (Paris). This same guild, in the reign of Emperor Tiberius (14–73 AD), dedicated a pillar to Jupiter, which was discovered beneath the Notre-Dame chancel and is now exhibited here in the museum part. The Boatman's Pillar (or *Pillar des Nautes*) is Paris's oldest sculpture and features both Celtic deities and gods from the Roman pantheon.

> **Musée des Thermes et de l'Hôtel de Cluny**: 6 place Paul-Painlevé. Tel. 43 25 62 00. M St Michel/Cluny. Open 9.45 am–12.30pm, 2–5.15pm, Mon, Wed, Sun. Admission 18f adults; 8f 18–25s, OAPs; free under 18s.

Due south is the shabby **place Maubert** where, in the Middle Ages, open air lessons were given – the name Maubert is possibly a corruption of Maître Albert, a Dominican teacher at the University who held his classes in the open air. Later on gruesome public executions took place there – though there's hopefully no connection between recalcitrant students and the capital punishment. Today the only punishing activity in *la Maube* is all the heavyweight shopping that goes on in the morning market on Tuesdays, Thursdays and Saturdays when the low prices lure the crowds.

Off *place* Maubert, slender, medieval streets stretch down to the Seine. In one of them, **rue de Bièvre**, heavily guarded by police, there's the private home of President Mitterand, where he still spends quite a lot of time when not officially ensconced at the Palais de l'Élysée residence. In the adjacent rue de Maître Albert, is the Paris branch of the PDSA, a small animal clinic donated by the Duke of Windsor to his adopted city. (For a description of the area to the east of here, see the **Jardin des Plantes** p.382.)

Returning to the rue St Jacques, if you turn towards the Seine and then left into the pretty **rue de la Huchette**, you'll find another slice of old Paris. On the left is the **Caveau de Huchette** jazz cellar and a little further on is the tiny **Théâtre de la Huchette** where a double bill of one act plays by Ionesco has been running non-stop for over a quarter of a century – a record only *The Mousetrap* in London's West End can beat. At number 10, in 1795, lived the young Napoleon, unemployed, unpaid, and not yet glorious. The narrowest street in Paris, the dark rue de Chat-qui-Pêche, runs off down to a quay, but if you continue to the corner of the rue de la Harpe, you'll end up in the souk.

Carry on to the fountain in the populous **place Saint Michel**. It's a famous meeting and pick-up place, and the starting point of the thoroughfare that is synonymous with the Latin Quarter, its "High Street", the **boulevard St Michel**, aka *boul' Mich*. Tree-lined, busy with cafés and bookshops, it slips down to the Luxembourg Gardens. At its junction with the great lateral artery of the left bank, the boulevard St Germain, is the **Cluny Museum** (see box), with its entrance on place Painlevé.

On the other side of the *place* in the appropriately named rue des Écoles, along which are the undistinguished – architecturally not intellectually – buildings of the Sorbonne, Collège de France and Lycée Louis Le Grand. The **Sorbonne** looks more like a jail than a great seat of learning: a sentence that will reek of blasphemy to most Parisians. Apparently plans are in the pipeline to restore it. The austere edifice was mostly rebuilt in the 19th century; that's with the exception of the elegant chapel which was finished in 1642 and is all that

The Police Museum
The small **Musée des Collections Historiques de la Préfecture de Police** is one of the very few Parisian museums that's free, the only snag being that you have to go right through the 5th *arrondissement* police headquarters to get to it on the second floor. The history of the Parisian police force is traced from the 16th century up to the present day and it's all more fun than it might sound, despite the deeply unimaginative presentation. There's a sinister assembly of weapons and other artefacts, including souvenirs and warrants for the arrest of famous conspirators like Danton from the Revolution.

Find the museum at 1 bis rue des Carmes. Tel.43 29 21 57, ext 336. M Maubert-Mutualité. Open 9am–5pm, Mon–Thur; 9.30am–4.30pm, Friday.

remains of Cardinal Richelieu's rebuilding of the Sorbonne. These days it's used for temporary exhibitions (which is also the only time you can visit it) rather than services. Paris loves relics and Richelieu's ceremonial red hat dangles from the Sorbonne chapel ceiling; he is also buried here. The façade of the chapel dominates the east side of the attractive, traffic-free **place de la Sorbonne,** whose lime trees, bookshops and cafés make it a favourite studently meeting place.

AROUND THE PANTHÉON

Smack in the centre of the University area, the bulging rue Soufflot opens on the left to the **place du Panthéon.** On the north side at number 10 is one of the richest and most famous libraries in France, the **Ste Geneviève Library** (open to readers' ticket holders and students only) with its collection of original manuscripts and almost 3 million books. It is on the site of the once infamous Collège de Montaigu where, from the 16th to the 18th centuries, young men endured a spartan – and frequently flagellatory – "education".

Opposite, dominating the summit of the Montagne Saint

Cluny Museum

Chastity belts, spurs, sculpture, stained glass, bronzes, even 12th century shoes — you'll find all these and much more medievalia in one of the very best collections of arts and crafts from the Middle Ages in the world. They're housed in 24 rooms of a stunning 15th-century residence in the Hôtel de Cluny. Along with that of Sers and Jacques Coeur's house in the Marais, it's one of the three large private houses dating back to the 15th century left in Paris.

To get you straight into the spirit of the place, spouting gargoyles greet you in the flamboyant Cour d'Honneur. Duck through low doors to enter beamed rooms with tiny mullioned windows.

The new, light and airy Notre-Dame de Paris gallery contains fragments of sculpture, spoils from Notre-Dame vandalised during the Revolution, including 21 heads of Kings of Judah. They were unearthed at a construction site in the 9e and date from the mid-12th to the mid-13th century.

The highlight of the museum, though, must be the tapestries. These are beauties — full of rich colours and detail, including the stunning series *La Dame Aux Licornes*, or Lady and the Unicorn, displayed upstairs on the first floor in a skylit rotunda. Woven at the end of the 15th century for the Jean Le Visite family from Lyon, whose coat of arms with three golden crescents recurs throughout the design, five of the six tapestries depict allegories of the senses. The sixth, *À Mon Seul Désir*, remains unexplained. The lion (chivalric nobility) and the unicorn (bourgeois nobility) stand on either side of a richly-clad lady.

Steps lead down from the ground floor of the Hôtel to the Roman building housing the thermal baths — for details see box feature **Latin Paris**.

Cluny Museum: 6 place Paul Painlevé. Tel. 43 25 62 00. M St Michel. Open 9.45am–12.30pm, 2–5.15pm, Mon, Wed–Sun. Closed Tue. Admission 18f adults; 8f 18–25s, OAPs; free under-18s. No credit cards.

Geneviève, sits the imposing **Panthéon**, its grandiloquent dome presiding over the wind-blown square. Remains of the illustrious lie in little rooms in the lugubrious and labyrinthine crypt which extends under the whole building. There are guided tours every 15 minutes. Amongst those celebrated in death are Resistance leader Jean Moulin; Louis Braille,

inventor of braille; Rousseau. Some make odd room-mates
– like Victor Hugo and Émile Zola. Before they changed
their minds and threw his body into an open sewer, Marat
was here too. Gambetta's heart still is – thankfully – in an
urn. Built as the Church of Ste Geneviève, the patroness
of Paris, as a gesture of thanks to her from Louis XV
for his recovery from a serious illness, the Panthéon was
originally destined to be a more glorious shrine to her
than the old abbey church of that name which was later
demolished. The ambitious architect, Soufflot, masterminded
the project and Louis XV himself laid the first stone in 1764.
But before construction had been completed, the Revolution
had swept over Paris; 42 of the windows were blocked up
and the new government turned the whole building into the
gloomy Panthéon, a secular mausoleum for the nation's great
and good.

Climb the circular stairs for a good view of the interior.
At the time of writing (1991) there's substantial restoration
work in progress, but you can get a neck-craning glimpse
of pale pillars, which lift the eye upwards towards the
chaste, cream-coloured masonry and the curvaceous cupolas. In 1788 the erection of the dome, and possibly some
minor ground subsidence, caused cracks in the walls. Legend
has it that the architect, brokenhearted, died a couple of
years later.

A stunning series of paintings by the 19th-century symbolist, Puvis de Chavannes, shows scenes from the lives of Ste
Geneviève and St Germain d'Auxerre and there are some
awful frescoes by Cabanel.

A second set of stairs takes you to the gallery; from there
you get a bird's eyeful of the interior and may look down on
the statuary and columns and appreciate the intricacy of the
carving. Up the third flight and you'll find yourself outside,
facing a view of Paris that is almost as impressive as that
from the Eiffel Tower, yet at half the price. Gaze across to
St Étienne du Mont, or see if you can make out Sacré-Coeur
in the bleary distance or, better still, climb one more dizzy
storey to a *terrasse* and a 180-degree view of the skyline;
helpful plaques are inset into the wall to show the locations
of the landmarks ahead.

The Panthéon: rue Clothilde. Tel. 43 54 34 51. M Cardinal-Lemoine Luxembourg. Open April–Sept. 10am–6pm, Mon, Wed, Sun. Oct–March, 10am–4pm, Mon, Wed–Sun. Admission charge for crypt; half-hourly guided tours from 10.30am–5.30pm.

Just behind the Panthéon, to the east, the small place de Ste Geneviève opens out in front of one of the most interesting churches in Paris, the church of **St Étienne du Mont**.

Mainly built in the 16th century, its combination of styles shows the transition from Gothic to Renaissance architecture – look for the hints in the stylistic diversity of the façade in particular. The ground plan is Romanesque, the basic style Gothic, but there are Renaissance influences too, as in the little dome. A more coherent architectural style is found inside the church. The interior is strikingly clean and flooded with light – it's immediately apparent that this is a cherished, well cared for monument. The rood screen (1545) is the only one left in Paris. In the 15th and 16th centuries all major churches had rood screens from which the sermons were delivered and the gospels were read. But because they obscured the congregation's view of the ceremonies performed in the chancel, all the ones in Paris were sooner or later, removed. This one got away since the wide arch still affords the congregation a good view.

On either side of the entrance to the Lady Chapel are commemorative plaques to Pascal and Racine who are both buried in the church. On the right of the choir is the church's most venerated monument – the shrine of Ste Geneviève, patron saint of Paris, whose miracle-working credentials include having saved the city from attack by Attila the Hun. Her remains were destroyed during the violent anti-clericalism of the Revolution and all that's left of her is a bone or two, preserved in a reliquary.

St Étienne du Mont: place St Geneviève. No phone. M Cardinale-Lemoine. Open 7.30–11.45am, 2.15–7.15pm, Mon–Sat. Closed July, Aug. Admission free.

After leaving the church you may fancy a wander in the surrounding villagey streets, or slipping into one of the many cafés in the neighbourhood. Or you could even, if you're feeling homesick, try the English pub down on rue Descartes

– it's called the **Mayflower** and it sells draft beer. Also on rue Descartes is the Lycée Henri IV, a renowned school. It is not open to the public, which unfortunately prevents access to the remains of the ancient Abbey of Ste Geneviève, founded in 510 AD by King Clovis.

RUE MOUFETTARD

Behind the Lycée Henri IV is the tiny **place de la Contrescarpe**, renowned as a hangout for tramps and dossers, but equally littered with students and tourists. Recently renovated, with terraced cafés like **La Chope** and the **Café des Arts** to detain you, the *place* was once a rendezvous for artists and writers like Hemingway. An upward glance at the buildings' top-most storeys, which remain untouched, is all it takes to transport you eerily back a couple of centuries. At number 1 an inscription recalls the cabaret described by Rabelais as Pomme-de-Pin.

From here you could set off down one of the most atmospheric streets on the left bank, the sinuous **rue Mouffetard**. It starts as a pullulating shopping street lined with towering, slimline, ancient houses before sloping down and spreading out at rue de l'Epée de Bois into a raffish, aromatic outdoor food market – one of the oldest, and most famous, in Paris. In "**rue Mouffe**", and its animated even narrower satellites, streetwise French shoppers badger proprietors into giving them the best cuts of meat, the firmest vegetables, the plumpest fruit from their canopied stalls. There's a pretty flower market, purveyors of the most exotic supplies and dozens of mouthwatering restaurants – every other one of which seems to be a taverna. Try **Le Jardin d'Artemis** at number 34 (Tel. 45 35 08 11) which offers "nouvelle cuisine Grecque", with menus for under 80f. There's no shortage of characterful watering holes either – like the **Caves St Thareel**, a lovely pungent wine bar with wooden fascia, yellowed floor and counter. The street is at its most crowded on a Saturday morning or evening when buskers add to the cacophony of bargaining.

Rue Mouffetard ends with a splash at the fountain in the Square St Médard. On the left of the street is the

Église St Médard, a church which was started in the 15th century, completed in 1655, and is a curious combination of styles; flamboyant, Gothic, Renaissance, 17th-century and 18th-century.

In the early 18th century, an intensely devout Jansenist deacon, Abbé Pâris, died at the age of 36, was buried in the churchyard and declared a saint by the Jansenists. The church became the centre of a noisy cult. When sick, followers called *Convulsionnaires* came to pray and writhe by his tomb, eat earth in manic devotion, and then appear miraculously cured. To restore peace to the area, Louis XV had to decree an end to the hysteria so in 1732 he had the following directive nailed to the cemetery wall: "By Order of the King let God no miracle perform in this place!" He also closed the graveyard where the tomb lay. Today the former cemetery is a garden and the only screeches come from the kids as they whizz down the slide outside the church.

VAL DE GRÂCE QUARTIER

At the south-western edge of the 5e, tucked away off the rue Saint Jacques and just south of St Médard, is the church of **Val-de-Grâce**, which, with its adjoining buildings, is the best preserved 17th-century group in Paris. At that time, the Valley of Grace *quartier* was a thriving centre of women's religious orders, many of which were founded by Anne of Austria, wife of Louis XIII. They were disbanded during the Revolution but reminders of their existence cling to street names like rue des Urselines and rue des Feuillantines. The Queen founded a Benedictine convent on this site in 1622 which she used as a retreat.

Remarkably, the Abbey buildings still remain, including a double-arcaded cloister. The **Church of Vâl de Grâce** was added by Anne in thanksgiving for the birth of a son, Louis XIV, after 23 years of childless marriage and it was he who in 1645, aged eight, laid the foundation stone.

Designed by Mansart and continued by Le Mercier, and finally Le Duc and Le Muet, the church strongly resembles those in Rome. The pedimented façade is dominated by a decorative dome, its architects (Le Muet et Le Duc) having been inspired by the dome of St Peter's. The same baroque style runs through the interior. During the Revolution the convent was left intact but unoccupied until 1793 when, at the instigation of Napoleon, it was turned into a military hospital which it remains, incorporating a museum about the history of military medicine (closed at the time of writing, due to alterations) and a medical school conferring degre es on military doctors and pharmacists. In fact, the entire *quartier* is very medical nowadays, with its large hospital and all the various medical institutions thereabouts.

Val de Grâce: 277 rue St Jacques. Tel. 43 29 12 31. M Port Royal. Open 8am–6pm.

Heading a little way north along the rue St Jacques, you come to the **Institut Océanographique** at number 195, and a museum set up by Jacques Cousteau. Denizens of the deep are displayed in a dozen aquariums and other exhibits explain Cousteau's work in helping to develop aqualungs. An accompanying film is shown on Wed, Sat, Sun, at 3pm and 4pm.

Institut Océanographique: 195 rue St Jacques. Tel. 46 33 08 61. M Luxembourg. Open 10am–12.30pm, 1.15pm–5.30pm, Tue–Fri; 10am–5.30pm, Sat, Sun. Closed August. Admission 15f adults; 9f 4–18s, students under 25; free for under 4s. No credit cards.

AROUND THE JARDIN DES PLANTES

To the east of the Latin Quarter on the quieter side of the 5e, by the Seine, is the **Jardin des Plantes,** a formal garden-cum-botanical station of historic trees, parrots and rare blooms. A haven of peace, quiet and natural beauty, the gardens are also the place you'll find the Natural History Museum and the oldest public zoo in the country, which dates back to the 19th century. Some of the wretched animals look almost as old themselves. The botanical garden was originally planted in 1626 by Louis XIII's physician as a medicinal herb garden; it opened to the public 24 four years later. Over the years it has expanded to encompass a wide variety of European and tropical plants as well as an inescapable-from maze added by its greatest curator, the French naturalist Buffon, who ran the gardens from 1739 until he died in 1788. By the exit on rue Cuvier is a famous Cedar of Lebanon planted in 1734 by the botanist Jussieu. Legend has it that he brought it all the way back from Syria under his hat, keeping it moist from his water ration, but the truth is it was raised from a seed sent across the Channel from Kew Gardens.

Along the south-eastern edge of the park is a row of buildings housing a quartet of departments of the **Natural History Museum** – a tribute to the 19th-century's meticulous attention to the natural world. It is ordered into sections as follows:

- Palaeontology: kids love it – dinosaurs (skeletons and casts); pickled organs human and animal); bones galore.

- Palaebotany: exhaustive collections of academic, fossily collection of petrified plants etc.

- Mineralogy: precious stones, crystals, yet more fossils.

- Entomology: Innumerable insects from all corners of the world.

- Frequent temporary exhibitions are also held by the Museum in a nearby annexe.

In the laboratories close by, in 1896, Henri Becquerel discovered radioactivity and a couple of years afterwards the Curies discovered radium.

Jardin des Plantes: 57 rue Cuvier. Tel. 40 79 30 00. M Jussieu Monge Gare d'Orléans-Austerlitz. Open dawn-dusk daily. Includes the following: *The Menagerie* (live animals), open winter 9am–5pm, Mon–Sat; summer, 9am–6pm, Mon–Sat; 9am–6.30pm, Sun. *The Winter Garden*: open 1–5pm Mon, Wed–Sun. *The Botany School*: open 8–11am, Mon–Fri; closed on public holidays. *The Alpine Garden*: open April–Sept. *Minerology Gallery*: open 10am–5pm, Mon, Wed–Fri; closed on public holidays. *Entomology Gallery*: open 2–4.50pm, Mon, Wed–Sun; closed on public holiday. *Anatomy & Palaeontology Gallery*: open 10am – 5pm, Mon, Wed–Fri, Sun; 11am–6pm Sat; closed on public holidays. *Zoological Gallery* (museum of stuffed animals) will be reopening in 1992 after refurbishment.

Behind the Jardin des Plantes, poking itself unexpectedly towards the skyline, is the 100-foot tiled minaret of Paris's only **mosque**. Paris has around a quarter of a million believers in Islam and this mosque was built between 1922 and 1925. Gleaming and white on the outside, plush on the inside, the religious buildings wrap themselves around a patio based on the one at the Alhambra in Granada. You can take a guided tour (in French) or take yourself straight to North Africa by sipping a coffee or mint tea on a divan seat in the traditional Arab café. In fine weather you can enjoy your honeycake, sitting outside by the fig trees and fountain.

The Café de la Mosquée de Paris: open 10am–9.30pm; Closed Fri.

As well as its *salon de thé* and restaurant the mosque also houses a library and the hammam – or Turkish bath, reputed to be the best in Paris and very good value.

The Hammam de la Mosquée: 19–39 rue Geoffroy-St-Hilaire. Tel. 43 31 18 M Jussieu/Censier Dauberton. 14. Open (Women) 11am–7pm, Mon, Wed; 11am–9pm, Thur; 10am–7pm, Sat. (Men) 11am–7pm, Fri, Sun. Closed August. No credit cards.

The Mosque: place du Puits de l'Ermite. Tel. 43 35 97 33. M Monge Censier Daubenton. Open guided tours 9am–noon, 2pm–6pm, Mon–Thur, Sat, Sun. Closed to visitors during Muslim holidays.

The new **Institute of the Arab World** (Institut du Monde Arabe) by the river close by, at 23 quai Saint Bernard, was commissioned by the French government and 20 Arab countries. Architecturally, it's remarkable with its windows made up of giant lenses that open and shut with the sun. Arab culture past and present is the underlying point of the permanent and temporary exhibitions and there's a library, museum, resources centre and a restaurant – serving *French* food!

The Institute of the Arab World; 23 quai Saint Bernard. Tel. 40 51 38 38. M Jussieu Cardinal Lemoine. Open 1–8pm, Tue–Sun. Admission to exhibitions varies. Phone for info.

Nearby, on the quai St Bernard in the riverside park called

Les Bouquinistes

The *bouquinistes*, or secondhand booksellers, whose green-painted stalls line the riverside *quais* at the northern tip of the 5e and 6e, opposite the Ile de la Cité and Ile Saint Louis, are as Parisian as Notre-Dame and the Eiffel Tower. Browsings might begin at quai de la Tournelle for a novel or detective story. Don't expect bargains though — long gone are the days when an antiquarian volume or rare first edition could be carried off for a song. Along a little, on the **quai St Michel**, stalls seem to specialise in old postcards, prints swaddled in cellophane and reproduction posters. Once upon a time the *bouquinistes* (whose embankment book-vending tradition goes back to the 17th century when the old city's river edge was lined with market stalls), could be counted on as a source of erotica and naughty novels. For years they were among the few places where an unexpurgated version of *Lady Chatterley's Lover* could be bought. Works of literary merit aside, ardent rummagers will still be able to find risqué numbers. Most *bouquinistes* open around lunchtime and close at about 6.30pm or 7pm.

Jardin Tino Rossi (in memory of the Corsican singer) is an open air sculpture museum. On a fine day it's a pleasant place to stop for a loll or a picnic, taking in the pieces of modern sculpture, some messy, some minor masterpieces, depending on your point of view. At the western (Pont de Sully) end is *Naissance des Formes* (1958) by Zadkine. More of his work can be seen at his own museum — see the section on the 6e.

THE CHIC 6E

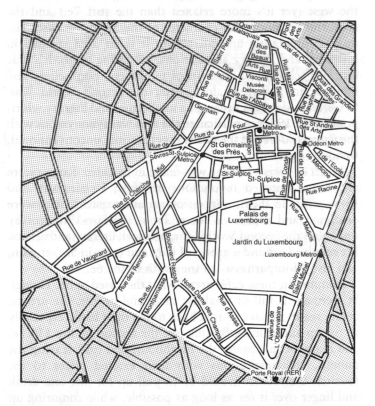

Stretching from the river down to the busy boulevard du Montparnasse, the 6e *arrondissement* is the heart of the fashionable left bank. The northern half is one of the most fascinating areas of Paris to explore, the St-Germain-des-Prés *quartier*. St Germain was somewhat separate from the rest of Paris until the 17th century. But when Louis XIV began work on the Louvre, stones had to be brought from a quarry to the south. The ferry was too slow a means of transportation, so the **Pont Royal** was built, bringing an end to St Germain's isolation. Today, with its even more exclusive neighbour the Faubourg (suburb) St Germain, in the 7e, St-Germain-des-Prés is reckoned to be one of the most desirable (and most expensive) parts of Paris to live in.

In many respects the 6e combines the best of the two adjacent *arrondissements*: the sedate elegance of the 7e to the west (yet it's more relaxed than the stiff 7e,) and the colourful cosmopolitan character of the 5e to the east. The mix is stimulating and attractive. It is an area steeped in historical and literary associations, yet raring to go. It's chic but also scholarly, a domain of publishers, booksellers and binders, art galleries galore. After the Second World War, St Germain-des-Prés became an intellectual and literary whirl-pool. In the 1950s in particular, the area was synonymous with the *jeunesse dorée* of the postwar generation: unconventional, trendsetting, radical chic.

Much of Paris's history was made in its cafés: Robespierre and Lenin hatched revolutions in them; Hemingway and Joyce wrote in them; impressionism and existentialism were discussed and organised there. From the late-19th-century until after the Second World War, political, literary and artistic life revolved around a group of bars and cafés in St Germain, and also Montparnasse, to the south of the 6e.

Admittedly, these cafés aren't what they used to be. Though St Germain is full of wealthy, successful people, the artistic centre seems to have shifted back to the right bank, especially to the up-and-coming Bastille (see the section on the 11/12e) and many people prefer the neighbourhood café, leaving the famous, chic institutions with their exalted prices to the tourists. Our advice would be to pull up for just one drink and linger over it for as long as possible, while conjuring up the legendary ghosts.

Not surprisingly, this is a very popular area with tourists, so the usual caution is required when picking hotels and restaurants – avoid the over-priced, overcrowded variety. But there are also many small, family hotels offering the charm of the left bank atmosphere, combined with proximity to the major sights on the other side of the Seine – the Louvre, the Champs-Élysées, and the Tuileries.

ST-GERMAIN-DES-PRÉS

The most interesting segment of the 6e is roughly bounded by the boulevard St Germain and the river, by rue des Saints-Pères to the west, rue Mazarine to the east. Allowing for coffee and museum stops, it would comfortably fill a morning or afternoon to stroll around this compact but fascinating area, taking in some of its sights and streets.

A good place to start is the St-Germain-des-Prés Métro by the cobbled place St Germain, the hub of the *quartier*. The square at St Germain is shadowed by the historic church of the same name. The **Church of St-Germain-des-Prés** is the oldest in Paris, founded in 542 when King Childebert returned from Spain with what he claimed were the tunic of St Vincent and a piece of the True Cross. He built a church on the site to house the relics, and it was later named after St Germanus, the Bishop of Paris, who consecrated it in 558 and is buried there.

For hundreds of years the church stood in open meadowland (*prés*). It weathered many storms, including Norman attack. Except for a few capitals and columns, nothing that can be seen in the church is any earlier than 11th-century – it's a real mixture of different periods. In a side chapel is the tombstone of Descartes, the "I think, therefore I am" philosopher.

The small, south-facing square – a refuge from the busy boulevard – is the site of a monks' cemetery. While relaxing in this little oasis of calm, shaded by chestnut trees, you might remember that it was also the site of a massacre in 1792 when 318 priests and monks were killed here. The great tower is all that remains of the Benedictine monastery which also occupied the site. You can study it from a pavement seat in the *niveau* of the area, **Les Deux Magots**, for generations a centre for intellectual debate and gossip.

You can enjoy a similar buzz from the **Café Flore** next door on the boulevard St Germain. It's very expensive. If you're rash enough to order a couple of gin and tonics, you'll receive four glasses (two with plain water), nuts, an ice-bucket, mats, swizzle sticks. It'll cost about £10.

Across the road is the snooty **Brasserie Lipp**, which, like its neighbours, is open until the early hours of the morning. Dinner at the Lipp – Art Nouveau tiles, plain wooden tables, and waiters swathed in stiff white linen – is a crowded and serious business. The Lipp waiters regularly perform that very Parisian trick – just when you think they really hate you, they smile. Two courses and some brilliant wine will cost about £30 for two (see box).

Outside, in the evening, fire eaters and sword-swallowers enjoy their own consuming passion. Those in search of further excitement should head for **Le Mazet** at 61 rue St-André-des-Arts, a bouncy bar which is always crowded with buskers and students, in spite of the exorbitant prices.

The **place St-Germain-des-Prés** is like a magnet – all roads seem to lead to it. There are some tempting shops along this stretch of the boulevard, but you can remove yourself from them by making a detour at the gardens of the Ukranian Church, turning right into the rue des Saints-Pères, marked by the eyesore of the façade of the faculty of medicine. Watch out for cheap eateries catering for the university medical school at this end of the **rue Jacob,** a smart little street of bars, decorations, good bric-à-brac shops and galleries, where Wagner and Stendhal once lodged.

The first left goes into tiny rue de Nesle and then first right leads into gaunt rue de Nevers, where the south end of the street is crossed by the wall of a house – it stands on the line of the medieval city wall built by Philippe Auguste. You emerge from the ancient scenario to face the Seine on quai de Conti, by the **Pont Neuf.** This is the bridge that, despite its name, is the oldest of the bridges spanning the Seine, completed in 1607 under Henry IV. It glides effortlessly over the river at its widest point in the city, to land on the quayside.

Mint Condition

On quai de Conti is the magnificent **Hôtel des Monnaies** which has been the Mint since the end of the 18th century. The actual business of coin production is now handled at a new mint, set up in 1973 near Bordeaux, but security at the old building remains tight as weights and measures, medals and limited edition coins, are still produced here – but you can visit the workshops on Tuesdays and Fridays. There is also a museum showing coins and medals from the Renaissance to the present. Round the corner, the Mint has its own shop, at 2 rue Guénégaud.

La Monnaie de Paris: 11 quai de Conti. Tel. 40 46 56 66. M Pont Neuf. Open: Museum 1am–5pm, Tue, Thur–Sat; 1–9pm, Wed. Workshop: 2.15–3pm, Tue and Fri. Admission 10f. No credit cards. Shop open 9am–5.30pm, Mon–Fri; 10am–1pm, 2–5.30pm, Sat.

If you do like to make the most of being by the quayside, there are all the pleasures of browsing amongst the stalls of the *bouquinistes* for old books, cartoon porn, postcards, posters, guides – but do negotiate the price first. Next along the quai is the impressive semi-circular façade of the domed **Institut de France**. This is where the great minds of France think. Of the five scholarly academies which comprise the Institute, the best known is the **Académie Française** where 40 members meet to ensure that the French language remains undefiled by modernisms, anglicisms and sloppy thought.

Institut de France: 21–5 quai de Conti. Not open to the public except cultural groups by arrangement. M Pont Neuf.

Facing the Institut is the **Pont des Arts**. This lovely wooden footbridge was built so that students at the École des Beaux Arts to the right could cross to look at artworks in the Louvre. Students from the School of Fine Arts still drift along nearby bridges and *quais*, sketchpads and pencils poised for action. Since the early 19th-century it has been a hothouse for some of the best French painters. You could drift into the school courtyard to see casts and copies of statues from the old Museum of French Monuments which were once stored here, or catch one of the temporary exhibitions of professors' and students' work: entrance through the gate at 14 rue Bonaparte.

This is the north-western tip of the 6e. If you slip south down the rue Bonaparte you'll end up back to the starting point, the St-Germain-des-Prés Métro. If you're still in a meandering mode, you could wander a little further along the waterfront to **quai Voltaire**–where the *maître* died at number 27 on 30th May, 1778. Nearer Pont des Arts, at number 19, is the **Hôtel du quai Voltaire**. Here Wagner, Baudelaire, Sibelius and Oscar Wilde all at some time or other lived and worked. Corot and Delacroix had a studio at number 13 and, while he was a professor at the École des Beaux Arts, Ingres lived at number 11. At number 9 the novelist Anatole France spent his boyhood, as his father kept a bookshop there.

There's more history if you go down rue Bonaparte and take the first left. You'll be in **rue des Beaux Arts** – Oscar Wilde died at number 13, now a very chic hotel. On rue Bonaparte again, take a left into **rue Visconti**, known in the 16th century as "little Geneva" because of the Prot-estant ghetto that it became. The tragedian Racine lived at, number 24 until his death in 1699; Balzac set up a

Cafés of St Germain

Haussmann slashed a boulevard through St Germain during the Second Empire and at the crossroads, outside the Church of St-Germain-des-Prés, three of the best cafés in Paris came to be established ...

Café Flore was the first, opened in 1865. Jean-Paul Sartre once said, "it was like home to us", and it's often credited with being the womb of existentialism. Like its rival across the road, Les Deux Magots, it has a long roll call of deceased famous clients. Simone de Beavoir wrote part of *The Second Sex* here. The second floor was comparatively secluded and, most important, the Flore was always *warm*.

Les Deux Magots. Only in France would a café offer an annual literary award. Le Prix des Deux Magots was created in 1933. The café is newer than its neighbours, the Flore and Lipp, having been here since 1875, but seems the most welcoming and yet the most venerable. It has played (to quote the menu) *"un rôle important dans la vie culturelle de Paris"*. Picasso came here, along with Rimbaud, Verlaine, Mallarmé, Gide, Léger, Hemingway, Saint-Éxupery, Sartre. They didn't have to shell out 30f for a coffee! It's not cheap, though the sandwiches and patisseries are admittedly delicious and beautifully served. You can linger here for a couple of hours with a book and a coffee and feel that this, at last, is really Paris. The hot chocolate, served foaming in little jugs, is wonderful, best enjoyed very late at night, not on the goldfish bowl terrace but in a cosy mahogany booth inside.

Lipp is a celebrated plotting den of left bank publishers and left-wing politicos. François Mitterand often used to end up here after late sittings, the National Assembly being just a few blocks down the boulevard. After the Germans crushed the Second Empire in 1870, a number of refugees from occupied Alsace came to Paris, among them Leonard Lipp, who opened, across the boulevard from the Flore, a little brasserie. Its Alsatian plum tart is famed. So too are the clientèle — it has always been popular with celebs and politicians and its walls are decorated with giant mirrors which conveniently assist the people-watching.

Even back in the '40s, a visit to Lipp or Flore was special. For hanging around, there were always cheaper places — the Royal, the Café Bonaparte (Sartre lived for a time above this one) or Mabillon. Today's would-be intellos like the café in rue Bonaparte, immodestly called **Le Prés aux Clercs** (the meadow of intellectuals, being a rough translation) where *the* style accessory is a 6-inch thick book with no pictures in it. Some leading heavyweights of modern French intellectual life prefer the **Twickenham**, an "English pub" round the corner from Lipp at 70 rue des Saints Pères.

A neighbourhood café that wears its literary links lightly is the pre-war Café de la Mairie in place St Sulpice, just a few minutes north of the Luxembourg Gardens. William Faulkner was a regular and Saul Bellow used to enjoy a tipple here, though these days it has become a bit fancier.

Café Flore: 172 boulevard St Germain. Tel. 45 58 55 26. Open 7am–1.30am daily. M St-Germain-des-Prés.

Les Deux Magots: 6 place St-Germain-des-Prés. Tel. 45 48 55 25. M St-Germain-des-Prés. Open 7.30am–1.30am daily. Closed 2nd week of January.

Lipp: 151 boulevard St Germain. Tel. 45 48 53 91. M St-Germain-des-Prés. Open from 9am–1am. Main meals from noon. Closed first 2 weeks over Christmas and New Year.

printing shop at number 17, and Delacroix worked here from 1836–44.

At the end of rue Visconti is **La Pallette** (actually at 43 rue de Seine), a popular hangout for "Beaux Art" types, while all around the café, above the tiles and mirrors, large paintings do their own hanging out from the walls. It's open daily until 2am. The nearest Métros from here are either Mabillon (due south) or back again to St-Germain-des-Prés.

It's fun to potter about the streets criss-crossing this patch, full of antique, book and art shops. Pick up a hot dog with melted cheese (a French refinement) or a *croissant aux abricots* as you wander.

From rue Jacob, turn south towards the Church of St Germain again, into the quiet and pretty **rue de Furstemberg** – a charming old street with globe lamp-posts which was first built in 1699, based around a monastery stableyard. At the corner of place de Furstemberg, at number 6, you'll find, if you look carefully, the **Eugène Delacroix Museum** in a tiny backwater.

It's not a brilliant museum by the usual standards, containing a thin collection of sketches and other work by the artist, but it's steeped in atmosphere and Delacroix's vast studio is a very fit setting for those rippling, heroic canvasses. Most of his paintings though are in the nearby Musée d'Orsay. The garden at the rear of the studio, while no Giverny, is a pleasant and peaceful spot. One of the great Romantic painters of the 19th century, Delacroix spent the last 5 years of his life at this apartment-cum-studio, living in hermit-like seclusion. He died in the bedroom here in 1863, at the age of 65.

Delacroix Museum: 6 rue Furstemberg. Tel. 43 54 04 87. M St-Germain-des-Prés. Open 9.45am–12.30pm, 2–5.15pm, Mon, Wed–Sun. Closed Tue and some holidays. Admission 10f adults; 6f 18–25s, OAPs; free under 18s. No credit cards

Delacroix was a passionate painter of religious themes – one reason he moved to place de Furstemberg was so that he could be nearer to the **Church of St Sulpice** on the other side of the boulevard St Germain, where he was painting the ceiling and frescoes in a side chapel. You catch a glimpse of the towers of St Sulpice on the right as you squeeze through the ancient streets of rues de l'Abbaye and de Bourbon le Château (left off Furstemberg), taking you to the gastronomic **rue de Buci**, a wonderful, aromatic street market (though *not* the cheapest in Paris) which continues into rue de Seine. **Boulangerie Boudin**, at number 6 (after 10.30am, not Mondays), have moreish *fougousse* (rich flaky pastries); at number 26 there's a *salon de thé* owned by Christian Constant, whom many say is the best *pâtissier* in town.

At 27 is **Le Muniche**, one of the most popular St Germain brasseries – there's nothing Bavarian about the cuisine; the best value is the *prix fixe* menu. Last orders are not until well after midnight and there's a downstairs jazz club, **Le Furstemberg**. You're advised to book (Tel. 46 33 62 09). Under the same management, at 25, **Le Petit Zinc** is smaller, nicely old-fashioned, and also stays awake until the early hours serving hearty regional dishes. **Layrac** at number 29, have great terrines, quiches, salads, wine and other goodies to take away at all hours, i.e. 9am–3am every day of the week.

The main market comes to an end in carrefour de Buci. Running south from here is **rue Grégoire du Tours**. Style vultures swoop on **Le Mouton à Cinq Pattes** where designer clothes can be purchased *degriffé* (with the label ripped out). Here a £300 Giorgio Armani jacket can be picked up for £30. In theory these are reject garments, but at those prices most people can put up with a loose thread or two. (More of this in the shopping section.)

This same street is full of Greek restaurants. At number 4, the wonderful **Orestia** is a fast and fashionable little dive where you won't pay more than £20 for two for a great deal of food and wine.

One of the waiters who has been pouring retsina there for close on 40 years tells a story about Picasso (who lived in the rue des Grands Augustins where he painted "Guernica"). Apparently the great man was found scribbling on a tablecloth. Would he mind signing his doodles? "*Mais non*," snapped Picasso (or words to that effect). He was paying for his meal, he grumbled, not the entire restaurant.

The street running parallel on the right is **rue de l'Ancienne Comédie**: the Comédie Française played here in the 17th century, which is when the district began to be known as a cultural and literary hotbed. **Le Procope** at number 13 is where Molière, Corneille and Racine drank their coffee (see box below).

At number 10 rue de l'Ancienne Comédie there's a 24-hour boulangerie. The St Germain pub on the same street is unaccountably popular with young Parisiens. It claims to sell over 100 beers, but they seldom have the one you want, and most English people go there only once.

This is an animated quarter, day or night. Rue de l'Ancienne Comédie leads into **rue St-André-des-Arts**, which, like its neighbouring streets, holds loads of antiquated charm. Off the rue St-André-des-Arts, the **cour de commerce St André** with its ancient houses, is also worth a look. It was outside number 9 that the first guillotine was constructed. There are many bars and restaurants in this web of streets. The **Bistro Rive Gauche** in the cour de Commerce St André, with its Art Deco interior, does a good English breakfast for 42f and serves light meals all day. **À la Cour de Rohan** at 59—61 rue St-André-des-Arts is a pretty tearoom – the chintzy variety with flounced tablecloths, perfectly at home

---

Le Procope

The oldest café in Paris, possibly the world, **Le Procope** has been operating on the Rue de l'Ancienne Comédie since 1686. Chaps like Voltaire, Rousseau, Balzac and Benjamin Franklin had their elevenses here. Later came the Revolutionaries: Robespierre, Danton, Marat, Napoleon. Violently refurbished in 1988, with the addition of a tinkly piano, it's now a Michelin-rated restaurant, and no bargain.

Le Procope: 13 rue de l'Ancienne Comédie. Tel. 43 26 99 20. M Odéon. Last orders 1am. Closed July.

---

in an 18th-century alley. (A special tea menu is 24f; set lunch 85f.)

Towards the river you'll find **rue Dauphine** where **Le Tabou** used to be a jazz cellar frequented in the post-war years by Juliette Greco, but has now been turned into a popular, mostly reggae, disco, though the look of an old Paris cellar has been retained.

St Germain is still a good area for jazz, though – there are three clubs on **rue Saint Benoît**, west of rue Bonaparte. Off to the right is a street called **rue Christine**: Gertrude Stein lived with her paintings at number 5, looked after by Alice B. Toklas. Film-buffs should note that the Nouvelle Vague flourishes at the **Action Christine** cinema in the rue Christine (it runs down to the rue des Grands Augustins). There are several "Action" cinemas in Paris, good repertory houses with a particular fondness for French films of the '50s and '60s.

SOUTH OF BOULEVARD ST GERMAIN

South from the boulevard St Germain the streets tend to be calmer, more upmarket. An exploratory amble could start from Mabillon Métro, taking in the attractive **rue Mabillon** which runs off rue du Four, passing **Carpentiers** at number 10. The name of this popular restaurant comes from the fact that the Guild of Master Carpenters and Cabinet Makers had its HQ next door – and what did embryonic carpenters eat to keep their strength up? Given that the menu hasn't

altered much in years, you can see the answer: slap-up
meals involving pigs' trotters, roast duck, stuffed cabbage
and melting *clafoutis*, sadly at less than artisan's prices
these days. Drinks are served from a long, old-fashioned
bar with a traditional zinc counter. (Tel. 43 36 30 05.
Closed Sun).

At the end of the street is the **Church of St Sulpice**, built in
and around 1700. It's no great shakes architecturally, but it
does have two Delacroix frescos and one of the largest organs
in the world, with 6588 pipes, on which recitals are often
given. In the crypt you can see the foundations of an earlier
church.

St Sulpice: place St Sulpice. Tel. 46 33 21 78. M St Sulpice. Open
7.30am–7.30pm, Mon–Sat.

The **St Sulpice place**, with its fountains and trees, is a
pleasant place to pause for a restorative cup of coffee at
the popular **Café de la Mairie**. The **Yves Saint Laurent Rive
Gauche** fashion boutique is also in the *place*.

All around St Sulpice is a maze of narrow streets: opposite
the church is the aged **rue des Canettes** (Duckling Street)
– there are ducklings over the door of number 18, which
sneaks into the tiny Italian-flavoured **rue des Ciseaux** with
its pizzerias. In **rue Princesse**, parallel to rue des Canettes,
is a pally American bookshop, **The Village Voice**, where you
browse sustained by coffee and snacks. **Castel's**, at number
15, is the most exclusive nightclub in Paris, overseen by Jean
"Sun King of the Paris Nightlife" Castel. He has now opened
Puzzle next-door (number 13), a late night grocery/bistro/jazz
club (Tel. 46 34 55 80).

East from the square is **rue de Vieux Colombier**, lined
with liturgical bookshops. You join the **rue du Cherche
Midi**, a classy and affluent part of the 6e, selling classy
and pricey clothes, antiques and other consumer desirables.
Affordable by all though is bread from **Poilâne** at number
8 – arguably the best in Paris – and that's really saying
something. Heading south, the street has a marvellous variety
of typically left bank cafés, restaurants and shops. It is crossed
by the **rue Saint Placide** – on the left it leads to **Au Bon
Marché**, the department store on the border of the 7e. The

rue St Placide is worth exploring for cheap – that is, last season's – fashion.

In fact, it's a shopper's heaven just south of St-Germain-des-Prés, bordered by the Métro stops of Sèvres-Babylone, St Sulpice, Mabillon and Odéon. This is where young Paris shops for clothes and the range is very wide, depending on your taste and finances.

Further along the rue du Cherche Midi at the corner of rue Jean Ferrandi, on the left, is a restored 18th-century mansion, the **Hôtel Montmorency**. This is a one-man museum, devoted to paintings and drawings of Ernest Hébert (1817–1908). While the artist never lived in this house it's a perfect setting for the work of the very orthodox Hébert, a member of the Institut and professor of the École des Beaux Arts, who flirted with the symbolist movement.

Hébert Museum: 85 rue du Cherche Midi. Tel. 42 22 23 82. M Vaneau. Open 2–6pm, Mon, Wed–Sun. Admission 10f adults; 5f students, OAPs; free under-18s. No credit cards.

Leaving the Hébert museum, you are now in the south-west corner of the 6e. Walk along rue J. Ferrandi, cross the longest street in Paris, rue de Vaugirard, entering **rue Blaise Desgoffe**. You leave the calm of these residential retreats when you join **rue de Rennes**. On either side of rue Blaise Desgoffe shoppers head for **Tati**, an emporium packed with bargain wearables, or **FNAC** at number 136 for best price cameras, stereos, cassettes, etc. Walk along up this busy street to get to place St-Germain-des-Prés, or take a right back on the Vaugirard to come to the **Jardin du Luxembourg**.

In the 13th century you wouldn't have gone footloose in the **Luxembourg quartier**. The area was terrorised by a notorious highwayman known as Vauvert who lived like a hunted animal. His violent reign ended in 1257 when the Carthusian Order built a huge monastery, effectively policing this dreadful wilderness.

As far as Henri IV (1553–1610) was concerned, levels of violence hadn't improved much by the 17th century. On May 14th, 1610, while riding in his carriage along the rue de la Feronnnerie (not far from the Pompidou Centre), he was killed by the assassin Ravaillac. A pity, because as kings go he wasn't a bad one.

After his death, his grieving widow Marie de Medici decided to build herself a palace which would remind her of the happier days of her youth in Tuscany. In 1612 she bought a mansion belonging to Duke François of Luxembourg and a plot of adjoining land. By 1615, the architect Salomon de Brosse began work on what was to become known as the **Palais de Luxembourg**, stylistically not unlike the Pitti Palace of Florence. By 1625 the dowager queen had moved in, but Cardinal Richelieu – a man who lived to plot – was keen to see her moved out of Paris altogether. He had influence with her son, King Louis XIII, and in 1630 poor Marie was banished to Cologne where she died in 1642. During the Terror (1793–94) this "des. res." on the left bank became a prison, then a parliamentary building. In the first half of the 19th century, Chalgrin (architect of the Arc de Triomphe) revamped the interior and Alphonse de Gisors enlarged the

Cafés of the boulevard du Montparnasse

At the southernmost edge of the *arrondissement*, on the main boulevard du Montparnasse, which divides the 6e and 14e, there is a cluster of more illustrious cafés. As a broad generalisation while the literati tended to favour St Germain, the arty preferred Montparnasse.

Le Select, at 99 boulevard du Montparnasse, of all the Montparnasse cafés, has changed least since the days when it was used by Erik Satie, and it's refreshingly untrendy, a true café with not an oyster in sight. Across the road, and thriving on its past association as a favourite loitering-hole of Modigliani, Stravinsky, Hemingway and Picasso, is **Le Dôme**, at 108 boulevard du Montparnasse. Tarted-up in 1986, the days when it offered cheap eats must be confined to memory.

Facing it, and much changed from when Lenin and Trotsy were there, **Le Rotunde**, at number 105, is now more of a bourgeois restaurant than a café. Five minutes further along the boulevard is a famous bastion of left bank café-culture, **La Closerie des Lilas**, standing on the corner of boulevard St Michel at 171 boulevard du Montparnasse. It opened in 1907 and was another of the very thirsty Hemingway's watering holes — he was here so regularly that a brass plate commemorates his preferred place at the bar and his face ornaments the menu. Not surprisingly, you can order a *steak au poivre Hemingway*. (Baudelaire, Verlaine and Appolinaire are also remembered, but not on the menu.) While the arty set still like the bar and brasserie, the main restaurant, which is horribly expensive, attracts a very much more bourgeois lot.

palace considerably with the addition of some wings and pavilions.

The Palace is now the seat of the French Upper House – the Senate – and is open to visitors between 1 January–31 March and 1 July–30 September, when the Senators are elsewhere. During the sessions, guided tours are available on Sundays. Much of the later work is grand, but not particularly distinguished. Make a bee-line for the Golden Book Room where the panellings and paintings date back to Marie de Medici's day. The series of 24 paintings she commissioned from Rubens commemorating her life now hang in the Louvre.

The Luxembourg Gardens

Open from dawn to dusk daily, the Luxembourg Gardens are, like the Luxembourg Palace, in the Italian style which fell out of favour in the 18th century when the English look caught on. They are formal, and give the illusion of great space, and airiness.

In a more leisurely age, you might have met Watteau, Baudelaire or Verlaine among the statuary. These days, you meet mostly the French equivalent of 30-something yuppies – trying to look relaxed as they set out on a Sunday constitutional. There are places to sit and stare and places to play in this un-touristy park. One lawn is set aside for children under 6 years, who make a charming picture, romping like puppies in their smart little outfits. Older children can go-kart, roller-skate, and ride donkeys. Sailing boats can be hired on the large pool in the centre of the gardens. There are the traditional municipal attractions of slides, sandpits, tennis courts and roundabouts, and the performances of the Théâtre du Luxembourg – a marionette theatre – on Wednesday, Saturday and Sunday afternoons at 2.30pm. There's boules too. Are these players for real, or do they come from Central Casting? They look too French to be true.

Contrasting with all this bustle is the Medici Fountain, a slightly sombre Italianate construction, dominating a shady pool with dark niches full of classical figures in the grip of ignoble passions.

The Luxembourg Gardens: entrances on boulevard St Michel/rue de Vaugirard. M Odéon. RER Luxembourg. Open dawn–dusk daily.

Luxembourg Palace: rue de Vaugirard. Tel. 42 34 20 00 for information, details of tours, etc. M Odéon.

Stretching out in front of the palace are the Luxembourg gardens where, in another era, artists, poets and writers would go on walkabouts (see box).

Look up, look west, and you're back in the tail end of the 20th century with a full view of one of Paris's controversial architectural follies, the **Tour Montparnasse** – a composition in concrete, glass and aluminium. The entrance nearest the Luxembourg Palace is on rue de Vaugirard, but the main entrance to the gardens is on the famous **boulevard St Michel**

which marks the eastern edge of the 6e. People of a certain
age who can't get that Peter Sarsted song out of their heads
— "Where do you go to my lovely?" — will remember that
the girl in question had an apartment on the **Boul' Mich**
where she kept her Rolling Stones records and her friends
of Sasha Distel.

The **rue Michelet**, which runs west off the southern part of
the boulevard St Michel, leads to another one-man museum,
in this case devoted to the works of the cubist sculptor, Ossip
Zadkine. It is in the house-studio-garden where he lived and
worked until his death in 1967 and there are drawings,
gouaches, prints and, naturally, sculptures.

Musée Zadkine: 100 bis rue d'Assas. Tel. 43 26 91 90. M Port-
Royal/Navin. Open 10am – 5.40pm, Tue–Sun. Admission 10f adults;
7f students; free on Sundays. No credit cards.

Skirting the northern edge of the Jardin du Luxembourg,
rue de Vaugirard spills into the **place de l'Odéon** where the
17th- and 18th-century houses have all been listed as historic
monuments. At number 1 lived the Revolutionary, Camille
Desmoulins; at number 2 was the literary Café Voltaire
where Hemingway and Scott Fitzgerald supped and sipped.
The Théâtre de l'Odéon was opened in 1908.

Théâtre National de l'Odéon: place de l'Odéon. Tel. 43 25 70 32. RER
Luxembourg. Open 11am–6.30pm daily. No show Mon.

Directly north, off place de l'Odéon, is the sloping, somno-
lent **rue de l'Odéon**, full of publishers and booksellers. If you
happen to be ready for lunch, there's a favourite restaurant
street east, in the parallel rue Monsieur-le-Prince. **Polidor** (at
number 41) has an excellent value set lunch (Mon–Fri only)
but it pays to go early as it's everyone else's favourite too —
Verlaine, Valéry and Joyce used to eat here (Tel. 43 26 95 34)
and the chances are that Pascal would have done too if it had
been around when he lived at number 54.

The Odéon Métro is back on the boulevard St Germain, at
the top of the rue de l'Odéon.

7E:
Affluence and Aristocrats
behind closed doors

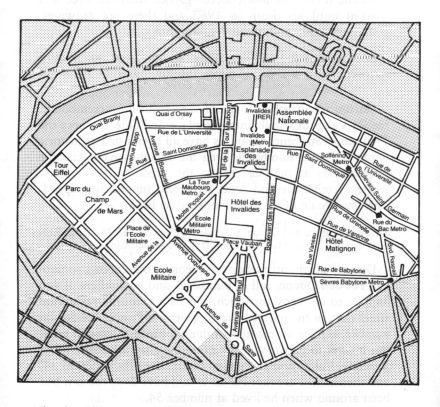

The dignified 7e *arrondissement* makes an inverted fat triangle, its northern edge traced by the Seine, with the Esplanade des Invalides driven through its heart.

Compared to its eastern neighbour, the more extrovert 6e, it's an inhibited, rather haughty district, bound by the kind of diplomatic reticence appropriate to an area full of grandiose mansions sheltering ministries and embassies.

While much of the *arrondissement* is very private, with all the pretty places secreted behind high walls or in clandestine courtyards, the 7e does have three of the city's most magnetic tourist attractions: the massive **Eiffel Tower**, the imposing **Invalides** where Napoleon is buried, and the impressive **d'Orsay Museum**.

MUSÉE D'ORSAY

The **Musée d'Orsay** on the Seine, just east of the Pont Solférino, now houses the Jeu de Paume's impressionist and the Palais de Tokyo's post-impressionist collections, and the work of artists born at the end of the 18th century, like Delacroix, Ingres and Corot, thus bridging the gap between the Louvre and the Beaubourg, both artistically and chronologically. Fine arts, sculpture, decorative arts, architecture and photography are also covered.

Formerly the Orsay railway terminus, built in the late 19th century by station architect Victor Laloux, this remarkable building was saved from demolition in 1973. The façade has been conserved, while the innards have been removed and replaced by artworks. Milan-based Italian architect, Gae Aulenti, was responsible for the design of the several thousand square metre exhibition space.

You enter the museum from a wide esplanade – plenty of time while you queue to look at the monumental statues rescued from museum cellars and demolition sites. Inside, there's a stridently modern, still station-like, main hall where instead of an Awayday to Versailles you can get your admission ticket.

The exhibition itself is staggering. Wandering through the galleries you seem to encounter every single one of those impressionist masterpieces which are so much a part of the modern consciousness.

Works are arranged in a chronological order over three levels (although some collections are exhibited together) and are generally separated according to the techniques used. If it's the impressionists you're after, you'll make a beeline via the back escalators for the top floor. Post-impressionists (Cézanne, Seurat, Gauguin, Toulouse-Lautrec, Van Gogh) are here too.

Early work by Manet, including *Le Déjeuner sur l'Herbe*, and works by Monet and Renoir are on the ground floor along with early 19th century sculpture. On the middle level there's late 19th century sculpture, including Rodin (a lot more of his work to see at the **Musée Rodin**, see p 409), decorative arts and interiors, including three rooms of Art Nouveau *objets* furniture and paintings, which demonstrate the transition to the moderns to be seen at the Beaubourg.

Nudging these works, on the top floor, is the handy Musee d'Orsay Café, behind the face of the massive station clock. Its views over the Seine towards Montmartre and the Sacré Coeur make it worth fighting the crowds for a *café crème* by a window. There's a Belle Époque restaurant at the museum too, gleaming with gilt and chandeliers, where it's essential to book. (It's so popular it even opens when the museum is closed; you can make a reservation for the **Restaurant du Palais d'Orsay** by telephoning 45 49 42 33.)

Musée d'Orsay: 1 rue de Bellechasse. Tel. 40 49 48 14. Recorded information 45 49 11 11. M Solférino/RER Musée d'Orsay. Open 10am–6pm, Tue, Wed, Fri, Sat; 10am–9.45pm, Thur; 9am–6pm Sun. Between June 20–Sept. 20, the museum opens at 9am. Admission 23f adults; 12f 18–25s, OAPs; free under-18s. Credit (bookshop only): AE, MC, V. Free guided tours in English daily except Sun at 11am, 2pm; presented at 12.30 is "A Work to See". NB: tickets are sold until 5.15pm; 9pm Thur.

NEAR THE MUSEUM

You may well feel a little punch-drunk after a long, preliminary visit to the d'Orsay. The little bars and cafés behind the museum are full of dazed tourists examining their postcards. One of the best (if museums make you hungry) is **La Solange Crêpèrie**, 8 rue de Bellechasse. French crêpes make English equivalents seem like wet flannels.

Previous occupants of the fine Palladian-style **Hôtel de Salm**, next to the d'Orsay, include the writer Madame de

Staël and Napoleon, who created the Order of the Legion of Honour in 1802. The mansion now houses the **Musée de Légion d'Honneur**: French and foreign decorations, insignia, regalia and documents on display, with a special section devoted to the Légion d'Honneur itself. Rodin, Utrillo and Colette were amongst those who received it.

Légion d'Honneur Museum: 2 rue de Bellechasse. Tel. 45 55 95 16. M Solférino. Open 2–5pm, Tue–Sun. Closed Mon. Admission 10f. No credit cards.

If you were to follow the embankment further west (with the river on your right) you'd come to a fine, pillared mansion facing the Pont de la Concorde – the **Palais Bourbon**. Originally built by the Duchess of Bourbon, a daughter of Louis XIV, no sooner had it been completed than the French Revolution erupted and the building was taken over and altered by the State. This is where the lower house of the French Parliament meets (called the National Assembly or Chamber of Deputies) in an ornate red, gold and white room. Visitors are allowed to see the library, decorated with frescoes by Delacroix, charting the history of civilisation. You must apply in writing if you'd like to attend an Assembly debate, but seats are very limited.

Palais Bourbon: 126 rue de l'Université. Tel. 42 97 64 08. M Assemblée Nationale. Entry at 33 quai d'Orsay. Visit on application to the Office of Administrative Affairs, 33 quai d'Orsay, in person.

FAUBOURG ST GERMAIN

The north-eastern corner of the 7e contains the noble and rather intimidating **Faubourg St Germain**. It's a world away from the hubbub and shopping opportunities of the adjacent *quartier* St Germain-des-Prés, even though it's only just across the rue des Saints Pères. There's less of a true left bank atmosphere in the Faubourg than in the 6e. Even the link between the two areas, the boulevard St Germain, which further along becomes cosmopolitan and bustling, is, while it lingers in the 7e, more sedate.

In the 18th century the Faubourg (suburb) St Germain developed into a rival of the Marais as a fashionable and desirable residential area. While Louis XIV ruled, aristocrats tended to cluster round the court at Versailles, but with Louis XV on the throne they felt free to live in Paris again. The land to the east of Les Invalides then became their building site.

Today, dozens of dignified mansions line streets like rue de l'Université, rue St Dominique, rue de Lille, rue de Grenelle and rue de Varenne. The **Hôtel Matignon** at 57 rue de Varenne is the office and home of the Prime Minister. In the rue de Grenelle is the attractive 18th-century **Quatre Saisons** fountain, and along the street, at 110, is the fine **Hôtel de Courteilles**, now the Ministry of Education.

One of the few mansions of the Faubourg that may be visited is the beautiful Hôtel Biron, on the corner of the boulevard des Invalides and now the **Rodin Museum**. The rococo Hôtel was built by Gabriel the Elder in 1728–31 for a prosperous wig-maker. It was owned towards the end of the century by Marshal Biron, who was beheaded in 1793. Much of its exquisite painted and gilded panelling was removed by the nuns when it later became a convent, but has now been partially restored.

There is a good view from the garden of the Rodin Museum of the graceful, gilded dome of Les Invalides, gleaming above the tree tops.

LES INVALIDES

Just a stone's throw to the west of the Rodin Museum, **Les Invalides** shows Paris at its most imperial. It was dreamed up in a very grandiose manner in the 1670s by Louis XIV and his architects as a home for up to 4000 destitute, invalided soldiers. The idea was to save them from a life of beggary – an embarassing reminder of the price of war. Libéral Bruand was the architect responsible for most of the building, which was topped with the dramatic cupolas of the Dôme chapel by Jules Hardouin-Mansart.

Everything about Les Invalides is on a grand scale, glorifying 17th century militarism. The Hôtel des Invalides takes

up over 30 acres; the noble façade is 645 feet long and faces
a wide, landscaped grassy esplanade (designed by Robert de
Cotte) which stretches right down to the Seine and the gilded
Pont Alexandre III. Separating the monumental *Hôtel* from
the esplanade are suitably impressive fortifications: a moat,
numerous batteries of bronze cannon.

Only a few dozen soldiers live in Les Invalides today. The
rest of the space is taken up by bellicose museums and, the
big tourist draw, **Napoleon's tomb.**

The Hôtel des Invalides: M Invalides/Varenne/Latour Maubourg/RER
Invalides. Open 7am–7pm daily. A *son-et-lumière* in English is held in
the main courtyard on evenings throughout the summer.

Housed in the main cobbled courtyard of Les Invalides, the
massive **Army Museum** has one of the finest collections of

arms, armour, uniforms, model soldiers and militaria in the
world, from the Middle Ages to World War II. You can see
the cannon ball which killed Turenne, Napoleon's campaign

Rodin Museum

Early this century the state bought the elegant Hôtel Biron and let it be used by artists, Auguste Rodin included. He had a ground-floor studio here from 1907 until his death in 1917.

The Thinker, Adam and Eve, The Cathedral, The Burghers of Calais, the statues of Balzac and Victor-Hugo — you'll find all Rodin's greatest works here. The temptation to touch the statuary is almost irresistible.

There are 7000 of Rodin's drawings, prodigiously august sculptures and paintings, from early days onwards, all handsomely arranged, including *The Girl in the Flowered Hat* and the bust *Mignon*, both reputed to be modelled on his long-suffering lover Rose Beuret who bore him a son and whom he married 2 weeks before her death; Rodin himself died in the same year. Some of the work is sensual, some becomes very official-seeming and bombastic.

The collection also includes some of Rodin's own favourite artworks, including those by his distinguished contemporaries, including Monet's *Paysage de Belle-Isle*, a Renoir, and two of Van Gogh's most celebrated canvasses, *Le Père Tanguy* and *The Harvesters*.

The gardens are lovely too, and, as an extension of the museum, provide a perfect setting for some more of Rodin's most famous statuary. Just past the former chapel is *The Thinker* (1880), cast in bronze, paid for by public subscription, set up in 1906 in the place du Panthéon and transferred in 1922 to the Rodin Museum. Further on is *Balzac* (1891–7), and to the left of the forecourt the group of *The Burghers of Calais*, the first casting of which was set up in Calais in 1895. Further on is the bronze masterwork *The Gates of Hell* (1880–1917), cast only in 1937 and framed by two figures in neo-Michelangelesque vein, *Adam and Eve*.

Musée Rodin: Hôtel Biron, 77 rue de Varenne. Tel. 47 05 01 34. M Varenne. Open 10am–5pm, Tue–Sun. Admission 20f adults; 10f 18–25s, OAPs; free under-18s, art students; half price; Sun. Credit (bookshop only): V.

tent — and in fact wherever you look, there's Napoleonic memorabilia — even his dog (stuffed).

Passing through the main entrance, you come into the Cour d'Honneur where you're confronted by ancient cannon ranged along the walls. The statue of Napoleon in the centre once stood on top of the column in the place Vendôme. The collection is divided into two sections, one housed on the east side of the courtyard and the other on the west.

The story of the French army is related in the east wing. On the ground floor are two huge rooms which once served as refectories – the Salle Turenne has a collection of flags while the Salle Vauban has cavalry exhibits, including life-size dummies of soldiers on horseback.

Upstairs, on the second and third floors, is an enormous array of military memorabilia covering different periods of history. Weaponry and armour fills the ground floor and former refectories of the west wing, while above, on the first and second floors, there are good sections on the first and second World Wars.

Musée de l'Armée (Army Museum): Hôtel des Invalides, Esplanade des Invalides. Tel. 45 55 37 67. M Varenne/Latour–Maubourg./École Militaire/Invalides. Open 10am–5pm daily. Admission (valid for 2 consecutive days) 25f adults; 13f children; free under-7s, soldiers in uniform. No credit cards. Cinema (films on First World War at 2.15pm; Second World War II at 4.15pm). Shop.

Musée des Plans-Reliefs – located within the army museum, on the fifth floor of the right hand wing – is an unusual collection of miniature versions of French forts from the time of the strongholds built by military architect Vauban in the 17th century. Originally it was the brainchild of Louvois, Louis XIV's Secretary of State for War, and later régimes carried on the practice of making detailed scale models up to the end of the 19th century. Access through the Army Museum with the same ticket.

Entered via the north-west corner of the main courtyard is the **Museum of Two World Wars** (not the Army Museum). Temporary exhibitions around military themes are held here and there's a small permanent collection of relics from the two World Wars.

Same ticket as for the army museum. Open summer 10am–6pm, winter 9am–5pm. Closed Sun, Mon.

Created by General de Gaulle to honour those who made an outstanding contribution to the freeing of France, the Order of Liberation is celebrated via photographs and mementoes in the **Museum of the Order of Liberation**.

Separate from the Army Museum, the entrance to the **Museum of the**

Order of Liberation is at 51 bis boulevard de La Tour-Maubourg. Tel. 47 05 35 15. Open 2–5pm. Closed Sunday.

There are two churches within Les Invalides. Designed by Mansart, **St-Louis-des-Invalides** was the original church of the Invalides. It was on the fine 17th-century, 4800-pipe organ here that the first performance of Berlioz's *Requiem* was given in 1837. The Dôme church was built on to the end of the St Louis and shared a common altar, but was blocked off from it in 1793. They're now separated by a glass barrier.

Inside the church of St Louis (which is also known as the Church of Soldiers), the bones of famous military leaders are interred. Tattered, captured enemy flags flutter along the aisles. Boards attached to the pillars explain the trophies which stand out as landmarks in French history.

Church of St Louis: 2 rue de Tourville. Tel. 45 55 92 30. Open Apr–Sept, 10am–6pm daily; Oct–Mar, 10am–5pm daily.

Having completed Les Invalides, Louis XIV decided that it needed an extra dash of grandeur. The result was the **Dôme** church, very different in style to the church of St-Louis-des-Invalides, and generally considered to be one of the finest churches built in France since the Renaissance. To find out whether you agree, or think it too pompous, you can get to it through the Army Museum (using the same ticket).

Designed by Hardouin-Mansart, added on to the end of the St Louis between 1677 and 1735, most people visit it because it is also Napoleon's final resting place. His ashes are interred in the circular crypt in six coffins, one inside the other, all encased in a red porphyry sarcophagus which looks like a huge chunk of bakelite.

Tourists cluster round to gawp down on the monstrous tomb from the upper gallery which encircles it. This has to be the highest profile mausoleum in Europe. Both crypt and tomb were designed by Louis Visconti in a grand style which France's most powerful Emperor would have approved of – after all, it's the way he lived. All round the tomb are bas reliefs commemorating Napoleon's achievements, and the names of his victories are carved in stone: Wagram, Friedland, Iéna, Austerlitz, Rivoli.

The tomb is sited under the impressive painted dome.

In the side chapels are tombs of other military heroes: World War I hero Marshal Foch has a great black warlike sarcophagus, held up by soldiers; Turenne is here, as is military architect Vauban, whose heart was brought to Les Invalides on Napoleon's orders.

THE QUARTIER ST DOMINIQUE

Just west of Les Invalides the 7e becomes more down-to-earth. There's an animated little gaggle of a *quartier* midway between the two obligatory tourist sights of the *arrondissement*, the Eiffel Tower and Les Invalides, sectioned off by the blank boulevard de La Tour-Maubourg, avenue Bosquet and avenue de la Motte-Piquet.

Within the web of 19th-century streets are good places to eat and stay. Comparatively few tourists sleep in this segment of Paris, although there are many quiet hotels and the location is very central. At **Thoumieux,** for example, in the rue St Dominique, you can do both. This 1920s-style restaurant with rooms has been in the same family for three generations: the fixed price lunch menu (under 60f) gives the best value. The streets ranging south from St Dominique are less formal than other parts of the 7e. The pedestrianised, paved, distinctly foody **Rue Cler** for instance, is the sort of terrific market street you find in provincial French towns, scented by baking bread and fresh charcuterie. You can buy excellent picnic fodder here.

Tarte Julie, at number 28, is a spotless all-white pâtisserie where you can pick up a whole, huge quiche or a lunch size one-portion slice of smoked salmon quiche at 24f. (It's open from 9am–7pm, Mon–Sat; 9am–1pm, Sun). Over the road at number 37 is **Charcuterie Breton** where you can get the rest of your picnic – stuffed tomatoes, all kinds of cold meats and salads; next door is a branch of **Léonidas,** the superior purveyor of chocolates and at number 47 **Le Lutin Gourmand** is another chocaholic wonderland. There are excellent greengrocery shops in rue Cler for those with less sweet teeth: piles and piles of melons and tangerines that never seem to look so vibrantly colourful in markets at home.

North of the rue St Dominique, heading towards the Seine, you'll come across a small museum where smoking is forbidden even though it's the subject of all the exhibits. **Jean Nicot** (as in nicotine) introduced the deadly weed to France in 1561 via his diplomatic bag and the history of tobacco is traced via displays of smoking paraphernalia: pipes, pouches, snuff boxes, and so on. The museum was set up by SEITA, the French version of BAT, a state-run tobacco company and major sponsor of artists and designers.

Seita (Tobacco) Museum: 12 rue Surcrouf. Tel. 45 56 60 17. M Invalides/LaTour-Maubourg. Open 11am–6pm, Mon–Sat. Closed Sun and holidays. Admission free.

The **American church** is very near – continue from the SEITA museum to the river and it's at 66 quai d'Orsay. (Tel.

The Sewers (Les Égouts)

It helps to have a de-sensitised olfactory organ to enjoy a tour of the Paris sewers – not that you actually see anything yucky, you understand, but then again you can hardly expect the capital's waste system to smell of roses.

There are 1305 miles of subterranean passages, some delving under the Seine, which each year cart off enough solid waste to build a six-storey building. These astounding facts and many more are reeled off during a tour of a tiny section of the labyrinth, the entrance to which is by the Pont de l'Alma. The only boring bit is the exhibition of historical documents and the rather dated audio-visual presentation (in English for groups on request) on how the system works. Then it's off through drippy, damp, spooky tunnels – following in the footsteps of Victor Hugo who came down here to plot Jean Valjean's route in *Les Misérables*. The Résistance was based down in the sewers during the war – one of the service chambers served as a clandestine hospital – and a new respect emerges for their endurance after you've experienced conditions for yourself. Kids love it.

The Sewers (Les Égouts de Paris): place de la Résistance, entrance at corner of quai d'Orsay and Pont de l'Alma. Tel. 47 05 10 29. M Alma-Marceau. Open 11am–5pm, Sat–Wed. Closed Thur, Fri. Admission 20f; 10f, under-10s; free under 6s. No credit cards. Shop.

47 05 07 99; Open 9am–10.30pm, Mon–Sat; 9am–8pm, Sun. Services 11am, Sunday.)

From here you can walk along the quays to the **Eiffel Tower** – no need to tell you which direction to turn – passing at the corner of quai d'Orsay and Pont de l'Alma, the entrance to the *égouts* or sewers (see box). Across the river, the Pont de l'Alma, on the right bank, is where you can hop on one of the big motor boats known as *bateaux-mouches*: to get to it go along the avenue Rapp and cross the bridge (see p. 425)

THE EIFFEL TOWER

If a job hadn't been found in 1909 for the Eiffel Tower there'd have been a very good chance that it would have been demolished. As it happened, the city's most famous landmark, known the world over on ashtrays, T-shirts and tea towels, was saved by becoming a transmission tower for radio (and later, in 1959, television), and it played a strategically vital military rôle in the First World War.

The tower's future had been in doubt ever since the time it went up in 1889. Erected as an exhibit for the World Fair, which was held to commemorate the Centenary of the Revolution, it initially had a bad press. "Vulgar" was amongst the many terms of abuse hurled at it by critics.

More recently, the Eiffel Tower has been treated with appreciation and affection: in 1964 it was finally declared a national monument and it got a total sprucing up for its 100th birthday in 1989 – new lifts, refurbished restaurants, the works. Someone had the idea of lighting the Tower from the inside, so now it blazes beacon-bright in the night sky.

Each year around 4 million people go to see it – and it may well feel as if they're all there at the same time as you stand in a never-ending line waiting for your turn. If you're really fit and feel it, you can climb the stairs to the first two platforms. Alternatively, take the lift – the third and top-most stage, which can only be reached by lift, has a bar, souvenir shops and the office where its creator, Gustave Eiffel, worked. More than a 100 million vertigo-braving visitors have whizzed up and down the latticework over the years to admire the brilliant

PICTURE 9

panoramic views – on the clearest day you'll see for 42 miles. When it was completed it was the tallest building in the world, at 984 ft (300m); today its height, including aerials, is 1052ft (320.75m)

A brilliant feat of engineering, the most staggering fact of all is that the total weight of the structure, an estimated 7000 tonnes, ends up on the ground as a dead weight per square inch of no more, it is said, than the pressure on the legs of an armchair with an average man sitting in it. This is due to the load being so well dispersed – between the bases of the arches is an area of more than 2 acres. Perched high on the second floor of the Tower is one of the poshest nosheries in Paris, the revamped **Jules Verne** (Tel. 45 55 61 44) with its own private elevators to the sky-high prices. Not a tourist trap, expect to

The Eiffel Swindles

There were an unscrupulous few who tried to capitalise on the Eiffel Tower's uncertain future. When one of the 20th century's most cunning swindlers, Victor Lustig, read in 1925 about the financial difficulties encountered in plans to restore the famous tower, a wicked scheme took shape in his audacious brain.

He convened a meeting of the five most powerful ferrous metal buyers in his suite at the Hôtel Crillon. To add credibility to the proceedings he demanded in the name of the President that secrecy be maintained regarding the meeting. Lustig then revealed to the five that Paris could no longer afford to keep the Eiffel Tower and wanted to sell it to the highest bidder. A Monsieur Poisson jumped at the chance and handed over a cheque (for an unknown sum) made out to the middle-man, Lustig, whom he believed was acting as legal negotiator.

By the time that Poisson had discovered the swindle Lustig had escaped to the USA. Realising he'd become the laughing stock of Paris if news of his deception got out, Poisson never did file a complaint.

Incredibly, in 1960, exactly the same trick worked again and a David Stimson managed to pocket a cheque for 50 million francs, having once more "sold off" the Eiffel Tower to a gullible would-be purchaser.

book your seat 2 or 3 weeks in advance, like buying an airline excursion ticket.

The Eiffel Tower: Champs de Mars. Tel. 45 50 34 56. Recorded information 45 55 91 11. M Bir Hakeim/École Militaire/Trocadéro. Open summer, 9.30am–midnight daily; winter, 10am–11pm daily. Admission by lift 14f–35f adults (depending on floor); 6f–20f under-12s; free under-4s; by stairs to 2nd floor, 7f adults; free under-4s. Group discounts available.

Grazing around the feet of the Eiffel Tower are the gardens of the **Champ-de-Mars** – called the "Martian Field" because of its use a century ago for military training. It is always busy here – dotted with camera-clicking hordes, parked cars, ice cream and chip sellers, players of *pétanque* on the gravelly parts – and lively even at night when footballers come to kickabout by floodlight.

A small, green woodland pavilion near the end of avenue

UNESCO

Just south of the École Militaire are buildings housing the Ministry of Health and UNESCO. While it looks far from daring now, the concrete and glass UNESCO structure is another edifice that caused a rumpus when it opened, in 1958. Designed by the American Breuer, the Italian Nervi, and the Frenchman Zehrfuss, UNESCO called on the great artists of the 156-member nations to decorate the buildings. There are two huge ceramic works by Miró, tapestries by Le Corbusier, frescoes by Picasso; Henry Moore's *Figure in Repose* is visible from the avenue de Suffren. Regular exhibitions are held here which the public can attend, and the main hall is used for various events. Phone for details.

UNESCO Building; 7 place de Fontenoy. Tel. 45 68 10 00. M Ségure. Open 9.30am–6pm, Mon–Fri. Admission free.

Barbey-d'Aurevilly is one of several Parisian theatres which stage traditional puppet shows – Punch and Judy *à la française*. Performances last about 40 minutes. (Telephone Marionnettes du Champ-de-Mars on 45 74 69 75 for times and programme details. Tickets are around 14f.)

The chief architect to Louis XV, Jacques-Ange Gabriel (he who designed place de la Concorde), laid out the Champ-de-Mars as a military parade ground and from 1867 world fairs were held here. Gabriel also built the 18th-century École Militaire facing the Champ-de-Mars, at 43 avenue de la Motte Picquet, whose most famous old boy was Napoleon Bonaparte (his leaving report stated that he showed "great promise"). It's still a military academy, a kind of French Sandhurst, so you won't get to see beyond the classical façade unless you enrol for the School of Advanced War Studies, or the Higher School of National Defence.

THE SOUTHERN TIP OF THE 7E

Across the avenue de Breteuil, the southern boundary of the 7e is formed by the busy rue de Sèvres. **Au Bon Marché**, at number 38, on the corner of rue de Sèvres and rue du Bac, was founded in 1852 and is the oldest of the Parisian department stores. House specialities include Oriental carpets – which the store has been trading in since 1871; food – it has the biggest food store in Paris on the ground floor, including takeaways; haberdashery; and, some say, the best selection of ladies' undies in town. Children's clothing is less pricey here than in the more chic Au Printemps or Galeries Lafayette. Eiffel – the very same engineer who left his mark so blatantly on the other side of the *arrondissement* – designed the metallic structure.

Rue de Babylone

Rue de Babylone, running west off Raspail, is one of the restrained Faubourg St Germain *quartier's* most animated streets and it has two extremely good value eateries. **Au Babylone** at number 13, characterful, inexpensive and very old-fashioned, is open only for lunch, which need not cost more than 50f. Then there's **Au Pied de Fouet**, at 45, with simple home cooking to enjoy – if you can get in. It is tiny, with just a handful of tables, open from noon for 2 hours and 7–9pm, Mon–Fri, and for lunch on Saturdays. Slightly more expensive, **Bistro de l'Empereur** at number 54 has a handy 58f menu. At number 56, **Le Temps de Lire** is an inviting bookshop, while next door at 58 there's a slim shrine to order in the tiny Filofax shop. **Lili Blei** at number 54 has fashionable, pretty shoes.

Taking you by surprise at number 57 bis as you plod up rue de Babylone is a Japanese pagoda. That's right – the genuine 19th-century article, with a pointy roof, **La Pagode** was shipped to France at the height of the Oriental vogue in 1896 and reassembled here in the Faubourg St Germain. The client was a Doctor Morin, the head of the nearby Au Bon Marché department store, who presented it to his party-loving spouse as a venue for her fancy dress balls, masquerades and transvestite knees-ups. So visually exciting were they that rents shot up for rooms with balconies overlooking the Pagoda which gave a good view of the jollies. Converted into a cinema in March 1931, the Pagoda also has a tea room with tables outside in summer. (See **salons de thé**; also **cinemas**.) Across the road from the Pagoda at 68 rue de Babylone is **Ciné-images**, a treasure trove of movie collectibles, postcards and posters.

Au Bon Marché: 38 rue de Sèvres. Tel. 45 49 21 22. M Sèvres-Babylone. Open 9.30am–6.45pm (food shop 7.30pm). Closed Sunday. Credit: AE, DC, V.

A little further on is the wide boulevard Raspail which slashes through the 6e. At number 45 (and just in the 6e) is a *hôtel* which actually *is* a hotel – of the de-luxe variety. A curvy masterpiece of early Art Deco, the **Hôtel Lutétia's** guest rooms were smartened up in 1989 under the direction of designer Sonia Rykiel, and no one would ever guess that it had seen less fortunate years as Gestapo HQ during the Occupation. De Gaulle, who spent his wedding night here, was just one of its illustrious former guests. The statues adorning the façade of the hotel are by Paul Belmondo, Jean-Paul's papa.

The Hôtel Lutétia: 75007 45 boulevard Raspail. Telephone 45 44 39 10.

8E:
Commerce and Couture

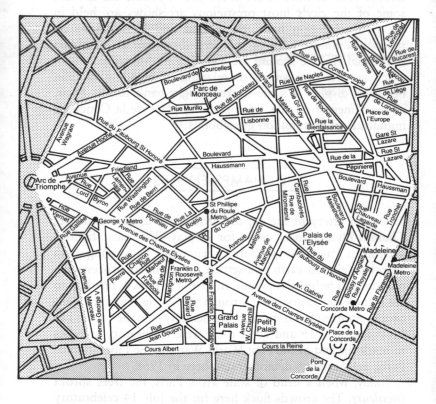

A large, opulent *arrondissement*, the 8e is stylish, slightly snooty, exclusive, yet distinctly lacking in neighbourhood ambience, apart from its atypical easternmost edge around St Lazare. The money shouts in the ultra-smart streets, including the superlatively chic rue du Faubourg St Honoré, with its art galleries and haute couture salons. There are plush hotels, posh restaurants – Maxim's for one, the Lucas Carton for another – great fragrance houses and upmarket jewellers. The sightseeing attractions are mostly of the monumental not museumeological kind.

French presidents live in the 8e, in the un-Republican-sounding Élysée Palace; the huge Madeleine Church, flanked by a flower market, looms over the luxury goods in the French equivalent of Fortnum & Mason, Fauchon – while tarts of another kind flaunt in the streets behind the church; some of the city's most prestigious art shows are held in the two exhibition halls, the Grand and Petit Palais; on the northernmost edge of the *arrondissement* is the smart residential enclave around the bucolic Parc Monceau.

It's an area less suited to relaxing or blending in than being on display. It's the heart of right bank tourist Paris, its monumental Arc de Triomphe and place de la Concorde immortalised in a million guidebooks.

THE CHAMPS-ÉLYSÉES

The main artery of the 8e, the broad, tree-lined **avenue des Champs-Élysées**, was made for display. The most famous avenue in Paris has probably seen more flagwaving than anywhere else on earth as a setting for countless processions, parades and political marches. In 1840 the crowds lined up to see Napoleon's hearse pass through the Arc de Triomphe – his own monument to his military invincibility – on the way to Les Invalides; in 1919 and 1944 there were celebratory marches to mark the end of the First World War and the Liberation of Paris, and students demonstrated here in 1968.

Today, when a head of state visits Paris, the trees sprout *tricoleurs*. The crowds flock here for the July 14 celebratory goings-on when tanks roll down the avenue again, and for the finish of the Tour de France cycle race on the second to last Sunday in July. And when the Christmas lights go on, it's glued up by a steady, treacly stream of car-bound sightseers.

The beginning of September 1991 saw the start of a

long overdue effort to recapture some of the heady pre-war grandeur of the avenue. For the Champs-Élysées is not what it was – whatever glamour it had has been all but engulfed by the car fumes, the car showrooms, airline offices, cinemas and other urbanisms. The mayor of Paris, Jacques Chirac, has put Pierre-Yves Ligen, the city planner who masterminded the 5-year restoration of the Louvre, in charge of rescuing the Champs. They hope to restore former glory by doubling the number of trees, making pavements wider and toning down the more gaudy shop fronts. Strict architectural standards are to be imposed and development zones set up to attract a better class of business. A new range of urban furniture (benches, streetlights, waste bins) has been designed by architect Jean Michel Wilmotte, who also wants the bus stops to double as flower stalls, to help make the Champs-Élysées, in the words of Mayor Chirac, "once again the most beautiful street in the world".

CONCORDE TO ROND POINT

The Champs-Élysées begins at an imposing and impressive square, **place de la Concorde**. People used to be guillotined here and it's still murderous for pedestrians. The largest by far of all the squares in Paris, there are great views from Concorde in every direction: through the western gateway formed by Guillaume Coustou's Marly Horses Statue, up the Champs-Élysées to the distant Arc de Triomphe; east over the Tuileries to the Louvre; north across the rue Royale to the colonnaded place de la Madeleine and south over the Seine to the equally colonnaded **Chambre des Deputés**, or French lower house of Parliament.

Try to dart safely over to the centre because this is the best spot from which to survey all its embellishments. Not that you can miss the granite 75-foot high obelisk from the ruins of the temple at Luxor. Over 3 thousand years old, it was a gift from the Egyptian Viceroy Mehemet Ali to Louis-Philippe. The king saw it would make a suitable non-political centrepiece and had it erected in 1836. (Models showing the obelisk's arduous journey to France are on view in the Maritime Museum.)

Concorde's Bloody History

The architect Jacques-Ange Gabriel laid out the place de la Concorde in 1757–72 and named it after its centrepiece, a bronze statue of the then King, Louis XV.

No sooner had the Revolution flared up than down came the statue, to be replaced by the guillotine, and the square was renamed place de la Révolution. Between 1793 and 1795, over 1300 necks were chopped, including those of Louis XVI (ironic, really, since the place had been built to honour his grandfather, Louis XV), Marie Antoinette, Madame du Barry, Charlotte Corday, Danton and Robespierre.

At the end of The Terror, in 1795, perhaps out of wishful thinking, the square received its present name, Harmony Square (it really does sound better in French). Nowadays, the only life-threatening goings-on are due to the death-defying manœuvres of the terrible traffic.

The fountains on either side were modelled on those in St Peter's, Rome, and the eight statues on pavilions represent allegorically the French provincial towns of Lyon, Marseille, Bordeaux, Nantes, Lille, Brest, Rouen and Strasbourg. On the north side are Gabriel's two palace-like buildings dating from the 1770s. The one on the left is the prestigious Le **Crillon** luxury hotel, while the one on the right houses the **Ministère de la Marine**. The decoration of the square was completed in the reign of Louis-Philippe by the architect Hittorff who also designed the Gare du Nord.

Considering what a thundering great thoroughfare it is, the Champs-Élysées from Concorde to the Rond Point traffic circus is surprisingly verdant. Laid out in the late 17th century by Louis XIV's landscape boffin, Le Nôtre, it is laced by park-like strips which slip down to the Seine on the southern side. Parents bring their children here in fine weather to play on the swings and roundabouts or go walkies under the horse chestnut trees with their dogs.

Grand and Petit Palais

The two grandiose buildings poking above the greenery, facing each other across the avenue Winston Churchill (a turning off the Champs-Élysées at place Clémenceau) are the **Grand and**

Petit Palais, built for the Paris exhibition of 1900, just like the nearby Pont Alexandre III bridge.

The show-offy Grand Palais makes a fitting shelter for blockbuster temporary exhibitions and amongst the other large scale events held here is the annual October international modern art fair, **La FIAC** – when at least 100 galleries exhibit. (The dates vary so it's best to telephone to check.)

Grand Palais: 1–3 avenue du General Eisenhower. Tel. 42 89 32 13. M Champs-Élysées-Clemenceau.

In the west wing of the Grand Palais is the **Palais de la Découverte** or Palace of Discovery – the science museum before it was eclipsed by the high-tech Cité des Sciences et de l'Industrie at La Villette (see the **19e**). It has a very practical, educational approach and is much used by schoolteachers who can let loose their charges on the games that help to bring alive principles of science and physics.

Embryonic genetic engineers might enjoy the scientific experiments held at 11am and 3pm. A world away, the **Planetarium** has shows (at 2pm, 3.15pm and 4.30pm, with extra ones during school holidays and weekends) where different aspects of the universe are projected on to a hemispherical dome. There are also film shows (2.30pm and 4pm) and guided tours.

Palais de la Découverte: avenue Franklin D. Roosevelt. Tel. 40 74 80 00 /recorded information Tel. 43 59 18 21. Open 10am–6pm, Tue–Sun. Admission: 20f adults; 10f under-18s, OAPs. Planetarium: 13f adults; 9f under-18s, OAPs. No credit cards.

Over in the scarcely less flamboyant Petit Palais the **Beaux Arts museum** contains a little-known mélange of 19th- and 20th-century paintings. It's good for Courbet and Bonnard (you'll find *Le Sommeil* by the former and *Nu dans le Bain* by the latter) and also has works by Cézanne, Monet, Delacroix and Pissarro. Other myriad bits and pieces include Greek pottery, 18th-century furniture and Beauvais tapestries. Temporary exhibitions are also held here from time to time.

Musée du Petit Palais: avenue Winston Churchill. Tel. 42 65 12 73. M Champs-Élysées-Clemenceau. Open 10am–5.40pm, Tue–Sun.

Admission 15f adults; 8.50f 7–18s, students; free under-7s; additional charge for temporary exhibitions. Credit (bookshop only): V.

Paris de Luxe

West of the Grand Palais, and continuing to remain south of the Champs-Élysées itself, streets of biscuity-coloured apartment blocks lead to the quiet place François 1er. From here you are poised to enter a Bermuda Triangle of awesome wealth formed by the line of the Champs-Élysées on the right, with the avenues George V and Montaigne making up the other two sides. Along with the typically 8th *arrondissement* elements – a few embassies (China, Mexico, Canada), three palatial hotels (George V, the Plaza Athenée, Prince de Galles), even a popular night spot, the Crazy Horse Salon (see **Night clubs and Discos** section), countless banks, business offices, chic cafés and restaurants – there are more couturiers to the metre here than anywhere else in Paris except perhaps, the rue du Faubourg St Honoré. Wandering up and down the avenues George V and Montaigne, pressing your nose against the sparkling shop windows, you get a whiff of what Luxury Paris is all about. It's the world of serious money and spending it.

Ted Lapidus and **Pierre Balmain** are in rue Francois 1er. **Guy Laroche, Givenchy, Chanel, Valentino, Thièrry Mugler, Nina Ricci, Balenciaga,** are amongst the other names beside the doors; **Christian Dior**, at number 11 avenue Montaigne, has the largest couture boutique in the world – over 15,000 square feet of it.

On a more accessible note, both avenue George V and avenue Montaigne decant into place de l'Alma, and, almost on the place itself, is the **Théâtre des Champs-Élysées**, the city's main concert hall. One of the first reinforced concrete buildings to be built in Paris, it was completed in 1913, the work of Auguste Perret, the French architect who adored concrete and prefigured the International style. The bridge, **Pont de l'Alma,** is an embarkation point for the *bateaux-mouches.*

ROND POINT TO ARC DE TRIOMPHE

Resurfacing from this heady diversion, at the top of avenue Montaigne, you come to the **Rond Point** where six avenues

Bateaux-Mouches

The Pont de l'Alma is the embarkation point for the bulky, glass-enclosed motor boats known as *bateaux-mouches*. A multilingual commentary accompanies the trip as it heads east to the Ile St Louis and then back west, past the Eiffel Tower as far as the midstream Allée des Cygnes.

The literal translation of *bateaux-mouches* is "fly boat" – at the turn of the century, small pleasure craft went by the name of "fly-weight boats". Another theory has it that the "Mouche" referred to a district of Lyon where the boats were originally manufactured.

Expensive lunch (300f), afternoon tea/concert (60f), and even more expensive dinner (500f) cruises are also laid on, but you'd be better off taking the boat trip (30f) and enjoying a leisurely, commentary-free meal ashore.

Bateaux-Mouches: port de la Conférence. Tel. 42 25 96 10 or 43 59 30 30. M Alma-Marceau. Departures April-mid Nov every half an hour, 10am–9pm daily; mid Nov–March 11am, 2.30pm, 9pm daily. (Embark 30 mins before departure.)

drop in to say hello to the ten-lane Champs-Élysées. No ordinary car-crazed traffic circus, the Rond Point is prettied up with fountains, flowers and trees. Providing you're not driving, try to take a look at the restored façade behind the big black and gold railings of the *Jours de France* buildings.

At the Rond Point, too, you could slip off the street into **Galéries-Élysées,** one of the brash shopping malls that lead off the upper half of the avenue, where the tinkle of fountains vies with the tinkle of muzak to keep you spending pennies.

Out in the daylight, the commercialism of this far-from-Elysian stretch of the Champs is no less evident. The line up is of massive cinema complexes, touristy shops, fast fooderies, banks, rocket-priced restaurants and cafés, and as many gleaming car showrooms as you'd find at a motor show.

This is *not* the best value area to eat out, but if you are dying of thirst after your march, or determined to have a tipple on the Champs-Élysées, then your best bet is **Le Fouquets,** the famous café on the corner of avenue Georges V. Fouquet's was where Churchill, de Gaulle and Roosevelt lunched, and where James Joyce dined nearly every night. It was threatened with demolition a few years ago but saved when it was declared a national monument, on the grounds that it had "historical associations". The cocktails are excellent, with prices up in the stratosphere, but service is fast and friendly

and you can make the most of your investment by doing some serious people-watching from the terrace. The most serious people-watching of all goes on after the César ceremony (the French equivalent of the Oscar awards) when the stars pour in here for the official dinner.

Nearer the top of the Champs-Élysées, on the left as you approach the looming Arc de Triomphe, at 127, is the main **Office du Tourisme** where you can pick up free advice, brochures and maps on the sights in Paris, the suburbs

---

Arch History

Since 1923, the Arc de Triomphe has been the spot for national events and on all major festivals and state occasions, a huge *tricoleur* billows inside the arch. There was already a grassy crossroads here when, in 1806, Napoleon (who else?) decided he wanted a monument to his military successes and commissioned Chalgrin to build a triumphal arch.

The fall of the Empire put the work on hold for so long that it became a standing joke for Parisians. Eventually, some 10 million francs and 30 years later, the Arc de Triomphe was opened by King Louis-Philippe, who dedicated it to the armies of the French. Haussmann added his own dash of grand scale town-planning to the *place* 8 years later, with seven more avenues to complete the 12-pointed star.

---

and the rest of France. It's worth making a mental note, too, of the **Drugstore Publicis** at number 133 (Tel. 47 23 54 34), in case you suddenly crave a packet of cigarettes or a magazine at one o'clock in the morning (it's open from 9am–2am, Mon–Sat and from 10am–2am on Sunday. There's also a branch at 1 ave Matignon, 8e, open the same hours.)

The Marble Arch of Paris sits in all its squat majesty at the junction of the 16th, 17th and 8th *arrondissements*, a dozen symmetrical avenues fanning out from it – hence the name **L'Étoile** (the star) which sticks, despite the fact it was called **place Charles de Gaulle** after the President's death in 1970.

A fitting climax to the Triumphal Way, the colossal **Arc de Triomphe** (164 feet high and 148 feet wide), is the main symbol of French power and patriotism – though it is doubtful whether this is uppermost in the minds of the heroic Parisian motorists as they attempt to negotiate this hazardous intersection.

Of the sculptural decorations on the pillars of the arch, Rude's *La Marseillaise* is the best: the frieze commemorates Napoleon's campaigns with hundreds of larger-than-life figures in battle. Beneath the arch lies the **Tomb of the Unknown Soldier**, where a flame is kept burning (lit daily at 6pm) over the remains of the anonymous Frenchman who fell at Verdun and whose body was brought here in November, 1920, to commemorate the dead of the First World War. You may, queues permitting, sooner or later take a lift to the top of the arch from which point there is a brilliant panoramic view all the way down the Champs-Élysées beyond Concorde to the Carousel Arch at the Louvre. Looking west, in the other direction, there's an equally unobstructed view down the avenue de la Grande Armée towards the high-rise city of **La Défense** with its modern triumphal Grande Arche, glass and concrete skyscrapers (see box below).

La Défense

To call the overgrown office blocks at the westernmost end of the avenue de la Grande Armée "Manhattan-sur-Seine" is to do New York a serious injustice. There is nothing uplifting about the futuristic skyscraper city development of La Défense, although to be grateful for small mercies, at least it's on the outskirts.

To venture out there is to get a glimpse of an architectural playpen of modernist profligacy.

Begun at the end of the '60s, it's a crazed concrete and glass paean to commercial and consumer values – the Quatre Temps hypermarket is the largest in Europe, containing twice the area of all the shops in the Champs-Élysées.

In the towering slabs are the offices of major and multi-national companies, and there are also hotels, restaurants, cinemas, a station and bizarre apartment blocks with coloured tiled exteriors – not that many people live here. Of the 100,000 who work at La Défense, only about 20,000 stay to rest their weary heads. Arty additions dot the podium and open terraces including works by Agam (monumental fountain) and Joan Miro (*Les Deux Personnages*).

Consolidating Mitterrand's reputation as a "Builder President", yet another of his *Grandes Travaux* is the awesome and rather awful triumphal arch, or **Grande Arche of La Tête Défense**. A sleek, business centre, it is an office block-monument. Designed by the late Danish architect Johan Otto Von Spreckelsen, the huge cube (each side measures 380 foot) is aligned with the Arc de Triomphe, the Champs-Élysées and the Louvre.

Grande Arche: Tête Défense. 2km/1.2 miles from Paris. RER La Défense. For more information Tel. 47 96 24 24.

Arc de Triomphe: place Charles de Gaulle (access via pedestrian subway). Tel. 43 80 31 31. M Étoile. Open 10am–5.30pm (5pm in winter) daily. Closed public holidays. Admission to viewing platform: 22f adults; 5f under-17s; 12f OAPs, students.

THE MADELEINE AREA

At the heart of the affluent 8e is the Church of Ste Marie Madeleine, known to all as **La Madeleine**.

Inside, the church is windowless – gloomy or atmospheric depending on how you like your churches – crepuscular light leaking through the three shallow domes. Once your eyes are accustomed to the dimness, you'll be able to drink in the unexpectedly rich details: the marble murals, gilt columns and fine sculpture including the central group on the high altar by Marochetti, the *Ascension of Mary Magdalen*.

The church has a superb organ – Saint-Saëns was appointed organist here in 1857 when he was 22 and stayed for about 20 years, writing music almost every day. Some years later his

---

Madeleine History

Looking like a Greek temple with its rows all round of 75-foot-high Corinthian columns, La Madeleine took 80 years to finish and was eventually consecrated as a church in 1842.

In the intervening years it was very nearly chosen as Paris's first railway station – (this honour went instead to another site, what's now the Gare St Lazare, just up the road) and, before that, initial plans for a church had been dumped in favour of a bank, a theatre and the Temple de la Gloire, a memorial to Napoleon's armies. It has to be said that from the outside, at least, it could still pass for a very grand bank. A long flight of 28 steps takes you from the square to the door of the church. From the top there's a good view down the upmarket rue Royale, across the place de la Concorde with the French House of Commons, or Palais Bourbon in the background. Some of the most fashionable weddings in Paris take place here, the monumental steps providing the backdrop.

For Foodies

In a city full of excellent food shops, this, one of the smartest shopping areas of all, has its fair share of outstanding ones. **Fauchon**, at 26 place de la Madeleine, is to foodies what the Sistine Chapel is to Catholics. If you can't afford to join the gastronauts who pay the cosmic prices for take-out luxuries, at least have a look at the windows full of Food as Art: wonderfully coloured terrines and *pâtés*, glossy fish, boned poultry. Venture inside and you'll get lots of gourmet gift ideas: fragrant oils, exotic mustards, spices from the ends of the earth. A kilo of goose *pâté* with truffles, perhaps? Yours for £250.

Fauchon have an excellent cellar too — not just for fine vintages, but also for inexpensive bottlings. Across the street is their stand-up cafeteria, well worth sharing with the crowds to enjoy some of the best coffee in Paris, terrific cakes and sarnies.

Still in the place de la Madeleine, **Kaspia** at number 17, has caviar galore (with an upstairs restaurant to sample the *specialités de la maison*), and no prizes for guessing that **La Maison de la Truffe**, number 19, is *the* place to try the freshest truffles (November–March is the season). At number 21, **Hédiard** is another temple of the tummy whose floor-to-ceiling shelves groan with yummies: jars of preserves, cherry juice, condiments with exotic names, vintage sardines packed straight from the sea, coffee roasted daily. Upstairs is a small, elegant, *not* inexpensive restaurant. **Marquise de Sévigné** at number 32 is for chocaholics. The tradition for posh nosh continues just around the corner in rue Vignon where **La Ferme St Hubert** at number 21 sells cheeses of every sort. Next door is a little restaurant where you can nibble the cheeses or try a cheesy dish. **La Maison du Miel** at number 24 buzzes with activity when the honey season starts (yes, there is one) in September: stock up on the miniatures and let your taste buds tell you the difference between the diverse honeys.

pupil, Gabriel Fauré, who in turn taught Ravel, became organist at La Madeleine. And while we're name dropping, Chopin's funeral service was held here, with Mozart's *Requiem* playing to a packed congregation and performed by the entire choir and orchestra of the Paris Conservatoire. Concerts are still held here every month.

La Madeleine: place de la Madeleine. Tel. 42 65 65 17. M Madeleine.
Open 7.30am–7pm, Mon–Sat; 8am–1pm, 4–7pm, Sun.

Outside, one of the church walls is flanked by flower sellers and, on the west side of the square, is the handy **Kiosque Théâtre** which sells half-price theatre tickets on the day of the performance. (It's open Tue–Sat, 12.30–8pm, Sun 12.30–4pm. Closed Monday and July and August.)

At number 9 place de la Madeleine is one of the smartest restaurants in Paris, the **Lucas-Carton**, a Belle Époque landmark with prices to match its reputation. The set menu is about 800f.

Catering to rather different bodily needs, but at a fraction of the cost, it's worth descending the mosaic staircase leading from the square, to see the very elegant Art Nouveau lavatory, built in 1905. The Gents was converted recently into a control room for the national telephone company so the Ladies looks after both. The stained glass panels, and the original wooden fittings, make it more of a museum piece than a public convenience. (Open 9.30am–11.30am, 12.30–7pm, WC. 2.20f; shoe shine 8.80f. 13.20f for boots.)

Straight in front of the Madeleine Church and linking it with the pace de la Concorde is **rue Royale**, a tree-shaded, introspective street lined with exclusive shops. At the end of the 18th-century the writer Madame de Staël lived in number 6 and the architect Jean Gabriel (who designed the place de la Concorde a few hundred yards away) in number 8.

Maxim's, with its velvety Belle Époque dining room, is at number 3. **Lalique,** the grandest name in crystal in the world, is at number 11. You can have the most exclusive afternoon tea in town at Maxim's – not in the restaurant but at the Maxim's flower shop right next door! Only three tables are set every afternoon for a maximum of a dozen customers. No chance of getting a seat if you just turn up – you need to book well in advance. Set aside around £6 for a slice of cake from Maxim's kitchen and take solace from the scents of the surrounding flower arrangements, all of which are for sale, at a price.

THE FAUBOURG ST HONORÉ

Halfway down the rue Royale from the Madeleine is a crossroads – on the left is **rue St Honoré**, a long narrow street of shops and offices. On the right, it becomes one of the poshest streets in Paris, the **rue du Faubourg St Honoré**, where you'll find wall-to-wall luxury, palpable in the art galleries, jewellers, perfumiers and emporia of the fashion houses. At number 22 is **Lanvin**, number 24 is **Hermès**, at number 73 the colourful boutique of **Christian Lacroix**, the more traditional **Louis Féraud** at 88.

Continuing along the rue du Faubourg St Honoré towards the place Beauvau, on the left is the **Palais de l'Élysée**, the official Paris residence since 1873 of the French President and, as you'll guess from the guards, not open to the public. Built in 1718, restored in 1753 for Madame de Pompadour, later enlarged, it became a dance hall during the Revolution. Napoleon signed his abdication here in 1815 after Waterloo. François Mitterrand, soon after moving in (1981), enlisted the help of leading designer Philippe Starck in redecorating the Presidential apartments. (See more of Starck's work in the Café Costes, a trendy spot near the Beaubourg.)

Few of the other elegant mansions (once lived in by the aristocracy after the Faubourg took over from the Marais as the in place to live) are private residences these days. The **British Embassy** is at number 35 in the mansion built by Pauline Bonaparte; the residence of the **American Ambassador** is at 41; and at number 96, the **Ministry of the Interior**, built 1770. Further along, at number 112, is **Le Bristol**, one of Paris's finest hotels and conveniently located for the visiting heads of government who stay there, just down the road from the Élysée Palace.

Much further on, the rue du Faubourg St Honoré meets the beginning of the wide **boulevard Haussmann** where the emphasis on the finer things in life is carried into the lavishly furnished **Jacquemart-André Museum**. Housed in an elegant mansion, the collection was created by a banker, Edouard André, and his wife, a portraitist, Nelie Jacquemart, who bequeathed the house and contents to the Institut de France. Works by Rembrandt, Rubens, Titian, Watteau and Uccello, plus Della Robbia terra-cottas, Donatello bronzes. Temporary exhibitions are also held.

Musée Jacquemart-André: 158 boulevard Haussmann. Tel. 45 62 39 94. M Miromesnil St-Philippe-du-Roule. Open noon-6.30pm daily; permanent collection closed Mon, Tue. Admission 35f adults; 25f children. No credit cards.

MONCEAU QUARTIER

The Jacquemart-André Museum is just one of several Parisian museums which were originally private houses and collections. Two others are found directly north, at the border with the 17e, in one of the city's smartest residential areas, the Monceau *quartier*. Follow the rue de Courcelles north from near the Jacquemart-André Museum on boulevard Haussmann and you'll come to the boulevard de Courcelles and the main gate of the **Parc de Monceau**.

Many of the fine mansions surrounding the park are still lived in by the French aristos. Two that have been willed to the State and are now museums are the Cernuschi and the Nissim de Camondo.

Parking Space

The Parc de Monceau was designed originally by the painter Louis Carmontelle in 1778 as a garden for Philippe Egalité, Duke of Orléans, and it still has formal touches: romantic mock ruins, as well as a duck pond and children's playground. The young Marcel Proust played in the sandpits here with his little friend Antoinette Fauvre, and so have a great many high-ranking Parisians since, watched over by their uniformed nannies.

A mild sensation was caused here in October 1797 when the first parachutist, Garnerin, jumped out of a balloon 3000 feet up and landed in the middle of it all. One gets the impression that nothing as exciting has happened since.

Parc Monceau: entrance in boulevard de Courcelles. Tel. 42 94 08 08. M Monceau. Open dawn-dusk daily. Admission free.

The **Cernuschi Museum** has a small, well-preserved collection of Chinese art, bequeathed to the nation, along with the house, by a Milanese banker (Cernuschi) in the late 19th-century. Exhibits range from neolithic pottery to paintings by modern Chinese artists. Specialists who want more of the same should seek out the Musée National d'Arts Asiatiques Guimet in the 16e.

Musée Cernuschi: 7 avenue Velasquez, entrance at 111 boulevard Malesherbes. Tel. 45 63 50 75. M Villiers/Monceau. Open 10am–5.40pm, Tue–Sun. Admission 15f adults; 7.50f students, OAPs; free under-7s; extra charge for temporary exhibitions. No credit cards.

Around the corner, in an elegant 1910 house bequeathed, like the Cernuschi, with its contents to the State, is the **Musée Nissim de Camondo**. The interior is sumptuous and a bit intimidating – it's easy to feel as if you're trespassing on private property, namely that of the collection's rich creator, Count Moïse de Camondo, a man with a passion for 18th-century decorative art. He built the house in the style of the Petit Trianon at Versailles and recreated the lavish interior of an 18th-century Louis XVI Parisian mansion, dating from the last days of the *Ancien Régime*. On display is the family's collection of vases, sculpture and antique furniture. The tapestries are from the great workshops of Gobelins, (see the 13e) Beauvais and Aubusson, while the porcelain room is crammed with Sèvres, Chantilly and Meisson.

Musée Nissim de Camondo: 63 rue de Monceau. Tel. 45 63 26 32. M Monceau Villiers. Open 10am-noon, 2–5pm, Wed–Sun. Admission 15f adults; 8f 18–25s, OAPs; free under-18s. No credit cards.

Both museums are on the east side of the park; the adjacent boulevard Malesherbes runs alongside down to the place St Augustin and then continues to the Madeleine. This is the model Parisian boulevard, as conceived by Mr Boulevard himself, Haussmann, complete with all the signature details: pregnant balconies, bulging from buildings built from 1860–80, with sculptured façades.

The **Church of St Augustine** is bulky and not very beautiful, with a heavy dome containing frescoes in need of a clean by a popular 19th-century French artist called William Bougureau.

> ## 8e and beyond – by bus
> An economical, lazy way to sightsee is by bus and a par-
> ticularly good route, number 24, starts at St Lazare (every
> day except Sun), whisking you round place de la Madeleine,
> into Concorde, along the Seine beside the Tuileries, past the
> Louvre. It crosses by Pont Neuf to the Ile de la Cité for a
> view of Notre-Dame before slipping over to the left bank and
> going on to the quai de Bercy.

The engineer Baltard (who had just used iron to build the
market halls at Les Halles) used metal girders to hold up this
Italian Renaissance-cum-Byzantine church, obviating the need
for external buttressing.

QUARTIER ST LAZARE

From the place St Augustin, going a little way east along
the boulevard Haussmann (towards l'Opéra), you come to
the quiet, green **square Louis XVI**, a former cemetery where
many victims of the revolutionary guillotine were buried,
including Louis XVI and Marie Antoinette, until Louis XVIII
had their bodies taken to St Denis, in 1815. In the vaults of
the necropolis-like Expiatory chapel, are statues of the royal
twosome. (Open 10am-noon, 2–5pm or 6pm.)

A few steps from here is one of the world's largest railway
stations. The **Gare St Lazare** is at the eastern edge of the 8e,
north of boulevard Haussmann. It's the end of the line for
trains from Normandy, the western countryside and suburbs.
The Norman link is evident all around the terminal (place du
Havre, Relais Normand, Bar de Dieppe) with the restaurants
in rue de St Lazare, just a crab's crawl from the station,
specialising in seafood brought in on early morning trains
from the Norman coast. In the ultra-chic 8e, this down-to-
earth *quartier* is the most downmarket and most untainted
by tourism. There are neither monuments nor buildings of
any particular architectural or historical value. But there's
rich local colour and it's not a bad idea to consider staying
round here if you want to be within walking distance of the

big shops, and central sights; there's no shortage of hotels of the smaller, family-type: choose carefully, though, there are also some very dubious establishments.

The streets spreading out from the station up the hill to Montmartre and radiating out from place de l'Europe are named after European cities, rather arbitrarily it would appear. Heaven knows what the Hungarian tourist would make of the porno cinemas and omnipresent prostitutes of rue de Budapest. More appropriately located is **Androuët** at 41 rue d'Amsterdam, one of the best cheese shops in Paris. At their midday or evening (7pm) *dégustations* you can, for a nominal sum, get a crash course in cheese lore.

9E AND 10E:
Shops, Stations, Culture and Crystal

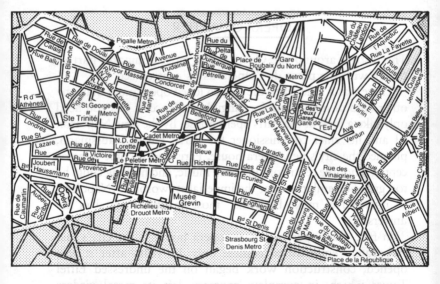

Covering a large chunk of northern central Paris, this area stretches from the opulent Opéra at the eastern edge to the city's major canal, St Martin, over in the west. The 9e and 10e are bounded in the south by the *grands boulevards* – really one long street which changes its name en route.

Culturally, and architecturally, the 9e is very mixed. The part around the Opéra and busy boulevard Haussmann with the major department stores is a tourist zone. The northernmost part of the 9e slips towards the sleaze of Clichy and Pigalle and the junkified, red-light district. There are plenty of hotels around here which you may well want to avoid.

In the 10e are two of the city's largest railway termini, the Gare du Nord and the Gare de l'Est, and it's in this part of town you'll be deposited if you come in from the ports by train – not an auspicious first sight of Paris, but quite an authentic one as it has remained a backwater, except for the main boulevards. It is sometimes shabby, a bit drab, there are few sights to see. But its lack of tourist lustre – and the fact that it has never become fashionable – means that there are lots of budget-priced places to stay.

OPÉRA QUARTIER

The district around the Opéra is the most upmarket part of the 9e with the **place de l'Opéra** as its centrepiece.

There was a time when the French loved opera more than any other kind of music, and for tangible evidence of this you need only take a look at the Paris opera house. By the time Napoleon III and his chief commissioner for Paris, Baron Haussmann, planned the city's new opera house, Paris had become a major centre, if not *the* centre of European music, and nothing could be too grand or ambitious for the imperialist twosome. (Napoleon III intended to make Paris the "most beautiful capital in the universe".)

In fact, the hyperbolic Paris opera house is the city's last elaborately embellished edifice; only 12 years after it was opened, construction work began on the undressed Eiffel Tower which, in complete contrast, left its metal girders exposed, structurally naked.

Whatever you think of the Opéra it is hard not to be impressed. Henry James wrote, in 1877: "It (the avenue de l'Opéra) stretches straight away from the pompous façade of the Opéra to the doors of the Théâtre Française, and it must

Garnier and the Paris Opéra

An open competition was held to find the architect of the Paris opera house, and from 171 submitted designs (including one from the Empress Eugénie) an unknown 35-year-old architect called Charles Garnier was unanimously chosen by the jury to head the most important building project of the Second Empire.

The foundation stone was laid in 1862, but by the time the Opéra was completed, the Second Empire had fallen, a victim of the Franco-Prussian War. Although it opened in 1875, under the Third Republic, it is really a symbol of the exceptionally materialistic society of the France of Napoleon III, an era dominated by a very affluent bourgeoisie.

A lot was expected of Garnier and he plundered any source where there was a tradition of unrestrained splendour for inspiration. When asked by the Empress Eugénie to describe his jackdaw-like profusion of styles, Garnier replied that it was neither Louis XIV, Louis XV, nor Louis XVI, but something wholly new — Napoleon III.

Garnier wanted to make the ornate sculptured façade of the Opéra a work of art in itself. Certainly the symbolic group by Carpeaux representing the Dance, facing the place de l'Opéra, won critical acclaim — the present sculpture is a copy, the original having been carted off to the Louvre, to escape extremes of weather and pollution.

be admitted that there is something fine in the vista that is closed at one end by the great sculptured and gilded mass of the former building."

Two main threads run through the story of the development of opera — an Italian one and a French one. From time immemorial, the Italian opera has stressed the importance of the music, while the French opera has put its emphasis on theatrical action. So it's appropriate that the Paris Théâtre National Opéra should be so theatrical; the building itself stands for grandeur and operatic grandiloquence.

Its architectural extravagances were the perfect backcloth for the gorgeously trussed and dressed up Parisian theatre-goers of the 19th century. For the Opéra was used for State occasions including balls — when ceremonial pomp, being seen and making a dramatic entrance, eclipsed the excitement of the show. And the Grand Foyer is a hard act to follow with its statuary, white marble and onyx Grand Staircase and great sweeping balustrades.

Then again, there is nothing low key about the opera house; covering 3 acres, it's gigantic. During the 13 years it took to build, every major French artist and craftsman of the day was involved at some time or other. It still has the largest stage in the world – it can hold 450 performers. And while we're number-crunching, the building has 1606 doors, 7593 keys and 450 chimneys. The Opéra is 185 foot high, 568 foot long, 333 foot wide. A 12-mile maze of halls and corridors crawls over several levels. Since a large proportion of the space was given over to the public rooms and stage, the auditorium only seats a comparatively modest 2158 – Milan's La Scala seats 3600, for instance. The auditorium itself is a five-tiered red velvet and gold leaf confection with a 6-ton chandelier dripping from the ceiling. Traditionalists were shocked in

1964 when André Malraux gave artist Marc Chagall *carte blanche* to paint a tableau on the auditorium ceiling. You can decide for yourself whether Chagall's ceiling fantasy clashes with the ornate surroundings, or adds a touch of lightness to the plushness.

These days the Opéra has nothing to do with operatic productions – they've moved into a new home at the Bastille (see the 11e and 12e), but it remains the home of the Paris Opéra Ballet. Until 1989 Nureyev was director here and he helped to bring back international stars and glitter to l'Opéra. He was succeeded by the present director, Patrick Dupond, aged just 32, one of the most brilliant dancers in the Opéra ballet company's recent history. The best way to see the Opéra is to go to a performance, but unless you queue for hours, ticket prices are very steep. During the day you can visit the interior and there are guided tours. In the basement is a grotto – the underground stream inspired Gaston Leroux to write *The Phantom of the Opera*, which later became a classic horror movie and an Andrew Lloyd Webber musical.

Opéra Garnier: place de l'Opéra. Tel. 42 66 50 22. M Opéra. Open 11am–4.30pm. Closed public holidays. Tours do not take place every day, call for exact times. The box office is open from 11am–7pm daily.

Next to his edifice, on the rue Auber side, is a gilded bust of the architect, Charles Garnier. Opera and ballet aficionades will enjoy the little **Musée de l'Opéra** (19th-century models to scale of opera sets, a wonderful collection of Diaghilev memorabilia, Debussy's desk, Nijinsky's sandals, Pavlova's tiara, busts of composers and performers).

Musée de l'Opéra: 1 place Garnier, entrance on rue Auber side of Opéra. Tel. 40 17 33 33. M Opéra. Open 10am–5pm, Mon–Sat. No credit cards.

Directly opposite the Opéra is the **Grand Hôtel** which, when built in 1860–1, was the largest in Europe. Its long frontage stretches along the boulevard des Capucines and also overlooks rue Auber and rue Scribe. When it first opened it offered comfort on a hitherto unknown scale, with all mod cons including 15 bathrooms. The still intact **Salle des Fêtes** is ringed by a double colonnade of Corinthian columns and is lit by a giant stained glass skylight, like a flower with overlapping petals. Skylights of this size and style aren't unusual in French buildings of the period and similar ones can be found nearby in the Galeries Lafayette department store and also in the banking hall of the Societé Générale on boulevard Haussmann.

Opened in 1891, the **Café de la Paix** at 12 boulevard des Capucines is a Parisian landmark and tourist trap. It's named after the rue de la Paix, close by, lined with swish jewellers and fashion houses. But you might think it is worth splashing out on a cup of coffee (and prices are far from cheap) to see the Second Empire frescoes and décor by Charles Garnier, whose Opéra is across the road. Outside is where you brave the car fumes to sit and watch the world and his wife on the busy boulevards. In winter the enormous terrace is glassed-in and heated, so you can do so comfortably. (The café is open from 10am–1.30pm, 2.30pm–midnight, daily.)

The Opéra is the middle of Paris's busiest shopping centre. Only yards behind it are two of the city's largest – and oldest – department stores: the **Galeries Lafayette** and **Au Printemps**, both on boulevard Haussmann.

It's worth dropping in on one to get another perspective on *la Vie Parisienne* – and both have handy restaurants. Both Au Printemps and Galeries are sophisticated temples to consumerism and try very hard to lure you through their portals. They pride themselves on the attractiveness and originality of their window displays. These are especially striking at Christmas, transcending the needs of advertising to provide elaborate audio-visual and kinetic entertainment in themselves. It's not just the kids who have their noses flat against the windows watching electronic toys mime fairy tales or fantastic creatures landing on earth.

The family-owned Galeries is to Paris what Bloomingdales is to New York or Harrods to London. Built 30 years after Printemps, it has to be the most fashion-oriented and prettiest of Parisian stores with its sweeping staircase and elegant dome of stained glass and wrought iron. You name it, they do it – sell theatre tickets, cut keys, change money, stash heavy bags in their basement *consigne*.

The Opening of the Stores

The opening of Au Printemps in 1865 caused a sensation; it was not long before others followed and it became clear that department stores were in Paris to stay.

The reaction of the city's small shopkeepers was a bit like that of the corner shop owner who discovers that Tesco's are setting up next door. They saw their customers deserting them for the new, one-stop fashion — and fashionable — shops which offered a wider range of merchandise at more competitive prices than they could ever do. (Zola, in his novel *Au Bonheur des Dames* or *The Happiness of the Ladies*, vividly describes their despair.)

Au Printemps: 64 boulevard Haussmann. Tel. 42 82 50 00. M Havre-Caumartin St Lazare Opera/RER Auber. Open 9.35am–6.30pm, Mon–Sat.

Galeries Lafayette: 40 boulevard Haussmann. Tel. 42 82 34 56. M Chaussée d'Antin Opéra/RER Auber. Open 9.30am–6.30pm, Mon–Sat.

Back on Haussmann, there's a huge branch of **Monoprix** and, at number 35 (just across from Au Printemps and Galeries Lafayette), there's a more luxurious branch of **Marks & Spencer** than you'll see in London. Anglophiles and expats alike crowd into the ground-floor food department for such delicacies as bacon, cottage cheese, crumpets and muffins. The bacon goes on for yards and you can get an *oeuf et cresson* sandwich for 18f. (Open from 9.30am (10am Mon) – 6.30pm. Closed Sun.)

Shops sneak all around the giant department stores: the Rag Trade decants into the surrounding warren of streets with outlets offering cheap kids', womens' and leather wear.

THE GRANDS BOULEVARDS

The southern edge of the 9e and 10e is marked by a wide *grand boulevard* that changes its name eight times in the space of two *arrondissements*.

There are many boulevards in Paris, but the *grands boulevards* are the ones which, under 11 different names, link in a sweeping semi-circle the city centre from the Madeleine to the place de la République and the Bastille: Capucines, Italiens, Montmartre, Poissonière, Bonne Nouvelle, St Denis, St Martin, Temple, Filles de Calvaire, and Beaumarchais. The smarter end is near the **Opéra,** further east it becomes tawdry. Once a fashionable promenade, their original character has been engulfed by offices, shops, ubiquitous fast food outlets and couscous eateries.

Haussmann (see box) gave the boulevards their utilitarian appearance of today but the *grands boulevards* (which soon became known just as The Boulevard) had in fact originally been laid out under Louis XIV on the site of the city's obsolete ramparts and moats. (*Boulevard* was a military term for rampart terrace.) In the middle of the 18th century they became walks: Parisians would come and sit under the trees to watch the world go by.

While the streets around the Opéra and the Madeleine became fashionably residential, further east the working people's district bustled with street entertainers. From around 1825, when the first street lights replaced gas lighting, the boulevard was *the* meeting place for lively Parisians – and it remained so, on and off, until the First World War.

Throughout the latter half of the 19th century the boulevards were extremely fashionable. Elegant society flocked to the Opéra: the politicos, arty and literati thronged the pavement cafés, mingling with the dandies, their courtesans and dodgy members of the demi-monde, as recorded in Balzac's novels.

The streets were lined with theatres right along to the edges of the place de la République. The *café-concerts*, – or early music halls – were very popular. A few even survived until the 1920s and 1930s which is where stars like Piaf and Chevalier started their careers.

Today, cinemas have overtaken most of the theatres, but the *grands boulevards* are still a main area for entertainment. The **Opéra Comique** recaptures the atmosphere of the boulevard theatre and is found just off the boulevard des Italiens, a street which actually took its name from an older theatre specialising

---

Haussmann the Boulevard-maker

The wide, spacious boulevard is the signature of Baron Haussmann, the administrator from Alsace put in charge by Napoleon III of turning squalid central Paris into a modern metropolis.

Like his empire-building uncle, Napoleon Bonaparte, Napoleon III had massive ambitions for Paris — *and* the money to realise them, since this was a period of economic buoyancy and industrial expansion. He wanted a majestic capital and the humourless single-minded Haussmann, as the faithful executant of his commands, set about urbanising great chunks of the still partly-medieval Paris — the greatest transformation the city has ever known.

From 1873–18, Haussmann demolished, designed, constructed and conquered the insanitary, narrow, tortuous streets, crowded with a growing population. His new thoroughfares made great gashes through the city and solved several problems simultaneously. They were cleaner, eased the flow of traffic, and assisted riot control as they were easy to attack while being difficult to barricade, as insurgents tended to do. The draconian scheme was imposed without thought of preserving historic buildings which had outlived their usefulness, or preserving any ancient individuality — today you have to walk around the Marais to get a glimpse of medieval Paris. Haussmann earned his name as a vandal by destroying two-thirds of the Ile de la Cité, leaving only Notre-Dame and the place Dauphine out of what had been a maze of ancient streets and churches. But when it comes to passing judgement on Haussmann, the jury's still out. You may see him as culpable, a philistine who should have known better. On the other hand, if he had not forced his "Plan" on to Paris, the city might not have had such a major rôle in the modern world.

---

in light Italian opera — of which Rossini was briefly musical director.

TO PARADISE AND BACK

An exploratory amble along the following lines (allow a couple of hours) takes in much of the 9e and some of the

New Athens

Over in the western part of the 9e, north of the rue de Châteaudun, in the deep "V" beyond the junction of rues Notre-Dame-de-Lorette to the west, and rue d'Amsterdam to the east, is a little-known patch which came to be known as "New Athens" in its heyday, in the early to mid-19th century.

At the time it was an epicentre of literary and artistic life, comparable to St Germain, although from its undisturbed and relatively undistinguished appearance today, you'd never guess.

Walk around it and you'll see 19th-century architecture in all its diversity — particularly rues de la Tour-des-Dames, La Bruyère, d'Aumale, Henner and Ballu. In the late 18th century many stars of the theatre lived between rue Blanche and rue des Martyrs and between Ste Trinité and the boulevard Clichy. They were followed by the musicians, writers and many painters who'd meet up in a café in place Pigalle called La Nouvelle Athènes. Chopin, Liszt, Ingres, Millet, Delacroix were amongst them but it's Georges Sand who gets all the attention in the exhibition at the small **Museé de la vie Romantique**. Exhibits include her jewels and drawings, as well as drawings by Delacroix and Ingres. A programme of changing exhibitions highlights creative life in the 19th century.

Musée de la Vie Romantique (Museum of Romantic Life) (formerly Musée Renan-Scheffer) 16 rue Chaptal. Tel. 48 74 95 38. M Pigalle/St Georges. Open 10am–5.40pm, Tue–Sun. Closed Mon. Admission 15f adults; 7.50f students; free under 16s.

Musée Gustave Moreau: 14 rue de la Rochefoucauld. Tel. 48 74 38 50. M Trinité. Open 10am–12.45pm, 2–5pm, Mon, Wed, Sun. Admission 16f adults; 8f 15–18s, OAPs; free under-15s. Half price Sundays. No credit cards. Bookshop. Library (by appointment only).

The house where reclusive symbolist painter Gustave Moreau (1825–1898) lived, painted and taught Matisse and the Fauves, contains 11,000 of his drawings and dreamlike paintings, including *"Salomé"*.

10e in the hinterland of the *grands boulevards*. Starting point is by the Rue Montmartre Métro.

Just past the point where boulevard Haussmann merges into boulevard Montmartre is the **Musée Grévin**, the main Paris waxworks inspired by London's Madame Tussaud's, but nothing like as good. It was founded in 1882 by the caricaturist Grévin and it has been pulling in the crowds ever since.

This museum concentrates on imitations of famous personalities (a newer branch of Grévin in Les Halles recreates Paris of the 1900s) but it's more a total Palace of Fun than just a waxworks – the words over the entrance at 10 boulevard Montmartre say *"cabinet fantastique"*. A conjuring show, a Palais de Mirages, funny mirrors all add to the japes. The Théâtre Grévin is one of the prettiest in Paris – it's where the mine artist Marcel Marceau made his début.

Museé Grévin: 10 boulevard Montmartre. Tel. 47 70 85 05. M Rue Montmartre. Open termtime 1–7pm daily; school holidays 10am–7pm daily. No admissions after 6pm. Admission 46f adults; 32f 6–14s; free under-6s. No credit cards.

Unobtrusively connecting the traffic-swept boulevard Montmartre with rue du Faubourg Montmartre are two pedestrianised 19th-century shopping arcades or *passages* (lots more lie to the south of boulevard Montmartre in the 2e – see that chapter for more details).

Above the **Passage Jouffroy** is the date 1846. It's the place to come for walking sticks, umbrellas, theatrical antiques, secondhand books. There's even an inexpensive hotel – the **Chopin** at number 46 where you're not likely to be kept awake by traffic. Round the double bend in the arcade, at 43–53, is **Cinédoc**, a treasure trove of cinemabilia: books, postcards, stills.

Across the road is the **Passage Verdeau**. **La France Ancienne** at number 26 has a great selection of old postcards, prints and engravings; **Librairie Farfouille** specialises in secondhand books, at number 29; **Photo Verdeau** (numbers 14–16) deals in old cameras. **Verdeau** at number 25 is a superior, inexpensive baked potato restaurant – a very useful lunch stop. It's not open after 3pm or on Sundays.

Nearby is another invaluable address – for gourmands rather than gourmets – the cavernous **Chartier** is a Paris institution. If you're going to remember just one address for a simple, affordable, meal, let it be 7 rue du Faubourg Montmartre. Yes, it's on the tourist trail but it's not touristy. They serve 2000 meals a day – the waiters are friendly but fast, so rehearse what you want to order before they swoop. The restaurant was founded by the brothers Chartier who, in the last years of the 19th century and early part of the 20th, built up a chain of quick service eateries. (Under the same management are **Le Drouot** in the 2e and **Le Commerce** in the 15e, but neither have the character of this one).

While we're talking food, continuing along the rue du Faubourg Montmartre, at number 35 is a wonderful delicatessen called **A La Mère de Famille**. The interior dates from the turn of the century and has original wooden display stands with enamel labels, and fortress-like cash kiosk. It passes the authenticity test by closing for the month of August. Their own label preserves or boxes of *bon-bons* make delicious presents – or treats.

Straight ahead is **rue Cadet** and at number 16, at the back of a Masonic Temple, there is a small museum displaying documents and ceremonial objects connected with the Society. (The Musée de la Franc-Maconnerie – i.e. Freemasonery is open from 2–6pm, Mon–Sat. Admission free. Tel. 45 23 20 92.)

Back at the junction, to the right, along **rue Richer**, is an old Jewish quarter with kosher butchers, shops and synagogues. Next to a synagogue is the mythical **Folies-Bergère**, the oldest of the Paris cabarets and, like all the others, more than a little behind the times. There are still plenty of folk (incredibly) who'll pay over the odds for the tarnished tits-and-tinsel spectacle they provide (every night except Monday in the case of the Folies). Cancan, extravagant plumage, glitzy cabaret routines – the theatrical review at the Folies-Bergère has hardly changed in 120 years, but is still packing 'em in every night. It's a little cheaper than the other cabarets so if you can't resist trying one out this is probably your best bet.

If we now cross the **rue du Faubourg Poissonnière** (so called because it was the old route of fishmongers travelling to the

> ### Pots and Glass in the 10e
>
> The tableware trade settled in this workaday corner of the 10e because it was within shunting distance of the Gare de l'Est, the delivery point for glass arriving from the Vosges where the great glassmaking firms of St Louis and Baccarat started. Porcelain and faïence ware from Nancy and Strasbourg also goes to the Gare de l'Est.

Les Halles market), we move from the 9e into the 10e and continue along the **rue des Petits Ecuries** – jazz fans make a mental note of the **New Morning Club** at numbers 5–7, a venue which attracts the top international names.

Go up rue Martel and you'll be in the **rue de Paradis**, the main street in a neighbourhood of china and glass emporia. Tableware, whether it's glass, china or silver, in every shape and form, as well as gift and decorative items, are to be found at the best prices in Paris in this area. That doesn't necessarily mean *cheap*, but if you scour the outlets well, you can often find reduced prices and sales.

At 30 rue de Paradis, **Baccarat**, one of the most celebrated French crystal houses, have a museum featuring glass items from the early-19th-century to the present day – strictly a look-don't-touch affair.

Musée du Cristal (Baccarat Museum): 30 bis rue de Paradis. Tel. 47 70 64 30. M Château d'Eau. Open 9am–5.30pm, Mon–Fri; 10am–noon, 2–5pm Sat. Closed Mondays. Admission free. Credit (shop only): MC, TC, V.

If by now you're clutching some precious purchases, you may be only too keen to find the nearest Métro – at the eastern end of rue de Paradis turn right into the rue du Faubourg St Denis. The Métro (Château d'Eau) is on rue du Château d'Eau, the next turning on your left.

If you continue down the rue du Faubourg St Denis you'll pass at number 16, **Julien**, a brasserie with a resplendent Art Deco interior that's somehow at odds with the seedy street. Where the rue meets the boulevard St Denis, there's an unexpected, triumphal arch built in the 1670s in honour of Louis XIV's victories. There's another, slightly less fancy,

Railway Stations of the 10e

There's a pair of fine hulks of imposing 19th-century architecture in the shape of two main railway termini in the 10e. To the west of the Canal St Martin is the grand Gare de l'Est, its cast iron structure tucked away behind a massive, stately, stone façade.

The introduction of cast iron in the 19th century had tremendous impact, but many architects thought that to leave the frame uncovered was too undignified — too industrial, in fact. Consequently, they took elaborate steps to hide the use of metal in buildings, especially railway stations.

Within shunting-distance of the Gare de l'Est, in the northwest of the 10e, is the even grander Gare du Nord. Stations were seen as prestigious sites and their grandiose design celebrates the idea of travel, gives it status, importance. (Never mind that behind the glorious façades there's chaos and confusion as the buildings try to adapt to 20th-century demands, outside all is serene and orderly.)

Architect of the Gare du Nord was Hittorf who embellished the place de la Concorde. He added all types of columns to the façade and dotted the station's skyline with nine symbolic statues, dignified women crowned with a small castle, each representing a spirit of one of the cities served by the railway. To ensure the passenger was in no doubt he was at the right place, Hittorf placed several big "Nords" across the front too.

two streets along, on boulevard St Martin. The **Portes St Denis** and **St Martin** replaced a couple of fortified gates which had vanished with the old city wall.

On the other side of the street is a Métro station, Strasbourg St Denis. If you feel up to continuing your explorations, you're very near the Canal St Martin.

AROUND THE CANAL ST MARTIN

The 10e is bisected on its eastern side by the Canal St Martin which can be explored between 1 April and 4 November by catamaran. Failing that, a stroll alongside the calm, tree-lined canal on the cobbled *quais* is an untouristy pleasure. You'll

take in the sweeping, hump-backed iron footbridges that punctuate the gaps between locks, the side alleys, warehouses, workshops and barge-workers' cosy brown cafés. Atmospheric, authentic, there are spots on the northern side which have slipped straight out of 19th-century industrial Paris. The most attractive part though is at the southern end and it's especially seductive between the square St Frederic Le Maître and rue Bichet.

If you're a film buff this will be familiar territory: the canal provided the setting for Marcel Carné's *Quai des Brumes* and, at 102 quai de Jemappes is the now defunct Hôtel du Nord (smothered in scaffolding at the time of writing) which starred in the '30s movie of the same name, with Jean Gabin and Arletty.

Built by Napoleon I in the 19th century to link Paris with the northern French and Belgian waterways, and still a working canal, it curves up to the Bassin de Villette at the place de Stalingrad in the north and vanishes underground beneath boulevard Richard Lenoir in the south, re-emerging south of the Bastille.

Beyond the place de Stalingrad (now in the 19e *arrondissement*) is the Bassin de la Villette dock – a reminder that Paris was once the first port in France, but a quiet spot these days, lined by anglers. At the far end, the run-down rue de Crimée crosses a 19th-century hydraulic bridge – Pont de la Rue de Crimée – operated by canal water.

The movie *Diva* was shot in the dismal and decrepit streets around here. Several years ago the late President Pompidou wanted to fill in the Canal St Martin and build an autoroute over it. Vociferous public dissent stopped that. But it's worth catching this neglected corner while you can, for it's doubtless only a matter of time before the tempting canal frontage beckons more developers.

St Martin Canal: M République/Jaurés. For details of barge services along the canal, tickets and information, contact the following: Canauxrama (Canal St Martin), 13 quai de la Loire. Tel. 46 07 13 13. Paris Canal, 19 rue d'Athènes. Tel. 48 74 75 30.

11E AND 12E:
Bastille to Bois de Vincennes

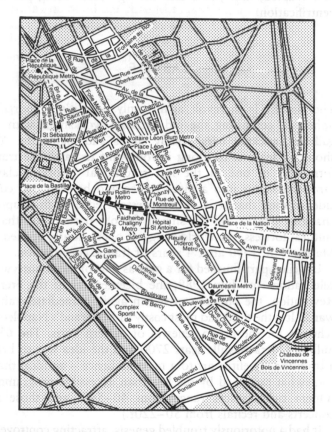

Slipping these two *arrondissements* together makes sense: together they give a long slither of eastern Paris ignored by many guide books. It's not that they're geographically or socially suburban, more that they've always been the shabby underside of the city and not worth showing off. But major projects of considerable national and municipal pride (not to mention cost) are set to put the area on the up and up.

In the north-eastern corner of Paris, in the 19e, the extraordinary new high-tech development at La Villette is almost complete; down in the south of the 12e, the chilly concrete utopia at Bercy is taking shape. But it's on the eastern edge of the Marais, in the 11e, where the French Revolution first erupted, that you'll find the "g" force being put into gentrification.

BASTILLE

The **Bastille** is in revolt again, only now it's a bourgeois upheaval, colonising the old artisinal workshops with art galleries, cocktail bars, trendy shops and nightclubs. You shouldn't leave it too long if you want to catch the transformation of one of the last traditional "working-class" *arrondissements* into a place to see and be seen. No coincidence then that it is on the western edge of this rapidly changing district, on the site of the old Bastille jail, that a cultural fortress, the world's biggest opera house, opened on March 17th, 1990 after 4 years of frantic construction.

Unveiled part-finished for a gala as part of the countrywide celebrations for July 1989, the bicentennial of the French Revolution, the builders moved in again immediately afterwards. It is the third and most costly of Mitterand's Napoleonic schemes for the urban renewal of eastern Paris. The £300 million **Opéra Bastille** seats 2700 and the idea was to bring a traditionally elitist art to a mass audience – an ideal that's somewhat tarnished by the less than accessible programme. (Opera ticket prices range from 40–540f and those for concerts and recitals from 50–220f.)

It had a notoriously troubled genesis, attracting controversy from the moment when an unknown Venezuelan-Canadian, Carlos Ott, won the architectural competition to design the building – the judges apparently believing the anonymous entry to be from the respected American, Richard Meier.

Architecturally, the glass-encased edifice is an unromantic, ungainly, but very practical opera house with an impressive spaciousness about it, from the leg room between the seats to the enormous ceiling. There's an unobstructed view of the stage from every seat, faultless acoustics and no fewer than six moving stages. The latter feature is something that the old Palais Garnier could never claim, but then again it's impossible to imagine a Phantom of the Opéra Bastille.

Musical director of the Bastille is the 36-year old Korean-born pianist and conductor, Myung-Whun Chung, who took up his post in 1989 following the tumultuous dismissal of Daniel Barenboim. Other operatic stars protested with boycotts: "What's the difference between the new Opéra and the *Titanic*?" went Paris's favourite joke at the time, "The *Titanic* had an orchestra".

The Opera House pushes out on to the south side of the vast, untidy, traffic-ridden **place de la Bastille**. Here, you can't miss the giant **July Column** topped by *la Génie de la Bastille* or "Spirit of Liberty" (re-gilded for the bicentennial celebrations). While it marks the site of the infamous old prison, symbolically destroyed during the French Revolution, the Column was actually erected to commemorate those killed in the July uprising of 1830, which replaced the repressive Charles X with another monarch, the hardly more liberal "Citizen King", Louis-Philippe, who was to be the last. When, 14 years later, Louis-Philippe himself was ousted, in a bloody re-run of 1830, the names of a few of the Parisians killed in the 1848 fighting were added to the column.

After the workers' revolution of 1848, France was a republic once again – but not for long. A provisional government abolished slavery in the colonies and the death sentence for political crimes, introduced universal male suffrage, and guaranteed jobs for all workers. However, an unsympathetic view was taken of such radical reforms by the provinces and by those who had benefited from the 1789 revolution and, in May 1848, general elections brought a conservative commission to the head of the Republic.

Out went the jobs for all clause, seen as too costly and too egalitarian. Out again came the desperate workers in revolt, but this time the insurgents got the worst of it. All of eastern Paris was barricaded, with some of the most

The Storming of the Bastille

Events hardly justify the sense of glory that the name "Bastille" evokes. Nothing remains of the massive medieval fortress, protected by eight towers and a wide moat, that was built by Charles V in the late 14th century to guard the eastern entrance to the city.

For its last 400 years the infamous Bastille was used as a prison, rather like the Tower of London, almost exclusively for political opponents of the establishment: Voltaire, the Marquis de Sade, and the mysterious Man in the Iron Mask were all incarcerated here.

It is generally said that it was because of the role it played in political oppression (and prisoners were nearly always held by order of the King) that the Bastille became the first purely symbolic target of the Revolutionaries, at 5.30 in the afternoon of 14th July, 1789. Purely symbolic because the Bastille had already fallen into disuse and was scheduled for demolition. It's likely though that the symbolic interpretation was added later and that the storming had a much more pragmatic objective — to enable the mob to get their hands on the guns and cannon which they knew they'd find there.

After a few hours' siege, sporadic firing and futile nego- tiation, the governor, de Launay, simply flung open the gate and the frenzied mob streamed in. They streamed out again hours later with his head on a pike, and paraded it through the streets. Rivazol, a French political writer of the time, put it rather callously when he recorded that de Launay had lost his head before it was even cut off.

There were only seven prisoners in the dungeons at the time — including an Irishman who thought he was God — all of whom were triumphantly displayed and then promptly locked up again the next day.

Very soon afterwards, the fortress was actually demolished — a job for the experts since the walls were over 2 foot thick. Some of the original stones were carved into miniature facsimiles of the Bastille and sent to the provinces for sale, as a reminder of royal oppression. Other stones tracing the outline were set into the surface of the place de la Bastille.

"The Storming of the Bastille" was believed to epitomise the power of the populace and so the *quatorze juillet* (July 14th) became the national day, celebrated with nationalistic pride throughout France, and reaching a crescendo beneath clouds of *tricouleurs* in the place de la Bastille itself.

bloody confrontations on the rue du Faubourg St Antoine. The rebellion was quelled harshly, and the massacres even continued after combat was over.

Today the locals protest vigorously, but less violently, about the changes to the area. Across the square, in a backstreet at number 5 rue de la Bastille, is an ancient brasserie (one of the oldest in Paris) which doesn't acknowledge change beyond varying its menu – its maroon and gold Belle Époque interior remains reassuringly the same and, some would say, is more consistently impressive than the food. Be that as it may, **Bofinger** has been around long enough to have a very local clientèle, supplemented these days by opera-loving yuppies and media persons, many of whom drift in from **La Mousson** next-door, Bastille's first jazzy cocktail bar and restaurant. On the corner, by the Opéra Bastille, is a cavernous brasserie, expensively decked out in very mock Belle Époque, **La Tour d'Argent**, which is absolutely *not* to be confused with the gastronomic temple of the same name on quai de Tournelle.

Another sign of the yuppie times, the Bastille now has a refurbished marina, complete with thousands of boats and attractive terraced gardens. From the **Bassin d'Arsenal** – actually on the western edge of the 12e – you can take a barge north up to La Villette or to explore the canals.

Running off the square is **rue de la Roquette** where you'll find some of the most trendy places to eat in the Bastille – if you can get in. They're always busy, so do book in advance at places like **brasserie Balthazar** (number 13 – expensive cocktails, reasonable food), the ultra-in **1929** (number 90), the très Bastille part-restaurant part-gallery, **Lance Roquette** (number 53). **Rival** (number 59) is a coffee shop serving American-style brunch at weekends.

Fed up with all this bionic *branché?* Bastille not so long ago was the main hangout for Parisian Hell's Angels and bikers – and they haven't all left it behind. The stragglers can be found at **Café Rotonde** (number 17) and **Phify's** (number 74). If you haven't got your biker's gear with you, perhaps the next best stuff to be seen in would be the designer-surplus/banana republic clothing on sale at the **Comptoir du Désert**. A trendy present-trove is **Fragile** (number 40), while **L'Usine** (number 9) has what the French call *objets et créations*, on sale at lower

Bastille Nightlife

Some very serious revelling goes on in this area: there's a lively night culture of clubs, restaurants, late shows and bars. Parisians might well kick off with aperitifs at 6 and keep up the jollies until grabbing a freshly-baked croissant from the local boulangerie at daybreak.

The rue de Lappe really comes alive after dark. It's the chic high-tech **Cactus Bleu** (number 8) for cocktails or dinner; or **El Barrio**, a sleazy Spanish bar (number 43), for sangria; **La Tchaïa** (number 7) is a trendy Russian eatery, **Tapas Nocturne** (number 17) does what it says and stays open until 2am, or you can get fish and chips *à l'Anglais* at **Hamilton's** (number 51). In this street there's also a reminder of the very Parisian *bals musettes*, traditional music halls of the 1930s, where Piaf, Jean Gabin and Rita Hayworth hung out. You can't miss the large neon sign at the best known dance hall — a dark and glittery grotto called the **Balajo** (number 9), open continuously since the 1930s. You can join in the dancing there or at **Chapelle des Lombards** along the street (number 21), the city's top spot for African and Latin American bands. Both **Le Petit Lappe** (number 20) and **Bastide** (number 10) stay open for late-late-night alcoholic revivers.

Just off rue de Lappe in the passage Louis-Philippe, is the **Café de la Danse**, a café by day which turns into a cabaret theatre after dark. (Call 43 57 05 37 for programme info.)

A loyal yuppie clientèle frequents the ultra-chic cocktail bar at **L'Entrepôt**, 14 rue de Charonne. It has the best décor of any of the Bastille bars and is also the place to be seen, *if* you're still in a fit state, in the early hours. Expat Brits nurture their beer-bellies at **Café de la Plage** (number 59) in the same street.

No shortage of places to eat in the area, but **Au Limonaire**, 88 rue de Charenton, is an inexpensive bar-cum-bistro with live accordion music; **Bastille Corner** (number 47) serves Tex-Mex nosh and margaritas; in the same street is **Magnum and Cie**, a noisy Brit-run wine bar, and next door (number 27) **El Merengue**, a pricey late-opening cocktail bar.

Piaf Museum

Rue de la Roquette stretches all the way east to the Père Lachaise cemetery in the 20e, where Edith Piaf is buried. Piaf pilgrims might like to make a preliminary detour to the small private museum dedicated to her, housed in an old apartment block in the north-eastern part of the 11e (near Ménilmontant Métro) where mementoes of her life — tiny clothes, shoes, letters, posters, photos, paintings — are displayed. Visits are by appointment only and, while you're scanning the exhibits, the caretaker sets the scene by playing her haunting records.

Edith Piaf Museum: 5 rue Créspin-du-Gast. Tel. 43 55 52 72 M *Ménilmontant St Maur*. Open by appointment only, 1–6pm, Mon–Thur. Closed July. Admission: voluntary donation. No credit cards.

prices than the similarly covetable collectibles in nearby rue de Charonne. One of the *quartier's* many contemporary art galleries is **Galerie Franka Bendit** (number 4).

There are many more in the narrow, semi-seedy **rue de Lappe** running off rue de la Roquette and almost bursting at the seams with night clubs, bars and art and with rural courtyards, strewn with leaves leading off it. **Galérie Bastille** (number 20) was the first; **Caïre Currus** (30–32), **Guthurc-Ballin** (47) **Galérie Carlihan** (51) and **Galérie de Lappe** (53) all show new and often unconventional artists' work.

The rue de Lappe keeps up its tradition for nightlife; only the *bals musettes* which used to pull revellers east to mix with the city's low life have all but gone. (See section on **Bastille Nightlife** below.) At number 51 is **Hamilton's Fish and Chips**. Imagine, Paris, the world's gastronomic capital, hadn't got a single fish and chip shop before this one opened in 1987. French *BCBGs* flock to it for generous take-outs (from 35f).

Rue Keller which, going east, also leads off rue de la Roquette, has more art galleries per square foot than anywhere else in the *arrondissement*. Diverse exhibitions are featured in its galleries – **Antoine Candau** (number 17) and **Galérie de la Génie** (number 23) to name but two. Rest your eyes at **Café Moderne** (number 19), a '50s-style bar with billiard tables and leather-jacketed locals.

Both rue Keller and rue de Lappe lead into **rue de Charonne**, the place to come for retro Deco. Names to watch for are **Axis** (number 13), owned by a carpet designer who accessorises the display of her work with glasses, tableware and so on.

One-off pieces abound in **Galerie Hervé Hogan** (number 32) and Galerie Clara Scremini (number 39); **La Dolce Vita** (number 25) and Pirouette have pricey pieces from the '30s and '40s; while **French Line** (number 29) specialises in '50s and '60s–abilia; **Géométrie Variable** (number 26) is good for presents. Andy Warhol's last Parisian show took place at **Lavignes Bastille** (number 27).

The present day plethora of crafts on show in these streets echoes the area's artisinal past. Until the 17th century the district east of the Bastille was outside the city walls. Many craftsmen, to avoid the strict rules set by their guilds, came and settled here in the village then known as St Antoine.

Up until recent years, their descendants lived and worked in the streets between the Faubourg St Antoine and the rue de Charonne, making mostly furniture and other fittings. You can still see some of the workshops if you poke about in the alleyways; elsewhere in the *arrondissement*, other workshops specialised in metalwork.

Today there's nothing at all charming about the **rue du Faubourg St Antoine** in the 12e, with its tacky furniture shops catering to those with more dosh than taste. Slip off the main street through a gap at the Bastille end, and you'll find a secretive creeper-lined courtyard with two interesting galleries. **Michel Vidal** specialises in work by young French artists and established names from the '60s and '70s, while the **Comptoir de la Photograph** has a good selection of works by leading contemporary photographers. A little further along the rue du Faubourg St Antoine, the rue Antoine Vollon leads to one of the Bastille's rare green patches, **square Trousseau**.

Nearby is the **place d'Aligre** where there has been a street market since 1843. Sprawling fruit and vegetable stalls supply many Parisian restaurants; for indefatigable rummagers, there are also junk and antique stalls as well as newish and cheapish clothes – it's a more copeable-with alternative to the fleamarket at Clignancourt and one of the best markets for bargains.

Reached by a continuation of the rue du Faubourg St Antoine, due east of the Opéra Bastille, is a junction you're bound to cross if you're exploring the city by bus or car. This is the **place de La Nation**, eastern Paris's answer to the Arc de Triomphe, with the busy street of cours de Vincennes providing a more mundane equivalent of the Champs-Élysées.

Place de la Nation was originally known as place du Trône, but a name like Throne Square didn't stand a chance of making it through the Revolution. A bronze group in the *place* depicts the Triumph of the Republic. It was here in 1794 that a guillotine was set up and over 1300 heads rolled. Many of the victims' bodies are buried around the corner in the **Cimetière de Picpus** at 35 rue Picpus. The American General La Fayette is buried in a vault near the gate, identified by its US flag. The cemetery is open Tue–Sun, 2pm–6pm (2pm–4pm winter). M Nation/Picpus.

BERCY

Engulfed in nondescript sprawl, the rest of the 12e is less rewarding than the 11e to explore on foot. Better to hop on a bus or take the Métro down to **Bercy** if you want to see for yourself evidence of the vast programme for the urban renewal of eastern Paris.

For some years now, developers have been having a field day, ripping apart docks, depots and 19th-century houses, grabbing prime land for pricey multi-storey offices. In this zone are two of the most gigantic buildings you've ever seen.

Ousted from its palatial quarters at the Louvre, the Ministry of Finance is now installed in the monstrous edifice on the left – the one that looks like a gleaming wall, jumping over three roads and settling down on the embankment at quai de la Rapée. Set on a former industrial site, the **Bercy Office Complex** – designed by the French architect Paul Chemetor

---

Gare de Lyon

Earlier this century, at the first sign of winter, travellers would come here to catch an overnight *wagon lit* to the warmer, more hedonistic south. To set them up for the journey they'd dine in style – which is how the Gare de Lyon came to be endowed with the most opulent station restaurant in Paris, **Le Train Bleu**, now officially declared a national monument. Even if you don't want to splash out and eat there (around £50 for two), the Belle Époque interior is worth seeing and you could always have a drink at the bar.

---

and his Chilean partner Borja Huidobro – is the largest of its kind in Europe.

Another Mitterand-special, and source of great municipal pride, is the behemoth on the right, the **Palais Omnisports**. Essentially an efficient multi-purpose stadium for a Bruce Springsteen concert or perhaps an ice hockey match, it's surrounded by acres of wide concrete steps, and the near-vertical outside is covered by real grass, a weird effect that leaves you wondering how on earth you'd ever push a lawnmower up, or control one coming down for that matter.

This is not an area where you can rely on a map, such is the pace of change. East of here, and at the time of writing probably about to be bulldozed, is a crumbling, ghost-like area, bisected by the rue de Dijon, of tiny empty cobbled street with names like cour Margaux, cour St Émilion, cour St Julien and rue de Pommard – once the centre of the Paris wine trade. This is the site of the proposed new **Cité des Vins**, a hi-tech wine museum due to open in the near future in the former Bercy Wine Market.

To the east, behind the Ministry of Finance, and almost smothered by the office blocks, is the classic 19th-century **Gare de Lyon**, *not* about to be bulldozed.

BOIS DE VINCENNES

The Bois de Vincennes to the south-east of Paris makes a scenic excursion, particularly if the weather's fine. It's no more difficult to get to than its better known counterpart to the west of the city, the Bois de Boulogne (bus 46, Métro to Porte Dorée) and there's plenty to see and do – from boating on its lakes, to taking a look at its **royal castle** and the **zoo**. More than enough to fill a day.

Centuries ago the Bois de Vincennes was, like the Bois de Boulogne, a royal hunting ground. Later, in 1860, Napoleon gave the park to the citizens of Paris and had it landscaped in the style of an English park with lakes, pathways and streams. Its 2458 acres of greenery are not so car-full as the other Bois, but Vincennes still gets crowded, especially at summer weekends.

You could preface your explorations of the Bois by visiting one or two of the local museums – they're often overlooked by tourists.

Right by the main entrance is the **Musée des Arts Africains et Océaniens**, easily spotted by the huge bas relief on the façade paying homage to colonialism. Originally built for the Éxposition Coloniale in 1931, the museum is a masterpiece of Art Deco architecture and interior decoration – the remarkable **salon Paul Reynaud**, named after a former Minister for the Colonies, with its floor of inlaid ebony and ivory door handles, is perhaps the most complete interior of its kind in Paris. There's a superb collection of culture and creatures – masks from New Guinea, Aborigine bark paintings, and, in the basement, one of the best tropical aquariums in Europe, complete with crocodiles in a pit.

Musée des Arts Africains et Océaniens (Museum of African et Oceanic Art): 293 avenue Daumesnil. Tel. 43 43 14 54. M Porte-Dorée. Open 9.45am–noon, 1.30–5.15pm, Mon, Wed, Fri; 12.30–6pm, Sat, Sun. Admission 23f adults; 15f 18–25s, OAPs; free under-18s. Half price Sunday. No credit cards. Bookshop.

A little further south of here, in the avenue de Ste Marie off avenue Daumesnil, is a nostalgic **Museum of Urban Transport**, housed in a former RATP bus depot and run entirely by keen amateurs. Old Parisian omnibuses are a speciality but there are also unlikely exhibits from other countries too – including, for instance, a Glasgow corporation tram.

Musée des Transports Urbains: 60 avenue de Ste Marie, St Manele. Tel. 43 28 37 12. M Porte Dorée. Open Sat, Sun, April 15-Oct. 31, 2.30–6pm. Closed weekdays.

One other little visited, intriguing museum in the area is devoted to bread – the **Musée de Pain**. This is on the south side of the Bois de Vincennes, a stone's throw from Charenton Écoles Métro. It opens on Tuesday and Thursday afternoons and deals with everything to do with its subject – shop fronts, model ones, knives, cartoons, manuscripts.

Musée de Pain: 25 bis rue Victor Hugo, Charenton Le Pont. M Charenton Écoles. Open Tue and Thur pm. Admission free.

Within the Bois, close to the château are 70 fragrant acres of the **Parc Floral**, renowned for seasonal displays of azaleas, roses and herbaceous plants which attract lots of green-fingered admirers. A great spot for kids – the **Astral Theatre** presents children's shows at weekends and public holidays (ring the main office for details on 43 43 92 95)

Château de Vincennes

Surrounded by its moat and drawbridge the fortified château of Vincennes does not look too friendly, reflecting perhaps its less than cheerful past. Henry V of England died of dysentery here in 1422; the Marquis de Sade was imprisoned here; and in 1944 it was the scene of the execution of 26 members of the French Resistance by the Nazis, who also destroyed parts of the castle.

Now restored, at different times parts of it have been used as a royal residence, prison, arsenal and a fashionable porcelain factory — which became so successful it moved to Sèvres. Architecturally, it's a sandwich of buildings of different periods. The story of the castle is told in its museum, housed in the impressive keep (*donjon*). The only medieval keep in greater Paris, it can be seen with a guide along with the Gothic **Ste Chapelle** opposite. Modelled on its namesake on the Ile de la Cité, the chapel has five rose windows and attractive stained glass. Across the courtyard, two 17th-century pavilions face each other: Louis XIV spent his honeymoon in one in 1660. After Versailles was built, however, he went completely off Vincennes and abandoned it.

The Château de Vincennes: open 10–11.15am, 1.30–5.15pm (4.30pm in winter). Closed Tuesday.

and a miniature train chugs round the garden (4f a go). In summer, clowns, puppets and magicians add to the more usual playground thrills. (Métro Château de Vincennes then 112 bus to Parc Floral or a 15-minute walk.)

Further east, encircled by a little ring road, are the **Minimes Lakes** with three islands, a restaurant, boating facilities and lots of ducks to feed. Nearby is the garden of the School of Tropical Agronomy with its temple commemorating the Indo-Chinese killed in the First World War.

Turning south, to the south-eastern corner of the woods, there is an arboretum and the Breuil School of Horticulture (more pretty gardens which may be visited on written application to the director). Alongside is the Vincennes Racecourse and to the west, back near the main entrance, cycling tracks and **Lake Daumesnil** where you may hire a bike or a boat, or dive into yet another café.

The fenced-off part on the southern side of the lake is a

Vincennes Zoo

On the northern side of the lake is the largest of Parisian zoos, stretching for 17 acres, where you can see exotic animals galore in sympathetically authentic-looking surroundings.

There are a couple of cafés and at the centre of the Parc Zoologique is a 235-foot-high artificial rock from the top of which there's a great view over the whole menagerie, the Bois to the east and Paris to the west.

Vincennes Zoo 53 avenue de Saint Maurice. Tel. 43 43 84 95. M Porte Dorée/bus 46. Open 9am–6pm daily in summer, till 5pm in winter. Admission 30f adults; 15f 4–9s; free under-3s; family discounts. No credit cards.

Buddhist Centre with a Tibetan temple containing the largest effigy of a Buddha in Europe, made of glass fibre and covered in gold leaf. (Admission is 15f. Telephone 43 41 54 48 Open every day 9am–4pm.) The temple only accepts visitors making up a group of ten or more, except on the first three Sundays of September, and October, when visitors are welcome to join in the religious celebrations. It is closed in August.

Bois de Vincennes: M Château de Vincennes Port Dorée/bus 46, 56, 86. Open 9.30am–7pm, Mon–Sun Apr–Oct; 9.30am–6pm, Nov–Mar. Admission free. Arboretum. Boating lakes. Boules. Cafés. Riding School. Zoo.

13E, 14E, 15E:
Tapestries and Tower Blocks

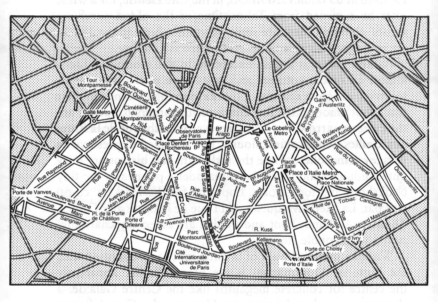

The huge area covered by this trio of *arrondissements* includes the southern outer zones of Paris within the Périphérique, bounded by the Seine on the west as it curves to the south. Of all of them, the most visited by tourists is **Montparnasse** (14e) which has been called the left bank's answer to Montmartre.

13E

Until post-war developers struck a mighty hammer-blow at this part of Paris, the 13e was well known for its strong working-class identity. The roots of its close community went back to the 18th and early-19th centuries when it was the home of the poorest and most rebellious of Parisians. The spread of workshops and small factories in the area hastened the 19th-century sprawl of cottages, bars and cafés in narrow lanes. It was here that the consumption of horse meat became institutionalised: Paris's first horse butcher set up shop in the 13e in 1866.

A flourishing artists' colony attracted painters like Gauguin. He lived at 65 boulevard Arago, in the Cité Fleurie, for a while after he returned from Tahiti. One of the oldest surviving artists' colonies, there are some 30 studios built in the 1880s, set in a tangled garden. Nearest Métro is Glacière.

Pockets like this are an exception in the moribund 13e – almost all of the cottages and lanes have now disappeared, towering concrete apartment blocks looming gloomily in their place. But amongst the few characterful corners to savour are the maze of narrow, one-way streets around the rue de la Butte aux Cailles, which, miraculously, has managed to preserve its villagey atmosphere. Here the little bars and bistros are busy until midnight and a general camaraderie permeates the tiny bookshops and food stores. Look out for the workers' co-op jazz bar, La Merle Moqueur, at 11 rue de la Butte aux Cailles. The rues Alphand, Buot and Michal are especially charming, paved with cobble stones.

Within 5 minutes' walk of la Butte (not to be confused with the Butte of Montmartre) is the place d'Italie, apparently the centre for concrete megaliths like the Centre Galaxie, a shopping complex. Its new neighbour is the Grand Écran, a nine-storey, state-of-the-art audio-visual complex. Nearest Métro is M Place d'Italie.

Part of this *arrondissement* has become the cultural centre for south-east Asians in Paris: in the area bordered by rue de Tolbiac to the north, boulevard Massena to the south and the avenue d'Italie in the west there are over a hundred south-east Asian restaurants. A packed, noisy street market between the avenues de Choisy and d'Ivry would do justice to any commercial quarter of Hong Kong (it's there daily, except Mondays).

It's in the Tolbiac district that President Mitterrand intends to build the city's latest construction wonder: two pairs of glass towers containing the world's biggest library, or **très grande bibliothèque**. For more on this see page 9.

MONTPARNASSE

Three hundred years back there really was a hill here and successive generations of resident poets, painters, writers and musicians did justice to its namesake, Mount Parnassus, seat of Apollo and the Muses.

Modigliani, Utrillo, Max Jacob, Apollinaire, Chagall, Klee, Picasso and his friend, the customs officer Rousseau, all lived and worked in an area which was to peak as an artistic honeypot in the '20s and '30s. Here were the stars of café society – Hemingway, Gertrude Stein, Henry Miller – and their firmament, the boulevard du Montparnasse (the building of which, incidentally, removed the hill). Despite the recent brutal development of Montparnasse, the boulevard itself, and some of its more celebrated cafés, remain intact.

When Montparnasse reached its zenith during the 1920s, Hemingway used to sit in **La Closerie des Lilas** at 171 boulevard Montparnasse. It is still favoured by Parisian writers, artists and journalists, a true brasserie where art posters for local exhibitions cover the walls. It had been a lilac-shaded country tavern during the 17th century. Later it was frequented by luminaries like Verlaine, Mallarmé, Baudelaire and Lenin. At 102, **La Coupole**, which opened in 1927, rapidly became the intellectual centre of the left bank. People came to look and to be seen. Regulars here included Cocteau, Stravinsky, Hemingway, Lawrence Durrell, Samuel Beckett, Gertrude Stein and Henry Miller. Now restored to its original Art Deco interior, including frescoes and flamboyant tiles, its the largest restaurant in Paris, with a largely yuppie clientèle. Nearby are the Dôme, Select and Rotonde – more famous arty pothouses.

Some *arrondissements*, like the 14e, are better for entertainment than others. The **boulevard Montparnasse** comes

Tapestry Art

Tapestries have been made in this *quartier* since the 17th century, when the now subterranean river Bièvre ran brightly, polluted by the carpet-makers' dyes. The name of the 15th-century Flemish dyer Jean Gobelin lives on in a workshop that became a national institution and, more recently, a working museum. You can watch craftsmen painstakingly making tapestries by hand and see textiles of around 17,000 different hues woven on looms little changed since the factory first opened here in 1662.

Manufacture Nationale des Gobelins: 42 avenue des Gobelins. Tel. 48 87 24 14. M Gobelins. Visits are by guided tours only on Tue, Wed and Thurs, 2pm and 3pm. Admission: 22f.

into its own in the evenings, when pavements crowd with cinema-goers, for which the whole area has become a centre. In the day time, it's rather a dreary thoroughfare, the massive, rectangular **Tour Maine-Montparnasse** dominating one end, the side streets that once housed a tangle of artists' studios now interspersed with soulless '60s and '70s apartment blocks.

The rebuilding of the Montparnasse station and the commercial development that followed the Tour has destroyed most of the old streets around the station, and the charm that went with them.

Theatres and *café-theatres* are found throughout the district. The **rue de la Gaîté** is worth a visit. It's narrow, seedy, dotted with fast-food joints and neon-lit sex shops (a sign above one narrow doorway welcomes "heterosexuals, homosexuals, bisexuals and transvestites"), but the **Théâtre Montparnasse** and, almost opposite, the **Théâtre Gaîté-Montparnasse** provide sufficient cultural cachet to remind patrons of the kind of gaiety for which the street was originally famous.

Rearing into the skyline at one end is the extraordinary concrete edifice of the **Amphitheatre**, a residential complex by Ricardo Boffil so stark that it adds poignancy to the crumbling rue de la Gaîté. Choose your bench and neither Tour nor Amphitheatre is visible in the tiny, tree-lined park in **rue du**

Maine, just off the rue de la Gaîté. This little triangle of quiet has a handful of sandwich bars and modest restaurants. **Les Mousquetaires** at 77 avenue du Maine, behind Montparnasse station, a terrific, barn-like café and billiard hall combined, attracts a young crowd.

Since the **Gare Montparnasse** is the point of arrival from Brittany, crêperies and cider-filled Breton cafés proliferate in the side streets around **place Edgar Quintet** (look out for rue d'Odessa, rue du Montparnasse and rue Delambre).

The **Montparnasse Cemetery** in boulevard Edgar Quintet is neither picturesque not pretty but it does have some illustrious inhabitants, including Baudelaire, de Maupassant, Saint-Saëns, the industrialist Citroën, Sartre and de Beauvoir. Ask the attendant at any of the gates for a guide if you're name-spotting. There's the usual French confection of ornate sepulchres, sculpted marble and, in distant corners, rather alarming empty holes in the ground. One Auguste Rubin is commemorated by a bronze cherub whose left buttock glistens after repeated fondling by visitors. Built in 1824, it's the third largest Parisian cemetery.

Montparnasse Cemetery: boulevard Edgar Quinet. M Edgar Quinet. Open 8am–5.30pm, Mon–Fri; 8.30am–5.30pm, Sat; 9am–5.30pm Sun and holidays. Admission free.

Beyond the south-east corner of the cemetery there's the quiet, grassy **square Georges Lamarque.** Good for a picnic this, especially if you're waiting for the nearby **Catacombs** (see box) to open at 2pm. The nearby pedestrianised **rue Daguerre** is nice to shop in – buy speciality bread from **Le Fournil de Pierre,** cheeses, hams, sausages, and fruit from the stalls in the street market.

The 14e *arrondissement* has something rare in Paris: an almost entirely informal park. True, it is manmade (the engineer committed suicide when, upon its opening in the 1870s, the lake sprang a leak and drained dry), but it's endearingly irregular in shape and populated by swans and ducks. The **Parc Montsouris** takes its name from the mice attendant on the granaries that once stood on this spot. Today there are more pigeons than mice, rushing to feed on the crumbs left by picnickers attracted by the shaded grassy slopes, the informal clumps of trees and well-rolled lawns.

The park is divided by the RER line station (Cité Universitaire) with little footbridges across the railway. Due south of the park, across the boulevard Jourdan, lies the residential complex of the **Cité Universitaire**, a series of hostels

The Catacombs

Marooned on what amounts to a traffic island in the place Denfert-Rochereau, the last remains of the city wall's Barrière d'Enfer (Hell's Gate) provides public access to the municipal ossuary, a macabre labyrinth 60 foot underground.

Gentrification of Les Halles had the local populace complaining about the squalid, overcrowded Cimitière des Innocents, Paris's central burial ground, and in 1785 the first of the old graves were exhumed and the bones deposited in what had been Labyrinthine Gallo-Roman quarries.

The tour of the Catacombs begins modestly enough — the gradual descent down gloomily-lit tunnels, past floodlit chambers, carved rock. Then suddenly a sign says *"Arrête! C'est ici l'empire de la mort"*. (Stop! Here is the Empire of Death).

Transporting the 10 centuries-worth of remains from the old cemetery took 15 months. Later on many other city cemeteries were cleared in the same way.

Bones and skulls are stacked in bizarrely neat patterns, lining tunnel walls for over a quarter of a mile. There are an estimated 6 million skeletons, including those of La Fontaine and Madame de Pompadour, but you could never, of course, begin to guess which was which.

Once down here, there's no turning back. The trail runs for about half a mile, ending in a steep climb up a circular staircase (100 steps), to emerge from a discreet doorway in a side street. It's no surprise to learn that the Catacombs were used by the French Resistance. Final climb apart, they are at least cooling on a hot summer's day. Too chilling for some. Turn right to meet the avenue General Leclerc. The Métro station Alésia is 2 minutes' walk to your left.

The Catacombs: place Denfert-Rochereau. Tel. 43 22 47 63. M Denfert-Rochereau. Open 2–4pm Tue–Fri; 9–11am, 2–4pm, Sat & Sun. Closed on public holidays. Admission 15f adults; 8.50f under-18s. Lecture every Wed at 2.45pm, 20f plus entry fee.

To Observe

South of the Luxembourg Gardens the dome of the Observatory swells into the skyline. You must make an appointment to visit the small Observatory museum at 61 avenue de l'Observatoire, but it's enough of a treat simply to gaze at its exterior. Built by Colbert in 1667 for Louis XIV, it is the oldest astronomical institution in Europe. Its four façades are aligned with the four compass points and its southern wall is the determining point for the city's official latitude. Astronomers at the Observatory have achieved several "firsts", including calculations for the true dimensions of the solar system, the mathematical discovery of the planet Neptune and the calculation of the speed of light. You can go into the pretty garden behind the Observatory for free (entered from boulevard Arago), but to arrange an appointment to visit the museum (which is only open on the first Saturday in each month) apply to the Secretariat in writing, enclosing a stamped addressed envelope.

The Observatory: 61 avenue de l'Observatoire. Tel. 43 30 12 10 M Port Royal.

for students of all nationalities. Some of the buildings are themselves of interest. Both the **Swiss Foundation** and the **Franco-Brazilian Building** were designed by le Corbusier.

Actually within the Parc Montsouris is a towering reproduction of the Bey's Palace at Tunis, originally made for the exhibition of 1867. It was long used as an observatory, but on a recent visit we found it decked in scaffolding. By the end of 1991 it will have been transformed into a permanent **Tunisian Cultural Centre**.

The Parc Montsouris is open daily from 7.30am to 1am in the summer, 8am until dusk in the winter. There's a restaurant close to the lake, **Le Jardin de la Paresse**, open from May to October. It caters for kids too, with a children's lunch menu. A neighbouring children's playground has a sandpit and swings.

In the summer you can catch a performance of the **Marionettes de Monstsouris** in the park on Wednesday, Saturday and Sunday at 3pm and 4pm. (Tickets 10f.) Performances are near the lake, close by the park entrance at the eastern end of the avenue Reille.

The little streets west and north-west of the park were once the haunt of impoverished artists. On the whole, modern-day pilgrimages are unrewarding. **Rue des Artistes**, up steep steps from the busy avenue René Coty, is a quiet cul-de-sac where the lofty studio windows breathe a decidedly yuppie ambience. The restaurant where Mata Hari, Lenin and Sartre dined, **Le Pavillon Montsouris,** is expensive. If you're determined to pursue the artistic past, you're better off wandering the pathways of the Parc Montsouris, much painted by Rousseau, or the backstreets around Alésia.

In the triangle formed by the rue d'Alésia, rue Raymond Losserand and the avenue du Maine there's a maze of small streets, narrow passages and studio cottages that have survived the developers' onslaught and are still the stamping ground of many contemporary artists. It's best to take the Métro to Alésia (five stops from Montparnasse), walk up the avenue du Maine and then take the first left into the winding **rue du Moulin Vert,** very much the centre of the contemporary artistic scene.

The **rue d'Alésia** itself and some of its satellite streets are worth exploring if you're on the trail of marked-down designer wear (see too **Shopping,** pp. 231–271). Most outlets are open until 7pm but closed on Sundays.

When Lenin was forced out of Russia before the Revolution, he came to Paris accompanied by fellow revolutionaries including Trotsky. Lenin lived for a time at 4 rue Marie Rose, which is south of the Alésia Métro. It has now been turned into a museum covering his years in Paris. It's open by appointment only.

Lenin's House: 4 rue Marie Rose. Tel. 43 22 82 38. M Alésia.

15E

The 15e is vast and untrendy, sprawling to the south-west and the banks of the Seine in anonymous fashion and attracting little in the way of tourism. George Orwell worked in the lively rue du Commerce and described how it was in the 1920s in *Down and Out in Paris and London.*

Sunday Junk-et

The region around the **Porte de Vanves**, in the south-west corner of the 14e, is good for weekend browsing among market stalls. Head for the avenues Marc Sangnier and Georges Lafenêstre for bric-à-brac, old clothes, book, records, antique furniture, glass, silver ... all kinds of flea-sized or tatty treasures including what *may* be a bargain (if your French is good enough, do try haggling). You won't see too many tourists here. The market on avenue Marc Sangnier is the junkier. After lunch on Sunday it becomes a *marché aux fripes* — that's *real* junk. (M Porte de Vanves.)

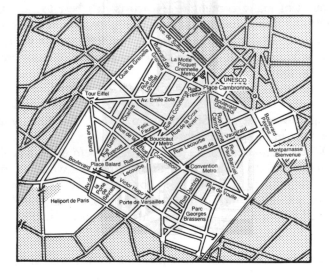

It's best known for the area around the modern Gare Montparnasse, which of course includes the famous tower, the spiky 59-storey **Tour Maine-Montparnasse**. The city's first skyscraper, it opened in 1973 and is still the only tall building for miles. The best thing about the view from the top, goes an old joke, is that you can't see the Tour Montparnasse. On a clear day, views from the 56th-floor observatory extend up to 30 miles. An illuminated frieze runs around the top of the observatory wall and there's a multi-language commentary on landmarks. The 56th floor also has a bar and restaurant and the bold can climb two floors higher to the roof top for an open-air view. Beneath are layer upon layer of offices and a vast Galeries Lafayette on the first floor. A high speed lift whizzes you to the 56th floor in less than 40 seconds. The ride is free if you're going to eat or drink; otherwise admission is 32f. (Open 9.30-11pm daily. M Montparnasse Bienvenue.)

As well as a brash shopping complex round its skirts, a couple of museums stand in the shadow of the Tour. The **Musée de la Poste** is cleverly laid out and extensive in its coverage. Visitors start on the fifth floor, gradually descending through a series of 15 rooms where exhibits (letter boxes, stamps, printing techniques, postmen's uniforms and designs for stamps) automatically light up as you enter the room. This is the story of postal delivery through the ages, with occasional exhibitions of contemporary artists whose work has appeared on French stamps.

Musée de la Poste (**Museum of Postal Service**): 34 boulevard de Vaugirard. Tel. 43 20 15 30. M Montparnasse Bienvenue. Open 10am–5pm, Mon–Sat. Closed holidays. Admission 15f; 10f for those aged 18–25; free under 18s. No credit cards.

A couple of streets away, the studio of Emile Bourdelle, who studied under Rodin, has been transformed into the **Musée Bourdelle** without losing the ambience of a sculptor's home and workplace. There are over 100 sculptures on display, plus scores of sketches and maquettes. Visitors can wander into a pleasantly tangled little garden.

Musée Bourdelle: 16 rue Antoine-Bourdelle. Tel. 45 48 67 27. M Montparnasse Bienvenue/Falguière. Open 10am to 6.40pm daily except Monday. Closed holidays. Admission 18f; 12f students, OAPs; free under-7s. No credit cards. Reference library (researchers only).

Allée des Cygnes

The dull western edge of the 15e faces the Seine, from the Port de Javel to the Eiffel Tower. Out in the middle of the river opposite Port de Grenelle is a slender island, the **Allée des Cygnes**, where it's pleasant to take a midstream walk under the shady chestnuts, which run from end to end. Hard to imagine that it used to be a dump for the bodies of dead horses, an earlier version of today's breaker's yard. The island was laid out in the 1830s with the same ruthless rigidity as the Champs-Élysées. A scaled-down Statue of Liberty stands at the downstream end.

If you have time to spare, it's worth exploring the area between the rue de Vaugirard and the wide band of railway track that terminates at the Gare Montparnasse. Largely residential, there are little pockets of charm, like the cobbled, somewhat dilapidated streets around the **place Falguière**, and the **Parc Georges Brassens** on the rue des Morillons, which stands on the site of the old Vaugirard abbatoir. Recently landscaped, this park has a tiny vineyard and a garden of scents created for the blind.

Just beyond the park, at 52 passage Danzig, a strangely shaped building with a pagoda-style roof accommodates around 200 artists' studios. This is **La Ruche** (the beehive), which owes its existence to the sculptor Boucher. He apparently acquired some of the buildings from the 1900 World Fair in Paris and had them reconstructed here by the same team who erected the Eiffel Tower. It opened as an artists' colony in 1902. Chagall, Soutine, Léger, Zadkine and Modigliani all lived here. Contemporary residents are tolerant of the curious who wander past the vast Art Nouveau gates.

Bird's eye Paris

There are cheaper ways of seeing Paris for sure, but if you're heli-mad then you can go up, up and away. Don't forget your map — and read this book first as there's no commentary owing to the propeller-noise. Prohibitively pricey at around 560f per person for a 20-minute flit round the city, or about 840f per person to take in the city, La Défense and Versailles. If you get really hooked, you can go further afield — and dig further into your pocket accordingly.

A minimum pay-load of four passengers is required and you should telephone in advance.

Hélifrance: based at the Héliport de Paris, 4 avenue de la porte de Sèvres, 75015. Tel. 45 54 95 11. M Balard. Open 9am–5pm daily. Credit: AE, CB, DC, V.

16E AND 17E:
Airs and Graces

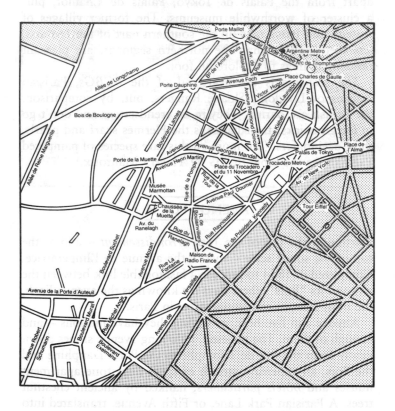

A very large *arrondissement*, the *seizième*, or 16e, is *le beau quartier*, not because it is an outstanding attractive part of Paris, but because it's the *only* area (with the possible exception of the 7e) where people who are particularly vain about their addresses are proud to live. Snooty, exclusive, it's not a neighbourhood that's particularly accessible to outsiders. It stretches from the top of the hill at place Charles de Gaulle down to the southern part of the Bois de Boulogne and the Seine. To its north is the staid, solid, monotonously genteel 17e, which has no major sights and is understandably well off the tourist circuits.

Embedded in these opulent districts are elegant shops, especially in the boulevard Victor Hugo, and some excellent and expensive restaurants, but there's little to draw tourists, apart from the Palais de Tokyo, Palais de Chaillot, plus a cluster of worthwhile museums. The former villages of Auteuil and Passy take up the southern part of the 16e and, less metropolitan than the northern segment, are pleasant residential areas to explore on foot.

The *seizième* is the heartland of the *BCBG*s, Parisian cousins of London's Sloane Rangers, but, by comparison, the British are daring. They're no trendsetters and don't go in for gimmicks; their badge is the Hermès scarf and pearls, the Gucci loafers. (For more on this rare species of pampered Parisian see the bible *BCBG* by Thierry Mantoux.)

AVENUE FOCH

Starting at the top of the 16th *arrondissement* – and at the top of the social scale – there's the avenue de l'Impératrice. Completed in 1854 to provide a fashionable link between the city and its "Bois", these days it's known as the **avenue Foch**, the most famous residential street in Paris.

Anyone can live here, providing they have millions – and enough of them. The majestic, mile-long avenue slopes down gently from the Arc de Triomphe to the Porte Dauphine and the Bois, an expensive stretch of sprawling stone apartment houses and *hôtels particuliers*, flanked by ancient chestnut trees. A Parisian Park Lane, or Fifth Avenue, translated into the stately architectural elegance reserved for the French élite. The buildings present a uniformly staid front which belies their sometimes OTT interiors. Gone are the former glories of the *ancien régime*, when it was the most chic street in France with royalty on parade, yet property prices continue to soar. The long-established remnants of the French aristocracy, discreet and dusty, live alongside the loudest and most louche of the *nouveau riche*.

The Rothschilds own buildings in the avenue Foch, as did Adnan Khashoggi; Christina Onassis used to give gargantuan feasts there; Prince Rainier of Monaco has a house there. Many more of the Great and the Good play dodge-the-paparazzi between the pavement and their front doors.

Apart from breathing in the rarefied airs and graces of the *quartier*, there's little to snare the visitor, with the exception perhaps of two nearby museums which open intermittently. The **Musée Fondation Dapper** at number 50 avenue Victor Hugo (Tel. 45 00 01 50) has exhibitions of African art, chosen by theme or region, but the museum is closed between exhibitions. A specialist library can be visited by appointment. (M Étoile). Admission is 15f adults, 7.50f others. Across the way from the avenue Foch RER station (nearest Métro Porte Dauphine) is the unusual **Musée de la Contrefaçon** at 16 rue de la Faisanderie. An impressive array of forgeries shows how widespread, ancient and lucrative the counterfeiting biz is. Admission is free and it's open Monday and Wednesday afternoons from 2–4.30pm, and Friday morning from 9.30–12 noon. (Tel. 45 01 51 11. Nearest Métro Porte Dauphine.)

THE CHAILLOT QUARTER

If you're feeling museological, you'll want to make frequent stops according to what takes your fancy, along the itinerary suggested here.

You'll pick up a flavour of part of the 16e if you start at Alma Marceau Métro and take the dull avenue du President Wilson to the **Palais de Tokyo**, a massive '30s "brave new world" building erected for the World Exhibition of 1937, which now looks about as modern as a tin can. Now that some of its art collections have been stashed away in the Beaubourg or d'Orsay, part of the building has become the **National Centre of Photography** exhibiting the work of past and present photographers.

In 1993 the Cinémathèque's extensive film library and

collection of stills will be housed under one roof here, along with screening facilities – the Cinemathèque is currently based a few streets further on, in the Palais de Chaillot.

Centre National de la Photographie (National Centre of Photography): Palais de Tokyo West Wing, 13 avenue du Président Wilson. Tel. 47 23 36 53. M Alma Marceau/Iéna. Open 9.45am–5.15pm, Mon, Wed–Sun. Admission 25f adults; 15f 18s–25s, OAPs; 12f 10–25s; free under 10s. No credit cards.

The **Museum of Modern Art of the City of Paris,** housed in the lofty east wing of the Palais de Tokyo, looks a bit like a set from *Batman*. No longer the home of the National Museum of Modern Art, it has been somewhat emasculated by the Beaubourg, yet it's far less crowded and there is, nevertheless, a strong selection of Cubists and Fauvist paintings here. Most dramatic are the huge works by Robert Delaunay that he did in the 1920s and the giant painting, *"La Fée Electricité"* (the Good Fairy Electricity), that wraps round all four walls of a room, by Raoul Dufy. Commissioned by the Paris Electricity Board for the Palace of Light at the 1937 Exhibition, and measuring about 200 feet by 35 feet, it could well be the largest painting in the world.

A large room is given over to Art Deco furniture and *objets* (1920–37), where lavish gilt and lacquered panels by Jean Dunand gobble up several feet of wall. Works by Braque, Utrillo, Modigliani, Dufy, Léger, Chagall and many others are also featured in the collection.

At the well-stocked downstairs bookshop, specialising in 19th- and 20th-century art and architecture, you'll find a good selection in English. Excellent temporary exhibitions are also held at the Museum.

Musée d'Art Moderne de la Ville de Paris (Museum of Modern Art of the City of Paris): Palais de Tokyo West Wing, 11 avenue du Président Wilson. Tel. 47 23 61 27. M Alma Marceau/Iéna. Open 10am–5.30pm, Tue–Thur, Sun; 10am–8.30pm, Wed. Closed Mon, holidays. Admission 35f adults; 20f students; free under-7s, OAPs.

Set in a garden opposite is the Palais Galliera, used for temporary exhibitions of dress through the centuries from the **Musée de la Mode et du Costume** (Tel. 47 20 85 23.) and on the same side, some 300 yards away at 6 place d'Iéna, the **Musée National d'Arts Asiatiques Guimet** (This used to be known just as the Musée Guimet.) Wealthy Lyonnais industrialist and traveller Émile Guimet gave the bulk of his collection of Indian and Far Eastern art to the State in 1884, but since the museum has become a national one it has been considerably augmented to create one of the richest treasure troves of Far Eastern art in the world.

Buddhas are thick on the ground floor where renowned Cambodian Khmer sculpture is displayed, along with Vietnamese, Indonesian and Thai varieties. It was here that Tibetan llamas came when they were expelled from Tibet, to re-establish their tradition, and copy their sacred art and texts. Indian sculpture spanning different centuries from 3rd BC onwards is featured on the first floor, as well as an outstanding collection of Chinese bronzes, dating back as far as 2000 BC. Elsewhere in the museum are Chinese and Japanese religious works, porcelain and lacquer pieces. The museum has a reference library and organises talks and films about the Far East.

Musée National d'Arts Asiatiques or Musée National Guimet: 6 place d'Iéna. Tel. 47 23 61 65. M Iéna/Boissière. Open 9.45am–5.10pm, Mon, Wed–Sun. Admission 23f. **adults; 11f students; half price Sunday. Library.** Photographic archive reference section.

At the end of the avenue du President Wilson is the semicircular, monumental **place du Trocadéro,** with half a dozen big avenues fanning out from it. (The unusual name comes from an obscure fort in Spain, conquered by the French

in 1823.) The patch of green between avenue Georges Mondel and rue du Cdt Schloesing is the **Passy Cemetery** where Débussy, Gabriel Fauré and Monet lie buried.

The view from the terraced cafés in the place du Trocadéro may be tempting, but the prices aren't – better for the health of your pocket to avoid. By way of compensation, the view of western Paris and over to the Eiffel Tower from the huge terrace between the wings of the Palais – if you can pause to enjoy it between attempts to slice you in two by roller skaters of amazing skill – is wonderful.

Like the Palais de Tokyo, the present **Palais de Chaillot** in the place du Trocadéro dates from 1937, having been built to replace an earlier Moorish-style Palais, designed for the 1878 World Exhibition. Two great curved sandstone wings face each other across the terrace, and each contains two large museums. In addition there's the **film library of the Cinémathèque Française** and the **Theatre National de Chaillot** with an auditorium seating over 2000. More than enough to keep you busy for hours and hours.

In the south-west wing are the **Musée de l'Homme** and the **Musée de la Marine.** In the north-east wing are the **Musée des Monuments Français** and the **Musée du Cinéma.**

The history of mankind in the **Musée de l'Homme** is traced through a wide range of extraordinary exhibits. Anthropological and ethnological wonders include Easter Island cult carvings, a mummified Inca from Peru, Maori earrings and African masks, even Descartes' skull. There's a prehistory section too: watch out for the skeleton of the Menton Man in the paleontology section. The collection is outstanding, if not always helpfully explained.

Musical instruments from all over the world are taken from their museum cases and used in public performances on certain Sundays; film shows are also held during the week (2.30pm, Wed–Sun) and there are kids' activities.

Musée de l'Homme (Museum of Mankind): Palais de Chaillot, place du Trocadéro. Tel. 45 53 70 60. M Trocadéro. Open 9.45am–5.15pm, Wed–Mon. Closed Tues. Admission 16f; 8f children, OAPs, students. Free under-4s. Credit: AE, EC, V (Bookshop only). Restaurant, café. Guided tours.

Parc du Trocadéro

Below the Palais, the Parc du Trocadéro slopes down to the quays of the river and the fountains look even more dramatic when floodlit. A grotto on the left as you walk down shelters an **aquarium** (open 10am–5.30pm winter, until 6.30pm summer) full of all the kinds of freshwater fish found in France.

This commanding hill overlooking the Seine has always been a much favoured spot. It was here that Catherine de Medici built a country house in the 1580s, which later on became a convent, and was subsequently destroyed during the Revolution.

Napoleon singled out the hill as the place to build a kind of second Versailles, a magnificent palace for his son, the future King of Rome. As he explained: "I want to create, in a work, a Kremlin a hundred times more beautiful than the one in Moscow. It will be my Imperial City, the Napoleonic city." The aforementioned heir was born on 20th March, 1811 and the foundation stone of the new project laid on 15th August, 1812. The Fall of the Empire put paid to his scheme and for years after that the hill was undeveloped.

The **Navy Museum** portrays all things maritime: scale models, cannons, navigational instruments, figureheads, plus a large collection of salty paintings. Not surprisingly, it's French seafaring achievements that are highlighted. There's an interesting reconstruction of how they shipped the Luxor obelisk to the place de la Concorde and you can see Napoleon's plush barge propelled by 28 oars.

Musée de la Marine (**Navy Museum**): Palais de Chaillot, place du Trocadéro. Tel. 45 53 31 70. M Trocadéro. Open 10am–6pm. Closed Tue. Admission 20f adults; 10f 5–12s, soldiers, sailors; free under-5s. Credit (bookshop only): V. Guided tours. Lectures.

The **Musée des Monuments Français** is far more fascinating than its unpromising name suggests. The idea for this unusual museum sprang from the indefatigable 19th-century architect-restorer Viollet-le-Duc, who needed scale models from which to work. Statues, frescoes, buildings are all meticulous copies – in the course of an hour or two you can travel France, getting a glorious overview of the triumphs, styles and periods of monumental sculpture. There are chunks of sculptured wizardry from cathedrals at Chartres, Amiens and Reims represented, gargoyles from Nantes, carving from Limoges, and whole vaulted ceilings have been copied. For an introduction to French medieval architecture, it couldn't be bettered.

Musée des Monuments Français (Museum of French Monuments): Palais de Chaillot, place du Trocadéro. Tel. 47 27 35 74. M Trocadéro. Open 9.45am–12.30pm, 2–5.15pm, Wed–Mon. Admission 15f adults; 8f under-25s, OAPs; free under-18s. No credit cards.

The **Musée du Cinema** (Henri Langlois), a shrine for *cinéastes*, tracing the early days of film technology from magic lanterns to the present day, is in the basement of this wing. Special attention is paid to Méliès with a reconstruction of his studio. Cinemabilia – including the private collection of Henri Langlois who founded the Cinémathèque, photos, posters, décors, scripts, projectors, costumes galore – is comprehensively displayed. You can even see the garb worn by Rudolph Valentino in *The Sheik*.

It is open only for guided tours (in French) which take about an hour and a half and also feature some clips of movies. If this whets your appetite for more, the adjoining **Cinémathèque Française** has a daily varied programme of distinguished films – consult the box office or press for details. (Box office 47 tel: 04 24 24. See also section on **Cinemas**.)

Musée du Cinema Henri Langlois (Cinema Museum): Palais de Chaillot, place du Trocadéro. Tel. 45 53 74 39. M Trocadéro. Open: guided visits at 10am, 11am, 2pm, 3pm, 4pm, Mon, Wed–Sun. Admission 20f. No credit cards.

PASSY-LA-MUETTE

If by now you've od'd on museums, Trocadéro Métro is your escape route. If not, you're well placed to press on into Passy-La-Muette, to soak up more of the airs and graces of the 16e, and take in some or all of yet more diverse museums. In the 13th century Passy was a humble woodcutter's hamlet.

Health-giving spring waters were found here 500 years later and rich Parisians began to build summer residences.

From place du Trocadéro, head left along rue Franklin, passing stately turn-of-the-century apartment houses. At number 8, the **Musée Clemenceau** is where the Prime Minister who led France to victory in the First World War lived from 1896 until his death in 1929. Everything's as he left it; mementoes recall his career as a journalist and politician. (Tel. 45 20 53 41. to check opening hours; afternoons Tue, Thur, Sat, Sun only.)

Go on from here, down rue de l'Alboni, to the right of the Passy Métro station. Trains rattle out across the Seine by the "double bridge", the **Pont de Bir-Hakeim**. If you walk a little way over the bridge, there's a good view of the Eiffel Tower and the modern **Maison de Radio-France** – the biggest single building in France when it was constructed in 1963. Looking back over your shoulder there's Passy on its steep hillside, as seen through the bedroom windows in Bertolucci's *Last Tango in Paris*, a movie which was filmed around here. Returning to Passy Métro (by escalator), you come to square Charles Dickens, and below the station, the appropriately named **rue des Eaux**, where Parisians used to come to take the ferruginous Passy waters.

From here you could turn on to **rue Raynouard** (really a continuation of rue Franklin) which has had its fair share of famous residents, including Balzac and Rousseau. Benjamin Franklin lived at number 66 from 1775–85. Apart from his politics, he was interested in physics and installed on his house the first lightning-conductor seen in France. The present building is less than a century old and only has TV aerials.

Balzac lived at number 47 from 1840–47 in what was, in those days, a comparatively remote part of town – probably so he wouldn't run into the debt collectors whom he tried to keep at bay by furiously scribbling. He finished his *La Comédie Humaine* series here and a big bas relief in the garden commemorates the fact. He called the house *Ma Cabine* and rented it in the name of Louise Breugnot, his housekeeper, to avoid unwelcome attention.

Overlooking the end of Balzac's garden, numbers 1–5 rue Raynouard is an ugly, modern block of flats built by the

Balzac's House

The entrance is through a gate set into the wall, down a flight of steps through a lugubrious garden. The museum is immensely intimate – it's easy to imagine Balzac churning out the words in his study, fuelled by dizzying doses of black coffee. The coffee pot is there, on its spirit lamp, along with loads of photographs of his women and even more unpaid bills and summonses. There is also a library here – containing nearly as many books written by the prolific Balzac as ones about him.

Maison de Balzac: 47 rue Raynouard. Tel. 42 24 56 38. M Passy/La Muette. Open 10am–5.40pm, Tue–Sun. Admission 15f adults; 10f students, OAPs; free under-7s. No credit cards.

French architect August Perret or King Concrete. Even more surprising is the fact that he lived there himself. He also died there, in 1954.

At the back of Balzac's house there's a "secret door" – a useful escape route for him from the bailiffs – opening out at a lower level on to the rue Berton, a rustic alleyway. With its cobbles, ivy-covered wall and gas lights you could have entered an 18th-century time warp, but for the gendarmes armed with sub-machine guns guarding the Turkish Embassy further down the lane.

Leaving Balzac's house, if you turn right and cross into sleepy rue de l'Annonciation you'll catch another whiff of old Passy. At the junction with place de Passy (the old village square), you join **rue de Passy** (the old village high street), a slick line-up of *BCBG* retail outlets, one of the few shopping areas in the 16e.

If you need an escape route now, La Muette Métro is just to your left; if not, just by the station at the top of avenue Mozart there's a quirky museum that will amuse all myopics. Another of Paris's idiosyncratic private collections, the **Spectacles Museum** in a posh optician's, has 3000 monocles, reading glasses, binoculars, and other focusing devices on display. There's even the obligatory celebrity selection: Sarah Bernhardt's gold monocle, and specs that have belonged to Sophia Loren and the Dalai Lama to name but two pairs.

Wine Museum

Number 5 rue des Eaux marks the original entrance to a quarry. In the cellar there is now a wine museum whose vaulted *caves* connect with the former quarry tunnels (not viewable). The museum has been built under the old Abbey of Passy (demolished 1906) whose monks were dedicated viticulturists, growing vines on local hillsides that must have seen more sun centuries ago than they do now — street names like rue Vineuse and rue des Vignes are the giveaways. Wine-making secrets are revealed using audio-visuals and waxwork models, and there's a *dégustation* (wine tasting).

Wine Museum (Musée du Vin): 5 rue des Eaux. Tel. 45 25 63 26. M Passy. Open 12–6pm, Tue–Sat. Closed holidays. Admission 25f (to include wine tasting).

Musée des Lunettes et Lorgnettes de Jadis: 2 avenue Mozart. M La Muette. Open 9am–1pm, 2pm–7pm, Tue–Sat. Closed Aug. Admission free.

At the main junction follow avenue du Ranelagh and you'll come to the leafy **Jardin du Ranelagh**.

Across from the gardens, the 19th-century mansion of art collector and historian Paul Marmottan, now the **Marmottan Museum**, reveals a spectacular array of impressionist paintings, probably the best in Paris after that of the d'Orsay. In 1932 Marmottan bequeathed both house and collection to the Institut de France. There was already a fine collection of Monets when in 1971 Michel Monet bequeathed 65 of his father's paintings, including many studies of the waterlilies in

Jardin du Ranelagh

If Ranelagh Gardens sounds un-French that's because it was named after the celebrated Chelsea pleasure gardens set up in London by Lord Ranelagh. An earlier, more raucous version has vanished, leaving today's tranquil gardens which were laid out in 1860. It's a pleasant spot to rest your weary feet and there's still a curiously British feel to the gardens with their felty lawns, which you can actually *walk* on (unusual in French parks), unruly chestnut trees, and a bandstand. The donkey rides are popular with local children.

the pond at Giverny. The bequest also included works by some of Monet's friends, including Renoir and Sisley, which are in a specially-built gallery, along with some of Monet's personal effects, like his pallette and letters he wrote from Giverny. There's an unhurried, uncrowded feel to the Marmottan, perfectly suited to looking at misty Monets. Tragically, the painting that gave the impressionist movement its name – *Impression Soleil Levant* – was pinched, along with a fistful of other famous works, in a robbery in 1985.

Apart from all the fine major pieces, there's the Wilderstein collection of European (Flemish mainly) 13th- and 14th-century illuminated manuscripts and miniature paintings. A further series of rooms is devoted to furniture and works of art of the Napoleonic era.

Musée Marmottan: 2 rue Louis-Bouilly. Tel. 42 24 07 02. M La Muette. Open 10am–5.40pm, Tue–Sun. Admission 25f adults; 10f 10–25s, OAPs; free under-18s. No credit cards.

AUTEUIL

In the southernmost segment of the *seizième*, stretching to the city limits, Auteuil is another des res district. It didn't become part of the city of Paris until the second Empire and even managed to keep some of its rural character up until the end of the 19th century, being a Haussmann-free zone. Many of the detached houses still have their private gardens and there's much of interest architecturally, especially if you like Art Nouveau and Art Deco.

The *Eglise d'Auteuil* Métro is a convenient starting point for your meanderings. Off the main *place*, rue d'Auteuil, the narrow old village high street leads to *place* Jean Lorrain where there's a lively Saturday market. Running north off the *place* Lorrain is *rue la Fontaine*, so called because of a spring which fed Auteuil village.

Here you can see buildings by the Art Nouveau architect Hector Guimard who designed so many of the distinctive curly, canopied entrances to the Métro stations. (Most of these have now disappeared but you can see restored ones at Porte d'Auteuil Mirabeau and Eglise d'Auteuil in this vicinity.) At 14 rue la Fontaine is Guimard's best-known apartment block, Castel Beranger (1894–98); at number 25 is the Studio Building de Sauvage (1926) while number 60, begun in 1911, is reckoned to be one of his finest. There are more examples of his work around here: in nearby rue Agar, at 34 rue Boileau, 192 ave de Versailles. At 122 avenue Mozart is the house he built for himself in 1910.

Rue Raffet and rue Jasmin have their moments of Art Deco, the style that dominated architecture in the '30s.

Off rue La Fontaine, to the left, is rue Poissin where gates give on to **Villa Montmorençy**, a very *seizième* (i.e. exclusive) residence. An enclave of Art Deco, the **rue Docteur-Blanche** runs behind it and at numbers 8 and 10 **square du Docteur-Blanche**, right in a cul-de-sac, are two modernist villas designed and built by Le Corbusier in the '20s. Both number 10, which was originally built for modern art collector Raoul La Roche, and its twin are owned by the **Le Corbusier Foundation**, but only the former is generally open to the public. Inside all is rigidly arranged: no surplus furniture or meaningless bric-à-brac to spoil the clean, sharp lines. As well as a library there's a collection of paintings and sculptures by the architect.

Fondation Le Corbusier: 8–10 square du Docteur-Blanche. Tel. 42 28 41 53. M Jasmin. Open 10am–12.30pm, 1.30pm–6pm (5pm Fri), Mon–Fri. Closed Aug. Admission 5f. No credit cards.

Nearby, the **impasse Mallet-Stevens** is a collection of houses in cubist style, built in 1927.

To round off the walk, take rue de l'Assomption all the way back to the massive, concentric **Maison de Radio-France**. The entrance is round by the river at 116 avenue Président Kennedy. Statisticians love this tubular construction – $1/3$ mile in circumference, it houses 3500 personnel in 1000 offices. A museum on the second floor of the building traces the history of radio and TV.

Musée de Radio-France: 116 avenue du Président Kennedy. Tel. 42 30 21 80. M Ranelagh Passy. Open for guided tours only at 10.30, 11.30, 2.30, 3.30, 4.30, Mon–Sat. Admission 10f adults; 5f students. No credit cards.

Jardin d'Acclimation

There's plenty here to spend a great deal of time and francs on, from the moment you board the toy-town train which rumbles gently along to the amusement park. Animals, both the exotic types and more familiar, roam the zoo; there are radio-controlled model boats, a maze, donkey rides, a fine collection of antique dolls at the **Grande Maison des Poupées**, a ginormous helter skelter, boat rides on a "magic river", go-karts, a farmyard, miniature golf, places to eat ... you name it, it's here.

Some of the attractions have separate entrance fees, averaging 5–8f, including the educational **Musée en Herbe** (13f; 6f excluding garden; 18f supervised workshop) where Astérix explains life in a Gaulish village. Lively temporary exhibitions are held, and in the workshop *les enfants* can paint or draw impressions of what they have seen (Tel. 40 67 97 66. for details of events).

Amongst the free attractions is the **Guignol** theatre (Tel. 40 67 90 82; shows from 3pm, Wed, Sat, Sun, every day in school holidays).

Jardin d'Acclimation: Bois de Boulogne. Tel. 40 67 90 80. Short walk along rue des Sablons from M Sablons, or miniature train from outside Mé Porte Maillot. (Train leaves from behind L'Orée du Bois restaurant. Runs every 10 minutes throughout the day, on Wed, Sat, Sun, public holidays, and from 1.30pm during school holidays). Admission: *Train*: 7f adults, 3.50f under-16s. *Jardin d'Acclimation*: 7f adults, 3.50f under-16s. *Combined ticket*: single journey plus admission 10.50f adults, 7f under-16s; return journey plus admission 14f adults, 10.50 under-16s. No credit cards.

THE BOIS DE BOULOGNE

Just west of the 16e, and not strictly part of it all, is the **Bois de Boulogne**, over 2000 acres of former royal hunting forest which Louis XIV opened to the public and Napoleon III presented to the city. To the north lies the Porte Maillot with affluent Neuilly beyond, and to the west is a large loop of the Seine.

During his time in exile in London, Napoleon III had been impressed by the informality of English parks. On his return

Bagatelle

It's not unusual to see people squatting by the flowers here, trying to inhale their scent or even peering at them through magnifying glasses. In spring it's carpeted with tulips, hyacinths and daffodils; in May there's a stunning display of iris in the walled garden, and in June there are roses and water lilies. One enclosed garden within the Bagatelle has a whole wall, some 200 foot long, cloaked in various varieties of clematis.

In the late 18th century the rich were folly-mad. The future Charles X constructed a villa in less than 70 days, the result of a bet with his sister-in-law Marie Antoinette – they always tried to outdo each other in extravagance. He won his wager and the **Bagatelle**, as it came to be called (the word means "trifle"), is the resulting folly in the middle of the park, now named after it. It subsequently belonged to English collector Sir Richard Wallace (his treasures, the Wallace Collection, are in London) who was responsible for many of Paris's fountains.

There's also a restaurant tucked away in the garden, and art exhibitions are held in the Orangerie and Trianon.

to Paris, after the Revolution of 1848 (he became Emperor 4 years later), he wanted to keep the Bois as natural-looking as possible, like open countryside. The maze of shady walks, cycling and riding tracks, artificial lakes and waterfalls are reminiscent of London's Hyde Park or Central Park in New York and make it a welcome retreat from the city. Less idyllic are the many roads criss-crossing it and the ubiquitous parked cars.

Maps are helpfully provided at most entrances and there's a bus (244) which goes diagonally through the Bois from Porte Maillot.

Here we give a brief résumé of the delights of the Bois, all of which, with the exception of the restaurants, should be enjoyed by day. The Bois de Boulogne after dark should carry a government warning – entering parts of it can seriously damage your health.

Rent boys crowd around the infamous Porte Dauphine circle and inside the Bois, against a black backdrop of trees, wild transvestite hookers parade along the condom-strewn perimeter, illuminated by car headlights. Only the most confident *travestis* work the main strip – the less convincing bodies lurk in the side roads. Like the rent boys, most come from South America where the Bois is seen as the Mecca of European prostitution.

More innocent pleasures are to be found in the extreme north of the Bois at the Jardin d'Acclimation (see box).

Very near the Jardin d'Acclimation is the **Museum of Popular Arts and Traditions**, which is full of the joys of rural life from the Iron Age to the 20th century. Folk art, culture and skills are well illustrated – there are lots of working models, knobs to turn, buttons to press, but no descriptions in English. Reconstructed interiors include a clairvoyant's room complete with crystal ball. Craft techniques are demonstrated.

Musée des Arts et Traditions Populaires (Museum of Popular Arts and Traditions): 6 avenue du Mahatma Gandhi. Tel. 40 67 90 00. M Sablons/Porte Maillot. Open 9.45am–5.15pm, Mon, Wed–Sun. Admission 15f adults; 9f 18–25s, OAPs; free under–18s. No credit cards.

Enclosed within the Bois is the magnificent **Bagatelle**, a garden famous for its flora, where no cars are allowed (see box).

Entrance: Route de Sèvres at Neuilly or off Allée de Longchamp. Bus 244 or Pont de Neuilly. Admission 5f. Open 8.30am–7.30pm, daily.

East of the Parc de Bagatelle, across the Allée Longchamp in the centre of the Bois and beyond two small lakes, is another mini-park, the **Pré Catelan**. There's a copper beech here whose branches span almost 600 square yards, which must make it the largest tree in Paris. In 1953 the so-called **Shakespeare Garden** was planted with as many of the trees, flowers and plants mentioned in the Bard's works as possible. There are guided tours at 11am, 3pm and 4.30pm. (Route de la Grande Cascade. Bus 244 or M Porte Dauphine.)

Elsewhere in the Bois, you can go roller skating or jogging, hire a bike from the northernmost point of the lake (one of the most pleasant ways to make your way around – there are 59 miles of roads and paths in the park), go

---

The Paris Experience
The story of Paris is told in the capital's latest attraction, **Paristoric** in the 17e — an audio-visual tour through the history and treasures of Paris. The 40-minute show, available in seven languages, uses 27 projectors to flash thousands of images on to the panoramic screen. Open 365 days a year, from 9am–6pm, Paristoric is at Espace Hebertot, 78 boulevard des Batignolles. Tel. 42 93 93 46. M Rome.

---

boating on Lac Inférieur, perhaps row over to one of the central islands. The south-west corner is particularly good for walking, and here too is the **Hippodrome de Longchamp** (M Porte d'Auteuil, then shuttle bus on race days) where the Prix de l'Arc de Triomphe is held. It's one of three horse-racing tracks in Paris. The Hippodrome d'Auteuil is at the south-eastern tip of the Bois (M Porte d'Auteuil) and the third is on the Bois de Vincennes. As well as two racecourses, the 16e also has the major tennis and football stadiums – Roland Garros on the edge of the Bois, and Parc des Princes.

17E

You might find yourself deposited in the western – more affluent – half of the 17th *arrondissement* if you catch the Air France bus from Charles de Gaulle airport. It drops passengers at the **Palais de Congrès** on a busy spaghetti junction near the *périphérique* at Porte Maillot. Built in 1974 the Palais itself, a landmark on the Louvre-Champs-Élysées-La Défense axis, provides a good, but charmless, home for concert and conference-goers (seating 4000 in its multi-purpose hall) and is the base of the Paris symphony orchestra. There are also four cinemas, a couple of discos and two circular floors of shops in the complex (know as the **Centre Internationale de Paris** or CIP), along with the massive 1000-room Concorde La Fayette hotel.

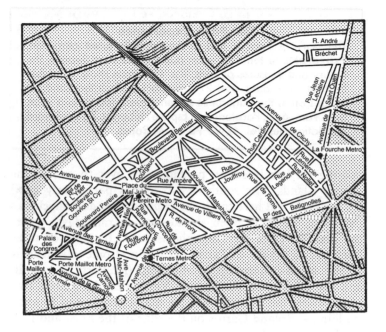

The nearby **Meridien Hotel** in boulevard Gouvion is a well-known jazz venue (see **Jazz**).

More interesting for the visitor is the eastern sector of the 17e. North of the parc Monceau is the great bustling food street market of rue de Lévis (everyday of the week except Monday) leading from the junction of the avenue de Villiers and boulevard de Courcelles. It's a good area too for restaurants – at all prices. A turning on the right into rue Legrande leads to the Sainte Marie church, which sits behind the unexpected, attractive **Square des Batignolles**, really a small park with gravel paths and a duck pond.

Running south from here is the main artery of this villagey *quartier*, the rue des Batignolles.

Another glimmer in the rather colourless 17e (though it's just been enlivened by "Paristoric" – see box) is the one-man **Henner Museum**, just by the Malesherbes Métro – a visit could be combined with a wander in the Monceau park and the Nissim de Camondo and Cernuschi Museums in the neighbouring tip of the 8e. Hundreds of paintings and drawings by the Alsatian artist Jean-Jacques Henner (1829–1905), whom Dégas called "a two-bit Leonardo" but who became very popular in the late 1800s, are featured.

Musée Jean-Jacques Henner: 43 avenue de Villiers. Tel. 47 63 42 73. M Monceau. Open 10am–noon, 2–5pm, Tue–Sun. Admission 12f adults; 7f under-15s, students, OAPs. No credit cards.

18E:
Montmartre, Parisian village

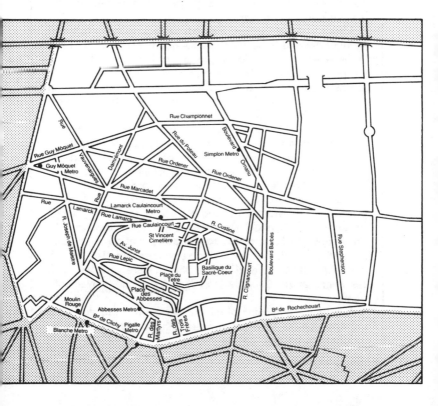

Uniquely in Paris, Montmartre has managed to retain the
style and amenities of a real village. The northernmost of
the city's perimeter hills, the "Butte" or hill of Montmartre
stands 423 feet above sea level, a jumble of narrow streets
and tiny, secretive squares. Elegant 19th-century buildings

Montmartre Artists

Parts of Montmartre are so little changed that you may well recognise views and street corners from famous paintings. A faithful tour of artistic haunts, however, needs some guidance: to make use of the following notes you'll need a detailed street map.

The first major artist to live in Montmartre was **Berlioz**, who in 1833 took up residence at 4 rue du Mont-Cenis. There, he and his English wife entertained many well-known friends, including Liszt, Chopin, Alfred de Vigny, Dumas and Gautier. More artists later followed: rents were cheaper than on the left bank, the light better.

After his arrival in Paris, **Renoir** settled on the outskirts of Montmartre and remained there for nearly 40 years. He lived in the rue Cortot, rue Tourlaque and at the Bateau-Lavoir in the place Émile Goudeau, before settling in greater style at Château des Brouillards. **Utrillo** also lived for some time in the rue Cortot, with his mother Suzanne Valadon, herself a talented artist.

Dégas lived in the rue Victor Masse and died in the boulevard de Clichy. The Italian painter and sculptor **Modigliani** rented a studio in what was one of the wildest parts of Montmartre at 7 place Jean-Baptiste Clement. Stand at the bottom of the rue Norvins, look up towards the Butte and rue St Rustique, and you'll see the Consulat bar looking pretty much as **Manet** painted it. Neo-impressionist painters **Seurat** and **Signac** worked in adjoining studios at 128 boulevard de Clichy. **Braque**, **Picasso** and others shaped the birth of cubism at the Bateau-Lavoir studios. The French poet **Apollinaire** also kept a studio there and his book *Les Peintures du Cubisme* (1913) mapped the movement's significance.

Around the beginning of this century many artists started to quit Montmartre for Montparnasse although its reputation as a bohemian nesting spot remained.

tower over a warren of cottages, alleys and stairways. The hill was relentlessly quarried for what the world knows as Plaster of Paris, producing such a labyrinth of underground passages that 19th-century developers passed it by. The original village clustered around a religious refuge, the walls of a Benedictine abbey, of which all that now remains is the church of St Pierre.

From early medieval times, the windmills of Montmartre ground corn harvested on the rich agricultural plains to the north. By the second half of the 19th century most of its mills had become dance-halls and the area acquired a growing notoriety for raffish and exotic nightlife.

All this is alluring enough, but the added *cachet* of being an artistic haunt, the setting of many a famous painting and many a famous liaison, makes Montmartre highly marketable as a tourist honeypot, and at times it sinks into a pastiche of its former self.

If you must visit Montmartre on a summer's weekend, get up at the crack of dawn, for when tourism peaks in Paris, the streets around the hill's summit are unbearably crowded. It's a steep climb to the top and those who want to conserve energy, should take the 30-second Funiculaire ride from one corner of the place St Pierre (M Anvers), open daily 6am to 12.45am.

It costs 5.20f or a Métro ticket. Another soft option is the diminutive Montmartrobus, which winds a circuitous route between the place Pigalle and the *Mairie* (town hall). For a real tourist trip, pick up *le petit train* from its departure point outside the Moulin Rouge on the place Blanche. For 25f (10f for children under 12) you'll get a 40-minute guided tour of the winding slopes of Montmartre from an open-top, slow-moving carriage. It operates daily between 10am and midnight.

A MONTMARTRE WALK

A much more satisfying, but more time-consuming approach to Montmartre is a meandering route beginning in the compara- tively peaceful countrified **place des Abbesses**. The Abbesses Métro station still has the decorative Art Nouveau entrance designed by Guimard, architect of most of the original Métro stations. A short walk down rue Yvonne le Tac brings you to the **Chapelle des Auxiliatrices du Purgatoire**, where lie the remains of the patron saint of France. St Denis and two prelates were beheaded on La Butte in the year 250. Thus, so one story goes, giving the region its name: mountain of the martyrs. St Denis is purported to have picked up his head and wandered around with it for some time (see **St Denis**, page 523).

Due north of the place des Abbesse, the quiet, modest little **place Émile Goudeau** looks an unlikely place of pilgrimage. A concrete building at number 13 is the modern replacement for the famous **Bateau-Lavoir**, once the home of many an impov- erished artist. Braque, Picasso, Gris, Modigliani and the poet and painter Max Jacob lived here – it was Jacob who coined the name of the old building. Its shape resembled a ship, he said, and its paint-splattered scruffiness suggested a perpetual need of a good wash. Another version of the story has com- pared it in shape to the laundry boats – *les bateaux lavoirs* – on the river. In 1970, just when Le Bateau Lavoir had achieved the status of historical monument, it was burnt down.

The replacement, built to the original design by Charpentier, houses contemporary artists, and is not open to the public. Never mind – the cobbled square overhung by chestnut trees is

Montmartre Markets

The circumference of La Butte is a long and unlikely trek studded with markets. Just north of the Métro station Anvers, the **rue de Steinkerque** provides a good hunting ground for cheap clothes and fabrics. A street market in **rue Paul Albert**, one street due east of Sacré-Coeur, sells similar fare (daily except Monday).

In the area bordered by the boulevards Barbès and de la Chapelle, there are plenty of cheap cafés and restaurants. The district is known as the *Goutte d'Or*, or drop of gold, the name deriving from a medieval vineyard. The character of the place derives from North African immigrants; it's not a place in which to wander comfortably at will, except on Wednesday and Saturday when crowds are drawn to the market in **boulevard de la Chapelle**.

The flea market that runs along the northern end of **rue du Mont Cenis** provides more entertainment than bargains (watch out for pickpockets). An ancient fruit and veg market survives at the southern end of **rue Lepic** – just about the only saving grace in a part of Montmartre where the commercial pursuit of a reputation for relentlessly raunchy nightlife is uninspring.

charming, and the cafés moderately priced and un-touristy. **Chez Camille**, at the bottom of place Émile, is a century-old, laid-back café which has provided a dash of local colour in several movies.

Rue Orchampt or the tiny, steeply stepped rue de la Mire brings you to **rue Lepic**, one of the main roads in the *quartier*, where Montmartre's two remaining windmills rear strangely up against the skyline. **Moulin de la Galette**, on the corner of rues Girardon and Lepic, was once the infamous music hall painted by Renoir. The gardens, where artists dallied with dancing girls, unfortunately are not open to view.

Running almost parallel to the rue Lepic, the more modern, thoroughly bourgeois avenue Junot embraces a secret little part of Montmartre, uncrowded except for the occasional clutch of people on the trail of fast-talking guides. A small side gate leads from the southern end of avenue Junot into a tranquil public garden, complete with a boules station, fountain and a fine statue of a martyr carrying his own head.

Tumbling lilac, low-hung tiled roofs with little dormer

Montmartre's Vineyard

Covering a very small part of the last rise of Montmartre's hill is Paris' sole surviving commercial vineyard, the Vigne de Montmartre. It produces a rather thin white wine, whose diuretic qualities gave rise to a jolly piece of doggerel: *"C'est du vin de Montmartre. Qui en boit pinte en pisse quarte."* (Drink a pint, piss a quart.) The grape-harvesting festival is a moveable feast, usually held early in October.

Montmartre Vineyard: corner at rue de Saules and rue Saint Vincent. M Lamarck Caulincourt.

---

windows and painted picket fences – this hardly feels like Paris. If you walk through the gardens to the place des Quatres Frères Casadesus and turn right, you'll reach the **allée des Brouillards**. Here you can see what is left of the **château des Brouillards**.

It's all private property around here, but 100 yards up the hill there's a part of historic Montmartre which you can enter. The cabaret bar **Le Lapin Agile** at 22 rue des Saules, (tel. 46 06 85 87, M Lamarck-Caulaincourt) was the haunt of Verlaine, Renoir, et al. Miraculously, its 1860s interior is intact and the atmosphere relatively unsullied by commercial tourism. It's open until 2am and admission is 90f, 70f for students, and includes one drink. Its curious name (the nimble rabbit) comes from the original sign which once swung outside and now rests in the Musée de Montmartre. This shows a laughing rabbit jumping out of a saucepan, bottle of wine in hand. Since the patron's name was Gill, the place was quickly dubbed "lapin à Gill". Say this with your best French accent and it becomes *lapin agile*. Opposite Le Lapin Agile, Utrillo's burial place is to be found in the tiny **Cemetery of St Vincent** (entrance in rue Lucien Gaulard).

If you continue north on the **rue des Saules**, crossing the wide, bustling rue Caulaincourt, and scramble down yet more steps, you'll find the small **Musée d'Art Juif** at number 42. The steep return climb up the hill is justified by some remarkable exhibits that include paintings by Pissarro and Marc Chagall.

Musée d'Art Juif (Museum of Jewish Art): 42 rue des Saules. Open 3–6pm, Sun-Thurs. M Lamarck-Caulaincourt. Admission 15f; 10f students, children.

SACRÉ-COEUR

The basilica of Sacré-Coeur, the massive white edifice that crowns La Butte, is an extraordinary sight, part fairy-tale, part monolith. The vast building took 18 years to complete, and was not consecrated until 1919. Financed initially by private Catholic funds, it soon became a national votive offering. A competition was held to find the winning architect and out of 78 entries the design of one Abadie was chosen.

Architecturally it remains a white elephant, the marriage of Romanesque and Byzantine styles, the cluster of oriental domes attracting derision and scorn. The inside is rather gloomy, but this adds to the beauty of the golden mosaic, the focal point of the interior above the high altar. It's one of the largest in the world, and shows Christ exposing a golden heart to worshippers grouped around him, include the Virgin and Joan of Arc – the church is dedicated to the cult of the Sacred Heart, the vision of Christ literally opening his chest to reveal his heart.

The Dead

Montmartre Cemetery is not the most atmospheric, nor at 25 acres the biggest of Parisian cemeteries, but it's fairly bursting with famous names. The nearest entrance from Métro Blanche is on the avenue Rachel. Ask for a plan at the lodge. Among the most illustrious buried here are Degas, Stendhal, Offenbach, the Russian ballet dancer Nijinsky, Alfred de Vigny, Alphonsine Pléssis (of *La Dame aux Camelias* fame), Zola, Berlioz, the Guitry family, and Adolphe Sax, inventor of saxophones.

Montmartre Cemetery: avenue Rachel. M Blanche/Lamarck-Caulaincourt. Open 8am–5.30pm, Mon–Fri; 8.30am–5.30pm, Sun.

The views from the upper galleries (admission 10f) are spectacular. For a further 12f you can visit the austere crypt, view the tombs of cardinals and watch an audio-visual history of the church.

Basilique du Sacré-Coeur: 35 rue Chevalier-de-la-Barre. Tel. 42 51 17 02. M Abbesses/Lamarck-Caulaincourt. Open April–Sept 9.15am to 1.30pm, 2 to 6.30pm, daily. Oct-Mar 9am to noon, 1 to 5pm, daily.

Emerge blinking from the dark church, and you'll see that the views south over the capital from the place du Parvis-du-Sacré-Coeur are almost as good as those from the dome, especially at night . . . and they're free.

AROUND THE BASILICA

The steps and little streets around Sacré-Coeur attract hordes of visitors and at peak visiting times it's barely possible to move through the throng. Fifty paces due west will bring you to the peace and quiet of the more modest church of **St Pierre de Montmartre**. One of the oldest in the city, the church was built in the 12th century as part of a Benedictine monastery and has all the grace and tranquillity wanting in its more famous neighbour. Much has been sympathetically restored or rebuilt. The fine stained glass dates from the 1950s. The church also has its enigma: two pairs of black marble columns surmounted by Gallo-Roman capitals. One theory identifies these as part of a Roman temple that is supposed to have stood on the Mount of Mercury – *mons mercurri* – from which the name of Montmartre could also be said to derive. In the Revolution the church of St Pierre became the Temple of Reason and was used as a station for a new aerial telegraph link between Paris and Lille. The station remained until the 1850s.

The **place du Tertre** (*tertre* means hillock) is familiar the world over from countless paintings. It was the setting for Puccini's *La Bohème*, the meeting place of Communards and the heart of the Montmartre bohemian café society. Such a glamorous history unfortunately sealed its fate as a tourist target and visual cliché. The bars that line the square are mostly overpriced and unremarkable, and the talent peddled by the licensed pavement artists of equal

---

Montmartre Museum

There are no truly great works of art in this museum, but it has bags of charm. Founded in 1886 by a group of collectors committed to preserving the artistic heritage of Montmartre, the museum occupies an 18th-century manor house, at different times the home of Renoir, Dufy and Utrillo.

You can wander freely among the rooms hung with paintings, portraits, framed letters and photographs of bygone Montmartre. A small room contains the well-worn zinc bar from M. Baillot's café in the rue de l'Abreuvoir, now demolished. There's an irony here, for Utrillo, whose studio still stands in the courtyard of the museum, was one of Baillot's best customers.

Examples of the Clignancourt porcelain made in the 18th century in a local pottery, cartoons by Poulbot, original Lautrec posters and the original sign for the Lapin Agile, memorabilia from the office of the composer Gustave Charpentier ... this is an eclectic assembly, probably irritating to some. Undeniably charming, however, are the peaceful gardens and view over Montmartre's famous vineyard. The Old Montmartre Society holds public lectures and discussions groups here, with a regular open meeting every Saturday at 5.30pm.

Musée de Montmartre: 12 rue Cortot. Tel. 46 06 61 11. M Lamarck-Caulaincourt. Open 12.30–6pm, Tue–Sat; 11am–5.30pm, Sun. Admission 20f; 10f under-18s and students; free under-8s. No credit cards.

mediocrity. Unless you're in Montmartre on a winter's day, when with luck it might have reverted to a quiet village square with uninterrupted views south over Paris, you will miss nothing by turning instead to the highest street in Paris, the cobbled passage, **rue St Rustique**, that runs parallel to the place du Tertre. In the tangled thread of streets where the rues St Rustique, Norvins, Lepic, des Saules and Poulbot meet, you'll find Utrillo's Montmartre little changed.

The tumbled run of buildings in rue Poulbot includes **L'Historial**, a little wax museum which provides an effortless introduction to the history of many of Montmartre's more infamous and famous characters. (Open daily 10am to 6.30pm, admission is 24f.) At one end of rue Poulbot is the quiet, unhurried little **place du Calvaire** with another knock-out view across Paris.

If you descend from the Basilique du Sacré-Coeur via the terraced steps to square Villette around 100 feet below, you'll come to the **Max Fourny Museum of Naive Art**. A changing exhibition of naive paintings is hung in the cool steel pavilion of the Halle St Pierre. The venue is shared by the conservationist **Musée en Herbe**.

Max Fourny Museum of Naive Art and Musée en Herbe: 2 rue Ronsard. Open 10am–6pm, Sun–Fri; 2–6pm, Sat. Admission to Max Fourny: 22f. Admission to Musée en Herbe: 13f adults and children; free if under 3; 11f OAPs, parties, families with 3 children. Open 10am–6pm, Sun–Fri; 2–6pm, Sat.

PIGALLE

The area goes downhill and downmarket as it slips into Pigalle. The boulevard de Clichy and place Blanche are thoroughly seedy. By day it's strangely anomalous to see mums pushing prams, people relaxing on benches or carrying their shopping, against the tawdry neon backdrop of sex shops and porno movie houses. By night the fumes from the parked coaches fill the place Blanche as they decant their occupants into the mythical epicentre of Paris nightlife. You can still watch the cancan at the **Moulin Rouge**, but it's more tired Las Vegas than the verve and nerve chronicled in the 1890s by

Toulouse Lautrec. Across the road, a sign invites punters to view the Pornossimo Ciné Sex. In the Moulin Rouge you pay a minimum of 365f to see bare breasts and tights; from 530f for dinner and dance.

The Moulin Rouge: 82 boulevard de Clichy. Tel. 46 06 00 19. M Blanche. Open 8pm–2am, daily.

East of Pigalle the gaudy boulevard de Clichy changes its name and its character. The scruffy boulevard de Roche-chouart is the 18e's boundary with the 9e. The ribbon of shows and showbizzy places thins out and simple diversions take over – there's a funfair in the middle of the boulevard or you can buy hot chestnuts or high fashion at cut prices. Further east, for the rest of its run in the 18e, the thoroughfare becomes the no less scruffy boulevard de la Chapelle, with the decrepit *quartier Goutte d'Or* to the north of it.

19E & 20E, EASTERN PARIS:
Science, Cemetries, Villages

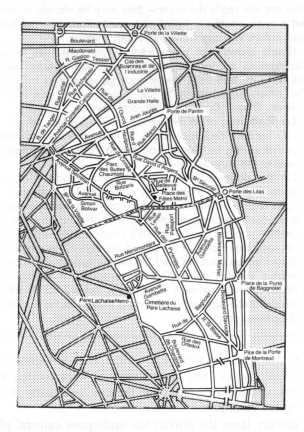

The unfashionable, hard-working area just south of the Porte de la Villette in the north-easternmost corner of Paris, has not in the past been on the main tourist track.

In the early 19th century, the area was densely populated. Rapid industrialisation had come with the construction of the

La Géode

La Géode is a dazzling, spherical, OMNIMAX cinema, over 100 feet high, seating 370. The ultimate state-of-the-art movie show is achieved by projecting films with a special camera and a 70mm horizontally progressing film onto the curved inner walls: the largest cinema screen in the world. Spectators are dunked in images and six-track multidirectional stereo sound, spiked with special effects from lasers and holograms. The films are not really the point – they may be visually stunning but they're essentially trivial and are in French – but given their nature you might find that rarely matters.

Hourly shows take place from 10am–9pm Tues to Sun. Reservations are advisable. (You can buy a ticket which will get you into both the science museum and a Géode film; otherwise admission to the Géode only is 45f, 35f for students. Open 10am–7pm Tuesday–Sunday.

La Géode is at 26 avenue Corentin – Cariou. Tel. 40 05 06 07 for recorded information. M Porte de Pantin is nearer if you're visiting La Géode first, but M Porte de la Villette is closest to the museum.

On the slope just to the west of the Géode is a giant dragon that winds through the playground. Strictly for the kids, its a popular slide made from recycled bits and pieces. The surrounding park sprouts sculptural offerings and nearby is Zenith – you can't miss it – there's a red aeroplane balancing on its roof. Less than half the size of the city's other major pop and rock venue (Bercy in the 12e) the auditorium of this Zenith inflatable stadium still appears cavernous – it seats 6500. **Zenith** is at 211 avenue Jean Jaurès, Tel. 42 45 91 48. M Porte de Pantin. Concerts are once a week. (Phone for details and opening times).

waterways (the Canal de L'Ourcq, Canal St Denis, Canal St Martin) and in 1867 more new jobs were created in the new main slaughter houses for the city and cattle markets built at La Villette.

A century later, the district has undergone cultural plastic surgery as the chosen foster home of a 136-acre (55 hectares) cultural and communication complex dedicated to science, technology and industry. The facelift has swallowed £1/2 billion of public funding to date and redevelopment work is still in progress. The **Parc de la Villette** on the site of the old abattoirs and surrounded by two canal basins, stretches from the Porte de la Villette to the Porte de Pantin and it takes about 20 minutes to get there from central Paris. Some of the area still looks like a building site, but its all destined, sooner rather than later, to be bullied into covered galleries, restaurants bars, swimming pools, shops and other paraphernalia of regimented leisure, as well as apartments.

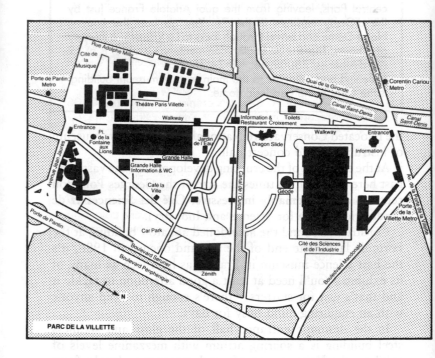

Across the Canal de L'Ourcq, the longest of the former 19th-century cattle market halls, the **Grande Halle** (designed by Baltard, the engineer of the graceful Les Halles buildings which were destroyed when the market was moved) is now used for exhibitions (open Wed–Mon 10am–5.50pm Tel. 42 49 77 22.). Nearby, close to Porte de Pantin Métro is a theatre and cinema and the **Cité de la Musique**, which accomodates

La Villette by Barge

If you want to reach the science museum by barge, Canaux-rama cruises go along the canal Saint Martin and canal de L'Ourcq, leaving from the Port de L'Arsenal near the place de la Bastille, or from the Basin de la Villette, quai de la Loire (weekends only). The journey takes 1 1/2 hours. M Jean-Jaurès. Contact Canauxrama, the Basin de la Villette, 13 quai de la Loire 75019. Tel. 46 07 13 13.

Alternatively, you might travel on the Quiztour barge from central Paris, leaving from the quai Anatole France just by the d'Orsay museum in the 7e. You go past the Louvre, Notre-Dame and travel through locks to La Villette – a journey of 3 hours. There is an English commentary. Quiztour is at 19 rue d'Athènes, 75009. Tel. 48 74 75 30.

Behind and adjacent to the main science museum building, is the Géode, the geodesic dome.

the relocated Conservatoire National de Musique, its museum of instruments and concert hall.

At the epicentre of the erupting development is the vast—and vast here equals three times the size of the Georges Pomidou centre – and undeniably impressive, **Cité des Sciences et de l'Industrie** (Centre for Science and Industry).

Constructed round the abandoned abbatoir building at the Porte de la Villette end of the site and opened in 1986, it's the best science museum in France, as high-tech as many of its exhibits. You'll need at least a good afternoon to tackle it and that's just for starters – there's enough to keep anyone with an enquiring mind busy for days.

In the dramatic entrance hall of the glass and stainless steel building is a soaring atrium with mezzanine levels of exhibits. Satellites, spacecraft and astronauts dangle from the roof, while computer and video displays called **Explora** cover recent and future technology, with audio-visual exhibits and computer terminals within finger-flicking distance to encourage you to join in. Explora has four themes: Earth, Adventure of Life, Matter and Human Labour, Language and Communication.

The futuristic system of walkways and levels within the centre can be baffling – you'll have to watch out if you

nd yourself being deposited from the main
r without having seen unmissable exhibits
a or **Flight Simulator**.

e museum generally are well presented and
planations are given to most. There are bro-
s available in English. On the second level of
the museum you'll find the cafeteria and a **planetarium** (you
can reach it via a transparent lift). Commentaries are in French
with sessions at 10.30am, 12.30pm, 2pm, 3pm, 5pm. Lower
levels house a multi-media library (**Mediathèque**) – a current
events room and a large area for temporary exhibitions with
scientific or industrial themes.

On the ground level of the science museum is a special
section, called the **Inventorium**, a DIY discovery centre for
kids with two exhibitions. One caters for the 3-to 6-year-olds
and has a real stream running through it, and the other is for
the 6 to 12s. Entertainment and information are dished out
in equal doses via push-button games. Inventorium sessions
are every 90 minutes from 11am to 3.30pm Tues, Thurs, Fri;
12.30–5pm Wed, Sat, Sun. By the end of 1992 there'll be
an enlarged facility called **La Cité des Enfants** (the Kingdom
of the Children) encompassing all the experiments currently
featured in the Inventorium.

Centre for Science and Industry La Villette, 30 avenue Corentin-Cariou.
Tel. 40 05 27 72   or for round -the- clock recorded information
Telephone 46 42 13 13. M Porte de la Villette/Corentin-Cariou.
Open 10am–6pm Tues, Thurs, Fri. Wed 12–9pm. Sat, Sun, public
holidays 12–8pm. Admission: Cité day pass: 35f adults; 25f students,
schoolchildren; free under 7s. *Planetarium*: 10.30am, 12.30pm, 2pm,
3.30pm, 5pm. 15f extra. *Géode* open 10am–7pm Tues–Sun 45f adults;
35f concessions. Combined ticket with Cité 70f, 60f concessions
[available from Géode only].

BELLEVILLE-MÉNILMONTANT

The **Buttes Chaumont park** straddles the neighbouring twin
quartiers of the former village of Belleville and its hamlet
Ménilmontant. Moving south from Buttes Chaumont into the
20e, the first main street you come to is the **rue de Belleville**,

Parking Space

A short walk south from La Villette, at the heart of the 19e is one of the least visited and prettiest parks in Paris, the secluded **Parc des Buttes Chaumont**. Bounded by rue Manin and rue Botzaris (where you'll find the main gate) it comes as a complete surprise and breaks the urban monotony.

The **Buttes Chaumont park** has a colourful history. During the Middle Ages, it was the site of the Montfauçon gallows where gruesome public executions were held. It was subsequently used as a slaughterhouse for horses; later, its disused plaster quarries became a refuge for thieves and a stinking rubbish dump. By the time the indefatigable urban planner Haussmann got his hands on the area, after the incorporation of the outlying villages into Paris in the 1860s, it was a menacing desolate place, justifying its name *Monts Chauves* which literally means "bald hills".

At the request of Napoleon III, who admired Hyde Park and English gardens, he sculpted it into 60 curvaceous verdant acres, exploiting the torn terrain to turn bits of it into rock gardens *à l'anglaise*. He created a lake around a craggy central island crowned by a delicate, now-classical temple, which is reached either by a suspension footbridge or by the **Pont des Suicides**.

From the temple top there are good views across the park to Sacré-Coeur and beyond. The park has cascades, crags, a grotto of stalactites, rustic châlets, fish ponds (get a permit from the *gendarmerie*) puppet shows in summer, a children's playground and a couple of restaurants.

Parc des Buttes Chaumont: rue Botzaris, 75019, M. Buttes Chaumont Botzaris. Tel. 42 41 19 19. Open dawn–dusk daily.

The park is a perfect place to loll on the grass or stroll and there's no better way to wind up your perambulations than by dropping into the **Sorbet de Paris** at 34 rue des Alouettes (Tel. 42 09 99 25. open 9am–7pm, closed Sunday) where you can choose from over 40 flavours of sorbet.

which skirts one of the city's most heterogenous immigrant areas. Edith Piaf was born here – on the steps of No. 72 – a memorial plaque marks the spot and she is buried in the local cemetery, Père Lachaise, her grave marked with her real name, Madame Lamboukas. Piaf began her singing career on the pavements of the neighbouring boulevard de Belleville.

This was at a time when it was thought that to come from Belleville made one particularly *Parisian*. Historically a poor, working-class area, it provided asylum initially for not very well off Jews. Other races followed. Arabs and North African Jews in particular, and in more recent years an influx of South-East Asians have added to the multi-ethnic melting pot. Not surprisingly, prodigious injections of culture, customs and cuisine colour the neighbourhood ambience. It's *the* place to come for exotic flavours: Vietnamese and Chinese restaurants dominate the lower end of the rue de Belleville – Belleville's "Chinatown". Only the poshest parts of Paris lack their neighbourhood couscous restaurants, but you won't find a greater concentration of North African eateries anywhere else in Paris.

You can feast cheaply too, with numerous take-aways selling everything from snacks like Sandwich Tunisien (basically tuna on French with olives, salad, peppers, doused in hot sauce) to the stickiest pastries ever pastried. For real French bread, pop over to 150 rue de Ménilmontant to **Ganachaud**, one of the best bakeries in town, selling at least 30 varieties straight out of a wood burning oven. (It's open from 2–8.30pm on Tues, 7.30am–8pm Wed–Sat; 7.30am–1.30pm Sun. M Ménilmontant. Tel. 46 36 13 82). There's a market with a tropical flavour at the **place des Fêtes**, the former village green, just off the rue de Belleville.

Belleville's street life is at its most exhibitionist on a Sunday morning. Ethnic foodstalls, news-stands, posters; Art Deco cinemas showing karate movies, exotic spice shops are the backdrop to the indolent men who spill onto the pavements to loll, saunter, sip coffee, spit, kiss and hiss at each other. The accents you'll hear are those of a dozen Arabic dialects, Yiddish or French peppered with words of both languages.

To catch the down-at-heel delights of Belleville at all, you'll have to hurry. In parts it still has the kind of dilapidated charm that used to be so typical of Paris, but as has happened in other *arrondissements*, it's being rapidly usurped by modernity, conformity and yuppy-dom.

The fraying buildings are being torn down fast to make way for further high-rise, low-income housing of the most mundane, concrete kind. But you can still get a glimpse of the Paris that has all but vanished – just take a walk beginning at either the Belleville or Ménilmontant Métro stations and follow a wide semi-circle to join the other station. A stone's throw from Belleville Métro are rue Dénoyez and rue Ramponeau (where the last Communard on the last barricade held out single-handedly) and a network of small passageways that the developers have so far missed.

South of rue Ramponeau, at 83 rue Couronnes, at the end of the cobbled passage Plantin, is one of the last surviving **villas** (ie little cul-de-sacs of terraced houses) in Belleville. Through the wrought iron gate you can see an overgrown garden and brilliant houses where French film director Francois Truffaut shot a few scenes of *Jules et Jim*. There's more of the same kind of down-at-heel cottages with unkempt gardens over to the right, off the rue de l'Ermitage, at the Villa de l'Ermitage. Nearby, in the rue de la Mare, a door, number 32 takes you to a secret lane of terraced houses.

The area in and around Ménilmontant was known as **Ménilmuche**. Maurice Chevalier started off here – there's a *place* named after him off rue Ménilmontant. With its large paving stones, the serpentine rue des Cascades (again, off rue Ménilmontant) is one of the better preserved parts of the district; the rue des Amandiers is the wide main road of the "village". Alleyways creep in between old, crooked houses, to open into small courtyards or narrow into stairways and lead to roads with names which evoke the area's long-distant history as a place of orchards and market gardens: *pruniers* (plum trees) *mûriers* (blackberry bushes); rue des Champeaux, rue des Grands–Champs.

Parts of the area might remind you a bit Montmartre and, in fact, Belleville is on the second highest hill in Paris after Montmartre, hence the terrific views over the rest of the city.

PÈRE LACHAISE

Of the dozen or so cemeteries which lie within the city limits, the biggest, best-known and best for browsing is Père Lachaise, burial ground of the great, the good and

---

Charonne

For ages Charonne, the old Parisian village nestling just between the Père Lachaise cemetery and boulevard Davout in the 20e escaped the property developer's beady eyes. Then they came, marauding the little roads, squares, cul-de-sacs of attractive two- and three-storey houses with adjoining workshops and gardens. Somehow the former main village road, church, a few pretty passages – and their charm – survived: take a look at the old houses along rue Saint Blaise which leads towards Montreuil, and, in rue de Bagnolet, the small Hermitage pavilion at number 148 dates from 1734 and the house at number 137 is also 18th century.

Further on, at 4 place Saint Blaise, enveloped by the city, is the former country church of Saint Germain de Charonne. Built in the 11th century, reconstructed in the 15th, renovated in the 18th and 19th, it has kept a sturdy 12th-century belfry and, apart from St Pierre in Montmartre, is the only Parisian church to have retained its own graveyard. The sculpted foliage decorating the inside pillars and the bunches of grapes symbolising the old Charonne Vineyards date back to the 15th century. Saint Germain de Charonne (M Porte de Montreuil/Gambetta/Porte de Bagnolet) is open from 9am–12 noon and 2pm, Sun 3–7pm.

---

the glorious. You get the feeling only the unimportant are allowed there if still breathing.

One of the largest open spaces in the city, it is particularly atmospheric if you catch it at its most defoliated and dilapidated on a steely-skied winter's day. It is a place to wonder, wander and wallow – and we don't just mean tourists – Parisians come to this curiously secular cemetery for revivifying Sunday strolls. They follow in a long tradition: "I go out but rarely but when I do take a walk, I go to cheer myself up in Père Lachaise," wrote Balzac in a letter to his sister in 1819.

It was laid out in 1804 and named after Louis XIV's Confessor, Father La Chaise, who had given generously to a Jesuit house of retreat on the site. To advertise the opening of the cemetery, the supposed mortal remains of medieval lovers Abélard and Héloïse were transferred here, as well as the graves of Molière and La Fontaine to attract custom. It worked – this cemetery became so popular that in 1850 it had to be enlarged.

Père Lachaise is circuited on two sides by the avenue Gambetta and the boulevard de Ménilmontant with the main entrance on Ménilmontant. You can get a map which shows the sites of the distinguished corpses from any one of the officially appointed custodians at the gates. You'll definitely need this, because it's a vast place with around a million graves and not as systematically laid out or as easy to follow as it might at first appear.

The necropolis is criss-crossed by a converging network of tree-shaded cobbled paths. The tier upon tier of 19th- and 20th-century tombs and sepulchres are like houses, arranged in numbered diversions. To visit the famous resting places, you have to do a bit of irreverent poking about among the tightly-packed tombstones. Some are rather decrepit, some are well cared for; some are ugly-awful, some downright spooky. Some graves are surprisingly simple: dramatic actress Sarah

Death in the Cemetery

The cemetery has not always been as peaceful as it might. Fierce fighting took place amongst the graves during the last stand of the Paris commune in May 1871. After the battle, at dawn, 147 surviving *Commuard* insurgents were lined up against the *Mur des Fédérés* in the far south-eastern corner of the cemetery and shot. They were buried where they fell dead in a mass grave — a spot visited each year by many political pilgrims.

Bernhardt is commemorated by a small, granite slab with just her name and date inscribed; beneath modest tombstones, La Fontaine lies next to Molière. Above all though, Père Lachaise is an incredible open air museum of 19th-century statuary. Some of the famous sculptors who worked on monuments in Père Lachaise now lie buried there themselves. Gustave Doré did a bust of an actress, Rodin a bust of René Piault, D'Angers a bronze for Balzac.

While you're struggling to stay unlost, you might well stumble across the Hugo family mausoleum, the sentimental memorials to Abélard and Héloïse or the graves of Nijinsky, Cyrano de Bergerac or Isadora Duncan. Buried here too are composers (Rossini, Bizet, Cherubini, Chopin — minus his heart, which is in Warsaw — who is buried next to his friend Bellini); artists (Modigliani, Delacroix, Corot, David, Ingres, Géricault, Seurat) writers and poets (Apollinaire, Balzac, Colette, Paul Eluard, Proust, Gertrude Stein). One of its most recent residents is the actor Yves Montand who died at the end of 1991.

The liveliest spot is the grave of rock star Jim Morrison. It's also one of the easiest to find. In different parts of the cemetery, fans have chalked arrows marked "Jim" on less well known graves to direct would-be pilgrims. Jim's graffiti-strewn tombstone was stolen in 1989 but draped on and around his grave is a perpetual congregation of guitar-strumming, latter-day hippies.

Just as in life, you can tell a lot about a person by the company they keep, so you can guess who's buried where by noting who's hanging around the tomb. Poetry readers prop

---

Montreuil Flea Market

Right out at the Porte de Montreuil is one of the city's best flea markets. It is in full swing from daybreak on the Paris side at rue Dejerine. every weekend and Monday. The likelihood of getting food bargains decreases during the day. As well as a terrific selection of second-hand and discounted clothes stalls sell furniture, tools, gifts, *objects* of all sorts. (M Porte de Montreuil.)

---

themselves up on Oscar Wilde's striking Art Deco/Egyptian memorial (designed by Jacob Epstein) while soulful-looking Piaf-ites cluster around the songstress's simple resting-place hoping to soak up some of her *outre-tombe* vibes.

But the cult centre tomb that attracts more disciples than any other belongs to spiritualist Allan Kardec, leading exponent of the art of communicating with the dead. The graveside inscription summing up Kardec's credo "To live, to die, to be reborn again, continual progression, that is the Law", was all but erased in July 1989 when a bomb exploded on the tomb. The bombing was widely believed to have been carried out by orthodox Christians as a retaliation attack on the revival of macabre occult practices in Paris. When the monument had been rebuilt, Mayor Jacques Chirac had a notice displayed there pointing out that "it is strictly forbidden to treat (Kardec) as a prophet or a founder of some esoteric cult".

While we wouldn't recommend you staying there as long as its residents, do allow enough time to explore – it'll take the best part of a morning or an afternoon just to uncover the main sites. Amongst the people you *won't* find resting there are Dumas (père) Stendhal, Berlioz and Baudelaire – all of whom are tucked up in the Cimetière de Montmartre in the 18e.

Père Lachaise: boulevard de Ménilmontant. M Gambetta/Père Lachaise. Open from 8am–6pm Mon–Fri and 8.30am–6pm Sat; 9am–6pm Sun and public holidays from 16th March–5th November and 8am–5.30pm, November 6th–January 15th. From January 16th–March 15th it's open from 8.30am–5.30pm Mon–Sat. on Sundays and holidays from 9am–5.30pm.

OUT OF TOWN:
Les Environs and
L'Ile de France

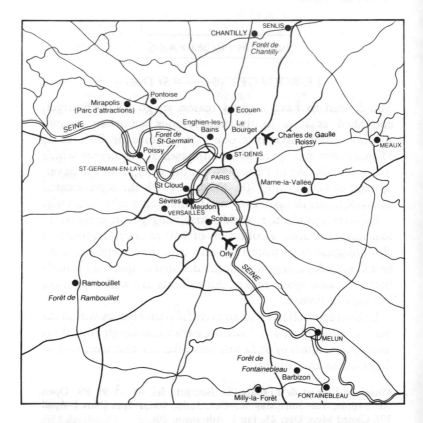

The suburbs aren't usually "must sees" for any visitor to a city, least of all Paris, but you may want to get out of town, get a breath of air, a new perspective or follow up an interest. Here are suggestions for accessible excursions to local sights, half or whole day trips on the fringes of the city, some of which could well be combined. All are less than an hour away from the centre of Paris, by the efficient public transport network – Métro, rapid-transit RER, train or bus. We've given brief suggestions for eating out with details of which credit cards are accepted when available, but we do suggest that you phone first to check opening times.

If you've time to head further than the outskirts, the section after this one details other possible excursions within the Ile de France region.

NORTH FROM PARIS

LE BOURGET (*Seine – St Denis*)

You'd need to have a good reason to go to Le Bourget, enmeshed as it is in the monotonous suburban sprawl. Aviation enthusiasts have one – the **Musée de l'Air et de l'Éspace** (Air and Space Museum) based at the airport which was the main one in Paris between the wars, until the development of Orly in the '50s. Then, in 1974, the sophisticated Roissy/Charles de Gaulle opened to share air traffic with Orly.

Exhibits include the world's first hang-glider, early aeronautical structures, a collection of 140 aircraft, arranged in chronological order from 1919 onwards, the cramped-looking first Concorde, and in the hangar devoted to space is France's first successful space rocket. All exhibits are well explained, but only in French.

Le Bourget itself has had an eventful past. History was made here on 22nd May, 1927 when Charles Lindbergh landed his monoplane, *Spirit of St Louis*, here after the first west-to-east flight across the Atlantic.

Musée de l'Air et de l'Éspace, Le Bourget. Tel. 48 35 99 99. Open 10am–6pm, Tue–Sun (May 1st–Oct. 30th); 10am–5pm (Nov.1–April 30). Closed Mon, Dec. 25, Jan 1. Admission 20f.

How to get to Le Bourget

9m (15km) from Paris.
By train: RER from Gare du Nord to Drancy; from Drancy station

go along avenue Francis-de-Pressensé as far as the main road. Take a left and at the first crossroads, take bus 152 to Le Bourget/Musée de l'Air.

By bus: 350 leaves Gare du Nord, Gare de l'Est, Porte de la Chapelle, or get a 152 from Porte de la Villette.

ÉCOUEN (Val d'Oise)

Admittedly not the easiest place to get to by public transport – although it's only half-an-hour north of Paris. If you're seriously into discovering more about the Renaissance architecture and fine art of the Ile de France, a visit to the château housing the **Musée Nationale de la Renaissance** (**Museum of the Renaissance**) will be very rewarding.

The magnificent château was one of two built during the 16th century for one of the most powerful French dynasties. Constable Anne de Montmorençy was François I's friend and ally (Despite the name, Anne was a man.) The other château was Chantilly.

Inside you'll see some of the original interior decoration, featuring splendid fireplaces, a gold-and-cerulean tiled floor, grand staircases. Perhaps the most impressive work is in the **Galerie de Psyche**, the outstanding series of 16th-century Belgian tapestries depicting the story of David and Bathsheba. There are also examples of the best of the decorative arts of the 16th and early-17th centuries on display from Italy, France and the Netherlands, largely drawn from the Cluny museum in Paris.

Écouen sits sedately on a high point surrounded by moats and steep walls with sweeping views over the Ile de France. Nearby is a forest for a nature walk, a bosky ramble or a picnic.

Musée Nationale de la Renaissance: Écouen. Open 9.45am–12.30pm, 2–5.15pm, Wed–Mon. Closed Tue. Telephone 39 90 04 04 for admission prices, further details.

How to get to Écouen

13m (21km) from Paris.
By train: from Gare du Nord (*banlieue*) – approximately 20 minutes, then bus. Or Métro to St Denis and bus 268C.

Where to Eat

Campanile Écouen: hotel restaurant on RN16. Tel. 39 94 46 00. Open 12–2pm, 7.30–10pm. Menus 71f–94f, children 39f, or allow 100f *à la carte*. Traditional cooking plus house specialities to try.

ENGHIEN-LES-BAINS (Val d'Oise)

Enghien is the nearest spa to Paris, only 8 miles (13 km) north of the city. A visit could be combined with seeing the basilica in the industrial town of St Denis (see below).

Thermal baths were established on Lake Enghien in 1821 and it became a popular 19th-century excursion from Paris: country houses and a casino were built. The latter is still there, along with a racecourse, and there are good boating facilities on the lake around which the town is built. The waters of Enghien, said to be the most sulphurous in France, are used in the treatment of skin ailments and rheumatism.

Tourist information: Office du Tourisme, 2 boulevard Cotte. Tel. 34 12 41 15.

How to get to Enghien-les-Bains

8m (13km) from Paris.
By train: from Gare du Nord. By road: N14 Porte de Clignancourt.

Where to Eat

Auberge Landaise: 32 boulevard d'Ormesson Tel. 34 12 78 36. Closed Sun evening & Wed, Aug. Michelin-recommended menus from 160–250f.
Grand Hotel (restaurant in hotel): 85 rue du Général-de-Gaulle. Tel. 34 12 80 00. Open 12–2pm, 7–9.30pm. Menus 160–200f. View from hotel grounds over the Lake d'Enghien. Pleasant terrace.

ST DENIS (Seine-St Denis)

It's well worth making your way to this heavily industrialised, working-class suburb, a bastion of the Communist Party, to see its famous 12th-century Gothic cathedral, erected around the tomb of St Denis, first bishop of Paris.

If you're coming by car to or from Charles de Gaulle airport you could pull off the motorway, or else it's simple to get to by Métro, as the cathedral is close to the St Denis Basilique station exit.

As the first-ever large-scale Gothic building, begun by Abbot Suger, friend of Louis VII, in the 12th century, St Denis was widely copied and provided a model for the great cathedrals of the Ile de France, Chartres included. The emergence of the pointed arch, slender graceful lines and ribbed vaulting of the new style is seen clearly in the choir; the rose window in the west front was the first of its kind in France.

Traditionally the place where French kings were entombed, it's the burial place of all but three. The royal monuments create a museum of lavish funerary sculpture. Louis XVI and Marie Antoinette share the Bourbon family vault down in the crypt. NB: there's an extra charge for admission to this part of the church (open 10am–6pm daily).

Doubtless the kudos of being buried near the relics of a saint made the cathedral an apt choice for a royal necropolis.

St Denis was named after the French national saint who is also buried here. As the first bishop of Lutetia, St Denis evangelised the Parisii in the 3rd century, and was reputedly arrested after knocking pagan statues off their pedestals. As a punishment, the Roman governor sentenced Denis to be decapitated on the Mount of Martyrs in Montmartre in the year 250. Having been executed, the story goes that Denis picked up his head and kept on walking, head in hands, chanting psalms, finally falling at a spot north of Paris where he was buried by a Christian woman.

According to legend, the **Basilica** dedicated to him stands on the exact spot where his body lies buried.

Basilique de St Denis: place de la Légion d'Honneur St Denis. Tel. 48 20 15 57. Open 10am–5pm, Mon–Sat; noon–5pm, Sun. Closed 1 Nov, 11 Nov, 25 Dec, 1 Jan, 1 Mar. Guided tours at 10.30am, 3pm daily. Admission 22f to include headphones with French, English or German commentary.

A collection of documents relating to the history of the Abbey and the town, plus archaeological exhibits and medieval ceramics, are all stashed away in the **Musée d'Art et d'Histoire**, a short stroll away on rue Gabriel-Péri. Go down rue de la Légion d'Honneur and take the third turning on the right. Housed in a carefully restored former Carmelite convent it has won a European Museum of the Year award, and also has items on the Commune uprising and on the life and work of Communist poet, Paul Éluard, who was born in St Denis in 1895.

If you happen to feel like walking back to Paris, the most interesting way to do it is to follow the Canal St Denis (1½–2 hours to Porte de la Villette) whose towpath takes you through the tired landscape of a down-at-heel neighbourhood. (To reach the canal follow rue de la République from the Hôtel de Ville to the Church, turn left towards the canal bridge.)

Musée d'Art et d'Histoire de La Ville de St Denis: 22 bis rue Gabriel-Péri. Open 10am–5.30pm, every weekday except Tue; 2pm–6.30pm, Sun. No admission charge on Sundays.

How to get to St Denis

6m (9km) from Paris.
By Métro to Saint Basilique. By bus: 153, 154.

Tourist information: Office du Tourisme, 2 rue de la Légion d'Honneur.
Tel. 42 43 33 55.

Where to Eat

Flunch: centre commercial St Denis Basilique, 1 place du Caquet. Tel.
48 09 27 41 or 48 09 27 43. Open 11am–2.30pm, 6.30–9.30pm. Allow
45–50f per person. Self-service restaurant, non-smoker's area and kids'
menu 19f. Credit: V.
Le Gaulois: Hôtel Fimotel Saint Denis, 20 rue Jules Saulnier. Tel. 48
09 48 10. Open 12–3pm, 7–10pm. Set menus 72f, 94f, 125f plus *à
la carte*. Traditional cooking. Credit: AE, V.
Grill St Denis: 59 rue Strasbourg. Tel. 48 27 61 98. Open for lunch and
dinner Mon–Sat (except Sat lunch). Closed Sun; 29 April–8 May. Menus
in ground floor restaurant 140–250f. Michelin awards 2 knives and
forks to the *Grill* for comfortable surroundings. Credit: AE, MC, V.

SOUTH-WEST FROM PARIS

ALBERT KHAN GARDENS (Boulogne-Billancourt, Hauts-de-Seine)

Standing out from the amorphous sprawl of suburbs at
the south-west edge of the city, is this splash of greenery,
named after Albert Khan, a turn-of-the-century adventurer
and diamond merchant. Across from St Cloud park (see
below) on the Paris side of the river, it's a very cosmopolitan
garden – or really a series of gardens – incorporating strict
French landscaping, rolling English parkland and a Japanese
garden with waterlilies and footbridges. The **Maison de la
Nature** (House of Nature) organises activities and exhibitions
relating to the environment for children, and those aged 7–14
are welcomed every Wednesday into the kitchen garden to see
how things grow. Albert Khan built up a collection between
1910–30 of photographs and films ("archives of the planet")
now on display in his home in the middle of the park. They can
be seen by appointment at the Photothèque-Cinémathèque.

How to get to Albert Kahn Gardens

Find them at 1 rue des Abondances (or they can be reached through the Maison de la Nature) in Boulogne-Billancourt. Tel. 46 03 33 56. By Métro: Pont-de-St-Cloud. By bus: 52, 72. Open 15th March–15th November, daily 9.30am–12.30pm and 2–7pm (6pm Oct, Nov). Maison de la Nature: open daily 9am–12.30pm, 2–6pm, admission free. Photothéque-Cinémathèque: 10 rue du Quatre-Septembre. Tel. 46 04 52 80 for details.

MEUDON (Hauts-de-Seine)

Like St Cloud (p. 530), Meudon used to be in the country, but is now firmly a residential town with the big asset of being on the edge of a magnificent forest (with walks and play areas), just south of Sèvres (see below). In Meudon there's a small **Rodin Museum** (an annexe of the one in Paris) and the house, **Villa des Brillants**, where the sculptor spent his last years. (He is actually buried in the garden.) This is at 19 avenue Rodin, off rue de la Belgique and is open 1.30–5pm, Sat and Sun.

High above the town is an **Observatory** and also the terrace of the town's former château, open from 8.30am–5.30pm. There's a very good view of Paris, but it's quite a hike to get to without transport. More accessible is the small historical museum in the 17th-century house of Molière's widow at 11 rue des Pierres, but it's only open on Sundays and Mondays from 2–6pm. It houses souvenirs of architects Mansart, Gabriel, and royal landscape gardener Le Nôtre. Rabelais was once curé here and Wagner wrote his *Flying Dutchman* at Meudon. On the edge of Meudon forest is the **Musée et Jardin de Sculptures de la Fondation Jean Arp** at 21 rue des Châtaigniers, the former home and studio of Jean Arp and Sophie Taeber with examples of their work dotted around the house and garden. It's open 2–6pm. Fri–Sun.

How to get to Meudon

7m (11km) from Paris.
By train: from Montparnasse; RER C5/C7 lines By bus: 36, 169, 179.

Where to Eat

Lapin Sauté: 12 avenue le Corbieller. Tel. 46 26 68 68. Open for lunch and dinner Tue–Sat, and Sun lunch. Closed Aug. Menu 150f. Michelin awards a couple of knives and forks.

ST CLOUD (Hauts-de-Seine)

When you feel like you need a lungful of oxygen, some good views and woody walks, travel 8 miles (13km) out of town to the park of St Cloud. It lies on the slopes of a hill overlooking the river, high above the suburb of Boulogne, near Sèvres (see below).

Along with the Parc de Sceaux, the **Parc de St Cloud** is one of the most pleasant open spaces within easy reach of the city centre. Steep paths drop down to a tiered Grand Cascade, designed by Hardouin Mansart in the 17th century. There are ornamental fountains, patios and the park spreads out to the west.

How to get to Saint Cloud

8m (13km) from Paris.
By Métro: Porte-de-Sèvres; Boulogne-Pont-de-St-Cloud, then walk across the river: or take a train from St Lazare to St Cloud and make your way south. By bus: 52, 72, 144, 175.
(To get to Sèvres porcelain factory from here, follow N187 road to the south east of the park.)
Saint Cloud is just 6km from Malmaison, 16km from St Germain and 10km from Versailles so if you have transport, it's easy to combine a visit to these as well as to Sèvres (below).

SÈVRES (Hauts-de-Seine)

On the edge of the Parc St Cloud, which stretches away to the north and west (see above), is the **Musée National de la Céramique** (National Ceramics Museum). It's easy to get to – a Métro ride to Sèvres, cross a bridge across the Seine to the left bank, and you're at the Porcelaine de Sèvres workshops, which have been based here for over 200 years.

Originally a private business, the porcelain factory was eventually nationalised. Exhibits include not only Sèvres porcelain but early Islamic and Chinese pieces and work from other European centres. There's also a shop and show-room.

Musée National de la Céramique de Sèvres (National Ceramics Museum: (place de la Manufacture): 92310, Sèvres. Tel. 45 34 99 05. M Pont de Sèvres. Open 10am – noon, 1.30–5pm, Mon, Wed-Sun. Admission 15f (special exhibitions 22f) adults; 8f (13f) 18–25s, OAPs; free under-18s. Credit (porcelain showroom only): DC, MC, TC, V.

How to get to Sèvres

7.5m (12km) from Paris.
Sèvres is the next station along the line from Meudon (see above).

Where to Eat

Au Lapin Frit, 36 avenue Gambetta Tel. 45 34 02 18. Open until 9.30pm. Closed Sun pm, Monday. Not the easiest place to find, on the edge of Parc de St Cloud, but worth seeking out if you like rabbit. Menus from 130f.

SCEAUX (Hauts-de-Seine)

Sceaux has a fine park and château, and the Museum of the Ile de France. The original 17th-century pile was rebuilt in 1856, a pastiche of the earlier version which had belonged to Colbert, Louis XIV's financial whizz.

In it is a museum, **Musée de l'Ile de France**, covering the folk culture, history and topography of the region. A pictorial record is presented, evoking the countryside's vanished lovelies. Paintings by artists who worked in the region are featured and there's a fascinating collection of miscellaneous domestic bits and pieces.

The surrounding *grand siècle* **park** is magnificent, with all the Le Nôtre signature details: noble avenues of trees with long perspectives, terraces, sweeping steps, ornamental waterfalls, fountains and lakes. What "Capability" Brown did for 18th-century English landscape, Le Nôtre did in his very different way for the French in the 17th century.

Dahlia time (Sept-Oct) is the only time you're allowed to visit the **Hanover Pavilion**, a building transported here from the boulevard des Italiens in Paris, where it had been built for

Richelieu. It was in this pavilion that Louis XV first met Jeanne Becu, later well known as Madame du Barry. At summer weekends concerts are held in the pretty Hardouin-Mansart (1685) **Orangery** and in the 17th-century **Aurora Pavilion** designed by Claude Perrault. (Details from the museum, or contact the Direction des Musées de France, Palais du Louvre, Cours Visconti, 34 quai du Louvre, Paris 75001.) On the outskirts of the Park is an open-air swimming pool, so if the weather's nice you could take your togs and make a day of it.

Musée de l'Ile de France: Tel. 46 61 06 71. Open 2pm–5.30pm, Mon and Fri; 10am–noon, 2pm–5pm, Wed, Thur, Sat, Sun. Admission 9f adults, 4.50f students, OAPs, free under-16s.

How to get to Sceaux

7m (11km) from Paris.
By train: RER to Parc de Sceaux then a walk of 5–10 minutes to the château gates – take a left, then right into avenue R de Launay from the station. Then turn right into avenue Le Nôtre. By bus: buses that pass include 128, 194 from Porte d'Orléans.

Tourist information: Office du Tourisme, 68 rue Houdan Tel. 46 61 19 03.

WEST OF PARIS

A short ride out on the RER A1 line brings you to **Malmaison**, once the home of Josephine Bonaparte, and **St-Germain-en-Laye,** for centuries a royal retreat, now a museum. You could combine a visit to both in one day.

MALMAISON (Hauts-de-Seine)

Despite its name, Malmaison isn't a bad house; modest, yes, and not particularly distinguished architecturally. The *mal* part suggests a place with a "bad" name and it's possible that there was once a leper colony here – which explains why it was avoided by the aristos until the end of the 18th century.

In 1799 Josephine Bonaparte rebuilt much of the existing château and spent weekends here when Napoleon was Consul. When he later divorced her, after he'd become Emperor, she retreated to Malmaison where she died in 1814.

Napoleon seemed to like it here. "Nowhere, except perhaps on the battlefield," wrote his secretary, Bourienne, "have I seen Bonaparte more happy than in his gardens at Malmaison."

Josephine loved her garden, especially the rose garden, and it manages to eclipse the house in beauty. What you do get from the interior of the château is a good idea of Empire-style decoration, furniture and paintings. It's in the bedroom, in Josephine's apartments, that we can get the best picture of how the house actually was. In 1867, 53 years after Josephine died, the Empress Eugénie had this room restored, using a watercolour as a reference. The bed is the actual one in which Josephine died. There's more Napoleonic memorabilia in the **Bois-Préau museum annexe.**

Château and the Bois Préau Museum: open 10am–12.30pm, 1.30–5.30pm daily. Closed Tue. Guided tours only. No admission charge on Wednesdays.

Admission to museum, inc. Château 22f, 12f Sun & holidays. Half-day coach tours are available from Paris.

How to get to Malmaison

About 9 miles (14.5km) from Paris.

By train: RER A1 line to Reuil-Malmaison and then a walk. By bus: take bus 158A to Malmaison-Château from La Défense – a journey of about 25 mins and then there's a 10 minute walk to the Château.

Where to Eat

Plat d'Étain: 21 rue Marroniers (in Rueil-Malmaison) Tel. 47 51 86 28. Open Tue-Sat, Sun lunch. Closed Aug. Menus 100f (lunch only except Sat) 150f. Traditional French fare. Credit V.

ST-GERMAIN-EN-LAYE (Yvelines)

The town itself, a bourgeois residential suburb 19 miles (30km) from central Paris, with crooked, medieval streets, is easy to get to. Its massive **château** (almost opposite the RER Station) contains not period furnishings or furniture but a museum devoted to prehistoric and medieval times, created by archaeology buff Napoleon III in 1862. Amongst the well-displayed artefacts are the oldest remains found on French soil, the Gallo-Roman collection, and a life-sized replica of the Lascaux cave drawings.

Le Château de Saint Germain was, for 5 centuries, one of the main royal residences, before it was relinquished in 1682 for the greater glories of Versailles. Henri II, Charles IX and Louis XIV were born here. Mary Queen of Scots spent a decade of her childhood here and James II died here, having sought refuge with his cousin Louis XIV – his heart is buried in the parish church.

The splendid terrace gardens facing the Seine were designed by Le Nôtre (yes, him again) in the mid-17th century. You can walk, rent deckchairs, sit under the centuries-old trees admiring the view of the wiggly Seine with the Eiffel Tower on the horizon. It's a scene that inspired impressionist painter Sisley.

The immense forest, the former royal hunting ground, is criss-crossed by many pleasant walks and is a favourite picnic place. The "enlaye" bit of the place name, by the way, is derived from the Roman *lidia* – Latin for "woods".

The composer Claude Debussy was born at St Germain and Alexandre Dumas wrote *The Three Musketeers* and *The Count of Monte Cristo* near here: he built the pseudo-Renaissance château of Monte Cristo in 1846.

Château and Museum: open 9.45am–12 noon, 1.30–5.15pm, daily except Tuesday and public holidays. Admission 20f. Tel. 34 51 53 65.

How to get to St-Germain-en-Laye

19 (30km) from Paris.
By train: RER 1 line to St Germain-en-Laye.

Tourist Information: Office du Tourisme, 38 rue Au Pain. Tel. 34 51 05 12.

Where to Eat

La Forestière: 1 avenue du Président Kennedy. Tel. 39 73 36 60. Actually a hotel with 24 very comfortable rooms and six suites, on the edge of the forest. There's also a smart restaurant, *Cazaudehore* (Tel. 34 51 93 80) Michelin recommended, acclaimed locally, but you'll need to allow 280–350f. Closed Mon and public holidays. Open until 10pm. Hotel rooms are from 600f. Expensive, but it's a lovely spot. Credit: MC, V.

Campanile St-Germain-et-Laye (Hotel restaurant): Route de Mantes, RN13. Tel. 34 51 59 59. Open 12–2pm, 7.30–10pm. Menus 71–94f. Children's menu 39F. Traditional cooking. Credit: V.

Des Coches: 7 rue Coches. Tel. 39 73 66 40. (Ring for opening times) Set menus from 100–22f.

THE ILE DE FRANCE

Culturally, and politically, Paris has always been the power-house of France. Hardly surprising then that the surrounding district known as the Ile de France (see box) with the tips of the neighbouring provinces (Oise, Eure et Loire) became the

Practical Information

General information about the region, including accommodation, camp sites, etc. may be obtained from individual tourist offices whose addresses are given after each excursion suggestion, or else by writing to the following:

ILE DE FRANCE: Comité régional de Tourisme (CRT), 19 rue Barbet-de-Jouy 75007 Paris. Tel. 45 51 09 92.

ESSONNE: Comité départmental de Tourisme (CDT), 4 rue de L'Arche 91000 Corbeil-Essonnes. Tel. 60 89 31 32, ext. 254.

EURE-ET-LOIRE: CDT, 7 place des Epars BP6728000 Chartres. Tel. 37 21 39 99.

HAUTS DE SEINE: CDT, 1 rue Trosy 92140 Clamart. Tel. 46 42 17 95.

OISE: CDT, 1 rue Villiers-de-L'Isle Adam BP 222, 60008 Beauvais Cedex. Tel. 44 45 82 12.

SEINE ET MARNE: CDT, Château Soubiran, avenue H. Barbusse 77190 Dammarie-les-Lys. Tel. 64 37 19 36.

SEINE-SAINT-DENIS: CDT, 2 ave Gabriel-Péri 93100 Montreuil. Tel. 42 87 38 09.

VAL DE-MARNE: CDT, 11 avenue de Nogent, 94130 Vincennes. Tel. 40 08 13 00.

VAL D'OISE: Union départemental des OTSI BP23, 95290, L'Isle-Adam. Tel. 34 69 09 76.

YVELINES: CDT *préfecture* 78010 Versailles, Tel. 39 41 82 00, ext. 2697.

SAMU—EMERGENCY MEDICAL SERVICE: Eure-et-Loire, Oise and Essonne: Tel. 17. Val d'Oise and Yvelines: Tel. 15. Seine-et-Marne: Tel. 64 37 10 11

Remember that to telephone outside Paris from the capital you must dial 16 before the number.

rest and recreation ground of the royals, their acolytes and other movers and shakers.

Rich châteaux, vast oak and beech forests (formerly royal hunting grounds but now owned by the State and enjoyed by all), affluent, attractive old towns and villages, magnificent cathedrals and churches, are all signature details of an area that's often called "a living museum".

These trips are all within a radius of around 100km (about 60 miles) of Paris. They're only a small selection from a vast

The Ile de France — départements

The region covers eight *départements*

Paris	(75)
Seine-et-Marne	(77)
Yvelines	(78)
Essonne	(91)
Hauts-de-Seine	(92)
Seine-St-Denis	(93)
Val-de-Marne	(94)
Val d'Oise	(95)

The area immediately around Paris is known today, as it has been since it became the centre of Frankish settlement in the 5th century, as the Ile de France. It was mainly encircled by water in the shape of three big rivers (Marne, Oise, Seine) — hence the name "Island of France".

Largest of the *départements* is Seine et Marne, spread around the two great rivers to the east of Paris. The shimmery light and landscape of river and woodland drew many artists, impressionists included, to work here. The artists' village of Barbizon, royal palace and forest of Fontainebleau and château of Vaux-le-Vicomte are in this *département*.

Clustering around Paris are Val-de-Marne, which includes Orly airport as well as peaceful, wooded riverside stretches; Hauts-de-Seine with residential and industrial blocks; and Seine-St-Denis, to the north of the capital, now urbanised but once one of the most fertile farming areas of the country. North of Seine St Denis is the unspoilt, wooded Val d'Oise, nudging Yvelines to the west, carpeted with forest and farmland and including the presidential residence at Rambouillet, castles and museums at St-Germain-en-Laye and Versailles, and the pretty Vallée de Chevreuse. On its eastern border, Essonne has attractive towns (like Étampes) and riverside villages.

variety of excursion possibilities, accessible by train, bus or car. Many private companies catering for tourists organise day and half day tours, including Cityrama, Paris Vision and America Express. (See **Getting Around**, p 48, for telephone numbers and addresses).

Pariscope and other weekly guides list the museums of the Ile de France. Contact the following too for details of guide-accompanied excursions:

Caisse Nationale des Monuments Historiques et Sites: Bureau des Visites, Hôtel de Sully, 62 rue St Antoine 75004 Paris. Tel. 48 87 24 14/15. Publishes a small booklet listing all forthcoming tours.

Tourist Services of the RATP (Paris's public transport service): place de la Madeleine 75008 Paris. Tel. 26 53 11 8; or 53 quai des Grands Augustins 75006. Tel. 43 46 42 03. Both offices are open daily.

For further information on how to get to various destinations, call the *SNCF* on 42 60 51 51 or **France Information Loisirs** (42 96 63 63; for information in English 47 20 88 98).

NORTH OF PARIS

CHANTILLY (Oise)

Synonymous with whipped cream and handworked lace; with a famous racecourse, an elegant château and substantial forest, Chantilly attracts fewer sightseers than the blockbuster sites of Versailles or Fontainebleau. Nevertheless, it does get pretty crowded on Sundays and if you want to visit the château, avoid days when the horseraces are held because it'll be closed then.

Its setting makes Chantilly perfect for an out-of-Paris jaunt and footloose *flâneurs* (strollers) could combine it with an excursion to the old world town of Senlis, a few miles to the east (by bike, bus or foot).

There are, in fact, two châteaux joined together, the Grand and Petit, great cylinders of stone with domed corner turrets lapped all around by a lake-like, fish-filled moat.

Much of the original, 16th-century **Grand Château** was destroyed during the Revolution – it symbolised the privilege, power and wealth of the owners, the Montmorency and Condé families. In the 19th century the original castle was restored and bequeathed to the Institut de France.

Needless to say, the history of Chantilly is enmeshed with that of the French court. The Grand Condé, a celebrated general, friend and relative of Louis XIV, devoted a lot of his energies upon his retirement to making Chantilly magnificent. In 1622 he employed the ubiquitous 17th-century landscape gardener Le Nôtre to do his stuff on the grounds, giving them great stone steps, shimmering expanses of water, vast parterres, all sheltered by avenues of limes.

There is a prototype of the toy village or *hameau* of Marie Antoinette, later installed at Versailles, and a statue of Le Nôtre taking a rare rest on a bench just by the Terraces.

As befits a fairytale castle like Chantilly, there are many gruesome and intriguing stories attached to it. One of the best known is of the former *genre* and shows how seriously the French take their gastronomy.

In 1671 the redoubtable Grand Condé held a party lasting 3 days for King and Court at Chantilly. No mean feast this, there were hundreds of guests, accommodated in marquees, local inns and villas. The great royal chef Vatel was in charge of feeding this lot three times a day; he didn't sleep for 12 days before the first banquet – and on that first night there were two tables without roasts. The brilliant but sensitive Vatel was deeply upset. He felt such a failure. On the following day the fish didn't turn up from the coast. Exhausted, the chef ran a rapier through his heart rather than face the anger of his hungry King. But doubtless the King – and courtiers – didn't starve.

The château is crammed with the treasures of the Musée Condé, the lavish collection of the Duc d'Aumale who inherited the castle in the 19th century. There are paintings (works by Raphael, Botticelli, Poissin, Watteau, Ingres and others), tapestries, stained glass, ancient relics and precious stones – including the celebrated Grand Condé pink diamond, one of the largest sparklers in the world. The *pièce de résistance* is the priceless 15th-century illuminated manuscript of *Les Très Riches Heures du Duc de Berry*.

Near the château, beyond the ornamental gate, are the palatial 18th-century **Grandes Écuries**. The duc de Bourbon, grandson of the Grand Condé, was fantastically rich and lavished a lot of his loot on these extravagant stables. It's said that he believed in reincarnation and thought that he might return to earth as a horse. Even the most fussy equine tastes couldn't have found fault with these quarters. They held 240 horses with a staff of 89 to look after them, plus kennels for more than 400 hounds for the stag and boar hunts. The stables are still in use and live horses nibble away

Abbaye de Royaumont (Val d'Oise)

About 5m (8km) south-west of Chantilly is one of the most lovely Gothic buildings in France, the Cistercian Abbey at Royaumont, founded by the saintly King Louis IX (1226–70). He was married in the church here in 1234 and regularly made self-chastising visits to the abbey where he served the monks at table. There are accompanied half-hour tours April–October daily except Tuesday in winter months, weekends and bank holidays. To reach the abbey direct from Paris, it's 25 miles (40km) north on the N1/D909.

next to wooden statues in the **Musée du Cheval** (Museum of the Horse).

Horse racing in Chantilly began in 1834. The famous racecourse adjoins the stables and it's here that the French equivalent to the Derby (the Prix du Jockey Club) and to the Oaks (the Prix de Diane) are run every June.

You can saunter through the 16,000 acre (6300 hectares) Chantilly forest where the French monarchs once went hunting. There are hiking trails and, to the south, ponds – **les Étangs de Commelle** – culminating in a pretty hunting lodge, **Le Pavillon de la Reine Blanche**.

Château de Chantilly, Musée Condé: Tel. 44 57 08 00. Answers weekdays 9.30am–12.30pm. Telephone information 44 57 03 62. Open April–Oct: 10am–6pm, Mon, Wed–Sun. Nov–March: 10.30am–5pm, Mon, Wed–Sun. Admission 30f adults; 7f under-12s. Park only: 12f adults; 7f under-12s. Credit (bookshop only): V.

The Musée du Cheval: Tel. 44 57 13 13. Open 10.30am–6.30pm, Mon, Wed–Fri; 10.30am–7pm, Sat–Sun, April–Oct; 2–4.30pm, Mon, Wed–Fri; 10.30am–6pm, Sat–Sun, Nov–March. There are horse training demonstrations April–Oct daily at 11.30am, 3.30pm, 5.15pm. Admission to the museum and show 35f; students, children, OAPs, 28f.

How to get to Chantilly

30m (50km) from Paris.

By road: Autoroute du Nord, A1 from Paris exit at Survilliers. By train: Gare du Nord to Chantilly. You can rent a bicycle outside the train station for around 25f–38f per day.

Tourist information: Office du Tourisme, 1 avenue du Maréchal Joffre,

Chantilly. Tel. 44 57 08 58. Open Mon and Wed–Sat. 8.30am–12.30pm, 4pm–6.30pm; Sun 9am–2pm.

Where to Eat

Château: 22 rue Connétable Tel. 44 57 02 25. Closed Mon evening, Tue. Michelin recommended; menus from 90f.

Les Quatre Saisons: 9 avenue Général-Leclerc. Tel. 44 57 04 65. Open noon–2.30pm, 7–10.30pm. Closed Sun evening. Michelin recommended; set menus are best value, ranging from around 120f.

COMPIÈGNE (Oise)

The dense forests found in the countryside all around Paris help maintain the temperate, humid climate. An hour to the north-east of the capital, the historic town of Compiègne sits between the Oise river and one of the largest forests in France. "My great delight in Compiègne," wrote Robert Louis Stevenson in his *Inland Voyage*, "was the Town Hall". This ornate **Hôtel de Ville** was also singled out by the 19th-century restorer Viollet-le Duc as the most beautiful example of civil architecture in the north of France.

Although Compiègne was badly damaged during the Second World War, the Hôtel de Ville, right in the town centre, managed to harm escape. It was built of the finest stone in France between 1499 and 1509 and has a famous belfry which contains the original bell, dating from 1303, and little early 16th-century figures known as *picantins* strike the hours. Next door is the **Musée de la Figurine Historique** (open 9am–12noon; 2–6pm, 5pm in winter) with close on 100,000 tin soldiers modelling military uniforms throughout the ages, from Roman legionnaires to modern day paratroopers. (You can arrange a guided tour with the Compiègne tourist office, tel. 44 40 01 00.)

Compiègne is deeply enmeshed in French history, having had strategic – and therefore political – importance since the days of Charlemagne. The remains of a tower, known as the **Tour Jeanne d'Arc**, a little to the west of the bridge, and the **Porte Chapelle** to the east are all that's left of the old fortifications. Other than these there are no suggestions of its former importance.

Joan of Arc was imprisoned here before her execution; Napoleon chose it as the place to wed Marie-Louise before he took her to the capital; the Empress Eugénie made it the political and social centre of France.

Compiègne's **château**, or royal palace, built by Louis XV as his third most important residence, is only upstaged in splendour by Versailles and Fontainebleau. (Tackling the château's *appartements historiques* is almost as daunting too – procure a thick, detailed guide if you want to wring all you can out of a visit.)

The castle's austere façade on the town side belies the sumptuous interior – the best collection of First Empire furnishings in the country – and the impressive view over the incredible forest. Not surprisingly, the original château was used as a royal hunting lodge. Louis XIV often stayed there, despite moans that at Compiègne, he was "housed like a peasant".

It was Louis XV and Louis XVI (who first met Marie Antoinette here), who transformed it into a palace. But the castle is be remembered for the 19th-century feasts and frolics hosted by Napoleon III and the Empress Eugénie, abruptly terminated by the Franco-Prussian War.

There is also a **Musée de la Voiture**, with a hetereogenous collection of horsedrawn vehicles dating from 1740, including the coach that carried Napoleon to and from Moscow in 1812, early cycles and vintage cars. The palace park (modified by Napoleon for Marie-Louise) adjoins the enormous forest where there are a number of things to see and do – boating lakes, cycle paths. Walk to Les Beaux Monts for a good view of the château and the Oise.

Château (Royal apartments, Second Empire Museum, Musée de la Voiture): place du Général de Gaulle, Compiègne. Open 9.30am–noon; 1.30–5pm, Mon–Wed, Sun. Admission 21f adults; under-18s free. Guided tours only. Park open dawn to dusk. Telephone **44 40 02 02** for more information.

In the forest (N31 from town, direction Soissons) about 5 miles (9km) from the town, there are many good walks. Take avenue des Beaux Monts to visit the **Clairière de l'Armistice** (or Armistice Clearing) where, in a railway carriage, the 1918

Armistice between France and Germany was signed; there's a small museum devoted to the First World War. On 14th June, 1940, in the same carriage, Hitler received the French capitulation during the Second World War. It was taken off to Berlin where it is believed that it was destroyed in bombing raids.

Musée de l'Armistice: open 8am–noon; 1.30–6.30pm daily in summer; and 9am–noon; 2–5.30pm, Wed–Mon in winter. Closed Tuesday.

With your own wheels, there are yet more possibilities for sylvan explorations – to the village of **Vieux Moulin** for example, and the **Étangs de St Pierre**, the favourite fishing hole of the Empress Eugénie. She and her husband had an unusual hunting castle nearby, about 5 miles or 9 kilometres from Compiègne but still within the forest, the pseudo-mediaeval **Pierrefonds**. It could have been transported from *Cinderella* but actually is the work of Viollet-le-Duc who rebuilt it from rubble, between 1861 and 1884.

Pierrefonds: open 10am–noon, 1.30–6pm, Mon–Sat; 9.30am–1pm, Sundays and public holidays. Telephone 44 42 80 77 for more information.

How to get to Compiègne
52m (84km) from Paris.
By road: Autoroute du Nord A1 from Paris, exit Compiègne.
By train: from Gare du Nord (it takes about 50 minutes)

Tourist information: Office du Tourisme, 1 place Hôtel de Ville, Compiègne. Tel. 44 40 01 00.

Picnic fare

Compiègne is a pleasant place to shop. For your picnic fodder it's worth visiting the excellent morning food market (through an arch leading off the place de l'Hôtel de Ville) or check out **Au Fermier Normandier**, 3 rue Napoléon for an excellent selection of local cheeses.

Where to Eat

Golden Horse: 2 rue Bouvines Tel. 44 23 20 56. Closed Saturday lunch. Michelin recommended. Close to rue Jeanne d'Arc and the river. Menus from around 80f.

Senlis *(Oise)*

Municipal pride envelops Senlis, a small town that feels as though it ought to be a lot further from Paris than it actually is. Plaques reliably proclaim any accomplished former resident; the whole place looks as if it has been newly washed, like the pristine, pale stonework of the exquisite 12th-century cathedral, a contemporary of Notre-Dame.

This is an affluent town (as a glance into the local estate agents windows show), easy on the eye, but not in the schmaltzy, rose-smothered, Cotswoldy sort of way — Senlis has a crisper, cleaner, kind of charm. There are so many hairdressers for such a small town, it's almost as if the residents feel they have to keep themselves as preened as Senlis itself.

The old town centre spreads out from the Cathedral and its crooked, cobbled narrow ways weren't made to be explored except on foot.

From the 5th century until the reign of Henri IV in the 17th, Senlis was a royal residence and you can see the ruins of the castle. The original château was built on the foundations of an ancient royal palace.

Château Royal: place du Parvis de Notre-Dame. Open 10am–noon, 2pm–6pm; 5pm Oct–Mar. Closed Tuesday all day, Wednesday am and from 3rd week in December to 3rd week in January.

Next door is an historic cluster of buildings, formerly part of the royal castle and now housing a Hunting Museum. Even if blood sports turn your stomach, it's worth forking out the entrance fee to explore the group of dilapidated buildings. The kings of France, when not cavorting with their mistresses, spent a great deal of time on *la Chasse*. The **Musée de la Vénerie** is open the same hours as the Château Royal, and also contains the King's retiring chamber plus fine paintings.

Dominating the parvis is the 12th-century **Cathédrale de Notre-Dame**, with its 200-foot high 13th-century spire. Cleaning of the masonry was completed in 1987 and the stunning, soaring, glowing white interior is in sharp contrast to the lugubrious ones we usually see. On a severe 12th-century base, there are a lot of later Gothic embellishments or additions. The Romanesque Grand Portail; consecrated to the Virgin Mary, was later copied in Chartres cathedral and Notre-Dame in Paris; another outstanding feature is the beautiful gallery which runs high above on either side of the nave and choir.

How to get to Senlis

31 miles (51km) from Paris.
10km east of Chantilly, 12km from 18th century château and park of Ermononville, so a visit to two or all three could easily be combined. By road: on A1 from Paris. By train: from Gare du Nord, RER or banlieue lines to Chantilly, transfer for SNCF bus for last few miles – a 20 minute or so ride.
Tourist information: Office du Tourisme, place du parvis Notre-Dame. Tel. 44 53 06 40. Open April–Nov, Mon and Wed–Fri 2–6pm, Tues 10am–6pm, Sat–Sun, 10am–noon, 2–6pm. Conducted walking tours start from the Tourist Office, contact them for details of times, prices, themes of tours.

Les Jardins d'Eugénie: 23 place de l'Hôtel de Ville. Tel. 44 40 00 08. Open daily 12 noon–midnight.
Conveniently located right in the town centre. Don't expect great gastronomy but down to earth, homely cooking. Menu at 98f, or allow 200F.
La Rôtisserie du Chat-qui-Tourne, (Hôtel de France): 17 rue Eugéne-Floquet. Tel. 44 40 02 74. Open daily noon–2pm, 7.30pm–9pm.

In the town centre, by the Hôtel de Ville, where there's been an inn on the same site since the 17th century. Excellent set menus start around 150f and you get a lot for your money.

WEST AND SOUTH-WEST OF PARIS

GIVERNY (Vallée de la Seine)

Suffering from a surfeit of châteaux? Giverny is an out-of-Paris excursion with a less formal flavour, technically in Southern Normandy, halfway between Paris and Rouen, but easily reachable from the capital. A Norman by birth, Claude Monet (1840–1926) couldn't tear himself away from the soft sensations of Seine Valley light and he lived and worked here for 43 years, until his death. He is buried here, too, by the church apse. By 1900 Monet's sales had shot up, bringing him over 200,000 francs a year. His wealth allowed him to develop his land at Giverny into a horticultural paradise, with the help of a handful of full-time gardeners.

At its very best in late spring, at cherry and apple blossom time, images of Giverny are immortalised in thousands of reproductions. When not painting, Monet was an indefatigable gardening experimenter and, in his view, the Giverny garden of earthly delights was his greatest achievement – a personal world of his own making, giving *in situ* inspiration.

It's a true painter's garden: a cheerful orgy of colour, texture, shape, all artfully arranged to give a profusion of flowers from early spring to late autumn. Across the road is the famous waterlily garden, the model for his *Nymphéas* series. Water lilies obsessed him; you can see the actuals in the pond, but must head back to the Orangerie in Paris to compare them with the virtuoso paintings. In fact, none of Monet's own paintings, apart from reproductions, are in the faithfully – restored brick farm house and three studios, though you can see his collection of Japanese prints. All rooms have been restored to their former design: every piece of furniture is original, faithfully renovated, with the guidance of old black-and-white photographs for its positioning. Visitors might easily forget that it's a museum and that the occupants are all dead.

Musée Claude Monet: open from April to October, Tuesday–Friday, 10am–noon, 2–4pm; 10am–6pm, Sat–Sun. The gardens are open from 10am–6pm. Tel. 32 51 28 21 for more information.

How to get to Giverny

51m (82km) from Paris.

By road: A13 from Paris to Vernon, exit D181, cross River in Vernon and follow D5 to Giverny. By Train: Gare St Lazare to Vernon (it takes 50 minutes), change to private bus or walk or taxi (fare approx 6f) remaining 3.5m (7km).

Boat and bus tours on the Seine are organised by Confiens Sainte-Honorine, to include lecture and lunch. Contact Hors Cadre, 17 rue Custine, Paris. 75018. Tel. 42 52 27 27.

Guided Tours: half or full day tours from AMEX, 11 rue Scribe, 75009 Paris. Tel. 42 66 09 99 and enquire at the RATPE offices at place de la Madeleine 75008, Paris or 53 quai des Grands-Augustins 75006.

Tourist information: Office du Tourisme 36 rue Carnot, Vernon. Tel. 32 51 39 60. (Next to the Église Notre-Dame). Vernon itself is a good touring centre for the Seine and Eure valleys.

Where to Eat

Beau Rivage: 13 avenue Maréchal Leclerc, Vernon. Tel. 32 51 17 27. Closed Sun eve, Mon, 2 weeks in Feb and Oct. Riverside restaurant. Set menus from 100f. Credit: AE, DC, MC, V.

RAMBOUILLET (Yvelines)

Encircled by a massive forest of oak, pine, beech and birch, the **château at Rambouillet** is not nearly as grand or imposing as some of the royal residences. It was never intended for long stays, as the king and court came here to kill the deer and boar in the forest, not loll around the estate.

Rambouillet suited Francois I (although he did breathe his last here in 1547) Henri III and Charles X, but Marie Antoinette hated it (she called it a "Gothic toad-hole"), except when she was up to her pastoral games in the Queen's Dairy where she liked to play milkmaid. You can visit her 1783 *Laiterie* and *Bergerie*.

After the Revolution the castle was emptied. Napoleon spent his final night here before being exiled in 1815, and today the treasures to be seen are the Emperor's small, private apartments and formal dining room.

President Mitterrand holds state dinners here, but when he is not playing host, this and the rest of these rooms are open to the public. It's his official summer residence though there's little chance of seeing him inspecting his flowerbeds as the house and grounds are usually closed when he's home.

Château de Rambouillet: place de la Libération. Open 10am–12 noon, 2–6pm (5pm in winter), Wed–Mon. Guided tours only. Closed Tuesday, state occasions, and when the President is in residence. For further information telephone 34 83 15 93.

How to get to Rambouillet

36m (54km) from Paris.
Rambouillet is 31km from Versailles; a visit to both could be combined – if you have the stamina for it! By road: N10 from Paris. By train: from Gare Monparnasse *(banlieue)*.

Tourist Information: Office du Tourisme at the Hôtel de Ville. Tel. 34 83 15 93.

Where to Eat

Relais du Château: 2 place de la Libération Tel. 34 83 00 49. Open Wed-Sat noon–2.30pm, 7pm–10.30pm, Sun lunch. Closed Mon, Tues, Sun pm and Jan 1 to mid-Feb.

A restaurant which overlooks the main square of Rambouillet right outside the Château, weather permitting you may eat out on the terrace. Modestly priced set-price menu (around 100f) Credit: AE, V.

VERSAILLES (Yvelines)

Versailles is royal egomania run riot, a monstrous monument to absolutely divine rule, the architectural equivalent of the *oeuvre* of Busby Berkeley. It has had a bad press but whether you are over- or under-whelmed by the whole extravaganza, you certainly won't forget it.

Of all the bizarre aspects of Versailles, the choice of site is the most surprising. It was, we are told by the Duc de Saint-Simon, whose memoirs of the life and times of Versailles run to a 37-volume opus: "the most dreary and barren of places". Nevertheless this inhospitable spot must have appealed to Louis XIII. In 1624 he built a hunting lodge there.

Louis XIV, the Sun King, around whom life at Versailles was later to revolve, didn't show any interest in the place until 1661. He used to nip over from the official seat of the court at St-Germain-en-Laye for secret (or not so secret, since he was always accompanied by a band of courtiers) trysts with his latest mistress, Louise de la Vallière.

Versailles was convenient for him for another reason too – he wanted his power base to be well removed from the rabble of the city and St-Germain-en-Laye was certainly not big enough to absorb a court of acolytes and their servants. Seething jealousy played a part as well. Louis XIV felt he had been upstaged by the glorious new residence of his financial whizz, Fouquet, at Vaux-le-Vicomte (see page 554 for more details). Having attended a housewarming soirée there on 17th August, 1661 – which historians claim was the most flash party in the history of France – Louis XIV was so put out by the ostentation, he repaid Fouquet's hospitality by having him imprisoned. The 23-year-old King Louis filched

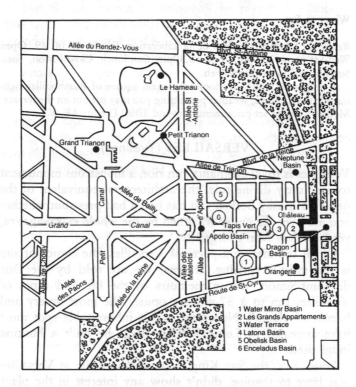

1 Water Mirror Basin
2 Les Grands Appartements
3 Water Terrace
4 Latona Basin
5 Obelisk Basin
6 Enceladus Basin

the big name triumvirate that had created Vaux-le-Vicomte: architect Le Vau, decorator Le Brun, landscaper Le Nôtre, and got them working on Versailles. For the rest of the year, historians tell us, the moving wagons were kept busy on the road between Vaux and Versailles.

If Versailles sprang very much from a whim, it was not made concrete overnight – building work went on for half a century. After Le Vau died, 32 year old Jules Hardouin Mansart took over as architect. At one point some 36,000 men and 6000 horses were employed in the creation of the palace and park. Not content just to have a roof over his head, the King wanted, and got, 25 acres of it.

For over a century Versailles was the capital of France, right up until the Revolution.

The King's decision in 1682 to make Versailles the court

residence and seat of government meant that it had to accommodate a vast number — 1000 or so aristos, as well as their retinue and hangers-on. When Louis died at the age of 77 in 1715, many thousands of people lived in the palace, revolving like satellites around the Sun King, a monarch who spent all his time in public yet allowed no one, except his brother, to sit down in front of him.

Many aspects of court life were most odd and it's worth delving into those memoirs of Saint-Simon, or digging into the history books, to get a clear idea just how odd. Nancy Mitford's *Sun King* is colourful background reading.

The Palace

Three main roads, from Saint Cloud, Sceaux and Paris, converge at the place d'Armes, with the royal stables, built by Hardouin-Mansart, on the right and left. The great wrought-iron palace gates open on to the **Minister's Courtyard**, named after Louis XIV's ministers who had the two wings of the château on each side of it. A second gate leads into the **Royal Courtyard**, where access was once granted only to the privileged few. These days coach-loads of visitors will be disgorging themselves into the palace at the same time as you.

"When you arrive at Versailles," wrote Voltaire, "from the courtyard you see a wretched, top-heavy building with a façade seven windows long, surrounded by everything which the imagination could conceive in the way of bad taste. When you see it from the garden, you see a huge palace whose defects are more than compensated by its beauties." He has a point: you could be forgiven for thinking the two sides aren't the same building. But then Versailles always was a very two-faced sort of place.

A doorway off the courtyard leads to the light, cool chapel, the last of its kind to be built within a palace in France and constructed of a special white stone known as *Blanc Royal*.

From here you are poised to penetrate the palace. It's so massive, you really have to decide in advance what you want to see. There are various guided tours to help you make sense of it all. The most popular tours are those including the series of **state apartments** leading into the astonishing **Galerie des Glaces** (Hall of Mirrors) with its tall, arched windows overlooking the gardens, matched on the opposite wall by mirrors. Lavish Louis Quatorze style even permeates **La Chapelle** where the 16-year-old prince, the future Louis XVI, married Marie Antoinette in 1770. (You'll also see the bedroom where she spent her last night at Versailles before trying to run away from the angry revolutionaries.)

The **Grands Appartements** were mainly used for State occasions. Less formal are the **Petits Appartements** featured in a second tour. You'll be able to see where the King actually lived with his endless aides, servants, and sometimes his mistresses, Madame de Pompadour and her successor, thoughtfully chosen for him by Madame de Pompadour, Madame du Barry. It was here that Mozart, as a child prodigy, played before the court on an early European tour.

Or you could take a tour of the **Museum of French History** (paintings, historical items from the 15th to the 20th centuries, and *objets d'art*). A fourth tour has as its themes the **King's Apartments** and the Louis XV interiors. The **Royal Opera**, which is set in the end of the north wing, can also only be visited on a guided tour. An opera house in miniature, in the first oval room in France, it was built by the architect Gabriel for Louis XV in 1770.

Château de Versailles Tel. 30 84 74 00. Open: Château: 9.45am–5pm Tues–Sun; closed Bank Holidays; *Gardens*: times vary, usually dawn-dusk daily. Admission: *Château*: 23f; *Gardens only*: free. For details of guided tours telephone 39 50 58 32 or write to Service des Visites, Château de Versailles, 78000.

The Gardens

The 250-acre statue-filled grounds are an integral part of the microcosmic utopia Louis XIV conceived. The Sun King metaphor, a solar force around which everything revolves, just as the state revolves around the monarch, is an underlying theme throughout.

In the gardens, landscaped by Le Nôtre, nature is tamed and limited by a complicated series of terraces, dotted with lavish fountains, gilded statues, and parterres. Louis XIV is represented as Apollo in the gardens, as in the **fountain of**

Apollo where he drives his chariot out of the water, just as the sun is driven out of the sea at daybreak.

There are fountains all over the place – and only switched on on *Grand Eaux* days when more than 6000 cubic yards of water flings itself into a splashy spectacle. (For details of times and tickets for displays, telephone 39 50 36 22.) Beyond the Fountain of Apollo is the *Grand Canal*, said to remind Louis XV of Venice, he liked to glide down it in a gondola. The more prosaic alternatives offered to today's visitors are hired rowing boats.

At one end of the *Petit Canal,* a mile or so from the palace, stands the pink marble, elegant **Grand Trianon**, built in the 1680's by Mansart for Louis XIV. It is used these days as a guest house for visiting VIPs. The original furniture has mostly been replaced by the 19th-century Empire style. Madame de Pompadour died here in 1764 instead of in the nearby Petit Trianon, which was built for her in the 1760s by Gabriel, but not completed before her death.

Marie Antoinette preferred it here to being in the main

château, even more so when she could give the court formalities the slip completely to play in her *hameau*, or mock-rustic hamlet, where she and her attendants would dress up and act out unlikely bucolic fantasies – they even had a specially groomed flock of perfumed lambs.

The Town

Versailles *ville*, being synonymous with its château, tends to be overlooked by tourists, understandably perhaps, as they're probably all so flaked out after trotting round the palace and park.

The town itself won't disappoint you as long as you bear in mind that it's one of the earliest examples of town planning and specifically laid out as an adjunct to the palace. While it was all planned some 3 centuries ago, it has yet to assert a personality over the severe, grid-like streets. It's snobby and rather soulless, and yet was an inspiration behind the design of such cities as St Petersburg.

There are fine 17th- and 18th-century streets and a couple of churches worth visiting: **Notre Dame**, built by J.H. Mansart in the 1680s, and the **Cathédrale St Louis**, built in the mid-18th century by Mansart's grandson.

How to get to Versailles

15m (24km) from Paris.
By road: N10 from Pte St Cloud. By Métro: to Pont de Sèvres, then bus 171, or train from Gare St Lazare to Versailles Rive Droite, then bus to the château. The Rive Gauche station is nearer the château and so the easiest route is to take the RER line C5 from Gare d'Austerlitz, quai d'Orsay, Pont de L'Alma to Versailles Rive Gauche – take the train described as "Vick" as others turn off before Versailles.

Inclusive half or whole day tours by coach are organised by amongst others, Cityrama Tel. 42 60 30 14. and Paris Vision Tel. 42 60 30 01.

Tourist information: Office du Tourisme, 7 rue des Reservoirs Tel. 39 50 36 22 Open Nov–April: 9am–4.15pm Mon–Fri; 9am–5.30pm Sat. May–Oct: 9am–7pm Mon–Sat 9am–5.30pm Sun.

Where to Eat

La Boeuf à la Mode: 4 rue au Pain Tel. 39 50 31 99. Open 12–2pm, 7.30pm–12.30am. Traditional cooking – allow 100–150f per person. Credit: V.

La Boule d'Or: 25 rue Maréchal Foch Tel. 39 50 22 97. Open until 10pm. Closed Sun eve, Monday. The oldest (late 17th century) restaurant in town, specialising in shellfish. Excellent set menu weekdays, but not cheap, at around 150f per person.

Potager du Roy: 1 rue Maréchal Joffre Tel. 39 50 35 34. Closed Sun, Mon. Owned by the former chef of Les Trois Marches. Fresh, inventive cuisine. Menus from 150f. Michelin-recommended. Reservations advised.

Vert Galant: 85 rue Paroisse Tel. 39 21 76 50. Closed 10–31 August; Wednesdays. Michelin-recommended; menus from 85f. Credit: AE, DC, MC, V.

Trois Marches: 3 rue Colbert. Tel. 39 50 13 21. Closed Sun, Mon. We mention this expensive restaurant because it's the best in town, with innovative cooking from a top chef. Michelin guide bestows a couple of stars. Weekday lunch menu at 230f. Reservations necessary.

Where to Stay

Although Versailles is an easy day-trip from Paris, it's worth considering it as a weekend or short break base, particularly if you want to delve deeply into the history and mysteries of Versailles.

Trianon Palace: 1 boulevard de la Reine, Tel. 39 50 34 12. The poshest in town, the four star luxury hotel is just 3 minutes from the Palace. A grand Edwardian edifice, it is very busy year round, there's a health club and guests can borrow bicycles. Rooms from 580–1165f per night. Credit: AE, DC, MC, V.

Hôtel de la Chasse: 2–4 rue de la Chancellerie, Tel. 39 50 00 92. The only *logis* in town, 2 stars, 18 rooms and you must book ahead, especially in the summer. Rooms from around 200f. Restaurant.

SOUTH-EAST OF PARIS

VAUX-LE VICOMTE (Seine-et-Marne)

The elegant 17th-century **château Vaux-le-Vicomte** was built for Louis XIV's filthy rich finance minister Nicolas Fouquet at the height of his power in 1655. Just like the greedy Richelieu and his mentor, Cardinal Mazarin, the able and ambitious Fouquet had built up a conspicuous personal fortune.

Sparing no expense, he employed three of the biggest talents in France – royal architect Louis Le Vaux, royal landscape gardener André Le Nôtre and the painter-decorator Charles Le Brun. Along with around 18,000 labourers, they set about creating an opulent stuccoed palace complete with moat, pool and Grand Canal into which 1200 fountains splashed. But Fouquet's aspirations were to backfire on him.

All the time the castle was being built, Jean-Baptiste Colbert, who later became Finance Minister, was attempting to convince the young king that Fouquet was power-hungry and dishonest. Then on a summer's night in 1661 Fouquet held a shamelessly extravagant housewarming fête; there was a sumptuous banquet fit for a king, with a solid gold dinner service; Molière and his troupe performed in the open-air theatre; a state-of-the-art fireworks display followed. Not one to enjoy being outshone, less than 3 weeks later the Sun King had his upstart finance minister arrested for peculation. After a lengthy trial he was imprisoned and died in captivity 19 years later.

The lavish contents of the château and the garden statuary were confiscated (much of its booty found its way over the ensuing years to Versailles) and Vaux-Le-Vicomte began to slither into dilapidation. Louis XIV appropriated the artistic triumvirate Le Vaux, Le Nôtre and Le Brun and set them to work on his own magniloquent château at Versailles.

A sugar magnate and arts patron Alfred Sommier rescued the neglected property in 1875 and devoted much of his immense fortune to restoring it. As no major alterations or extensions have been made to the château or park, the impeccably preserved Vaux-Le-Vicomte is one of the best examples of a substantial 17th-century property to have survived.

As well as the château and gardens, you can also visit, in the former stable block, a **carriage museum** with displays of sporting vehicles, travelling and town carriages with dummies decked out in formal livery.

In theory, you could, if you're up to it, "do" Vaux-Le-Vicomte in the first half of the day and proceed by train from Melun to Fontainebleau.

Vaux-Le-Vicomte: Tel. 60 66 97 09/60 66 97 11. Open 10am–12.30pm, 2–6pm daily (gardens 10am–7pm), April 1–Oct 31. 11am–12.30pm, 2–5pm, Nov 1–Mar 31. Admission: 42f (gardens only 17f). There are fountain displays on the second and last Saturday of each month, 3–6pm, April–Oct. Candlelight tours Sat and Sun, May–Sept, 8.30–11pm. (Telephone for more details.)

How to get to Vaux-Le-Vicomte

37m (60km) from Paris.
By road: Autoroute A6 from Paris to Fontainebleau exit; follow signs to Melun or take A4 to Melun exit, then N36 and D215 east. Vaux-Le-Vicomte is on the D215. By train: from Gare de Lyon to Melun, change for Maincy then bus, taxi, bike 4m (6km) to château. Buses also go to the château from Melun.
  Paris Vision organise half day/day trips from Paris.

Tourist information: Office du Tourisme, 2 avenue Gallieni. Tel. 64 37 11 31.

Where to Eat:

See *Ibis*, Melun below.
Fort de l'Eau: 1 avenue Thiers, Melun. Tel. 64 37 04 14. Open 12 noon–2.30pm, 7–10.30pm. Lunch menu for 75f, otherwise allow 120f per person. Couscous a speciality.

FONTAINEBLEAU (Seine-et-Marne)

Like Compiègne to the north of Paris, Fontainebleau found royal favour as a hunting base, melting as it does into the endless bronze and green of a fine forest.

In 1528 François I took the neglected royal manor and transformed it into a majestic Renaissance palace fit to entertain his mistress, the Duchess of Étampes. A battalion of Italian artists came to paint, sculpt, fresco and stucco and the Fontainebleau School was born. Apart from being a rake and a military man, François I was a discriminating and avid collector and amassed jewellery, weapons, sculptures and loads of artworks – including the Mona Lisa, now encased behind bullet-proof glass in the Louvre.

As you'd expect, subsequent rulers all left their stamp on Fontainebleau until, in 1789, the revolutionary mob swept in and left theirs.

Napoleon renovated the interior, kept Pope Pius VII a prisoner here, and in 1814 signed his own abdication at Fontainebleau. The finest collection of Empire furniture, Napoleonic relics and memorabilia from various national museums are on permanent display in his apartments and those of Josephine.

The main entrance, the **Cour des Adieux**, is where the pint-size despot said goodbye to his retinue before being packed off to exile in Elba. To the right of the eye-catching, double horseshoe staircase, an arch leads into the most beautiful part of the palace, the inmost sanctuary of the royal court, the **Fountain Courtyard** by the Carp Pond (some of these fish are said to be over 100 years old). The gilded door (through another arch to the west) is one of the most famous features of the palace; the **Cour Ovale** is the oldest and most interesting courtyard and here you can see the **medieval dungeon**. It's worth allowing a good hour or so to wander through the formal gardens, designed by André Le Nôtre in 1664.

To get the most from your visit you'll need a good 2–3 hours inside the palace. (Some might fancy making a weekend of it.) There are three separate sections – **Les Grands Appartements**, the **Musée Napoléon** and **Les Petits Appartements**.

Of the three, the one part not to miss if you have to ration your time is the **Grands Appartements** which contain the famous **François I Gallery**. This was decorated by Rosso Il Fiorentino (one of the Italian artists specially imported for the work) and his team, during the years 1534–37. Frescoes surrounded by rich, decorative stucco work illustrate events or allegorical subjects linked with the reign of François I: one shows, for example, an elephant decorated with fleur-de-lys as an allegory of the wisdom of the king. This section also includes a vast Renaissance-style ballroom and **Napoleon's private suite**. Symbols and emblems that pop up throughout include the Napoleonic bee emblem of industry and all over the building the fire-breathing salamander that was the trademark of François I.

Fontainebleau is wonderful. Unlike Versailles, it's rarely overcrowded, although it obviously receives legions of visitors. Whereas Versailles is imposing, formal in its open setting, Fontainebleau is more subtle (what wouldn't be?), with a pleasing disunity of plan and surrounded by its beautiful, vaporous forest. Stretching over some 42,000 unspoiled acres, the forest has sandy clearings, straight *allées*, quiet glades, rivers and outcrops of rock which make it a popular training site with climbers. Plunge into it on foot or on a bike – it's criss-crossed by walking and cycling trails (all well signposted and marked on Michelin map 196–*Environs de Paris*, or buy a map from the tourist information office). Bikes may be hired from the tourist information office (see below); mountain bikes from Folies, 246 rue Grande (Tel. 64 23 43 07). Would-be horse-riders, contact Société Hippique Nationale, avenue de Maintenon (Tel. 60 72 22 40), who'll let you have details of accredited riding centres. For the less energetic, bus tours run from the town into the forest.

Château de Fontainebleau: Tel. 64 22 27 40/64 22 41 80. Open 9.30am–12.30pm, 2–5pm, Mon, Wed–Sun. Admission 23f adults; 12f 18–25s, OAPs; free under-18s. Sunday 12f for all. Guided visits by appointment.

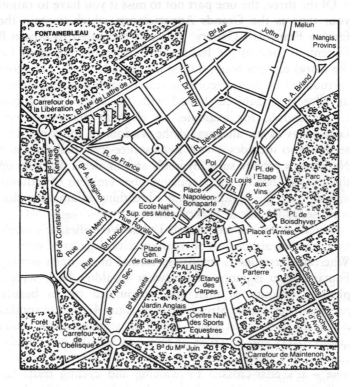

The Town

Quiet, self-contained, snug, the well-heeled little town of Fontainebleau is fairly typical of the more affluent urban environs of Paris. It has many hotels and restaurants, but if transport isn't a problem you might prefer to stay outside if you're in the area for longer than a day trip.

How to get to Fontainebleau

41m (65km) from Paris

By road: 16 to Fontainebleau exit, then N7.

By train: from Gare de Lyon to Fontainebleau-Avon station (it takes 50 minutes) then take the bus A or B – there's a regular service to the castle.

Paris Vision, Cityrama and other companies run excursions from Paris to Fontainebleau combined with Barbizon.

Tourist information: Office du Tourism, 31 place Napoléon. Tel. 64 22 25 68. Open Mon–Sat 9am–7pm, Sun 10am–noon, 3pm–7pm. From Oct–April closed 12–2pm and Sunday pm.

Where to Eat

Arrighi: 53 rue de France Tel. 64 22 29 43. Open noon–2pm, 7–10pm. Closed Monday. Near the Palace, well-priced and pleasant, excellent fish dishes with set menus around 90f.
Le Dauphin: 24 rue Grande Tel. 64 22 27 04.
Moderately priced menus, around 120f
The Franklin Roosevelt: 20 rue Grande Tel. 64 22 33 14. Excellent value, set menus from 60f.
Le Grillardin: 12 rue Pins. Tel. 64 22 36 83. Set menus from 75f.
Le Gaullois: Hôtel Fimotel Avon (see below). Open 12–2.30pm, 7–10.30pm. Set menus at 74f, 92f; allow 100–150f *à la carte*. Childrens menu 35f. See **hotels** section below for address etc.

Around Fontainebleau

The impressionist painters loved this neck of the woods. **Barbizon**, 4 miles (7km) along the N7, set on the edge of the Forest of Fontainebleau, is a pleasant if touristy village that was the centre, in the 19th century, of the *plein-airiste* school of landscape artists who liked to paint out of doors, and whose work pre-figured impressionism.

The founders of the Barbizon School were Millet and Théodore Rousseau whose studio you can visit, just off the rue Grande. This traffic-clogged stretch is the main street, and is lined with art galleries. The landscape painter Corot also lived here from 1830–35. You can nip into the artists' local watering hole and meeting place, **Pierre Ganne's Inn**, now an art gallery.

Musée Auberge du Pierre Ganne: 92 rue Grande. Open Wed–Mon, 10am–5.30pm. Wed, Fri, Sun only in winter. Admission free.

At 25 rue Grande is the **Millet Museum and Studio** (Open 9.30am–12.30pm, 2–5.30pm, Mon–Sat. Admission free). Millet – the first French artist to put peasants in his landscapes – bought the house in 1849 and lived here until his death in 1875. His work and that of others of the Barbizon School is featured in some of the rooms and you can also buy work by today's local artists.

The countryside around Barbizon is good for walking, notably through the **Apremont Gorges,** just inside the Forest of Fontainebleau. You can get to the *gorges* by driving – or cycling – half a mile (1km) out of Barbizon along rue Grande to the Carrefour du Bas Bréau where you park. From here there's a signposted trail to the rocks. After a gentle climb you come to the top platform from where there's a view of miles around.

About 10 miles (16km) away through the forest is the sleepy town of **Milly-la-Fôret** whose buildings include the 12th-century Eglise Nôtre Dame and covered market place made entirely of oak (1479). More recently, Milly acquired a well-known honourary citizen, the French artist and poet Jean Cocteau, who lived here until his death in 1963. He is buried in the small stone **Chapelle St-Blaise-de-Simples,** which he restored and decorated with his own frescoes. (The Chapel, on route D948, is open 10am–noon, 2.30–6pm, Wednesday–Monday. Closed 5pm winter.)

How to get to Barbizon

35m (56km) from Paris; 6m (9.5km) from Fontainebleau Barbizon is not accessible by train.

Tourist information: Office du Tourisme, rue Grande. Tel. 60 66 41 87.

EAST OF PARIS

EuroDisney see page 288 (**Paris for Kids**)

MEAUX (Seine-et-Marne)

Meaux is cheese-ville, the capital of the rich farming district of northern Brie, on the Marne and the Canal de l'Ourcq. Brie cheese has been produced here since the 13th century and although you cannot visit the *boutiques* (which is what they're called) where it's manufactured, the town is a good place to buy it inexpensively. The three types of Brie are the classic *Brie de Meaux*, the stronger *Brie de Melun*, and the less fully fermented *Brie*. This is also the place to pick up a jar of strong Meaux mustard.

Chief non-gustatory attraction of the town is the great **Cathédrale de St Etienne** – a text-book illustration of the different kinds of Gothic styles. (Only the left tower was completed in the original flamboyant Gothic) The stained glass dates from the 14th century.

Next door is the former bishop's palace, a heavily restored 17th-century building now housing the **Musée Bossuet**. It has a wide range of exhibits: paintings, 17th-century apothecaries' vessels, pre-history, local history, plus memorabilia of the 17th-century religious writer and preacher Jacques-Bénigne Bossuet, Bishop of Meaux from 1681–1704.

Musée Bossuet: Tel. 64 34 84 45. Open 10am–noon, 2–6pm, Wed–Mon. Admission free.

How to get to Meaux

34m (54km) from Paris
By road: A4 and N36 From Paris. By train: every 30–40 minutes from the Gare de l'Est.

Tourist information: Office du Tourism, 2 rue Notre Dame. Telephone 64 33 02 26. Open Tue–Sat 10am–noon; 2–6.30pm (restricted hours in winter).

SOME
RECOMMENDED BOOKS

A selection of fiction, non-fiction and photographs.

FICTION

Down and Out in Paris and London, George Orwell (1933) (*Penguin, 1989*).

Maigret, Georges Simenon. Atmospheric Paris with crime in the 1950's (*Penguin, 1992*).

Les Misérables, Victor Hugo (*Penguin, 1982*).

A Moveable Feast, Ernest Hemingway (*Cape 1964/Panther 1977*).

Nadja, André Breton (*out of print*).

Nana, Émile Zola (*Absolute Classics, 1990*).

Quiet Days in Clichy, Henry Miller (1955) (*Allison and Busby, 1988*).

Sentimental Education, Gustave Flaubert (1869) (*Penguin*).

A Tale of Two Cities, Charles Dickens (1849) (*Armada, 1992*).

Thérèse Raquin, Émile Zola (1867) (*Absolute Classics, 1988*).

Tropic of Cancer, Henry Miller (1934) (*Panther, 1965*).

NON FICTION

Expatriate Paris: A Cultural and Literary Guide to Paris of the 1920's, Arlen J. Hansen (*Arcade 1990/Littlebrown 1991*).

France in Modern Times, Louis Wright (*New York, 1987*).

France in the 1980s, John Ardagh (*Penguin, 1988*).

The French, Theodore Zeldin (*Collins Harvill, 1988*).

French Army and Politics 1870–1970, Horne (*Macmillan, 1984*).

French Blues Paul Rambali (*Minerva, 1989*).

Handbook of French Popular Culture, edited by Horr. (*Greenwood Press, 1991*).

Inside Paris, Joe Friedman, photographs by Jerome Darblay (*Phaidon, 1989*).

The Journals 1931–74, Anaïs Nin (*7 rois, Quartet, 1973–82*).

A Literary Companion, Littlewood (*J. Murray 1988*).

Makers of the Twentieth Century: Charles de Gaulle, Julian Jackson (*Cardinal Books, 1991*).

Mythologies, Roland Barthes (*Paladin, 1973*).

Paris, John Russell (*Thames and Hudson, 1983*).

Paris Anthology: In Transition (*Secker & Warburg, 1990*).

Paris: Architect's Guide to 101 Buildings to See in Paris, Salvadori (*Butterworth Architecture, 1990*).

Paris Art Guide, edited by Fiona Dunlop (*Art Guide Publications, 1988*).

Paris a Century of Change 1878–1978, Norma Evensen (*Yale U.P., 1981*).

Paris Notebooks, 1968–85, Mavis Gallant (*Hamish Hamilton, 1989*).

Roads to Freedom Trilogy, Jean-Paul Sartre (1945–49) (*out of Print*).

Reflections on Contemporary French Art and Culture, Porter (*Oxford U.P. 1987*).

Sam White's Paris: The Collected Despatches of a Newspaper Legend (*N.E. Library, 1983*).

PHOTOGRAPHS

Paris: Magnum Photographs 1935–1981 (*Aperture Inc. New York 1981*).

Paris After Dark, Brassaï (*Thames and Hudson, 1987*).

The Secret of Paris of the 30s, photographs by Brassaï (*Thames and Hudson, 1978*).

A Vision of Paris, Eugène Atget (*Macmillan, 1963; reissued 1980*).

MAPS: *see* **When in Paris** section.

INDEX

Apart from a few of the most famous, such as the café Les Deux Magots, individual hotels, cafés, shops are not in this index since they are listed alphabetically in their appropriate section. The main sections of this book are in the index.